Manchester

ENGLAND

London

Amsterdam

NETHERLANDS

Lyon

FRANCE

Bordeaux

Marseille

PORTUGAL

SPAIN

Lisbon

Lagos

Seville

Cádiz

Treaty of Tordesillas
Demarcation line, 1494

SENEGAL

SIERRA
LEONE

GHANA

BENIN

Accra

Lagos

São Tomé

Recife

WEST
CENTRAL
AFRICA

Luanda

BAHIA

Rio de Janeiro

Cape Town

Interwoven Globe

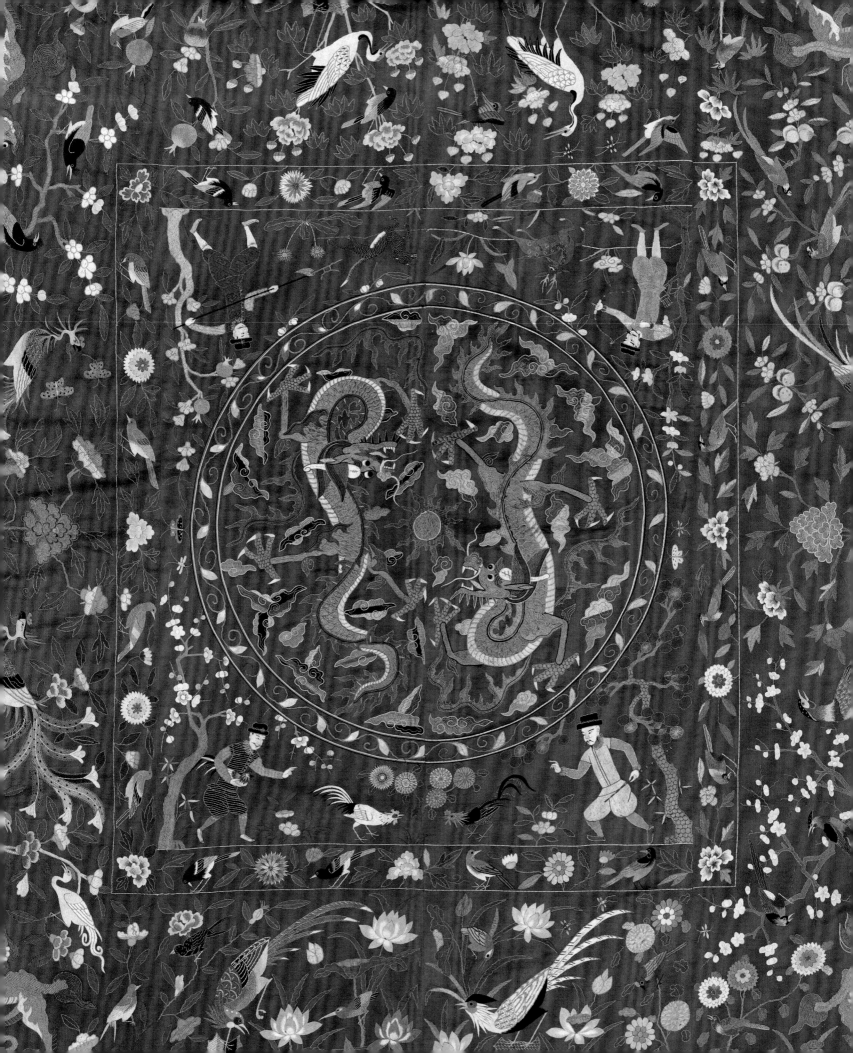

Interwoven Globe

THE WORLDWIDE TEXTILE TRADE, 1500–1800

Edited by AMELIA PECK

With contributions by

AMY BOGANSKY, JOYCE DENNEY, JOHN GUY, MARIA JOÃO PACHECO FERREIRA, ELENA PHIPPS,

MARIKA SARDAR, CYNTHIA V. A. SCHAFFNER, KRISTEN STEWART, AND MELINDA WATT

With 360 colour illustrations

Thames & Hudson

Photographs of works in the Metropolitan Museum's collection are by The Photograph Studio, The Metropolitan Museum of Art, unless otherwise noted; new photography is by Anna-Marie Kellen. Additional photography credits appear on p. 350.

Cover illustrations: (front) Detail of Bedcover (cat. 10B); (back) Detail of Coverlet (cat. 26)
Endpapers: (front) Map of European Maritime Trade Routes to the Americas in the Early Modern Period; (back) Map of European Maritime Trade Routes to Africa and Asia in the Early Modern Period
Frontispiece, p. i: Detail of Bedcover (cat. 10B)
Frontispiece, p. ii: Detail of Coverlet (cat. 26)
Frontispiece, p. 1: Detail of Wedding Coverlet (Colcha) (cat. 23)

This catalogue is published on the occasion of the exhibition "Interwoven Globe: The Worldwide Textile Trade, 1500–1800," on view at The Metropolitan Museum of Art, New York, from September 16, 2013, through January 5, 2014.

The exhibition is made possible by The Andrew W. Mellon Foundation, the Diane W. and James E. Burke Fund, The Coby Foundation, Ltd., The Favrot Fund, the Gail and Parker Gilbert Fund, and the Quinque Foundation.

This publication is made possible by the Diane W. and James E. Burke Fund.

Published by arrangement with The Metropolitan Museum of Art, New York

First published in the United Kingdom in 2013 by Thames & Hudson Ltd, 181A High Holborn, London WC1V 7QX

Edited by Cynthia Clark
Designed by Jean Wilcox, Wilcox Design
Production by Jennifer Van Dalsen
Bibliography by Penny Jones
Image acquisitions and permissions by Jane S. Tai
Maps by Anandaroop Roy

Typeset in Sabon and Syntax
Printed on 150 gsm Galaxi Supermatt
Separations by Professional Graphics, Inc., Rockford, Illinois

British Library Cataloguing-in-Publication Data
A catalogue record for this book is available from the British Library

ISBN: 978-0-500-51716-1
Printed and bound by Graphicom S.R.L., Verona, Italy

To find out about all our publications, please visit www.thamesandhudson.com. There you can subscribe to our e-newsletter, browse or download our current catalogue, and buy any titles that are in print.

Contents

Director's Foreword

The golden age of European maritime navigation in search of spice routes to the East, beginning in the sixteenth century, brought about the flowering of an abundant textile trade. Often used as direct currency for spices and other goods, textiles (and their designs) made their myriad ways throughout the globe via ports of call in the Middle East, India, Asia, Southeast Asia, the Americas, and northern and southern Europe. Blending the traditional designs, skills, and tastes of the cultures that produced as well as purchased them, these beautiful and historically fascinating fabrics also served as conduits of information, sparking ideas of imagined exotic lands and peoples both East and West.

Interwoven Globe: The Worldwide Textile Trade, 1500–1800, includes works from across the Metropolitan Museum's collection (augmented by several key domestic and international loans) to make worldwide visual connections and to highlight an important design story that has never been told from a truly global perspective. Seven Museum departments participated in the exhibition, bringing together luxurious Asian embroidered silk hangings, exquisitely painted and dyed Indian cottons, boldly patterned American quilts, rare English and French tapestries, and richly embellished costumes and religious vestments in addition to paintings depicting the popularity of borrowed styles and the use of trade textiles throughout the world. And while more than three-quarters of the textiles on display in the exhibition and catalogue are from the Metropolitan's own holdings, many have rarely, or indeed never, been exhibited in the galleries, as they often are difficult to contextualize with more traditional works of art made domestically for a particular culture or country.

Interwoven Globe is the product of a team of curators and scholars, all with special knowledge of a particular part of the world, who worked together for more than three years to bring the exhibition and publication to fruition: Amelia Peck, Marica F. Vilcek Curator of American Decorative Arts, The American Wing; Melinda Watt, Associate Curator, European Sculpture and Decorative Arts Department, and Supervising Curator, Antonio Ratti Textile Center; John Guy, Florence and Herbert Irving Curator of the Arts of South and Southeast Asia, Asian Art Department; Joyce Denney, Assistant Curator (retired), Asian Art Department; Elena Phipps, Senior Research Scholar; Marika Sardar, Senior Research Associate, Islamic Art Department; Kristen Stewart, until recently Research Associate, the Costume Institute; and Amy Bogansky, Research Assistant, American Decorative Arts, The American Wing. They are all to be thanked for their vision, patience, and collegiality. The Textile Conservation Department staff, under the leadership of Florica Zaharia, Conservator in Charge, must also be acknowledged for the extraordinary care and effort they put into preparing these fragile objects for display.

An exhibition of this scope also requires a consortium of donors, and for that we thank The Andrew W. Mellon Foundation, the Diane W. and James E. Burke Fund, The Coby Foundation, Ltd., The Favrot Fund, as well as the Gail and Parker Gilbert Fund and the Quinque Foundation. We are also grateful for the Diane W. and James E. Burke Fund's support of this catalogue.

THOMAS P. CAMPBELL
Director, The Metropolitan Museum of Art

Acknowledgments

Our work on *Interwoven Globe: The Worldwide Textile Trade, 1500–1800*, showed us that research on trade textiles demands an international journey, both literally and figuratively. For our exploration of the history and meaning of textiles that traveled around the globe, we enlisted a worldwide network of colleagues. Without the many people listed below, the project would not have been such a rich, at times even exhilarating, experience. The visual and historical connections we were able to discover while learning about the textiles were mirrored by the wonderful personal associations we made throughout the global community of curators, scholars, and collectors and by the ties strengthened with our coworkers closer to home.

One author does not appear on the title page of this book: Alisa LaGamma, Curator in Charge of the Department of the Arts of Africa, Oceania, and the Americas here at the Museum, kindly wrote the entry for the African ivory saltcellar. Cynthia Clark, Senior Editor, shepherded this multiauthor, multipart publication into print. Anna-Marie Kellen, Associate Chief Photographer, produced the fine pictures that help make this book as handsome as it is informative.

Many other colleagues and friends at the Metropolitan Museum were integral in helping the catalogue and exhibition grow and thrive. We extend our wholehearted appreciation to the following: Thomas P. Campbell, Director, Jennifer Russell, Associate Director for Exhibitions, and Carrie Rebora Barratt, Associate Director for Collections and Administration, Office of the Director; Christine Begley, Deputy Chief Development Officer for Government and Foundation Giving, and Sarah Higby, Deputy Chief Development Officer for Corporate Programs, Development Office; Mark Polizzotti, Publisher and Editor in Chief, Michael Sittenfeld, Peter Antony, Jane S. Tai, Jennifer Van Dalsen, Elizabeth Zechella, Hilary Becker, Dale Tucker, and Josephine Rodriguez-Massop, Editorial Department, along with Margaret Aspinwall, Erin Barnett, Margaret Donovan, Joanna Ekman, Richard Gallin, Nancy Grubb, Penny Jones, Fronia Simpson, Richard Slovak, Mary Sprinson de Jesus, Russell Stockman, Sylvia Tidwell, mapmaker Anandaroop Roy, translator David Auerbach and Eriksen Translations, and designer Jean Wilcox of Wilcox Design; Barbara J. Bridgers, General Manager for Imaging and Photography, and Einar J. Brendalen, The Photograph Studio; Staci Hou, Paco Link, and Eileen M. Willis, Digital Media Department; Linda Sylling, Manager for Special Exhibitions, Gallery Installations, and Design, Michael Lapthorn, Sophia Geronimus, Clint Ross Coller, and Richard Lichte, Design Department; Allison Bosch, Registrar's Office; Giovanna P. Fiorino-Iannace, Senior Manager, Eva H. DeAngelis-Glasser, Toma Fichter, Isabel Kim, Eva L. Labson, and Kieran D. McCulloch, Antonio Ratti Textile Center; Florica Zaharia, Conservator in Charge, Rebecca Beyth, Julia Carlson, Cristina Carr, Giulia Chiostrini, Emilia Cortes, Min Sun Hwang, Kristine Kamiya, Sarah Pickman, Janina Poskrobko, Yael Rosenfield, Wendy Wood, and Olha Yarema-Wynar, Textile Conservation; Nancy Britton and Pascale Patris, Objects Conservation; Marco Leona, David H. Koch Scientist in Charge, Federico Carò, Federica Pozzi, and Nobuko Shibayama, Scientific Research; Robyn Fleming, Watson Library; Joseph Loh, Jennifer Mock, and Jacqueline Terrassa, Education Department; Morrison H. Heckscher, Lawrence A. Fleischman Chairman, Elaine Bradson, Sean Farrell, Dennis Kaiser, Chad Lemke, Kelly Mulrow, Mary Beth Orr, and Leela Outcalt, The American Wing; Donald J. La Rocca and Morihiro Ogawa,

Arms and Armor; Christine Guintini and Julie Jones, Arts of Africa, Oceania, and the Americas; Maxwell K. Hearn, Douglas Dillon Chairman, Imtikar Ally, Laurie Carrier, Alison Clark, Jennifer Cuminale, Denise Patry Leidy, Shi-yee Liu, Luis Nuñez, Beatrice Pinto, Sunny Wang, and Hwai-ling Yeh-Lewis, Asian Art; Harold Koda, Curator in Charge, Andrew Bolton, Elizabeth Bryan, Joyce Fung, Marci Morimoto, and Sarah Scaturro, The Costume Institute; George R. Goldner, Drue Heinz Chairman, Stijn Alsteens, and Femke Speelberg, Drawings and Prints; Keith Christiansen, John Pope-Hennessy Chairman, Katharine Baetjer, and Andrea Bayer, European Paintings; Luke Syson, Iris and B. Gerald Cantor Curator in Charge, Elizabeth Cleland, Jacob Goble, Daniëlle Kisluk-Grosheide, Jeffrey Munger, Juan Stacey, and Denny Stone, European Sculpture and Decorative Arts; and Sheila Canby, Patti Cadby Birch Curator in Charge, Walter Denny, and Navina Najat Haidar, Islamic Art.

Many of the authors were ably assisted in their research here at the Museum by graduate-student interns and Museum fellows. Our gratitude goes to Lauren Arnold, Luke Baker, Nynne Christoffersen, Billy DeGregorio, Ruthie Dibble, Sylvia Houghteling, Jennifer Johnson, Michelle Labrague, Erin Leary, Pengliang Lu, Haneen Rabie, Mei Mei Rado, and Katy Werlin.

This project could not have been conceived and created without the help and support of our colleagues at museums all around the world, who so kindly lent objects, information, and enthusiasm to the endeavor. Many thanks to Anna Jolly, Abegg-Stiftung, Riggisberg; Kristen Mable and Jan Riley, American Museum of Natural History, New York; Daniel Walker, Erika Morris, and Jonathan Taveras, Art Institute of Chicago; Natalie Dubois, Arthur van Mourik, Ninke Bloemberg, and Martine Kilburn, Centraal Museum, Utrecht; Feng Zhao, China National Silk Museum, Hangzhou; Louise Mackie, Robin Hanson, and Gretchen Shie Miller, Cleveland Museum of Art; Linda Baumgarten, Colonial Williamsburg; Kirsten Toftegaard, Designmuseum Danmark, Copenhagen; Chris de Bruyn, Dordrechts Museum / Huis van Gijn, Dordrecht; Rosemary Harden, Fashion Museum, Bath; Madelief Hohé, Gemeentemuseum Den Haag, The Hague; Deborah Emmons-Andarawis and Mary E. Doehla, Historic Cherry Hill, Albany; Tess Fredette, Amanda Ricker, Oliver Tostmann, and Amanda Venezia, Isabella Stewart Gardner Museum, Boston; Susan Braunstein and Stacey Traunfeld, The Jewish Museum, New York; Aki Yamakawa, Kyoto National Museum; Sharon S. Takeda, Ilona Katsew, Kaye Spilker, and Amy Wright, Los Angeles County Museum of Art; Barbara Karl, MAK (Museum für angewandte Kunst), Vienna; Teresa Morna, Museu de São Roque, Lisbon; Elisabete Rodrigues, Museu do Caramulo; Coronel Albuquerque, Museu Militar de Lisboa, Lisbon; José António Martins, Museu Municipal Dr. José Formosinho, Lagos; Teresa Pacheco Pereira, Museu Nacional de Arte Antiga, Lisbon; Pedro Ferrão, Museu Nacional de Machado de Castro, Coimbra; Pamela Parmal, Meredith Montague, Kim Pashko, Dennis Carr, Lauren Whitley, and Diana Zlatanovski, Museum of Fine Arts, Boston; Pip Dodd, National Army Museum, Chelsea; Peter Larocque and Bruce Thomson, New Brunswick Museum, Saint John; Isabel Stauffer and Deborah M. Straussman, New York Public Library; Karina Corrigan, Sarah Chasse, Karen Kramer Russell, Elisabeth Mansi, and Paula Richter, Peabody Essex Museum, Salem; Dilys E. Blum, Laura Camerlengo, and H. Kristina Haugland, Philadelphia Museum of Art; Menno Fitski and Elsie Janssen, Rijksmuseum, Amsterdam; Sarah Fee and Barbara Rice, Royal Ontario Museum, Toronto; Karen Zelanka Baker, Katherine Luber, and Marion Oettinger, Jr., San Antonio Museum of Art; Sumru Belger Krody, The Textile Museum, Washington, D.C.; Clare Browne and Rosemary Crill,

Victoria and Albert Museum, London; Linda S. Eaton, Joy Gardiner, Katie Orr, and Jeanne
Solensky, Winterthur Museum, Garden, and Library, Delaware; Timothy Goodhue, Cassandra
Albinson, Abigail Armistead, and Amy Meyers, Yale Center for British Art, New Haven.

One of the many compelling motivations to pursue this project was the desire to bring together
in one volume information about the cross-cultural nature of trade textiles. Parts of this story have
been told by many wonderful scholars. We are grateful for the generosity and knowledge of our
academic colleagues, including Michele Majer, Bard Graduate Center, New York; Jessica Hallett,
Carla Alferes Pinto, and Nuno Senos, Centro de História de Além-Mar, Universidade Nova de Lisboa,
Lisbon; Miyeko Murase, Columbia University, New York; Daniel Baugh, Cornell University,
Ithaca; Sophie Desrosiers, École des Hautes Études en Sciences Sociales, Paris; Masako Watanabe,
Gakushūin University, Tokyo; Thomas Yuho Kirchner, Hanazono University, Kyoto; Iwao Nagasaki,
Kyōritsu Women's University, Tokyo; Masako Yoshida, Kyoto City University of Arts; Larry Wolff,
New York University; Paul A. Van Dyke, Sun Yat-sen University, Guangzhou; Yuko Fukatsu, Tama
Art University, Tokyo; Luisa Elena Alcalá, Universidad Complutense de Madrid; Kate Smith, University
College, London; Birgitt Borkopp, University of Bern; Gregory P. A. Levine, University of California,
Berkeley; Sanjay Subramanian and Kevin Terraciano, University of California, Los Angeles;
Sir Christopher Bayly, University of Cambridge; John Styles, University of Hertfordshire, Hatfield;
Teresa Leonor Vale, University of Lisbon; Shigeo Fujiwara, University of Tokyo; and Giorgio Riello,
University of Warwick, Coventry.

Finally, we thank the independent scholars and collectors who gave advice and support and
the private lenders to the project who trusted us with their precious works of art: Sjoujke
Colenbrander, Amsterdam; William Dalrymple, New Delhi; Francesca Galloway, London; Kobori
Geppō, Ryōkō-in, Daitokuji, Kyoto; Mr. Gobalakichenane, Paris; Titi Halle, New York; Ebeltje
Hartkamp-Jonxis, Amsterdam; Florence and Herbert Irving, New York; Alan Kennedy, Westport,
New York; Peter Lee, Singapore; Vivian Mann, New York; Julia Meech, New York; Lisa Monnas,
London; Linda Pomper, New York; Midori Sato, New York; Milton Sonday, Brooklyn; Karun Thakar,
London; Lori van Houten, New York; Janny Venema, Albany; James C. Y. Watt, New York; John C.
Weber, New York; Junnaa and Thomi Wroblewski, London; and Luís Eduardo Wuffarden, Lima.

THE AUTHORS

Lenders to the Exhibition

American Museum of Natural History, New York
The Art Institute of Chicago
Centraal Museum, Utrecht
Cleveland Museum of Art
Cora Ginsburg LLC, New York
Historic Cherry Hill, Albany, New York
Isabella Stewart Gardner Museum, Boston
The Jewish Museum, New York
Alan Kennedy, Westport, New York, and Junnaa and Thomi Wroblewski, London
Los Angeles County Museum of Art
Museum of Fine Arts, Boston
New Brunswick Museum, Saint John, Canada
The New York Public Library
Philadelphia Museum of Art
Royal Ontario Museum, Toronto
San Antonio Museum of Art
Karun Thakar, London
John C. Weber, New York
Winterthur Museum, Garden, and Library, Delaware
Yale Center for British Art, New Haven, Connecticut

Contributors to the Catalogue

AB   Amy Bogansky, Research Assistant, Department of American Decorative Arts,
      The American Wing, The Metropolitan Museum of Art, New York
JD   Joyce Denney, Assistant Curator (retired), Department of Asian Art, The Metropolitan
      Museum of Art, New York
JG   John Guy, Florence and Herbert Irving Curator of the Arts of South and Southeast Asia,
      Department of Asian Art, The Metropolitan Museum of Art, New York
AL   Alisa LaGamma, Curator in Charge, Department of the Arts of Africa, Oceania, and
      the Americas, The Metropolitan Museum of Art, New York
AP   Amelia Peck, Marica F. Vilcek Curator of American Decorative Arts, The American Wing,
      The Metropolitan Museum of Art, New York
EP   Elena Phipps, Senior Research Scholar, The Metropolitan Museum of Art, New York
MS   Marika Sardar, Senior Research Associate, Department of Islamic Art, The Metropolitan
      Museum of Art, New York
KS   Kristen Stewart, Curatorial Assistant, The Caroline and H. McCoy Jones Department of
      Textile Arts, Fine Arts Museums of San Francisco, de Young Museum
MW   Melinda Watt, Associate Curator, Department of European Sculpture and Decorative Arts,
      and Supervising Curator, Antonio Ratti Textile Center, The Metropolitan Museum of Art,
      New York

Interwoven Globe

Trade Textiles at
the Metropolitan Museum

A HISTORY

Amelia Peck

Before the early modern period under investigation in *Interwoven Globe: The Worldwide Textile Trade, 1500–1800*, textiles had been traded between Asia, the Middle East, Africa, and Europe for hundreds of years, along lengthy routes that were traversed primarily over land until the mid-fifteenth century, when the fragmentation of the Mongol Empire signaled the end of the vast Silk Road. When in 1453 the Ottoman Turks captured Constantinople (present-day Istanbul) from the Byzantine Empire, an additional barrier was imposed for European trade with Asia. Until this time, Asian goods (particularly spices), after traveling great distances by land, had been shipped by Arab traders across the Indian Ocean and the Red Sea to the Levant, where European traders purchased the products and brought them first to the ports of the Mediterranean (chiefly Venice, where much of the spice trade was controlled between 1200 and 1500) and then to the rest of Europe. In the face of this disruption in trade, at the end of the fifteenth century the Europeans set sail in search of an ocean route to the Spice Islands of Southeast Asia and found exotic textiles to trade along the way. The newly discovered sea routes that directly connected Europe to the rest of the world enabled the creation of the first truly global trading community, and as the Europeans found that textiles were welcome currency for other goods (including human cargo in appalling numbers), the scope of the textile trade expanded significantly.

These textiles, whether luxurious silks or simple cottons, served purposes beyond such purely practical functions as clothing a person or covering a bed. In addition to their economic impact, textiles functioned as the primary category of object that engendered widespread ideas of what was desirable and fashionable in dress and household decoration. They served as status symbols for their owners, advertising the wearer's sophistication and knowledge of the wider world. New textile fabricating techniques and both woven and printed designs, many previously unknown to cultures in either the East or the West, were imitated, stimulating markets and production. This publication and the exhibition that accompanies it make the case that more than any other type of object, highly sought-after trade textiles, accessible to many in all economic levels, influenced the visual culture of the locations where they were marketed as well as produced. Because the scope of the textile trade was so widespread by the mid-seventeenth century, the constant interchange of exotic design motifs, fibers, and dyes between these now interconnected markets brought into being, for the first time, a common visual language of design that was recognizable throughout the world.

Trade textiles, which by definition traveled between cultures, often reveal a conglomerate of design and technical features from several different lands. Indeed, while working on this project, we (the curatorial team) found that some trade textiles display design characteristics and production techniques that are so complicated that even after months or years of study, the origins and dates of certain objects could not yet be firmly assigned. In fact, this exploration would not even have been conceived without the puzzling attribution of one particular type of textile: eighteenth-century blue-resist-dyed cotton fabrics that for the last century have defied the experts as to where they were made.[1] Their story is worth recounting. This type of cloth, patterned with commonplace European-style floral and bird motifs—but dyed in a method first perfected in India and East Asia—is almost always found in America and had even been thought to have been the earliest type of American-made printed fabric. By the mid-twentieth century these textiles were assigned to English producers on the basis of a single piece with an English export mark in an American museum. None, however, had ever been found in England.[2]

This type of textile came to intrigue me in 2005, when the Metropolitan Museum held the exhibition "Matisse: The Fabric of Dreams—His Art and Textiles." Several of Matisse's paintings in the exhibition had in the background a piece of blue-resist fabric in a familiar pattern that was well known in American collections, including the Metropolitan's (figs. 1, 2). Matisse had apparently bought his fabric in a junk shop in Paris in 1903. The curators of the exhibition asked for my help in describing the fabric in the display labels for the paintings, and discussions about its origins ensued. This was the first time that a piece of this particular type of blue-resist fabric had been located in France.[3] Like other American textile scholars before me,[4] I began to search the world for examples of textiles with similar traits. First came the resist-dyed batiks of Indonesia, which were predominantly made beginning in the nineteenth century and had very different overall patterns. Turning to India, where the resist-dyeing technique had been used for hundreds of years, there was no evidence of anything like the European-type patterns of the "American" textiles on the cotton fabrics designed for the Indians themselves. But in reading more, it became increasingly clear to me that there were huge numbers of textiles that were produced by Indian artisans for export to other parts of the world. Looking next at the European countries that were most actively trading with India in the eighteenth century, I found (in a book on Indian chintz in the Rijksmuseum, Amsterdam)[5] the first piece of Indian resist-dyed and painted textile that looked close to the American examples, brought to Holland by the Verenigde Oost-Indische Compagnie (Dutch East India Company, also referred to as the VOC), the powerful mercantile company that controlled a huge portion of the trade with India and East Asia in the seventeenth and eighteenth centuries (fig. 3). I wanted to know more about the relationship between these textiles, India, Europe, and America; the world beckoned to me, a lifelong Americanist, much as it had to the explorers who set sail in the fifteenth century. The cultural and artistic connections that I believed could be made through following the roots (and the routes) of textiles during the early modern era proved irresistible, and the idea for the exhibition "Interwoven Globe: The Worldwide Textile Trade, 1500–1800," was born.

The story of the worldwide textile trade is a complicated, multistrand narrative. Apart from the intermingling of design traditions from different countries and cultures found in these objects, many of which appear on the surface simply to be objects of great beauty and craftsmanship, some tell a story that is not always benign. In fact, the imagery on some of them speaks quite literally of the conflicts of conquest that came with the European quest for control of land and markets. Notable examples include the seventeenth-century Indian embroidered hanging for the Portuguese market (cat. 104) that shows a battle scene with masses of armies under different flags fighting each other, including images of carnage in the center of the field, or the more triumphal eighteenth-century Indian painted hanging celebrating the win of the British over the French for control of Pondicherry, a major trading post in India (cat. 105). Others were clearly meant as propaganda, like the Indian hanging embroidered with a monumental arch, erected in 1619, commemorating the entry into Lisbon of Philip III of Spain, who also ruled Portugal as Philip II (cat. 8), or the small piece of cotton (cat. 107A) printed with images of Native Americans carrying a woman—the personification of Spain—on a litter that bears the words "Triumfa España en Las Americas" (Triumph of Spain in the Americas). Some proselytize more quietly, such as the rich and glorious fabrics made in China to be used in vestments for the Catholic Church. Still others tell a subtler story, which can only be understood by following the fabric's path around the world to its ultimate purpose, such as the cloths found in the sample book of striped and checked textiles woven in Manchester, England, meant to clothe slaves in the West Indies (cat. 108).

Collecting objects that illustrate this complex story can be a challenge, especially for an art museum like the Metropolitan. Their "in-between" quality—straddling not only cultures but also the line between artifact and art—can make trade textiles a hard fit within the traditional cultural and geographical department structure at the Museum, an institution that preferences works of beauty over those that are primarily of historical interest. In the American Wing, for example, the collection prioritizes objects created by North American makers that illustrate clear American design characteristics over objects made in China or India for export to the United States. Yet trade textiles have traditionally found a home in the American Wing's period rooms, which are furnished to reflect American taste in home decoration: the Meetinghouse Gallery, first opened to the public in 1924,[6] displays the earliest American decorative arts in the Museum's collection, which date primarily from the mid-seventeenth to the early eighteenth century. Due to persuasive evidence discovered in the early twentieth century that East Indian textiles were used in the homes of the first settlers (a subject that is expanded upon in an essay in this publication), the curators at that time decided to hang three lovely Indian palampores against the walls of the brightly sunlit gallery (fig. 4).[7]

Working at the Metropolitan Museum, with its long and illustrious history of scholarship and collecting, today's curators recognize that they are metaphorically standing on the shoulders of those who preceded them. The Metropolitan has mounted many groundbreaking exhibitions in the field of textiles. Most have dealt with a particular type of textile, such as lace or tapestries, or textiles from a certain part of the world, such as China or Peru.[8] Surprisingly few have investigated textiles from a global perspective. Yet there were two important exhibitions shown at the Metropolitan Museum during the first half of the twentieth century, "Painted and Printed Fabrics" in 1927 and "The China Trade and Its Influences" in 1941, that investigated aspects of the textile-trade story. With these two exhibitions, the Museum's collection of textiles that were either trade goods or that illustrated the visual annexation and interpretation of the designs of Eastern cultures by the West garnered attention, encouraging the expansion of the collection in new directions. "Interwoven Globe" includes textiles shown in both of these exhibitions or collected afterward, perhaps because of their influence.

"Painted and Printed Fabrics" was the brainchild of the Metropolitan's extraordinary first curator of textiles, Frances Morris (1866–1955). Morris was initially associated with the Museum in 1896,

Fig. 3
Wentke. Constructed in the Netherlands. Textile: India (Coromandel Coast), ca. 1750–75. Cotton, resist painted and printed, dyed. Rijksmuseum, Amsterdam (BK-NM-4515)

Opposite:
Fig. 1
Henri Matisse (French, 1869–1954). *Pansies.* Oil on paper mounted on wood, ca. 1903. The Metropolitan Museum of Art, New York, Bequest of Joan Whitney Payson, 1975 (1976.201.22)

Fig. 2
Panel (detail). Probably India, ca. 1750. Cotton, resist painted and printed, dyed. The Metropolitan Museum of Art, New York, Gift of Mrs. Lawrence W. Scudder, 1952 (52.112.1a, b)

when she worked part-time assisting with the cataloguing of a collection of musical instruments given by Mrs. John Crosby Brown in 1889. In 1905 she was also asked to organize the cataloguing of the lace collection, the first textile collection of importance gathered by the Museum. Promoted to assistant curator in 1910, Morris was put in charge of the new Textile Study Room, a place where designers and students could go to study and be inspired by almost nine thousand textiles that had been collected; having art readily available for designers to study was in accordance with the Museum's original educational mission (fig. 5).[9] She was also responsible for the textile displays in three adjoining galleries. From 1910 until she left the museum in 1929, Morris oversaw the Museum's collections of textiles and musical instruments, both of which were part of the Department of Decorative Arts.[10] In a 1923 article about the Textile Study Room, Morris noted, "It is not so many years back that the American designer of textile fabrics who could not afford a trip abroad was obliged to content himself, in his search for inspiration, with publications such as Owen Jones' *Grammar of Ornament* . . . but today every advantage accorded to students in foreign museums is available in New York."[11] The same article states that by 1923 the Museum's textile collection contained "some 12,000 specimens." Apparently still not satisfied with the holdings, Morris was inspired to collect eighteenth-century printed textiles following the 1924 opening of the American Wing: "The widespread interest in the American Wing . . . is reflected on every side in the increasing demand not only for American furniture, but as well for the accessories that played so important a part in creating an effective setting for the maple and mahogany of our ancestors. This is especially true of the materials used in America's eighteenth-century houses, and today the American textile industry and the schools of design are turning to the Museum collection for inspiration . . . there is daily an increasing number of calls for 'Georgian' and 'flowered' patterns. Of these, the Museum has but a very limited supply."[12]

In a 1926 letter to Museum trustee William Sloane Coffin, Morris wrote, "When in Paris two years ago eighteenth-century printed cottons were still available at reasonable prices. Realizing the value of such material to the American Art student . . . I decided to duplicate, as far as possible, the finest pieces in the collections of the Musée des Arts Décoratifs and in the Bibliothèque Forney at my own expense, hoping that our Museum would sometime realize the importance of such documents."[13] A deal was made between the Museum administration and Coffin that he would contribute two thousand dollars both to reimburse Morris's expenses and to help purchase more printed textiles, some English, all 145 of which were given to the Metropolitan in December 1926 as the "Gift of William Sloane Coffin."

Morris used these printed textiles as the basis of her 1927 exhibition.[14] But realizing that the Museum's new collection of French and English printed textiles told only part of the story, she borrowed textiles from museums and collections around the United States and England; when the show opened on May 16, there were representative examples from most European countries, including Russia, as well as pieces from Armenia, India, Java, and Peru. She was aware that "what is particularly valuable in an exhibition of this scope is the opportunity it affords for studying the interrelation of the Oriental model and its European interpretation."[15] Although the exhibition was heavily weighted in favor of eighteenth-century French toiles, the textiles that received much of the public's attention were the painted Indian fabrics from the collections of textile producers G. P. Baker (at the time the world's leading expert on the subject) and Harry Wearne.[16] It was certainly Morris's intention to show the influence of Indian trade textiles on European design: "The gallery has been arranged with Indian fabrics hung on the end walls; on the south wall a small interior shows the eighteenth-century method of applying these decorative fabrics to household furnishings. The Italian *mezzari* are used as panels and bed hangings, while several *indiennes* from the collection presented by Mr. Coffin show the French interpretation of Indian patterns."[17] Morris also wrote an article in the July 1927 volume of the Museum's *Bulletin* discussing "Chinoiserie in Printed Fabrics" and tracing the sources of the European fascination with Chinese-inspired textile designs.[18] Accompanying the exhibition were a small, unillustrated checklist compiled by Morris and a Museum publication of Morris's English translation from the French of Henri Clouzot's history of the Jouy manufactory and other French textile printing workshops, funded by trustee Coffin. This volume also included "Notes on the History of Cotton Printing, especially in England and America, by Frances Morris" and black-and-white photographs of many of the objects in the show.[19]

"The China Trade and Its Influences" of 1941 was conceived by Joseph Downs (1895–1954), who was then curator of the American Wing; he had arrived at the Museum in 1932 as assistant curator. In his previous scholarly work, Downs was primarily concerned with eighteenth-century American furniture, so this exhibition might have seemed quite a leap for him. However, his years of study of Queen Anne and Chippendale furniture, both of which were influenced by Chinese precursors, undoubtedly gave rise to an interest in the transmission of Asian design to Europe and America.[20]

Although "The China Trade" began its exploration with the same time period (the mid-sixteenth century) as "Interwoven Globe," it included materials dating well into the nineteenth century. Photographs of the exhibition, with whimsical fabric-hung ceilings and pagoda-topped doorframes, reveal the flavor of the show. Downs's description of the exhibition's appearance, of which he was almost certainly the designer, is informative: "To provide an appropriate setting for this immense variety of colorful objects, the three rooms of Gallery D6 have been transformed into oriental interiors as a chinoiserie designer of the eighteenth century—Chambers, Thomas Chippendale, or the brothers Halfpenny—might have visualized them. The west room has a pagoda-shaped ceiling of sheer blue in the pale tint of clair-de-lune porcelain, through which the light shines on the walls of melon pink—a color often found in Eastern silks. The oval middle room has a yellow pagoda ceiling—yellow was once sacred to the Imperial Court—and, like the famous chinoiserie rooms of Claydon House in Buckinghamshire, celadon green walls. The third room has a pale coral red ceiling and yellow walls. In each room the doorways are framed by latticed pilasters and pagoda shaped hoods."[21]

Clearly the design of the exhibition was meant to reinforce the idea of the visual fantasies that informed the European (and American) understanding of "The East," a main theme of the exhibition.

To this end, most of the textiles Downs presented were chinoiseries—European textiles romantically decorated with what were perceived of as scenes of everyday Chinese life, including some from the Morris-Coffin collection (fig. 6). Downs included two mid-sixteenth-century pieces of silk woven in China by Chinese craftsmen for the Portuguese trade (as we have in "Interwoven Globe"; see cats. 15, 16). But mostly he displayed objects made in Europe in the "Chinese Taste." As might be expected, there are some objects that overlap this earlier exhibition and "Interwoven Globe." Because the Metropolitan had not yet acquired its Vanderbank tapestries (cat. 85), Downs borrowed two from Yale University (fig. 7). Judge Irwin Untermyer's French needlepoint curtain (then on loan, later a gift to the collection) figures prominently on the right in figure 8 (cat. 84). There were ninety lenders to "The China Trade and Its Influences." At that time, the Museum's collection could not support a show on the theme of East–West trade; today, more than 80 percent of the objects in "Interwoven Globe" are from the Metropolitan's own collection. Surprisingly, for a show on the China trade, Downs requested the use of several Indian palampores (acc. nos. 17.89, 28.78.1 and .2), a figural *kalamkari* (20.79), and a rumal (28.159.1), as well as the Armenian cope made of Safavid velvet (cat. 64) from what was then called the Department of Near Eastern Art. These objects did not end up being included in the show.[22] Do these requests for Indian and Iranian textiles mean that at one point Downs was planning an exhibition meant to encompass the subject of trade beyond China to Europe and America? In the end, only a single Indian palampore (30.96.2) was used as the backdrop for an American japanned high chest (fig. 8), still very much in keeping with the 1924 installation of the Meetinghouse Gallery.[23]

When compiling a list of objects for inclusion in "Interwoven Globe," many pieces from the 1926 Morris collection/Coffin Gift were examined, as were others that were exhibited in both "Painted and Printed Fabrics" and "The China Trade and Its Influences." There are textiles on display in "Interwoven Globe" that were loans to one or the other exhibition that were later given as gifts.[24] Was there a specific collecting policy in place at the Museum to systematically gather trade textiles during the era of these exhibitions? In the early twentieth century textiles were purchased for the Metropolitan's collection in far greater numbers than they are today (owing to availability, price, interest, and the Museum's goal to build its collection), yet it is hard to discern a specific collection goal toward increasing the representation of trade textiles. Objects were probably collected in a manner such as that described in correspondence between Morris and her boss, Joseph Breck, the head of the Decorative Arts Department. When Morris was in France researching and collecting the printed fabrics that would eventually form the majority of the William Sloane Coffin Gift as well as her 1927 exhibition, she was also shopping for whatever else interested her along the way. Writing to Breck in 1924 to describe her findings, Morris gives us a glimpse of the Museum's collecting style at the time: "Marian Hague writes me that you have purchased some of the Indian textiles for which I am duly thankful and we ought to have them. I'm also thrilled over the Persian piece. . . . When you reach Paris please see the waistcoat at Mme. Marie's—I decided I couldn't tie up the necessary amount to purchase it—but I've since spent quite as much on a bunch of fine Persian

Fig. 6
Chinoiserie-printed cottons exhibited in "The China Trade and Its Influences." The Metropolitan Museum of Art, New York, 1941

pieces that I have found in a shop here." [25] Sometimes Breck seemed to put the brakes on Morris's collecting of non-European textiles, as when he wrote, "I am afraid I cannot make any recommendation regarding this embroidery until I know more about it. The photograph shows many unusual features—particularly in the costumes. The general character of the work suggests the Near East. But where and when? As the chief interest of the fragment seems to be archaeological, rather than artistic, we must be quite clear about those matters before taking any action." [26]

Investigating the provenances of a few of the trade textiles in "Interwoven Globe" does point out certain patterns. Purchases outweigh gifts by about 2:1, and monies from the Rogers Fund, a Museum purchase fund set up in 1904 with five million dollars from the bequest of Jacob S. Rogers, an American

Fig. 7
Vanderbank tapestry exhibited in "The China Trade and Its Influences." The Metropolitan Museum of Art, New York, 1941

Fig. 8
Palampore and needlework curtain exhibited in "The China Trade and Its Influences." The Metropolitan Museum of Art, New York, 1941

locomotive magnate, were used to acquire the majority of the textiles.[27] Some of the trade textiles that came into the Museum as both purchases and gifts were clearly hard for the curators to fit into the art historical canon typically told in the galleries, which usually offer a linear progression of the design aesthetic of a particular world culture. Many were rarely (or never) displayed, although some have been in the Museum's collection for decades. The European Sculpture and Decorative Arts Department, for instance, owns three very large-scale (each about twelve by sixteen feet) seventeenth-century Chinese embroidered hangings for the Portuguese market that illustrate scenes from the series the Story of Troy (cat. 14). All three came into the collection as gifts and had been owned by financier and philanthropist Henry G. Marquand, president of the Museum from 1889 to 1902, until they were auctioned off in 1903 after his death. The first, *The Prophecy of Calchas* (50.97.2), arrived in 1950 as the bequest of Eleanor Cross Marquand, in memory of her husband, Allan Marquand, Henry's son. The second, *The Sacrifice of Polyxena* (51.152), was the bequest of Roderick Terry Jr. in 1951. The final hanging, *The Abduction of Helen* (cat. 14), was the gift of Louis E. Seley in 1979. Only two (51.152 and cat. 14) of these three extraordinary hangings have ever been seen by the public, when they were displayed for about a year in 1984–85.[28]

In other instances, related objects of the same origin sometimes found themselves in different departments, among them the early seventeenth-century Indian natural gold tussah silk embroideries for the Portuguese market; the cape (cat. 7) is owned by the Department of Islamic Art, while the embroidered coverlet (cat. 6) in the same technique was acquired by the Department of European Sculpture and Decorative Arts. Some textiles traveled between departments, as did the Chinese embroidered hanging modeled after an Indian palampore, which was initially gifted to the American Wing in 1947 but was later claimed by the Department of Asian Art (cat. 120). Even today, Indian painted cottons are collected by three different departments (Asian Art, Islamic Art, and European Sculpture and Decorative Arts), depending upon their intended market.

Textiles of all types entered the Museum's collection from 1910 to the 1980s, first under the auspices of Morris and then supervised by other dedicated curators. The Textile Study Room was never its own curatorial department and remained part of the Decorative Arts Department, today the Department of European Sculpture and Decorative Arts.[29] As time passed, textiles were no longer overseen by a single textile curator as in Morris's day, although there was always a Study Room curator to help visiting textile scholars or designers. By the 1980s the collection had long since outgrown the original Textile Study Room and the three galleries installed in 1910. Sometime after the 1950s a gradual process of decentralization took place, as various curatorial departments withdrew their textile collections and sought to store them separately, so that they would be more accessible to the departmental curators. The conditions within these storage facilities varied widely. Textiles other than tapestries have traditionally been undervalued as works of art, overlooked sometimes because they fall into the domestic sphere, their makers often anonymous and frequently female. Not every relevant department at the Museum has always had a curator with expertise in collecting and caring for textiles, so the growth of the textile collections in some departments has been more haphazard than in others. In 1989 planning began on a new centralized textile storage and study facility to replace the Textile Study Room. In a 1995 Museum *Bulletin* published in celebration of the new Antonio Ratti Textile Center, Director Philippe de Montebello explained the perceived benefits of textiles acquired and cared for by individual departments: "The primary advantage to maintaining varied curatorial responsibility rather than segregating textiles in a separate department—using the medium as the governing principle—is that the textiles have been selected and studied, and their significance understood, in the full context of knowledge of all the arts of the civilizations from which they came. Thus, for example, Asian garments have been acquired and displayed in the context of other Asian art forms, and European carpets, in the context of the finest European furniture and furnishings of the appropriate periods."[30] While it is true that many textiles benefit from being viewed within their own cultural context, this ideal neglects to take into consideration the textiles, like those in "Interwoven Globe," that do not fit comfortably into the narrow precepts described above and can be properly understood only when studied with textiles from other lands. A second issue made clear in 1995 was that not every department had been equally interested in the care of its textile collection. Both of these issues were acknowledged, at least in part: "Nonetheless, a disadvantage of department-by-department collecting is that the textiles have been cared for and housed in widely dispersed facilities, with very different methods of access and storage. Anyone wishing to compare examples from several departments in the course of a single inquiry will encounter considerable difficulty, and it has compromised the availability of the textiles to visiting scholars, colleagues, and members of the general public."[31]

A team of conservators, curators, and administrators worked for several years to see the Ratti Center come to fruition. Notable among the team were Nobuko Kajitani and Elena Phipps in the Textile Conservation Department and curators Barbara Boehm and Tom Campbell. The effort was led by Philippe de Montebello, with associate directors Penny Bardel and Jennifer Russell. Today the facilities remain state of the art, run with great competence by Supervising Curator Melinda Watt, Senior Manager Giovanna Fiorino-Iannace, and Assistant Manager Eva Labson. The Museum's textiles are immaculately stored there; owing to its three large viewing rooms and a wonderful staff of textile handlers, both the public and the staff have easy access to the actual works.

Another aspect of the new Ratti Center that made it so useful when it opened in 1995 was its fully computerized catalogue of all the textiles stored in the facility—one of the first areas in the Museum to have such a system.[32] Digital catalogues are today commonplace in most museums but were groundbreaking twenty years ago. Researchers could now search for textiles between departments, by country of origin, culture, time period, materials, techniques, and so on, with the ability to see large images, many in color, of almost every object. When our investigation into trade textiles began, these capabilities greatly facilitated our planning in the early stages of the project. It was incredibly helpful to be able to electronically sort through the collection of almost forty thousand textiles, country by country, looking for those that were clearly meant to be sold in foreign markets.

The attention focused on the Ratti Center project brought about a renewed interest in and understanding of textiles at the Metropolitan. With this new awareness of the importance of our textile collection by the Museum's administration came new staff members, hired because of their expertise in textiles. Having a supportive and congenial group of textile experts on staff was an integral factor that led to this exhibition. The curatorial team for "Interwoven Globe," who worked together cohesively for almost four years, included Melinda Watt of the Department of European Sculpture and Decorative Arts, a highly knowledgeable curator of European furnishing textiles; the Asian Art Department's John Guy, an expert in Indian printed cottons (among many other things); and, until her recent retirement, Joyce Denney, a specialist in Japanese and Chinese textiles. I have been overseeing the American Wing's textile collection since 1984, in the last ten years with the invaluable assistance of Cynthia V. A. Schaffner. The project team also benefited immensely from the inclusion of several younger scholars: Marika Sardar of the Department of Islamic Art, Kristen Stewart of the Costume Institute, and Amy Bogansky of the American Wing. In addition to this in-house group of "textilians," we were lucky to enlist the expertise of retired Metropolitan Museum Senior Textile Conservator Elena Phipps, whose work on the tapestries of the colonial Andes is renowned, and rising Portuguese textile scholar Maria João Pacheco Ferreira. All of our work was supported by Florica Zaharia, Conservator in Charge of the Textile Conservation Department, and her highly professional team.

The final circumstance that made this exhibit possible was the appointment of Tom Campbell, once the tapestry curator in the Department of European Sculpture and Decorative Arts, as Director of the Metropolitan Museum, succeeding Philippe de Montebello in 2009. A textile curator for fourteen years and the first Supervising Curator of the Ratti Center, Tom immediately understood the appeal of these diverse and influential textiles when "Interwoven Globe" was first proposed to him. In addition, the exhibition fits into his vision of the Museum as an integrated whole, with objects and scholarship shared among all departments and staff members. We are grateful for his support and hope that "Interwoven Globe" will be just the first of many twenty-first-century exhibitions—and publications—that will look across cultures to explain the global nature of art to the Metropolitan's visitors. We feel assured that the pivotal role that textiles have played around the world and throughout time will continue to be studied and that these beautiful and complex objects will be collected, cared for, and exhibited in the tradition begun more than a century ago by the Museum's first textile curator, Frances Morris.

"One Thing Leads to Another"

INDIAN TEXTILES AND THE EARLY
GLOBALIZATION OF STYLE

John Guy

he trading world of the Indian Ocean around the year 1500 was on the cusp of a revolution that would reverberate to the present day. The Asian exchange system overwhelmingly employed Indian textiles to barter for the spices from the eastern Indonesian islands of the Maluku (Moluccas), ensuring a steady supply of these prized condiments to the markets of India, West Asia, China, and Europe. Increasingly, European powers sought to capture some of this lucrative trade for themselves. The conversation that ensued over the next three centuries between diverse cultures spanning from England to Japan produced a new phenomenon: the globalization of style in textile design.

CLOTH FOR SPICE:
THE DYNAMICS OF MEDIEVAL ASIAN TRADE

That Indian cloth was the key to this trade is documented not only by textile finds from Southeast Asia and West Asia but also by archives of commercial correspondence relating to the Mediterranean–India spice trade from as early as the mid-eleventh century, preserved in the Geniza records of the Fustat (Old Cairo) synagogue.[1] These Judeo-Arabic texts (Arabic in Hebrew script), written by the scribes of Jewish merchants, demonstrate conclusively that "the India trade was the backbone of medieval international economy."[2] The Fustat records indicate that Fatimid Cairo served as the terminus both for the Mediterranean and the western India trade in this period. Typical of this exchange were the commercial dealings of Joseph Lebdi, a merchant from Tripoli, Libya, whose activities were preserved in court records of 1097–98: departing Egypt via Yemen to trade in India on his own account and on behalf of others who entrusted their goods to him, all was lost at sea and a claim was made against his estate.[3] Trade lists compiled from the Geniza records show that this commerce was largely a transit trade in which Indian Ocean goods—most notably spices, aromatics, dyes, Indian silk and cotton textiles, iron and brass goods, pearls and cowries, Chinese porcelain, Yemeni ceramics, African ivory and hardwood timbers—were distributed to the eastern Mediterranean. In return India demanded payment in gold or silver and sometimes processed metals, especially copper to service her famed bronze industry.[4] Among the few witnesses to this trade are the Indian textiles that have survived in Egypt and the Red Sea ports (cats. 2, 3). Two centuries later the Moroccan traveler Ibn Battuta (1304–1368/69) would provide one of the few firsthand accounts of this exchange from the Arab perspective.[5]

In 1498 Vasco da Gama's Portuguese fleet arrived on the Calicut coast of southern India, the first successful European conquest of the long sea passage following the loss of reliable overland caravans in the wake of Constantinople's fall to the Ottomans in 1453. In 1510 the European presence in India began in earnest when Afonso de Albuquerque, commander of the Portuguese expeditions, seized Goa and thus secured a foothold on the west coast of India (fig. 9).[6] He rapidly established a series of forts along the Indian coastline, the beginnings of a chain of fortified trading stations that would ultimately link Lisbon to Nagasaki in what the Portuguese titled their *Estado da India* (State of India) (figs. 10, 11). Within two years Albuquerque had seized the Malay entrepôt of Melaka (Malacca) and sent an ambassador to the Siamese court of King Rama Thibodi II at Ayutthaya.[7]

The dominant role of Indian textiles as the single most important exchange commodity for spices endured. The trading system that linked Southeast Asia to the Coromandel Coast, Malabar (Calicut, modern Kozhikode), Gujarat (Cambay/Khambhat), and the Arabian ports of the Indian Ocean at

OCOVERNADOR·AFFONÇO·EALBOQVERQVE·SVCEDEO·NAJNDIA
ADOM·FRANCĪSCO·EALME·92······IDA·EM·NOVEMBRO·DE
1509·TOMOV·DIAS·VEZES······ACIDADEEGOA·EASDMALA
STEORVZEFEZAFORTALEZ····ABCALECVTEFOIAPERCIAEAO
ESTRETO·DEORMVZ·E·····MAR·ROXO

Fig. 9
*Portrait of Afonso de Albuquerque,
Governor-General of Estado da
India.* India (Goa), early 16th
century. Paint on panel. Museu
Nacional de Arte Antiga, Lisbon

the beginning of the sixteenth century was vividly described by Tomé Pires, who served in Albuquerque's administration in Goa and Melaka in the years 1512–15, during which time his seminal account of Asian trade, *Suma Oriental,* was written.[8] From Pires and others it is clear that India and Southeast Asia were closely linked through Melaka and the major western Indian port of Cambay. Cambay and its successor port in the seventeenth century, Surat, served as the principal commercial centers for the gathering and exchange of products along the international trade routes of Asia. The merchants of the Red Sea, Arabian Peninsula, and Persian Gulf would gather in Cambay each year, bringing with them goods in demand in India and the East. They would form companies and hire Gujarati ships for the journey to Melaka. A great variety of goods traveled those routes, but the premier items for the voyage east were cotton cloth and dyestuffs employed in textile production and, on the return, spices, especially cloves and pepper. For the Indian textile trade, Cambay was the crucial link in a chain of exchange that stretched from the Mediterranean to Southeast Asia.

For over a century the port city of Melaka had served as the commercial hub of Southeast Asian exchange, making it a necessary conquest for the Portuguese in establishing their Asian commercial network. A significant prize, Melaka gave access to the spice and forest products trade of Southeast Asia. To ensure its supply of spices, the city cultivated regional diplomatic relations, particularly with the northern Sumatran sultanate of Aceh for pepper and the north coast ports of Java through which the cloves, nutmeg, and mace of eastern Indonesia were channeled. In addition, it nurtured its long-distance links with India to assure its supply of cotton goods with which to barter for spices and with China, a major market.

The early decades of the sixteenth century are remarkably rich in firsthand accounts of the Indian textile trade in the Indian Ocean, in marked contrast to the preceding three centuries, for which archaeological evidence affirms the importance of the textile trade, but contemporary, written descriptions are scarce.[9] However, as early as the thirteenth century accounts of foreign trade began to appear, written by harbormasters at China's southern ports, the most famous of which is Zhao Rukua's *Zhufanzhi* (Description of Barbarian Peoples) of 1225. He provides a record of Indian cotton goods available in his port of Guangzhou and displays an unprecedented knowledge of their places of origin, naming Gujarat and Malwa in western India and the Malabar and Coromandel coasts of southern India as important sources of cotton goods for the China market.[10] The ongoing nature of this trade is affirmed a century later by another commentator on China's overseas trade, Wang Dayuan, who describes in his *Daoyizhiue* (Brief Account of the Barbarian Isles) of 1350 patterned cloth imported from Nagapattinam, the premier port of southern India during the Chola dynasty.[11] Wang was a contemporary of Ibn Battuta, whose chronicle of his own extraordinary adventures in the second quarter of the fourteenth century gives the most detailed description of life in India, Southeast Asia, and

China of that time.[12] In his writing, Battuta makes passing references to the high value of cotton in Southeast Asia and China in the 1340s, noting that in insular Southeast Asia an elephant load of aloeswood could be purchased with a single cotton robe, while in China "a single robe of cotton is sold for the price of many of silk" and is worn by the wealthiest of merchants.[13] These sources suggest that although Indian patterned cloth (woven or painted is not clear) was available in both Southeast Asia and China, it was relatively scarce compared to Chinese silk and accordingly highly priced. In the course of the later fourteenth and fifteenth centuries this situation changed radically, with significant quantities of patterned Indian cotton goods, as well as, we may assume, plain muslins and *patola* silks, entering into the cloth-for-spices trade.

Detailed accounts of commercial life in the early sixteenth century are provided by Pires and his contemporary, fellow Portuguese Duarte Barbosa, whose insights into the commercial life of the merchants who dominated the Indian Ocean trade in this era are unrivaled. In Barbosa's description of Indian Ocean countries and their trade, written in 1518, he describes "a certain merchant there [in Cambay] who alone will discharge three or four ships laden with every kind of valuable goods and re-laden them alone from his own stock."[14] Consortia of investors and merchants generally shared in the lease of a vessel, thus spreading the ever-present risks of piracy and loss at sea, to which the earlier Geniza documents testify.

Of the Asian trading communities the most successful were the Gujaratis, as witnessed not only by Pires and Barbosa but also by a variety of other sources. All confirm that merchants from the Gujarati community routinely held the most senior post open to an expatriate trader, that of *shahbandar* (controller of maritime trade). This is widely recorded, by Zhao Rukua in his *Zhufanzhi* (1225), on a Muslim tombstone dated 1450 at the north coast Javanese port city of Gresik, and at the Siamese court of Phra Narai at Ayutthaya in the late seventeenth century.[15]

The community of merchants that stretched from Egypt and West Asia to Melaka and Java created a shared market, a trading diaspora whose reach is evidenced by the many Indian trade cloths discovered in Southeast Asia that are analogous to those found in Egypt. Historical Indian textiles found in Egypt range in date from the eleventh to the fifteenth century and have been excavated at the metropolitan center of Fustat, at the transshipment site of Quseir al-Qadim bordering the Red Sea, and at the Nubian trading posts of Qasr Ibrim and Gebel Adda in Upper Egypt, indicating a significant degree of dispersal.[16] Study of these fragments has established beyond doubt their place of manufacture as Gujarat (cats. 2, 3).[17] Arab and Gujarati merchants dominated the Red Sea–Cambay trade, and the traffic in Indian cloth astonished the Portuguese Barbosa: "It seems an impossible thing that they should use so much cotton cloth as these ships bring from Cambaya."[18] These same communities were also the principal players on the Cambay–Melaka route to Southeast Asia and the Spice Islands of eastern Indonesia, the Maluku. The commercial and religious alliances formed during this time facilitated both a dynamic trade in textiles and a new awareness within Southeast Asia of Arabic and western Indian Muslim culture, whose impact on the region is yet to be fully evaluated. The textile trade was key to this dialogue and remains an entrée to understanding the nature of cultural reciprocity between the Malay world, Muslim India, and West Asia.

During Tomé Pires's residence at Melaka he reported up to four ships arriving annually from Gujarat, carrying up to thirty varieties of cloth.[19] He added, "All the cloths and things from Gujarat have trading value in Melaka and in the kingdoms that trade with Melaka."[20] The primacy of Gujarati cloth to the exchange system is clear. But what did these cloths look like? Pires and others fall short of descriptions, saying at most that the cloth was plain or patterned and sometimes naming a

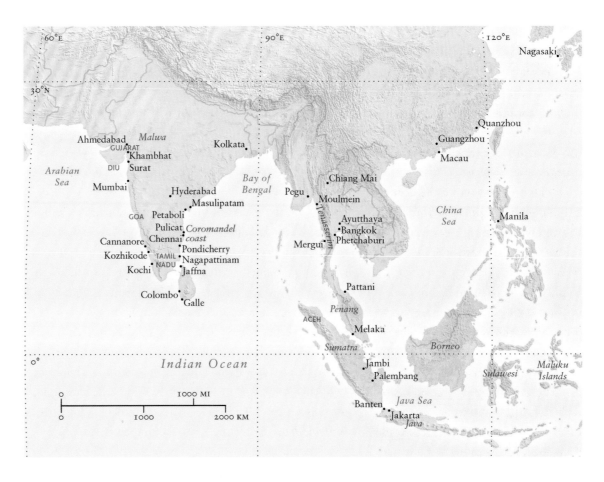

Fig. 10
Indian and Southeast Asian trading
centers

dominant color. The identity of these textiles has been a major lacuna in Indian textile studies that has only recently been addressed. Research undertaken in the past fifteen years has given us more secure evidence of what some of these Gujarati textiles actually looked like in the period leading up to the moment Pires was writing. Through accelerated radiocarbon (RC-14) testing it has been possible to obtain reliable dates for many of the Indian textiles recovered from Southeast Asia. These have been proven to date predominantly from the fourteenth and especially the fifteenth centuries. The range of designs and styles represented may reasonably be assumed to be among the thirty varieties referred to by Pires at the start of the sixteenth century. Thus we can begin to envisage the reality of the commodities traded.

Indian textile trade to Southeast Asia in the fifteenth century included a heavy, coarse Z-spun cotton cloth of large dimensions. In many instances the designs were intended to continue over two identical lengths of cloth, joined along the selvage to create a pictorial field measuring some two and a half yards by almost five and a half yards (about two by five meters). Such cloths were clearly not intended for dress, and we are left to speculate as to their precise function, symbolism, and social significance.[21] The range of designs on these textiles is spectacular, extending from landscape compositions to figurative motifs in which large repeat patterns are printed in iron black and then infill-painted with a combination of mordanted chay red and resist-dyed indigo blue (cat. 3A). Among the earliest designs to occur in both West Asian and Southeast Asian markets is the *hamsa*, a repeat-block design in mordant of the ancient Indian mythical-goose motif (fig. 12). The so-called Gujarati courtesans composition was particularly popular and can be traced through several generations of designs.[22] Another recurrent theme is that of equestrian warriors and elephants with howdahs; these

are a feature of Gujarati export cloths of this and later periods, again showing evidence of an evolution in the treatment of the motif. Among the earliest are block-printed cloth fragments surviving
from the Red Sea trade to Fustat.[23] All of these cloths share a color range limited to red, blue, and
black, in some cases black and one of the primaries. The colors are applied either as hand-painted
dyes—mordant or resist dyed—or as block-printed (again mordant or resist dyed) or as a combination of the two. There is no evidence of reactive dyeing being used at this time—that is, of applying one color over another to produce a third, such as yellow on blue to produce green, or red on
blue to create purple.

A notable survivor of this fifteenth-century genre is a painted cotton decorated with a densely
realized wooded landscape (cat. 3B). The motifs that dominate this composition—variegated flowering and fruit-bearing trees framed in a distinctive pearl-border device—belong to a shared repertoire characteristic of Gujarati architectural decoration and manuscript painting of the fourteenth and
fifteenth centuries. Tombstones from Cambay provide some of the closest visual analogies and have
the advantage of being dated; one such example, the cenotaph of Parviz Malik, preserved at the Jami
Masjid, Cambay, is dated 1333 (fig. 13). These headstones were produced for distribution around the
Indian Ocean to serve the needs of the Gujarati diaspora community.[24] Together with the painted
textiles of this period, they share a common visual language whose origins can be traced to the
architectural ornamentation of the Solanki dynasty of eleventh-century Gujarat.[25]

The European presence in India was dominated throughout the sixteenth century by the Portuguese.
It was another century before other European powers followed, establishing trading companies in
quick succession at the beginning of the seventeenth century. First came the English, establishing
the East India Company (EIC) in 1600, which was restructured in 1708 and renamed thereafter the
United East India Company (UEIC). They were followed by the Dutch East India Company (Verenigde
Oost-Indische Compagnie, or VOC) in 1601 and the French Compagnie des Indes Orientales in
1664.[26] The French traveler and occasional physician to the Mughal court François Bernier
(1620–1688) remarked in 1665, somewhat enviously, that "I have sometimes stood amazed at the
vast quantity of cotton-goods of all sorts, fine and others, tinged [colored] and white which the
Hollanders alone draw from thence and transport into many
places, especially into Japan and Europe, not to mention what
the English, Portuguese and Indians merchants carry away from
these parts."[27]

Fig. 11
Portuguese Carrack. India (Bengal),
late 16th century. Carved terracotta
brick, from a temple decoration. A
Portuguese presence in Bengal, centered at Hooghly from 1536, provided opportunities for local artists
to study this distinctive type of
Portuguese vessel. Present location
unknown

The trade in which successive European trading companies participated was dominantly intra-Asian. Their quickly
realized profits were most readily secured by interregional
Asian exchange rather than by an exclusive focus on the
long-distance Asia–Europe trade. Jan Pietersz Coen, director-
general of the newly formed VOC, wrote from Banten, in
western Java, to his directors in Holland in 1619 that great
commercial opportunities awaited the company in Asian
waters: "Piece goods [cloth] from Gujarat we can barter for
pepper and gold on the coast of Sumatra; rials and cottons
from the [Coromandel] coast for the pepper in Banten; sandalwood, pepper and rials we can barter for Chinese goods and
Chinese gold; we can extract silver from Japan with Chinese

Fig. 12
Textile with sacred goose (*hamsa*)
design. India (Gujarat), for the
Indonesian market, 15th–early 16th
century. Cotton, mordant- and resist-
printed, dyed. The Metropolitan
Museum of Art, New York, Gift of
Robert Coffland, in memory of
Mary Hunt Kahlenberg, 2012
(2012.445)

goods . . . and rials from Arabia for spices and various other trifles—one thing leads to another." [28]

The mechanism by which Indian textiles contributed to the control and regulation of the spice trade was straightforward. When Captain James Lancaster, commander of the English company's first fleet to Southeast Asia, seized a Portuguese carrack (fig. 11) loaded with Indian cotton goods in 1601, he readily traded his pirated cargo for pepper in the great mart of Banten. In 1603 Lancaster established the first English factory in Southeast Asia at Banten, which he stocked with Indian cloths for the purpose of bartering spices in Maluku, and dispatched a party to establish an English presence on Ambon, the commercial center of the Spice Islands. [29] Sir Henry Middleton, who commanded the East India Company's second fleet in 1604–6, reported from Banten that 52 fardels (bundles) of Indian textiles in stock were sent to Banda island in Maluku, with the expectation that they would be "sufficient, with a large overplus, to lade the 2 shipps we have [there] with mace, cloves and nutmegs." [30]

The Portuguese and Dutch were particularly interventionist and, in the case of the Dutch during the seventeenth century, aggressive in trying to secure a monopolistic control of the supplies of spices at their source, notably cloves, nutmeg, and mace in Maluku and pepper from Sumatra. [31] Trade, diplomacy, and coercion were skillfully combined: sometime after 1657 the VOC commissioned a portrait of Sultan Saifuddin of Tidore (r. 1657–89), depicted in part-European dress, to celebrate a highly prized alliance with the ruler of one of the Maluku islands richest in cloves and nutmeg (fig. 14), providing us a rare glimpse into seventeenth-century spice-trade diplomacy. Exotic textiles—predominantly Indian but also including Chinese and European fabrics—had long been reported as a distinguishing feature of court life in Southeast Asia. As early as 1579 the English navigator Francis Drake, on his reception in Maluku at the court of Sultan Babullah of Ternate (r. 1570–83), remarked on the richness of dress of the sultan and the display of wealth in the reception hall evinced by the variety of textiles to be seen. [32] This remained the case a century later with the commissioning of this portrait, in which the "King of Tidore," as the Dutch dubbed him, is represented in a jacket, presumably a VOC commission, styled to reflect mid-seventeenth-century Dutch fashion. It is tailored in an extravagantly luxurious fabric, most probably with embroidered or appliqué floral decoration, possibly from Safavid Iran, where the VOC was also active in the seventeenth century. [33] The sultan is wearing a jeweled gold chain, also undoubtedly a gift of the VOC, as well as gold hair ornaments of local production. [34] Exotic textiles, however, did not always remain the reserve of the ruler alone: in 1668 Sultan Saifuddin requested his annual compensation from the VOC for trade concessions in the form of 2,000 *rijks-daalders'* worth of cloth, which he distributed to his populace, so ensuring strong allegiances. [35]

Pursuing a similarly monopolistic strategy in southern India and Sri Lanka, in 1602 the Dutch admiral Joris van Spilbergen established a VOC presence in Sri Lanka and immediately embarked on trade negotiations with the Sinhalese king Wimala Dharma Suriya (fig. 15). Within fifty years the VOC had secured a monopoly over the Sri Lankan foreign trade, exchanging Indian cotton textiles for Sri Lankan spices and even attempting the transfer of textile technology and artisans from southern India to Sri Lanka.[36] A legacy of this may be seen in a number of large narrative cloth paintings and state and military banners, which have been identified in recent years in Sri Lanka. They are crudely painted compared to the work of the majority of southern Coromandel Coast cloth painters, yet are valuable documents in the history of Sri Lanka, with some containing fascinating and unique images, such as that of a Sinhalese king making an offering of a VOC coin into a large urn, an acknowledgment of the wealth that the Dutch presence brought to the rulers, whose cooperation the VOC needed to successfully trade in the island's natural wealth (fig. 16).

PICTURING THE SEVENTEENTH CENTURY

Although Indian textiles are the single most-discussed commodity in the plentiful European sources from the seventeenth century, as with earlier periods our understanding of which surviving textiles match those referred to in the sources remains tenuous. Visual sources are scarce and little studied, but two sets of paintings, one Indian, one European, help open up this study to more precise definition. In 1619 the order of the Jesuits at the church of São Roque in Lisbon commissioned a cycle of twenty paintings from the Lisbon artist André Reinoso (active ca. 1610–ca. 1650) to chronicle and celebrate the conversions and miracles of Francis Xavier.[37] These present a hagiography of Francis Xavier's life through his healing and missionary activities in India (Goa and Comorin), Sri Lanka, Melaka, Maluku (Ceram), Japan (Kagoshima and Yamaguchi), and China. The scenes relating to Goa and Sri Lanka, in particular, provide an unmatched visual record of South Indian textiles at the beginning of the seventeenth century. In the painting *Francis Xavier Preaching in Goa* (fig. 17), a bare-chested man (left) is wearing a black-and-white checked *lungi* (skirt cloth) with yellow stripes on the border, of typical South Indian cotton design; he is flanked by another figure wearing what appear to be Portuguese-style trousers of red with bands of gold thread, with a sheen suggestive of silk. Two women seated before him wear white blouses and *lungi*, one with a design of white floral arabesques on a red ground, the other with red geometricized floral motifs on a blue-black ground. Both these patterns find direct parallels in Indian trade cloths from Gujarat and from the Coromandel Coast, respectively. These are no artist's invention, but rather convincing representations of fabrics that must have been available to Reinoso in Lisbon in the 1620s. In all probability they were secured by the Jesuits in Goa and sent to São Roque in Lisbon. Portuguese church inventories as early as 1508 record the use of cloth from Cambay (Gujarat) and Calicut (coastal western India) in the tailoring of ecclesiastical vestments, intended principally for use in the churches of the East, with some also destined for Lisbon.[38]

Fig. 14
Sultan Saifuddin of Tidore. Maluku, late 17th century. Oil on panel. Czartoryski Museum, Kraków

Opposite:
Fig. 13
Cenotaph of Parviz Malik, Jami Masjid, Cambay (Khambhat), India. Marble, 1333

Fig. 15
*VOC Admiral Joris van Spilbergen
Being Received by the Sinhalese King
Wimala Dharma Suriya in 1602.*
Netherlands (Delft), 1605.
Engraving. Rijksmuseum,
Amsterdam (RP-T-1904.1). The
Sinhalese king wears a skirt cloth
(*tuppotiya*) with a floral border and
a sawtooth pattern at each end; the
tumpal motif came to dominate
Indian trade cloths for the Malay-
Indonesian market.

Fig. 16
*Sinhalese King Donating a VOC
Coin at a Shrine* (detail). Sri Lanka,
18th century. Cotton, painted resist
and mordant, dyed. Collection
Karun Thakar, London

Contemporary commentaries, read in conjunction with the visual evidence of Reinoso's paintings, allow us a reasonably clear understanding of the types of clothes then fashionable in southern India. The Dutch traveler and historian Jan Huyghen van Linschoten (1563–1611) recorded in his *Itineraris* of 1596 a description of women's dress there during the 1590s: "They likewise make clothes thereof for women to put about them from their navels downwards, bound about their bodies, which they wear within the house, very finely made, the best sort are named clothes of Sarasso, some being mingled with threads of gold and silver and such like stuff of a thousand sorts very beautiful to behold."[39] Linschoten could be describing the garments depicted in the São Roque paintings themselves.

Less securely datable is a series of Nayaka-period temple mural paintings preserved in the gateway (*gopura*) of the Shiva temple dedicated to Sri Narumpunatacami at Tiruppudaimarudur, Tirunelveli district, Tamil Nadu, on the Tambraparni River, not far from the great port city of Nagapattinam on the southern Coromandel Coast. They can be assigned to the first quarter of the seventeenth century or slightly later.[40] This exceptional set of paintings, commissioned by a branch of the Vijayanagara royal household, depicts alongside familiar religious themes a number of scenes of merchants engaged in commerce, notably assemblies of traders (*nagaram*), among them both foreign merchants—the most readily identified being the Arab and Portuguese horse traders— and local merchants (*vanikesan*). Prosperous gem traders, probably members of one of the powerful merchant guilds such as the Ayyavole, are depicted seated on a cloth with their precious wares laid out before them, engaged in a transaction (fig. 18).[41] A pair of panels depicts hanging textiles, each with a stepped-geometric design ground, one with a pair of lotus buds in the center field, the other with a serpentine tree motif (fig. 19).[42] Another mural panel depicts an Arab dhow delivering a cargo of horses to a southern Indian port, a unique record of the region's international trade connections.[43]

All of the murals are painted in a robust, direct, and summary style. The costumes of the Vijayanagar nobility and attendants and the Arab and Portuguese merchants, full of descriptive detail, present a vivid snapshot of social life and dress in this Nayaka court. The great variety of *lungi* and *dupata* (women's shawls) depicted, along with the distinctive headdress of each group, textile canopies above seated royalty, and so on, suggest that the mural artists were experienced in painting textiles—the confidently handled silhouetting technique and the blocking in of the background color are all suggestive of a painter trained to use the *qalam*, the hot-wax applicator for resist-dyed *kalamkari* textiles.[44] Similarly, the elevation views of temple architecture and the use of tiered registers is reminiscent of large-format painted temple cloths.[45] The dominant designs of small floral motif repeats and striped-and-checkered designs are consistent with the earlier cycle of murals at a number of Vijayanagar-period temples, most famously the Shiva temple at Lepakshi.[46]

The Tiruppudaimarudur murals are distinct from others of the Vijayanagar-Nayaka periods because of their singular focus on a secular theme, commerce. Contemporary Portuguese sources wrote extensively of the economic and military importance of the western Asian horse trade to southern India, a theme uniquely depicted in these murals.[47] The fact that two panels are devoted to representations of hanging textiles underscores the commercial importance of cloth. The nearby port of Nagapattinam served not only as an important production center for plain and painted cotton textiles but also as a major assembly point of products intended for the export trade.[48] Its role in the cotton-export industry was promoted by the EIC in the later seventeenth century, as it encouraged the shift of the textile industry from the northern Coromandel Coast to centers south.[49]

In the early seventeenth century both the Coromandel Coast and Gujarat were renowned as the premier sources for chintz and other dyed cloths of the highest quality, which combined fine cotton fabric with the most refined brushwork and skill of dyeing to achieve an unrivaled brightness and fastness of color. These may be identified in the company records by a great variety of names that appear in the course of different periods. Primarily based on the technical characteristics of a cloth, the names provide little or no clue as to their design beyond the occasional addition of such terms as striped, checked, or patterned, plain or dyed, and their suitability to a particular market. Among the many types of textiles documented are *baffetas*, *boxshales*, *chatars* or *chintes* (chintz), *longcloth*, *mores*, *palampore*, *percallaes*, *pitcharies*, *sarassa*, *salampores*, and *tappe* or *tapichindaes*.[50]

Fig. 17
André Reinoso (Portuguese, active ca. 1610–ca. 1650). *Francis Xavier Preaching in Goa*, 1619–22. Oil on canvas. Church of São Roque (Sacristy), Santa Casa da Misericórdia, Lisbon

The centers of painted- and dyed-cotton production relo-
cated over time, reflecting the shifting political fortunes of
competing European companies, so that by the 1660s the
English trading center at Fort St. George, Madras, was chal-
lenging Dutch-dominated Masulipatam as the epicenter of the
painted-cloth trade. Skilled weavers and cloth painters were
encouraged to migrate south, introducing skilled Telegu-
speaking artisans from Andhra Pradesh into Tamil Nadu. It is
significant that makers' marks on the borders of cloths originating in Tamil Nadu from this period on are often written
in Telegu rather than Tamil, reflecting this shift of artisans.

These weavers, painters, and dyers were highly proficient
practitioners of hereditary craft skills, renowned for their
ability both to replicate motifs as required by a client and to
synthesize design elements to create new and complex compositions. Designs and more often single motifs originating in
English, French, and Dutch pattern books published for
domestic consumption were introduced to Indian cloth makers
by company officials via their commissioning agents. On occasion the borrowings were very direct and uncompromised by
any filtering through an Indian aesthetic, as seen with the
southern Coromandel painted imitations of the early eighteenth-
century French flame-stitch wool and silk loom-woven designs
(fig. 20). Very few examples of these painted imitations survive, and all have been reported found in Indonesia, where
they would have been intended, in the first instance, for the
European expatriate and *mestizo* (mixed descent) communities.[51] A painting of Batavia's (modern Jakarta) Kali Besar
market with panoramic views of Castle Batavia, painted by
Andries Beeckman while resident there about 1657, captures
the cosmopolitan community of races that prospered in that
city less than forty years after its creation by the Dutch in 1619 (fig. 21). Commissioned by the
VOC, the painting was sent to Amsterdam, where, from about 1662, it hung in the boardroom at
East India House in the Hoogstraat.[52]

Floral-motif designs in the European manner, radically different from the Mughal renderings, were
widely disseminated and were incorporated in Indian chintz and palampores for the European markets.[53] An unexpected means of verifying the reception and dating of these patterns in India is provided by the decorative designs depicted on VOC gravestones, many of which are still preserved at
crematories located at the former sites of Dutch company factories, such as Pulicat and Batavia.[54]

Dated or datable paintings furnish another means of assigning Indian textiles. A miniature portrait of a woman and child, in which the round-back chair can be securely ascribed to the 1770s, is
one such instance (fig. 22). The product of a European-trained artist working for a client in one of
the great cosmopolitan trading cities of eighteenth-century Asia, this miniature painting probably
depicts a Dutch child with his nurse, the latter perhaps a member of the *mestizo* community in

Batavia, Melaka, or, more likely, Colombo. The woman wears a patterned chintz of large blue flowers and pineapples with red and yellow highlights, reserved on white, with a lozenge border, a sophisticated and complex asymmetrical design of European derivation. This design relates closely to a floral chintz skirt cloth worn by a senior Sinhalese company servant (*mudaliyar*)—seen at left foreground (and probably an adviser to the VOC governor seated at the head of the table)—in a contemporary painting recording the reception of a Sinhalese embassy from Kandy at the VOC headquarters in Colombo in 1772 (fig. 23).[55] The process whereby European stylistic elements were absorbed into Indian chintz design was complex and protracted. Continuous exchange and response produced a synthetic style that was the product of both Europe and India, the result of a long conversation. Pattern books, designs, musters, and sample cloths all circulated, fueling this process. Outside the European arena, nowhere in the history of Indian trade-textile design is the process of commissioning better documented than in the case of cloths produced to order for the kingdom of Siam.

Fig. 20
Flame-stitch design long cloth (detail). India (Coromandel Coast), 18th century, in the style of an early 18th-century French woven design. Cotton, painted mordant, dyed. TAPI Collection, Surat, India (TAPI 04.66)

Fig. 21
Andries Beeckman (Netherlandish, active Dutch East Indies). *Castle Batavia Viewed from Kali Besar*, ca. 1656–57. Oil on canvas. Rijksmuseum, Amsterdam (SK-A-19). This view is from the West Market on the Ciliwung River.

"A PITTIFUL CASE WHEN KINGS BECOME MERCHANTS": COMMISSIONING TEXTILES IN SEVENTEENTH-CENTURY SIAM

The painted cottons produced for use by the Thai court of Siam in the seventeenth and eighteenth centuries rival in their technical finesse and artistic achievement any produced for the markets of Europe.[56] They also demonstrate the degree of market specialization that was operating in the Asian textile trade and the responsiveness of the Indian producers to market needs. Designs ordered for specific regional markets appear in the EIC and VOC records from the first decades of the seventeenth century, and from the growing frequency of trade-record references thereafter, this had become the norm by the second half of the century. Understanding the specific nature of seventeenth-century Indian painted textiles for Asian markets was a necessary skill that all European merchants had to learn to compete with the established Asian and Arab traders in the Indian Ocean. Indeed, such was the market sensitivity of the designs that cloths commissioned for one locale proved virtually unsalable in another. Peter Floris, a Dutchman in the service of the English who captained the *Globe* to India and Southeast Asia in 1611–15, learned this lesson when he attempted to sell fine and well-colored Coromandel Coast fabric from Petaboli to the Malays at Pattani: "But a great oversight has been committed . . . a little white edge [has been added] and the upright Malay cloth must be without it, as the cloth of Paleacatte [Pulicat]

was. . . . If I had not now found it by experience, I had never believed it, that so small a fault should cause so great an abatement in the price. . . . The Malays say they be Siam sortes, so that I shall be compelled to send them there, as also the red yarne, which will not sell here." [57] The VOC merchant Jeremias van Vliet, who effectively directed the company's interests in Siam from 1633 to 1642, the last four years as director of the Ayutthaya factory, recounted a similar experience. In 1641–42 he traveled south to Pattani, where the VOC had long had a presence, to discover that their factory was stocked with Indian textiles "not of the Patanese fashion" and therefore largely unsalable in that market. [58]

Thai-market Indian textiles are the only category of Indian trade cloths for which we have corroborated historical sources detailing consumption from the sixteenth century onward. The first documentation of a trade in Indian cloths produced to Thai taste was reported by Tomé Pires in 1515. He stated in his *Suma Oriental* that among the goods traded from Melaka to Thailand were "wide and narrow muslins, and Kling cloths in the fashion of Siam." [59] The Indian imports were identified as "Kling," that is, goods traded by Indian merchants from the Coromandel Coast, expressly for Siam. Pires recorded that Siam traded with both Bengal and Gujarat via its southern coastal port of Tenasserim, on the Bay of Bengal. [60] Duarte Barbosa, observing this trade about the same time, reported in 1518 that Gujarati textiles were much prized in Siam. [61] He stated that the ports of Siam and the kingdom of Pegu in lower Myanmar (Burma) received large quantities of Indian textiles from both Pulicat on the Coromandel Coast and Cambay in western India and that these Indian textiles were highly valued.

A century later Thai-market Indian textiles continued to be singled out for mention. Henry Middleton, who captained the English company voyage to the Spice Islands in 1604–6, reported that in 1603 their agent in Banten was holding, in addition to 3,000 bags of pepper, "480 fardells of callicoes, viz. 8 canisters [probably bundles of cloth secured in matting] of pinthadoes and 117 fardells of checkered stuffes, 51 fardells of long Malocogirdles [waistcloths], 59 *fardells of girdles for Syam* [Siam; author's italics], 110 fardells of Java girdles, 13 chests of fine pinthadoes, 6 chests of divers sorts of comodities, 42 fardells of browne [i.e., unbleached] callicoes, and in loose pinthadoes about 80 fardells at the least of all sortes." [62] That one-tenth of the company's warehoused stock in Banten was apparently designed to Thai taste is surprising at such an early moment in European trading interests in Southeast Asia, when the focus was still firmly on using Indian textiles to secure supplies of eastern Indonesian spices.

VOC sources are particularly illuminating for seventeenth-century Southeast Asia and allow an understanding of the commissioning process not possible for less documented Asian markets. In 1608, seven years after the establishment of the VOC, the company ship *Eendracht* sailed from the port of Banten for the Coromandel Coast with detailed instructions to commission specific types of textiles required for the VOC's new markets in Southeast Asia. Along with the written instructions for their agents in India were fabric samples to indicate the specific designs required by the various markets. [63]

Dutch diplomatic relations with the court of Siam started promisingly, with the first Thai diplomatic mission to Europe posted to the Netherlands in 1608. The court at Ayutthaya (north of

Fig. 22
Miniature Portrait of a Mother and Child or Nurse and Child. Probably Sri Lanka, ca. 1770. Gouache on paper. Collection of Mr. and Mrs. Lee Kip Lee, Singapore

present-day Bangkok) continued to engage diplomatically with Europe throughout the century, most spectacularly with its third mission, sent by Phra Narai (r. 1656–88) to the court of Louis XIV at Versailles in 1686 (fig. 24).[64] The presence of the Siamese delegation at court—they were granted two audiences—and their social visibility in Paris, where they were in residence for many months and much feted, contributed to the "orientalist vogue" that became such a force in fashion in seventeenth- and early eighteenth-century France. The reciprocal embassies led to a strong French presence at Ayutthaya, richly described in a number of contemporary accounts. Louis XIV's numerous gifts—globes and telescopes were much favored—included six French master craftsmen who no doubt left their own legacy, which is yet to be traced.

It was a measure of the political sophistication of the Siamese court and strength of its state that no single European power came to dominate the Siamese trade. All were subservient to royal authority and subject to fixed market rates of exchange that allowed only very low profits. Writing in 1613, a Mr. Lucas of the English factory at Ayutthaya lamented the state of affairs in the textile market there, namely, that "other shopkeepers dare not be so bolde as to buye one piece of cloth till the King bee furnished and his price agreed," adding, "The King, not liking the prices of the taken goods, hath given it all back again, after having kept it for two months in his house [i.e., royal warehouse]. A pittiful case when Kings become merchants."[65]

Fig. 23
Carel Frederik Reimer (German, died 1796). *Reception of a Sinhalese Embassy from Kandy at the VOC Headquarters in Colombo, 1772.* Watercolor. Rijksprentenkabinet, Rijksmuseum, Amsterdam (RP-T-1904.18)

Afbeelding der plegtige Audientie verleent door ZYN WELEDELE, GROOTAG'TBAARE de Heer GOUVERNEUR en DIRECTEUR van 't Eyland CEYLON, etc. etc. *aan 't jaarlykse Gesandschap van den Koning van* Candia, te COLOMBO; *in den Jaare,* 1772.

All persevered because of the promise of greater trade with China, to which Ayutthaya was seen as a key hub. These economic constraints on foreign trading interests in Siam were also reflected in the purity of Thai traditional textile design. Unlike the growing hybridity to be witnessed elsewhere, most notably in India and China, Thai design was largely resistant to unbridled external influences, from East or West. Critically, the Siamese court through its Ministry of Trade closely controlled and regulated both the commissioning and trade of painted cloths from India. This level of centralized control was unique within Asia and akin to European company purchasing practices.

Direct evidence of a royal commission employing supplied samples from the Siamese court is preserved in EIC records of 1662. A company merchant stationed at Ayutthaya wrote in December of that year to his superiors at company headquarters at Surat in western India with an order placed on behalf of the "King of Siam." The order itemized the Indian cloths desired at the Siamese capital—red-ground chintz, "long cloth and most sorts of cloth from the Coast [i.e., Coromandel] . . . sad [dark or somber] coloured chints for lungees [waistcloths]"—and further stated that "The King of Siam expects those puttelaes to be made according to those patterns Mr Bladwell carried to Surat; if not to be procured, those patterns to be returned."[66] This directive confirms that pattern samples, or musters, were both in use and commercially sensitive.[67] The year, 1662, indicates that this order came from the court of King Narai; it is the earliest such evidence directly linking the Siamese court with the commissioning of textiles, a practice frequently alluded to, mostly in derogatory terms, by Dutch and French commentaries later in the century, as they struggled to make a profit in this highly regulated royal-monopoly market.

The bulk of the Thai-market commissioning took place on the Coromandel Coast, as the ports of Masulipatam, Petaboli, Pulicat, and others were easily reached by ships owned by or in the direct employ of the Siamese court. Sailings were made from the ports of Mergui or, most importantly, Tenasserim on the Andaman Sea. Thai-market cloths feature less prominently in European trading records precisely because the bulk of that trade was directly in Thai control. This remained the case until the later eighteenth century, when English country-traders like Francis Light began to participate and supplied the Siamese peninsular ports, where clients included provincial governors wanting high-grade textiles appropriate for part of their annual tribute to the court in Bangkok.[68] The VOC director at Ayutthaya, Jeremias van Vliet, reported that painted cottons from Coromandel and Surat were imported in great quantities via the Masulipatam–Tenrasserim route by Hindu and Muslim traders.[69] William Methwold, writing in 1626 of his experiences of trade in Golconda, recorded that [from Masulipatam] "To Tannssery [Tenasserim] they carry red cotton yarne, red and white beethyles [muslin], paintings [Portuguese *pintados*, i.e., patterned goods] of severall sorts befitting that countries weare."[70] The Siamese court also had its own agents who operated from Masulipatam and elsewhere on the northern Coromandel Coast, commissioning designs and chartering ships to conduct trade on their behalf. On a number of occasions the king's agents employed English or Dutch mariners, typically former company employees, to captain their vessels, most famously Samuel White, who was in the employ of King Narai.[71]

Fig. 26

Whose Sleeves? (Tagasode) (detail), late 16th century. Folding screen; ink, color, and gold on gilt paper. The Metropolitan Museum of Art, New York, H. O. Havemeyer Collection, Bequest of Mrs. H. O. Havemeyer, 1929 (29.100.494). The textiles seen here include an imported Indian painted cotton (*sarasa*) with floral repeat pattern and sawtooth (*tumpal*) end-border design.

The specificity of Siamese court textile designs must be seen against a complex hierarchy of court etiquette and protocol in which categories of imported textiles were restricted in their use under sumptuary regulations, thus serving as important denoters of rank (fig. 25). Imported Indian textiles were one of a number of prestige items used as expressions of royal favor, both within the court, where they were employed to secure and maintain loyalty, and beyond, where they were used in diplomatic and other forms of gift exchange. Many were also traded, with significant numbers destined for the Japanese market (fig. 26). The rules governing the design and wearing of Indian textiles for the Siamese court persisted well into the nineteenth century, culminating in one of the longest chapters in the history of Indian textile production in the service of a foreign client.

The legacy of the Indian textile trade to the development of an international language of design was long lasting and profound. It was perpetuated in new forms of hybridity that evolved through the dynamics of design exchange and the interpretation (and misinterpretation) of external ideas and imagery, and it was propelled by the forces of commerce. Throughout the sixteenth, seventeenth, and eighteenth centuries India retained her pivotal place—center stage—in the story of global textile design.

Opposite:
Fig. 24

J. Hainzelman (French, 1641–1693). *Portrait of Kosa Pan, the Siamese Ambassador of King Narai to France.* Engraving, 1686. Cabinet des Estampes, Bibliothèque Nationale de France, Paris. The ambassador is dressed in a tunic and conical hat denoting noble rank.

Fig. 25

Pha-nung, skirt cloth, design with celestial worshippers. India, for the Thai market, 18th century. Cotton, drawn resist and painted mordant, dyed. The Metropolitan Museum of Art, New York, Gift of Thomas Murray, in honor of John Guy, 2009 (2009.513)

The Iberian Globe

TEXTILE TRADITIONS AND TRADE

IN LATIN AMERICA

Elena Phipps

n 1494, with the Treaty of Tordesillas, Pope Alexander VI divided the world beyond the borders of Europe into two: half for Spain and half for Portugal, "like an orange," according to a letter written to Charles V ten years later.[1] The demarcation of the division, adjusted over time, lay along a certain meridian passing through the Atlantic Ocean: the lands to the west encompassing most of the Americas were for Spain, and the lands to the east, including Africa, India, Asia, and part of Brazil, were for Portugal (fig. 27). This monumental treaty signified the fundamental role that these two powers would play during the ensuing years in establishing a global context for textiles and trade. In the Americas, the different approaches to the process of colonialization and trade taken by the Spanish and the Portuguese, in concert with the indigenous response and engagement, resulted in divergent courses of social, political, and economic development from the sixteenth through the eighteenth century.

The Spanish enterprise in the Americas began with the quest for a western route to India in search of the spices and other treasures of the East. Columbus explored the Caribbean beginning in 1492, and by the early sixteenth century Spanish explorers arrived in Mexico and Peru, which together became known as the Indies. There they engaged not only in the acquisition and trading of gold, silver, jewels, and other riches of the New World but also, within a broader context, the expansion of the Spanish Empire.

By 1535 the Viceroyalty of New Spain had been established to govern the regions that are now Mexico, Guatemala, the Caribbean, and western North America; it was followed, in 1543, by the Viceroyalty of Peru, with boundaries that encompassed present-day Peru, Bolivia, Ecuador, parts of Colombia, Venezuela, Chile, Argentina, and western Brazil. Spain imposed governance under the rule of Spanish law (overseen by the Council of the Indies), by the adoption of Castilian as the language for administration in the region, and by the reconfiguration and building of new towns and cities according to Spanish models of town planning. Central to this program were the Catholic Church and its institutions, backed by the forces of the Inquisition; Spanish clergy were brought in to organize town parishes and archbishoprics and to oversee the conversion and the spiritual lives of the indigenous peoples, which included campaigns against idolatry that sought to eliminate all traces of native religious practice.[2] The discovery of silver in 1545 in Cerro Potosí (present-day Bolivia), which would become the world's largest silver mine, and the development of a mining industry to exploit silver deposits in northern Mexico at about the same time, would spur global trade networks and fuel the Spanish economy for centuries.

The Portuguese, by the time they arrived in South America, had already established long-distance trade with Africa and Asia via maritime trading forts (called factories) located strategically along the *Carreira da India* (India fleet) sea routes around the Horn of Africa to the east. Portugal's primary focus remained its Asian and African trade; in Brazil (most of which lay within the longitudinal domain delineated for Portugal by the treaty of 1494) Portugal turned to harvesting the region's natural riches. Initially this centered on logging brazilwood, which produced a highly desired red dye used in the European textile industry and which became the country's namesake;[3] later the focus was on gold and emeralds, along with the spread of Catholicism. In the early sixteenth century colonial activity in the region was undertaken primarily by private individuals,[4] with concessions of land and trade rights awarded by the Crown as "captaincies"; this resulted in the founding of small forts and trading posts in harbors along the southeastern coast of Brazil. Sugar, which was introduced by the Portuguese, was cultivated and processed starting in the early part of the sixteenth century and soon became the

principal export from Brazil to Europe. African men and women were brought to Brazil in the 1560s
by the Portuguese slave trade, which expanded during the seventeenth century both to replace the
indigenous population devastated by European diseases introduced by the settlers and to supplement
Indian labor in the mines and sugar mills.

During this period the production of and trade in textiles in the Americas evolved in concert with
the many changes that transformed the region. The social mixing of races and cultures in the colonial
era—a consequence of various factors, including the Portuguese and Spanish slave trade that eventually delivered hundreds of thousands of Africans to both Central and South America and the influx of
European administrators, clergy, artisans, and merchants, among others who established themselves
within all parts of Latin America—resulted in hybrid traditions of dress and textile use. After a brief
introduction to Brazil and the Portuguese, the following pages relate these changes primarily to the
textiles of the Spanish Americas, especially Mexico and Peru; while each has distinct historical and
social characteristics, under the Spanish rule of law they shared a similar process of colonial development. Many of the same aspects of colonial textile production and import also apply to the area
controlled by Portugal, particularly during the seventeenth and eighteenth centuries.

INDIGENOUS TEXTILE TRADITIONS IN THE AMERICAS

In the Portuguese territory of Brazil, the textile traditions of the nomadic Tupi and Tapuia tribes—
which occupied the coastal and tropical regions of the Amazon at the time the Portuguese and then
the French, English, and German traders arrived—were not significantly developed from a European
perspective. Numerous accounts describe the "nakedness" of the indigenous populations, who wore
body paint and animal-skin cloaks, as well as scant garments made of tropical-plant fibers created by
knotted, looped, and simple weaving techniques.[5] In one area they excelled: the making of featherwork jewelry and accoutrements from the wing and chest feathers of Amazonian birds.

Europeans were fascinated by the colorful feathered cloaks of the Tupi people, many specimens
of which were collected for the *Wunderkabinett*s of the royal houses of Europe, among them a red
feather cloak acquired by the king of Denmark in 1689.[6] The extraordinary technique called

tapirage—which altered the color of the new feathers as they grew on the living bird—was described in the late sixteenth century by Portuguese explorers and others.[7] Other early indigenous textile traditions were lost because of the devastation of the Tupi by disease and by the harsh conditions of slave labor imposed by the Portuguese. In addition, the Jesuits quickly introduced European-style clothing for the native populations living in the mission villages they established in the sugar plantation zones and in the less settled tropical interior of the Amazon region, which had a major impact on local textile production and garment traditions.

The Spanish, arriving in Mexico in 1519 and Peru in 1532, encountered a very different cultural situation with the highly complex, stratified societies of the Aztec and Inca empires. Here textiles played a major role in the lives of the native people, serving as important factors in the political process, tribute, and trade, as well as markers of status and identity integral to the social, political, economic, and spiritual aspects of the societies. In Mexico, tribute lists document the hundreds of mantles made of cotton and ixtle fiber (derived from the native maguey plant), feathered garments, and bags of cochineal, among other textile-related items, produced for the Aztec emperor Moctezuma II (r. 1502–20) in the first quarter of the sixteenth century, prior to the Conquest. Tribute items were required to be given on a regular basis, fueling the economy and contributing to the considerably ritualized activities of the Aztec Empire. The *Matrícula de Tributos*, a manuscript produced on native paper before 1521, documents that every six months eleven towns in the central valley, for example, together owed four hundred each of quilted-cotton garments, of red-and-white-striped mantles, of black-and-white-striped mantles, of loincloths, and of women's skirts and huipils (upper garments). In addition, once a year they had to contribute eight hundred bundles of long green quetzal feathers, forty bags of cochineal, two feather shields, twenty bowls of gold dust, and two strings of greenstone (see fig. 113).[8]

These lists reflect an extensive production of both coarse and fine cloth made according to local design traditions and using local materials. Unfortunately, the survival of these textiles is rare, owing for the most part to the consumption of textiles in Aztec rituals and battles, to the extensive destruction that resulted from the Conquest, and to the climate, which has not favored their preservation. As a result, it is primarily only through the documents that record their existence that we can glimpse the beauty and technical skill of pre-Spanish Mexican textiles (fig. 28).[9] Eyewitness accounts by Hernán Cortés, the Spanish conquistador in charge of the expedition to Mexico and the defeat of the Aztecs, attest to his appreciation of them. His gifts sent to the king of Spain on July 10, 1519, included garments of fine cotton; Cortés noted that "in no other part of the world is there such weaving as these, and there are bedcovers made of silk in other regions that do not compare."[10] Though listed in the royal inventories, these textiles have not survived.

In contrast, the ancient textile traditions of Peru can be traced through thousands of examples that have been preserved, especially in burials along the desert coast, providing evidence of remarkable

Fig. 28
Nezahualpilli, Ruler of Texcoco. From the Codex Ixtlilxochitl, Mexico, early 17th century. Bibliothèque Nationale de France, Paris (Ixt folio 108r). This drawing from the manuscript features an Aztec tie-dyed mantle.

Fig. 29
Man's tunic (*uncu*) with *tocapu*
design. Peru, Inca period, early 16th
century. Tapestry weave, cotton and
camelid fiber. Dumbarton Oaks
Research Library and Collection,
Washington, D.C. (B518)

achievements in weaving, dyeing, and embroidery. By the end
of the fifteenth century, the Inca Empire (which extended from
present-day Ecuador to southern Chile) had developed
extraordinary weaving techniques to produce specially woven
garments called *cumbi*, a term that refers to their high quality.
A hallmark of Inca culture, they provided a tangible link
between the king and local leaders in a hierarchy defined by
the reciprocal exchange of *cumbi* for loyalty (figs. 29, 30).
Specialists were selected from across the empire to weave
these textiles (produced primarily in tapestry weave) for
royal consumption and gifting; citizens were also required to
spin and weave more ordinary cloth for various official uses.[11]
This entailed highly organized state distribution of fibers and
other materials to individual households, which were obliged
to produce tribute goods from them—a system that was
taken over by the Spanish. This *tasa de tributo*, or labor tribute, continued well into the sixteenth century (and even into
the seventeenth century in some regions); thousands of textiles
were owed to administrators each year.[12] By 1570, however,
Francisco de Toledo, viceroy of Peru, lamented the loss of
the Inca-trained specialty weavers who could produce the
very finest tapestry-woven *cumbi* cloth, and he mandated
that a survey be conducted in the highland region to locate
the weavers and encourage them to continue.[13] Tapestries
with coats of arms and other European designs were commissioned by Spanish administrators,
who admired the skills of these weavers (cat. 21). Cloth made of vicuña, using the silklike fiber from
those wild animals native only to the highlands of the Andes, was especially prized as bedcovers in
Spain.[14] These and other special textiles were often sent to Spain as testaments to the unique
achievements of Mexican and Andean culture.[15]

PORTS AND IMPORTS

Shortly after the Spanish established a base in the Americas, goods, people, technologies, ideas, and
aesthetic influences from Europe flowed into the region. Moving in the other direction were the wealth
and resources of the indigenous cultures, including gold, silver, and jewels, as well as precious dyestuffs such as indigo, cochineal, and annatto, along with the prized textiles described above. Other
local commodities favored in Europe included cacao, quinine, sugar, tobacco, and large quantities
of cotton.[16]

All goods coming to the Americas from Spain arrived in ships that had departed from Cádiz, the
port of Seville. The New Spain fleet with goods for Mexico would land at Veracruz, Mexico; the
Tierra Firme fleet to South America would arrive at Cartagena, Colombia, and Portobelo, Panama.[17]
By the last quarter of the sixteenth century, goods coming from Asia via the Philippines would arrive
at the Pacific ports of Callao (the seaport for Lima, capital of the Viceroyalty of Peru) and Acapulco,

Mexico. At all these ports, the goods would be off-loaded from the ships to seasonal markets and then transported overland to major cities north and south. In the case of Panama, goods were literally carried across the isthmus and then reloaded onto ships in the Pacific port. The markets, and the economy, revolved around the arrival of these annual Spanish treasure ships.

Markets in Mexico City and Lima thrived, becoming permanent features of city life. In his 1553 history of the Conquest, Francisco López de Gómara, chronicler of Cortés's experiences in Mexico, devoted an entire chapter to the sixteenth-century markets of Tenochtitlán (now Mexico City), with their textiles of all types, including vendors of yarns spun from rabbit hair, cotton, or maguey, as well as sellers of feathers and dyes (fig. 31).[18] In Peru one *visitador* (official inspector) remarked in 1562 on the fact that Indians did not exchange large quantities of goods: "In the time of the Inca there were no merchants in bulk as there are with the Spanish, only the Indians of the *tiangues* [markets] who just sold food to one another, and clothing was not bought because everyone made what they needed."[19] By the mid-sixteenth century this was no longer the case with Lima and its port, Callao, where goods from Europe were plentiful. Martín de Murúa, Mercederian friar and author of the *Historia general del Perú* (produced in Cuzco, in various manuscripts between 1590 and 1616), described Lima and its market in more detail: "they sell everything precious and valued that England, Flanders, France, Germany, Italy, and Spain produces, works and weaves, . . . when man desires the cloths, brocades, velvets, fine cloth, rags, damasks, satins, silks, . . . , fringes, they have all here, at the measure that one wants, as if one were in the richest and most frequented fairs of Amberes [Antwerp], London, Lyon, Medina del Campo, Seville, and Lisbon."[20] By the seventeenth century, whole portions of Lima had become permanent markets for the merchandise coming from the Spanish fleets, and in the Calle de Mercaderes (Street of Merchants) luxuries from Europe and Asia were available in forty different shops.[21] In the eighteenth century, additional storage facilities were erected along the southern coast of Peru to hold the overflow of goods awaiting their turn at market.[22] During the last quarter of the eighteenth century, exports to Spain from the Americas included approximately 13 million reals' worth of vicuña wool, 461 million reals of cochineal, 45 million reals of cotton, and 560 million reals of indigo.[23]

TEXTILES FROM SPAIN

More textiles were shipped from Spain to the Americas than any other item. As Felipe Guáman Poma de Ayala, Andean author of *The First New Chronicle and Good Government* (1612–15)—which he addressed to Philip III of Spain (r. 1598–1621)—succinctly put it: "From the Indies, silver, from Castile, cloth."[24] The range of textiles shipped from Spain included bolts of cloth, fabricated clothing items, and furnishing fabrics, for personal use and for resale. Woolen cloth was essential, and in a decree of 1572 the king of Spain encouraged shipping to the New World "as much woolen [cloth] as possible."[25] According to a ship's manifest from as early as 1554, two passengers bound for New Spain, Diego de Carvajal, a resident of Seville, and Francisco

Fig. 30
Martín de Murúa (Spanish, active Peru). *Capac Ypanqui, Inka King.* From *Historia general del Perú.* Peru, 1590–1613. Laid rag paper, ink, and pigments. The J. Paul Getty Museum, Los Angeles (83Mp159, folio 30v)

Fig. 31
Woven ecclesiastical band (detail). Probably Mexico, 16th–17th century. Spun feather and rabbit hair. Cooper-Hewitt, National Design Museum, Smithsonian Institution, New York, Gift of John Pierpont Morgan, 1902 (1902-1-374-a).

Bernal, were each transporting (among many other textile items) a bale of "rruanes"—one consisting of 448 varas (one vara is roughly equivalent to a yard, or 36 inches) and the other of 443 ¾ varas.[26] *Ruan*—a lightweight woolen textile produced in Rouen, France, and often made with fleece from Spain—is of particular interest in terms of cross-cultural trade. Sale of this material in the Americas was a concession that had been in the hands of Spanish families in France who had ties both to shipping and to the wool industry in Burgos, Spain, a primary source for the fleece.[27]

In spite of an earlier edict of 1509 declaring that "in the Indias they are not allowed, under penalty, to use garments of silk nor other costly materials,"[28] quantities of silk—threads, yarns, floss, and fabrics—were imported from Spain. For example, included in that 1554 shipment from Diego de Carvajal of Seville to New Spain were "2 pounds of silk (one pound each of spun and unspun thread), 3 pounds of 'Portuguese' thread, and 50 pounds of golden thread."[29] The metallic thread, which was essential for both embroidery and weaving, had likely been produced from silver and gold that had previously been shipped to Spain from the Americas as part of the Royal Fifth—the king's tax on all goods. Pounded into thin sheets of metal in Spain, cut into strips, and wrapped around a silk (or some-times linen) core, it was reexported back to Mexico and Peru, where it became a prized commodity.[30]

Imported cloth—the silks, damasks, velvets, and brocades used for garments and household furnishings in the Americas—initially came solely through Spanish merchants. Shipping manifests indicate that by the end of the sixteenth century more than six million reals' worth of cloth and clothing were arriving from Spain each year.[31] Lace from Spain and Belgium was extremely popular, along with ribbons, trim-mings, and metal edging tapes used as embellishments (fig. 32). Even with the opening of trade routes to the East, which provided new sources for silk from Guangzhou (Canton), in China, the importation of Spanish silk to the Americas continued actively throughout the colonial era, and by the eighteenth century silk imports from Valencia to Lima alone neared fifteen thousand pieces in one year.[32]

TEXTILES FROM CHINA

With the establishment of the Manila galleons— annual ships from the Philippines to Acapulco (starting in 1579) and to Lima (starting in 1581)— goods from China became part of the vocabulary of textiles and dress in the Americas. Initially, the importation of Chinese silk was prohibited, a restric-tion that was repeated at various times throughout the seventeenth and eighteenth centuries, when trade with China became too competitive with Spanish luxury goods.[33] But silk remained in high demand by colonial society, and it continued to be the primary export from China, in exchange for American silver. Silk arrived in various forms: as raw materials; as reeled fibers, floss, unspun and

spun yarns and threads; as bulk fabric lengths, both undyed and dyed; and as embroidered, painted, and woven pieces, both new and previously used. Some of the silk goods had been produced specifically as finished items for export, including embroideries and weavings made for the European and American markets, to be used as decorative and furnishing fabrics as well as garments both secular and ecclesiastical (see the essay by Maria João Pacheco Ferreira in this publication). Others came as secondhand items, such as cast-off decorative elements from Chinese garments, notably Mandarin squares, or rank badges—embroidered or woven emblems with animal designs symbolic of office and rank—that had been worn by administrative officials on the fronts and backs of their robes at the Ming dynasty court (1368–1644). After the fall of the dynasty, these decommissioned items became subject to trade, arriving along with other items in the Manila galleons. That the Ming textile designs inspired Andean weavers can be clearly seen in a group of tapestries woven in Peru whose designs and compositions are based almost entirely on these emblematic Chinese flora and fauna (fig. 33; cat. 28).[34] In a powerful interplay of symbolic and decorative elements, mythical horned and winged animals, phoenix, deer, and dragons of Chinese origin cavort among Christian symbols such as the Pelican in Her Piety and familiar colonial elements like the Spanish double-headed eagle or crowned lion (cat. 71).

Once trade relations were fully established between Asian producers and Spanish merchants in the Americas, Chinese embroiderers were commissioned to embellish traditional Andean and Mexican garments as well as those of European origin. An eighteenth-century poncho, for example, was

Fig. 33
Tapestry with Asian designs. Peru, colonial period, late 17th–early 18th century. Tapestry weave, wool, silk, cotton, and linen. Museum of Fine Arts, Boston, Denman Waldo Ross Collection (11.1264)

Fig. 34
Poncho with Asian and European motifs. Embroidered in China, for the Peruvian market, 18th century. Cotton or wool (?), embroidered with silk and metal-wrapped thread. Museo Histórico Nacional, Santiago, Chile (1981-259)

embroidered with colorful phoenix motifs at the base of the neckline, front and back (fig. 34).[35] The embroidery had likely been done in China, commissioned for this garment, which may have been fitted with its neckline and completed as a poncho once it arrived in Lima. In other cases, garments were constructed first, then sent to China to be embroidered. After Philip V, king of Spain (r. 1700–1746), adopted the French Bourbon style of wearing elaborately embroidered waistcoats and breeches, the fashion took hold in the Spanish colonies as well. This prompted the observation that in Mexico "great men, many of them, . . . send their garments to China . . . to be embroidered."[36] In addition, Asian craftsmen were brought to Mexico and Peru to execute specialized work not only in textiles but also in other decorative arts, including painted screens and furniture.[37]

Other exotic textiles—notably, East Indian calicoes—came to the Americas via secondary markets in the global trade network. These colorful, lightweight, dyed-and-printed cotton textiles, already popular in Europe, were used for garments and furnishing fabrics in Mexico and Peru between the sixteenth and the eighteenth century, though few examples have been preserved. One rare fragment of a two-color Indian block-printed cotton textile with characteristically delicate floral and geometric designs was excavated recently in Lima, from a sixteenth- to seventeenth-century Spanish-style house (fig. 35).[38] In the absence of other examples, the taste and fashion for hand-painted, resist-dyed, and printed Indian imports can be witnessed in the seventeenth- and eighteenth-century portrait paintings of Mexican ladies and gentlemen that frequently present their subjects wearing garments made of these fabrics.[39]

Fig. 35
East Indian textile excavated from the foundation of a Spanish house, "Huaca Tres Palos." Rimac Valley (Lima), 16th–17th century. Cotton, block-printed resist and mordant, dyed. Museo de Arqueología "Josefina Ramos de Cox," Instituto Riva-Agüero, Lima (I-0564)

ARTISANS FROM EUROPE

Just as fabrics came to the Americas from around the world, so too did craftsmen, who established textile industries modeled after European methods. The emigration of skilled artisans was encouraged by the Spanish government, which provided tax relief for those who established themselves in the New World. Arriving with the tools of their trade, these artisans included weavers, embroiderers, tailors, and specialists in spinning, fulling, and other aspects of textile production, among them those who specialized in the preparation and weaving of silk. By 1533 there were twenty silk weavers and spinners in Mexico City.[40] In Lima there were forty tailors, weavers, and hosiers by 1549, and by the 1560s, more than one hundred fifty of them.[41]

EMBROIDERERS

Master embroiderers were among the earliest to bring their skills from Spain. One of the first to arrive was Pedro Jiménez, who went to Mexico in 1526; the passenger list of a ship going from Cádiz to New Spain in 1538 includes embroiderer Diego Alemán and his wife, María de Gante.[42] Such master embroiderers from Spain produced their most refined and resplendent artworks for the Church in New Spain and Peru (figs. 36, 37). Emigrating primarily from Seville and Toledo, they brought with them the tradition of European silk and gold embroidery, using stitching techniques that originated in Italy as well as Spain. They also brought the European tradition of guilds, which became powerful social organizations representing all segments of textile work, including silk weaving and embroidery.[43] Many of these artisans were anonymous, but the archives of the cathedrals in Mexico City and

Puebla record the names of master embroiderers who created vestments for the priests as well as altar
frontals and other church textiles between the
sixteenth and the eighteenth century.[44] These
records reveal a pattern (the same as in Spain) in
which generations of a family of embroiderers would
assume, over time, the role of Master of the
Vestments, responsible for producing and maintaining the textile inventory of a cathedral.

   Less is known about the methods and organization of embroidery workshops in Peru than
about those in Mexico. However, two embroiderers in Cuzco, Domingo Guaman Suyo and
Juan Guaman Vilca, were commissioned on
April 19, 1596, to produce a red velvet
cover for a cross as well as two dalmatics
and a cassock. They were given the gold
and silk needed for the work; for the
cross cover they were paid 35 pesos,
for the dalmatics, 45 pesos, and for
the cassock, 25 pesos, plus "the
meals during all of the worktime."[45]
Another contract from Cuzco
records that in September 1600 one
Pedro Martin officially apprenticed
"with a master embroiderer named
Baltazar Aucca Poma, for a period of
three years during which he would be
trained in embroidery, and would be

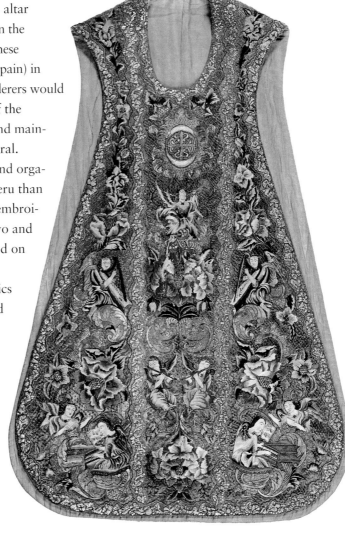

Fig. 36
Chasuble with angels. Dominican
Convent of Santa Rosa de Lima,
Puebla, Mexico, ca. 1750. Silk,
embroidered with silk and metal-
wrapped thread. Museo Nacional
del Virreinato, Instituto Nacional de
Antropología e Historia, Tepotzotlán,
Mexico (AA383041)

Fig. 37
Detail of angels from fig. 36

given food and medicines, and for each year he would be given a garment of *pano de quito* [a
woolen cloth from Ecuador], one hat, three shirts, shoes, and at the end of three years, a frame,
scissors, thimble and needles, and some patterns and other curiosities that will aid in his work."[46]
The fact that the name of the master is Andean, or at least a mix of Spanish (Baltazar) and Quechua
(Aucca Poma), suggests that by the turn of the seventeenth century Spanish-style embroidery was in
the hands of Andean master artisans.

TAPESTRY WEAVERS

In Peru, former Inca *cumbi* weavers, with Spanish oversight, created a new hybrid medium that became
the major textile art form of the region. The function of tapestry-woven textiles changed from the
fine, modest-size garments used by the Inca to large-scale wall hangings in the European manner.
European influence can be seen in the narrative content of the pictorial imagery as well as in the use
of a central field with concentric borders, similar in design to both Flemish tapestries and

Right:
Fig. 38
The Creation of Eve. Southern Andes, early 17th century. Tapestry weave, cotton and camelid fiber. Círculo de Armas, Buenos Aires

Top:
Fig. 39
Detail of fig. 38, showing the skillful, delicate rendering of shading by Andean tapestry weavers

Bottom:
Fig. 40
Baltasar Jaime Martínez Compañón (Spanish, active Peru). Colonial innovation in spinning using a foot-powered wheel. From *Trujillo del Perú*, Peru, 1782–86. Hand-drawn manuscript. Real Biblioteca, Palacio Real de Madrid (11/345)

Hispano-Moresque carpets.[47] Subtle modification of indigenous tapestry-weaving techniques resulted from local training by European weavers or close observation of European models. Hatching, for example—a weaving method used in Europe to achieve subtle shading through the interpenetration of colored yarns into adjacent areas—can be seen in some Andean colonial tapestries for the first time. This is particularly notable in a series of narrative tapestries made in Cuzco in the seventeenth century, which depict biblical scenes such as the Garden of Eden and the Creation of Eve (figs. 38, 39).[48] To provide European aesthetic and technical guidance to skilled native craftsmen (and craftswomen), in the eighteenth century the Jesuits brought two Flemish tapestry weavers, Philip Ossemayer and Thomas Semiller, to the art academy they had established on the outskirts of Santiago, Chile.[49] There likely had been other experts before them, though we do not know their names.

NEW METHODS AND MATERIALS

Traditional native materials and methods of cloth production persisted in some regions of Mexico and Peru during the colonial era, especially within small isolated communities remote from the centers of colonial power. In other areas, the old ways were completely altered by the arrival of the Spanish. Artisans coming to the Americas applied European approaches to the local crafts of spinning, weaving,

Fig. 41
Samples of printed cottons (*Indian-illas*). Mexico, 1793. Archivo de Indias, Seville (MP-TEJIDOS,15). These were accompanied by a letter dated August 30, 1793, from the viceroy of New Spain, Juan Vicente de Güemes Padilla Horcasitas y Aguayo, Count of Revillagigedo, Mexico.

sewing, and embroidery and brought new equipment and ways of working (fig. 40). The hand spindles traditionally used for cotton in Mexico and Peru and for camelid-hair spinning in the Andes continued in native use, while the introduction of hand-operated and water-powered spinning wheels increased the production of yarn.[50] As early as 1545 Spanish craftsmen brought with them tools that included large European-style foot-treadle looms with multiple shafts, used for weaving long lengths of patterned cloth, as well as such small items as metal pins, needles, and scissors.[51] These contrasted with the traditional Andean backstrap, ground-stake, and upright looms that had been used in the region for centuries.[52]

By the mid-sixteenth century the introduction of new materials—sheep's wool from Spain, silk from both Spain and Asia, metallic yarns from Europe—had a major impact on textile production in Latin America. Some of these goods came in the form of raw or partially prepared materials, such as woolen fleece or spun-silk yarns. But in many cases, the sources themselves were introduced as part of the Spanish enterprise. Merino and Churro sheep, for example, were imported from Spain early in the sixteenth century to establish a wool industry in ranches and pastures throughout the Americas.[53] A fifteen-year program to plant mulberry trees in Huejotzingo, Cholula, and Tlaxcala, begun in 1536, was the first step in introducing silk production to Mexico, on the orders of Antonio de Mendoza, viceroy of New Spain (r. 1535–50). Establishing these trees was essential because fresh mulberry leaves, consumed daily, were (and are to this day) the cultivated silkworms' only sustenance.[54] Raising the silkworms from "seeds" (actually eggs) shipped from Spain was a delicate matter, requiring knowledge as well as luck for them to survive the long sea voyages, and the processing of the precious filament they extruded to form the cocoon (the silk fiber), as well as the spinning and weaving, had to be done by specialists.

In Peru another European fiber, linen, was introduced in 1545, following dictates from Spain to establish a linen and hemp industry.[55] A staple of the Spanish textile industry, linen—or rather the flax plants whose long stems provided the linen fiber—had been expected to be cultivable in Peru. However, the forbidding environment of the coastal deserts could not sustain the fragile plants, which required substantial water to thrive.

COLONIAL TEXTILE PRODUCTION

The cultivation of sheep's wool, silk, and linen was necessary to establish textile production on a broad scale aligned with European custom. The knowledge of how to process, spin, and weave these materials, each with its own requirements, was equally critical to ensuring a viable textile industry. Although Andean and Mexican weavers excelled in their native craft traditions, by the mid-sixteenth century textile workshops, or *obrajes*, modeled after those in Spain, were established in both Mexico and Peru.[56] They primarily created lengths of utilitarian cloth, in bolts thirty varas long (approximately thirty yards).[57] This was an entirely different approach to textile production, as traditional Latin American weavers generally produced one single item or garment at a time, conserving the cloth that was used without cutting.[58] Woven on European-style foot-powered treadle looms, these simple, somewhat coarse textiles became a colonial staple. They included *sayal* (lightweight woolen sackcloth), bayeta (woolen flannel or felted cloth), and *jerga* (woolen twill).

Spanish law regulated both the method of production and the quality, which was specified in terms of the number of threads per unit of measure that were set up on the loom, such as fourteen, eighteen, or twenty-four.[59] The 1548 *Cortes* of Valladolid, one of a series of regulations that governed guild production of textiles in Spain and the colonies, specified that *obrajes* in the Americas could not produce fabrics finer than a twenty-four count.[60] The textiles made in the *obrajes* were intended mostly for domestic consumption, as noted by Luis de Velasco, viceroy of Peru (r. 1595–1607): "principally they make clothing that the natives use and blankets and not valuable cloth."[61] Workshops varied in size, including the number of looms and weavers, and so did the scale of production, which influenced whether the textiles were consumed locally or were traded regionally. Mexico, for example, developed major production centers for both cottons and woolens and maintained an active regional trade, exporting cloth to Peru. Dyestuffs were also part of this extended trade network; by the eighteenth century, one large *obraje* in Cuzco, Peru, was using indigo from Guatemala.[62]

The woolen industry, in particular, took hold in both Mexico and Peru. Bayeta cloth made in Spain was known for its dense felted surface and deep colors, produced with dyes of Mexican cochineal and Guatemalan indigo. Wool cloth like bayeta, which was also made in England, France, and Holland, was used for barter and trade throughout the world (cats. 30, 110); the red and blue cloth was also imported into the Americas (see fig. 111). Recent excavations in the sixteenth-century church of Magdalena de Cao Viejo, on the northern coast of Peru, uncovered a fragment of blue felted trade cloth.[63] Mexican *obrajes* produced bayeta based on the Spanish model and traded it within the region extending from the southwest of North America to southern Peru. A special version of bayeta was also produced in Peru, where brushing the woolen cloth after weaving created an unusually long-haired, even shaggy surface. A rare sample book of *bayetones* (a variant of bayeta) made in the Moxos region of eastern Peru in 1795 shows a number of variations of this cloth.[64]

Cotton cloth was one of the most important products made in the New World, used locally and exported both regionally and internationally.[65] Workshops that specialized in the spinning and weaving of coarse and fine cotton were developed on a large scale. The native cotton (*Gossypium barbadense*) grown in Peru and Mexico both before and after the Conquest had an unusually long staple and yielded extremely fine, silklike fabric.[66] Printed cotton textiles called *Indianillas* were made in Mexico as a local counterpart to the popular imported East Indian calicoes (fig. 41). They were produced in sizable building complexes (also referred to as *Indianillas*) that were specially constructed to house the printing and dyeworks. By the second half of the eighteenth century, these East Indian–style fabrics made in Mexico became part of the global trade in textiles.[67]

Though not native to the New World, silk became essential to colonial society, and, as noted above, a silk-weaving industry was successfully established in Mexico.[68] Along with the raising of silkworms, which took place specifically in central Mexico, the various processes related to silk—including reeling the silk from the cocoons, preparing the yarns, dressing the loom, and actually weaving the fine cloth—required specialized craftsmen and equipment, including the sophisticated European-style drawloom for weaving complex designs. The industry flourished especially in Mexico City and Puebla, though it was diminished during the seventeenth century by the availability of imported Chinese silk, by a downturn in the economy, and by the Spanish Crown's prohibition in 1634 of the lucrative export of Mexican silk fabrics to Peru.[69]

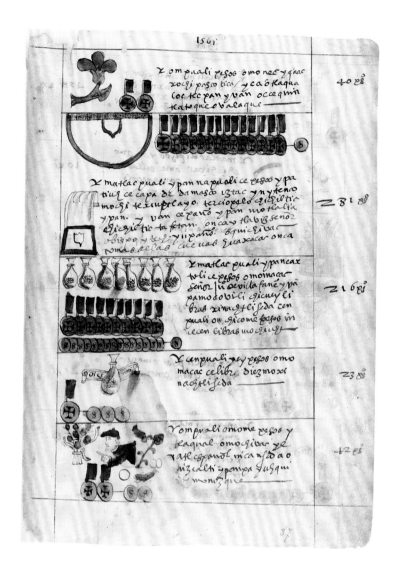

Fig. 42
Codex Sierra, folio 37. Mexico, 1550–61. Hand-drawn manuscript. Rare Manuscripts Collection, Biblioteca Histórica "José María Lafragua," Autonomous University of Puebla, Mexico. This folio shows orders from 1561 that include a white damask cope to be made by Tomás de las Cuevas, eight bags of silk eggs, and Spanish food.

TEXTILES AND THE CHURCH

In Mexico and Peru the Catholic Church was one of the largest consumers of silk (and of gold and silver threads) as well as the leading patron of the textile arts. The Church's need for luxurious textiles to serve as vestments for priests and furnishings for altars contributed to the development of global networks for both raw materials and finished goods. Contracts for the embroiderers, seamstresses, and tailors from Spain, China, and the Americas who made the ecclesiastical furnishings document the ways in which these global networks intersected. In a combination of Nahuatl and Mixtec text and pictographs, a sixteenth-century book of accounts from the rural community of Santa Catalina Texaupa—a town in the mountains in Oaxaca that raised silkworms—provides a remarkable glimpse into the process. The book, referred to as the Codex Sierra, records the yearly expenditures made between 1550 and 1564 for church furnishings, which include various copes and chasubles, altar frontals, canopies, covers for the cross, curtains, and other items. It also notes the income to the town

Fig. 43
Unku santo, tunic for a statue of the
Christ Child. Bolivia (Lake Titicaca
region), late 16th–early 17th cen-
tury. Tapestry weave, camelid fiber,
silk, and metal-wrapped thread.
Museo Nacional de Etnografía y
Folklore, La Paz (316)

from the sale of their locally raised silk, which was periodically taken to be sold in Mexico City. There,
gold threads and silk yarns and other specialty items were obtained, among them an altar frontal
"made by Diego Gutiérrez of red velvet with silver embroidery with many figures, fringes, and yellow
satin" and a white silk damask cope with red velvet borders, lined with red taffeta and made by
Tomas de las Cuevas, purchased in 1555 for 436 pesos and in 1561 for 281 pesos, respectively
(fig. 42).[70] These transactions, which involved the sale of local silk cocoons for funds to purchase
Spanish and Chinese silk cloth and finished items, included clear specifications of style and color,
along with the unspoken preference for European-style tailoring and sewing. That these transactions
were conducted by this one small town just thirty-some years after the Conquest is extraordinary.

   From a slightly later period, a contract for a set of vestments for the convent of Santa Clara in
Mexico City provides similar specifications and, in addition, provides details about the origin of
some of the materials. The order—which included "two dalmatics, a chasuble, choir cope, a pulpit
cope, a lectern cloth, a chalice veil, sash, three maniples, two stoles, and a corporal burse, all fourteen pieces on a white background of Cantonese silk and lined with crimson taffeta from Bengala, with

gold and silk fringes"—was commissioned in the seventeenth century for twelve hundred pesos.[71] White silk "from Canton" is specified in numerous documents of the period, especially in commissions for the Church (cat. 68).[72] The reference in this order to linings of Indian (Bengal) crimson silk taffeta are notable because the crimson color was likely produced with the famous cochineal dye from Oaxaca, exported to Asia and India.[73] Combining these materials imported from Europe, Asia, or India with the artistry of local or foreign craftsmen resulted in textiles whose composite origins can be difficult to identify or assess.

The growth of the Catholic Church in the Americas beginning in the sixteenth century was concurrent with the suppression of native religions. Nonetheless, native religious practice persisted, and imported trade textiles penetrated into its realm. At the same time, traditional Andean textiles found their way into Christian celebrations. In spite of efforts by Spanish priests in the sixteenth and seventeenth centuries to "extirpate idolatry" from the Andes (a term used by the clergy in the sixteenth century), native worshippers would use special imported silk cloths in ritual contexts, such as covering huacas—natural stones or other objects honored as sacred.[74] They also gave fine indigenous *cumbi* cloth as offerings to huacas, and in 1552 several of these textiles were confiscated by Augustinian friars and made into altar frontals.[75] Used native garments were sometimes donated to churches, among them a "primrose-colored satin woman's mantle with gold trimming" belonging to María de Amores, from Quito, Ecuador, which she left in her will of 1596 to be given to the convent of Nuestra Señora de los Remedios in Quito so that it could be remade into a chasuble.[76] And, with encouragement from the Jesuits, native garments were sometimes produced especially for the Church, in the form of miniature Inca-style tunics woven in silk and gold to clothe statues of Christ (fig. 43).[77]

COLONIAL DRESS AND IDENTITY

In the sixteenth century, dress in the viceroyalties was regulated through official decrees issued by the king of Spain, which were part of the Laws of the Indies that governed both native and nonnative behavior. Continuing a long tradition of Spanish sumptuary laws, these edicts had an impact not only on the style of garments but also on the materials permitted for use in making them. Initially, a royal cedula pronounced that the Indians "are forbidden to dress themselves like us."[78] Later, though, in the Andes—both at the end of the sixteenth century and again in the eighteenth—Inca-style tunics were banished for political reasons, and the populace was instead required to conform to Spanish-style dress.[79]

After the traditional *anacu* was declared indecent in the 1570s because the wrapped garment exposed women's legs as they walked, dress codes in Cuzco required that they be stitched up the sides; at the same time we find the petticoat was introduced.[80] The materials of women's garments, as well as their shape, were also regulated, including the use of silk and metal threads and the number of pieces of lace.[81] These costly materials were incorporated into native women's garments, particularly those of high status, often as small design elements, such as mermaids or flowers; at other times, they were used to weave the entire garment. Andean weavers also created new kinds of hybrid fabrics, inspired by expensive European textiles and materials. For example, *tornesol* (as it was known in Spain) was a type of luxury cloth—"shot" or "changeable" silk—produced in Europe, India, and Asia, in which yarns of two different colors create a shimmering effect. Sometime after the mid-sixteenth century, weavers of the southern Andes created their own version of this iridescent fabric, called *pechuga*

De Eſpanolyd'India, Meſtiſa.

de paloma (dove's breast).[82] It was composed of extremely fine, highly twisted alpaca yarns, with black in the warp and pink in the weft, woven into simple but spectacular rectangular mantles and dresses that would shimmer in the sunlight, comparable in luster and fineness to any European satin.

In both Mexico and Peru during the seventeenth and eighteenth centuries, painted portraits of native women wearing traditional-style garments celebrated each culture's rich textile heritage and accentuated the wearer's status by means of the artist's detailed depictions. These portraits are generally in the context of a union with a Spanish or Creole male partner (fig. 44). These unions were important features of colonial life, as they created a new hybrid society with new social orders.[83] That this mixed heritage was reflected in textiles can be seen in documents such as wills and testaments.

Spanish inheritance law applied to the inhabitants of the viceroyalties, who passed down textiles and garments—along with jewelry, furniture, land, animals, and even slaves—as property. María de Amores from Quito (whose bequest of a mantle was mentioned above) had been married twice to Spanish husbands, and her 1596 will included the following items: "a Chinese lijilla . . . / a lijilla of green Castilian damask with golden edging / an anaku of green Castilian satin with golden edgings / a lijilla of primrose colored satin with needlework, and golden edgings."[84] The "lijilla" (*lliclla*), a traditional woman's shoulder mantle or shawl, and the "anaku" (*anacu*), or wrapped dress, were Andean women's garments from Inca times. The bequest of a Chinese shawl by 1596 is remarkably early, considering that only a few Manila galleons had brought silks to the Viceroyalty of Peru by that date. In addition, the use of Castilian damask, satin, and metallic trimmings for traditional native garments offers a glimpse into the worlds negotiated by this woman.

Such a mix of materials and cultures was not limited to women, as seen in a testament dated August 3, 1584, from a gentleman of Quechua origin, Juan Quispe from Trujillo, Peru. It mentions European-style garments in a variety of fabrics: "one *jubon* [waistcoat] of *mediñaque* with its buttons, old; a manta of Ruan with its fringe; a piece of clothing, the colored *camiseta* of *cumbi*."[85] This means that he had a European-style waistcoat made of a fabric, *medriñaque*, that is possibly of Philippine origin (perhaps referring to Chinese embroidery brought via the Philippines),[86] a fringed mantle made of cloth from France, and a piece of Spanish clothing described in Inca terms as *cumbi*, indicating high-quality cloth. The composite nature of one man's possessions acquired within fifty years of the Conquest indicates clearly that textiles that were part of the global trade found their way into the households of a great variety of social circles in sixteenth-century Latin America.

In 1602 Gaspar de Zúñiga, fifth count of Monterrey, viceroy of New Spain (r. 1595–1603) and subsequently of Peru (r. 1604–6), observed about the population of the region, "All these people live most luxuriously, all wear silk and of the most fine and costly quality."[87] This luxury continued into the eighteenth century, when it was noted by travelers such as Amédée-François Frézier (1682–1773), who traveled through Peru in 1712–14. As he described it: "Both men and women are equally inclined to be costly in their Dress. The women not satisfy'd with the Expense of the richest Silks, adorn them after their Manner, with a prodigious quantity of Lace. . . . The Fashion whereof, which amounts to very much, ruins the Husbands and the Gallants" (see fig. 32).[88]

The desire for silks, velvets, and other luxury or exotic goods was shared by much of society within the viceroyalties, a society composed of indigenous inhabitants, Europeans, Africans, and even Asians. From the early phases of contact and conflict through the establishment of the structures of colonial life, the transformation of the cultural landscape in this vast region between the sixteenth and the eighteenth century was reflected in the value systems, identities, lifestyles, and politics of every stratum of colonial life. Throughout this period, the Americas participated in the international exchange that fueled the global trade networks, not only as a primary supplier and source of some of the most precious and sought-after materials but also as a major consumer of the international products that traversed the oceans.

Chinese Textiles
for Portuguese Tastes

Maria João Pacheco Ferreira

ortugal's involvement in Asia began with Vasco da Gama's voyage to Kozhikode (Calicut), India, in 1497–98. After the Portuguese conquered Melaka (Malacca) in 1511, the significance of the Chinese market in terms of interregional trade became evident to them, motivating an increased interest in the Far East.[1] The Portuguese Crown, hoping to benefit from the unimaginable wealth that trade with China might bring, sent an embassy to the Chinese kingdom.[2] The first official trip to China took place in 1513, under the command of Jorge Álvares (d. 1521). In 1516 the Portuguese apothecary Tomé Pires (1465–1524?), who was considered to be "the best European collector of information on Asia,"[3] was sent to China from his home in a Portuguese colony in India by Manuel I (r. 1495–1521) to serve as ambassador. Arriving first at Guangzhou (Canton), the newly appointed emissary traveled with his official entourage to Beijing, where the emperor refused to receive them, the embassy having suddenly fallen out of favor. Its members were imprisoned or killed, and the Portuguese were prohibited from entering Chinese waters by imperial decree of the Ming dynasty (1368–1644) as part of its broader ban on foreign trade.

Direct commerce between the Portuguese and Chinese merchants from the coastal areas of Zhejiang, Fujian, and Guangdong became a reality in the 1520s, albeit secretly, via bribery and contraband. In 1554 a new era of Sino-Portuguese relations began when Leonel de Sousa succeeded in signing an agreement with the provincial authorities of Guangdong that legalized Portuguese trading activities in China through the payment of taxes. This settlement was influenced in part by Portuguese collaboration in removing Japanese pirates from Chinese waters and by their development of trade with Japan (where the Portuguese had arrived in 1542), centered on exporting Chinese silk and importing Japanese silver. By 1557 the Portuguese had received authorization to establish a permanent settlement in Macau, which would expand gradually over the following years.

By the mid-sixteenth century the Chinese from the southern coastal provinces—still barred by the Ming court from engaging in private maritime trade—were eager to foster foreign relations and sought out intermediaries to assist them. Having established a foothold in Macau, the Portuguese were quite familiar with the main trade routes of the Asian seas. They thus assumed a privileged position as key partners with the Chinese in what would soon become an immensely lucrative enterprise. Despite the periodic conflicts during these early years, Chinese and Portuguese merchants forged close ties, and Macau swiftly became a successful commercial port.[4]

In addition to serving as a trading post, Macau quickly assumed strategic importance for religious organizations, particularly for the Portuguese-based Society of Jesus (active in India beginning in 1542, and in Japan beginning in 1549), who were hoping to begin the spiritual conquest of China originally conceived by Francis Xavier (1506–1552; see fig. 17). The Jesuits, who did not receive authorization to enter mainland China until 1582, had established a residence in Macau in 1562 and organized a religious community there that remained dominant until the 1630s, when other religious orders—notably the Dominicans (1631) and the Franciscans (1633)—began to arrive from Europe, particularly from Portugal, Spain, and Italy. The Jesuits were pivotal as the intellectual and religious standard-bearers for the newly formed Macanese society, serving in conflict mediation, teaching, charitable works, and diplomacy. They also offered support to the Macanese in their relations with the provincial Chinese authorities as well as with the court in Beijing, where a Jesuit mission was established by Matteo Ricci (1552–1610) in 1601.

The founding of the Portuguese colony in Macau marked the beginning of Chinese trade with Europe, eventually making Chinese goods available to many other nations beyond Europe. Multicultural

Macau became a hub for the circulation of people, products, and knowledge that included such diverse fields as music, medicine, painting, astronomy, and watchmaking.

EARLIEST EVIDENCE OF CHINESE TEXTILES IN PORTUGAL

Benefiting from an increasingly more consolidated network of trading posts and contacts in various Asian trading centers—such as Macau, Melaka in Malaysia, and Kochi and Goa in India (the final ports of call for trading ships bound for Lisbon)—the Portuguese now had access to a considerable range of products. In terms of textiles, trade focused on both raw materials and finished products, including cloth yardage sent to Portugal to be cut and assembled according to Western styles. In 1518 alone, more than two and a half tons each of Chinese silk and other Chinese fabrics were shipped from Kochi to Portugal.[5] In the *Crónica do felicíssimo rei D. Manuel* (Chronicle of King Manuel), published in Lisbon in 1566, Damião de Góis describes the Chinese cloth that Fernão Peres de Andrade brought back from Asia to the royal palace in Évora in 1520. This book, which contains the oldest known reference to Chinese textiles in Portugal, mentions fabrics that were richly adorned with depictions of landscapes, orchards, and figures of Chinese deities, including Matsu, the goddess of the seas and "Patroness of Sailors."[6] De Góis may have been describing Chinese silk tapestries, or *kesi*, which, if indeed the case, would have been the first of their kind to reach Portugal (fig. 45).

Fig. 45
Panel with a phoenix in a rock garden. China, Ming dynasty (1368–1644). Silk and metallic thread tapestry (*kesi*). The Metropolitan Museum of Art, New York, Seymour Fund, 1960 (60.1)

The earliest articles of clothing and other items made entirely from or incorporating pieces of Chinese textiles survive only in written descriptions, such as the Chinese brocade liturgical vestment that appears in a 1522 inventory of King Manuel's wardrobe.[7] As evidenced by a similar inventory from 1534, João III (1502–1557) shared his father's tastes and had among his possessions pieces crafted from Chinese silks, including a set of three flags, one in damask bearing the Portuguese coat of arms and two in white taffeta adorned with the cross of the Order of Christ.[8] The same document mentions more than 100 yards of gauze and over 4 yards of satin, also from China. The 1528 inventory for Catherine of Austria (1507–1578), queen of Portugal, records some 35 yards of white Chinese silk among her possessions.[9] By the second quarter of the sixteenth century, Chinese silks figured as feasible alternatives to European textiles in the creation of clothing, vestments, and hangings.

Although these early pieces have not survived, there is sufficient evidence remaining today to give us an idea of the importance of Chinese textiles from the sixteenth to the eighteenth century in Portugal. Examples of Chinese fabrics are found in churches and public and private museums throughout Portugal, most prominently in the Museu Nacional Machado de Castro in Coimbra and the Museu Nacional de Arte Antiga in Lisbon. These collections are noteworthy for preserving some of the finest examples of works created in China to suit

Portuguese tastes, a large number of which are in the form of liturgical vestments and other ecclesiastical accoutrements.

THE INTRODUCTION OF NEW PRODUCTS FOR EXPORT

By the mid-sixteenth century, fully aware of the economic potential behind trade with the Portuguese, the Chinese began making textiles for this new market, imitating designs or reproducing iconography that were essentially foreign to their own aesthetic principles, largely copied from European engravings and decorative objects. The Jesuit missionary Luís Fróis (1532–1597) offered eloquent proof of this when describing, in one of his letters to Portugal, the use of Chinese textiles embellished with Christian imagery in feast day observances at Saint Paul's College in Goa, India, in the late 1550s: "I will tell you something very humorous about the Chinese: [after] they were informed how the Portuguese worshipped their God and made their processions in Goa using images, the Chinese, as skilled as they are, decided not to lose the opportunity to profit, which is their main interest."[10] Although relations between Portugal and China were still in an embryonic stage, Chinese craftsmen demonstrated a tremendous flair for imitation and had already become quite conversant in the preferences of the Portuguese in a broad range of artistic media.[11]

On the basis of documentation and material evidence relating to Chinese textiles in Portugal, we now have a relatively clear image of the newly formed Sino-Portuguese artistic universe. The objects analyzed reveal an extraordinary interweaving of European and Chinese references. This is true not only from a material and technical standpoint but also with regard to visual imagery, in terms of iconography and ornamentation, all of which follow aesthetic principles culled from both artistic traditions. The inventoried corpus of works shows a majority of articles fashioned with silk textile supports that are almost always embroidered or painted, the most common methods used to pattern Chinese silks for export. These techniques predominate from the seventeenth century on, due to the relative ease of producing such pieces.[12] In the sixteenth century, however, patterned woven silks, manufactured following Chinese traditions, were produced for the Portuguese and were generally used for both furnishings and liturgical vestments. Particularly noteworthy are the examples scattered among various international collections of a silk lampas yardage decorated with patterns dominated by crowned, double-headed eagles set above heart-shaped vases pierced with arrows (see detail p. 46; cats. 15, 16). Despite the double-headed eagle's obvious associations with the Habsburgs, and the pierced hearts' affiliation with the religious order of the Augustinians, this particular motif's appearance in textiles for the Portuguese market should mainly be understood as the adoption of one of the most popular and widely disseminated elements in European iconography, in use from the time of the Roman Empire. Its continued presence and acceptance are otherwise difficult to understand in the Portuguese world after 1640, when Portugal regained the political sovereignty it had lost in 1580 to Spain and the Habsburgs. The same decorative motif of eagles clutching crossed arrows that pierce what appear to be heart-shaped vases can be seen in three velvet panels likely of Chinese manufacture from the second half of the sixteenth century, which are today in a Portuguese museum (fig. 46).

A core group of embroidered specimens, mostly dating from the seventeenth century, represents the essence of Sino-Portuguese textile manufacturing, again characterized by the interchange of concepts and technical approaches from both cultures. This synthesis is even found in the design of the

Fig. 46
Panel. China, for the Portuguese
market, second half of the 16th century. Silk velvet. Museu Nacional
de Arte Antiga, Lisbon (2178-2180)

Fig. 47
Curtain. China, for the Portuguese
market, 17th century. Silk velvet,
embroidered with gilt-paper-wrapped
thread. The Metropolitan Museum
of Art, New York, Bequest of Mary
Anna Palmer Draper, 1914 (15.43.314)

Opposite, top:
Fig. 48
Rank badge with a crane. China,
Qing dynasty (1644–1911), late
17th–early 18th century. Silk satin,
embroidered with silk and gilt-paper-
wrapped thread. The Metropolitan
Museum of Art, New York, Fletcher
Fund, 1936 (36.65.10)

specific stitches and manufacturing techniques adopted.[13] The procedures identified, which generally follow Chinese embroidery and East Asian artistic notions, sometimes also reference European embroidery techniques. This is the case with the use of gilt-paper-wrapped thread, a characteristic East Asian material that was employed together with filling materials (rolls of paper or thick cotton threads) to give a three-dimensional appearance reminiscent of European couched work (fig. 47).

Many decorative elements with obvious European origins, taken from Christian, heraldic, mythological, or ornamental sources, appeared in Chinese textiles, some of them seeming to be entirely European (with the exception of occasional technical or material aspects). In other cases, the compositions indicate a coexistence of European and Chinese themes. In a sixteenth-century blue and gold damask (cat. 16), such essentially Chinese design elements as stylized lotus blossoms balance ornamentation that would appeal to European tastes, in this instance double-headed eagles and elephants.

Sometimes European motifs were composed in a Chinese manner. The double-headed eagle is generally represented with open wings and an extended tail, as if it were inscribed within an imaginary circle. In some circumstances, this suggestion is further enhanced by the representation of the tail as an open fan. A similar treatment of birds within circles can be observed in Chinese rank badges and other textiles from the Ming and the beginning of the Qing dynasties (1644–1911), particularly in the emblems of high-ranking officials represented by the image of the crane (fig. 48). Occasionally the eagle is elongated, particularly in the beak, neck, and wings, thus suggesting a strong similarity to the Chinese phoenix symbol, and the scales along the length of the eagles' necks and heads resemble a sort of crest. The visual power and decorative versatility of the resulting eagle image contributed greatly to its popularity, as did the concurrent meanings associated with the eagle and the phoenix, in the West and in imperial China, as symbols of power and courage or of strength and solidity,

respectively.[14] This may explain the appearance of double-headed eagles on pieces for domestic use, such as hangings or coverlets (fig. 49), as well as on textiles for religious use. Of particular note is the presence of this motif in the center panel of one of the chasubles in the Metropolitan Museum's collection (cat. 72), which is the only example of the double-headed eagle known among the liturgical vestments the author has studied. The same process of adaptation by craftsmen in transforming European imagery into something more familiar to them can be seen in an embroidered coverlet (cat. 25) in which Chinese facial features appear on figures clearly meant to represent Europeans.

In contrast to the Europeanizing tendency evident in many pieces, in some there persist numerous Chinese elements. On the same coverlet, there is abundant imagery representing Chinese flora and fauna. In other examples, such as a chasuble in the Museu Nacional de Arte Antiga, Lisbon, and a dalmatic in the Treasury of Braga Cathedral, plant stems appear as a dominating compositional element, with leaves, tendrils, flowers, or fruit often coiling sinuously upward, virtually covering the entire surface of the fabric.[15] Peony branches, which became an important element in the Chinese thematic repertoire in the late seventh century after the plant's cultivation was encouraged by Empress Wu Zetian, abound.[16] Animals also play a prominent role in Chinese imagery, with birds and mammals depicted almost always in pairs. Noteworthy within this particular context is a type of embroidered panel with a central composition dominated by pairs of rotating phoenixes surrounded by a dazzling array of other animals (cat. 28).[17] Such panels must have been enormously popular and were exported not only to Europe but even farther afield, becoming the model for several Peruvian tapestries (fig. 33). The great esteem in which Chinese textiles were held, along with the difficulty of obtaining them, undoubtedly fostered the creation of similar products outside China. Under such circumstances, in which the final product often embodies what John Irwin termed "Chinoiserie," or the application of a Chinese manner or style by another culture, it is not always easy to distinguish the boundary between what is and what is not authentically Chinese.[18]

The growing enthusiasm for Chinese textiles overseas surely contributed to the steady development of workshops and an increase in the number of craftsmen involved. The specific approach that the craftsman would adopt was determined by the quantity and variety of patterns, the interests and tastes of customers, and the nature of the commissions or orders received. Along with commissions that came with explicit specifications (we know these existed because of the number of works bearing the coats of arms of noble families and Portuguese religious institutions; fig. 50), many other orders were far less detailed and simply requested Chinese fabrics, in keeping with the rising popularity in Europe for all Asian goods, which were associated with refined taste and status. This was as true for textiles destined for religious use as it was for those for secular use. In some cases decorative compositions reveal a prior conception

Fig. 49
Hanging. China, for the Portuguese market, early 18th century. Silk satin, embroidered with silk and gilt-paper-wrapped thread. Museu do Caramulo, Portugal (270)

Fig. 50
Hanging. China, for the Portuguese market, early 18th century. Silk damask, embroidered with silk and gilt-paper-wrapped thread. Museu Nacional de Arte Antiga, Lisbon (1754)

and subsequent production carried out entirely in China, while other items appear to have been crafted using Chinese silk yardage that was painted or embroidered overall with repeating patterns and then assembled in China or wherever the yardage ended up being sold (fig. 51). Chinese craftsmen became accustomed to producing work for foreigners and to working within a modular structure that allowed them to provide great variety in large quantities, following rigorous quality standards, with high turnover and low production costs.[19]

Chinese craftsmen's use of relatively few resources to suggest a diverse assortment of media and effects is well known. There were, however, varying qualities of execution depending on the end purpose of the textiles produced. Sometimes techniques were employed that while highly visually effective were also faster to produce and therefore more profitable, such as the use of mixed-colored threads to achieve the effect of shading (fig. 52). Alternatively, these more "shorthand" techniques may also have been in response to the instructions, issued by Chinese rulers in the 1520s at the start of Portugal's contact with China, that were intended to impede access by foreigners to the most sophisticated Chinese works.[20]

The exact location of these workshops in China is still not known, nor is it known at what point they became exclusively oriented to production for Western customers.[21] Some scholars suggest Macau as a probable center, specifically for woven fabrics like those decorated with double-headed eagles,[22] which is corroborated by the fact that in 1609 António de Morga mentions the arrival in Manila of furnishing fabrics made in Macau, followed by reports of some Chinese weavers residing there who worked on Portuguese commissions after the Portuguese expulsion from Japan (1639).[23] Nevertheless, evidence in support of this has so far not been found. Aside from the development of certain crafts-related industries, specifically in metal- and stonework, Macau functioned primarily as a commercial port, in keeping with the provisions of its charter of 1588.[24] Macau has also been proposed as a center of production for embroidered fabrics, since the city's craftsmen were known to occasionally produce liturgical vestments to satisfy the needs of local religious orders.[25] The religious communities residing there included members from various countries, including China. Some of the community members were highly skilled and functioned as artists and architects; hence, the suggestion that there were missionary members who also worked as embroiderers is hardly surprising. This could explain the existence of a set of three quite similar vestments decorated with various representations of apostles, saints, and the Virgin Mary. Those figures are painted in ink and surrounded by embroidered branches of peonies that have little in common with Chinese style or technique and thus could possibly have been decorated instead by Europeans in Macau (fig. 53). In general, however, it is more likely that these religious communities had access to outside Chinese workshops.

A production center more probable than Macau would be Guangzhou, although it is not known if the merchandise obtained there reflected local manufacture or was only marketed there. The Portuguese traveled regularly to this city and also traded there through intermediary Chinese merchants, who not only made transactions on behalf of customers from Macau but also often financed Portuguese dealings. This successful trading helped to further consolidate the links between customers,

Chinese middlemen, and the crafts workshops themselves, which, in turn, fostered loyal patronage over the years.

Fig. 51
Cope. Textile: China, 18th century. Silk, painted. Museu Municipal Dr. José Formosinho, Lagos, Portugal

Fig. 52
Mixed-colored silk embroidery on coverlet (detail of cat. 26)

THE RECEPTION OF CHINESE TEXTILES IN PORTUGAL

After gradually becoming familiar with the refined works produced in Asia in the sixteenth century, the Portuguese became steadfast consumers of prized Chinese textiles; this was especially true for embroidered textiles. There are noteworthy commentaries lauding the expensive materials such as silk and gold, and the "curiosity," beauty, and sophistication of the execution of the pieces and their decorative schemes. The very origin of these works—the distant and mythical China—merited great praise. One contemporaneous account of the magnificent appearance of a set of Chinese satins of various colors installed in the Carmelite church in Lisbon following the canonization of Saint Mary Magdalene of Pazzi in 1669 declared, "Suffice it to say that it was from China."[26]

Some authors from the period emphasized the tremendous innovation and meticulous detail evident in the decoration of Chinese fabrics. Novelty was certainly an important component when appraising any highly coveted luxury

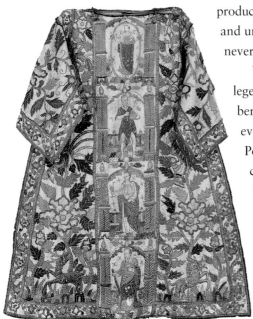

Fig. 53
Vestment. China (Macau?), 17th
century. Silk, painted with ink,
embroidered with silk and gilt-paper-
wrapped thread. Museu Nacional de
Arte Antiga, Lisbon (2276)

product. In 1586 the Augustinian friar Juan González de Mendoza commented on the precious and unfamiliar Chinese gold-paper-wrapped thread, which he believed was "spun in a way never before seen in Christendom."[27]

While it might be surmised that access to Chinese textiles was limited to a small, privileged segment of Portuguese society, these works have been linked, surprisingly, to members of nearly all social classes—from the royal family and the nobility to the Church and even to the middle class. This wide availability reflects a new era in seventeenth-century Portugal marked by increasingly frequent contact with and demand for a myriad of foreign commodities. It also attests to a profound cultural transformation in terms of the consumption of Asian goods and to a more materialistic attitude, one that extolled material wealth as a sign of status and well-being according to the precepts advocated during the Renaissance. No less important was the potential symbolic meaning associated with these (and other) Asian objects as images of the power of the Portuguese Empire, which undoubtedly further contributed to their positive reception and extensive dissemination.[28] In this context it is worthwhile to note the white taffeta canopy from China, embroidered in gold thread and multicolored silk with birds, branches, and flowers sent by King Henrique (r. 1578–80) to Abu Marwan Abd al-Malik, the Saadi sultan of Morocco, as ransom for some of the Portuguese noblemen imprisoned in Morocco after the defeat and death of King Sebastião (r. 1557–78) in the battle of Ksar el Kebir.[29]

Chinese textiles were quickly embraced in Portuguese ecclesiastical and civil life. Expressing taste, prestige, and ostentation, they were a preferred option for vestments and secular clothing, as well as for the decoration of homes, churches, and the cities themselves. This is confirmed by inventories and by accounts of both solemn and festive celebratory events, which contain references to the use of Chinese textiles as hangings or liturgical ornaments. Their overwhelming popularity can also be inferred from the tenor of some of the sumptuary laws against luxury goods, including an edict published in Porto in 1609; among the forbidden objects one finds various mentions of mantillas embroidered in China with gold and silk, in addition to coverlets, bedspreads, and curtains, all adorned with figures of birds and flowers.[30]

On important occasions, such as court ceremonies or the religious observances that filled the Catholic liturgical calendar, Chinese textiles were proudly loaned and exhibited. A splendid Chinese hanging, installed in the chapel of the royal palace for the baptism of the future king João V (1689), was embroidered with historical scenes, possibly similar in nature to a rare surviving work, the *Abduction of Helen* from a set of the Story of Troy (cat. 14). Another example is the ensemble made with Chinese gauze and decorated with gold flowers that literally covered all of the interior walls of the Church of Our Lady of Divine Providence (Saint Cajetan Monastery, Lisbon) for the canonization feast of Saint Andrew Avellino in 1713.[31]

Ongoing exposure to and greater awareness of these exotic goods, which continued in high demand, inevitably spurred the appearance of domestically produced imitations, some of which may have been the work of Portuguese artisans or of Asian slaves residing in Portugal.[32] Although there is not yet much known about the activities of these slaves, a 1578 letter from Florentine merchant Filippo Sassetti to Baccio Valore in Florence commented that among the slaves who landed annually in Portugal there were Japanese and Chinese captives. Sassetti wrote about them not because of their large numbers but because of their distinctive features and great skill: "From other places come the Japanese, greenish people with good acquaintance to practice all the arts; they have small faces and an average size. Chinese men are endowed with great intellect and also practice well all the arts."[33] Some slaves did specialize in embroidery work, as was the case with women coming from Cebu, one of the Philippine islands.[34] There were also captive female embroiderers brought from Kanyakumari (Cape Comorin, India) by Afonso de Albuquerque aboard the *Flor de la Mar* for Queen Maria (1482–1517).

A chasuble in this publication (cat. 71) could be included in the category of objects made in Portugal in the Chinese taste. The decorative floral treatments in the orphreys of this vestment resemble Portuguese tile designs from the seventeenth century that were also influenced by Chinese designs (figs. 54, 55). Such Portuguese-made articles could satisfy the desires of those who were seeking, through their attire, to adhere to these new precepts of taste without actually purchasing Chinese goods. Another example of a work made in Portugal in the Chinese taste is the antependium at the Museu de Aveiro (fig. 56), with its valance dominated by a composition clearly inspired by embroidered Mandarin squares or rank badges.[35] The appearance of this design is not surprising, given the 1569 account by Dominican friar Gaspar da Cruz (ca. 1520–1570) confirming the arrival of these badges in Portugal, where they were considered suitable for incorporation into Catholic church decorations and liturgical garments.[36]

Prior to the seventeenth century, well before the Dutch East India Company and the English East India Company were trading with China, the Chinese were producing textiles attuned to European tastes for the Portuguese. Until the mid-seventeenth century Portugal was China's main trading partner and, through the port of Macau, established concrete production guidelines in certain artistic spheres, of which embroidery is a prime example. No less relevant, the Portuguese controlled or participated in a large and complex network of routes that connected Macau to many other lands and trading partners—from Japan and the Philippines to Southeast Asia, India, Africa, Brazil, and Europe. The arrival of and competition from other European nations during the seventeenth and eighteenth centuries, however, had a dramatic impact on the market, and the Portuguese lost their leading position. Raw silk became one of the most sought-after textile commodities, particularly for the English market, and finished pieces made up a fraction of the goods transported.[37] In time, textiles manufactured in China became more broadly adapted to Western aesthetic tastes and gained an increasingly international character.

Fig. 54
Silk embroidery on chasuble (detail of cat. 71)

Fig. 55
Tiles. Lisbon, 1660–80. Painted faience. Museu Nacional do Azulejo, Lisbon (147 Az)

Fig. 56
Altar frontal (detail). Portugal, 17th century. Linen, embroidered with silk and metal-wrapped thread. Museu de Aveiro, Portugal (36/c)

Japan and the Textile Trade in Context

Joyce Denney

uring the sixteenth century, as international maritime trade began to link the world, three geographical areas developed voracious appetites for China's silk textiles and had the precious metals to pay for them: Europe, the Spanish colonies in the Americas, and Japan. Demand for luxury textiles—especially silks from China—grew rapidly in sixteenth-century Japan, amid an era of warring samurai that would culminate in the country's unification. Japan's silver mines (and innovative smelting techniques that improved production), combined with China's higher valuation of silver, created opportunities for trade—of Chinese silk for Japanese silver. The resulting sky-high profits provided an incentive for merchants from around the globe.[1]

Ming-dynasty China during this period maintained the position that all international trade conducted outside the framework of tribute constituted illegal piracy, a policy that made trade opportunities dependent on a country's submission to the Chinese court. (Restrictions were eased in 1567, when China permitted some private trade.) However one might define piracy, merchants from Japan, China, and other nations certainly stole goods and attacked ships and ports, for example in Ryukyu, more generally known today as Okinawa. Early in the sixteenth century the kingdom of Ryukyu served as a vital entrepôt in the trade, but in midcentury its participation declined, due in large part to widespread piracy.[2]

Viewing the Japanese as pirates, the Chinese outlawed direct trade with the country, even after 1567. Despite the ban, Chinese merchants actively carried on trade with Japan illegally, shipping goods from a number of ports in China to various Japanese ports, mostly on the island of Kyūshū, but also the port of Sakai on Osaka Bay and others on Honshū, going through intermediate ports in East and Southeast Asia (fig. 57).[3] With the mid-sixteenth-century establishment of Macau by Portugal, Portuguese merchants began to trade regularly with Japan. From the 1570s until 1617 they completed a nearly annual voyage from Macau of one enormous carrack, "the great ship of Amacon," which carried to Japan a fortune in Chinese silk, double or triple the size of a regular cargo shipment.[4] By the 1590s the Spanish had entered the trade in Chinese goods, initiating the triangular galleon route connecting East Asia, Manila, and Spanish colonies in the Americas. The Iberians also brought Christianity, which would later affect Japanese trade policies.

In Japan the era of the "red seal" ships began in the 1590s and lasted until the mid-1630s. Starting in 1604 the Tokugawa shogunate annually issued permits with red seals (*shūinjō*) to dozens of ships (*shūinsen*), both Japanese and foreign, in an effort to encourage and protect trade and to improve Japan's foreign relations, especially important after its disastrous invasion of Korea, a Chinese vassal state, in the 1590s. In 1600 the Dutch appeared on the scene, followed in 1613 by the English, but Japan's Asian trading partners—China, Korea, Ryukyu, and Southeast Asia—remained the most important. During the same period, the Japanese journeyed as never before, setting up expatriate communities, mostly in commercial ports in East and Southeast Asia, and even venturing, albeit very rarely, on tours to Europe and Mexico.[5]

By the mid-1630s Japan's shogunate desired more control over both trade and the people within its borders; the country's foreign policy was overhauled, with maritime restrictions imposed on the Japanese and their trading partners. Citizens were not permitted to leave Japan, and, if they did leave, returning became a capital offense. Christianity, which had come to seem a rebellious and subversive faith, was violently suppressed. Portuguese and Spanish traders were expelled; instead, the Dutch—nonproselytizing Christians—were chosen by the shogunate as their only European trading partner. Even as late as 1673, when the English tried to regain a share of the trade with Japan, their bid was

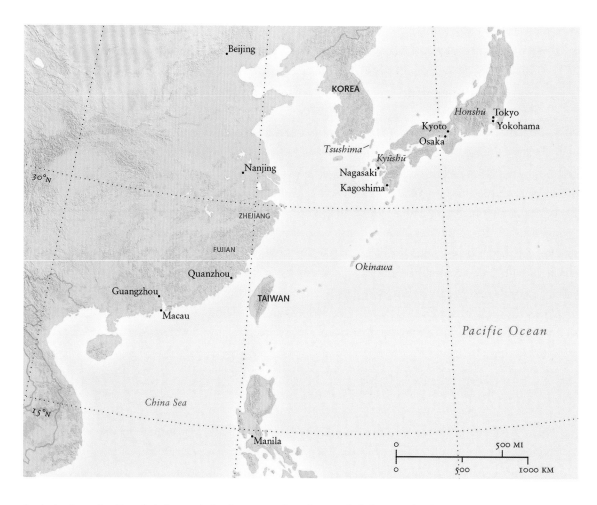

Fig. 57
Chinese and Japanese trading centers

denied when the Dutch informed the Japanese that the English king, Charles II, was married to a Catholic princess from Portugal, Catherine of Braganza.[6] In 1641 traders with the Dutch East India Company (Verenigde Oost-Indische Compagnie, or VOC) were restricted to the small island of Dejima in Nagasaki's harbor, where official VOC trade and an unofficial side trade by VOC employees were conducted. Of course, arrangements were made for merchants from Japan's most important trading partner, China, who also resided in Nagasaki but were far less restricted in their movements than the Dutch.[7] In addition, the shogunate permitted two *daimyō* families to engage in international trade: the Sō clan of Tsushima, located between Kyūshū and the Korean peninsula, continued the important Korean trade,[8] while the Satsuma family of Kagoshima, Kyūshū, traded with Ryukyu, with a focus on Chinese and South and Southeast Asian goods. (In 1609 the Satsuma had invaded and occupied Ryukyu, but to gain access to the kingdom's tribute trade with China, they maintained a convenient fiction in front of the Chinese that Ryukyu was solely a Chinese vassal state.)[9]

From the late seventeenth through the eighteenth century the Japanese shogunate gradually implemented a strategy of replacing imports with domestic products and protecting their supply of precious metals, needed for the increasing monetization of the Japanese economy: local sericulture was encouraged, imports discouraged, and exports of precious metals became more restricted. The lucrative trade of Chinese silk for Japanese silver declined, and these developments constrained the behavior of traders. Instead of cargoes of silk from China, extremely profitable in the early seventeenth century, for example, the official VOC traders of the early eighteenth century sent to Japan increasing amounts of sugar and sappanwood red dyestuff from Southeast Asia, while the long-standing unofficial private trade by VOC employees (overtly recognized and limited by the Japanese in 1685) struggled to find profitable products to import into Japan and in 1720 did not even reach its limit. The Dutch private trade did recover by tapping into a Japanese market for exotica, but until it went out of business at the end of the eighteenth century, the VOC had to calibrate carefully both its official and private imports to maximize the deteriorating profits of the Japan trade.[10]

Maritime restrictions that had been imposed by Japan in the 1630s lasted until the mid-nineteenth century and led to the Western perception of Japan as a "closed country"; this presumption lingers even today among nonspecialists. While it is true that the laws barred the Japanese from leaving Japan to conduct international trade themselves, scholarly opinion since the 1970s has offered a far more nuanced picture than that of a door slamming shut.[11] After all, Japan had multiple windows on the world: the presence of Dutch and Chinese traders, and relationships with Ryūkyū and Korea. In addition, vast quantities of goods (including nonreligious books) were imported from abroad, and the shogunate required a report about the outside world from every visiting ship.[12]

Indeed, the sheer amount of imported cloth on cargo lists shows that Japan was not closed, and the variety of fabrics gives testimony to the fact that the Japanese people were decidedly not closed-minded and clearly loved the rare, the exotic, and the new. Almost ubiquitous, imported textiles appeared in many contexts in Japan: in the art of tea, in religious vestments and festivities, in samurai clothing, and also in fashionable dress and accessories, as discussed in more detail below.

TEA

In Japan the art form of preparing and drinking tea (often translated as "tea ceremony") is focused on two types of tea.[13] The better known of the two, *chanoyu* (literally, "hot water for tea"), involves a beverage made by whipping powdered green tea (*matcha*) with water. The less familiar type, which became popular in the eighteenth century, uses steeped *sencha*, green tea in leaf form. Imported textiles play a role in both traditions. Within the context of *chanoyu*, certain textiles are considered *meibutsugire*, a term that first appeared in the late sixteenth to early seventeenth century but became common only in the Genroku period, about 1700. The *-gire* part of the word means cloth, while *meibutsu-* refers to famous named tea implements and vessels, considered masterpieces, that were wrapped in valuable imported cloth. In this context the textiles were secondary; they drew their importance from the objects they wrapped.

To ensure that the textiles would match the quality of the pieces they protected, tea practitioners developed a loose classification system for *meibutsugire*. To qualify, fabrics had to be associated with tea-related masterpieces, they had to be old (imported between the fourteenth and eighteenth centuries), and the judgment had to be made by an authoritative tea master.[14] *Meibutsugire* finally became codified in the late eighteenth century with the publication in 1787–95 of the tea-related compendium *Kokon meibutsu ruijū* (Classified Collection of Renowned Wares of Ancient and Modern Times) compiled by tea master Matsudaira Fumai (1751–1818). The work included two volumes of *meibutsugire* textiles illustrated in color with captions giving their names and some commentary.

Fig. 58
Kōdaiji *kinran* (detail). China, 16th century. Lampas, silk and metallic thread. Kyoto National Museum, Maeda Collection (IK110)

Fig. 59
Textile (*sarasa*) with lions and snakes (detail). India, 17th century. Cotton, painted resist and mordant, dyed, gilded. Kyoto National Museum, Maeda Collection (IK185)

By convention, *meibutsugire* were categorized according to textile type, based loosely on textile techniques, such as *donsu* (which refers to Chinese damasklike fabrics, frequently of two colors) and *kinran* (Chinese silks woven with gold patterns). The non-Chinese pieces were often grouped according to perceived origins or designs: *sarasa* (dye-patterned cottons of exotic—that is, not of East Asian—origin or pattern, usually from India), *kantō* or *kandō* (striped and lattice-patterned woven textiles thought to be from Southeast Asia), and *mōru* (woven textiles believed to be from Mughal India).

A tea master's perception of a textile was of primary importance, whether the perception was fact or not. Tea was a world unto itself, and the *meibutsugire* system was not a catalyst for the rigorous study of textiles. Yet the context of tea focused attention on imported textiles, created demand for imported textiles, and increased the desirability of imported textiles, including the unusual.

An affinity for the exotic was especially marked in the context of *sencha*, which began as a form of participation in Chinese literati culture. The popularity of *sencha* in the eighteenth century reflected a renewed enthusiasm for Chinese arts in Japan. Furthermore, it has been noted that "all foreign-made products came to be categorized as exotic, an aesthetic cultivated by *sencha* aficionados that allowed for the inclusion of non-Chinese foreign elements in ostensibly Sinophile *sencha* environments,"[15] including dye-patterned cotton cloth from India. *Sencha* would continue its rise in popularity during the nineteenth century.

During the first half of the seventeenth century, the third Toshitsune, head of the powerful Maeda family of Kaga province, was a *chanoyu* tea practitioner said to have been responsible for initiating the family's large collection of high-quality fabrics imported from China, India, and Southeast Asia. In 1637 he dispatched a vassal to the port of Nagasaki for the purpose of buying textiles. A Ming-dynasty Chinese example from the Maeda collection, with a scrolling floral pattern woven in gold on dark blue (fig. 58), bears the name "Kōdaiji *kinran*"—Kōdaiji refers to a temple in Kyoto, and *kinran* is the term used for textiles with woven patterns in gold thread (the origin of the textile's name is obscure, as is frequently true of the names of *meibutsugire*). The desirability of these tea-related Chinese textiles lived on: tea practitioners even collected small fragments of *meibutsugire* in albums.

The importation of *kinran* textiles continued, and perhaps textiles with the same or similar patterns were also produced in Japan for various uses. The pattern of the Maeda collection's *kinran* textile, for example, is remarkably similar to the white and gold cloth used for the lapels of the red wool sur-coat, or *jinbaori*, in the exhibition (cat. 30).

While the textiles most frequently classified as *meibutsugire* were Chinese, fabrics of other origins also received the honor: some dyed-cotton cloths from India were designated as wrapping cloths for tea implements associated with the *chanoyu* tea master Kobori Enshū (1579 – 1647).[16] The *sencha* context also made use of dyed-cotton cloths with exotic patterns, as seen in surviving seventeenth- and eighteenth-century examples of *fukusa*, which served such ceremonial purposes as the wiping of tea vessels.[17]

The tastes of the Maeda went beyond the usual Chinese woven silks to the collecting of Indian dyed cottons. One striking example features a particularly lively intercultural design with Western- and Chinese-style lions and cobralike snakes in a landscape (fig. 59). Applied gold leaf enhances the outlines and details of the repeating pattern (see cat. 13, which has also been enhanced with gold). Two other pieces with the same pattern survive; one is in the Fries Museum in Leeuwarden, Netherlands,[18] a location that suggests the cloth was widely disseminated. The other textile of the same pattern is mounted as a small, single-paneled standing screen (*tsuitate*), a format perhaps indicat-ing use as a brazier screen in the context of a *sencha* tea gathering.[19]

RELIGION

Centuries before 1500, imported textiles were in use for Buddhist vestments (*kesa*) in Japan. Buddhism came to Japan from the Asian continent and was widely practiced on the islands by the sixth century. The tradition of Buddhist vestments, made of textiles pieced together in a prescribed configuration, reached Japan with the religion. By the Kamakura period (1185 – 1333) continental textiles became especially desirable for vestments as a result of connections between Japanese clerics and their Chinese teachers or related temples; sometimes the vestments of high-ranking clerics were preserved with supporting documents and inscriptions. Three portraits of successive fifteenth- and sixteenth-century abbots of the temple Ryōanji, depicting each abbot in the same *kesa* made of Chinese cloth, confirm visually that *kesa* were passed down as lineage garments.[20]

The use of imported textiles in *kesa* continued from the sixteenth through the eighteenth century. Many vestments were made of imported fabrics bearing traditional Chinese or Chinese-style patterns, but some broke with this convention. An eighteenth-century *kesa* in the Metropolitan Museum was made from a Chinese dragon silk with a large-scale woven design intended for a Chinese court robe.[21] Another (cat. 62) is made from an eighteenth-century dress silk with a European-style pattern produced in China for the European market but instead employed in a Japanese *kesa*.

Other vestments incorporated textiles from farther afield, in keeping with the wider range of fab-rics that became available through increased international trade. A vestment that belonged to Kōgetsu Sōgan (1571 – 1643), the abbot of Ryōkō-in, part of the temple Daitokuji in Kyoto, was made from four different textiles of the late sixteenth to early seventeenth century (fig. 60), most remarkably a floral textile from Safavid Iran seen in the internal framework of the garment's design. It was woven with polychrome silks and a distinctive silver thread in which the silver strips, wrapped on a silk core, do not have the paper substrate found in East Asian examples. In Japanese tea circles textiles with

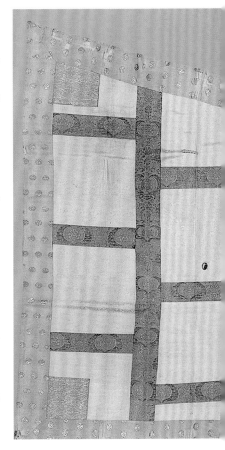

Fig. 60

Vestment (*kesa*) of Kōgetsu Sōgan (detail). Japan (1571 – 1643). Com-posed of four different textiles, three Chinese and one Persian. Daitokuji temple, Ryōkō-in subtemple, Kyoto

Fig. 61
Dōbuku of Uesugi Kenshin (died
1578). Japan, 16th century. Patchwork
of 16th-century Chinese textiles.
Uesugi Jinja, Yonezawa, Japan

comparable patterns were called *mōru*; the term was applied to woven textiles with a Middle Eastern
or Mughal Indian appearance. Kōgetsu Sōgan, a connoisseur of works of calligraphy used in the
adornment of tearooms, was, like many clerics and members of his family, a tea practitioner. The
creativity revealed in the tasteful yet surprising combination of textiles in his *kesa* is akin to the
dynamic combinations of vessels and implements, textiles and works of art, integral to the art of tea.

Religious institutions also used imported textiles as hangings and altar cloths for rituals and
celebrations. Several textiles similar to a lively Chinese embroidered hanging with birds, flowers,
and animals (cat. 28) are preserved in Japanese temple collections,[22] and other such pieces appear
among the draped decorations for the tall floats of the famous Gion festival procession,[23] celebrated
in Kyoto for hundreds of years since its founding in the ninth century.

SAMURAI

One of the most treasured sixteenth-century garments preserved in Japan is a *dōbuku* (a man's coat
worn over a kimono; fig. 61) that belonged to Uesugi Kenshin, an important samurai leader who
died in 1578 while preparing for yet another battle. While the design of the patchwork is Japanese,

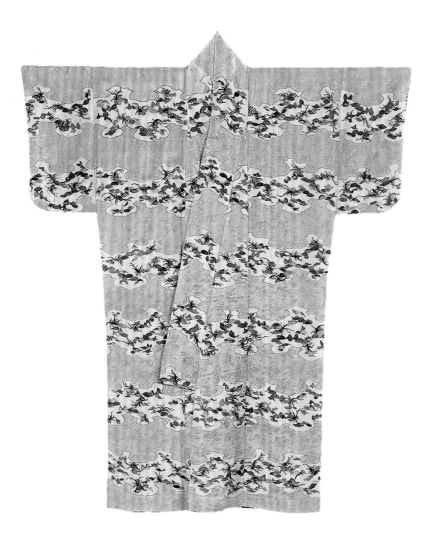

intensive study of the garment found that the 157 smaller pieces that make up the coat are from six-teen imported Chinese textiles of the sixteenth century that correspond to imported *meibutsugire* fab-rics used in Japan to wrap important tea utensils.[24] In this garment, they were used to wrap Uesugi Kenshin in a sumptuous statement of his power, wealth, and elevated taste. They also draw atten-tion to the high status accorded to Chinese imported textiles at the time.

Battle jackets, or *jinbaori*, surcoats worn over armor, were originally meant to keep a warrior warm and protected from the elements. Also a prime site for display, *jinbaori* were usually made of bold and luxurious, often imported, textiles. One silk velvet *jinbaori* (cat. 31), for example, has a European-style pattern, which must have seemed quite exotic to the Japanese; this elegant velvet was woven in China for the European market.

In November 1613 an English trader in Japan, Richard Cocks, expressed exasperation in a letter to the heads of the English East India Company as he explained his lack of success in selling woolen broadcloth: "But as yet they are soe addicted to silks, that they doe not enter into consideration of the benefit of wearing cloth. But tyme may altar their myndes."[25] Various types of European woolen cloth did enter Japan. Frequently mentioned are plain-weave wool with a napped surface (*rasha*, from the Portuguese *raxa*), twill-weave wool with a napped surface (*heruhetowan*, called *perpetuan* or *perpetuana*—and variants with other endings—in the Netherlands and England),[26] plain-weave

Fig. 62

Kosode with design of shells and sea grasses. Japan, Edo period (1615–1868), early 17th century. Float-patterned plain-weave silk, resist-dyed, embroidered with silk, applied gold leaf. The Metropolitan Museum of Art, New York, Gift of Mr. and Mrs. Paul T. Nomura, in memory of Mr. and Mrs. S. Morris Nomura, 1992 (1992.253). See detail p. 56

cloth woven with worsted yarns (*goro*, from the Dutch *grofgrein*), and felt.[27] The fabrics came in many vivid colors—red, black, yellow, blue, and green, among others (cat. 30).

Over the course of the Edo period (1615–1868), *jinbaori* were more and more frequently made of European wool cloth—as seen in the "uniforms" of the shogun's large security detachment, the prestigious *okachigumi*.[28] In the seventeenth century various regulations also restricted the use of woolen cloth: an edict of 1683, for instance, omitted woolens from the list of textiles permitted to *chōnin* (townspeople, including merchants and artisans). The list of permissible textiles was reissued frequently, but woolen cloth was never added; it does come up, however, in passages that describe elite dress in Edo-period novels popular among townspeople.[29] In general, until the Meiji period (1868–1912) European wool products found only limited use in Japan, mostly for samurai garments—notably *jinbaori* surcoats and clothing for firefighting.

FASHION

In fashionable Japanese dress, especially in the first half of the seventeenth century, Chinese textiles hide in plain sight. A rare Japanese garment in the Metropolitan's collection (fig. 62), nicknamed the seashell *kosode* for obvious reasons, provides a good example. Judging particularly from the textile's width, the robe's foundation fabric was almost certainly a Chinese import utterly transformed in Japan, using Japanese dye techniques, embroidery, and even the application of gold leaf (see detail p. 56). The single-color damasklike foundation cloth with a design of flowers on a diagonal fret is a type of textile called *saya*, characterized by a pattern in twill on a plain-weave background.

During the first half of the seventeenth century Japan imported annually from China a vast amount of lightweight monochrome woven silk, especially damasklike textiles such as *saya* and *rinzu*, which were prevalent in the clothing of the wealthy and the elite. According to extant cargo lists, even as late as 1641 more than 60,000 bolts of *saya* and more than 70,000 bolts of *rinzu* were imported from China in that one year, with each bolt presumably enough for one kimono.[30] (To help put such quantities in perspective, the entire urban population of Japan in 1600 is estimated to have been about one million people, and certainly not everyone wore silk.) These imported fabrics must have been made in China especially for the Japanese market to fill the demand created by the pressures of fashion and to attain the remarkable profits of the trade. Many *kosode* of this period that have been preserved in Japan were likely to have been made with lightweight imported Chinese cloth.

Later in the Edo period, mostly during the eighteenth and nineteenth centuries, colorful, exotic, dye-patterned cottons (*sarasa*) from India became especially popular among townspeople (see cat. 33), particularly for accessories such as small bags for personal items, including a small tobacco bag made from leather covered in *sarasa* from India, part of a smoking set (fig. 63). The tobacco bag's diagonal pattern is punctuated with a simple rosette at the intersections of its colorful diamond lattice. A very similar pattern is seen in a wrapping cloth in the tea-related collection of the Hikone Castle Museum, with some difference in color.[31]

Sarasa became so sought after that the Japanese began to make it themselves; a manual of *sarasa* designs (*Sarasa benran*) was published in 1781 with black-and-white illustrations and notations indicating the colors to be used (fig. 64). A textile with the same design and colors as the pouch illustrated here (fig. 63) must have served as a model for the illustration in the book: both pattern and indicated colors are almost identical.[32] Some of the illustrations in *Sarasa benran* correspond to the tea-related *sarasa* textiles of the Hikone Collection of the Ii family, now in Tokyo National Museum.[33]

Japan's all-consuming passion for Chinese silk textiles, coupled with its rich silver supply, prompted the arrival of merchants from around the world—East Asia, Southeast Asia, and Europe—with goods from even farther afield. Open to the possibilities, Japanese appetites broadened with the availability of new and unusual fabrics that were used domestically in diverse contexts—for tea gatherings, religious vestments and festivals, samurai garments, and fashionable dress and accessories. Japan's openness to foreign products and information heralded its transition in the second half of the nineteenth century to full economic and political participation in the world.

Fig. 64
Page from a Japanese manual of *sarasa* designs (*Sarasa benran*). Illustrated book, 1781. Paul T. and Betty M. Nomura, on loan to The Metropolitan Museum of Art, New York (L.1993.9.29)

Silk along the Seas

OTTOMAN TURKEY AND SAFAVID IRAN

IN THE GLOBAL TEXTILE TRADE

Marika Sardar

he territories of Turkey and Iran had for centuries been part of long-distance trade networks linking eastern Asia to Europe, but these routes required moving goods by a combination of land, river, and sea, and crossing territories belonging to many different ruling authorities—a costly, tax-heavy, and dangerous proposition. In the sixteenth century, an alternative path to Europe presented itself: an ocean route connecting directly with Asia. Discovered by the Portuguese explorer Vasco da Gama, this route traversed the Indian Ocean, rounded the southern tip of Africa, and continued north directly to the western European ports of Lisbon, London, and Amsterdam. It had the major advantage of eliminating the need to transfer goods to pack animals and cross the lands connecting the Indian Ocean to the Mediterranean Sea; from the European perspective, it had the added benefit of bypassing the territories of the Ottoman Empire, recently expanded with the capture of Constantinople in 1453.

For the neighboring regions of Turkey and Iran (fig. 65) the discovery of the sea route around Africa had different implications. Raw silk produced in Iran was the main textile-related product of the area, and so for the Safavid shahs (1501–1722) the route presented a potentially transformative opportunity. Though they possessed a valuable commodity, the shahs had previously had no direct way to reach their main market in Europe (lands to the east being supplied by China), and they were forced to reach it overland through the Ottoman Empire, their religious, economic, and political rival.

For the Ottoman sultans (ca. 1299–1922) who ruled those very lands connecting the Indian Ocean and Mediterranean Sea, this new route presented the real possibility of losing a major source of revenue. While those who transported the silk made profits upon selling it, the Ottoman sultans extracted taxes along the route, most notably at the entrepôts of Bursa and Aleppo and the ports on the Mediterranean and Red Seas where supplies of raw silk and textiles from points east were directed to markets west.

This was no small loss, for the silk trade was substantial and extremely profitable. In the early seventeenth century, Iran produced about 20,000 bales of raw silk each year (in modern terms, over 2,200 tons). The merchants who transported the silk from Iran to Turkey charged the European traders waiting at eastern Mediterranean ports double what they had paid for the silk in Iran (a sixteenth-century source quotes a return of 1,200 piasters on an investment of 600 piasters).[1] Those European traders in turn charged exorbitant prices at home; prices nearly tripled between 1550 and 1640 as demand grew. For the Ottomans, this meant a corresponding rise in taxes and an increased foreign market for the silk textiles produced in their royal workshops.[2]

This essay will explore the reactions of the Ottoman and Safavid rulers to the changing conditions of trade between the sixteenth and nineteenth centuries and will assess the final effect of the European-discovered sea route on how these polities conducted business. In turn, it will examine the textiles that were sent abroad during this period. While the impact of the great sea discovery can be debated, the textiles that traveled as a result of the period's diplomatic and mercantile relationships were themselves undoubtedly influential.

TRADE AND RAW SILK IN THE OTTOMAN AND SAFAVID REALMS

The geographical reach of the Ottoman Empire encompassed multiple conduits for trade, including ports on the Black, Mediterranean, and Red Seas as well as the overland routes that connected Europe,

Africa, and Asia. This was the result of careful strategy and planning, built on the legacy of the rulers of the Seljuq dynasty (1081–1307), who had vastly improved and assiduously maintained the land routes connecting Turkey to the silk-producing regions of Iran, providing safe and functional roads, bridges, and caravansaries to traders. Taking control of this region over the course of the fourteenth and fifteenth centuries, the Ottoman sultans further augmented this infrastructure[3] and, with the capture of the Crimea and its important ports in 1475, were also able to facilitate trade with Russia.[4]

Later sultans structured military campaigns with similar economic gains in mind. Süleyman I (r. 1520–66) conquered Rhodes in 1522, eliminating the threat of the Knights of Saint John to the Mediterranean trade; his 1534 campaign to Tabriz and Baghdad first interrupted and then strengthened the silk trade with Iran. He also initiated offensives against Venice (1537–40) for control of the Aegean and participated in the siege of Diu (1538) to limit Portuguese activities in the Indian Ocean. His successors continued efforts on the same fronts over the next several decades, with the Venetians, the Habsburgs, and the Safavids as the main antagonists.

Thus through the nineteenth century, Bursa and Aleppo, and later Izmir, were the main termini for land routes from the East and the primary collection and redistribution points for silk from Iran. It was a grueling journey for merchant and silk from Iran to Turkey's ports; an English merchant named Newbery, who traveled the route in 1581–82, reported that it required seventy-nine days just to cross from Kashan, in western Iran, to Bursa, the major Ottoman entrepôt near the Marmara Sea connecting to the Mediterranean.[5]

Many goods also arrived on ships that crossed the Indian Ocean and sailed up the Red Sea. After its capture in 1538 by the Ottomans, Jeddah became the main Turkish port in the region. Here cargo was loaded onto smaller boats heading to Suez, where goods were then carried over land and river to Alexandria.[6]

To continue their journey from these points, the goods were transported on ships by European merchants who had settled in the various port towns of the Ottoman Empire, living and working under the capitulations granted by the sultans to their respective countries.[7] Italians (from Venice, Ragusa, and Florence) initially controlled the Mediterranean trade, but during the sixteenth and seventeenth centuries Dutch and English companies increasingly dominated this arena. On land, Hungarian and Polish merchants took the goods into eastern Europe via the same routes developed in imperial Roman times. To reach Russia most profitably, goods were transported over the Black Sea to the Ottoman port of Feodosiya (Kaffa) in the Crimea and from there by river and land to Moscow.[8]

With Portugal's dramatic and swift takeover of Indian Ocean activity in the early sixteenth century, the Ottomans had to recalibrate their strategy, working aggressively to expand their exposure along the Red Sea. Without a naval tradition of their own, they recruited corsairs from the Aegean, as well as Christian merchants operating in the Mediterranean, to establish a navy and provide important shipbuilding and navigational knowledge. As a result of this policy, famous captains such as Hayreddin Barbarossa, Kemal Reis, and Pirî Reis got their start in the imperial Ottoman ranks. With the 1517 defeat of the Mamluk dynasty and the incorporation of Syria, Egypt, and the western coast of Arabia into the empire, several ports along the Red Sea were brought under Ottoman control. These were maintained with a steady presence throughout the period of Portuguese expansion into these realms.[9] The Ottomans also moved into the coastal regions of Ethiopia in the 1550s (though they were unable to hold these areas for long)[10] and captured the key Persian Gulf port of Basra, over which they exerted a more lasting control.[11]

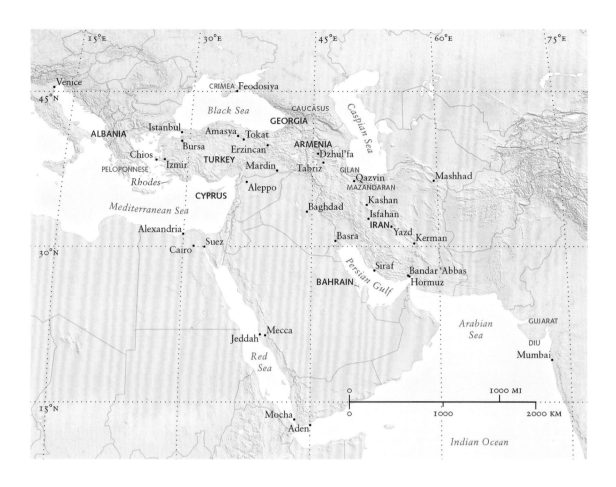

As additional European companies joined the Indian Ocean trade, Ottoman sultans continued to forge alliances, granting capitulations to the English in 1580 and to the Dutch in 1612. Selim II (r. 1566–74) also gave full trade privileges to the French in 1569.[12]

While Bursa had been a major transshipment point for Iranian silk in the fifteenth century, and an increasingly important area for sericulture in the sixteenth, by the later seventeenth century its role as a center for textile production declined, and the European mercantile situation shifted. With Venice's supremacy giving way to the Dutch and English Levant companies, which moved goods between Turkey, Syria, Egypt, and western Europe, Aleppo and Izmir became the primary ports at which the land routes ended and sea routes commenced.[13] In the eighteenth century Izmir became the most important port in the empire and, therefore, of utmost value to the silk trade.[14]

Naturally, trade operated only when the Ottomans and their trading partners were on good terms, and so trade with Iran was often restricted due to conflict. Selim I (r. 1512–20), during whose reign war with Iran was almost continuous, called a complete halt to trade with Iran and exiled its traders (although, unofficially, it may have continued to a certain degree).[15] Trade with Iran resumed under Süleyman but was interrupted by wars in the 1530s, 1540s, and 1560s. Similarly, various Italian merchants were alternately granted rights and stripped of them depending on political conditions. The ambitions of Venice, in particular, clashed with Ottoman interests; wars over Cyprus and other key trade points caused crises throughout the sixteenth century. During such moments the Ottomans simply utilized other trade partners—Florence, for instance, could also trade high-quality woolens for silk and textiles from Ottoman realms that could be sold in Europe.[16]

Fig. 65
Ottoman and Safavid trading centers

Fig. 66
Dalmatic with the Virgin Mary
and Christ Child. Textile: Turkey
(probably Istanbul), before 1583.
Silk (*kemha*). Kremlin Armory
Museum, Moscow (TK-2766)

These periodic interruptions—and their devastating economic effects—led Süleyman's grand vizier Rüstem Pasha to embrace raw-silk production as an area for economic reform. Whereas Süleyman attempted to conquer the silk-producing regions of Iran through war, Rüstem Pasha promoted the cultivation of the mulberry trees in which silkworms live, building on Selim's earlier attempts at native sericulture. Rüstem Pasha also established silk-textile workshops in the capital of Istanbul, many under direct control of the court. By the mid-seventeenth century, Bursa, Albania, Chios, and the Peloponnese were producing silk that was used in local textile manufacture.[17] Despite these efforts, Turkey's role as a trader of raw silk to the larger market, and as a producer of luxury textiles, remained largely predicated on a supply of raw silk from Iran, and as a result Turkish production and trade suffered during times of conflict with its neighboring state, or when seventeenth-century rebellions endangered trade lines through the Anatolian provinces. Although the Ottomans did what they could to maintain a full spectrum of trade mechanisms, their relations with Iran remained key because Iranian silk enjoyed the highest reputation for quality.

While the Ottoman sultans possessed the means of trade but not the most valuable materials, the Safavid shahs had the essential raw silk and weaving technology but no means to get products to Western markets. At the beginning of the sixteenth century the trade systems based on Iran's silk production that had operated intermittently since the thirteenth century had been shut down by wars, internal revolts, and the resulting dangerous caravan conditions engendered by the struggles that culminated in the rise of the Safavid dynasty. Once firmly in power, Isma'il (r. 1501–24), the first ruler of this line, was faced with a ban on the trade of silk established by his rival, the Ottoman sultan Selim I. This prohibition forced Isma'il to find a way for Iranian silk to reach Europe directly. The two options were to move the silk north—via the Caspian Sea and through Russia—or south to the Persian Gulf and then by sea to Europe. It was the choice between these routes that would continue to define the policies of his successors.

In pursuit of the northern route, Isma'il attempted to foster ties with the rulers of Russia, sending an ambassador to Vasily III (r. 1505–33), grand prince of Moscow, in 1521. Not much seems to have come of this embassy or of those subsequently sent by his successors, as each time other political factors intervened: on the Safavid side, relations with the Ottomans were constantly changing, and the later shahs were plagued by internal rebellions; on the Russian side, attentions were diverted to problems in the Baltic and the Crimea.[18]

The route south and thence to Europe appeared a more satisfactory option. In the initial years of Safavid rule, the lands of the new state did not extend to the southern coast of Iran, so there was no way for Iranian goods to connect with the European trading ships using the new sea trade routes. In 1515, however, the Portuguese captured the port of Hormuz on the Persian Gulf, which they used as the first stop on the way to Europe from India, bringing their ships right to Isma'il's door.[19] The Safavids attempted to take advantage of this opportunity, exchanging embassies with Portugal in 1513, 1515, and 1523. But, as with Russia, these missions—which traveled at a lumbering pace, reported back home slowly, and were incapable of adjusting to the quickly changing political scene—were unable to reach any agreement and were eventually abandoned.[20]

Isma'il's son Tahmasp I (r. 1524–76) faced the same economic conundrum. Repeated invasions and bans on trade by the Ottoman sultans led him to approach the Russians as well as the English Muscovy Company, which offered its services to complete the silk's journey from Russia to western Europe. There were several problems with these negotiations, among them the fact that neither the Russians nor Tahmasp had full control of the areas where the goods originated or subsequently traveled. Although Tahmasp repeatedly granted trade privileges to the Muscovy Company (in 1565, 1568, and 1570), he was unable to guarantee that there would be silk for the English to buy or that their caravans would be safe traversing his northern provinces.[21]

These were the issues that 'Abbas I (r. 1587–1629) attempted to rectify upon coming to power in the late sixteenth century. After reaching a peace agreement with Istanbul in 1590 and quieting rebellions in the east, he formulated a new economic policy with the silk trade at its heart. In 1592 he brought the silk-producing provinces of Gilan and Mazanderan under his direct control and classified their revenue to accrue to the crown purse. He placed in charge of these areas governors who were chosen from the *ghulam*s, specially recruited slave forces that were loyal to him and had been trained for such administrative positions. Finally, he stipulated that foreign merchants were permitted to purchase raw silk only at fixed prices from royal warehouses in the capital of Isfahan rather than directly from the producers in Gilan and Mazanderan.[22]

Another component of 'Abbas's plan was to resettle certain populations—in particular Georgians and Armenians—to areas in which they would be able to increase either silk production or its sale. These operations started in 1603, with the forcible move of tens of thousands of people.[23] Some were sent to Gilan and Mazanderan, where silk was cultivated. The Armenian inhabitants of Dzhul'fa (Julfa) were moved to the new Safavid capital at Isfahan, where they were given land—in a neighborhood that became known as New Julfa—as well as interest-free loans to restart their businesses. A crucial stipulation in the operation of these businesses, however, was that the Armenians, like the European traders, were forced to buy raw silk from the shah at fixed prices rather than from the silk producers directly.[24]

To open up new transit routes for the silk, 'Abbas seized the Portuguese-held coastal fort of Gombroon on the Persian Gulf, which he renamed Bandar 'Abbas, the port of 'Abbas. As much as possible, he forced trade traffic south to this outlet, strongly discouraging the northern and western passages that traversed Ottoman lands.[25]

In addition, 'Abbas sent ambassadors all over Europe, to Venice, Spain, Portugal, the Netherlands, France, Poland, Russia, and Sweden. They took with them samples of raw silk to sell, returning the money to the royal purse.[26] In response to these new economic opportunities, the English and Dutch East India companies established themselves in Iran. They succeeded in buying several hundred bales of silk annually, and in 1622 the English assisted 'Abbas in ejecting the Portuguese from their base at Hormuz; in reward they received an increased portion of the customs revenues from Bandar 'Abbas.[27] While negotiations with the Dutch proved more fraught, their trading company was granted several capitulations as well.[28]

To a great extent, 'Abbas's policies worked. Effectively blocking all silk shipments to the Ottoman Empire between 1603 and 1629, he was able to encourage the sale of Persian goods in European markets, now fueled by silver from the New World and an increasing taste for silk textiles. By the 1620s approximately 4,500 bales of Iranian silk were being sold in Europe annually; England bought 300–600 bales each year, while the Dutch purchased a record 1,200 bales in 1628.[29]

The system was completely changed by 'Abbas's successor Safi (r. 1629–42), who loosened restrictions on the silk trade and ended the royal monopoly. This rediversified the routes by which silk was exported and forced individual merchants and larger trading companies to adjust their ways of operating. Soon English involvement was almost nonexistent, and Dutch activity declined as well. In 1639, however, Safi was able to conclude a long-lasting peace with the Ottomans (albeit by ceding much territory in Iraq) that reopened land routes to the west, and the silk trade continued apace.[30]

After Safi's reign, both the quality of the silk and trade conditions worsened to such a degree that trade to western Europe almost stopped, although trade with Russia increased. A 1667 treaty with the Russians gave the New Julfa Company a monopoly on importing goods from Iran, thereby allowing Armenian traders to resume their role as the main purveyors of Iranian silk.

In 1722 Iran was economically devastated by the invasion of Afghan tribes under the leadership of Mahmud Gilzay, which also brought down the Safavid dynasty. While the silk trade did not stop completely, it was changed by the loss of the established Ottoman channel to the West, and new trade routes had to be developed.[31] A reorientation was confirmed by the accounts of British traders, among them an anonymous report to the English East India Company stating that almost no silk could be had in Ottoman domains, but that the route from Russia into northeastern Iran seemed to hold much potential.[32]

Ultimately, the Portuguese-discovered sea route had a limited impact on the way trade was conducted from Iran and Turkey. While various European states obtained colonies in Asia, Africa, South America, and Southeast Asia, their involvement in the Near East was circumscribed after the seventeenth century. The Europeans continued to operate as traders, but as the Safavid and Ottoman rulers resolved their internecine conflicts and secured the overland routes between their two territories, they no longer sought to ally themselves with foreign powers and instead dealt with each other directly. Most importantly, both preserved their sovereign status and were never conquered by European powers. By the end of the eighteenth century, commerce had returned to the earlier traditional combination of land and inland sea routes.

OTTOMAN AND SAFAVID TRADE TEXTILES

While finished textiles were but a small part of the trade story in the Ottoman and Safavid realms, as evident from the discussion above, products from both regions did circulate abroad and were sufficiently admired to have had an effect on design and fashion, especially in Europe.

Ottoman trade silks came primarily from Bursa, the city designated in the late fourteenth century as the empire's main entrepôt for the transshipment of raw silk from Iran to Europe and other parts of western Asia. By the early fifteenth century its role in the silk business had made it one of the most prosperous cities in the world. Under royal encouragement, a silk-weaving industry was also developed in the Ottoman capital of Istanbul in the 1500s by transplanting artisans and looms from Bursa. Other cities along the silk trade route, such as Erzincan, Amasya, Tokat, Mardin, and Maraş, were secondary production sites, as was the island of Chios, where some raw silk was cultivated.[33]

In the last quarter of the fifteenth century velvet was considered the preeminent luxury textile at the Ottoman court, and a velvet-weaving industry was established in Bursa in reaction to the popularity of Italian velvets from Venice and Florence. Soon the technical accomplishments of the Ottoman weavers reached great heights, with the production of complex designs with contrasting areas of raised and voided pile as well as brocading with metal-wrapped thread, and Ottoman velvet became the main luxury textile traded abroad.[34] Their designs were initially based on Italian velvets, but over time the two industries became mutually influential; Italian weavers utilized motifs created in Turkey (cat. 5), and Turkish artisans responded to new design developments in Italy.

Due to the rising costs of raw materials at the start of the sixteenth century, there was a sudden drop in the quality of the Bursa velvets. Weavers used lower grades of silk that were in turn not prepared in the necessary (and time-consuming) manner and not dyed with superior materials. It was about this time that Istanbul started to produce velvets (cat. 4), but the top end of the market switched to purchasing from Italy almost exclusively. The Italians shrewdly catered to these buyers; in 1512 a Florentine law set the width for export textiles to just under twenty-six inches (65.6 centimeters) so that they would be the same width as Ottoman velvets, and designs were formulated specifically for Ottoman taste. As a mark of their success in the Turkish market, the vast majority of velvet robes in the sultans' own collections were made of Italian velvet, local velvet being used mainly for furnishing fabrics.[35]

Turkish velvets remained popular in select markets abroad—Sweden, Romania, Bosnia, Poland, and Russia—though not in Italy.[36] In eastern Europe velvet was used in churches for altar frontals and reliquary coverings (as in the Rila Monastery in Bulgaria) or Bible bindings and vestments (as in the Trinity-Sergius Monastery near Moscow). Velvets were also used at court for Turkish-style robes and, in one exceptional case, the lining of a royal carriage in Transylvania.[37]

In the mid-sixteenth century fashions changed, and in clothing velvets were largely replaced by Ottoman-woven silk textiles made with a lavish use of metal-wrapped threads and executed in the complicated weave structures of *seraser* (*taqueté*) and *kemha* (lampas). This switch was likely the result of a program by the vizier Rüstem Pasha, who regarded the expensive foreign textiles that had taken over the court as a drain on the imperial budget. He also saw the adoption of Ottoman-made fabrics at court as a way to increase the foreign market value for these finished textiles.[38]

As a distinctively Ottoman decorative style emerged from the court workshops based in the Topkapı Palace in Istanbul, the design of textiles evolved alongside that of ceramics, tiles, carpets, and even drawing, as all of these media took up the same repertoire of motifs and arrangements.[39] In the mid-sixteenth century popular motifs such as pomegranates, artichokes, and tulips were set along undulating vines (cat. 95), placed in ogival lattices (cat. 69), or used to fill other motifs such as medallions (cat. 94).

Textiles like these were created with the local user in mind but were also very well received abroad. Eastern Europe was again the market where Ottoman textiles were most favored; the plentiful use of the color red and the large size of the motifs led to their success.[40] Inventories in Poland show the range of Turkish textiles (fabrics of metal-wrapped silk and velvet used for furnishings, clothing, and even Turkish costume) held by the nobility and the middle class. In Hungary, too, men's clothing at court was modeled on contemporary Ottoman fashion, and Hungarian princes, like Ottoman sultans and ministers, presented caftans to subordinates as a sign of favor.[41] At the Russian court, Ottoman silks draped palace walls, covered thrones and tables, and screened doorways and windows. There

Fig. 67
Metal-ground textile. Iran (Isfahan),
for the Thai market, early 18th cen-
tury. Silk, metal-wrapped thread.
The Textile Museum, Washington,
D.C. (3.313a, b)

are even descriptions of several hundred Russian courtiers wearing Turkish "cloth of gold" to ceremonies.[42] In Russian churches, numerous ecclesiastical garments were made out of imported Turkish silk fabric; these were often embellished with embroidery that imitated the motifs of the Turkish textiles on which they were sewn (cat. 63).

Because Ottoman-style textiles found many ready markets, there was little impetus for Ottoman weavers to adjust either the style or the techniques of the textiles produced for sale abroad. The only special production of the sixteenth to eighteenth century seems to be a group of fabrics made specifically for use in Orthodox churches. The standard design of these textiles consists of Greek crosses alternating with roundels enclosing a bust of Christ with his hands raised in the orant gesture and flanked by the Greek letters representing the phrase "Jesus Christ Victorious." Other textiles display a pattern of Christ Enthroned and the Virgin Mary holding the Christ Child overlooked by two angels; between these figures are Ottoman-style tulips and rosebuds encircling crosses (fig. 66).[43]

The connection with the Orthodox church in particular seems strong. Silks with typically Ottoman patterns were used for vestments throughout the Roman Catholic churches of Poland and in the Franciscan churches and monasteries of Croatia and Bosnia, but silks with Christian imagery are preserved in Orthodox churches in Russia, Greece, Romania, Bulgaria, and Moldavia.[44] These textiles were probably made to the orders of the Orthodox patriarchate in Istanbul.[45]

In Iran the raw silk that was traded so profitably abroad came from the provinces bordering the Caspian Sea—Gilan, Mazanderan, and the Caucasus—each of which produced several different grades of quality. Though quite difficult to estimate based on the available sources, it seems that Iran supplied an average of about 20,000 bales of raw silk annually, and possibly as much as 50,000 bales a year in the early eighteenth century.[46] In addition, cotton was grown almost everywhere in Iran, and wool was widely available.[47]

Using these raw materials, textiles of the highest quality were produced in Kashan, Yazd, Isfahan, Tabriz, and Mashhad, as attested by enthusiastic foreign traders who saw the wares on offer.[48] This class of textiles comprised velvets and other fabrics made in a great variety of complex weave structures such as samite and *taqueté* and which were quite different in flavor from contemporary Ottoman silks, featuring figural vignettes of hunters, animals in combat, lovers, and literary characters (rather than the large abstract or vegetal motifs of the Ottoman fabrics). A special group within this high-end production incorporated metal-wrapped threads, which were used to fill the areas between motifs. Common patterns for these textiles included single flowering plants repeated in rows (cat. 64) or trees with birds and deer (cat. 93A).[49]

Iranian velvets traveled abroad primarily as diplomatic gifts or products for sale in the Indian market, where they were prized at the Mughal court and elsewhere. (Indeed, a coach presented by the English East India Company to the Mughal emperor Jahangir [r. 1605–27] was originally lined in Chinese velvet, but Jahangir had the coach stripped and reupholstered with a metal-ground floral velvet from Iran.)[50] Floral silk brocades were also sent with envoys as well as with those who traveled to India at the accession of 'Alamgir (also known as Aurangzeb, r. 1658–1707).[51]

Other kinds of silks found their way west, primarily with Armenian traders who are credited with introducing the Persian vogue for wearing long sashes around the waist into Russia and Poland, where this fashion became popular in the eighteenth century. The type of sash imported from Iran was several feet in length, with a long field of stripes or a repeating motif set in rows and panels at either end with a design of full, flowering plants that would show at the front of the body when tied (cat. 101A). Soon, workshops were set up in Poland to produce sashes that imitated the Iranian originals; there were also factories that catered to this trade in Istanbul, run by Polish Armenians.[52]

Yet silk and velvet fabric from Iran more commonly traveled abroad as part of diplomatic presents, possibly because such a small quantity was made and most of it was purchased by the court. Another factor may have been cost; in the end, the foreign companies that might have promoted the sale of Iranian textiles abroad found that it was easier and cheaper to conduct trade with other cloth-producing regions, particularly India.[53] Therefore it is remarkable to find such examples as a pair of Iranian silk textiles evidently designed for sale in Thailand (fig. 67). While the weave structure and the palette combining blue, green, and salmon-orange are typical of eighteenth-century production in Iran, the design includes several elements of distinctly Thai origin, notably the elongated, flamelike motifs in the border (*tumpal*). The Thai market was particularly exacting in its commissions, specifying grade of cloth, design, and loom width.[54] A Dutch trader quoted in connection with the manufacture of such textiles provides the obvious reason why this market did not become a larger factor in Iranian trade: "The gold and silver stuffs for the King of Siam, of the required size, will demand one year of production according to the weavers. They will have to erect a separate loom for each design, and therefore they will become very expensive."[55]

Also unusual is a cloth now in the collection of the Kremlin Armory, Moscow, that bears the coat of arms of Venice. With rows of flowering plants and a metal ground, it is much like other seventeenth-century brocades save for the addition of winged lions (the symbol of Saint Mark) holding shields with the inscription PAX TIBI MARCE EVANGELISTA MEUS (Peace to you, Mark, my evangelist). A similar textile with Russian heraldic symbols also survives, but the circumstances of these two creations remain unknown.[56]

Fig. 68
Rudolph II's Envoy Presents a Clock to Sultan Murad III. Germany (Augsburg), 1694. Engraving. Special Collections, Charles E. Young Research Library, University of California, Los Angeles (DR 473 R96pG, fol. 228)

TVRCARVM IMPERATOR NOS QVOQVE
VESTIBVS DONAVIT.

Fig. 69

*Sigismund von Herberstein Wearing
the Robes Presented by the Ottoman
Sultan in 1541*, from *Gratae pos-
teritati Sigismundis liber Baro in
Herberstain*, 1560. National Art
Library, Victoria and Albert Museum,
London (86.B.67)

TEXTILES AND DIPLOMATIC EXCHANGES

The establishment and maintenance of these international trade connections
involved the exchange of many diplomatic missions. Representatives who
traveled back and forth negotiated not just the terms of trade and the rights
of the traders but also ensured that the political goals of all parties were
aligned. Logistics alone made these missions very complicated. The wait for
ships to become available and for the weather to cooperate could take years:
one Portuguese ambassador made it from Lisbon to Goa in seven months
but was delayed in India for three years before he could proceed to Iran.[57]
Travel conditions were rough: in 1597 a single Russian embassy was beset
by the deaths of three diplomats.[58] Even upon reaching their destination,
ambassadors could be stalled for months, first to be granted an audience
with the ruler and then to receive permission to return home once business
was concluded: it took one Dutch ambassador over a year to be released
from his position.[59]

One of the most important calculations in negotiations concerned which
gifts to send with the ambassador. If deemed too poor, discussion could be
scuttled immediately, but exactly the right item could open many doors.
Austrian clocks, for instance, figured prominently in exchanges between the
Habsburgs (and later the Holy Roman Emperors) and the Ottomans (fig. 68).[60]

Political wrangling added another layer of complexity. European rulers
complained that ambassadors from Iran and Turkey conveyed conflicting
messages and that the Eastern potentates did not make definitive decisions.
Yet dealings with the Europeans who presented themselves at the courts of
Istanbul and Isfahan were no simpler. Although the various European East India companies were
businesses run independently of the Crown, their agents presented documents signed by the sovereigns
of the countries in which they originated. Meanwhile, those same monarchs might send their own
representatives to Eastern courts. Despite the resulting confusion and ill will, trade flourished, and the
exchange of so many agents brought about some noteworthy presentations of textiles.

In one of the earliest assignments from this period, Sigismund von Herberstein (1486–1566)
was dispatched in 1541 to the Ottoman court of Istanbul. Serving as ambassador on behalf of three
emperors of the Holy Roman Empire, he participated in numerous missions; in this instance, his
task was to negotiate an alliance against the Habsburg kings. He visited the court of Süleyman I
when the sultan was camped at Buda and, after his audience, was presented with robes of honor, as
was the custom at Muslim courts. These robes are depicted among the portraits von Herberstein
had made as illustrations for his autobiography, which show the clothing that he had either worn
to see, or had received from, the monarchs of Poland, Russia, Spain, and Turkey. So detailed is the
engraving of von Herberstein wearing the robes given to him by Süleyman, it has been determined
that the inner robe was made of Turkish velvet and the outer robe was of Italian velvet tailored in
the Turkish style (fig. 69).[61] Interestingly, the robes he received in Moscow are thought to have
been made from Turkish silk.[62]

At about the same time, Sweden sent its first envoy to the Ottoman court, also to test the possibility of an alliance against the Habsburgs. In the seventeenth century the Swedish king Charles X

Gustav (r. 1654–60) sent a second mission to promote Sweden's interests in eastern Europe, an area in which Turkey was continuously involved. To this end, Charles X Gustav's representative, Claes Brorson Rålamb, arrived in Istanbul in May 1657, and another ambassador, Gotthard Wellingk, arrived in June. Rather miraculously, Rålamb was granted audiences with the sultan Mehmed IV (r. 1648–87) and his grand vizier within days of his arrival, but matters did not turn out well. Rålamb, forced to travel anonymously because he was passing through enemy lands, had not brought any gifts to present to the Ottoman sultan. In addition, the sultan and his vizier considered Sweden's alliance with Transylvania problematic in light of their own designs to conquer this area, and the arrival of a second ambassador from the Swedish king was thought puzzling. At the ambassadors' final visit to the court, Mehmed's vizier expressed the goodwill of the sultan toward the Swedish king—without committing to any alliance—and presented both ambassadors with robes.[63] The fabric from the robe given to Rålamb now survives as a chasuble made for use at the church on the family estate in Högsjö. Typical of *kemha*s of the early seventeenth century—if not of the best quality—the Turkish fabric bears a wavy-vine pattern on a red ground, its decorative motifs executed in gold and silver metal-wrapped thread (fig. 70).[64]

The Dutch also wanted to establish relations with Turkey, in part because of the Habsburg menace to their territories but also because of the increasing role of the Netherlands in the international sea trade and its dominance of the Southeast Asian and Japanese markets. In 1612 Cornelis Haga arrived in Istanbul, and his negotiations with Ahmed I (r. 1603–17) resulted in favorable trade concessions, which were reaffirmed by Murad IV (r. 1623–40) in 1634 and Mehmed IV in 1680. So successful was Haga, and so important was this trade relationship to both sides, that he remained as an ambassador in Istanbul for twenty-six years.

Dutch ambassadors continued to be posted to the Ottoman court through the eighteenth century, playing an important role in political negotiations with other European powers as well: in 1737, for example, Dutch ambassador Cornelis Calkoen mediated negotiations with Russia over the Crimea.[65] One of Calkoen's audiences with Ahmed III (r. 1703–30; fig. 71) is depicted in a painting by Jean Baptiste Vanmour, a French artist based in Istanbul. In it, the ambassador and his retinue wear Ottoman silk robes, presumably presented by the sultan, over their European attire. Vanmour also created for Calkoen a series of paintings of thirty-two Ottoman officials, capturing all the details of their dress (fig. 72a–d). These were later donated to the Directorate of Levant Trade and were hung in its meeting room.[66]

A source of raw silk as well as a potential ally against Ottoman expansion, Iran was attractive to many European powers, and it received its own share of visitors. In 1633 Friedrich III, duke of Holstein-Gottorp (parts of present-day Denmark and Germany), sent two ambassadors to Iran with the proposal of making his new city of Friedrichstadt the terminus of an overland trade route via Russia. Stopping in Russia to conclude the necessary treaties there, the two ambassadors continued on to Isfahan by sailing down the Volga and then crossing the Caspian Sea. Although they were

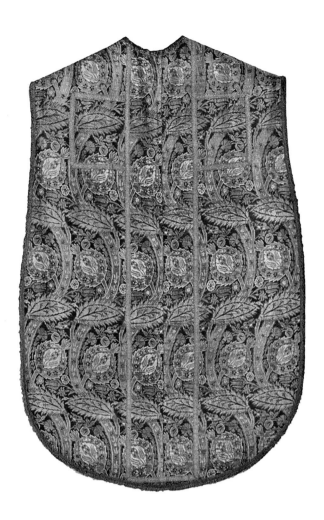

Fig. 70
The Rålamb Chasuble. Sweden, mid-to late 17th century. Textile: Turkey, mid-17th century. Silk (*kemha*). Museum of National Antiquities, Stockholm (33767)

received warmly by Safi and returned to Gottorp in 1639 with a representative from Iran, no definitive arrangements for trade were ever made.[67]

The textile legacy of these exchanges, however, is quite intriguing. A group of mid-seventeenth-
century velvets now in the collection of the Rosenborg Palace in Copenhagen are believed to have
been the gift of Safi's ambassador to Friedrich. The presence of velvets from Iran in Gottorp was
noted in several seventeenth-century inventories, which sometimes recorded where they were displayed. The velvets were likely transferred to Copenhagen about 1817, after the Rosenborg Palace had
become a royal storehouse of sorts. As part of the conversion of the castle into a museum in 1833,
the textiles were hung on the walls as a backdrop to paintings and furnishings associated with the
reign of Christian V (1670–99)—though by this time museum guides identified the velvets as Chinese
(fig. 73). It was only in the early twentieth century that the Iranian origin of the Rosenborg velvets
was recognized and connected to the velvets listed in the Gottorp inventories.[68]

Russia was directly involved in negotiations with Iran as well, including the ill-fated mission of
1597 recounted above. 'Abbas I was particularly keen to establish a northern route to Europe through
Russia, and multiple embassies were exchanged during his reign. Later, in the 1660s and 1670s, the
Russians were eager for this trade to flourish,[69] and in 1673 Alexis I Mikhaylovich (r. 1645–76) sent
Prince Andrey Priklonskiy as his ambassador to the court of Sulaiman I (r. 1666–94). This mission
was entirely successful on the diplomatic front, and the Russian ambassador even caught the imagination of Safavid artists such as 'Ali Quli Jabbadar, who painted his portrait (fig. 76). Numerous later
copies of this painting indicate the fascination the Russian prince continued to hold for local artists.[70]

The inventory of gifts that passed between the two states underscores the importance of these
relations. Among the textiles 'Abbas II (r. 1642–66) sent with his ambassadors to Russia in 1650 were
over three hundred pieces of velvet, damask, satin, and taffeta from Yazd and Kashan, in addition

72a

72b

72c

72d

to several sashes and fifteen carpets.[71] One of the finest items of clothing sent from Iran to Moscow was a robe of figural velvet that was later presented by Alexis I Mikhaylovich to Queen Christina of Sweden (r. 1632–54) (fig. 74).[72]

Although England played a role in the expansion of trade from Iran's Persian Gulf ports, diplomatic relations between the countries were almost comically complicated. The two most prominent characters in these exchanges were the brothers Robert and Anthony Sherley. Arriving in Iran with a group of Europeans in 1598, Anthony was sent back to Europe the following year to act as a representative for 'Abbas I, accompanied by several Iranians. Quarrels broke out frequently within the

Fig. 72a–d
Jean Baptiste Vanmour (French, 1671–1737). Four paintings from a costume series, 1727–30. Oil on canvas. Rijksmuseum, Amsterdam

72a: *The Great Effendi, Head of the Chancellery* (SK-A-2024);
72b: *Mehmed Kahya, Adjutant to the Aga* (SK-A-2026);
72c: *The Grand Vizier Nevşehirli Damat Ibrahim Pasha* (SK-A-2017);
72d: *Sultan Mehmed I* (SK-A-2014)

group, and some of the Iranians settled in Spain, having converted to Christianity. The aim of creating an alliance against the Ottomans went unrealized, and so 'Abbas twice sent Robert to Europe. He too failed, partly because 'Abbas separately dispatched an Iranian ambassador, one Naqd 'Ali Beg, who disgraced Robert during an audience with Charles I (r. 1625–49).[73]

Despite these missteps, Charles continued the negotiations, sending ambassadors to Iran to represent his commercial interests and also to collect antiquities and historical manuscripts.[74] Eventually, trade agreements were established, and the East India Company built factories in Iran, successfully entering the silk market and also managing to sell England's wool textiles in Iran. Most significantly, the English helped 'Abbas expel the Portuguese from Hormuz to benefit his own Persian Gulf port, Bandar 'Abbas.

While no surviving textiles appear to be connected with this exchange of ambassadors, there is evidence for the presentation of robes of honor. Like the portraits of Sigismund von Herberstein that record him in Ottoman dress, portraits of Robert Sherley show him in Safavid costume (fig. 75). These were not simply items worn at the sitting, for the many English travelers who met the brothers in Iran noted their ease in, and indeed their preference for, local dress,[75] in contrast to 'Abbas's ambassadors who traveled to Europe. Mehdi Quli Beg, who visited the court of the Holy Roman Emperor Rudolph II (r. 1583–1612) in 1604, is typical of that group in that he neither adopted any European habits nor changed his style of clothing during his travels abroad (fig. 77). Robert's portrait was painted by Anthony van Dyck during a stop in Rome in 1622, and it depicts him in the robe presented to him by 'Abbas, which was made of velvet with a design of spiraling vines encircling women holding wine bottles.

Gifts sent between courts were seen only by a limited few, and the number of finished textiles that moved from Iran and Turkey to the rest of the world was relatively small, yet these technically and visually innovative textiles had a strong impact. Eastern European fashion was heavily influenced by Ottoman design, and in western Europe the bizarre silks produced in the late seventeenth and early eighteenth centuries were inspired by Ottoman prototypes (cat. 43). Iran's bird-and-tree textiles (cat. 93A) caught the foreign imagination as well. Echoes appear in a variety of media, from Portuguese tiles and Indian palampores (cat. 118) to the American textiles that they in turn inspired (cat. 54).

Opposite page:
Fig. 73
Rosenborg Palace, Copenhagen.
Room 26 installed with Safavid
velvets ca. 1833; photo 1901

Fig. 74
Robe. Iran, 1630s. Brocaded velvet,
silk and metal-wrapped thread. Royal
Armory, Stockholm (3414)

Left:
Fig. 75
Anthony van Dyck (Flemish, 1599–
1641). *Sir Robert Sherley*, 1622. Oil
on canvas. National Trust, Petworth
House, Sussex, United Kingdom (38)

Below, left:
Fig. 76
'Ali Quli Jabbadar (Iranian, active
1642–late 17th century). *Portrait of
the Russian Ambassador, Prince
Andrey Priklonskiy*, from the *Davis
Album*, 1673–74. Ink, opaque water-
color, and gold on paper. The Metro-
politan Museum of Art, New York,
Theodore M. Davis Collection,
Bequest of Theodore M. Davis, 1915
(30.95.174.5)

Below, right:
Fig. 77
Aegidius Sadeler (Netherlandish,
1568–1629). *Portrait of Mehdi Quli
Beg, Persian Ambassador to Prague*,
1605. Engraving. The Metropolitan
Museum of Art, New York, The
Elisha Whittelsey Collection, The
Elisha Whittelsey Fund, 1949
(49.95.2202)

"Whims and Fancies"

EUROPEANS RESPOND TO TEXTILES FROM THE EAST

Melinda Watt

I n 1756 the third edition of a design manual titled *The Laboratory, or, School of Arts* was published in London by Godfrey Smith. In the chapter on designing for woven silks, the author praised the "excellent genius" of the Chinese, who "supply our imagination with vast varieties of whims and fancies," including motifs of "birds, butterflies, houses, fish, and many other things" that could transform an ordinary pattern into a marketing success.[1] By the middle of the eighteenth century foreign motifs were so thoroughly integrated into the European sensibility that a dress silk decorated with whimsical fish or tiny pagodas was deemed completely acceptable—albeit still associated with a foreign culture. This impact on English textile design is just one example of the shifts in taste and consumption that were stimulated by the increased importation of foreign fabrics from Asia into western Europe during the seventeenth and eighteenth centuries. Colorful Indian cottons and lustrous Chinese silks, along with coffee, tea, porcelain, and lacquer, captivated discerning consumers. These new fabrics were incorporated into decorating schemes and fashioned into garments that expressed a desire to escape to foreign lands and experience exotic cultures. While textiles and other imported goods were initially accessible only to the upper classes, by the middle of the eighteenth century consumers at all levels of society were participating in this trend.

Chinoiserie has become an accepted term to denote the incorporation of foreign (mostly Chinese, Japanese, and Indian) motifs into a new and uniquely European style.[2] Objects made in this style bore little or no resemblance to actual Asian objects made for their own domestic markets.[3] Contemporary evidence suggests that European consumers of goods imported by the various East India companies did not have a clear idea of the precise origins of these products. In the seventeenth century phrases like "façon de la chine," "Japan work," and "genuine Indian work" were used to describe not only imported objects regardless of their country of origin but also the European imitations of porcelain, lacquer, and textiles, which together constituted the most highly prized and popular decorative objects imported from the East.[4] Thanks in part to the wide dissemination of printed materials—travel accounts, studies of global dress, and designs published during the seventeenth and eighteenth centuries—modern scholars have been able to study chinoiserie as a pan-European phenomenon: successful printed works were quickly translated into multiple languages and distributed from the publishing centers of Antwerp, London, and Paris, among others.[5]

A love of things Turkish and Persian also gripped the fashionable world in the seventeenth and eighteenth centuries, with regional differences in taste and interests. The French and Austrians, who certainly participated in the vogue for chinoiserie, were at the same time more engaged with influences from the Ottoman Empire than the English and the Dutch appear to have been. This phenomenon, which has been termed *turquerie*, was closely associated with the masquerades, theater, and music of eighteenth-century high society, particularly in France (cat. 88). By the end of the eighteenth century, however, chinoiserie and *turquerie* had become domesticated, and floral patterns and motifs originally found on Indian chintzes and Chinese damasks were so completely incorporated into European textile design as to be unremarkable, while still retaining their fashionable charm.[6]

THE EUROPEAN TRADING COMPANIES
AND THE IMPORTATION OF TEXTILES

The taste for the exotic could not have spread beyond elite circles in Europe had it not been for the founding, in the early seventeenth century, of national trading companies that greatly expanded and increased the circulation of goods around the globe. Prior to this expansion, Europeans consumed only limited quantities of imported textiles from the Middle and Far East. Although many countries with aspirations to wealth and influence established their own companies to facilitate direct trade with India, China, and Japan, the Dutch and English companies were by far the largest importers of goods, including textiles, to Europe.

As John Guy writes in this publication, it was spices, not textiles or other commodities, that drove the earliest trade between the Indian textile producers and the Western traders, and the initial aim of northern Europeans, beginning with the Dutch, was to compete in that trade. Subsequently, they extended their interests to include textiles. The original goals of the English traders were actually twofold: to expand the market for English wool textiles into Asia and to compete with the Dutch and the Portuguese in the global spice trade.[7] The French also considered developing an East Asian market for their wool textiles. Not surprisingly, wool cloth had a limited appeal in the warmer spice-growing climates of the Indonesian archipelago and southern India—a region that produced its own relatively inexpensive cotton products.[8] Both England and France did have some success exporting wool cloth to the Levant. As might be surmised from the names for the French wool cloth that was intended for this market—Londres and Londrins—the English product was imitated by French manufacturers.

The English founded the Governor and Company of Merchants of London Trading in the East Indies[9] in 1600, during the last years of the reign of Elizabeth I (1558–1603). This name was unofficially shortened to the East India Company (EIC), and it then became the United East India Company (UEIC) in 1708. Active in India until 1858, the company was not formally dissolved until 1873.[10] Although the Dutch were trading in the East by the 1590s, they did not establish their official national organization, the Verenigde Oost-Indische Compagnie (the Dutch East India Company; VOC) until 1602; it was dissolved in 1800. Denmark soon followed, with the establishment of a company in 1616 under Christian IV (r. 1588–1648). The business operated until 1650 and was revived as the Asiatic Company between 1670 and 1729. The French lagged behind their neighbors, forming a centralized national trading company only in 1664, after Louis XIV (r. 1643–1715) appointed the ambitious Jean-Baptiste Colbert (1619–1683) finance minister. The Compagnie Royale des Indes Orientales (or French East India Company) operated until 1769, with a brief revival between 1785 and 1794.[11] In the first half of the eighteenth century, Austria and Sweden both established trading organizations. The Austrian Kaiserliche und Königliche Indische Kompanie (Imperial and Royal Indian Company), operating out of Ostend, sent more than thirty ships to the Far East during its brief period of activity, beginning in 1722. Its dissolution in 1731 as a condition of the Treaty of Vienna, which created an alliance between Austria and Britain, was proof of the highly competitive nature of the European trade with Asia.

Initially, a large portion of the textile-related trade was in raw materials and supplies for the industry: dyestuffs (see the essay by Elena Phipps in this publication), raw silk, and partially finished silk thread, as well as undyed cloth. Sir John Chardin (1643–1713), a French merchant who traveled to Iran (Persia) and India, recorded the huge quantities of raw silk that the Dutch shipped from

Iran in the 1670s via the Indian Ocean; this trade was tightly controlled by the Iranians (see the essay by Marika Sardar in this publication).[12] Not all of the textiles and related goods purchased by the European companies were bound for western European customers. In fact, the export of finished textiles back to Europe does not appear to have been a primary commercial goal until the mid-1600s. The textiles traded by the EIC in the mid-seventeenth century included fine cotton muslins for reexport to the Ottoman Empire and North Africa, as well as coarser cotton cloth, patterned with checks and stripes, for the West African market (for eighteenth-century examples of the cloth for this market see cat. 108).[13]

Fig. 78
Palampore with the arms of Christian VI of Denmark. India, for the Danish market, 1740–46. Cotton, painted resist and mordant, dyed. Designmuseum Danmark, Copenhagen (A31/1925)

Some finished textiles were brought back to Europe during the early years of the seventeenth century. Bengali embroidered quilts were well known in Portugal and, subsequently, in England (cats. 6, 8). The appearance of satins and rare damasks from China played a role in encouraging the silk-weaving industries in trading strongholds such as Greater London and Amsterdam.[14] After the restoration of the English monarchy in 1660, the EIC actively sought and received the support of Charles II (r. 1660–85), in part by bestowing gifts, including textiles, on him and other members of the Stuart court.[15] The English diarist Celia Fiennes noted in 1698 that the Queen's Chamber of State was decorated with "all Indian Embroidery on white sattin being presented to her by the Company."[16]

Although patterned textile imports are the focus here, it should be noted that much of the cloth imported by Europeans was monochrome—either dyed solid colors or imported plain white—to be printed or used plain. By the late 1600s, cotton fabrics from India accounted for the majority of the finished textiles imported into western Europe by the various East India companies. For centuries, Indian textile producers had made various grades of all-cotton textiles, and the most luxurious of these were patterned by a combination of hand-painted mordants (chemical fixatives that produced multiple colors in combination with madder dye) and resists (some sort of wax or paste). For second-tier goods, block-printed mordants and resists augmented or replaced hand-painted ones. After these were applied, the cloth was subjected to a series of dye baths (one for each shade), rinses, and finishing processes that took at least several weeks to complete.[17] Several names—most commonly "pintado," "chintz," and "calico"—were used to describe imported cloth with patterns more elaborate than simple woven stripes or checks. The word *pintado*, from the Portuguese for "spotted," was current from the late 1500s to about 1650; the term originally referred only to high-quality painted cloth. By about 1680 the English tended to use "chintz," "calico," and "painted calico" instead, as evidenced by inventories and wills that describe rooms decorated with patterned Indian cotton textiles.[18] Like "pintado," "chintz" originally referred only to the painted cloths, not to the less expensive types that were either printed or produced with a combination of printing and hand-painting. Rather confusingly, "calico" could refer to either patterned or plain cotton fabric. Inventories and merchants' orders often qualified the word with a color name or an indication of a pattern, as seen in the correspondence of American merchants (see the essay by Amelia Peck in this publication).

Cotton textiles accounted for a significant 73 percent of the overall value of EIC imports in the mid-1660s, and this figure rose to a high point of 83 percent in the mid-1680s, when they comprised more than 1.5 million pieces of cloth.[19] Not only were the English and Dutch companies supplying their buyers at home, but they were also competing for the rest of the European market.[20] Although Chinese and Indian silk textiles played a minor role compared to the great quantities of cotton being traded, they were nonetheless desirable commodities in Europe. Like cotton textiles, most of these fabrics were monochrome plain weaves and satins; only a small percentage were patterned on the loom or by painting.[21]

The most striking of the Indian cotton products that entered the European market must certainly have been the large bedcovers and hangings usually referred to as palampores. These panels measured up to nine feet (or almost three meters) in width, and most were decorated with luxuriant Tree of Life designs, images of single trees sprouting countless species of fantasy flowers (cats. 52, 118). The hybrid nature of these designs, which combined myriad motifs from both East and West, has been demonstrated by comparisons with earlier motifs of a multiflowering tree in Persian and Indian art, as well as in English embroidery of the early seventeenth century.[22]

By the end of the seventeenth century, the taste for chintz furnishings was well established, and palampores were being imported in large numbers. In 1695–96, for example, the EIC imported forty thousand palampores, as well as coordinating chintz yardage.[23] These imports, clearly produced in large quantities, reflect the preference for decorating rooms en suite, as exemplified by the chintz and embroidered ensembles associated with Ashburnham House in London (cat. 74). Ensembles for an entire bedroom could include the bed hangings, a bedcover or quilt, wall hangings, and sometimes covers for seat furniture (cat. 55).

A smaller number of palampores were decorated with European armorials rather than the Tree of Life. These were probably special commissions ordered by people connected with the East India trade. Two notable examples are in the Victoria and Albert Musuem, London: one displays the English Royal Stuart arms in a field of exotic animals and plants, and the other features the coat of arms of one J. C. Pielat (1692–1740), an official with the VOC.[24] A superb example in Denmark is presumed to have been made in the Danish colony of Tranquebar, on the Coromandel Coast of India (fig. 78).[25] The panel bears the royal arms of the Danish king Christian VI (r. 1730–46) and depicts scenes of daily life in the Danish colony in India. It displays a lively combination of European and Indian motifs (similar to those seen in cat. 105). These include Danish soldiers in authentic uniform, hunt scenes, and an Indian princess on horseback. A third style of palampore, less commonly exported to the West, used a composition based on carpet designs, with a central medallion or motif such as a bouquet of flowers that was repeated in the four corners of the field (cats. 10, 54).

Fears that imported cottons and silks would compete with European textiles—particularly the products of the well-established silk-weaving industry in France and those of the traditional wool and growing silk industries in England—resulted in a series of protectionist measures against the importation of foreign fabrics as well as the domestic production of imitations. Protests against imports and imitations began in both countries during the late seventeenth century. The protectionist policies that resulted from this outcry are understandable in light of the staggering statistics of importation between the 1660s and the 1680s; legislators had no way of knowing that imports would never again reach the peak they attained during this period.[26] Although the Netherlands did not ban the importation of cotton or silk textiles from Asia, their local industries did protest the activities of the VOC. As early as 1643, the silk weavers of Amsterdam lodged complaints against the company for its importation of textiles.[27] Protests from both weavers and thread producers continued into the late seventeenth century, in response to the VOC practice of sending European textiles and designs to their Chinese and Indian workshops to be copied and adapted.[28] The objections of the silk thread makers, or throwers, indicate the scope of the textile industries. The importation of materials in a finished state—such as silk that was already thrown (twisted into thread) or dyestuffs that replaced local traditional materials—threatened the livelihoods of those who labored in the professions that supported the work of the weavers.

From 1686 to 1757 Lyon silk manufacturers were prohibited from making imitations of banned Indian silk textiles "lest the genuine article should then be fraudulently imported."[29] The French also banned the importation of chintz in 1686, again for fear of harming the silk-weaving industry.[30] This ban marked the beginning of eighty years of prohibitions that finally ended in 1756.[31] In 1700, after several years of lobbying and even a riot by London silk weavers, the English Parliament passed a ban prohibiting the use of "all wrought silk, Bengalls, and stuffs mixed with silk or herba, of the manufacture of Persia, China, or East India, and all calicoes painted, dyed, printed or stained there."[32] This law was further strengthened in 1721, when domestic use of pure Indian cotton fabrics printed in England was prohibited as well. All restrictions against the importation and production of printed cotton for English consumption were not lifted until 1774.

Several crucial points are essential to understanding this legislation and its actual impact. First, restrictions on imports were often quite specific in regard to fabric names; therefore, importers could circumvent prohibitions by substituting another similar type of cotton or silk cloth. Restrictions on printing all-cotton cloth were bypassed by substituting European fabrics of linen or a mixture of linen and cotton (often called "fustian"). Second, especially in England and France, such restrictions did not apply to exports, so that the substantial Atlantic trade kept these producers in business. Finally, some people undoubtedly practiced smuggling, blatantly disregarding the bans on the use of printed cotton and imported Eastern silks. Indeed, government officials were not above trying to acquire desirable but illegal imported fabrics. In 1752 an administrator in Rouen had his shipment of Chinese and Indian silks and Indian painted cottons confiscated, but the fact that an official even attempted to order these imports implies that the success rate for such activities was worth the risk.[33]

The English writer Daniel Defoe (1660–1731), one of the most eloquent advocates for the European domestic textile industries, produced a number of pamphlets against the importation of Indian goods.[34] In 1708 he characterized the increased use of exotic textiles in terms that one might use to describe a disease, noting that "it crept into our houses, our closets and bedchambers; curtains, cushions, chairs, and at last beds themselves were nothing but Callicoes or Indian stuffs" and concluding that "everything that used to be made of wool or silk, relating to either the dress of women or the furniture of our houses, was supplied by the Indian trade."[35] Not everyone was of the same opinion, however, and an English pamphlet written in response to the violent protests of the Spitalfields silk weavers in 1719 actually praised the Dutch for their lack of prohibitions. According to the writer, the Dutch realized that "excessive duties are great encouragement to running [smuggling], and that prohibitions make people more eager for that which is forbid."[36]

EASTERN TEXTILES AT HOME IN THE WEST

Exactly how were these appealing but controversial new imports used? The creation of exotic-looking spaces came to be associated with leisure and the pursuit of pleasure. Luxurious fabrics from the East were primarily relegated to semiprivate spaces, either bedrooms or private closets (sometimes called *cabinets*). On a grander scale, exotic textiles and imitations of them were sometimes used within the freestanding garden pavilions built by European nobility as retreats from the formality of court life. The earliest pleasure palace built in the chinoiserie style was the Trianon de Porcelaine at Versailles, commissioned by Louis XIV for his mistress Madame de Montespan in 1670; it was decorated outside with porcelain vessels and tiles and inside with furnishings "in the Chinese manner."[37] One of the extant structures of this kind is the garden pavilion at Drottningholm, Sweden, which was built between 1763 and 1769 and is decorated with wall panels embroidered by Queen Louisa Ulrika (1720–1782). The edict issued when her son Gustav III (r. 1771–92) planned to spend time in the pavilion gives a sense of the exotic escape offered by the retreat: "If the King is to lunch in China and to spend the whole day there, this will be announced as soon as he awakens . . . carriages will gather on the grand terrace of the palace for the trip to China."[38]

The first chintz furnishings sold in Europe were those made for regional markets on the Indian subcontinent and imported to the West as curiosities. The English writer and diarist John Evelyn

(1620–1706) described painted cotton hangings in an account of a dinner at Lady Mordant's home in 1655: "Here was a roome hung with Pintado full of figures great and small, prettily representing sundry trades and occupations of the Indians, with their habits."[39] A small group of Indian figural hangings dated to the mid-1600s, which may have been made for a courtly setting in Jaipur or the Deccan, appears to correspond to Evelyn's basic description.[40] An early example of furnishing chintz made specifically for Europe can be found in the extraordinary dollhouse of about 1677 that belonged to Petronella Dunois (1650–1695) of Amsterdam (fig. 79). The miniature "lying-in" room is by far the earliest surviving interior that conveys exactly how chintz yardage was used. The walls and the bed hangings are of the same textile, trimmed with tassels and cords in coordinating colors. These furnishings are rare extant examples of chintz with a dark red background; though this was a standard Indian production at the time, white backgrounds came to be preferred by most Europeans (see cat. 118). The English diarist Samuel Pepys (1633–1703) and his wife apparently invested both time and money to furnish her study with an Indian cotton. He wrote in September 1663: "My wife and I to Cornhill and after many trials bought my wife a Chinke; that is, a paynted Indian Callico for to line her new Study, which is very pretty."[41]

Another type of furnishing was the collage chintz fabrics created by appliqué embroidery, seen mostly in France and Austria. Probably the most spectacular surviving example is the bedroom ensemble made for Prince Eugene of Savoy (1663–1736) for his hunting retreat of Schloss Hof, near Vienna. The wealthy and sophisticated Prince Eugene, raised in Paris, was an avid collector of art and exotic luxuries both European and imported, and he took advantage of his international connections to procure goods for his home.[42] The wall hanging in figure 80 is made of various patterned and solid-colored

Fig. 79
Dollhouse of Petronella Dunois, view of the lying-in room. Netherlands (Amsterdam), ca. 1677. Rijksmuseum, Amsterdam (BK-14656)

Fig. 80
Wall hanging with musicians from
Schloss Hof, Austria, ca. 1730,
appliquéd with various Indian
cottons. MAK Vienna: Austrian
Museum of Applied Arts / Contemporary Art (T8425)

cottons, all certainly Indian fabrics, cut out and applied to a cotton background. Several possible routes by which the prince may have acquired this extravagant suite of furnishings include purchase of the fabrics from the EIC, through the VOC, or, perhaps, via his position as governor of the Austrian Netherlands from 1716 to 1724, during which time the short-lived Austrian Kaiserliche und Königliche Indische Kompanie was in operation.[43]

Chinese silk damasks were the most popular Eastern patterned silks used for interiors. References to "Indian damask" in European inventories of the time presumably reflect ignorance regarding the actual provenance of the fabrics, which were probably all Chinese. An example of Chinese damask, most likely made for domestic consumption in China, survives as a backing on a sixteenth-century embroidered cushion at Hardwick Hall, Derbyshire, England,[44] and Portuguese and Spanish trade accounts list damasks as part of their cargoes throughout the seventeenth century.[45] According to the EIC records for the second quarter of the eighteenth century, merchants were ordering "bed damasks," among other types of silk.[46] This term probably referred to large patterns suitable for use as furnishings (not limited to bed hangings); smaller patterns would have been more appropriate for clothing. Silk damasks, both Chinese and European, also found great favor with wealthy North American colonists (cat. 121).

FASHION AND EXOTICISM

Along with the publication of illustrated travel accounts, the dissemination of costume books such as the Venetian artist Cesare Vecellio's *Habiti antichi et moderni di tutto il mondo* of 1598 helped to familiarize the European public with dress of other lands.[47] These compilations of regional and world costume emerged at a time when fashion and textile consumption was, in effect, being deregulated. The system of sumptuary legislation that had historically limited, by social class, what types of textiles could be worn was being dismantled.[48] Simultaneously, there was a rapid increase in the availability of fashionable and relatively inexpensive textile products. Indian fabrics found their way into the dress of the English and Dutch by the 1670s. As early as 1681 anxiety about the popularity of imported textiles was aimed specifically at their use in dress that crossed social strata. Objections were couched in the moralistic language of the medieval sumptuary regulations: "As ill weeds grow apace, so these manufactured goods from India met with such a kind reception that from the greatest gallants to the meanest Cook Maids, nothing was thought so fit to adorn their persons as the Fabrick from India."[49] Rapid changes in the fashion cycle were criticized, as well. Daniel Defoe proclaimed that "vice and luxury are now become essential to us" and found it "incredible" that clothes were discarded in England "not for their being worn out, but merely for their being out of fashion."[50] But Defoe and others who objected to the EIC trade did not represent all public opinion. Early proponents of free trade supported the vicissitudes of fashion as potential economic stimuli.[51]

The increasing use of chintz for dress, not just for furnishings, gave rise to product specialization. In 1683 the EIC asked its Surat factory to supply chintz of finer cotton to suit the tastes of upper-class women, since the Indian chintzes were already "the ware of Gentlewomen" in the Netherlands but only worn by "the meaner sort" in England.[52] This strategy appears to have been successful: the company reported in 1687 that chintzes were "the Ware of Ladyes of the greatest quality, which they wear on the outside of Gowns and Mantuoes [mantuas, or loose coats][53] which they line with velvet and Cloth of Gold."[54]

The last portrait of Madame de Pompadour (born Jeanne
Antoinette Poisson, 1721–1764), the mistress of Louis XV
(r. 1715–74), shows her at her embroidery frame in a small but
lavishly furnished room (fig. 81). She wears a striking floral gown
of Indian chintz, accessorized by many yards of French needle-
lace trimmings and striped silk ribbons, and lined with silk.[55]
Madame de Pompadour was an influential patron of the arts, as
well as an investor in the Compagnie Royale des Indes Orientales.

Evidence for the use of Indian chintz and English imitations across the English Channel at the other end of the socio-
economic scale survives in the records of the London Foundling
Hospital. The parents who gave up their children to the hospital between 1740 and 1770 left textile fragments as "tokens" by
which to identify the foundlings.[56] It is unknown whether the
garments from which these fragments were taken were purchased
as new, refashioned from adult clothing, or whether they were
acquired on the secondhand market. But clearly the parents,
people of very limited means, participated in the consumption of
both imported Indian cottons and the English printed textiles
inspired by them.

Numerous Europeans had their portraits painted while wearing versions of "Oriental" dress, some made of imported textiles
and others assembled from European fabrics. Many of these
depictions commemorate the sitters' travels and the costumes
they acquired as souvenirs. Early examples are the images produced for sixteenth- and seventeenth-century diplomats such as
Sigismund von Herberstein (1486–1566), whose memoirs
include illustrations of the European and foreign dress worn during his long career in service to the
Holy Roman Empire (see fig. 69).[57] Sir Robert Sherley (ca. 1581–1628), an English emissary to the
court of Shah 'Abbas in Iran, sat for at least three portraits in his Safavid finery: the work painted by
Anthony van Dyck is artistically superior (see fig. 75), but an unattributed portrait more carefully
delineates his dress.[58]

Arguably the most famous European woman to travel to the Ottoman territories in the eighteenth
century was the English noblewoman Lady Mary Wortley Montagu (1689–1762), whose husband
was named ambassador to Constantinople in 1716. She was painted in Ottoman dress first while in
Istanbul (Constantinople) but also numerous times after her return to England (cat. 92). One of
the most famous portraits of her is attributed to Jean Baptiste Vanmour (1671–1737), a French artist
who lived and worked in Constantinople intermittently from 1699 until his death (fig. 82). He was
the logical choice as portraitist for expatriate Europeans, particularly after his *Recueil de cent
estampes représentant différentes nations du Levant* was published in Paris in 1714 and enjoyed great
success.[59] Lady Mary often wore Eastern dress during her stay in Turkey, sometimes in an attempt to
appear less conspicuous,[60] and in her correspondence she often expresses admiration for the exquisite
manners and courtly behavior of her Turkish acquaintances. Nevertheless, female Turkish dress was
also associated with an amorous intent or loose morals in eighteenth-century Europe. The unfamiliar

Fig. 82
Attributed to Jean Baptiste Vanmour
(French, 1671–1737). *Lady Mary
Wortley Montagu with Her Son,
Edward Wortley Montagu, and
Attendants*, ca. 1717. Oil on canvas.
National Portrait Gallery, London,
Purchased, 1958 (NPG 3924)

seraglio system, whereby men had multiple wives, was anathema to Western customs, and the mere idea of it provided endless titillation. Thus, costumes that vaguely referenced Eastern dress in the use of feathers, jewels, and metallic trimmings remained some of the favorite disguises for English women who attended wildly popular masquerade entertainments in the eighteenth century.[61] Male masqueraders also adopted features of Ottoman dress, evoking the image of powerful Turkish leaders. An observer at a 1755 event hosted by the Russian ambassador at Somerset House in London likened the Duke of Cumberland to "Osman the Third . . . in the centre of his new seraglio."[62]

The vogue for Turkish styles was by no means confined to the English; as noted above, the phenomenon of *turquerie* was particularly strong in France and Austria. The somewhat eccentric Swiss artist Jean Étienne Liotard (1702–1789), who had lived in the Ottoman territories between 1733 and 1743, dressed as a Turk and styled himself "le Peintre Turc," as seen in his 1744 self-portrait, now in the Uffizi, Florence. Upon his return to Europe, he worked at the court of the Austrian empress Maria Theresa (r. 1740–80) and her consort Francis I, creating both traditional portraits and images of wealthy Europeans in Turkish dress.[63] Those who did not have the opportunity to travel to the mysterious East, or to sit for one of the era's successful portraitists, could affect a variation on Turkish dress by imitating fashion plates in late eighteenth-century journals such as *Galerie des modes*. An example from 1779, titled *Costume of a Sultane*, implies that the proper placement of feathers, tassels,

Fig. 83
Costume of a Sultane, from *Galeries des modes et costumes français*. France (Paris), 1779. Thomas J. Watson Library, The Metropolitan Museum of Art, New York (GT865. G35 1911, vol. 2, pl. 107)

Fig. 84
Joseph Vivien (French, 1657–1734). *Portrait of Clemens August, Elector and Archbishop of Cologne*, ca. 1722–25. Oil on canvas. Schloss Falkenlust, Brühl, Germany

and fur trim would suffice to create the illusion of Turkish splendor (fig. 83). One additional detail is interesting to note: the woman's petticoat has been draped between her knees so as to suggest what were called "drawers," like those Lady Mary Wortley Montagu actually wore in Constantinople.

The oeuvre of the English painter Sir Joshua Reynolds (1723–1792) includes many romanticized images of both men and women in various iterations of exotic dress. Some, like the portrait of Mrs. George Baldwin, who was born in Turkey, show apparently authentic Ottoman textiles or garments (cat. 100A). Others, like the portrait of Mrs. Horton, in a turban created by draping a fine Kashmir shawl about her head and shoulders, merely suggest an air of the exotic (cat. 100B).

The Kashmir shawl was to become indispensable during the Neoclassical period, when simple, light cotton dresses were the height of fashion. India still produced the best quality of the fabric favored for these garments: very fine, translucent white cotton muslin (cat. 76). Queen Marie Antoinette of France (1755–1793) was credited with popularizing the style, as seen in her 1783 portrait after Élisabeth Vigée Le Brun (1755–1842) in the National Gallery of Art, Washington, D.C. The queen, always controversial in her fashion choices, was criticized in this instance not for her usual extravagance but for neglecting both the dignity of the monarchy and the livelihoods of French silk weavers by wearing cotton.

Exotic dress entered the male wardrobe with the trend for wearing loose-fitting dressing gowns—variously called banyans, Indian gowns, morning gowns, nightgowns, or *japonsche rocken* (Japanese robes)—that was established in the mid-seventeenth century (cats. 96–98). An early reference to this fashion is found in the family correspondence of Thomas Howard, Earl of Arundel, in 1634, when the purchase of "an Indian warme Gown" (presumably one with padding for insulation) in Amsterdam is noted as being an expensive extravagance.[64] The vogue for wearing banyans is documented in numerous portraits of men from all over northern Europe and America. The Dutch artist Caspar Netscher (1639–1684) recorded a number of prominent citizens in their Japanese or Indian gowns, often in shades of medium brown silk, like the "Indian gowne" Samuel Pepys wore for his 1666 portrait (as well as the garments seen in cats. 98, 99).[65] The banyan was apparently such an essential item of the sophisticated male wardrobe that Pepys went to the trouble of renting one for his portrait sitting. In France, Molière's *Bourgeois gentilhomme* (1670) satirized the social-climbing M. Jourdain, the son of a cloth merchant who ordered new clothes, including an informal garment of chintz, because "my tailor told me that persons of quality dressed this way in the morning."[66]

The banyan also functioned as a prop in the theatrical setting of a chinoiserie interior in a portrait that may be the most evocative depiction of a man in such attire (fig. 84).[67] Not only does the sitter, Clemens August (1700–1761), elector and archbishop of Cologne, wear a banyan made of European "lace-patterned" or possibly "Persienne" silk (cat. 47), but he holds a Chinese export porcelain cup and saucer of the sort used for the consumption of tea, coffee, and chocolate, newly popular beverages from around the globe.[68] Moreover, this portrait survives in situ at Schloss Falkenlust, the elector's private residence used for hunting and small parties, in the "Indian Cabinet," a room decorated with lacquer panels. There Clemens August positioned himself as a sophisticated collector of all things fashionable and exotic.

IMITATION AND INSPIRATION

Diverse sources inspired European textile designers to produce tapestries, woven silks, embroideries, and printed textiles that imitated imported fabrics or incorporated exotic motifs. Numerous seventeenth-century illustrated travelogues provided images with a semblance of ethnographic accuracy. These illustrations rarely served as direct sources for textile designs, but during the eighteenth century they were adapted with great facility and success by artists and designers who made their reputations with publications of chinoiserie designs for the decorative arts, some of which inspired textile designers. Imported textiles themselves certainly provided much fodder for the imaginations of textile producers in Europe. Though specific instances of copying from textile to textile are more difficult to document, visual evidence of Eastern influence is often undeniable.

The tapestry series known as the Story of the Emperor of China, produced at the Beauvais manufactory in France, provides a rare example of the incorporation into a textile format of images derived from a European's direct observations in the Far East (fig. 85).[69] The designs for this series make use of a variety of print sources, most importantly those of Johannes Nieuhof that were first published in Amsterdam in 1665.[70] His illustrated travel account met with great success; it was translated and published in French later in the same year, in German by 1666, and in two English editions that appeared in 1669 and 1673.[71] The image of the Chinese emperor, among other figures in the series, was adapted from the frontispiece of Nieuhof's work (fig. 86). The inspiration for the tapestries may have been the appearance of French Jesuit missionaries from China at the French court in 1684; the Jesuits' scholarly endeavors, which allowed them privileged access to Chinese society, interested the French scientific community as well as the courtiers (cat. 60).[72] The purchase of sets of the tapestry series by the duc du Maine (1670–1736) and the comte de Toulouse (1678–1737), two of the legitimized sons of Louis XIV and his mistress Madame de Montespan, illustrates the vogue for the exotic at the French court in the late seventeenth century. Not only did

Fig. 85
The Audience of the Emperor, from the tapestry series The Story of the Emperor of China. Guy Louis Vernansal the Elder (French), Jean-Baptiste Belin de Fontenay the Elder (French), Jean-Baptiste Monnoyer (French), designers. Beauvais Manufactory, France. Designed ca. 1685–90, woven ca. 1685–1740. Tapestry weave, wool and silk. The Metropolitan Museum of Art, New York, Gift of Mrs. J. Insley Blair, 1948 (48.71)

Fig. 86
Johannes Nieuhof (Netherlandish, 1618–1672). Frontispiece from *Het gezantschap de Neerlandtsche Ost-Indische Compagnie, aan den grooten Tartarischen cham, den tegenwoordigen keizer van China*, Amsterdam, 1668. Engraving. Thomas J. Watson Library, The Metropolitan Museum of Art, New York (912.1. N55)

Fig. 87

Fabric with chinoiserie scene. England, in the style of Jean Pillement (French, 1728–1808), ca. 1765. Cotton, copperplate printed. The Metropolitan Museum of Art, New York, Rogers Fund, 1913 (13.133.1)

Fig. 88

Jean Pillement (French, 1728–1808), author and designer; Robert Sayer (English, 1725–1794), publisher. Plate from *Ladies Amusement: Or, The Whole Art of Japanning Made Easy*, 1760. Hand-colored etching and engraving. The Metropolitan Museum of Art, New York, Harris Brisbane Dick Fund, 1933 (33.24)

Nieuhof's images inspire the Beauvais tapestry series, but they were also adapted, more literally, to embroidery designs for a unique set of hangings in the Residence Palace, Munich, made about 1700.[73] Both the Beauvais tapestries and the Munich embroideries borrow images from other contemporary works, but Nieuhof's illustrations appear to have been the most popular and most accurate models.

Several names stand out among the mid-eighteenth-century artists whose work incorporated chinoiserie into the European Rococo style. François Boucher (1703–1770) was arguably the French artist most associated with the Rococo, and his chinoiserie images were unsurpassed in their impact. Few of his designs appear to have been directly translated to textile techniques other than tapestry, but his pastoral and chinoiserie scenes, along with those of Jean Pillement (1728–1808), indirectly inspired manufacturers of copperplate-printed cottons and linens in the second half of the eighteenth century. Boucher referenced both European seventeenth-century illustrated works on the East and, more surprisingly, a Chinese treatise on silk weaving and rice farming, Jiao Bingzhen's *Yuzhi genzhi tu* (1696).[74]

Pillement published numerous collections of exotic designs that were widely disseminated in Europe and were adapted as textile designs, particularly for printed fabrics (fig. 87). His influence was broadened by his peripatetic life and the frequent reproductions of his work in compilations such as the popular *Ladies Amusement: Or, The Whole Art of Japanning Made Easy* of 1760 (fig. 88).[75] This collection includes both unattributed floral designs and copies of Pillement's chinoiseries, as well as those by other artists.[76] Designs identified as "Indian" and "Gothic" in the collection demonstrate the continuing confusion over sources for Eastern motifs.

The seventeenth century saw a burst of creative interpretation of Eastern silks inspired by the textiles themselves. European floral silks referencing compositions of weavings from Safavid Iran and Mughal India appeared by the middle of the century (cat. 73), and a few French designs of this type survive from the 1660s and 1670s.[77] The so-called bizarre silks of about 1690 to 1720 are the most obviously exotic European woven fabrics of the period between 1600 and 1800 (cat. 43). In the

1730s elements such as overblown fantasy fruits and flowers similar to those in the Indian palampores continued to appear, though more naturalistically rendered than in the bizarre silks. Pagoda-shaped garden pavilions and other Eastern-inspired architectural features were incorporated into woven silks such as a French design of the 1730s (fig. 89), which calls to mind Godfrey Smith's praise for the "excellent genius" of the Chinese "whims and fancies" (see also cat. 65).

The Tree of Life pattern, so popular on palampores of the late seventeenth century, continued to evolve throughout the eighteenth century and was reinterpreted in other techniques, including embroidery. This widely disseminated design found purchase in a variety of cultures and in textiles such as Indian and Chinese embroidered hangings or bedcovers (cats. 75, 120). Large fantasy flora also influenced chintz designs for European garments such as banyans and waistcoats (cat. 51), Indian chain-stitch embroideries (cat. 39), and, finally, late eighteenth-century European printed cottons produced in Jouy and elsewhere (cat. 56). Indian armorial palampores similar to the Danish example illustrated earlier (fig. 78) must have been known to the English textile printer George Ormerod, who produced the magnificent bedcover dedicated to the EIC merchant John Vandermersch in 1752 (cat. 53).

Embroidered versions of the Tree of Life made in England and America were generally worked in wool threads, called crewel wool (cat. 115). Many of the early examples, such as a bed hanging in the Metropolitan Museum's collection that is one of several of the same design that survive (fig. 90), are particularly lively. As the eighteenth century progressed, English embroidered curtains became more subdued and the designs less densely populated, but the Metropolitan's fragile example retains the same exuberance as the Ashburnham hangings, with a collection of wild creatures included at the base of the flowering tree.

Perhaps because of the minimal setup required for a workshop, embroidery was one of the primary methods of interpreting foreign designs in both the East and the West. In the West, it was practiced by both amateurs and professionals. From grand commemorative hangings such as the Bengali embroidery copied from a print of a triumphal arch honoring Philip III of Spain (cat. 8) to the modest but charming late seventeenth-century panel of English chinoiserie figures (cat. 79), very possibly made by an amateur needlewoman for her own use, embroidery was arguably the most flexible of interpretive techniques.

Motifs for silk design—as with painted Indian palampores and chintzes—did not flow in one direction only, from East to West. During the first half of the eighteenth century, reproductions of European silk designs were being woven in China, both for the court of the Qing emperor Qianlong (r. 1736–95) as well as for export to the West.[78] Emperor Qianlong had a great fondness for European art, commissioning a series of buildings in Western style decorated with imported furnishings and textiles. A small number of woven Chinese silks related to the work of the English designer Anna Maria Garthwaite have been identified, in part by their unusual coloration and technical details (fig. 91).[79] Another instance of Chinese silk weaving copying Western-style textiles can be seen in catalogue number 62, where the Chinese-woven fabric was made into a Japanese priest's robe.

Fig. 89
Design for woven silk. France (Lyon?), 1730s. Gouache on paper. Musée des Arts Décoratifs, Paris (Collection Galais, vol. 5, 0003)

TEXTILE PRINTING IN EUROPE

The literature on the impact of the global cotton trade is vast, and the gradual adoption of the fiber around the world has been studied by both economic and textile historians. There can be no doubt that the introduction of large quantities of reasonably priced cotton textiles to European consumers changed fashions and patterns of consumption.[80] The global textile trade to Europe, and the Atlantic trade that supported European reexport of Indian cotton, resulted in an increasing uniformity of taste over a vast geographic area.[81] European printers took advantage of the burgeoning fashion for cotton fabrics and eventually substituted their own products for fabrics previously available only from Indian painters and printers.

It is important to note that printing on fabric was not unknown before the introduction of colorful and colorfast chintzes from India. Some of the earliest European printed textiles were produced as substitutes for more expensive goods; English block printing on fustian made in imitation of Italian silk damask is recorded by the late fifteenth century, and a few examples survive.[82] Decorative maps, printed on either paper or cloth according to the customer's preference, were advertised by Robert Walton in London in 1655 as "a most commodious ornament for every man's house."[83] Possibly the earliest instance of copperplate printing on cloth was recorded in 1630, when Margaret van de Passe of Utrecht applied for the first of several patents to print with copperplates on linen for men's nightcaps.[84]

The process used to make the colorful Indian chintzes—which required successive stages of painting resists and mordants on the cloth by hand—was not practiced or understood by Europeans, however. The apparently elusive technique was observed with wonder and admiration by Western merchants and travelers. François de la Boullaye-le-Gouz (1623–1668/69), for example, commented in the mid-seventeenth century that "hitherto it is not known how the natives apply so successfully the colours to the . . . '*toiles peintes*' in such a way that they lose nothing in the washing," and the French dyers who viewed his samples shared his high opinion.[85] The Indian cotton-painting process was recorded and analyzed in detail by several curious Europeans. An account of about 1734 by a French naval officer, M. de Beaulieu, survives complete with eleven cotton samples documenting stages in the process.[86]

The French port city of Marseille was an early leader in the nascent European textile printing industry in the late 1640s, and by the late 1660s Armenian traders involved in the Levant trade had settled there; they were said to understand cotton printing and "how it is done in the Levant and Persia."[87] The first recorded English printer was one William Sherwin, who applied for a patent in 1676; Dutch printers are documented in Amsterdam in the same year.[88] By the end of the century a flourishing industry had grown up around London, in Amsterdam, in several German cities, and in Switzerland.[89] There is very little evidence of what these early products looked like, though a group of relatively coarse but charming printed fragments may give some idea (fig. 92a, b).

Despite the clear admiration for Indian products in the West, there seems to be no evidence that European textile printers ever went so far as to imitate the hand-painted application of mordants and resists that was the foundation of the most cherished Indian cottons. Instead, they concentrated on developing formulas for the application of dyes to cloth by direct printing. These early entrepreneurs, who identified themselves as "calico printers," used wood blocks almost exclusively until Francis Nixon developed a successful method of colorfast printing with copperplates in Drumcondra, near Dublin, in about 1752. Nixon quickly sold his innovation to George Amyand, a London-based East India merchant.[90] The technique spread from there to other calico printers in the area, and then to the Continent (cat. 89). The copperplate process did not immediately supersede block printing. The Oberkampf manufactory used wood blocks to create its beautiful chintz-inspired floral prints (cat. 56) well into the 1780s, despite the fact that it had begun to use copperplates for certain patterns in 1770.[91] Nevertheless, the copperplate process encouraged the creation of European themes in addition to attractive florals, and unlike block

Fig. 91
Woven silk. China, after an English design, 1735–50. Abegg-Stiftung, Riggisberg, Switzerland (3995a)

92a   92b

Fig. 92a, b
Two block-printed textiles. Nether-
lands. 92a: early 18th century. Bast
fiber. The Metropolitan Museum of
Art, New York, Gift of Herbert P.
Weissberger, 1920 (20.47). 92b: 18th
century. Bast fiber. The Metropolitan
Museum of Art, Gift of The United
Piece Dye Works, 1936 (36.90.881)

printing it was practical for larger patterns.[92] The late eighteenth and early nineteenth centuries saw a huge number of designs reflecting the zeitgeist of contemporary culture, with motifs inspired by operas (cat. 88), popular literature, and the Montgolfier brothers' balloon flight of 1783. Even depictions of the deaths of prominent figures were printed on fabric, from the ill-fated British explorer and naval officer Captain Cook (1728–1779; cat. 106) to the French philosopher Jean-Jacques Rousseau (1712–1778), who is memorialized on two different French textiles in the Metropolitan Museum's collection.[93]

THE EXOTIC BECOMES TAME

Fig. 93
Antoine Raspal (French, 1738–
1811). *Un atelier de couture en
Arles*, ca. 1785. Oil on canvas.
Musée Réattu, Arles (868.1.130)

Patterned cotton textiles remain a mainstay of dress and decor to this day. Once seen as rare in the
West, fantastic floral motifs based on exotic species were quickly absorbed into the vocabulary of
fabric design, appearing on printed cottons, embroideries, woven silks, and woolens.[94]

European printers created products that competed successfully with the Indian floral chintzes for
dress and furnishings both at home and abroad (cat. 112). The album of dress fabrics kept by the
Englishwoman Barbara Johnson (1738–1825) attests to the market for such domestic products.[95]
Johnson, the unmarried daughter of a clergyman, lived a comfortable life on a fixed income supple-
mented by gifts from her family and friends. In her "fashion album" spanning the years 1746 to
1823 there are fifty-four silk samples and forty-four samples of floral and small geometric patterns
that are either cotton or linen or a mixture of the two.[96] Only one of these textiles, identified variously

as calicoes, linens, cottons, copperplates, and chintzes, appears to be an Indian fabric (a "chintz" dated 1778); the rest are presumably English, though they could be from the Continent. Notably, only one of the floral fabrics labeled as cotton from before 1774 (when the ban on printed cotton for domestic consumption was lifted, as discussed above) is printed on pure cotton fabric; the remainder are a mix of linen and cotton.[97] This means that all but one of the pre-1774 floral printed samples were perfectly legal at the time, because they were not printed on pure cotton. Clearly, English calico printers developed a product that was completely acceptable to fashionable consumers of the eighteenth century.

As noted earlier, the area around Marseille, in southern France, was a cradle of early textile printing. Southern French textile printers were known for their bold, rich colors, and these were worn by working women in the area. The seamstresses in a painting by Antoine Raspal of about 1785 (fig. 93) wear floral and striped fabrics that are most likely all printed textiles, as are their decorated kerchiefs. In 1766 the manufactory of J. R. Wetter in Orange printed cotton with a bold pattern featuring a trailing vine with white roses on a clear pink background. The cycle of influence appears to have come full circle when the pattern was copied in India soon afterward, using colors favored by the Dutch (cat. 50).

By the end of the eighteenth century, as Europeans developed their own colorful printed cotton and linen fabrics, the demand for Indian cottons declined dramatically. In the last decade of the century, British domestic consumption of printed cottons was supplied almost entirely by domestic makers, and imports accounted for less than 6 percent of the market.[98] This proportion is particularly astounding when we consider the heated debates a century earlier in England and France regarding whether Indian textiles would bring about the ruin of the local textile industries. As it turned out, domestic printers were able to produce fabric as cheaply, and to respond to changes in tastes and fashions more rapidly, than producers on the other side of the globe. These factors, combined with the transition to Neoclassical fashions in decoration and dress, which favored monochrome textiles, reduced European demand for foreign and foreign-looking patterned fabrics.

Indian and Chinese imported fabrics became an accepted part of global textile consumption and were perceived as less of a threat by European producers and governments. Certain luxury textiles, such as the extremely fine and sheer cottons and Kashmir shawls fashionable for Neoclassical dress, found a market in Europe, where such fabrics could not be reproduced in quantities sufficient to meet demand.

European printers never adopted the labor-intensive method of hand-painting mordants and resists for cotton dyeing, but good-quality block and copperplate printing still involved time-consuming processes. Jean-Baptiste Huet's fabric design, *Les Traveaux de la Manufacture* (The Activities of the Factory) of about 1784, composed of eighteen different vignettes, illustrates steps in the process of producing a printed cotton textile in late eighteenth-century Europe (fig. 94).[99] The design was commissioned by Christophe-Philippe Oberkampf to commemorate the visit of Louis XVI (r. 1774–92) to his factory at Jouy and its designation as a Manufacture Royale. The work is a fitting tribute to an artistic and scientific accomplishment in Europe that was precipitated by two centuries of global textile trade.

Fig. 94
Les Travaux de la Manufacture.
Jean-Baptiste Huet I (French,
1745–1811), designer. Oberkampf
Manufactory, France. Ca. 1784.
Cotton, copperplate printed. The
Metropolitan Museum of Art,
New York, Rogers Fund, 1926 and
1927 (26.233.8, 27.44.3)

"India Chints" and "China Taffaty"

EAST INDIA COMPANY TEXTILES

FOR THE NORTH AMERICAN MARKET

Amelia Peck

rom the time of the first English settlements in North America (Jamestown, Virginia, established in 1607, and Plymouth, Massachusetts, in 1620) until the end of the American Revolution in 1783, Americans received almost all of their textiles through trade with Britain. As early as 1651 the British government realized the benefits of keeping tight control over trade with the colonies.[1] The obvious advantages to the British included the receipt of raw goods such as wood, fur pelts, fish, and tobacco from the colonies and an essentially captive audience for British manufactured products. Through a series of restrictive navigation acts ensuring that only British ships had a right to trade in the colonies and repressive measures against colonial manufacturing, the colonists were kept almost wholly dependent on the mother country.[2]

Woven woolens, the production of which the British had perfected, constituted by far the majority of the textiles that arrived in the North American colonies from the 1600s on. Linens of all types and weights also found a ready market. Some of the linens were made in the British Isles, but many of them were imported from such European countries as Holland, Germany, and Russia, first to England and then to the colonies. While these wools and linens have been studied previously,[3] little has been written about the Indian and Chinese textiles that made their way to the colonies beginning in the seventeenth century. These cottons and silks sold by the English East India Company (EIC) were known as "East India Goods," whether they came from East or West India, China, or Southeast Asia, all locations where the EIC traded. Such goods seem to have made up a relatively small segment of the textiles imported to the colonies. Yet they had a disproportionate influence relative to their numbers. Patterned Indian calicoes and chintzes transformed European home and dress fashions in the seventeenth and eighteenth centuries (see Melinda Watt's essay in this publication). They were so popular, in fact, that they were deemed a threat to the native textile industries and by 1701 were completely banned for sale in England and France. However, to help keep the lucrative English East India Company in business, Indian painted and printed cottons were permitted to be exported to the colonies. This meant that rather than being out of touch with fashionable trends, American colonists had easier access to high-style Asian textiles than did their English and French contemporaries. Which Indian and Chinese textiles actually got to the North American colonies in the seventeenth and eighteenth centuries, which fabrics were most popular in the colonial market, and how did American merchants trade for these colorful silks and cottons?[4]

The earliest records of textiles shipped to North America, specifically to New England, can be found in extant port books from the 1630s for London and five other English shipping towns.[5] As might be expected, most of the textiles shipped were British woolens, such as "Norwich stuffes," "kersey," "broad says," "cheneys," and "perpetuanos," and European-woven linens like "holland cloth," "Germany buckrams," and "broad Silesia lynen." Surprisingly, the records also show evidence of such cottons as "Corse Callicoes," "gingham," and "dimity," which at this early date were produced only in India, and "Taffety" silks, most likely of Chinese or Indian origin.[6]

The Indian "callicoes" listed in inventories and advertisements in the seventeenth and eighteenth centuries could either be plain white, all-cotton yardage or the hand-painted or block-printed multicolored cottons that were dye-fast, making them highly desirable in Europe by the early 1600s. Produced mainly for clothing, these relatively inexpensive cottons were worn by all classes and, indeed, created something of a social revolution, since previously it had been easy to distinguish between the gentry, dressed in patterned silks, and the common folk, in plain wools and linens. When everyone could afford and preferred the fashionable, highly decorative patterned cottons, class lines blurred.

The expanded market for lightweight printed fabrics spurred British manufacturers in the last quarter of the seventeenth century to attempt to create patterned textiles with designs derived at least in part from those of India, which they marketed as "callicoes." Owing to the inability of British manufacturers to spin strong cotton warp threads until the middle of the eighteenth century, British calicoes were not made of domestically produced all-cotton fabric. Instead, they were printed on linen; on "fustian," a cotton-and-linen-blend fabric that did not take dye as well as all-cotton cloth; or on imported Indian plain cotton yard goods (fig. 95).[7] However, any calicoes mentioned in inventories before the end of the seventeenth century were most likely the real thing, produced in India.[8] Palampores (cats. 52, 118), large, hand-painted Indian bedcoverings and hangings made with the same techniques as those used to produce dress calicoes, also found a ready market in Europe and eventually the American colonies.[9]

A survey of seventeenth-century inventories of both merchants and individuals from several Massachusetts towns, New York City, and Albany, New York, reveals that EIC textiles were fairly common household goods by midcentury.[10] Boston merchants' inventories list many pieces of white (unprinted) calico as well as red and "blew" calico yardage and "calico neckcloths."[11] Some also list "Bengal tafety" and "Silk grogram," which were woven silks.[12] The inventory taken of the belongings of Thomas Hawley of Roxbury, Massachusetts, on August 22, 1676, included "5 Indian coates & one paire of breeches" valued at 1 pound, 10 shillings. These "Indian coates" may well have been men's dressing gowns or banyans, which were modeled on Eastern styles of dressing (cats. 96–99), but whether they were actually made of Indian cloth is impossible to know.[13]

The December 1, 1677–78, inventory of the estate of Edward Wharton of Salem, also in Massachusetts, has textiles listed under two different categories. Within the group "Valued Heare as Money in N. England" are such EIC goods as "5 white dimity wascoates, 2 ends of fine wt. callico, 2 peeces broade white callico, 2 peeces dimity, 1 callico table cloath, 2 callico painted table cloathes, 1 large

Fig. 95
Red and brown floral fabric (detail).
England or France, ca. 1725. Linen,
block-printed. The Metropolitan
Museum of Art, New York, Gift of
Everfast Industries Inc., 1971
(1971.270.6)

ditto." Under "Valued as Cost Here in New England" is "1 calico India carpett." The single most expensive item is the large calico painted tablecloth, likely a painted palampore, valued at 14 shillings. The cost of the "calico India carpett" is only 4 shillings, and since it is included in the "Cost" rather than "Money" column, it may have been old and worn out. The heading "Valued Heare as Money in N. England" is a reminder of the role textiles played as currency; textiles were often traded for other goods and, at some points, even for human cargo (cat. 108).[14]

Captain George Corwin (1610–1685) was a Salem, Massachusetts, merchant who exported colonial foodstuffs, fish, and timber to Caribbean and Iberian ports, receiving for those products funds with which he purchased English-made or other imported goods to sell back in Salem. Imported textiles were an important part of the merchandise he sold or traded for Massachusetts products. His inventory taken on January 30, 1684–85, lists an extensive array of EIC textiles, both in his store and in his home, including calico and silk yardage and calico bedcovers. In a rare documented example of a seventeenth-century colonial room completely decorated with Indian textiles, the "Hall Chamber" (one of the home's bedrooms) was furnished with white Indian calico bed hangings and slipcovers, listed as "2 pr. White Calico Curtaines, Valients, tester Clothes & 6 Covers for Chaires." These were likely summer hangings and slipcovers, the light, white cotton being preferable in the hot weather to the more common wool bed hangings and chair upholstery fabric.[15]

Margrieta Van Varick (1649–1695) was a New York City merchant who owned many exotic goods, in this case imported through the Dutch East India Company (Verenigde Oost-Indische Compagnie, or VOC)—items she probably acquired as a result of her travel from Amsterdam to the Dutch-owned trading colony of Melaka (Malacca) in Malaysia in the 1670s with family members who were merchants. There she married her first husband, also a merchant with the VOC. After some years back in the Netherlands, she settled in New York in 1686. Her 1695 inventory with bequests is an extraordinarily detailed eighteen-page document, in which she leaves her children gifts of Turkish carpets, an East India cabinet with "an Ebony foot wrought," "wrought silver East India boxes," and textile goods, such as "a sett of white flowrd Muslin curtens, one Chint flowrd Carpet," "callico nightgownes" for her daughters (women's dressing gowns, like banyans), calico quilts, calico neckcloths, and two especially luxurious textile items that would have been extremely unusual to find in the American colonies: "One flowerd carpet stitched with gold," which could be a Bengali hanging (like the one in cat. 6); and "One blew satten flowerd Carpet" (which could relate to cat. 104).[16]

Fellow New York merchant Joseph Tores Nunes imported textiles directly from London but also at times through Jamaica; from there, textiles shared the hold of his ship with fifty-five gallons of rum. In his inventory, taken on October 8, 1705, it seems clear that he specialized in East India goods such as muslin, calico, *romalls* (Indian handkerchiefs), and woven silks priced at 4 or 5 shillings per yard. His inventory also lists "25 lbs of Silk" valued at 36 shillings per pound. This was probably silk thread, which was commonly sold by the pound.[17]

Many of the same sorts of trade textiles continue to appear in eighteenth-century inventories, but with the rise of colonial printed newspapers came merchants' advertisements, which prove very useful for understanding the extent of EIC goods that were available to consumers. A survey of advertisements of textiles for sale in the three major East Coast cities (Boston, New York, and Philadelphia) in the period between 1711 (the earliest newspaper ad listing textiles found to date) and 1784, when direct trade between the United States and India and China commenced, shows that most textile merchants had at least some EIC goods in their stock.[18] These three cities were depots of goods for much of the rest of the settled colonies. Boston supplied most of New England, New York covered the Hudson River valley and New Jersey, and Philadelphia furnished goods to the Delaware River valley and many of the southern colonies. These advertisements demonstrate that merchants had a wide variety of EIC textiles for sale starting in the earliest years of the eighteenth century, and their popularity grew as the decades passed. The vast majority of the ads (100 of 130) listed EIC textiles for sale alongside European textiles. Many merchants made it clear they had EIC textiles for sale in the lead-in to the ad, such as Boston merchant Robert Jenkins's ad of 1750, which promoted his "large Assortment of EUROPEAN and INDIA GOODS."[19] Others simply advertised textiles imported from London and Bristol, but among the predominantly European goods also appear East India Company textiles, identifiable by their names (for example, *romalls*, *mullmulls*, *chelloes*) or by the fact that the merchant described his wares as "India Chints" or "China Taffaties." Some merchants had both British and Indian versions of the same type of fabric, such as those offering "Indian and English Chints"[20] or "English and India Damask of divers Colours."[21] Some ads are downright confusing,

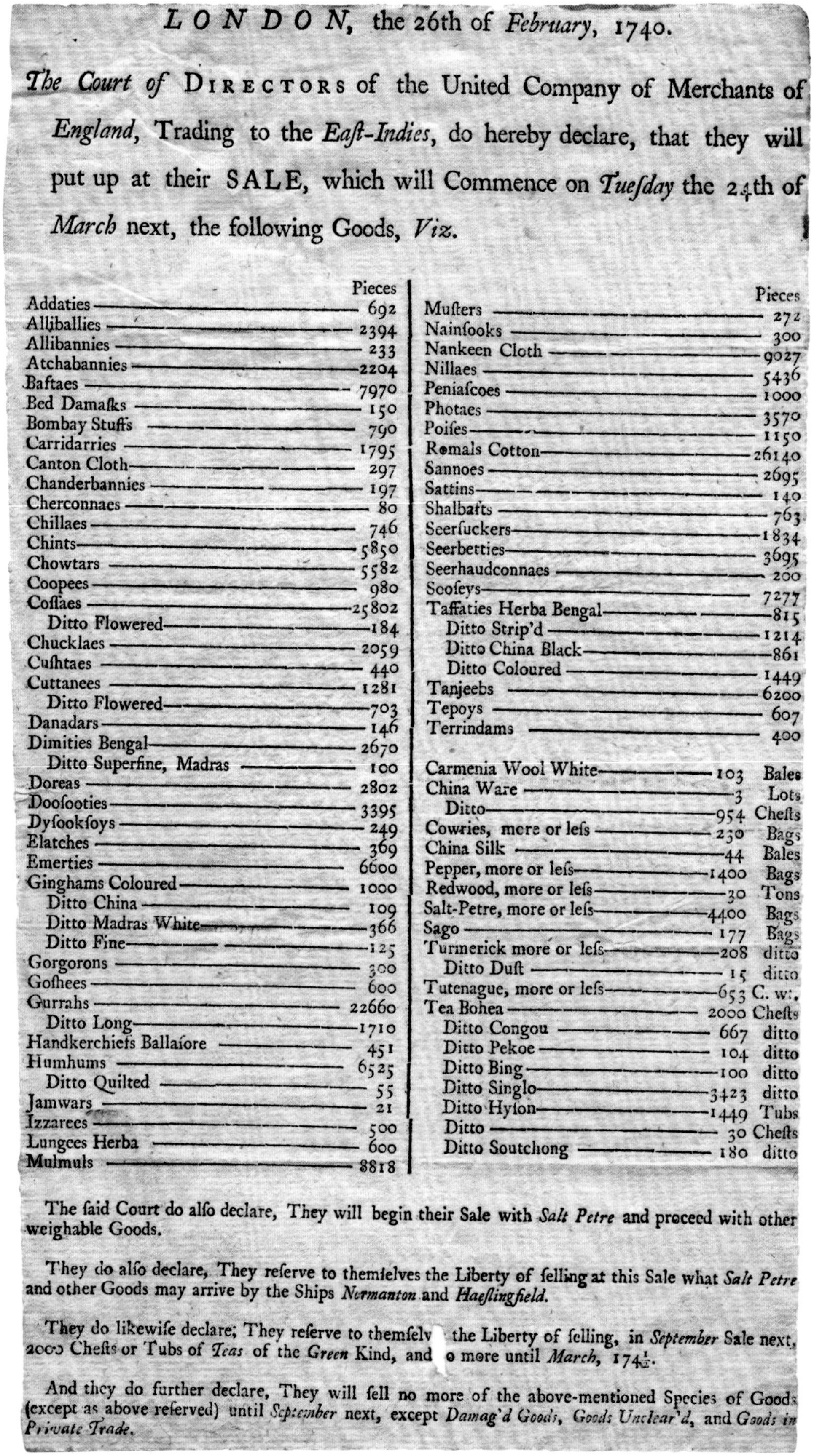

LONDON, the 26th of *February*, 1740.

The Court of DIRECTORS *of the* United Company of Merchants of *England,* Trading to the *East-Indies,* do hereby declare, that they will put up at their SALE, which will Commence on *Tuesday* the 24th of *March* next, the following Goods, *Viz.*

	Pieces			Pieces	
Addaties	692		Musters	272	
Alljballies	2394		Nainsooks	300	
Allibannies	233		Nankeen Cloth	9027	
Atchabannies	2204		Nillaes	5436	
Baftaes	7970		Peniascoes	1000	
Bed Damasks	150		Photaes	3570	
Bombay Stuffs	790		Poises	1150	
Carridarries	1795		Romals Cotton	26140	
Canton Cloth	297		Sannoes	2695	
Chanderbannies	197		Sattins	140	
Cherconnaes	80		Shalbafts	763	
Chillaes	746		Seersuckers	1834	
Chints	5850		Seerbetties	3695	
Chowtars	5582		Seerhaudconnaes	200	
Coopees	980		Soofeys	7277	
Coffaes	25802		Taffaties Herba Bengal	815	
Ditto Flowered	184		Ditto Strip'd	1214	
Chucklaes	2059		Ditto China Black	861	
Cushtaes	440		Ditto Coloured	1449	
Cuttanees	1281		Tanjeebs	6200	
Ditto Flowered	703		Tepoys	607	
Danadars	146		Terrindams	400	
Dimities Bengal	2670				
Ditto Superfine, Madras	100		Carmenia Wool White	103	Bales
Doreas	2802		China Ware	3	Lots
Doofooties	3395		Ditto	954	Chefts
Dysookfoys	249		Cowries, more or lefs	230	Bags
Elatches	369		China Silk	44	Bales
Emerties	6600		Pepper, more or lefs	1400	Bags
Ginghams Coloured	1000		Redwood, more or lefs	30	Tons
Ditto China	109		Salt-Petre, more or lefs	4400	Bags
Ditto Madras White	366		Sago	177	Bags
Ditto Fine	125		Turmerick more or lefs	208	ditto
Gorgorons	300		Ditto Duft	15	ditto
Goshees	600		Tutenague, more or lefs	653	C. wt.
Gurrahs	22660		Tea Bohea	2000	Chefts
Ditto Long	1710		Ditto Congou	667	ditto
Handkerchiefs Ballafore	451		Ditto Pekoe	104	ditto
Humhums	6525		Ditto Bing	100	ditto
Ditto Quilted	55		Ditto Singlo	3423	ditto
Jamwars	21		Ditto Hyfon	1449	Tubs
Izzarees	500		Ditto	30	Chefts
Lungees Herba	600		Ditto Soutchong	180	ditto
Mulmuls	8818				

The said Court do also declare, They will begin their Sale with *Salt Petre* and proceed with other weighable Goods.

They do also declare, They reserve to themselves the Liberty of felling at this Sale what *Salt Petre* and other Goods may arrive by the Ships *Normanton* and *Haeflingfield.*

They do likewise declare, They reserve to themfelv the Liberty of felling, in *September* Sale next, 2000 Chefts or Tubs of *Teas* of the *Green* Kind, and o more until *March,* 174½.

And they do further declare, They will fell no more of the above-mentioned Species of Goods (except as above referved) until *September* next, except *Damag'd Goods, Goods Unclear'd,* and *Goods in Private Trade.*

Fig. 96
Broadside for English East India Company public sale of goods, 1740. Many of the types of fabrics listed here were purchased in London to be sold in the American colonies. Joseph Downs Manuscript and Microfilm Collection, Winterthur Museum, Wilmington, Delaware (Shelf 65 x 510)

like that for the goods advertised for sale "Just imported from London" by Hamilton, Wallace and Company in Philadelphia in 1744. Some of the firm's goods were clearly British, some clearly Indian, but it also advertised oddities like "Spittlefield indians for gowns" and "superfine China Indian Persians" (fig. 96).[22]

The Indian and Chinese textiles mentioned in advertisements can be broken down into three major categories: cotton goods, silks, and handkerchiefs. Handkerchiefs were a large and important part of the market, as attested by ads as well as by merchants' orders. In the tables below, only those types of fabrics that were mentioned repeatedly are recorded, and only those that have enough descriptive evidence in the ad to be most likely of Indian or Chinese origin are included. There were also many types of Indian blended fabrics of silk and cotton available for sale in the period, such as the *cherriderries*, *pencascoes*, *teapoys*, and *sickersoys* that can be found in the ads under these and many alternative spellings. But they did not appear with the frequency of the all-cotton or all-silk fabrics.[23]

As can be seen (fig. 97a–c), mentions of types of cotton far outnumber other types of goods. Most were made in India, although nankeens, a Chinese plain-weave cotton, usually of a naturally yellowish hue, start to appear with more frequency later in the century and are a major import once direct trade between China and the United States began in 1784. Chintzes, calicoes, and muslins were all of primary importance, used for both home furnishings and clothing, although it is certain that the vast majority were used for clothing (fig. 98). Plain-weave, undyed cotton muslins came in all sorts of weights, with sheer *mullmulls* being the lightest (cat. 76), while *humhums* were quite coarse and sometimes used for toweling. Dimities were white cloths, often with woven stripes. Ginghams were checked, much as they are today; they were sometimes woven of silk and cotton combined, but usually they were all cotton. *Guinea cloths* and *chelloes* were both rough, striped or plaid cottons, used domestically to clothe slaves and for reexport to the West Indies (cat. 109).

COTTONS								
	Chintz	Calico	Dimity	Muslin Mullmull Humhum	Gingham	Guinea Stuffs and Chelloes	Nankeens	Indian Chintz Bedcovers
1710–19	1							1
1720–29		3		3		1		
1730–39	9	5	2	3	3	3		2
1740–49	8	12	4	13	9	12	4	
1750–59	11	12	6	16	7	2	3	
1760–69	10	10	3	12	2			2
1770–84	18	19	8	14	4		10	1
TOTALS	57	61	23	61	25	18	17	6

Fig. 97a–c
Tables showing the results of a survey of the textile advertisements in Boston, New York, and Philadelphia, 1711–84

SILKS

	Taffetas	Persians	Damasks	Satins	Peelong Satins	Gauzes	Misc. Silks
1710–19			1				1
1720–29	1						
1730–39	8	5	6	2			4
1740–49	15	11	3	2			9
1750–59	12	8	6	1			15
1760–69	8	9		6	10	3	7
1770–84	15	17	2	9	6	4	15
TOTALS	59	50	18	20	16	7	51

HANDKERCHIEFS

	Cotton Romalls	Silk Romalls	Lungee Romalls	Bandanoes	Misc. Handkerchiefs
1710–19					
1720–29		1			2
1730–39	2	1	1	2	12
1740–49	13	1	1	7	18
1750–59	9	6	6	15	13
1760–69	6	1	2	7	5
1770–84	3	2	1	4	16
TOTALS	33	12	11	35	66

Fig. 97a–c (continued)
Tables showing the results of a survey of the textile advertisements in Boston, New York, and Philadelphia, 1711–84

The silks most frequently imported, also primarily for cloth-ing, were woven in both China and India. "China Taffeties" are mentioned in almost every ad, as were "Persians," another vari-ety of taffeta, perhaps lighter in weight, which was sometimes used as lining fabric.[24] In the eighteenth century "Persian" was likely a name given to distinguish Indian taffetas from those woven in China. Both were lustrous, plain-weave silks, avail-able in a multitude of colors (fig. 99). Taffetas were frequently offered in changeable versions, with warps in one color and wefts in a contrasting color, making the woven fabric appear almost iridescent. In a few ads, Persians were specifically listed as "Indian Persians"; at the beginning of the eighteenth century, they were probably woven exclusively in the Bengal area in India, although Persians were also woven in England by the mid-eighteenth century and in China at the beginning of the nineteenth century, if not before (cat. 121).[25] The column Miscel-laneous Silks records textiles mentioned less frequently, such as *grograms*, *gorgorons*, *shagreens*, and *padusoys*. While it is hard to know if these were always EIC rather than European prod-ucts, fabrics of these names show up in merchants' orders for East India goods and on lists of fabrics available from the English East India Company. A 1756 advertisement placed in the *Pennsylvania Gazette* by the merchant Alexander Huston contains helpful information about the types of EIC silks he had available: "Indian silks, viz. damasks, padusoys, black and cloth colour'd taffeties, striped and plain Persians."[26]

Identifiable as Chinese-made by the width of the fabric and selvage marking (cat. 45), dress damasks were particularly trea-sured, and several eighteenth-century dresses made from these rich fabrics have survived that have histories of ownership in America (fig. 100).[27] Some of these damasks are in patterns that reveal their Chinese roots, while others are straightforward cop-ies of European silks. However, in ads where damasks are identi-fied with a place-name, puzzlingly, they are always called "India damasks."[28] There is no evidence that these damasks were woven in India; this nomenclature may point to preferences in marketing by merchants or a genuine confusion between Chinese and Indian goods that were all grouped under the large umbrella of "East India goods" because they were imported by the East India Company. Chinese *peelong* satins and gauzes, like Chinese cotton nankeens, appear in the later years of the century. Starting in the 1760s, both silks were offered in either plain or flowered ("sprig'd") versions and are likely the type of painted floral Chinese silks used for high-style dresses in this country (cat. 117).[29]

Fig. 98
Woman's jacket and gown worn by Ann Van Rensselaer, Albany, New York. Textile: India, ca. 1790. Cotton, painted mordant, dyed. Collection of Colonial Williamsburg, Virginia, Gift of Mrs. Cora Ginsburg (1990-10,1)

Fig. 99
Bundle of taffetas attached to order
from James Alexander to Messrs.
Collinsons, June 1, 1738. Manuscript
Collection, The New-York Historical
Society (Alexander Papers, Box 10,
Folder 5)

Fig. 100
Wedding dress. America, 1776.
Chinese silk damask. Brooklyn
Museum Costume Collection at
The Metropolitan Museum of Art,
Gift of the Brooklyn Museum,
2009; Gift of Edith Viele, 1949
(2009.300.731)

Handkerchiefs of many types, used for costume and personal needs, came from India—the most familiar today is the *bandano*, which was printed on silk in the eighteenth and early nineteenth centuries (fig. 101).[30] Less familiar cotton, silk, and "lungee romalls" were often striped or plaid woven handkerchiefs that made up a large percentage of the market (fig. 102; cat. 111).

To fully understand the range of East India Company fabrics that American merchants could obtain from London, it is particularly helpful to examine one order written in 1732 by the New York City merchant James Alexander (1691–1756)[31] to his London agent, Roderigo Pacheco, which is specifically for EIC textiles.[32] While other Alexander orders to Pacheco are for a mixture of European and East India goods, and some include nontextile items like porcelain and glass,[33] this order is inscribed on the reverse of the last page, "Invoice to Rod Pacheco/July 3d 1732 for/East India Goods for/Spring of 1733." Alexander asked for many types of textiles now familiar from the ads and inventories discussed above. He began with cotton "Demy Long Cloaths," printed blue (36 pieces), purple, or purple and red (65 pieces), in various floral, striped, and dotted designs. The term "Demy Long Cloath" likely refers to a half-length of a typical Indian "long cloth," a piece of fabric that usually measured about 37 yards.[34] He also ordered 126 "thirds Long Cloath" in similar colors, including 12 pieces of plain "white Callico." All these printed fabrics were probably referred to as "Callicos" in the ads of the day, as opposed to chintzes. After Alexander totaled the number of demy and third long cloths he ordered, he specifically asked for "12 pieces of best East India Chints 4½ yds Long Large + Close figures."[35]

At the top of the list for "Demy Long Cloaths" in Alexander's order above were requests for "12 ps fine Demy Long Cloaths two blues Pencil work with Large Stalks + running flowers four pieces of one figure fit for beds" and "2 Do [ditto] Striped for trimmings of beds"—details that may help to solve a long-standing debate about the origins of a particular type of well-known but puzzling printed cotton. The description of a textile patterned with a large floral in two shades of blue sounds like the indigo blue, resist-dyed fabrics often used for bed hangings and quilts, found in large numbers in America (see cat. 116). These fabrics were once thought to be the earliest American-made printed textiles, although in the past forty years they have been attributed to English manufacturers. However, only one small piece has been found in England to date.[36] Alexander's order seems to prove that these distinctive fabrics were produced in India rather than England, commissioned by the East India Company specifically for the American market. Putting these more expensive "Demy Long Cloaths . . . fit for beds" at the beginning of the order reveals that they were particularly valued. Not only are they listed first, but on the earlier draft of the order (May–June 1732) Alexander made an ink sketch of the type of pattern he was looking for, which shows a thick, serpentine vine bearing leaves and a flower, typical of the types of patterns common to blue resists.[37] Although no American garments made of blue resist have yet come to light, Alexander also ordered "4 ps Demy Long Cloaths two blews Pencil work with middling flowers fit for womens Gown" (see fig. 3).

The "two blews" mentioned above would have indicated darker and light shades of blue, which in this period were made by dipping cloth in an indigo bath, rather than trying to print indigo onto cloth.[38] This type of resist-printing technique was completely familiar to Indian dyers and had been practiced in India for hundreds of years before Europeans attempted to use indigo to make designs on cloth beginning in the seventeenth century (cat. 3). The large printed repeating figures on blue-resist fabric were made by first covering areas, such as the white ground, with wax, sometimes mixed with other ingredients such as clay, starch, and minerals, that blocked (resisted) the penetration of the indigo dye (see fig. 120). The largest areas of white were probably reserved by painting the wax free-hand onto the white fabric, which had been lightly marked with the pattern that was to remain clear of wax and therefore be dyed blue. The marking of the pattern may have been done with a wood printing block, in some cases, or with a stencil, in others. The first bath would dye the entire unmasked pattern a light blue. In most cases, the dyer then masked some of the light blue areas of the design and drew by hand with wax the fine lines that defined certain details. (This was the "Pencil work" mentioned by Alexander in his order.)[39] Some of these fabrics are also decorated with small white dot detailing, which was likely produced with wood printing blocks that had metal pins pounded into them in a pattern. The pinheads on the blocks were dipped in the wax and pressed onto the fabric, reserving the small dotted areas. After penciling with wax was completed, the entire piece went into the indigo bath a second time, which turned all the still-uncovered areas a darker shade of blue. For matching trim for bed hangings (such as those seen in cat. 116), blue patterns were dyed in repeating lines across a width of fabric and then cut into narrow strips.

Printed-paper sources such as illustrated books and engravings (fig. 103) were the most common way that designs were passed from one culture to another. However, it is also possible that European fabrics were sent to India to be copied in the larger, freer manner that appealed to the American colonists, especially, it seems, those of Dutch descent (fig. 104). Many of these blue resists

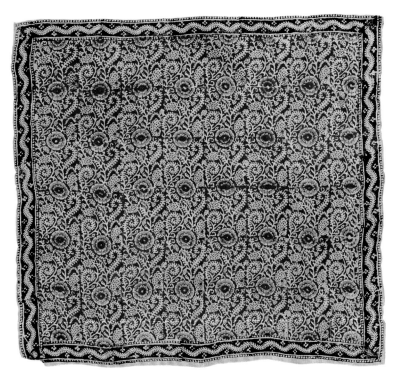

Fig. 101
Man's handkerchief. India, early 19th century. Silk, block-printed resist, dyed. The Metropolitan Museum of Art, New York, Bequest of Maria P. James, 1910 (11.60.483)

Fig. 102
Sample book. Book: England; Textiles: India, 18th century. Silk, cotton, and linen woven samples in leather binding. Cooper-Hewitt, National Design Museum, Smithsonian Institution, New York, Gift of Mrs. Samuel S. Walker (1936-46-1)

have been found in New York's Hudson River valley and Long Island, as well as along the Connecticut coast, all areas with vibrant Dutch populations in the eighteenth century.[40]

Proving that New Yorkers were fond of more traditional high-end dress and furnishing fabrics in addition to printed cottons, Alexander included a wide variety of East India Company silks in his order to Pacheco, including "China Taffeties," both single-colored and changeable, "india Damask" in single colors and several two-color versions with white grounds and showy colored flowers, as well as many colors of Persians.[41] Also included were silk "Shagreens" and "Gorgoroons" most likely to be made into men's suits.[42] At the end of the lists of textile yardage, Alexander attached samples for two grograms for suits and *shagreens* for lining and asked as well for buttons, trimming fabric, and silk hose to match. These were likely for himself; it was common for a merchant's personal request to be added toward the end of an order (fig. 105).

Alexander also ordered less expensive woven cotton goods, such as ginghams and "peniakoes," which were probably meant to clothe servants and slaves, possibly in the colonies or perhaps, after further trade, in the West Indies.[43] Instead of specifying a number of pieces, Alexander ordered "half a bale of guinea Stuffs" and stipulated, "let the most of them be of the blue + white sort." It would be interesting to know whether he requested blue and white because these colors were preferred by slaves or their owners, or because this simply colored fabric was the least expensive. After the "guinea Stuffs" he ordered handkerchiefs such as silk "Suaseys" (also spelled *sooseys*) in black, white, and yellow, and cotton *romall* handkerchiefs in blue and white and in red, blue, and white.

Certain extremely fine plain cotton muslins, used in the eighteenth century for delicate costume accessories such as neck stocks, fichus, and caps, seem to have been the most expensive fabrics

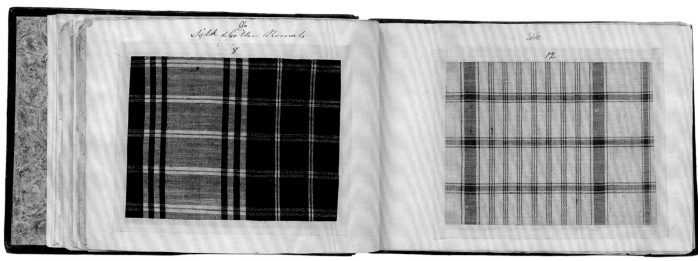

Alexander ordered. Although the pieces were of unspecified length, in comparison with the printed calicoes at the beginning of the order that cost about 30 shillings per demy long cloth piece, sheer muslin was 80 shillings per piece, "Gold End Muslin" was 75 shillings per piece, and the finest *mullmull* was 75 shillings as well. Five other types of less expensive muslins were also listed.[44]

Whereas Alexander's 1732 order for English East India Company textiles provides the most specific information about the types of fabric that were fashionable and available in New York City in the 1730s, the Beekman Mercantile Papers, dating from 1746 to 1799, give perhaps the best overall view of the trade in EIC textiles between London and America in the second half of the eighteenth century, since much of the full correspondence between the New York City dry-goods importer and distributor James Beekman (1732–1807) and his agents in London is extant.[45] These business papers are a wonderfully detailed record of the issues facing textile merchants in the period around the American Revolution.[46] Beekman's dry-goods stock included textiles and related items such as hats, stockings, threads, crewel wools, buttons, pins, scissors, and a small amount of tableware. He dealt with several London suppliers, each with a somewhat different specialty. For EIC textiles, Beekman turned to the firm of Pomeroys and Streatfeild (1753–57), later Pomeroys and Hodgkin (1757–71), then B. Pomeroy and Son (1771–75). After the Revolution, when Beekman again began to correspond with the Pomeroy firm, Bartholomew Pomeroy had retired, leaving his son Thomas in charge, with the financial associates (bill collectors) Thomas Streatfeild and Daniel Mildred. In reality, Beekman did little actual trading with the firm after the Revolution;[47] his finances at home were in disarray, and at the war's close he owed Thomas Pomeroy more than fourteen hundred pounds for goods he had purchased in the 1760s and 1770s and never fully paid for.[48] He spent the next fifteen years, until 1799, corresponding with the firm about ways to pay off his debt, which he eventually did.

The Pomeroy firm, in all of its iterations, was the only one that Beekman dealt with that consistently supplied him with large numbers of EIC textiles, although in addition to Indian cottons and

Fig. 103
Upright Baskets of Flowers. Jean-Baptiste Monnoyer (French, 1636–1699), designer and engraver; Nicolas de Poilly (French, 1627–1696), publisher. Engraving, before 1690. The Metropolitan Museum of Art, New York, Rogers Fund, 1920 (20.61.2[13–16])

Fig. 104
Panel (detail). Probably India, for the American market, mid-18th century. Cotton, painted and printed resist, dyed. The Metropolitan Museum of Art, New York, Gift of Mrs. Lawrence W. Scudder, 1952 (52.112.1a, b)

Fig. 105
Grosgrain samples attached to order from James Alexander to Roderigo Pacheco, July 3, 1732. Manuscript Collection, The New-York Historical Society (Alexander Papers, Box 5, Folder 1)

Chinese silks, it sold him linens such as cambrics, *osnabrigs*, and *garlix* from Silesia, Holland, Belgium, and Germany, as well as linens woven in Ireland. It supplied English as well as Asian silk yardage and English sailcloth. But Pomeroy did not deal in woolens, Britain's most important textile product, instead leaving that to other, specialized firms.

By March 1753, when the correspondence with James Beekman begins, the London supplier is already bemoaning the dearth of Indian cottons available to send: "Our calicoes were so very scarce that we could not complie with that part of Your order being obliged to reduce the orders of all our customers for that article. Cotton romalls being higher than formerly have only added five peices to your order. Guyney stuffs being too dear for your market are omitted. Instead of 6 New romalls we have sent you eight pieces and 4 lungee romalls that contain 16 hanks, and will make you more variety."[49] A letter in September of the same year explains that the scarcity of Indian printed fabrics has made the firm turn to English printers to make the patterns on the Indian-woven cotton calico: "In the choice of your Callicoes . . . [we] have conformed to your quantity and price as near as possible, but the alteration of prices every East India sale renders it impossible to be exact to your prices, the blue and white Callicoes are charged but 23.6 which you ordered at 28/ the six peices two purples 18 yards N[o.] 13 are not so clear, as we would have desired them, as we sent for them from our printers to finish our orders one week more would have brought them to a good colour, but they will improve with every washing. . . . As for the six peices you wrote for four colours, the Prints [printing blocks] are worn out, and no new Patterns cut, (and) instead of the 8 chints Patna we have sent but four as they are scarce and advanced (in price) and have sent you four ellwide english printed callicoes . . . which we esteem cheaper."[50] Patna chintzes, Bengali piece goods sold solely for exportation, were made in Patna, a city in northwestern India. It is telling that the dealers chose to replace the Indian-made chintz with English-printed calico. As the century progressed and the English calico industry grew, this would be the trend (fig. 106).

In 1757 Pomeroy and Streatfield explained to Beekman that the firm purchased plain white calicoes at the East India House sales and sent them to printers to be turned into colorful patterned calicoes.[51] Apologizing, Pomeroy and Streatfeild wrote: "We are sorry that we are obliged to omit so large a quantity of Your low printed calicoes, occasioned by the unavoidable misfortune of our East India Companys not having had a sale of callicoes last summer, which is our season for printing our goods for spring ships."[52] The printers used ran quite large operations, as attested by a letter from October 1775, which describes the delay of goods because of a fire: "We have endeavourd to conform to your orders as near as possible, but a providential disappointment hath renderd us incapable of executing your whole quantity, which was a dreadfull fire that happened at one of our printers about three weeks agoe, where we had one thousand peices of callicoes, many of which were promised to be brought home ready for these ships. As the workshops are burnt down, the printer is incapable of finishing them at present, and we are fearfull that many were destroyed by the flames."[53] It is doubly interesting to note that the workshop that burned was owned by "one of our printers" who had the capacity to print at least one thousand lengths of calico, indicating that the Pomeroy firm was not merely a middleman for already produced yardage but also commissioned patterned fabrics for its American customers. This was done by sending a sample book of swatches to the American merchants, in which each pattern was numbered for ease of ordering, as in the case of "N[o.] 13," mentioned above (cat. 108).

Fig. 106
English and Indian calico trim samples and textile order from Mary Alexander to David Barclay and Son, October 2, 1749. Manuscript Collection, The New-York Historical Society (Alexander Papers, Box 10, Folder 2)

Beekman sent an order to the London firm in September 1767 that shows the range of EIC goods he requested in addition to the English-printed calicoes. These included standards like "Spotted Bandanoes" in red and blue, striped muslin, silk "taffaty," and "30 pieces India Chintz handsome patterns at 30/." Orders for eighty-four other pieces of printed cotton calicoes, in all likelihood English-printed on Indian fabric, follow the request for "India Chintz."[54] As time went by and printing technology changed, Beekman grew increasingly specific in his orders for English-printed fabrics, some to be used for curtains or slipcovers (cat. 89). On December 6, 1770, he asked for "6 pieces China blue Furniture handsom figure" and "6 pieces China blue striped," while on December 22, 1773, staying on top of printing trends, he ordered "2 pieces of Copper Plate furniture Red and white handsome figure of Beasts and Birds" and "2 pieces Copper Plate furniture Blue and White." These must have been met with enthusiasm in the New York market, because in his next order, on May 7, 1774, a total of fourteen pieces of copperplate-printed furnishing fabrics (blue, red, and purple), each eighteen yards long, along with matching striped bindings, were requested.[55]

The firm sold Beekman silk yardage made in India or China as well as some produced in England. In some letters, silks are referred to as "China Silks" and "China taffaties." For the most part, the Asian silk was considered preferable to the British product. In 1759 a letter from Pomeroys and Hodgkin discusses both damasks and "taffaties" that have been sent to Beekman, saying: "We have endeavored to conform to Your colours in India damasks, but were obliged to send some in 18 yards. Your orders were for 20 black India taffaties which being scarce and dear have sent by both vessels six India and twelve English taffaties which are considerably cheaper."[56] (Here is evidence of one of the periodic shortages in London of East India textiles, especially silks.) In 1766 Pomeroys and Hodgkin reported, "As for India taffaties and damask Our East India Company have not imported any for several years,"[57] although in 1768 the supply of silks opened up again: "Our East India Company have lately made a sale of China silks, viz. black and coloured taffaties, Goshees and Powees 15 and 18 yards, Gorgorons and other silks which they have not imported for several years."[58] During shortages, "Persian taffaties" were woven in England: "the Narrow Persians You wrote for, Our Spittlefeilds Weavers do not keep them by them and it will take six weeks to make them."[59] But the English silks were not favored: "India China taffaties havin fallen ten shillings per piece since last sale (we) have omitted Your Spittlefeilds taffaties being so much inferior on quality."[60] It is telling that Beekman specified "India damask" furnishing fabric (the detailed description in the order indicating that it was likely for his own home) in his first order to Pomeroy in 1784, after the war's end, requesting, "Please add to my Memorandum, 3 pieces Crimson India Damask 15 yards each for furniture 16 tassels and Cord sufficient for four Windows."[61]

The Beekman Papers provide a fascinating look at the fluctuations in the affairs of textile merchants in England and the colonies, as they try to keep doing business in spite of the economic and political conflicts between their homelands. With the passage of the Stamp Act in 1765, the trade between Pomeroys and Hodgkin and Beekman grew rockier, though the tone of their letters was always cordial, and the British firm seemed apologetic for the actions of its government. Although their business together resumed after the Stamp Act was repealed in 1766, many of the letters detailed Beekman's struggles to find cash to pay for the goods he continued to order. However, on May 30, 1775, after the first battle of the Revolution at Lexington, a clearly distressed Beekman informs the firm "of the late unhappy as well as alarming Action at Lexington near Boston" and that "the present State of our Public Affairs has put a total Stop to Trade, as also to collecting in Debts, which renders it extremely difficult, and next to impossible for our Merchants to make Remittances Home. On which account I am prevented making that Payment which it was my Intention, and which I should otherwise have done. It is really a matter of Grief that our Divisions should be carried to such Lengths as to cause such mutual Distress in all Parts of the British Empire."[62]

After the war ended, Beekman did little trading with the English firm.[63] While this may have been due to his financial problems, it may also have come about in part because, after the Treaty of Paris was signed in September 1783, American merchants immediately began to fund the building of ships for direct trade with China and India. On February 22, 1784, the *Empress of China* sailed out of New York bound for Guangzhou (Canton) with a cargo of furs, lead, wine, tar, turpentine, ginseng, and silver coins, and returned a little more than a year later with tea, porcelain, silks, and nankeen cotton.

Her investors made a 25 percent profit on their investment. The *United States* left Philadelphia a month later, in March 1784, headed for India. It arrived in the French port of Pondicherry on the southeast coast in December 1784. These two voyages signaled the beginnings of a robust trade between the United States and Asia that was the source of many desired goods, especially textiles, for the American market. Unlike the pattern followed by the European countries two centuries earlier, Americans eschewed a national trading company.[64] Ships were privately financed by merchants, some of whom, such as Elias Hasket Derby of Salem, Robert Morris and Thomas Willing of Philadelphia, and John Jacob Astor of New York, amassed enormous fortunes.

The heyday of American direct trade was actually short-lived, owing to politics and international wars. Although the Jay Treaty of 1794 attempted to protect America's rights as neutral traders in the face of the war between England and France, both European countries continued to seize American ships and sailors, actions that finally engendered the Embargo Act of 1807, which, in an effort at self-defense, put a complete halt to foreign trading. It was enforced for only fourteen months, until March 1809, and proved highly unpopular with many merchants and shipowners. However, it did have the beneficial effect of stimulating American industrial growth.

The beginnings of American cotton production had already been seeded by this time. Eli Whitney's 1793 invention of the cotton gin, which separated cotton seeds from fiber much faster than was possible by hand, was a major breakthrough. Cotton thread spinning mills, such as the water-powered mill founded the same year by the British immigrant Samuel Slater in Pawtucket, Rhode Island, used technology pirated from England to further the American cause. The 1803 Louisiana Purchase brought with it tillable land in a temperate area that was perfect for growing cotton, and although the American transatlantic slave trade officially ended in 1808, those slaves already in the country were increasingly forced to work on enormous cotton plantations that brought huge wealth to their owners. The War of 1812 again put a halt to foreign trade, and by the time it was over in 1815 American mills, weaving cotton yardage from the raw cotton produced in the South, were opening in New England. These small mills were soon followed by large-scale, highly industrialized cotton mill complexes at places like Lowell, Massachusetts. Although Americans had been hand block-printing textiles since the eighteenth century (cat. 54), by the 1820s roller-printed textile yardage was factory produced, and by 1836 American mills manufactured approximately 120 million yards of printed cotton textiles annually.[65] Americans no longer had a need to go to India, or even Europe, for their printed cottons.

Silks were a somewhat different story. During the eighteenth and early nineteenth centuries, Americans had tried many times to establish sericulture in this country, but none of the attempts had proved particularly successful. Through the first half of the nineteenth century, therefore, woven Chinese silks continued to be imported. The U.S. government was determined to stimulate domestic silk manufacturing and passed a series of economic acts at midcentury to jump-start American silk production using imported raw silk.[66] By the 1860s firms like Cheney Brothers of South Manchester, Connecticut, were producing basic silk yardage from raw silk imported mainly from China; by the 1880s they were weaving complex silks that could compete with those from Asia and Europe. With domestically produced printed cottons and patterned silks available near at hand, for far less in cost, American demand for Indian and Chinese textiles essentially ceased, not to be reawakened again until the renewed global economy of the present day.

Global Colors

DYES AND THE DYE TRADE

Elena Phipps

I n September 1766 the Spanish frigate *El Nuevo Constante*, bound for the port of Cádiz, ran into a hurricane in the Gulf of Mexico and sank.[1] Part of an annual flotilla that traversed the Atlantic from the New World to Spain (see fig. 27), the ship had left Veracruz, Mexico, laden with valuable goods such as silver, copper, and gold.[2] In addition to precious metals, however, the ship's cargo contained a relatively new form of wealth: raw materials for the flourishing global trade in dyestuffs, including 2,896 pounds of indigo, 10,627 pounds of cochineal, 5,440 pounds of annatto, and 1,032 cut lengths of logwood weighing approximately 40,000 pounds (figs. 107, 108).[3]

As the manifest of the *Nuevo Constante* makes clear, dyes and colorants were among the first and most valued of the exotic products that stimulated long-distance trade across the Atlantic, Pacific, and Indian Oceans beginning at the end of the fifteenth century. Within this global network, indigo from India was exported to England, France, Italy, and the Netherlands, ultimately transforming the European textile and printing industries.[4] After indigo was discovered in Central and South America, the species native there was also extensively exported both within the American colonies and, by the sixteenth century, to Europe as well.[5] Cochineal, an insect used to make a brilliant red dye, was shipped from the Americas to Europe, Asia, and the Middle East over both land and sea routes.[6] Bernardino de Sahagún (1499–1590), a Franciscan friar active in Mexico in the mid-sixteenth century, observed that cochineal "is known in this land and beyond and there are great quantities of it [sent] to China and then to Turkey and from there all around the world, [where] it is appreciated and highly desired" (fig. 109).[7] Tropical dyewood trees such as the logwood that sank aboard the *Nuevo Constante* were another important source of color on the international market. In addition to certain species from Southeast Asia and India that had been valued commodities in Europe since antiquity, a motherload of related dyewoods was discovered in the Americas in the sixteenth century, significantly accelerating the growth of European textile industries (see detail p. 120; fig. 110).[8]

The crimson reds, deep blues, and wide range of purples, grays, and blacks achieved with these dyestuffs—raw materials that previously had been either unavailable to European dyers or found only in small quantities, and even then for high prices—were quickly incorporated into the palettes of the royal workshops of Spain and France and the extensive British and Dutch dyeworks. Arriving via carracks and frigates (and occasionally through pirate activity in the Atlantic) to the trading entrepôts of Lisbon, Seville, Antwerp, and London, they were then reshipped and distributed throughout Europe via local trade fairs and, after passing through other points of exchange, around the world.

Access to large quantities of foreign dyestuffs stimulated the transformation of the European textile industry into the center of what was becoming a truly global commercial network. Beginning in 1565, the fleet of Spanish ships known as the Manila galleons opened trade across the Pacific, sending silver mined in the Americas to Asia, where it was exchanged for Chinese silks and other goods. The silk was then shipped via the Philippines to Mexico and Peru and thence to Europe, resulting in a surge in the consumption of silk there and in the American colonies. Silk, which is easy to dye with an array of dyestuffs, arrived in Europe and Latin America either as undyed raw silk, cloth, or thread ready to be processed or as a finished textile already dyed and patterned with Asian colorants, including brilliant, fast yellows and highly saturated safflower pinks. Safflower had been used in China since at least the sixth century and was already known in Europe, having been introduced to Spain (where it was later cultivated) by the Arab rulers of Al-Andalus in the eighth century. It was eventually used in England to supply the color for the red tape used to tie legal documents, hence the phrase "red tape" to describe a cumbersome bureaucracy.[9]

European dyes and dyed goods also found their way to the Americas, as evidenced in an eighteenth-century Mexican table cover whose yellow silk was dyed with European weld, indicating that the silk was exported to Mexico already dyed (cat. 9). Perhaps no single dyed item from Europe contributed to the international exchange more than the "fiery" red woolen cloth produced in Spain, England, and the Netherlands, which was used as both economic and diplomatic currency (cat. 30).[10] Ironically, by the eighteenth century this cloth, which originally was dyed with local madder, was primarily being colored with dyestuffs that were themselves part of the global exchange, including lac from Southeast Asia (acquired by the Dutch from their regional trading partners) and cochineal from the Americas (used by the English and Spanish; fig. 111). It was in part the popularity of this red woolen cloth (referred to as "trade cloth") as a barter item that enabled European merchants to import the colorfully dyed Indian cottons and fine muslin that spurred a craze in the seventeenth century for such textiles and, later, for fabrics that mimicked or were inspired by Indian cottons but were made in Europe.

In the Americas, with their vast quantities of raw materials, European merchants and dyers were less interested in the ways in which these colors had been used in their native lands than in the dyestuffs themselves. A 1523 dispatch from Charles I of Spain (r. Spain 1516–56) to Hernán Cortés encouraged the conquistador to ascertain whether there was *grana* (the Spanish term for cochineal) in the New World and, if so, to gather as much of it as possible (fig. 112).[11] Cochineal, in fact, was among the exotic dyestuffs traders most desired, in addition to indigo, annatto, and the tropical wood dyes: the very treasures that sank aboard the *Nuevo Constante*. Along with gold and silver, these dyestuffs were not only an important focus of international trade, they were the basis of the colonial economy of the New World and contributed significantly to the financial stability and growth of the Spanish Empire in the sixteenth century, when it enjoyed a virtual monopoly on such trade from the Americas.[12]

Spanish imports of dyestuffs and all other goods from the Spanish colonies were processed exclusively through the port of Cádiz. From there they were sent to the Casa de Contratación, the custom-house in nearby Seville whence the raw materials were distributed throughout Europe and to eastern regions of the Mediterranean, Turkey, Persia, India, and Asia via regional merchant trade. By the late sixteenth century the French, Dutch, and English were all attempting to participate in the Spanish trade and undermine its monopoly by means both legitimate and illicit: by "force or stealth," according to English natural historian Mark Catesby.[13] The Spanish monopoly persisted until 1778, when reforms enacted by Charles III of Spain (r. 1759–88) opened both Spanish and American ports to foreign ships, which allowed French, English, and Dutch traders to engage in legitimate trade and largely forgo piracy and plunder.

Cultivation of dyestuffs in colonial territories, particularly cochineal and indigo, intensified after the mid-sixteenth century in response to surging worldwide demand and increased exponentially in the seventeenth and eighteenth centuries. As colonial administrations took hold around the world, new techniques of planting and cultivation were introduced to maximize production of these "renewable" resources. In Mexico, Guatemala, and South America, for example, the Augustinians and Jesuits introduced methods of increasing cochineal and indigo yields as well as seeds of particularly robust strains of plants. Similarly, engineers sent by the French government to its Caribbean colony of Saint-Domingue (modern Haiti) devised a means of increasing the efficiency of aerating indigo dye vats (fig. 118).[14] In India, English merchants and traders established a plantation system for growing indigo that supplanted much of the local crop production. Tropical redwoods of the Yucatán and Brazil were subject to intense logging by the Portuguese, Spanish, English, Dutch, and French.

As production of these dyestuffs escalated in the New World, it frequently had a corrosive effect on many of the local communities where it was practiced, acutely so when factoring in the decimation of native populations from introduced European diseases and the adoption of abusive labor practices. The scourge of slavery, moreover, was in part a direct response to the labor-intensive dye industry. The Portuguese slave trade brought hundreds of thousands of enslaved Africans to Brazil to work at first in dyewood harvesting and hauling and later in the sugar mills and mineral mines. The Spanish turned to slavery as a source of labor in the *obrajes* (textile workshops) of Peru after protective legislation in Spain prescribed "that the Indians not work in the cultivation of Indigo unless they volunteer."[15] In this regard, the worldwide trade in dyes and dyestuffs can be said to have forever altered the course and evolution of global human relations.[16]

SOURCES AND PREPARATION OF DYES

Until the second half of the nineteenth century, when synthetic dyes were developed, all colors used to dye cloth—from English woolens to Chinese silks to Peruvian camelid hair—came from natural sources. These dyestuffs ranged from plants whose roots, leaves, and flowers yield color, such as madder, weld, or indigo, to trees, including brazilwood and logwood, whose heartwood is the color's source. Certain animals, too, were important dyestuffs, from the tiny scale insects, such as cochineal, that yield a range of brilliant reds, to the *Murex* genus of marine snails and related species, which have a gland used since antiquity to make the famous Tyrian (or royal) purple.

For much of human history these plants and animals tended to be consumed locally, either within or near their native habitats. Kermes (*Kermes vermilio*), for example, a small insect that lives on the kermes oaks of the Mediterranean coastal shrublands, was a primary source of red dye for much of Europe from prehistory through the Renaissance. Lac (*Kerria lacca*), a different species of scale insect that yields a similarly brilliant red, is native to tropical regions of Southeast Asia and was relied on for red color throughout Thailand (Siam), Myanmar (Burma), India, and parts of China. This pattern of local consumption began to expand as early as the first century B.C., if not before, with the early Silk Road trade, which brought Asian goods, including dyestuffs, to the West, and it only increased in scope during the late medieval and early modern periods. Trade within Europe was particularly active among the cities of Kraków, Paris, and Antwerp as well as in the international fairs that traveled through Flanders, England, and France, while diplomatic activity between Venice and Constantinople often brought dyes, including cochineal, from as far away as the Americas to the East.[17]

With the onset of the worldwide sea trade in dyestuffs in the sixteenth century, the long-distance transfer of dyes and their varied applications to existing or developing textile industries increased substantially. The superior quality and

Fig. 107
Dried cochineal insects (*Dactylopius coccus*) from Peru, with typical silvery sheen

Fig. 108

Logwood billets from the Yucatán, Mexico, recovered from the galleon *Nuevo Constante*. Headed to Spain when it sank in 1766, the ship was salvaged in the 1980s. Department of Culture, Recreation and Tourism, Louisiana State University, Baton Rouge

Fig. 109

José Antonio de Alzate y Ramírez (Mexican, 1737–1799). *Cochineal Insects: Male with Wings and Female with Round Form, Front and Back*. Plate 2 from *Memoria sobre la naturalesa cultivo y benecio de la gana*, Mexico City, 1777. Pigment and ink on vellum. The Newberry Library, Chicago, Edward E. Ayer Manuscript Collection (Ayer MS 1031)

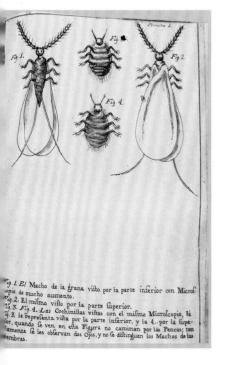

larger available quantities of certain regional dye sources, most notably the Indian species of the indigo plant and the American species of the cochineal insect, were immediately apparent to merchants, textile producers, and their customers. Cochineal, for example, yields its deep crimson color with greater ease than dyes made from kermes and lac, both of which contain resinous substances that necessitate additional, complex dyeing procedures. Moreover, cochineal can be cultivated, unlike the other wild species of scale insect, and contains a greater quantity of dye component per insect, thus requiring smaller amounts to be used in the recipes that measured dye ingredients per pound of cloth to be dyed. In the sixteenth century, when global trade made cochineal readily available outside its native range for the first time, it quickly overtook all other insect dyes as the premier source of red color in worldwide textile production.[18]

COCHINEAL REDS

"Cochineal" refers specifically to *Dactylopius coccus*, a parasitic scale insect native to South America and Mexico whose host plant is the prickly pear cactus (genus *Opuntia*). Prior to the arrival of the Spanish, cochineal had been cultivated for centuries in Mexico and Peru, where it was used to dye textiles and paper for both ritual and daily activities. The Oaxaca region of central Mexico, in particular, was a major center of cochineal production. Fifteenth-century documents record that certain towns paid a bimonthly tribute of forty bags of cochineal to the Aztec emperor Moctezuma I (fig. 113).[19] In Peru, although no written records predate the arrival of the Spanish, thousands of textiles dyed with the characteristic red of cochineal have been preserved, attesting to the dye's long history there. Recent analysis of Precolumbian textiles shows that cochineal was, in fact, the primary source of red cloth in the Andes by at least the fourth century A.D., if not earlier.[20]

In the great markets of Tepoztlán, Mexico—at the heart of the Aztec Empire—dyers traditionally prepared cochineal for sale by forming masses of dried insects into round cakes, which were then emended with other materials to increase their weight (fig. 114).[21] Spanish traders, mistrusting these subsidiary ingredients, insisted on shipping the individually dried insects "free of flour and stones and other materials."[22] José Antonio de Alzate y Ramírez (1737–1799), author of a 1777 treatise on cochineal cultivation, devoted an entire chapter to the "falsification" of cochineal, warning in particular against the addition of tiny pebbles, globules of chalk or clay, and beans. To detect impurities, he advised dropping samples of the dried cochineal into a glass of warm water or vinegar. So important to Spain was the cochineal trade—and so great a problem was the adulteration of the merchandise perceived to be—that in 1575 the king himself decreed that "nothing should be mixed with the cochineal" shipped from the New World.[23]

Another Spanish concern was the process used to dry the insects, which can affect the overall color derived from them (steaming the insects over a double boiler or oven drying them can turn them black, for example). In 1599 a manuscript was compiled at the request of the viceroy of New Spain to explain native methods of cultivating and drying cochineal. After surveying local cochineal farmers, the author recommended to all of the Spanish *encomenderos* (overseers) of cochineal-producing regions that the best method of drying the insects was to place them on a mat and leave them in the sun. Alzate, in the treatise noted above, further specified that the insects should ideally be harvested only when they had attained the size of "a fat lentil."[24] European dyers eventually became connoisseurs of American cochineal, able to select the finest-quality *grana* (or *granilla*, referring to a smaller

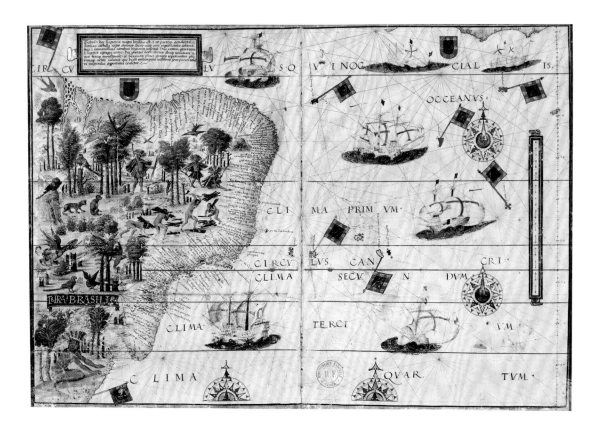

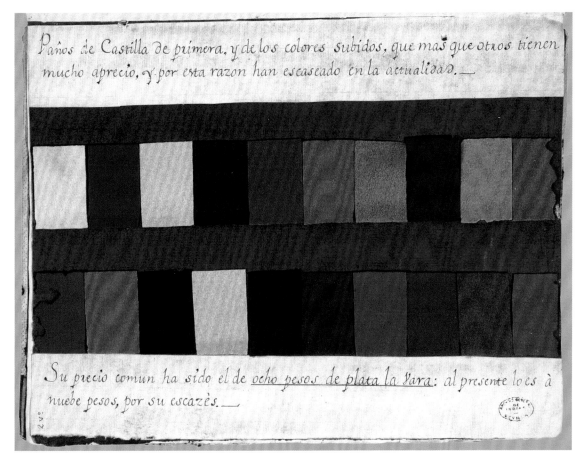

Fig. 110
Terra Brasilis (detail showing natives gathering brazilwood). From the *Miller Atlas*, Portugal, ca. 1519. Pigment, ink, and gold leaf on vellum. Bibliothèque Nationale de France, Paris (Ge DD 683 Rés, fol. 5v)

Fig. 111
Samples of high-quality Spanish woolen cloth (bayeta) sold in Quito for nine silver pesos per vara (yard). Spain, before 1780. From documents of the administrator of taxes to the President of the Audiencia of Quito, Ecuador. Archivo de Indias, Seville (ES.41091.AGI/26.25//MP-TEJI-DOS,14; fol. F2V, fig. 2/37)

Fig. 112
Harvesting grana, or cochineal.
Folio 85 from *Reports on The
History, Organization, and Status
of Various Catholic Dioces of New
Spain and Peru,* 1620–49. Pigment
and ink on paper. Newberry Library,
Chicago (Vault Ayer MS 1106 D8,
Box 1, Folder 15)

specimen of lesser quality) and to discern wild from cultivated insects and region of origin. A 1716 recipe for "French Scarlett" (a particularly popular shade of red) noted that "3 pounds of *campechiane* [cochineal from Campeche, Mexico] could be substituted [for] by only 1 pound of *mestique*,"[25] referring to a district in the state of Oaxaca considered the source of the finest-quality cochineal. In *The Art of Dying Wool, Silk, and Cotton* (1789), Jean Hellot, a French dyer, called specifically for *mestique* or *texcali*, likely referring to Tlaxcala, a town in the Puebla region, which was another important cochineal-producing area in Mexico in the seventeenth and eighteenth centuries.[26]

After being dried following the prescripts of the Spanish authorities, Mexican and Peruvian cochineal was normally shipped to Europe in leather sacks called *zurrónes*. Remarkably, a number of *zurrónes* aboard the *Nuevo Constante* survived for some two hundred years submerged in the sea, even as the thousands of pounds of cochineal they contained did not. So valuable was cochineal in the seventeenth century that it was often salvaged from such wrecks and remained an expensive commodity even when damaged.[27] Dried, it enjoyed a remarkably long shelf life, as noted by Hellot after he obtained a sample of dried Mexican cochineal from a Dutch supplier. Although the sample was "undoubtedly 130 years old," Hellot marveled that it was "entirely perfect" and still viable as a dye.[28] By the same token he cautioned against the sometimes unscrupulous practices of the merchants who dealt in damaged dyegoods and recommended scrutinizing dyestuff from shipwrecks, even if available at a cheaper price.[29] An additional problem faced by shippers of cochineal was the compounding of tariffs, as the dyestuff passed through numerous hands on its way to markets around the world. Sometimes it even made a return trip to the Americas, as lamented by Asa Ellis, an eighteenth-century dyer from Philadelphia. Cochineal, he wrote in his 1798 *Country Dyer's Assistant*, "is shipped to Spain, from Spain to England, whence we obtain it at a high price on the account of accumulated and heavy duties."[30]

The intensified production of cochineal that followed upon the worldwide upsurge in consumption quickly became a source of social unrest in the New World. Just thirty years after the Conquest, for example, Oaxaca experienced such a severe case of "cochineal fever" that local officials complained that the town's residents were not producing enough food and other staples, as they devoted all of their time to the insect, leaving agricultural fields fallow. The town council further admonished local producers of cochineal for indulging in "bad habits," including drunkenness and ostentatious displays of wealth. According to records of the Tlaxcalan town council (*cabildo*) from March 3, 1553, "Many sins were committed there and it is all because of cochineal."[31]

Other European countries soon sought to circumvent Spain's monopoly on the lucrative cochineal trade and its strict prohibition of the export of live insects from the Americas. These efforts included attempts to cultivate the cochineal insect abroad. In 1777 Nicolas-Joseph Thiéry de

Menonville (1739–1780), a French naturalist, collected live cochineal insects in Oaxaca and managed to slip his precious illicit cargo past the authorities as far as Saint-Domingue. Published accounts of his exploits detail how de Menonville evaded customs guards at the port of Veracruz by hiding the insects in his luggage, but he eventually succumbed to fever before his labors bore fruit.[32] The Spanish themselves brought cochineal and its host cactus to the Canary Islands, both of which successfully took to the island's rocky environment and thrive there to this day.[33] The English East India Company, betting that India would be a prime place to cultivate cochineal, smuggled in plant cuttings and insects acquired by a Captain Neilson in Brazil in 1794–95. Although the cactus died and the insects initially did not thrive, the project eventually succeeded, and by 1797 more than 36,000 pounds of "Madras cochineal" were being shipped to England.[34] In the nineteenth century Dutch traders cultivated cochineal on government plantations in Java and produced more than 80,000 pounds of it, primarily for the Chinese market,[35] while the French attempted to raise the insect in Algeria. The cochineal trade continued briskly until the late nineteenth century, when synthetic dyes supplanted the insect in the worldwide marketplace.[36]

INDIGO BLUES

Although blue color for cloth was derived from many natural sources, in terms of global and historical impact the most important of these, arguably, were a select few of the hundreds of species and subspecies of the *Indigofera* genus of plants, whose leaves are the primary source of a compound (indican) that can be chemically transformed to yield "indigo" blue (fig. 115).[37] The various species of indigo native to Africa, India, and the Americas all contain relatively high concentrations of

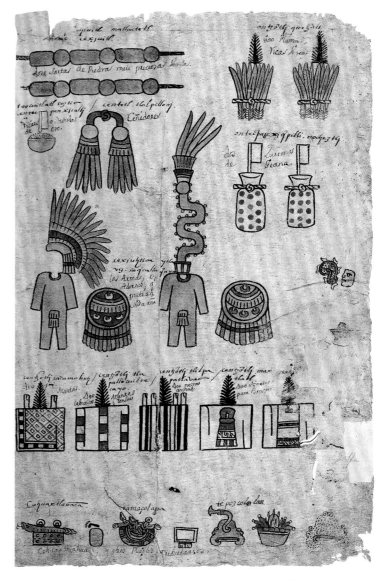

Above:

Fig. 113

Folio 23 from *Matrícula de Tributos*, showing the annual tribute owed by the towns of the Coaixtlahuacan region of northern Oaxaca. Mexico, early 16th century. Pigment on native paper. Biblioteca Nacional de Antropología e Historia, Mexico City (Codex 35-52)

Fig. 114

Bernadino de Sahagún (Spanish, 1499–1590). *Sellers of Cakes (Tortillas) of Cochineal*. From *Historia general de las cosas de Nueva España*, Mexico, ca. 1540–85. Ink on paper. Biblioteca Medicea Laurenziana, Florence (Mediceo Palatino 220, fol. 369r)

Fig. 115
John Gabriel Stedman (Netherlandish, 1744–1797). *Sprig of the Indigo Plant*. Plate 72 from *Narrative, of a Five Years' Expedition, against the Revolted Negroes of Surinam . . .*, London, 1791. Hand-colored engraving. Archive of Early American Images, The John Carter Brown Library, Brown University, Providence, Rhode Island (06944, vol. 2)

Fig. 116
Baltasar Jaime Martínez Campañón (Spanish, 1737–1797). Indigo vats. From *Trujillo del Perú*, 1782–86. Hand-drawn manuscript. Real Biblioteca, Palacio Real de Madrid (II/343)

indican. In Europe, however, the local source of the indigo compound used since prehistory was woad (*Isatis tinctoria*), a short, low-growing plant that contains comparatively smaller quantities of the dye. Color from woad was extracted through a slow process that involved fermenting balls of its macerated leaves. In this form, the woad leaves were difficult to transport because they required consistent levels of moisture and temperature. Woad was eventually displaced as the primary source of blue color in Europe because it could not compete with Indian indigo, with its greater quantities of colorant, which began arriving in Europe in the early sixteenth century via Portuguese traders and by midcentury through the Dutch.

In addition to its higher levels of indican, Indian indigo, which is formed into concentrated cakes for market, was also more convenient to ship than woad. During the last quarter of the seventeenth century alone the East India Company exported 1,241,967 pounds of the blue dye from Bombay and Surat to England.[38] The high demand for Indian indigo wreaked havoc with the long-established woad industry in Europe, sparking numerous political campaigns and legislation as local woad producers, facing the long-term collapse of their livelihood, protested the importation of what was referred to in Germany and England as the "devil's dye."[39]

The discovery in the sixteenth century of a species of indigo native to the Americas (*Indigofera suffruticosa*) greatly added to worldwide supply (fig. 116). Guatemalan indigo, especially prized, was exported primarily to Spain but was also traded within the Americas via Spanish merchants, who shipped it to the *obrajes* of Cuzco, thousands of miles south in Peru (fig. 117).[40] Central American indigo was also shipped to the North American colonies via England until the introduction of indigo cultivation in the late seventeenth and early eighteenth centuries in the southern United States, notably South Carolina, where it was a primary export to England before the American Civil War (indeed, the South Carolina indigo crop had contributed 35 percent of the total value of American annual exports to England by the time of the Revolution).[41] The French and British likewise introduced indigo cultivation to their colonies in the Caribbean, including Jamaica, Saint-Domingue, and Guadelupe (fig. 118). In 1771 exports of indigo from the French West Indies exceeded 1,800 tons.[42]

Concomitant with the intensive cultivation practices necessary to sustain such large quantities of indigo exports was a long history of abusive labor practices, resulting in periods of widespread social unrest involving both growers and merchants. Indigo was also intimately connected to the growth of slavery, which, as noted above, supplied much of the labor force needed to grow the crop, especially in the Americas. In the last quarter of the eighteenth century Bengali farmers in India were compelled by contracts with the English East India Company, which virtually governed the region, to grow indigo in most of their fertile ground, thus supplanting the rice crops needed to sustain the local population. The resulting famine and widespread resentment under the oppressive British plantation system led directly to the Indigo Revolt of 1859–60, which was resolved only when a charter was enacted stating that cultivators could not be forced to grow indigo against their will.[43]

DYEWOODS: RED, BLUE, PURPLE, AND BLACK

A number of tropical trees contain coloring compounds used to make dyes, from reds and blues to purples. Loaded onto ships, where they were often used as ballast, billets of hewn dyewood logs traversed the ocean, ultimately transforming the palette and color sensibilities of Europe while simultaneously fostering new trends in global fashion (fig. 108). Among the earliest traded dyewood species

is what we now refer to as sappanwood (*Caesalpinia sappan*), a tree native to India and Southeast Asia but known to Europe and the West by the eleventh century through imports from Ceylon and Sumatra.[44] African species of red dyewoods, such as camwood and barwood from Nigeria, Sierra Leone, and other regions, were traded to Europe after the Portuguese opened the sea route around the continent's southern tip, and they, too, eventually became part of the European and British dye palette, used, for example, to make the red and brown dyes for Scottish tartans.[45] The most sought-after dyewoods, however, came from the Americas, especially logwood from the Yucatán in Mexico and brazilwood from Amazonian Brazil, key species that, beginning in the sixteenth century, were exported to Spain, Portugal, France, Italy, and the Netherlands, where they became integral components of textile and tapestry production.

The tree known as brazilwood (*Caesalpinia echinata*) seeps an orange-red liquid when cut, hence its name, which derives from the Portuguese term *brasa*, referring to the color of burning coals. Somewhat confusingly, "brazilwood" was originally used to refer to the related Asian species sappanwood, noted above, which has similar characteristics. The modern country of Brazil, the wood's primary source, was in fact named after the dyewood; the Portuguese changed the country's name from Terra de Santa Cruz, or Land of the Holy Cross, giving rise to complaints that they "preferred a block of wood to the Holy cross and a red dye to the true blood of Christ."[46] The Portuguese began logging brazilwood in the northern Bahia region in the early 1500s, soon after explorer Pedro Álvares Cabral (ca. 1467/68–ca. 1520) loaded his ship with the precious wood and took the first logs back to Lisbon. To cut and haul the heavy brazilwood logs, the Portuguese traders who followed Cabral relied on the region's native Tupinambá people. The French soon established their own colony in Bahia and began logging there as well, and they, too, exploited the labor of the Tupinambá people living along the coast (see detail p. 120; fig. 110).

Fig. 117
Detail of 17th-century Peruvian tapestry with indigo-blue ground. The indigo dye was likely imported from Guatemala. The Metropolitan Museum of Art, New York, Purchase, Morris Loeb Bequest, 1956 (56.163)

Fig. 118
Indigo Processing in the Antilles, from *Histoire générale des Antilles habitées par les Français.* Jean-Baptiste Du Tertre (French, 1610–1687), artist; Thomas Iolly, publisher. Engraving. Paris, 1667. Archive of Early American Images, The John Carter Brown Library, Brown University, Providence, Rhode Island (01897)

From the 1620s to the 1630s the Dutch established a short-lived claim to a stretch of Brazilian coast near Recife and through the Dutch West India Company shipped tons of brazilwood back to the Netherlands.[47] To prepare the dyestuff, specialized workshops in Flanders and Bruges known as *tailleurs de brésil* cut and rasped the wood into chips.[48] Similar workshops existed in Italy, although the redwood imported through the port of Venice was primarily the Asian species. Called *verzino* in Italian, brazilwood was sold in Florence as both heartwood and "peelings" (*mondiglia di verzino*).[49]

Brazilwood dye was classified as fugitive, or false (*faux teinte*), by Jean-Baptiste Colbert (1619–1683), the French minister of culture under Louis XIV who in 1661 established dye regulations for the royal workshops. Used in Europe to impart color to silk and wool, brazilwood dye was understood not to have the same lightfast qualities of "true dyes" such as cochineal and madder.[50] Jean Hellot described the red derived from brazilwood as "an extractive dye in great abundance and tolerably beautiful, though evidently inferior to the cochineal." He further noted, however, that brazilwood red was "infinitely cheaper [and] consequently very much used."[51]

Equally fugitive is the dark bluish purple obtained from logwood (*Haematoxylum campechianum*), a large tree that grows in the boggy coastal wetlands of tropical Central America, in particular around the Yucatán Peninsula in a region that encompasses Mexico's Bay of Campeche (hence the Latin name of the species), Honduras, Belize, and Guatemala. In 1581 the British prohibited its use in textile dyeing, "forasmuch as the Colours made with the said Stuff called Logwood, alias Blockwood, is false and deceitful . . . Logwood shall be forfeited, openly burnd and no Cloth or Wool shall be dyed therewith."[52] When combined with a yellow dye and in some cases with a mordant (discussed below), logwood blue becomes black, a difficult color to achieve with natural dyes. Indeed, before logwood was available, producing black generally required multiple dyebaths and combinations of expensive dyes such as indigo and madder. After European dyers in the seventeenth and eighteenth centuries managed to stabilize logwood black, it became the most important component of black dye.[53] The combination of the vast quantities of logwood discovered in the Americas and the development of a method utilizing it to render true black had a tremendous impact on European silk and woolen production, notably supporting the ever-growing fashion for black garments spurred in part by the Protestant Reformation.

Logwood is so dense that it does not float. Large trees were thus cut into sections and shipped in pieces, which loggers either dragged to landing areas or ferried in small loads on canoes from the swampy regions of Mexico and Central America to the open seas. As English explorer William Dampier (1651–1715) observed, "when a [logwood] Tree is so thick that after it is logged, it remains still too great a Burthen for one Man, we blow it up with Gunpowder."[54] In the late seventeenth century Spanish vessels loaded with cut lengths of logwood were subject to frequent raids by English pirates. It was the English, in fact, beginning with acts of piracy—and in spite of their early prohibition of the dye—who eventually established the dominant North Atlantic trade in logwood via Jamaica, an English colony, where logwood was introduced and grown in the eighteenth century. From there it was taken to New England (especially Boston, one of the main ports for the logwood trade) as an intermediary stop before being shipped to England and to other parts of Europe.[55]

YELLOWS

One of the yellow dyestuffs often mixed with logwood to make black was "old fustic," a brilliant, strong yellow dye obtained from a tropical tree called "dyer's mulberry" (*Maclura tinctoria*), native to Central and South America and the Caribbean islands. Along with logwood, fustic was shipped north to Boston and thence to Europe, where it was used to make greens and khaki colors; it was even used to dye military uniforms during World War I.[56] Another highly regarded source of yellow, especially in England and France, was quercitron, a dye derived from the eastern black oak (*Quercus velutina*) of North America. The dye was developed by Edward Bancroft (1744–1821), a prominent American physician notable for being a double agent during the American Revolution. Bancroft, whose 1794 *Experimental Researches Concerning the Philosophy of Permanent Colours* addressed the history and science of dyeing, held exclusive rights to the import of quercitron into Europe in the late eighteenth century.[57]

Annatto is a yellow dyestuff derived from the seeds of achiote trees (*Bixa orellana*). Contained within a spiny pod, the seeds yield a bright orange or yellow used to dye foodstuffs and, in the tropical regions of the Yucatán and the Amazon, as a body paint (fig. 119). Like indigo, annatto was formed into cakes for shipping, and the more than five thousand pounds of annatto aboard the wreck of the *Nuevo Constante* were remarkably well preserved even after some two hundred years in the sea. French silk dyers made a paste from annatto seeds called *roucou*, which was not only a source of yellow but also a colorant used to "correct" the bright red of cochineal into an orange-red hue considered more fashionable in the eighteenth century.[58]

Turmeric (*Curcuma longa*), a rhizomatous member of the ginger family native to India and Southeast Asia, was imported to Europe as a spice but was also a key source of yellow color. Prior to the arrival of the Spanish and Portuguese in Southeast Asia, turmeric was one of the most important and widely traded colorants. Although in Europe turmeric's value as a food spice likely overshadowed its merits as a dyestuff, it was nonetheless understood as an important raw material in the global trade because Indian dyers used it to make their prized dye-painted cottons (fig. 121). In the traditional Indian dyeing process, turmeric was generally the last in a sequence of dyes and was often applied by hand over areas already dyed blue with indigo in order to create specific color details, such as the green of foliage. Georges Roques, an agent for the French Compagnie des Indes Orientales, recorded in a 1678–80 report on Indian dye-painted cloth production that final payments from the company to local dyers were made only after this turmeric-based green had been added.[59] Although the orange-yellow derived from turmeric is rather fugitive (like brazilwood, turmeric was classified as false in Europe), it nonetheless became a standard component of the French silk-dyeing industry, primarily as a modifier to scarlet reds. By the eighteenth century turmeric was mostly supplanted in Europe by annatto from the Americas, which served a similar purpose.

DYEING PROCESSES AND TECHNIQUES

Mastery of traditional dyeing techniques demanded a varied body of knowledge, from botany and chemistry to aesthetic principles. In addition to an intimate understanding of the special characteristics of dyes and their potential color ranges, the dyer had to know how to make colors fast, or permanent, rather than just stains or tints that would fade in sunlight or wash away in water over time. Creating

Fig. 119
Francisco Hernández (Spanish, 1514–1587). Achiote (annatto). From *Rerum medicarum Novae Hispaniae thesaurus*, Rome, 1651. Special Collections, The Getty Research Institute, Los Angeles, California (93-B9305)

specific shades and hues, moreover, often entailed sequential dyeing or overdyeing (dyeing on top of existing colors) rather than simply mixing powders, as we do today. The affinities of certain dyes for certain fibers—not every dye is suitable for every type of cloth—was another important consideration.

Unlike the pigments used in painting, which are composed of ground earths and minerals that in their natural rock or powder form can be used as colorants, the dye compounds in plants and animals generally require processing in order to be efficacious. The coloring materials first had to be extracted from a source (leaves, roots, or glands, for example) and then often immersed in hot or boiling water along with a mordant: an agent, such as mineral salts or certain metals, including aluminum, copper, and iron, that chemically enables the natural dye to bond securely to a fiber.[60] One of the most widely used mordants was alum, a mineral salt. In regions where deposits of alum did not occur naturally, plants whose leaves are rich in alum were burned to ash and then the ashes placed in water to leach out the salts. Soils rich in dissolved irons and tannins from decaying leaves were another early source of mordants. Iron could also be obtained from shavings of rust or scrap metal soaked in vinegar (or another type of "sour," meaning a natural acidic source), a technique used in India for part of the dye-painting process.[61]

A few dyes, including indigo and shellfish purple, do not require mordants and instead rely on different types of chemical transformations to impart their colors, which then bond permanently with the fiber or cloth.[62] Generally speaking, the first step in using indigo is to extract the colorant from the plant by crushing its leaves in water, which yields an almost colorless or yellow-green liquid containing the indican compound. As the indican comes into contact with oxygen through agitation of the dye bath or just being exposed to air, it turns blue and precipitates out of solution as the insoluble compound indigotin, which was often then shaped into cakes or blocks and dried. At this stage the indigo is actually a pigment. In order to be used as a dye, the insoluable indigotin must be returned to its soluable form in a second stage, known as vat dyeing, in which it is dissolved and reduced back to its yellow-green state; only then can it be absorbed into cloth or fibers. Many cultures around the world developed their own methods of bringing about this seemingly alchemical transformation in which the colorless liquid is absorbed into the fibers and oxidized, turning it the brilliant blue that is also extremely lightfast. Some methods relied on fermentation, for example, in which microbes assist the color change; others added stale urine or other strongly alkaline materials to the vat.

The chemistry of the dyeing process plays an important role in how colors bond with different fibers. Cotton and linen are difficult fibers to dye owing to the lack of affinity between the alkaline nature of plant fibers and the acidic nature of most natural dyes, which inhibits the formation of permanent bonds. (Animal fibers such as wool and silk do not have this problem and can be dyed comparatively easily with the majority of natural dyes.) Historically, most cultures that had indigenous cotton production, including those in Africa and the Americas, were able to dye it only with indigo blue or a variety of brown tannins. An exception was India, whose dyers found ways to produce a wider color range of dyed cottons, from reds and purples to yellows.

From the European perspective, the fine, colorfully designed and dyed cotton cloth from India, which had been produced there by at least the thirteenth century (but likely much earlier), was one of the marvels of the Indian Ocean trade in the early sixteenth and seventeenth centuries. These multi-colored textiles were known as "chints," or chintz, ultimately from the Sanskrit term *chitra*, meaning speckled, variegated, or spotted cloth (*pintados*, another term for them, derives from the Portuguese word for "painted").[63] To achieve this varied coloration, Indian dyers relied on an elaborate process

Opposite:
Fig. 120
Folio 5 from manuscript compiled by Antoine Georges N. H. de Beaulieu. This folio shows wax, colored with carbon so that the dyer can see its application, covering all areas of the fabric that will remain white, as a resist for the indigo-dye bath. Bibliothèque Centrale du Muséum National d'Histoire Naturelle, Paris (MS Beaulieu 193-1)

Fig. 121
Folio 11 from manuscript compiled by Antoine Georges N. H. de Beaulieu. This folio shows the last stage of the dye process with all colors present, including saffron-yellow details applied by hand over blue to make the green leaves. Bibliothèque Centrale du Muséum National d'Histoire Naturelle, Paris (MS Beaulieu 193-1)

that required weeks or even months to complete and used a number of different materials to override the inherent chemical hostility between cotton and natural dyes. First, the cotton was subjected to a repeated sequence of treatments with various oils and fats, described by European dyers as "animalizing" the cloth. These treatments were alternated with applications of astringents and mordants (animal dung and ash from alum-containing plants) followed by soaking in milk and washing and drying; between treatments the cotton was bleached in the sun. All of this was done even before any dyebath was involved. In 1734 French naval officer Antoine Georges N. H. de Beaulieu (1699–1764) observed a demonstration of Indian dyeing in Pondicherry, on the Coromandel Coast—center of the chintz trade—and cut samples of cloth at each of these stages (figs. 120, 121).[64] Once the cotton was ready to be dyed, each color was applied in a separate step. Sometimes color was achieved by immersing the whole cloth into the dyebath. Alternatively, either thickened color or a mordant could be applied directly to the cloth's surface with either carved wood blocks or a brush. Wax was also applied as a dye resist, reserving specific areas of the design (such as a white background) and maintaining the color of others (red flowers, for example). After dyeing was complete, the wax—which had to be applied to both sides of the cloth to ensure no dye penetrated it—was removed in hot water.[65]

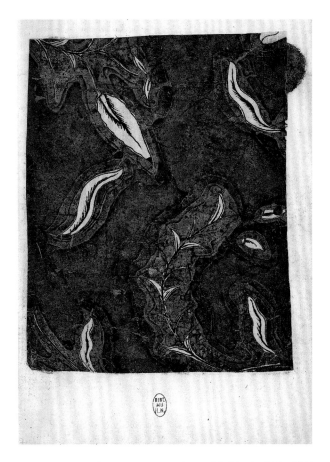

Although the sequence of steps was crucial in enabling the dyes to bond with the cotton fabric, Indian dyers also discovered how to achieve a variety of colors within a single dyebath immersion by applying different mordants (such as alum or iron), each thickened with gum, directly to various areas of the design. Areas treated with different mordants would come out as different colors or shades. In a dyebath of chay root, for example (the Indian form of madder red color used to create shades of red, pink, and purple), areas where an alum mordant was applied would turn red, those where iron had been applied would turn purple, and areas with no mordant would remain undyed, all within a red liquid dyebath.[66] To create blue was more cumbersome, as indigo will dye cotton even without a mordant. Where the color was not desired, Indian dyers covered the entire area with wax before immersing the cloth into the dye vat (fig. 120). The final dye application was turmeric yellow, which as noted above was used not only for its yellow color but as an overdye to the blue in order to create green.

The novel designs and nuanced polychrome palette of Indian chinztes proved irresistible to the European and American markets. The same was true of the lightweight cotton fabric itself, since the cotton plant did not grow in Europe (native linen and hemp made a much heavier and coarser cloth compared with fine handspun Indian yarns). Not surprisingly, shortly after the importation of these colorful fabrics to Europe began in earnest in the seventeenth century, European textile producers, seeking to achieve similar results—and profits, no doubt—investigated the Indian dyeing methods and how to reproduce them at home. Their initial approach was to gather

reconnaissance from travelers and agents of the East India companies, such as the detailed reports of Roques and Beaulieu.[67] European writers synthesized the crucial intelligence gleaned from these reports in various publications, among them *L'art de faire les indiennes* (1786),[68] which focused especially on helping the emerging cotton-printing industries of England, France, and Germany, among other countries, re-create bright madder-dyed red cotton, which was not produced in Europe until that time. Originally an Indian technique, this complex process resulted in a red cotton that became known as Turkey Red or Adrianopolis Red after dyers from Turkey and Greece were brought to Europe to help establish its industrial applications.[69]

This quest to understand and reproduce Indian polychrome cotton dyeing focused on developing new textile-printing techniques, not necessarily the use of Indian dyes themselves. Many materials essential to Indian dyeing, such as chay root, myrobalans (the dried fruit of the *Terminalia* genus of trees, which contributes to both the mordanting and tannin dyeing processes), buffalo milk, and sesame oil were not highly sought after since substitutes from local European plant sources were readily available. There were exceptions, however, notably indigo, whose efficacy and superiority to native woad were well established. In addition, some two thousand pounds of sandalwood salvaged from the Swedish East India Company's ship *Sveciai*, which sank in 1740 off the Orkney Islands on the return trip from Bengal, provides evidence of the importance of this redwood dye from Southeast Asia.[70] Christophe-Philippe Oberkampf (1738–1815), a German-born French printer and innovator in the European printing industry, is notable for having found inspiration in both the techniques and materials of Indian cottons, particularly in his famous copperplate-printed cottons and

Fig. 122
Louis XVI, Restaurateur de la Liberté (detail). Oberkampf Manufactory, France, 1789. Copperplate-printed cotton (toile de Jouy). The red dye used to print this cotton has been identified as Indian chay root. Whitworth Art Gallery, The University of Manchester, United Kingdom (1990.73)

linens with scenic designs known as toiles de Jouy, after the town where his factory was located. A recent scientific study of the 1789 Oberkampf cotton print *Louis XVI, Restaurateur de la Liberté* was found to have been printed with chay root (fig. 122).[71] Edward Bancroft, the chemist responsible for the widespread adoption of the yellow dye quercitron, mentions in his *Experimental Researches* that the French East India Company imported a substantial amount of the root to France and that trials with chay root took place in England possibly in the 1780s.[72]

Procedures for officially testing dyes had been established throughout Europe by dyers' guilds and textile organizations as early as medieval times, and these trials became part of a scientific process of assessing and regulating the growing textile industry in Europe in the seventeenth and eighteenth centuries.[73] Such experiments also served as a means of soliciting recipes for industrial use of new dyeing techniques, with organizations like the Royal Society of Arts, London, sometimes offering incentives in the form of annual prizes. John Wilson, a Manchester-based manufacturer of cotton velvets, submitted samples of his red madder-dyed cotton yarns to the society's Chemistry Committee on February 12, 1761, and won the prize offered that year.[74] Similarly, in 1811 Napoleon offered a prize of 20,000 livres "to the person who will find how to give wool by means of madder a solid vivid color as the most beautiful Turkey red and which most closely resembles cochineal scarlet."[75]

Although the global search for and cultivation of dyestuffs were first and foremost matters of commerce and profit, they also represented a quest for scientific knowledge, part of the gathering and "ordering" of the natural world that characterized the Age of Enlightenment. The travelers and naturalists who traversed the oceans from the sixteenth to the eighteenth century in search of such knowledge returned with plants and seeds that in some instances are still preserved in European botanical collections and gardens.[76] A specimen of the Asian pagoda tree (*Sophora japonica*), for example, whose seedpods are the source of a brilliant yellow dye used historically in China and Japan, was planted in the Jardin des Plantes, Paris, by French naturalist Bernard de Jussieu (1699–1777). Propagated from seeds sent home by a Jesuit priest in China, the tree, which is said to have flowered for the first time in 1779, still grows in the royal gardens today.[77] In many cases the collecting of plant specimens may have been motivated as much by their potential medicinal applications as their utility as dyestuffs, since many of the botanical sources of dyes were also used to treat illness.

By the late seventeenth and early eighteenth centuries, the spirit of scientific discovery and the advent of laboratory experimentation in Europe had greatly expanded the understanding of the chemical nature of color. Concoctions of metals and acids were invented that could produce brilliant hues such as Prussian and China blues.[78] Additionally, the discovery of essential dyeing aids such as industrial soaps and chlorine bleaches enabled the textile industry to color fabrics that previously had seemed impervious to dyeing.[79] These developments fostered an exponential expansion in European textile production, particularly in the dyeing and printing industries, much of which was in response to the abundance of raw materials available through the international trade and the high demand for Indian dyed and printed fabrics.

In the end, the history of dyes and colors from the sixteenth to the eighteenth century intersected with the evolution of global exchange on many levels. More than just commodities to be traded on an economic front, colorants were sources of cultural knowledge and identity as well as inspiration for creativity and ingenuity. The quest for these precious raw materials in turn spurred long-distance interactions, social transformations, scientific development, and artistic achievements whose profound implications are still being unraveled and understood today.

Catalogue

1. QUILT

Southern Europe, 17th century
Silk, with cotton filling
101 ½ x 87 in. (257.8 x 221 cm)
Winterthur Museum, Delaware,
Gift of Henry Francis du Pont, 1954.0049

At the center of this rare silk quilt a three-masted galleon plies the seas.[1] Is it a Genoese boat sailing through the Mediterranean on its way to the Levant? A Portuguese ship en route to India or China? Or perhaps a Spanish Manila galleon heading to South America? While we can say that this luxurious quilt was made in the seventeenth century in a southern European country, probably one under the rule of Habsburg Spain, the exact origins of this and several other quilts like it remain unclear. At first glance, the overall design and imagery seem to be related to the embroidered Bengali *colchas* of the same period, commissioned by the Portuguese for export back to Europe (cats. 6, 8). In addition, at twenty-nine inches the silk yardage is unusually wide, which might ordinarily indicate an Indian or perhaps even Chinese source for the fabric.[2] Nonetheless, the quilts are believed to be of European manufacture because the dyestuffs used to color the silk, when tested, were revealed to be dyes commonly found in Europe during this time, but not in India or Asia.[3]

There are three known yellow-silk ship quilts like this one.[4] All three were made using a corded quilting technique, with cotton filling, and two-ply silk thread to stitch the designs, and all have colored-silk backs that contrast with the yellow fronts. In each, galleons appear in a center circle, with a surrounding ring interrupted at top, bottom, and each side by four medallions of male heads in profile. As on many *colchas*, the imagery of these quilts features huntsmen, a metaphor for power and conquest. From quilt to quilt the profile heads vary, with some wearing European hats while others sport turbans. Two of the quilts in the group have Habsburg double-headed eagles stitched into the four corners, while this example shows men in turbans and cloaks in those positions.

Related to these three yellow quilts is one in green silk whose center circle has been split to make two half-circle arches, one atop the other.[5] Under the top arch a male figure plays a viola da gamba, flanked by two standing women, while the lower arch frames two facing ships (fig. 123). The cloaked men in the corners of the green quilt are the same as those that appear in this quilt. The depiction of the viola da gamba, a favorite Baroque instrument first invented in Italy but whose popularity soon spread throughout Europe, could be another reason to attribute this group of quilts to a European workshop.   AP

Fig. 123. Quilt (detail). Southern Europe, 17th century. Silk with cotton filling. Royal Ontario Museum, Toronto, Gift of Miss Betty Kingston (975.349)

1. Although this ship has been called a carrack in other publications, the flattened stern on the ship indicates it is a slightly later type of boat, the galleon, a shipping vessel for long sea voyages that was utilized by several European countries beginning in the second half of the sixteenth century.
2. Most European silk woven at the time was between nineteen and twenty-one inches wide.
3. The yellow silk was dyed with weld, and the pink side (once a darker red) was dyed with a redwood, probably brazilwood. For more on these quilts, see Eaton, *Quilts in a Material World*, p. 114, and Renner Lidz, "The Mystery of Seventeenth-Century Quilts," pp. 834–43.
4. The three yellow ship quilts under discussion are the present example in the Winterthur Museum, a quilt in the collection of Colonial Williamsburg (no. 2005-94), and a quilt in a private collection in England, published in Rae et al., *Quilt Treasures of Great Britain*, pp. 65–67.
5. For another related green-silk quilt with a row of ships at the bottom edge, see the exhibition catalogue Spink and Son, *The Glamour of Silk*, no. 5, "Hunters Quilt."

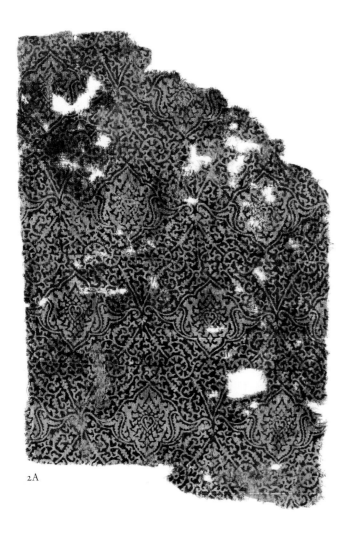

2A

2B

2A. TEXTILE WITH ARABESQUE AND
PALMETTE DESIGN

India (Gujarat), for the Egyptian market, 14th century
Cotton, block-printed mordant, dyed
9 ⅜ x 12 ⅝ in. (23.8 x 32.1 cm)
The Metropolitan Museum of Art, New York,
Gift of V. Everit Macy, 1930 30.112.28

2B. TEXTILE WITH LOTUS AND ARABESQUE DESIGN

India (Gujarat), for the Egyptian market, 14th–15th century
Cotton, block-printed resist, dyed
18 ⅛ x 8 ⅜ in. (46.1 x 21.3 cm)
The Metropolitan Museum of Art, New York,
Gift of V. Everit Macy, 1930 30.112.34

In this textile fragment (cat. 2A), elaborate vine tendrils form intricate symmetrical arabesques that enclose the signature motif of the design, a heart-shaped lotus bud in a palmette. The fabric is block-printed and mordant-dyed a dark red-brown or aubergine. Several variations of this design are known from textile finds in Fustat (Cairo), Egypt, and all have been identified as Indian imports from Gujarat.[1] No versions of this design have been recorded among Southeast Asian finds, and given the strong Islamic flavor of the design, it may be assumed to have been made in Gujarat as an inexpensive imitation of the woven luxury cloth produced in Egypt or Iran during the fourteenth century. This pattern is best known in silk and gold lampas, sometimes brocaded, associated with both Ilkhanid Iran and Mamluk Egypt (fig. 124). The Mongol conquests in West Asia resulted in the dislocation and sometimes forced resettlement of skilled weavers, directly contributing to an unprecedented hybridity of style and of weaving techniques and making secure attributions problematic.[2] Resonances of Mongol China are apparent in this textile, where the imported Chinese motif of the lotus-palmette has been reordered

Fig. 124. Textile with paired rabbit design. Egypt or Iran, 14th century. Lampas, silk and gold thread. The Metropolitan Museum of Art, New York, Fletcher Fund, 1946 (46.156.41)

3A. FRAGMENT OF TEXTILE WITH A FORESTED LANDSCAPE

India (Gujarat), for the Egyptian market, 14th century
Cotton, painted resist and mordant, dyed
16 x 12 ¼ in. (40.6 x 31.1 cm)
The Metropolitan Museum of Art, New York,
Gift of V. Everit Macy, 1930 30.112.42

3B. TEXTILE WITH A FORESTED LANDSCAPE

India (Gujarat), for the Indonesian market,
late 14th–early 15th century
Cotton, painted resist and block-printed mordant, dyed
38 ⅞ in. x 16 ft. 2 ¹¹⁄₁₆ in. (98.7 x 494.5 cm)
The Metropolitan Museum of Art, New York,
Purchase, Friends of Asian Art Gifts, 2005 2005.407

into a new symmetry by designers working in the Islamic tradition. A related fourteenth-century Chinese silk damask with the longevity character inset in a lotus, reportedly found in Egypt, confirms that contemporary Chinese silks were also in circulation at the time.[3] Egyptian Mamluk silks probably provided the immediate model for this printed cotton. Samples of such Mamluk woven cloth must also have been sent to western India, where this dyed-cotton version was produced for export back to Egypt.

A related fragment (cat. 2B), produced with the same mordanting technique, also shows a clear debt to Chinese models in the center field, whereas the border is very Indian, with its variegated banding and its square-and-star pattern evoking tie-dye (*bandani*). The center field pattern is that of a lotus flower in full bloom, viewed frontally, set in arabesque leaf-and-flower ogival enclosures—a motif and treatment that draw directly on Chinese designs of the Yuan period (1271–1368). This imagery is shared with blue-and-white porcelain of the period, most notably fourteenth-century Jingdezhen wares intended for the Islamic export market.[4] An early Yuan silk with frontally positioned lotuses provides one such textile model.[5] JG

1. Pfister, *Les toiles imprimées de Fostat et l'Hindoustan*, pl. xiib; Barnes, *Indian Block-printed Textiles in Egypt*, vol. 2, nos. 689, 769; and Gittinger, *Master Dyers to the World*, for variant types.
2. Komaroff and Carboni, eds., *The Legacy of Genghis Khan*, p. 262.
3. Metropolitan Museum, acc. no. 66.156.20.
4. See, for example, a faceted storage jar collected in Iran before 1876 and now in the Victoria and Albert Museum, London (no. 1599-1876). See also Guy, "China in India," forthcoming.
5. Metropolitan Museum, acc. no. 52.8.

Interlocking motifs of trees, leaves, vines, and flowers create complex design patterns in this small textile fragment (cat. 3A). These vegetal forms are reserved in white against a mordanted madder-red ground, with silhouetting outlines reserved in indigo blue and highlights in purple, achieved by superimposing red and blue. Many of the shapes are simplified to the point of abstraction, with only a signature leaf or flower motif to signal their identity. Nonetheless, it is clear that this fragment belongs to a Gujarati tradition of cloth painting in which a variegated forest landscape serves as the principal subject. The spectacular full-length cloth also seen here (cat. 3B) belongs to the same tradition. While the fragment was retrieved from a burial shroud in the sands of Fustat (Cairo), Egypt, this and several other versions, all measuring from four to five yards in length, have been recorded in eastern Indonesia. There they were prized by a number of communities, including the Toraja of central highland Sulawesi, who refer to them as Maa', or cloths of the ancestors.[1] The stylized vegetal forms in both of these textiles conform to recognizable Gujarati conventions of the period, present in carved marble cenotaphs (fig. 13), which are dated, and in western Indian Sultanate and Jain manuscript paintings, which generally are not.[2]

This long cloth (cat. 3B) is one of the finest examples to have survived. Like the other documented cloths, it has pearl-and-rosette border detailing on three sides only, a certain indication that it constitutes only half of the intended textile; an identical second half would have been joined to it longitudinally. As no two matching pieces have been recorded, it must be assumed that the halves were never united and in all probability were dispersed at the point of sale. The spectacular design is composed of a series of stylized trees, each species clearly identifiable, interlocking to form a densely forested landscape. It contains seven fruit-bearing trees

3A

and flowering plants, including mango, plantain, and palm; each is distinguished by a clearly defined silhouette, leaves, fruit, and flowers. Landscape—without a figurative or narrative component—is very rare in the history of Indian painting, making this series of Gujarati painted cloths a unique contribution. The block impression used to apply the madder red is repeated over two registers along the entire length of the cloth. Closely related examples are in the Victoria and Albert Museum, London, and the TAPI Collection, Surat.[3] These consistently radiocarbon-date to the early fourteenth century, indicating that the Cambay trade in these Gujarati-painted cotton goods to both the Egyptian and Indonesian markets was well established at least two centuries prior to when Portuguese apothecary Tomé Pires was writing his commentary on Indian Ocean trade, during his residence at Melaka (Malacca) in 1512–15.[4] While we have some understanding of the role these textiles played in Indonesia—both in mythology, as ancestor cloths, and in ritual displays associated with protection and with life transitions—we know little of their function in the Red Sea world of Mamluk Egypt prior to their end use as shrouds for the dead. Even in the dry sands of Egypt, few examples survived burial intact, whereas those in the tropical zones of Indonesia did endure, remarkably, as a result of the care extended to them as prized heirloom objects (*pustaka*).   JG

1. Nooy-Palm, "The Sacred Cloths of the Toraja," pp. 162–80.
2. Guy, "Indian Painting from 1100 to 1500," pp. 23, 25, 27, figs. 14–17.
3. Victoria and Albert Museum, London (no. IS. 96-1993), and the TAPI Collection, Surat (no. 00.175). See Guy, *Woven Cargoes*, p. 137, no. 44, and Barnes, Cohen, and Crill, *Trade, Temple and Court*, nos. 2, 3.
4. Pires, *The Suma Oriental of Tomé Pires*.

3B, detail

4. LENGTH OF VELVET

Turkey (Bursa or Istanbul), late 16th or early 17th century
Velvet, cut, voided, and brocaded,
silk and metal-wrapped thread
73 ½ x 26 in. (186.7 x 66 cm)
The Metropolitan Museum of Art, New York,
Rogers Fund, 1917 17.22.8b

From the late fifteenth century on, velvet was made in increasing quantities to meet the high demand of the Ottoman court. One grade was made for furnishings such as cushion covers and summer carpets. A higher grade was used for clothing, tailored into robes worn by the royal family and robes of honor presented to esteemed visitors to the court. In his travel account, the Frenchman Jean-Baptiste Tavernier, who passed through the Ottoman capital in the 1660s, also mentions particularly extravagant throne covers made of gold-brocaded velvet, as well as black, white, and violet velvets that had been embroidered with pearls, rubies, and emeralds.[1]

Despite the initial high quality of both technique and design of local velvets, standards dropped in the early sixteenth century, as the textile makers started to substitute cheaper materials, use less dye, or reduce warp and weft counts. As a result, velvet from Italy became highly prized. This shift in preference, evidenced by the great number of Italian-velvet garments preserved in the imperial collections of the Topkapı Palace in Istanbul, opened an extremely lucrative market to Italian manufacturers, who quickly adjusted the design and size of their fabrics to suit Turkish taste and usage.

In turn, contemporary velvets made in Turkey took on a strong Italian flavor. The preference for red grounds is said to come from this source. In Turkey the red was created with *Kerria lacca*, a crimson lac dye, that was used to tint the silk weft threads; once woven, the finished fabric was dipped in filtered indigo to augment the hue.[2] Brocaded designs of metal-wrapped thread, often gold, further enhanced the velvet, but weavers in Turkey never created the multiheight pile that remained a hallmark of Italian production.

With its double ogival lattice, this length of fabric represents the shared Italianate-Ottoman aesthetic that characterizes sixteenth-century velvets, but, about the time it was produced, official constraints on imports from Italy—enacted to bolster the local economy—stimulated changes. As locally made velvets once again gained a larger place in the market, their designs shifted along with those of other Ottoman decorative arts. Gradually, the ogival framework was replaced by motifs that became typical of the seventeenth-century Ottoman repertoire. Artichokes, pomegranates, carnations, tulips, and rosebuds were applied in large repeating patterns across the width of the fabric, and velvet started to appear in purple, blue, green, and other shades.   MS

1. Tavernier, *Collections of Travels through Turky into Persia,* quoted in Atasoy, Denny, Mackie, and Tezcan, *Ipek,* pp. 32–33.
2. A 1502 document records the complaints of master weavers that some workshops were substituting madder and unfiltered indigo for these costly materials. Quoted in Atasoy, Denny, Mackie, and Tezcan, *Ipek,* p. 163.

5. LENGTH OF VELVET

Italy (Venice or Florence), 16th century
Velvet, pile on pile, cut, voided, and brocaded,
silk and metal-wrapped thread
12 ft. 3 ½ in. x 23 ¼ in. (374.7 x 59.1 cm)
The Metropolitan Museum of Art, New York,
Rogers Fund, 1912 12.49.8

Precious silk velvets were among the most highly prized diplomatic gifts exchanged between the Ottoman and European courts during the late Middle Ages and the Renaissance. Both textiles and complete garments were given, following the Eastern tradition of presenting visiting diplomats with entire wardrobes appropriate to their station at court. These gifts were a crucial part of the displays of prestige and power, and their significance is emphasized by the fact that both the textile gifts and the quality of the garments worn by diplomats were carefully recorded in chronicles of the day.[1]

This length of velvet, a tour de force of the weaver's skill, is the type of textile that would have been valued in both Constantinople and the capitals of Europe. It displays all the features of the highest-quality European Renaissance velvets: multiple heights of silk pile, metal-thread brocading, and metal-thread loops, which create glittering highlights in the centers of the artichoke motifs. Variations on the design of this velvet have been catalogued as both Italian and Spanish. Among the examples that survive are a set of ecclesiastical vestments and an altar frontal, likely made for a Spanish Catholic bishop in the mid-sixteenth century, as well as a caftan in the Topkapı Palace, Istanbul, which is associated with Sultan Ahmed I (r. 1603–17).[2] The framework of pointed ovals, or ogees, surrounding a central floral motif appeared in European velvets by the late fifteenth century. However, the composition of this velvet references Ottoman textiles by creating a subtle double, or interlocked, series of ogees—a feature more common in the East. This is achieved by adding smaller artichoke motifs at the sides, along with pomegranates and Tudor roses, which together form a loosely connected curve echoing that of the central motif. In all of the other known examples of this pattern, the small pomegranate and Tudor rose are replaced

4, detail

5, detail

by more stylized flowers; these features are seen only in this velvet. While it is not known which of the variations was created first, the substitution of such changes indicates the weavers' adaptability to various tastes or markets.[3]   MW

1. See Monnas, "Textiles and Diplomacy: Ottoman Silks," forthcoming.
2. For the cope, chasuble, and dalmatic, see King and King, *European Textiles in the Keir Collection 400 BC to 1800 AD*, pp. 108–11; for another dalmatic and an altar frontal, see Monnas, *Renaissance Velvets*, pp. 120–21, no. 35; for another panel (possibly an altar frontal), see Mayer, *Masterpieces of Western Textiles from the Art Institute of Chicago*, p. 63, pl. 47; for the caftan, see Baker, Tezcan, and Wearden, *Silks for the Sultans*, pp. 196, 198, 199.
3. Thank you to Lisa Monnas for her comments on this phenomenon; an example was also documented by Michael Peter in his talk "The Velvet Hanging of Albrecht of Brandenburg in Halberstadt Cathedral."

6. COVERLET (COLCHA)

India (Bengal, Satgaon), for the Portuguese market,
early 17th century
Cotton, embroidered with silk
10 ft. 6 in. x 8 ft. 11 in. (320 x 271.8 cm)
The Metropolitan Museum of Art, New York,
Helena Woolworth McCann Collection, Purchase,
Winfield Foundation Gift, by exchange, 1975   1975.4

One of a group of textiles whose production is attributed to the area of Satgaon in Bengal,[1] coverlets such as this were made primarily for the Portuguese market, hence the Portuguese term (*colcha*) by which they are known. In the early seventeenth century they also fetched high prices at auctions in England and seem to have influenced the production of embroidery there (cat. 10). Characterized by the use of yellow tussah silk embroidery on a white cotton ground, they typically depict a combination of classical, biblical, and Hindu themes, although a few draw from other sources (cat. 8).

This *colcha* is embellished with a selection of vignettes found on several others, including an almost identical example in the Museu Nacional de Arte Antiga, Lisbon.[2] Successive bands around the border depict a hunt, the Labors of Hercules, and the story of Arion, while the center panel features the Judgment of Solomon surrounded by stories from the book of Judith: the siege of Bethulia (bottom right), Judith before Holofernes (top right), Judith beheads Holofernes (top left), and the severed head of Holofernes displayed from the walls of Bethulia (bottom left). Vignettes from classical mythology include Actaeon transformed into a stag by Diana (above the Solomon scene), Hercules shooting the Lernean Hydra (detail), and the story of Phaeton, who drove the chariot of the sun too close to Earth, scorching the planet and causing the animals to die (in the triangular panel below Hercules).

While the themes of these coverlets can be generally related to contemporary European tapestries and textiles, which also mix biblical and classical tales, the depiction of the protagonists in seventeenth-century Portuguese garb and the addition of Hindu imagery (such as the story of the Vishnu avatar Matsya, the fish-tailed figure in the second band from the center) must represent the traditions and imagination of the embroiderers who created them. The circulation of northern European prints and illustrated Bibles at the Mughal court is well documented, but the sources available to the Bengali embroiderers remain obscure and probably represent an entirely different category of material.

The inventiveness of the embroidery is further underscored by comparison to those made for the local market. Two pieces that likely date to the late sixteenth or early seventeenth century are embroidered in multicolored silk, and their design is composed of circular medallions enclosing lotus patterns, interlocking star shapes, and bands of human figures and animals.[3] Here, then, the switch to an almost monochrome yellow and white palette, the composition of concentric panels and bands, and the addition of foreign iconography were innovations for this particular type of export, which was produced only until the mid-seventeenth century.   MS

1. Irwin, "Indo-Portuguese Embroideries of Bengal," pp. 65–73.
2. Museu Nacional de Arte Antiga, Lisbon (no. 3692).
3. These are in Hardwick Hall, Derbyshire (see Crill, "The Earliest Survivors?: The Indian Embroideries at Hardwick Hall," pp. 245–60), and in the Museu Nacional de Arte Antiga, Lisbon (no. 3413) (Mendonça, *Embroidered Quilts from the Museu Nacional de Arte Antiga Lisboa*, no. 6).

6, detail

6

7. CAPE

India (Bengal, Satgaon), for the Portuguese market,
early 17th century
Cotton, embroidered with silk
39 ½ x 81 in. (100.3 x 206.1 cm)
The Metropolitan Museum of Art, New York,
Gift of Lily S. Place, 1923   23.203.1

Like the coverlet in catalogue number 6 and the hanging in catalogue number 8, this cape can be attributed to seventeenth-century Bengal and associated with the group of embroideries made there for the international market. These textiles are related in technique, material, and subject matter: they were embroidered with yellow tussah silk on a white cotton ground and were richly decorated with figural scenes and floral motifs.

While the coverlets and hangings survive in the greatest numbers, several types of clothing were made in the same manner. Jan Huyghen van Linschoten, a Dutchman who was in India from 1583 to 1589, wrote that the Bengali embroiderers produced "pillows, shaving cloths, and children's baptismal cloaks, like those which women in confinement wear round their shoulders, and they embroider them with leaf and flower-work and all kinds of Figures one can think of or imagine."[1] In addition, items known as "hair mantles," which might have been used to protect the shoulders during hairdressing, as well as capes of a type fashionable among Portuguese men in the early seventeenth century, are known in museum collections.[2] These capes and mantles have short collars and are constructed of trapezoidal panels sewn together to create a flaring shape, wider at the bottom than at the top.

The garment here is different in that it is constructed of a single panel of a semicircular shape and has no collar. A similar piece is at the Cooper-Hewitt, National Design Museum, New York.[3] On both, the decoration is arranged in bands around the edges of the garment and within and between two quarter-circular spaces inside the bands. The motifs include hunters riding on elephants and horses, rows of coursing beasts, and figures in European dress. On the Metropolitan Museum's example, the stitching that attaches the face of the garment to the lining is completed in a dense vegetal pattern that surrounds the figures and fills the background.

Because of their construction and shape, the Metropolitan and Cooper-Hewitt garments have usually been identified as copes, the full-length semicircular ecclesiastical vestments. Their roughly arm-length dimensions and decidedly unbiblical decorative motifs, however, argue against such an identification. Instead, they probably indicate that these items were yet another type of cape, a short, shoulder-length style worn by the Portuguese in India and illustrated in an engraving from Linschoten's *Itinerario*.[4]   MS

1. Linschoten served as bookkeeper to the archbishop of Goa and published his *Itinerario, voyage ofte schipvaert . . . naer Oost ofte Portugaels Indien* in Amsterdam in 1595–96; this translation in Irwin's "Indo-Portuguese Embroideries of Bengal," pp. 67–68.
2. For the hair mantles and their identification as such from a sixteenth-century inventory, see Wilckens, "Ein 'Haarmantel' des 16. Jahrhunderts," pp. 39–44. For the capes, see Maria Fernanda Passos Leite in Trnek and Silva, eds., *Exotica: The Portuguese Discoveries and the Renaissance Kunstkammer,* p. 182.
3. Cooper-Hewitt, National Design Museum, New York (no. 1951-41-1).
4. The engraving was also published in Mendes Pinto et al., *Vasco da Gama et l'Inde,* p. 146.

8. HANGING WITH TRIUMPHAL ARCH

India (Bengal, Satgaon), for the Portuguese market,
second quarter of the 17th century
Silk satin, embroidered with silk
105 x 83 in. (267 x 211 cm)
Isabella Stewart Gardner Museum, Boston, T20e4

Embroidered in white chain-stitched silk (now slightly discolored) on a blue silk ground, this magnificent hanging can be associated with similar textiles made in Bengal during the early to mid-seventeenth century by Indian embroiderers working under Portuguese commission. With its unique iconography, this example stands out, however, as being charged with political and aesthetic intent.[1]

Scholars recently identified an illustrated book published in 1622 by João Baptista Lavanha, a Portuguese mathematician and royal engineer, as the source of the hanging's design. It documents the ephemeral structures created for the triumphal entry of Philip III of Spain (who ruled Portugal as Philip II) into Lisbon in 1619.[2] In particular, the hanging depicts an arch known as the Flamand, which was erected by the community of Flemish merchants in Lisbon. The architectural details rendered here in embroidery, including the arch's articulated pediments and classical friezes, are all as described and illustrated in Lavanha's text (fig. 125).

Toward the top of the arch is Discordia, goddess of strife, standing between a divided disk, each side of which contains arms of the provinces of the Netherlands that at the time were engaged in a struggle for independence from Spain. The theme of the arch has thus been interpreted to represent the fraught political tenor of the era.[3] Another indicator of a political tone is the presence of the Portuguese royal coat of arms rather than those of the Spanish monarch, as seen in the engraving printed in Lavanha's book (the actual arch, when built, likewise displayed the Portuguese arms).[4] Although the engraving served as the model for the embroidered center field, other design sources informed the composition as a whole. Emanating from the arch, for example, are eight branches of a genealogical tree, each of which terminates in a portrait bust of a past Portuguese king. This suggests the embroidery was likely produced in the 1640s, during the restoration of the Portuguese monarchy.[5] A series of concentric borders surrounding the center field contain scenes of classical mythology, Christian religious subjects, fantastic sea creatures (including mermaids), and hunting scenes, all of which situate the embroidery within the iconographic program and design layout typical of Bengali production of the period (cat. 6).[6] Although these embroideries are often referred to as *colchas* (coverlets), this textile was clearly intended as a hanging and, given its stately theme, was likely a royal commission.   EP

1. See Carvalho, *Luxury for Export,* and Karl, "The Use of Growing Architecture as Propaganda," pp. 231–44.
2. See Carvalho, *Luxury for Export,* p. 13, and Lavanha, *Viagem da Catholica Real Magestade del Rey D. Filipe II. N.S. ao reyno de Portugal.* Two editions of Lavanha's book were published in 1622, one in Spanish and one in Portuguese.
3. Karl and Carvalho both discuss the role of the conflicts between and within rebellious Netherlandish groups as well as the conflict between Spain and the Netherlands as part of the struggle for independence from Habsburg rule, mirrored by similar conflicts between Portugal and Spain.
4. Carvalho, *Luxury for Export,* p. 13.
5. Carvalho (ibid., p. 19) interprets the last figure, who has no crown, as João IV (r. 1640–56), first king of the Bragança line, and uses this to date the embroidery after the 1646 restoration. Karl, in contrast, identifies the figure as João II (1455–1495) and proposes a date of about 1632, prior to the Mughal conquest of Hugli, the region where many of these embroideries originated (Karl, "The Use of Growing Architecture as Propaganda," pp. 242–43).
6. A set of bed hangings in the Bowes Museum, Barnard Castle, County Durham, U.K. (Emb. 283), which features portraits of kings, queens, and noblemen within roundels embroidered on a dark blue silk ground, is a composite made from a possibly related hanging. I thank my colleague Marika Sardar for bringing this compelling work to my attention.

Fig. 125. *The Arch of the Flemish from the Triumphal Entry of Philip III into Lisbon.* Etching. From Lavanha, *Viagem da Catholica Real Magestade del Rey D. Filipe II. N.S. ao reyno de Portugal . . . ,* 1622

9. TABLE COVER

Spain or Portugal, late 16th–early 17th century
Linen, embroidered with silk
97 x 66 ½ in. (246.4 x 168.9 cm)
The Metropolitan Museum of Art, New York,
Gift of Mrs. W. Bayard Cutting, 1945 45.114.12

Silk-embroidered linen covers were common furnishings in Iberian households. The proportions of this example indicate that it was used over a table rather than on a bed. The floral designs—elegant Renaissance-style scrolling vines with carnations, irises, and other flowers as well as hummingbirds seeking nectar—are constructed with brilliant yellow silk embroidered on a natural linen ground (outlines in brown tannin ink, drawn for the embroiderers to follow, are still visible in some areas). The golden yellow color, a favorite in Iberia for textiles, was derived from weld, a local dyeplant that thrived in the region and was relied on for its brilliance and durability.[1] Although the contrast between the yellow silk and the ecru ground echoes that of certain Indian embroideries made in Bengal and imported into Portugal and Spain in the sixteenth and seventeenth centuries (cats. 6, 7), the ease of the design and the variety in stitch type (including satin, chain, and stem as well as various kinds of knots and filling stitches) help identify this as a European cover.

The configuration of the cover's decorative elements constitutes a basic format that may have originated in Islamic Spain. In particular, the large central field with a series of outer borders, including a broad center border flanked, or "protected," by narrower guard borders on either side, was an established style for carpets throughout the Islamic world and one that influenced other regional textile designs, notably Spanish embroidery (the demarcation of the four outer corners in this example may, however, be more Iberian than Islamic in character). This design approach, in turn, was transmitted around the world via Spanish and Portuguese colonial administration and trade, from tapestries made by Andean weavers in sixteenth- and seventeenth-century Peru (cat. 20) to Asian and Indian embroideries intended for the European market (cats. 8, 26).

Given the shared heritage of Portugal and Spain, especially during the sixteenth century, when both countries were united under a single ruler, it can be difficult to differentiate the embroidery production of one from the other.[2] Both regions had long-standing traditions of fine textiles, from folk works to commissions made by professional guilds for the Church and royal court. This example lies somewhere in between: although the cover was intended for actual household use, its intricate style and high quality suggest that it was made for a person of means and status. EP

1. Nobuko Shibayama in the Department of Scientific Research, Metropolitan Museum, analyzed the yellow dye using High Performance Liquid Chromatography-Photo Diode Array (HPLC-PDA) and identified the source as weld.
2. For Spanish and Portuguese textile traditions, see May, *Silk Textiles of Spain, Eighth to Fifteenth Century*; Weibel, *Two Thousand Years of Textiles*; Réal, *Spanische und portugiesische gewebe*; and Vaz Pinto, *Bordado de Castelo Branco: Catálogo de desenhos,* vol. 1, *Colchas.*

10A. BEDCOVER

England, late 17th century
Cotton, embroidered with silk
62 x 60 in. (157.5 x 152.4 cm)
The Metropolitan Museum of Art, New York,
Rogers Fund, 1934 34.104.1

10B. BEDCOVER

England, 1725–50
Linen, embroidered with silk and metal-wrapped thread
79 x 67 ½ in. (200.7 x 171.5 cm)
The Metropolitan Museum of Art, New York, Purchase,
Everfast Fabrics Inc. Gift, 1970 1970.173

While the Portuguese were undoubtedly the first importers and consumers of the Indian embroideries made for the western European market (cats. 6–8), at least a few examples of these textiles did appear in England by the late sixteenth century. The 1601 inventory of Bess of Hardwick, Countess of Shrewsbury (1527–1608), included two quilts that were almost certainly products of this trade: "a quilt of yellow India stuff embroidered with birds and beasts" and "a quilt of India stuff embroidered with beastes."[1] Indian quilts of the type produced for the Portuguese market appeared with increasing frequency in London sales into the 1620s, when their value began to decline, perhaps because of diminishing novelty.[2]

The taste for Indian-style embroidery remained, however, and it is interesting to note that the English maker of catalogue number 10A used not only the Indian palette of golden yellow on white but also an imported Indian cotton as the foundation. The cover has rare seventeenth-century marks on the plain-weave cotton fabric: the initials G.C.E. (for the English East India Company's original name, the Governor and Company of Merchants of London Trading in the East Indies) as well as three other stamps whose significance has not yet been deciphered.[3]

On this bedcover, the embroidered designs draw heavily on such exotic motifs as pineapple-like vegetation and serrated leaves, but contemporary European sensibilities are also evident in the strapwork connecting the floral elements. Additionally, the three-dimensionality of the embroidery and the use of stitches with long floats that create a shinier surface to contrast with the matte appearance of the cotton ground diverge from the Indian prototypes, whose flatter chain stitches are less glossy. English bedcovers were usually part of coordinated sets that could include bolsters, pillows, and matching valances.[4]

In addition to the more common monochrome yellow-on-white embroideries, Indian polychrome embroideries also arrived

10A

10B

in England during the early seventeenth century. They, too, are described in sale records; for example, a 1614 sale included "a carpet or quilt embroidered upon calico with sundry silks."[5] The word "carpet" is probably used in its contemporaneous sense, that is, to signify decorative covers for a variety of furniture types, including beds. Catalogue number 10B, an English polychrome silk and metal-thread bedcover, is more obviously dependent on the stylistic composition of Persian and Turkish carpets than catalogue number 10A. By the eighteenth century, both embroidered and painted cotton textiles of this type, with a central medallion and smaller medallions in the corners of the central field, were being made in India for domestic consumption and for export (cat. 54, fig. 138).[6] These imported polychrome covers had a lasting influence on the production of English embroidered bed furnishings of the eighteenth century.   MW

1. Crill, "The Earliest Survivors?: The Indian Embroideries at Hardwick Hall," pp. 246, 260 n. 2; see also Levey, *The Embroideries at Hardwick Hall,* p. 390.
2. Crill, "The Earliest Survivors?: The Indian Embroideries at Hardwick Hall," p. 258.
3. Irwin and Brett, *Origins of Chintz,* p. 12. This East India Company mark first appeared in 1657, according to the India Office Archives; the other markings include one set of two Roman letters, and two symbols, at least one of which may be Tamil weaver's marks of the type that, according to Margaret Hall (quoted in ibid., p. 12), occur at one end of the cloth near a shot of red cotton used to mark length.
4. Catalogue number 10A has three coordinating pillows. In addition, there is a set with polychrome embroidery similar to catalogue number 10B in the Victoria and Albert Museum, London (no. T.48A–E-1967). One of its pillows (no. T.48E-1967) is illustrated in King and Levey, *The Victoria and Albert Museum's Textile Collection,* p. 99, no. 109.
5. Crill, "The Earliest Survivors?: The Indian Embroideries at Hardwick Hall," p. 250.
6. Ibid.; for another painted version for the European market, see Irwin and Brett, *Origins of Chintz,* p. 98, no. 77, pl. 75.

11. BEDCOVER

India (Gujarat), for the English market, early 18th century
Cotton, embroidered with silk
10 ft. 2 in. x 100 in. (309.9 x 254 cm)
The Metropolitan Museum of Art, New York,
Rogers Fund, 1968 68.61

During the sixteenth and seventeenth centuries, Gujarat, in western India, supplied embroideries of the highest quality to the Mughal court; these textiles became valued commodities in Europe as soon as sea trade with that region was established. The Portuguese were the first Europeans to enter this market, but most surviving Gujarati embroideries relate to trade with England, which increased in the early seventeenth century.[1]

Over the course of the seventeenth century, as the Gujarati embroiderers adjusted their output for the English market, they

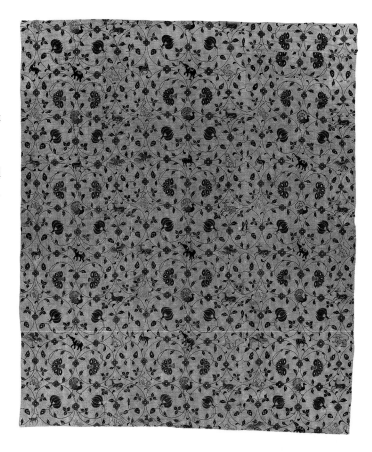

11, detail

adopted the common motif of pink flowers detailed in yellow that bloom from dark green vines with light green or yellow veins. In the background are spotted leopards, striped deer, squirrels, birds, and other chain-stitched beasts filled with bands of color or details in contrasting hues (detail). These elements are understood to have been culled from a variety of sources including English embroideries, examples of which must have been sent to India as models (cat. 74). But as English embroidery was itself responding to the influx of Asian textiles, incorporating and adapting many foreign motifs, the result was a mix of European, Indian, and Chinese imagery that then fed back to its original sources in a totally transformed state.

This piece, consisting of several panels that have been joined and then quilted to form a bed-size coverlet, includes the motifs found on seventeenth-century coverlets but must have been made in the early eighteenth century, when an overall pattern of rinceaux enclosing flowers became more common.[2] However, Gujarati production is remarkable for its variety; at the same time, embroiderers were also producing patterns related to French bizarre silks and palampore designs (cat. 75).   MS

1. For the involvement of different foreign traders in the region, see Irwin, "Indian Textile Trade in the Seventeenth Century: I. Western India," pp. 4–33, and Irwin, "The Commercial Embroidery of Gujerat [sic] in the Seventeenth Century," pp. 51–57.
2. See also the fabrics in the Victoria and Albert Museum, London (nos. IS 78-1955 and IS 79-1955).

12. COIF

England, early 17th century
Linen, embroidered with silk, metal-wrapped thread,
and spangles
9 x 17 in. (22.9 x 43.2 cm)
The Metropolitan Museum of Art, New York,
Gift of Irwin Untermyer, 1964 64.101.1258

Patterns of scrolling vines, or rinceaux, with flowers, birds, and insects—like the design on this coif, or cap—were extremely popular in England in the late sixteenth and early seventeenth centuries. By the 1580s portraits of Queen Elizabeth I and several of her courtiers show the sitters wearing embroidered sleeves decorated with an early version of this pattern in monochrome thread (usually black) on white linen.[1] Examples like this coif, made of linen embroidered with polychrome silk and metal threads, were first produced about 1600. This popular scrolling pattern appeared on both men's and women's headgear, women's jackets, and furnishing textiles. The design, which may derive from similar motifs found in Islamic Spain, remained fashionable in England at least until the 1620s.[2]

Features like the small diaper patterns used to fill the interiors of individual leaves and flower petals in blackwork embroidery and the striped or shaded leaves and petals like those seen here continued to be employed in English crewel embroidery of the later seventeenth century. These features are also found in some of the earlier surviving Indian chintz patterns produced for export to Europe. English embroidery patterns and Continental verdure tapestries were sources that contributed to the creation of the lush floral designs seen in late seventeenth- and early eighteenth-century Indian chintz.[3] A miniature version of a scrolling floral pattern appears in one of the earliest surviving Indian chintzes, found on the walls of the circa 1677 dollhouse of Petronella Dunois (1650–1695), now in the Rijksmuseum, Amsterdam (fig. 79).[4] A *sarasa* for the Japanese market (cat. 13), another type of Indian cotton, also displays this type of pattern, and a much larger-scale variation that includes exotic animals appears on an Indian embroidered bedcover (cat. 11).

Fig. 126. Bernhard Zan (German, active 1580–81). *Vegetal Scrollwork, Flowers, and Fruits*, 1581. Stipple engraving. The Metropolitan Museum of Art, New York, Rogers Fund, 1921 (20.8.1)

A number of ornament prints, such as the German artist Bernhard Zan's design of 1581 (fig. 126), could have served as models for European embroideries. Like the rinceaux design itself, ornament prints often had extended periods of use and were circulated and copied long after their original invention. While there is to date no concrete evidence that designs or textiles of this exact type were sent to Indian craftsmen to copy, the practice of sending patterns to India is well documented, and it seems likely that versions of such successful patterns as the European rinceaux with flowers influenced Indian textile production for the international market.   MW

1. See Arnold, *Queen Elizabeth's Wardrobe Unlock'd,* pl. 3, figs. 13, 14, 25, 37–39, 43–46, 66–68.
2. For a discussion of the origins of this style, see North, "'An Instrument of profit, pleasure, and of ornament,'" pp. 43–48.
3. Irwin, "Origins of the 'Oriental Style' in English Decorative Art," pp. 106–14.
4. See Hartkamp-Jonxis, *Sitsen uit India/Indian Chintzes,* pp. 10–13.

13. SARASA WITH GILDED FLORAL PATTERN
India (Gujarat), for the Japanese market,
first half of the 18th century
Cotton, painted mordant, dyed, with applied gold leaf
11 ¾ x 15 ½ in. (29.8 x 39.4 cm)
The Metropolitan Museum of Art, New York,
Funds from various donors, by exchange, 2010 2010.55

This textile fragment features a patterned scrolling-vine design inset with three alternating flower types, reserved in white against a mordant-dyed red ground, the flowers enhanced with painted gold; a textile with such decoration was known as *kin sarasa*. Gold appears as veins and edges of leaves and flower petals, along the stems, and as small dots on the red background. Both the major historical *daimyo* family collections of *sarasa*, the Maeda (Kyoto

National Museum) and the Hikone (Ii family; Tokyo National Museum), represent this type.[1] In the late Edo period surviving fragments of such cloths were routinely mounted in sample books, where they are known as *meibutsugire* (famed fabrics). This fragment is a survivor of that process, for most were probably cannibalized to supply sample books and to be tailored into tea utensil containers, display mats, tobacco pouches, scroll box covers, and other precious object wrappers.

Indian painted-cotton textiles entered Japan as early as the fifteenth century through the intermediary of Ryukyu traders. After some initial successes by the Portuguese, this trade came to be increasingly dominated by the Dutch East India Company (Verenigde Oost-Indische Compagnie, or VOC). Earlier variants of this scrolling-vine design are depicted in a costume worn on a Namban screen painted in Japan in the early seventeenth century.[2] A comparable cloth length in the Victoria and Albert Museum, London, bears a VOC/B merchant stamp, indicating that it was traded via Batavia, the company's Asian headquarters, probably in the first half of the eighteenth century.[3] The design relates to later seventeenth-century Mughal embroideries, which in turn drew part of their inspiration from earlier English silk and metal-thread embroideries (see cat. 12) that are presumed to have entered Mughal India as diplomatic gifts via Surat, the major port of Gujarat serving the Mughal court. Surat also served as the English East India Company's factory headquarters, supplying orders to Java and other destinations in the East.   JG

1. Ogasawara, *Hikone sarasa*; Ogasawara, *Sarasa*; Satoh et al., *Kowatari sarasa.*
2. Gittinger, *Master Dyers to the World,* p. 166, fig. 144.
3. Guy, *Woven Cargoes,* p. 100, figs. 128, 129.

14. THE ABDUCTION OF HELEN, FROM A SET OF THE STORY OF TROY
China, for the Portuguese market,
probably first half of the 17th century
Cotton, embroidered with silk
and gilt-paper-wrapped thread, pigment
11 ft. 10 ¾ in. x 15 ft. 9 in. (3.6 x 4.8 m)
The Metropolitan Museum of Art, New York,
Gift of Louis E. Seley, 1979 1979.282

Embroidered in China, this depiction of the abduction of Helen is monumental both in scale and in the freedom granted to the embroiderers, who included many Chinese motifs and interpretations within a purely Western narrative. A quintessential account in the Western classical tradition, the story of the Trojan War inspired large sets of European tapestries; the earliest documented set was presented to Charles the Bold in 1472.[1] This

embroidered hanging, too, was part of a large set, of which the Metropolitan Museum owns three, and four are preserved in other collections.[2] All have the same border, including an armorial at each corner that does not correspond completely with any known arms. Perhaps it is an erroneous rendering of the arms of the Mascarenhas family of Portugal; the nobleman Francisco Mascarenhas served as governor of Macau from 1623 to 1626.

The abduction of Helen ignited war between Troy and Greece; this version, in which Helen is forcibly seized, relies on postclassical sources.[3] Against a backdrop of European-style buildings with Baroque facades and struggling armored figures, a protesting Helen is carried off by two men, away from her white-bearded husband, Menelaus, and toward a boat on the right where the Trojan prince Paris awaits. No single print source has yet been found, but the subject matter and composition of the hanging were surely based on European sources.[4] The Chinese embroider-

14, detail

ers were responsible for many details from the Chinese decorative vocabulary, such as the waves in the background, the phoenixes in the center of the upper border, various details of the armor, the scales of the serpents and tritons in the border, and the lychee fruit seen outlined against the side of the boat (detail).

While most of the hanging is embroidered, the figures' faces and exposed limbs were painted directly on the cotton foundation cloth, probably also in China. Especially in the faces, the modeling of light and shadow for a three-dimensional effect, while naively done, shows an aspect of European-style painting that had reached East Asia with Jesuit missionaries in the sixteenth century. The Italian Jesuit Giovanni Niccolo (or Nicolao, 1563–1626) established an academy of painting in Japan in 1583 to train local artists to produce religious art. When the missionaries' relations with Japanese authorities deteriorated, Niccolo fled Japan, returning to Macau in 1614. Some of his students became active in China, including You Wenhui (baptized Manoel Pereira, 1575–1633), a young Chinese from Macau, and Ni Yicheng (also known as Jacopo Niva, 1579–1635), of Japanese and Chinese parentage. You Wenhui produced the only surviving painted portrait of the Jesuit leader Matteo Ricci (1552–1610).[5] The more highly regarded Ni Yicheng had studied at Niccolo's academy in Japan, and in China he "was in constant demand to paint works . . . both for the mission in China and the Jesuits' church in Macau."[6] Perhaps these artists or less well-documented colleagues were responsible for painting this textile.

Scientific analysis of the hanging's pigments supports this intercultural possibility: results show a blue-green pigment not used in Asia and a white not used in Europe. Furthermore, the white pigment occurs more frequently in Japanese than in Chinese contexts.[7]   JD

1. Campbell et al., *Tapestry in the Renaissance: Art and Magnificence*, p. 19.
2. The two others at the Metropolitan Museum are acc. nos. 50.97.2 and 51.152. Of the hangings in other collections, two are in the Musée des Beaux-Arts, Lyon (see Briend, *Les objets d'art*, pp. 76–77), and one is with Steinitz, Paris (see Courtin and Langeois, *Steinitz*, pp. 34–36). For additional details, see Standen, *European Post-Medieval Tapestries*, vol. 2, pp. 796–802.
3. Ibid., pp. 799, 802 n. 9.
4. Similarity to works of Marcantonio Raimondi was noted in Mailey, "European Sculpture and Decorative Arts: The Abduction of Helen." See also Standen, *European Post-Medieval Tapestries*, vol. 2, p. 799.
5. The painting is preserved in the collection of the Church of the Gesù, Rome. See Levenson et al., *Encompassing the Globe*, pp. 288–89.
6. Bailey, *Art on the Jesuit Missions in Asia and Latin America*, p. 96.
7. Report by Marco Leona, David H. Koch Scientist in Charge of the Department of Scientific Research at the Metropolitan Museum, August 23, 2012.

15. TEXTILE WITH CROWNED DOUBLE-HEADED EAGLES

China, for the Iberian market, second half of the 16th century
Lampas, silk
20 x 22 ½ in. (50.8 x 57.2 cm)
The Metropolitan Museum of Art, New York,
Rogers Fund, 1912 12.55.4

Crowned and splayed double-headed eagles, symbols of the Habsburg dynasty, are woven into this Chinese textile, one of a large group of related examples made for the Portuguese and Spanish market in the last part of the sixteenth century. The group represents an early production for export of complex woven silks that integrate both Iberian and Asian aesthetics and design. In this example, the eagle holds in its talons arrows that pierce a heart-shaped vase. The device of a heart pierced by arrows is associated with the Augustinian religious order, while representations of floral vases were popular motifs in China.

The conflation of pious and secular imagery seen here may be the result of free rein being given to the master weaver commissioned to produce the cloth. Although the pattern, colors, and general layout have a notable European character, a number of details point to an Asian hand in the design. The form of the oddly shaped leaf on the scrolling vines, for example, resembles Chinese floral patterns more than the European acanthus leaves we might expect to find, especially as associated with the grapelike fruit cluster motif that repeats throughout. Additionally, the stylized dark blue flowers are Chinese peonies; they alternate with the eagles, whose extended, erect neck feathers and patterned breasts recall the graphic means sometimes used by Chinese artisans to render the image of a phoenix. It could be that the weaver modified an original source (perhaps a European print) to incorporate these Asian elements within the overall European format.

A related group of silks, possibly from a different workshop, shares some of the design features seen here, including the arrow-holding double-headed eagles amid scrolling vines, although in that group the eagles are contained within narrow vertical panels delineated by leafy borders. Multiple examples of textiles with this design exist; in general, they have the same crimson red (lac dye) ground and are decorated in two colors, blue and yellow. In addition to silk, these fine woven textiles incorporate flat threads of gold leaf on paper, typical of East Asian works.[1] A complete cope (Royal Ontario Museum, Toronto) and a portion of a chasuble (Victoria and Albert Museum, London) made of this fabric confirm that it was used in Christian ecclesiastical vestments.[2] The exact location of production for this group of silks is unknown, but the combination of Iberian and Asian motifs and styles is typical of products exported through Macau, a major center of trade in the sixteenth century.

Although other Macau silks possess similar design elements, the color scheme of this example, with its pattern of green, blue, and yellow, is distinctive. It has been proposed, based on the motif of the arrows piercing the heart, that the fabric was made specifically for Augustinians active in the Philippines, but examples found in Spain, Portugal, and other European centers suggest it may have been part of the larger Iberian trade.   EP and JD

1. There are two examples in the Metropolitan's collection: acc. nos. 34.41.9 (red, blue, and yellow) and 34.41.1 (blue and yellow). The dyes used in this textile were analyzed by Nobuko Shibayama in the Department of Scientific Research, Metropolitan Museum, using High Performance Liquid Chromatography-Photo Diode Array (HPLC-PDA). The red color is lac dye, and the yellow is from the Asian pagoda tree (*Sophora japonica*). See also Digby, "Some Silks Woven under Portuguese Influence in the Far East," pp. 52–63.
2. For the Toronto silk (no. 973.422), see Vollmer, Keall, and Nagai-Berthrong, *Silk Roads, China Ships*, p. 19, and Mayer et al., *Raiment for the Lord's Service*, pp. 154–55. The London example (no. T215-1910) can be seen on the museum's website, http://collections.vam.ac.uk/item/O486944/fragment-unknown/. (Additional examples in the Victoria and Albert Museum include nos. T.217-1910 and T.169-1929.)

16. TEXTILE WITH ELEPHANTS, CROWNED DOUBLE-HEADED EAGLES, AND FLOWERS

China, for the Iberian market, second half of the 16th century
Silk damask
74 1/2 x 29 in. (189.2 x 73.7 cm)
The Metropolitan Museum of Art, New York,
Rogers Fund, 1940 40.27.2

A symbol of exoticism and power, the Asian elephant (identified by its small ears) shares the visual space of this finely patterned silk satin damask with a European double-headed crowned eagle beneath a stylized, oval-shaped lotus.[1] The elephant is shown with multiple tusks, three on one side and one peeking out on the other. As such, the animal seen here likely represents the Buddhist six-tusked elephant described in a fifth-century Chinese translation of a sutra as being resplendent and white and having lotuses, jade maidens, and other symbolic figures at the end of each tusk.[2]

Elephants have a long history in China. Given as tribute to the emperor by local rulers, particularly from neighboring Southeast Asian regions where they were raised, elephants were also presented as diplomatic gifts to important foreign kings. Apart from their use as work animals and army transport, they were sometimes tamed to provide entertainment in times of leisure, beloved by the royal courts. In sixteenth-century Europe, elephants held a similar fascination for royals and commoners alike, and they appear in the works of such artists as Dürer and Raphael. Shipped by boat from Ceylon to Lisbon, elephants were offered as gifts of the Portuguese kings to the courts of Spain, Austria, France, and England. In 1514, Manuel I of Portugal gave a white elephant (the famous "Hanno" known through Raphael's drawings) to Pope Leo X. An elephant given by the court of Lisbon to Philip II of Spain in 1581 was subsequently passed along to Henry IV of France. A year later, Henry, in turn, gave it to Queen Elizabeth of England, a brilliant re-gifting of an asset deemed too expensive to maintain.[3]

Here the combination of Buddhist symbols and Habsburg eagles produces a composite message of a religious and political nature that juxtaposes the two cultures of Asia and Europe. We do not know how this long-preserved length of fabric was originally used, but its delicate quality indicates that it may have been part of a garment or hanging.[4] Woven in China and likely exported through the port of Macau, this textile's blend of Asian and European taste and style was intended for a foreign market that may not have understood the Buddhist elements but nonetheless would have appreciated the fine weaving and exotic designs.   EP and JD

1. The textile is composed of a five-harness satin damask, with a blue warp and yellow weft. The blue color is presumably indigo, while the yellow dye was made from the Asian pagoda tree (*Sophora japonica*). Dye analysis was conducted by Nobuko Shibayama in the Department of Scientific Research, Metropolitan Museum, with High Performance Liquid Chromatography-Photo Diode Array (HPLC-PDA).

2. "The creature is colossal . . . and is whiter than the snows of the Himalayas. At the ends of his six tusks are six bathing tanks, in each of which grow fourteen lotuses. On each open blossom is a 'jade maiden' fairer than the damsels of Paradise, in whose hands are five spontaneously created lutes; each lute is accompanied by 500 other musical instruments, and 500 jewel-colored birds." *Guan Puxian pu sa xing fa jing* (Sutra on the Practice of Visualizing the Bodhisattva Samantabhadra), in Soper, "Literary Evidence for Early Buddhist Art in China," p. 223.

3. See Bedini, *The Pope's Elephant*, Gschwend and Bellet, *The Story of Süleyman*, and Lach, "The Elephant," pp. 152–58.

4. The panel comprises two widths of cloth seamed together: identical patterns that are somewhat mismatched at the join. A fragment of the white selvage with a blue stripe is preserved along the seam in two areas (visible at the back). Digby, "Some Silks Woven under Portuguese Influence in the Far East," pp. 55–56 and n. 11, notes that several Asian damasks from Macau have a white twill selvage with a stripe and that the structure of this selvage is distinct from other silks thought to be from Macau; the elephant silk conforms to the technical features of that group. Since we have little information as to the exact provenance of these textiles, technical features such as these can be important for identifying the potential locale of their production.

17. WOMAN'S WEDDING MANTLE (LLICLLA) WITH INTERLACE AND TOCAPU DESIGN

Peru, late 16th–early 17th century
Tapestry weave, cotton and camelid fiber
50 ½ x 45 ½ in. (128.3 x 115.6 cm)
The Metropolitan Museum of Art, New York,
Rogers Fund, 1908 08.108.10

Prior to the arrival of the Spanish in Peru, traditional attire for women of Inca nobility included a rectangular dress and a shoulder mantle that wrapped around the body and was held in place with silver pins. The mantle, or *lliclla*, was woven with the finest available materials, including silken hairs from the native alpaca, in a unique double-sided tapestry weave referred to as *cumbi*. Such *lliclla* were traditionally decorated with compartmentalized geometric designs called *tocapu*, which conveyed the noble status of the mantle's owner; indeed, the use of *cumbi* and *tocapu* was restricted to the family of the Inca king.[1]

During the colonial era, but particularly immediately after the Conquest, marriages between Spanish administrators and Inca noblewomen (known as *ñustas*) were formed as part of a strategic alliance aimed at legitimizing Spanish occupation of native domains, since land rights in the Andes followed matrilineal descent. As the wives of high-ranking Spanish men, *ñustas* were able to continue to dress in native-style garments; however, instead of the strict geometric aesthetic of the Inca, the designs of their colonial-era *lliclla* and other traditional forms of dress often incorporated elements of the Spanish decorative arts vocabulary.

The tripartite, horizontal orientation of this wedding *lliclla* follows Inca tradition, but the motifs in the two *pampa* (ground sections) above and below the center field contain a Spanish pattern of interlacing lattice, seen in a wide variety of colonial textiles, furniture, and metalwork beginning in the sixteenth century (cat. 18). The broad center band, in contrast, contains somewhat realistic designs of birds, which were traditionally associated with Inca queens (although Inca weavers generally would not have depicted them so literally). While the geometric *tocapu* are certainly of Inca origin, the manner in which they are used here—to outline the four borders as a decorative element—is unique to the colonial era. Thus, although the *tocapu* likely retained their symbolic meaning in this special garment, emphasizing the Inca lineage of the woman who wore it, their juxtaposition with Spanish motifs reflects the complexities of the Andean colonial milieu.[2]   EP

1. For *cumbi*, see Rowe, "Standardization in Inca Tapestry Tunics," pp. 239–64, and Phipps, "Garments and Identity in the Colonial Andes," pp. 16–39.
2. The use of single interlocking joins, the presence of chained warp selvages on the beginning end, and the cut-and-reentered finishing of the upper warp end of the mantle are typical Andean techniques derived from Inca weaving traditions. For a full technical description, see Elena Phipps in Phipps et al., *Colonial Andes*, pp. 204–6, no. 46.

18. VIRGIN OF GUÁPULO

Peru (Cuzco), ca. 1680
Oil on canvas
67 ¼ x 43 ½ in. (170.8 x 110.5 cm)
The Metropolitan Museum of Art, New York,
Gift of Loretta Hines Howard, 1964 64.164.385

Paintings of the Virgin Mary were produced in the Andes beginning in the early sixteenth century, shortly after the introduction of Catholicism to Peru by the conquistador Francisco Pizarro and the arrival of the first wave of Spanish Christians.[1] In the Andes, the Virgin was sometimes conflated with Pachamama, the Earth Mother worshipped prior to the arrival of the Spanish. Devotion to the Virgin, as a result, became an important factor in the conversion of native populations to Christianity.[2] This phenomenon of religious syncretism, in which two forms of belief are combined or analogized, is expressed in this painting through the wide, triangular shape of the Virgin's robes, which can be interpreted as the profile of a mountain, a visual metaphor seen in other colonial representations.

Numerous miracles were attributed to painted and sculpted likenesses of the Virgin, including protection from earthquakes and floods and the healing of the sick. This belief gave rise to a number of advocations of the Virgin—titles that honor specific manifestations of her and the miracles or places where she appeared, such as Our Lady of Cocharcas or the Virgin of Copacabana—and to the confraternities, or local groups, that were devoted to the maintenance of her shrines. Each advocation is generally represented with certain identifiable attributes or garments. The one depicted here, who holds a tasseled rosary and a blooming scepter of roses in one hand and the Christ Child in the other, is the Virgin of Guápulo, whose shrine is located outside Quito, Ecuador. The miracles attributed to the wood statue housed in the shrine—a copy after the famous statue of the Virgin of Guadalupe in Extremadura, Spain[3]—transformed Guápulo into a major, wealthy pilgrimage site, which in turn helped spread the cult of this Virgin throughout the Andes. That this painting is by an artist of the Cuzco school, in Peru, attests to the wide reach of her fame.

Three-dimensional statues associated with miracles were the object of fervent adoration in Andean Christianity and throughout the Hispanic world in general. In this respect, the Metropolitan's painting is a representation not of the Virgin herself but of the statue that resided at the Guápulo sanctuary. The porcelain-like features emphasize the Virgin's essential humanity, but the carved wood base visible below the hem of her garments underscores the fact that the subject of the painting is the statue itself.

The garments in which the Virgin and Child are dressed—matching European-style white silk brocades embellished with rosettes surrounded by ogival fretwork—reflect the Spanish tradition of dressing religious statues in the finest and costliest silks and laces, similar to elaborate ecclesiastical vestments.[4] Flower-covered lacework netting covers the Virgin's Spanish-style coiffure, and both figures have emerald beads, a cross of red coral, and jewel-encrusted gold crowns.[5] In the Andes the style and luxury of these garments would have linked the Virgin to Spanish culture, especially the nobility; that association in turn extended to the dress of the noblewomen of Cuzco, particularly those of Inca descent, who often incorporated designs from European fabrics (notably the interlacing fretwork motif) into their own garments (cat. 17). EP

1. I am grateful to Luís Eduardo Wuffarden and Luisa Elena Alcalá for their comments on this painting. For references to Pizarro's devotion to the Virgin, see Hall, *Mary, Mother and Warrior*. See also Teresa Gisbert in Phipps et al., *Colonial Andes*, pp. 259–61, no. 80.

2. See MacCormack, "From the Sun of the Incas to the Virgin of Copacabana," pp. 30–60.

3. The confraternity in Quito responsible for building the sanctuary commissioned the statue from Diego de Robles, a Spanish sculptor residing in Ecuador in the late sixteenth century (the statue was lost in a fire in 1830). For the Guápulo shrine, see Black and Gravestock, eds., *Early Modern Confraternities in Europe and the Americas*, pp. 206–12. See also Johanna Hecht in Phipps et al., *Colonial Andes*, pp. 261–64, no. 82

4. True to Andean tradition, the scale of the pattern is proportional to the overall size of each garment. See Phipps, "Garments and Identity in the Colonial Andes," pp. 16–39.

5. Certain visual oddities seem to indicate that the painter originally depicted the Christ Child at left and subsequently changed his position. Note, for example, the disjunctive rosary strand and the bows and teardrop pendants at the hem of the Christ Child's garment, which are repeated on the left side of the Virgin's cloak, as well as the awkwardly foreshortened sleeve cuff and hands.

19. ALLEGORICAL HANGING OR COVER

South America (?), third quarter of the 17th century
Cotton, embroidered with silk
9 ft. 4 ¼ in. x 7 ft. 9 ¼ in. (285 x 237 cm)
Alan Kennedy, Westport, New York,
and Junnaa and Thomi Wroblewski, London

The complex, exuberant embroidery that covers the surface of this large hanging includes courting ladies and gentlemen in Spanish dress, depicted from front and back and on foot and horseback; farmers with scythes and shovels; monkeys; centaurs holding a bow and arrow depicting the zodiacal figure Sagittarius; and winged putti. Nude figures swing among the swags of ribbons and tassels filled with fruits and flowers and visited by birds, bees, and butterflies. At the center is an allegorical representation of Africa, one of the Four Continents. She is dressed as a classical Roman

warrior in a short tunic, flowing cape, and laced sandals. On her head is a feathered turban (generally used to depict America in such allegorical contexts), and she holds a lion by a chain (see cat. 102). Alongside the border another vignette depicts a falcon with a bell attached to its leg with the inscription FAMA NOCET (Fame is harmful). This emblem is also found in a treatise on the principles of Christian governance by Diego de Saavedra Fajárdo (1584–1648), *Idea de un príncipe político christiano representada en cien empresas* (first edition, Monaco, 1640), with engravings by Johan Sadeler II, which was part of the social discourse on morality and ethics in the seventeenth century. Flanking the bird are two large lyrical and possibly mythical figures, with flowing short garments, holding bows and arrows; each has a white covering or halo at the back of the hair. Inside the lower border, these same figures flank a unicorn, with another emblem from Saavedra's treatise.[1]

There are three known embroideries that relate to this work: one panel with an inscription at the Musée des Arts Décoratifs, Paris; a large panel that may have been part of a bed or canopy hanging at the Museum of Fine Arts, Boston, embroidered entirely with brilliant cochineal-red silk on undyed cotton (fig. 127); and a long rectangular valance that appears to be part of the set of embroideries to which the Boston example belongs.[2] The workmanship on the Boston hanging and the related valance is more refined than that of the present example, with fine-line Spanish-style scrollwork borders and many highly detailed figures in Spanish dress; at its top, there is a personification of Africa with a short tunic, long cape, laced sandals, and a lion on a chain, much like the one here. Embroidered with the date May 1, 1661, it may have been produced first among these four related works, potentially serving as a model for our polychrome cover. All of these examples are embroidered on the same kind of broken-twill cotton ground cloth, which may be a key to identifying the origin of the group.[3]

The present cover was certainly produced within the sphere of Spanish influence, most likely South America.[4] Little has been published about embroidery made in the colonial Andes; we do know that guild embroiderers were established in workshops by Spanish embroidery masters in colonial Mexico as well as in Peru. Large textiles like this hanging, however, embellished with such particular imagination and creativity, would probably have been produced in convents for important marriages or major celebratory events. Although distinctly a product of the colonial world, this unique work—with its references to period sources from Spanish and Portuguese intellectual and religious circles—defies easy attribution. EP

19

1. Saavedra Fajárdo, "Fama Nocet," in *Idea de vn príncipe político christiano representada en cien empresas*, p. 64.

2. For the piece at the Musée des Arts Décoratifs, see Réal, *Tissus espagnols et portugais*, pl. 40. For the hanging at the Museum of Fine Arts, Boston, a 2006 analysis of the silk embroidery thread identified the red dye as cochineal. The third example has now been acquired by the Museum of Fine Arts, Boston (no. 2012.324).

3. The distinctive type of irregular weave structure of this ground cloth would have been produced on a European-style four-harness treadle loom; such looms were taken to Peru in the mid-sixteenth century by Spanish master weavers who went there to establish workshops. See Phipps, "Cumbi to Tapestry," pp. 72–99.

4. The previous owners, per family history, considered the hanging to be from Peru.

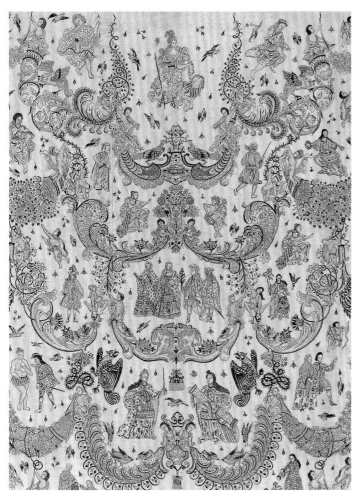

Fig. 127. Bedcover (detail). Probably Peru, 1661. Cotton, embroidered with silk, lace. Museum of Fine Arts, Boston, The Elizabeth Day McCormick Collection (52.1690)

20. TAPESTRY WITH FIGURATIVE SCENES

Peru, 17th century

Tapestry weave, cotton and camelid fiber

89 9/16 x 84 3/4 in. (227.5 x 215.3 cm)

The Metropolitan Museum of Art, New York,

Purchase, Morris Loeb Bequest, 1956 56.163

The varied iconography of this tapestry reflects the wide range of sources and ideas that informed the intellectual framework of colonial Andean society. Woven within its concentric borders and linked together through Renaissance-style scrolling vines and acanthus leaves are scenes from the Old Testament (Adam and Eve) and classical mythology (Leda and the Swan) as well as figures and episodes from popular fables, all part of the rich visual vocabulary of colonial decorative arts. Caryatids holding cornucopias and a king and queen seated beneath a canopied dais grace the corners of the outer border and center field, respectively. Beside the queen is a blue lion and what appears to be a white goat holding a brown elephant. The king is juxtaposed with a blue bull and a stylized shield or coat of arms surmounted by an animal head. Within the main outer border are hunters seeking game, women dressed in flared skirts holding babies or baskets (detail), and men shepherding animals.

The amorphous blue shape at center, which contains winged heads, has been interpreted as a rendition of a Chinese phoenix-and-dragon motif. In the top-left quadrant, three horsemen (possibly the Magi) are depicted wearing European-style garments: a ruffed collar resembling a Spanish *golilla* and a fitted tunic. Two riders are shown in profile, while the third, at center, is depicted frontally and foreshortened, visually linking them together as a group. Above their heads is the enigmatic phrase "Moussom Nessept," one of the few examples of a text associated with an Andean tapestry. Although the precise meaning of the phrase is not understood, "moussom" may derive from the Arabic *mawsim*, referring to trade winds that are favorable for sailing.[1]

The tapestry was made with traditional Andean materials and techniques, from finely spun and expertly dyed native camelid-hair yarns to the opulent cochineal red of the background.[2] The single interlocking joins at color changes and the presence of warp selvages at top and bottom are additional indications of the tapestry's Andean origins.[3] Although native tapestry weavers were sometimes commissioned by Spanish administrators to produce hangings for their homes both in the Andes and back in Spain, this example seems likely to have been made for the household of a mestizo scholar, descended from both Andean and Spanish forebears, who could have appreciated and perhaps requested the stories it tells. EP

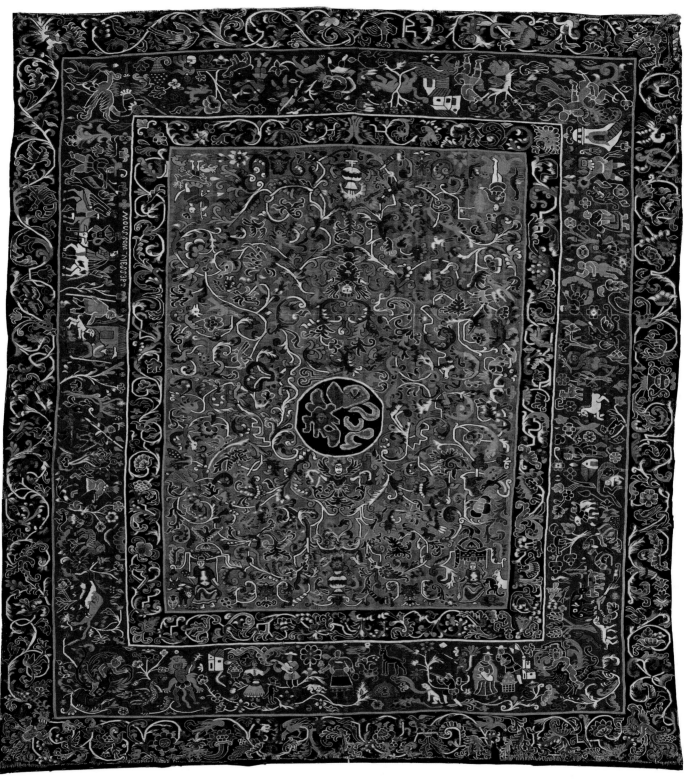

20, detail

1. See Elena Phipps in Phipps et al., *Colonial Andes*, p. 246 n. 2, no. 72.
2. In 2004 Nobuko Shibayama in the Department of Scientific Research, Metropolitan Museum, analyzed the tapestry using High Performance Liquid Chromatography-Photo Diode Array (HPLC-PDA) and determined that the red is cochineal, the blue is indigo, and the yellow is a flavonoid of rutin. See Phipps, Zaharia, and Shibayama, "Conservation and Technical Study of a Colonial Andean Tapestry," pp. 1–6.
3. For a technical description, see Elena Phipps in Phipps et al., *Colonial Andes*, pp. 243–46, no. 72.

21. TAPESTRY WITH CROWN AND ESCUTCHEON

Peru, late 17th–early 18th century

Tapestry weave, cotton and wool

11 ft. 4 ¾ in. x 11 ft. 6 ¾ in. (347.3 x 352.4 cm)

The Art Institute of Chicago,

Major Acquisitions Centennial Fund, 1979.507

During the Inca Empire, nobility and its attendant rights and privileges were signaled by the wearing of special garments. Woven in double-sided tapestry (*cumbi*) and embellished with sets of geometric designs (*tocapu*), such garments could be worn only by those who received them directly from the Inca king (see also cat. 17).[1] The Spanish likewise valued displays of their heritage bestowed upon them by their monarch, which took the form of armorial bearings, or coats of arms. In the colonial period, wall hangings woven in tapestry and decorated with Spanish arms were thus among the earliest works commissioned by Spanish administrators from the Andean master weavers known as *cumbi-camayos*, whose expertise and skill had once been the exclusive prerogative of the Inca king.

As colonial society evolved in the sixteenth and seventeenth centuries, generations of Spaniards living in the region—both Creole (someone of Spanish descent born in Latin America) and mestizo (a person of both Spanish and native parents)—faced an array of complex legal and social issues related to race and heritage. The establishment of bloodlines became a crucial factor in determining inheritance, land ownership, and social rights and privileges; it was also integral to the Spanish administration of the viceroyalties of the Indies, the territories of New Spain (Mexico and Central America), and Peru (including Ecuador, Peru, Bolivia, and Chile). Along with grants to titles, tapestries with armorial bearings numbered among the most important items produced not only for Spanish inhabitants of the colonial realm but also native clients claiming certain privileges within viceregal society.

The arms on this tapestry are characteristically European in design, with a central escutcheon surmounted by a crown and encircled by a laurel wreath filled with roses. The arms, consisting of horizontal brown and white bands, possibly belong to the Ribera, a family whose Spanish ancestors participated in the initial conquest of Peru and who subsequently gained prominence within seventeenth-century Limeño society.[2] The crown surmounting the escutcheon is that of a count, corresponding to the title granted by Charles II of Spain to Nicolás de Ribera on May 28, 1684 (count of Santa Ana de las Torres). The roses, moreover, suggest an association with the Virgin Mary and with the beloved Santa Rosa de Lima, patron saint of the capital city and the first native Peruvian to become a Catholic saint (she was canonized in 1671).[3] The field and borders display a variety of typical Baroque grotesques, from scrolling elements to intertwined figures with winged heads.

Little is known about the workshops that produced such tapestries. Although they were woven with Andean techniques and materials,[4] there is nonetheless a clear European influence in the overall template. We know that sometime after 1748 (and prior to their expulsion in 1767) Jesuits in Chile established an art academy near Santiago and imported Flemish tapestry weavers to oversee production.[5] There is no evidence for the use of full-scale cartoons or models in the Andes, as was the practice in Europe, so while the refined artistic abilities of the Andean weavers generally enabled them to replicate many foreign designs freehand, the complex iconography seen here would likely have required some type of design assistance, perhaps from those Flemish masters.   EP

1. On *tocapu*, see Phipps, "Garments and Identity in the Colonial Andes," pp. 16–39.
2. The attribution of the arms to Nicolás de Ribera came from an unnamed "Spanish authority on heraldry" per Mayer Thurman, "Large Hanging with Crown and Escutcheon," p. 359 n. 11. This was supported by information from scholar Luís Eduardo Wuffarden regarding the association of the Ribera family with the cathedral of Lima (email correspondence between Elena Phipps, Christa Thurman, and Wuffarden, 2006).
3. This observation was made by Wuffarden (email correspondence, 2006). On Santa Rosa, see Mujica et al., *Santa Rosa de Lima y su tiempo*.
4. These include three-ply cotton warp; weaving that progresses from bottom to top, with the design oriented in the same direction as the warp (as opposed to the European tradition, in which weavers construct tapestries sideways); and the use of sectional joins.
5. See Bailey, *Art on the Jesuit Missions in Asia and Latin America*, p. 49 and n. 192.

21

22. ARMORIAL HANGING

Mexico, 1771
Linen, embroidered with cotton and wool
93 1/8 x 90 1/2 in. (235.5 x 229.9 cm)
San Antonio Museum of Art, purchased with funds provided
by the Lillie and Roy Cullen Endowment, 2011.14

Inscription: SOI DEL GEN[ERA]ᴸ D[O]N FER[NAN]ᴰᴼ RUVIN DE
ZELIS PARIENᵀᴱ Y NORIEGA ALCAL [D]E I MAYOR DE LA CIVDAᴰ DE
S[A]ᴺ LVIS POTOSSI SEYZO EN EL ARMADILLᴼ ANNO DE 1771
(I belong to General Don Fernando Ruvin de Zelis Pariente and
Noriega Mayor of the city of San Luis Potossi [*sic*] made [se yeso?]
in Armadillo Year of 1771)

Professional Mexican needleworkers in the eighteenth century were
highly skilled guild artisans trained in part by Spanish masters, who
established in Mexico City and Puebla a European-inspired tradition along the lines of those of Seville and Toledo. These guilds
primarily made delicate and luxurious silk-and-metallic embroideries for ecclesiastical vestments (cat. 68). The style and technique of this armorial hanging, adorned with the arms of the
family of Fernando Ruvin de Zelis (both paternal and maternal
sides), however, represent a different approach.

Here, handspun wool and cotton yarns more often associated
with weaving than with embroidery completely cover the linen
ground cloth in a manner emulating the tapestry-woven armorial
hangings that graced the homes and palaces of the aristocracy in
Spain and in the viceroyalties of Peru and New Spain (cat. 21).
The linen ground cloth, undetectable except from the back, was
imported from Spain—although the cotton and wool embroidery
threads were most certainly local.[1] The long stitches, somewhat
randomly placed, create a variable surface that clearly articulates
the complex design of the quartered coats of arm as well as that
of the inscription, in which each letter is embroidered in a different color. The use of embroidery to create such a large-scale hanging is extraordinary, especially given that the white background
visible throughout the design is also entirely stitched. This type
of embroidery may be associated more closely with a tradition
familiar in the southwestern United States (which was part of
Mexico until 1820) used in the making of *colchas*, or bedcovers.

The embroidered inscription surrounding the central coat of
arms indicates that the hanging was made in 1771 in Armadillo
and "belonged" to Don Fernando Ruvin de Zelis (or Celis), the
mayor of San Luis Potosí. Near the present-day capital of San
Luis Potosí (which is also the name of the state in northeastern
Mexico) is a small municipality called Armadillo de los Infante,
where this piece was produced. In an archival document from

1771 (published in an 1894 history of the Sanctuary of Guadalupe
of San Luis Potosí), Don Fernando, along with eight other members of the *cabildo*, or town council, appealed to the local archbishop to designate the Virgin of Guadalupe as the patron saint
of the town and specifically to extend her protection to the local
mining and waterworks. They promised in exchange to venerate
her image annually "with all the magnificence, pomp and devotion normally committed."[2] Such celebrations no doubt involved
processions of the faithful carrying statues of the Virgin and the
saints from the church through the town. The Spanish tradition
of religious processions, adopted in New Spain and elsewhere
around the world, also included the display of tapestries and various cloth hangings from balconies. It is likely that this hanging
had been made to mark the acceptance of the Virgin as the patron
saint of the town and was perhaps hung from the balcony of the
mayor's home or office.   EP

1. The dyes used to produce the colors—red, blue, purple, yellow, brown, black,
and a peach hue—most likely consisted of cochineal red, indigo blue, and an
unknown yellow. The purple was probably achieved by overdyeing the red with
blue. Some of the browns are deteriorating, perhaps indicating an iron and tannin
dye. The black is in fairly good condition and may have been made from a natural
black wool.
2. Muro, *História del Santuario de Guadalupe de San Luis Potosí*, p. 15.

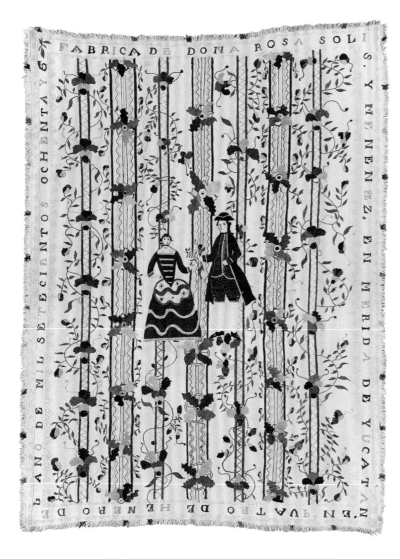

23. WEDDING COVERLET (COLCHA)

Doña Rosa Solís y Menéndez
Mexico (Mérida), 1786
Cotton, embroidered with silk
100 x 73 in. (254 x 185.4 cm)
The Metropolitan Museum of Art, New York,
Purchase, Everfast Fabrics Inc. Gift, 1971 1971.20

Inscription: FABRICA DE DOÑA ROSA SOLIS. Y MENEN[D/E]Z EN
MERIDA DE YUCATAN. EN QUATRO DE HENERO DEL AÑO DE MIL
SETECIENTOS OCHENTA Y 6
(Made by Doña Rosa Solis y Menendez in Mérida, Yucatán, on
four of January of the year one thousand seventeen hundred
eighty-six)

This Mexican embroidered coverlet, or *colcha*, embellished with
bright silk on a textured cotton ground, was likely made to celebrate the wedding of the couple depicted in the center. The vertical floral trellises that run behind and on either side of the couple
identify the event as a garden celebration. The pair's European-
style garments—the man wears a tricorn hat and buttoned waistcoat; the woman, wide skirts and a fitted bodice—reflect their
genteel status. Inscribed with the name of the maker, Doña Rosa
Solís y Menéndez; the date, January 4, 1786; and the location,
Mérida, Yucatán, the coverlet provides information that is often
missing from the records of colonial Latin American textiles,
which were generally made by anonymous artisans.

The texture of the handspun and woven cotton ground cloth
was created with rows of alternating thick and thin yarns.[1] This
monochrome striping effect can be seen in some types of industrially produced cotton textiles fashionable during the eighteenth
century and also derives from earlier Mexican cotton-cloth traditions, such as that of the *lienzos*, genealogical maps and documents of colonial history that were generally drawn by hand on
similarly textured cloth.[2] Locally grown cotton would have been
a suitable lightweight material for a coverlet in the tropical climate of the Yucatán. The region was rich in natural resources,
such as logwood for dyeing and mahogany for cabinetmaking;
both were exported extensively by the Spanish and the English.
It was also the primary point of embarkation for shipping
between Europe and the Americas.

The silk yarns used for the embroidery were brightly dyed in
colors of red (a pinkish shade), yellow, blue, and green.[3] Investigation into the sources of the dyestuffs found that the bright
pink contained carminic acid, indicating the presence of native
cochineal-red insect dye, and that the blue came from indigo
plants.[4] The source of the yellow was identified as weld (*Reseda
luteola*), a plant common in Europe, suggesting that the yellow
yarn had been dyed in Spain. The silk itself was likely a product
of China. Ships known as Manila galleons sailed regularly
between Asia and Mexico, landing on the west coast at Acapulco.
Goods destined for Europe were transported overland to ports on
the eastern shore for shipment along the Atlantic route via the Gulf
of Mexico. Thus the silk for the yellow-dyed yarn may have
traveled the seas from China to Mexico, then to Europe where
it was dyed, and back to Mexico to be embroidered into this
coverlet.   EP

1. The ground cloth of the coverlet is constructed in three selvage-to-selvage panels
stitched together. The manner in which the thicker woven elements were constructed
shows that all three panels were made to be used together. A woven fringe of cotton
and silk has been sewn to the edges.
2. See, for example, the Brooklyn Museum's mid-sixteenth-century *lienzo* from
Ihuitlan, in Fane et al., *Converging Cultures*, pp. 76–77, no. 1.
3. Brown ink is visible in some areas, indicating that the design was modified by
the embroiderer, who did not always follow the drawn pattern precisely.
4. Analyses of pinkish red, blue, and yellow dye samples were conducted in 2004
by Nobuko Shibayama at the Metropolitan Museum.

24. SHAWL (REBOZO)
Mexico, late 18th century
Silk, embroidered with cotton, silk, and metal-wrapped thread
30 ½ x 93 ¾ in. (77.5 x 238.1 cm)
Philadelphia Museum of Art,
Gift of Mrs. George W. Childs Drexel, 1939 1939-1-19

Rebozos, long rectangular shawls worn around the shoulders and sometimes used as head coverings or baby carriers, were readily adapted by Mexican women from Spanish-inspired models. Ubiquitous since the sixteenth century, rebozos continue to be worn in villages throughout Mexico as an integral part of traditional female dress.

In this example, rows of red ikat-dyed arrow or flame motifs woven into the cloth separate horizontal registers on which various scenes related to eighteenth-century Mexican society have been embroidered in silk and silver threads. A knotted silk fringe adorns the ends. A number of shawls embroidered with similar scenes of daily life have been preserved. They coincide with a period of French influence on elite Mexican fashion and culture, ushered in after 1700, when Philip of Anjou, grandson of the French king Louis XIV, ascended to the Spanish throne as Philip V.

Whether these delicate works were made to be worn, displayed, or given as part of a dowry or wedding trousseau is not known.[1] Most include images of courting couples and other figures enjoying leisurely pleasures in parks, amid flowers and fountains, and along idyllic waterways. The exterior scenes here depict Xochimilco, a favorite park where citizens of Mexico City went to drift in their flower-covered boats among the famous ancient "floating gardens," or *chinampa*.

Somewhat unusual are the interior scenes featuring details of furnishings, such as upholstered cabriole-leg chairs and curved-front tables, and servants offering tea. The people depicted in these intimate scenes span the range of Mexican society, from highly fashionable figures (indicated by their European-style dress and hairstyles) to servants in livery (including black men and others of uncertain ethnicity).[2] A Jesuit priest (identified by his distinctive pointed headwear, called a biretta) wearing a black cloak (rendered in a herringbone design) and a long blue silk scarf wafting in the breeze is shown in several scenes—always in the company of a lady. The prominent inclusion on this shawl of the Jesuit figure, a member of the powerful and wealthy Christian order, may indicate that the rebozo was made prior to the expulsion of Jesuits from Spain and the Spanish Americas in 1767. Alternatively, the somewhat flamboyant depiction of this priest—note the largeness of his cloak, his flowing scarf, and the presence of a constant female companion—could suggest a tongue-in-cheek critique of Jesuit behavior in Latin American society.   EP

1. Other similarly embroidered rebozos can be found in the Witte Museum, San Antonio; Museum of International Folk Art, Santa Fe (two examples); Parham Park, West Sussex, England (see Maríta Martínez del Río de Redo in Paz et al., *Mexico: Splendors of Thirty Centuries*, pp. 482–83, no. 235), Winterthur Museum, Delaware (no. 1969.4286); and in collections in Mexico, including the Franz Mayer Museum. See Castelló Yturbide and Martínez del Río de Redo, eds., *Artes de México* 18, no. 142 [*El rebozo*] (1971), pp. 3–96, cover ill., and Castelló Iturbide and Meade, "Rebozos mexicanos en el extranjero/Mexican Rebozos Abroad," pp. 70–71, 88. See also Ventura, "The Ikat Rebozos (Shawls) of Central Mexico," pp. 41–48.
2. The identification of race and social position within the multicultural society of Mexico during this period has been treated by a number of scholars; see Katzew, *Casta Painting*.

25. QUILT

China and Europe, 17th century
Central panel and outer border: China,
for the European market, 17th century
Silk, embroidered with silk and gilt-paper-wrapped thread
Inner border: Europe, second half of the 17th century
Silk damask
50 x 56 in. (127 x 142.2 cm)
The Metropolitan Museum of Art, New York, Rogers Fund
and funds from various donors, 1986 1986.152

The embroidered portions of this cloth were probably once part of a large marriage bedcover made in China for export. Later, the precious bedcover was cut up, and portions were pieced together with a delicate quilted European floral silk to create the panel as it appears today.[1] Its relatively small size indicates that it may have served as a christening or bearing cloth for a child being carried to the baptismal font for christening.[2]

At the very center of the textile are three bands from the original coverlet, one with a roundel containing a scene of a man and a woman flanking a tree, perhaps inspired by traditional depictions of Adam and Eve. The blossoming tree grows from a large container decorated with a continuous pattern of hexagons, a Chinese design suggesting longevity, and on the tree is a bleeding heart pierced with arrows, a secular symbol referring to love and devotion in Renaissance Europe.[3] The dress of the couple is generally consistent with that of late sixteenth- to early seventeenth-century Europe: the woman's unstructured clothing is typical of the early seventeenth century, while the man's hat conforms to late sixteenth-century examples.[4] Their garments are overembroidered with repeating Chinese patterns, as if made to resemble Chinese silk damasks.

The two other adjoining bands at the center of the panel were formerly one. If placed one directly above the other, they form a scene with a pair of ducks in a lotus pond (detail). Although the lotus pond is an enduring theme in Chinese textiles, here the pattern shows a heightened emphasis on flower centers, common in Chinese export textiles, and another type of duck has been substituted for the pair of egrets or mandarin ducks more frequently found in a traditional Chinese image.

Another part of the original coverlet was retained as the embroidered border of the present panel; while its sides were heavily pieced together, the ninety-degree corners were untouched in the piecing process, indicating that it served as a border in the original coverlet as well. The delicate, light peach-colored European textile chosen to surround the exotic portions of the cloth has a floral pattern typical of the last decades of the seventeenth century.[5] The panel is fully lined in a white monochrome woven silk with a small floral pattern on a continuous fretwork background likely woven in China. Cloth of this type, termed *rinzu*, was exported from China to Japan in large quantities during the seventeenth century to be used as the foundation fabric of luxurious dyed and embroidered Japanese kimonos, until the Japanese started producing it themselves in the mid-Edo period, starting in the 1680s.[6] JD

1. Chinese embroidered textiles on white silk were frequently used or reused in elite contexts in Europe. See Cammann and Blomqvist, *Spansk korkåpa av kinesiskt broderi/A Spanish Cope Made from a XVIIth Century Chinese Embroidery.* Cammann associates white grounds with manufacture in Guangzhou.
2. For further discussion of bearing cloths, see Cora Ginsburg LLC, *A Catalogue of Exquisite and Rare Works of Art . . . Winter 2011–2012*, p. 6.
3. Bayer et al., *Art and Love in Renaissance Italy*, p. 62.
4. For similar hats and facial hair in the dress of many of the male figures in a tapestry of 1597–99, see *Surprise Attack on Calais,* in Campbell et al., *Tapestry in the Baroque: Threads of Splendor*, p. 56.
5. See, for example, Metropolitan Museum, acc. nos. 09.50.1196 and 09.50.1581; see also a textile reproduced in Ribeiro, *Fashion and Fiction*, p. 253, fig. 160.
6. Gluckman and Takeda, *When Art Became Fashion*, p. 338. See also Ogasawara, *Some to ori no kanshō kiso chishiki*, pp. 243–44. The lining may be a later addition.

25, detail

26. COVERLET

China, for the European market, 17th century
Silk satin, embroidered with silk and gilt-paper-wrapped thread
84 x 79 in. (213.4 x 200.7 cm)
The Metropolitan Museum of Art, New York,
Rogers Fund, 1975 1975.208d

Embroidered in China with a dragon roundel at its center and four distinctive figures dressed in European garments in the surrounding field, this coverlet reflects the two disparate worlds of East and West and the contradictions that arose from artistic exchange between them. The men wear breeches and doublets, whose style and cut generally conform to late sixteenth- and early seventeenth-century European dress.[1] Yet these Western garments, depicted with detailed embroidery, bear certain characteristic Chinese motifs: one man has a dragon design on his doublet, while another's costume shows a typically Asian auspicious motif of intersecting diamonds within a diagonal lattice. In addition, the men's features—including wispy mustaches and beards—have an Asian character. While the embroiderer may have intended to represent Portuguese gentlemen, there is a certain mixing of imagery and types here that is seen in other decorative arts of the period that depict foreigners, such as the painted Japanese Namban screens showing the "barbarians" arriving in Japan.[2]

The basic design of the coverlet, which at some point was lined in a vibrant clamp resist-dyed silk from India (cat. 27), consists of a central roundel in a field surrounded by one or more borders; although this layout is frequently seen in works made for export, it also appears in domestic Chinese *kang* (daybed) covers.[3] Its imagery—including dragons flanking a flaming jewel, the birds and flowers of the border, and the Chinese-style lions in each corner—is common in Chinese textiles. Some of the details, however, are unusual, or are combined in unexpected ways, suggesting the involvement of a European trader or client unfamiliar with the selection and placement of motifs in Chinese iconography. The jewel between the dragons, for example, is uniformly surrounded by flames, resembling a Western sun more than the characteristic Asian flaming jewel. And the lotus pond at one edge of the border, which would normally be the backdrop for pairs of waterfowl, such as ducks or egrets,[4] instead features large pheasants, more often depicted in a dry, rocky setting. JD and EP

1. Arnold, *Patterns of Fashion*, pp. 69, 86.
2. See Henriques et al., *Portugal and the World*, pp. 354–55.
3. A Chinese textile with a central roundel, created for domestic consumption, is in the Metropolitan Museum (acc. no. 69.246).
4. The lotus pond with waterfowl was an important textile pattern and literary theme at the imperial court during the Yuan period (1271–1368); see Denney, "Mongol Dress," pp. 80–81. The pattern continues in the Ming and Qing dynasties; see Shan, *Zhixiu shuhua*, pp. 89, 246–47.

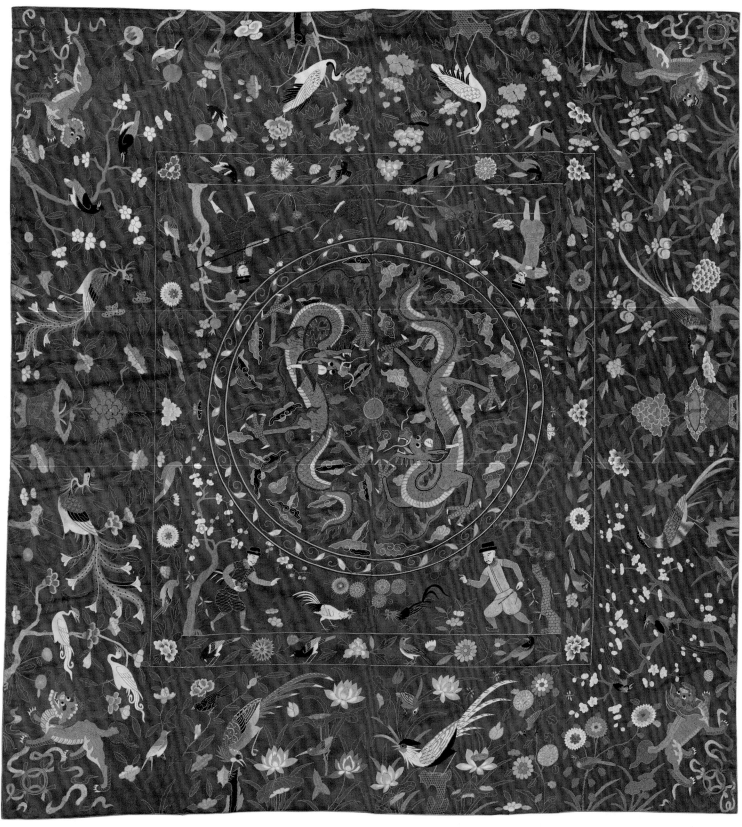

27. PATTERNED SILK

India, 17th century

Silk, clamp resist, dyed

96 x 44 in. (243.8 x 111.8 cm)

The Metropolitan Museum of Art, New York,

Rogers Fund, 1975   1975.208a

Clamp resist-dyeing is an ingenious, complex technique for producing polychrome designs on cloth.[1] Pairs of wood blocks are carved with mirror-image patterns, and the length of cloth to be dyed is folded and placed between the blocks. The blocks are clamped into place, and the whole unit is then immersed in a dyebath. Channels drilled within the wood blocks allow dye to flow into selected areas. (While some authorities believe that the dye is poured directly into these channels, the process actually varies according to the dyestuff being used, as most colors require immersion in a hot dyebath for proper penetration.) Multiple channels, each intended for a specific color, make it possible for several dyes to be applied in sequence, with the openings sealed or unsealed for each hue. In this textile, the white outlines against the red ground, with blue, yellow, and green floral and leaf designs, indicate that three different dyes were used.[2] Those pattern areas that have remained white (the silk's original color) must have been closely clamped by the blocks to physically resist the penetration of the colored liquids: red, yellow, and blue (the green color resulted from overdyeing yellow and blue). Repeating designs are characteristic of textiles created with this technique, and in the pattern here we can see the four-fold symmetry in the distribution of leaves and floral patterns.

Early evidence of this dyeing practice points to an origin in China and Central Asia, and examples have been preserved from as early as the seventh and eighth centuries.[3] Although less is known about the tradition in India, a cache of carved-wood blocks with channels was discovered within the walls of old houses in Ahmedabad, Gujarat.[4] Among them was an apparently mid-seventeenth-century block with a pattern of two men dressed in European clothing, including long baggy pants tied at the ankles, fitted waistcoats with flaring skirts, and feathered caps. Another, nearly identical in design to the Metropolitan's textile, follows the more traditional patterns that are also found in clamp resist-dyed fabric from Afghanistan and Tibet.[5]

This fabric was once used as a lining for the embroidered coverlet embellished with figures attired in Portuguese dress (cat. 26). The two parts—the embroidered coverlet and this dye-patterned lining—were likely produced in different locales. Although the date (and, in fact, the origin) of this clamp-resist textile is not clear, the two pieces were brought together somewhere in Asia.[6]

27, detail

Abrasions and holes in the dyed fabric that appear to predate its function as a backing to the embroidered cover suggest not only that it had a prior use but also that it is older than the embroidered cover, its precious color and pattern recycled for a second life.   EP

1. Extensive research on this dyeing technique and history was conducted by Alfred Bühler. See Bühler and Fischer, *Clamp Resist Dyeing of Fabrics*.

2. The dyes have not been tested. Nobuko Kajitani (personal communication, September 9, 2012) believes the red color is likely to be fresh chay root. The blue is indigo and the yellow could be any of a number of dyes.

3. See Bühler and Fischer, *Clamp Resist Dyeing of Fabrics*, pp. 50, 60–80. Fragments are preserved in the Royal Treasure House in Nara, Japan (see Matsumoto, *Shōsōin-gire*).

4. The blocks themselves were found by Alfred Bühler and published in Bühler and Fischer, *Clamp Resist Dyeing of Fabrics*, pp. 3–6, 8. Mattiebelle Gittinger has observed that the design of this textile is identical to that of a pair of blocks found by Bühler in Gujarat and on this basis concluded that the Metropolitan's example was produced in that region during the eighteenth century; Gittinger, *Master Dyers to the World*, pp. 154–55.

5. See Bühler and Fischer, *Clamp Resist Dyeing of Fabrics*, p. 9, fig. 2, and p. 108, pl. 2.

6. Gittinger, *Master Dyers to the World*, p. 155 n. 8.

28. PANEL WITH FLOWERS, BIRDS, AND ANIMALS

China, for the export market, 17th century
Silk, embroidered with silk and gilt-paper-wrapped thread
100 x 80 in. (254 x 203.2 cm)
The Metropolitan Museum of Art, New York,
Bequest of Catherine D. Wentworth, 1948 48.187.614

This large rectangular textile with Chinese motifs and embroidery techniques is part of an important but little understood group of related works made in China for export.[1] Described by various scholars as hangings, covers, or coverlets, all the textiles in the group share a common layout with a central roundel in a rectangular field, surrounded by multiple borders. This type of composition is often associated with the influence of Portuguese and Spanish models, although there are some earlier Asian examples that employ this format as well.[2]

Wholly Asian in subject and style, however, are the motifs. The pair of phoenixes at the center of the textile encircle a large peony. Similar dynamically posed birds are also seen in an architectural stone relief excavated from the Yuan dynasty (1271–1368) capital and now in the National Museum of China, Beijing, as well as in a corresponding textile in the collection of the Metropolitan Museum,[3] and peonies often figure in Ming rank badges, in which a pair of birds encircle a flower. Within the rectangular field are flowers and four more birds—two golden pheasants and two peacocks, which were used as insignia for the second and third civil ranks in both Ming and Qing China.

The multiple borders surrounding the central field include a wide border embroidered with various animals—rare creatures such as a tiger and elephant in addition to the familiar horse, deer, and goat, all of which are depicted side by side with such distinctively mythical Chinese beasts as a blue *qilin* and a white, single-horned *xiezhi*. A composite animal with hooves and usually a single horn, the *qilin* is mentioned in poetry as early as the Han dynasty (206 B.C.–A.D. 220);[4] its appearance was sometimes said to signal the birth of a sage, and it was used as a rank insignia for nobles. The *xiezhi* also appears in Han dynasty texts; known for its ability to distinguish virtue from evil, it used its sharp teeth and single horn to bite and gore wrongdoers, and it was the insignia for the censorate, which included judges. Here, both animals have flames shooting off their bodies, indicating their supernatural powers.

Embroideries of this type were made for export, and a number have been preserved in Japan and Europe in historical contexts. The oldest documented example is an altar cloth in Saikyōji, a temple in Kyoto; it was donated in 1616.[5] Another example, now in the Museo Diocesano, Chiavari, Italy, was donated to a church in Chiavari in 1651 and used as a baldachin, or canopy, for the clergy.[6] Others are preserved in museum collections.[7]

Chinese textiles and other goods came to the Americas via the Manila galleons' annual trips between Acapulco (and Callao, the port city of Lima) and the Philippines. While to date no preserved embroideries from this group have been found in Mexico or Peru, their influence was present there by the late sixteenth or early seventeenth century,[8] as evident in the similar layout and motifs of a Peruvian tapestry in the collection of the Museum of Fine Arts, Boston (fig. 33).[9]   JD

1. For a survey of textiles in the tradition of this piece, see Yoshida, "Saikyōji ya Honkokuji ni denrai suru kaki chōjū mon'yō shishū," pp. 101–19.
2. Chinese textiles that appear to have been made for the domestic market sometimes include central roundels with a pair of birds or animals and a four-directional layout. See, for example, the tapestry-woven silk textile, likely used as a *kang* cover, in the Metropolitan's collection, acc. no. 69.246.
3. Metropolitan Museum, acc. no. 1988.82.
4. Rawson, *Chinese Ornament*, p. 108.
5. See Yoshida, "Saikyōji ya Honkokuji ni denrai suru kaki chōjū mon'yō shishū," p. 103.
6. Failla, "Cielo di baldacchino processionale," p. 277, no. 156.
7. For a piece in Seville, see Yoshida, "Saikyōji ya Honkokuji ni denrai suru kaki chōjū mon'yō shishū," p. 109; for related pieces in New York, see Metropolitan Museum, acc. nos. 29.100.152–157 and 29.100.544.
8. Elena Phipps in Phipps et al., *Colonial Andes*, p. 250, no. 75.
9. Two other Peruvian tapestries that include East Asian animals are in the Textile Museum, Washington, D.C., and the Victoria and Albert Museum, London. For both, see Elena Phipps in Phipps et al., *Colonial Andes*, pp. 250–54, nos. 75–76.

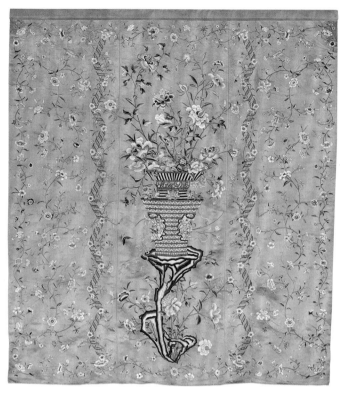

29. DOUBLE-SIDED HANGING
China, for the European market, second half of the 18th century
Silk satin, embroidered with silk
95 ¼ x 87 ¼ in. (241.9 x 221.6 cm)
The Metropolitan Museum of Art, New York,
Purchase, Friends of Asian Art Gifts,
in honor of James C. Y. Watt, 2011   2011.112

This hanging's double-sided foundation cloth is ingeniously woven with a red satin surface on one side and a yellow satin surface on the other, making its sale or trade abroad a violation of Chinese bans on the export of both red and yellow silk, which were reserved for imperial use.[1] Defiance of the color bans was extremely common, as are Chinese export silks of these colors in Western contexts (cat. 121). The violations were built into the Canton trade through systems of bribery and by timing shipments to avoid stringent searches.[2]

Consisting of three panels joined together, the piece's double-sided embroidery depicts a container of flowers resting on a distinctively Chinese garden rock stitched in blue and white, which would have appealed to the taste for the exotic in eighteenth-century Europe.[3] A minute detail of the container is strongly Chinese in flavor: the three rings perched on the rim are symbolic of achieving firsts in the three civil service examinations.[4] Overall, however, it is more productive to compare the vase with

European works in the Chinese style for use in European interiors, such as the vessel in the design of an embroidered fire screen in the Chinese Pavilion on the palace grounds at Drottningholm, Sweden (fig. 128), and, from the same collection, Chinese-style vases with diagonal ornament in inlay on a French *secrétaire*.[5]

The graceful blossoming embroidered vines throughout, as well as the bouquet in the central container, are punctuated by examples of flowers typical of Chinese work for export to Europe. By contrast with Chinese domestic textiles, the rendition of flowers in Chinese export work pays unusual attention to the flowers' centers, which frequently protrude dramatically and contrast sharply in color with their petals. These traits show the influence of Indian export printed and embroidered florals and of demand engendered by the export trade itself.

Theoretically, either side of the hanging could serve as the front, but judging from the contrasting yellow selvages that are visible at the seams of the red side, the

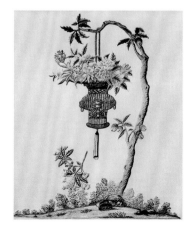

Fig. 128. Embroidered fire screen in the Chinese Pavilion on the palace grounds at Drottningholm, Sweden

front of the piece is the yellow side, which lacks this distraction, and the red side is the back. That does not preclude both sides' being visible; if the hanging was used as a bed curtain,[6] the yellow side would have been for the outside of the bed, the more public view. An example of a bed with Chinese export hangings in which the inside and outside views of the bed curtains are in contrasting colors is the early eighteenth-century state bed at Calke Abbey, Derbyshire, with an extremely dark blue for the outer view and white for the interior.[7]   JD

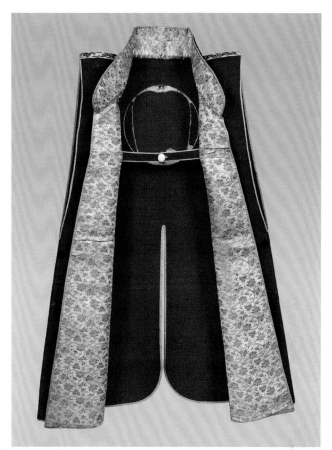

1. The bans were put in place during the reign of the Qianlong emperor (r. 1736–95).
2. See Van Dyke, "Weaver Suckin and the Canton Silk Trade," pp. 109–11, and Van Dyke, *Merchants of Canton and Macao*, p. 10.
3. The blue and white coloration of the rock is standard in eighteenth-century Chinese embroidered textiles. For a particularly close version in the Ashmolean Museum, Oxford, see Vainker, *Chinese Silk*, p. 188, fig. 120.
4. Cora Ginsburg LLC, *A Catalogue of Exquisite and Rare Works of Art . . . Winter 2010–2011*, p. 9.
5. The needlework of the fire screen is attributed to Princess Sophia Albertina of Sweden (1753–1829) and the year 1784. See Setterwall, Fogelmarck, and Gyllensvärd, *The Chinese Pavilion at Drottningholm*, pp. 114–15; the *secrétaire* is also illustrated, pp. 120–21.
6. A larger, faded piece with the same design appeared on the art market in 2004, thus supporting the hypothesis that the present piece was part of a set of bed hangings; Gerard Hawthorn Ltd., *Oriental Works of Art, 7 June–18 June 2004*.
7. Jackson-Stops et al., *The Treasure Houses of Britain*, pp. 442–43. The dark blue and the white of the Calke Abbey bed hangings are two different textiles, not the double-sided foundation cloth of the panel shown here. I am grateful to the staff of Cora Ginsburg LLC, New York, for confirming this information.

30. SURCOAT (JINBAORI)

Japan, probably 18th century
Body and crest: Europe, possibly Netherlands,
17th–18th century; wool
Lapels: probably China, 17th–18th century; lampas, silk
and gilt-paper strips
Shoulder pieces: Europe, 1760s; silk, brocaded with silk
and metal-wrapped thread
Length from shoulder 38 3/16 in. (97 cm)
John C. Weber Collection

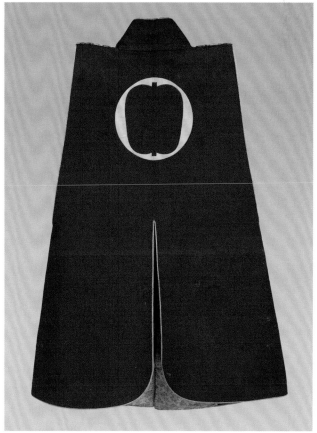

Woolen cloth was Europe's chief textile contribution to the worldwide trade. Wherever they sailed, European merchants (Portuguese, Spanish, Dutch, and English) sold or traded woolen cloth or used it as gifts to local elites. Surcoats (*jinbaori*) like this one, frequently made of European woolen cloth, especially in shades of red, were worn over armor by Japanese samurai.[1] Aside from wool's natural qualities of warmth and protection from the elements, the fabric was considered desirable for *jinbaori* because of its clear status as an import, since sheep were not raised in Japan. The highly prestigious rich scarlet of this example was also unmistakably of foreign origin: European dyeworks achieved the

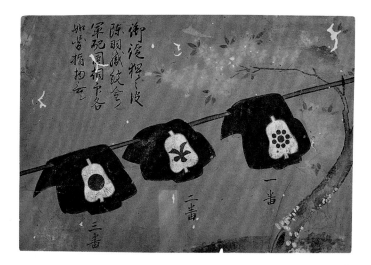

Fig. 129. "Kondō Yūzō kankei shiryō" (Materials related to Kondō Yūzō). Historiographical Institute, University of Tokyo, items 4-69 through 4-78, former number 7640

color through the combination of cochineal dyestuff from Mexico in the Spanish New World and a tin mordant developed in the first half of the seventeenth century by Dutch and British chemists.[2]

Two other imported textiles are included in this *jinbaori*—at the lapels and the shoulders. The white and gold lampas cloth of the lapels is likely to have been imported from China. Its small-scale floral pattern is similar to that of *Kōdaiji-gire*, in the group of textiles known as *meibutsugire* that were related to *chanoyu* (traditionally translated as "tea ceremony") and avidly collected by Japanese tea aficionados.[3] The shoulder pieces, a common feature of late Edo *jinbaori*, appear to be a later addition to the surcoat and are made of a European dress fabric with a floral design in silver metallic thread and silk. This cloth is comparable to a silk in the Metropolitan Museum's collection and to the fabric with a similar pattern (featuring gold instead of silver) on the gown worn by Isabella, Countess of Hertford, in a portrait of 1765.[4]

Demonstrating the continuing importance of imported woolen cloth to the system of samurai dress throughout the Edo period (1615–1868) is the development before the eighteenth century of wool *jinbaori* as the uniform of special groups of guards for the shogun, known as *okachigumi*.[5] The number of groups varied, starting out with only three to five units of about twenty-eight to thirty guards per unit but reaching as many as thirty units in the nineteenth century.[6] Membership in the *okachigumi* was desirable, for it gave men of lower rank and stipend much greater prestige and a pathway to promotion.[7] The identifying crest on the *jinbaori* of all units was a military fan of gilded leather, with an additional motif for each unit set within the fan. A set of illustrations (fig. 129) shows some of these *jinbaori* in scarlet with their golden crests.[8]

Probably coincidentally, the crest on the back of the present *jinbaori* is a military fan, but it is an appliqué of white wool, not of gilded leather. The family is not known.   JD

1. This example has been published in Rousmaniere et al., *Kazari*, no. 28, illus. p. 130. In his text for nos. 25–29 (p. 126), Nagasaki Iwao states that red *rasha* (thick plain-weave wool with a napped surface) was especially favored for the surcoats of wealthy samurai in the seventeenth century. Yuko Fukatsu's study of over one hundred woolen *jinbaori*, mostly from the late Edo period, included forty-seven red examples, almost as many as all the other colors combined; see Fukuoka Fukatsu, "Jinbaori no sozai to gihō ni kansuru kagakuteki bunseki to senshoku shiteki kenkyū," p. 75.
2. Results of dye and mordant analyses of the red wool of this *jinbaori*, performed by Nobuko Shibayama, Department of Scientific Research, Metropolitan Museum, July 27, 2012, and by Federica Pozzi and Federico Carò, July 26, 2012, respectively, indicate that it was colored with cochineal, likely from the Americas, and that a tin-based mordant was applied.
3. *Kōdaiji-gire*, however, is larger in scale, according to *Meibutsugire: Torai orimono e no akogare*, pp. 40–41.
4. Metropolitan Museum silk, acc. no. 33.39.52; for the portrait, painted by Alexander Roslin (Hunterian Museum and Art Gallery, University of Glasgow), see Ribeiro, *The Art of Dress*, p. 60.
5. See Fukuoka Fukatsu, "Jinbaori no sozai to gihō ni kansuru kagakuteki bunseki to senshoku shiteki kenkyū," pp. 14, 19–20 (explanation of illustration R5).
6. See Minami, "Edo bakufu okachigumi no fukusei ni tsuite," pp. 23–29, esp. pp. 23, 27–28. For nineteenth-century illustrations of several *jinbaori* with gold crests for *okachigumi*, see MS 208, Spencer Collection, New York Public Library, vol. 7 of "Shoyaku sashimono cho" (A book of designs showing the official position of samurai).
7. See Minami, "Edo bakufu okachigumi no fukusei ni tsuite," p. 24.
8. This illustration and nine others, showing a total of twenty *jinbaori*, are part of a collection of historical materials called "Kondō Yūzō kankei shiryō" (Materials related to Kondō Yūzō) housed at the Historiographical Institute, University of Tokyo, items 4-69 through 4-78, former number 7640. I am indebted to Professor Shigeo Fujiwara for the references and information he provided.

31. SURCOAT (JINBAORI)

Japan, 17th century
Body: China, for the European market, late 16th–17th century; velvet, cut and voided, silk
Lining: China, late 16th–17th century; silk damask
Lapels: Japan, probably 18th century; lampas, silk and gilt-paper strips
Length 36 ⅝ in. (93 cm)
The Metropolitan Museum of Art, New York, Friends of Asian Art, Purchase, Mr. and Mrs. Andrew Saul Gift, 1998   1998.190

Jinbaori surcoats, worn over armor by Japanese samurai, were frequently made from expensive and flamboyant imported textiles, such as the Chinese silk velvet of this example with its reddish pile pattern on a once-vivid yellow background.[1] The velvet's European-style "pomegranate" design features bilateral symmetry (mirror-imaged along a vertical axis) and a single direction of orientation.[2] Patterns of this type—rare in Japan—frequently appear in European textiles of the sixteenth to seventeenth century,

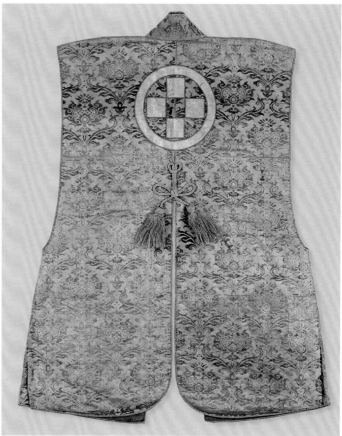

as seen in museum collections, fine European vestments, and portraiture of the elite.[3]

While this European-style velvet would have seemed quite exotic to the Japanese, no observant European would have mistaken it for a Western textile, as many details of the pattern reveal its Chinese origin. For instance, the edges of the main pomegranate motif, variously described as flame-, leaf-, or cloudlike, are commonplace in Chinese art and are long-standing decorative elements in floral patterns of Chinese blue-and-white ceramics and woven silk textiles of the Ming dynasty.[4] Technically, as well, the velvet conforms to the structure of Chinese velvets.[5]

The weaving of velvet in China was first explicitly reported in the West in 1592,[6] but it appears much earlier in Chinese sources. Textual evidence suggests that velvet production probably began at some point during the late Yuan to early Ming periods, between the fourteenth and early fifteenth century, and was completely developed by the mid-sixteenth century.[7] Chinese production of velvets for the European market was fully mature by the second half of the sixteenth century, as seen in a European cape (cat. 32) made of sumptuous Chinese silk velvet with a golden background.

An exquisite damask, also imported into Japan from China, with a floral pattern of tree peonies, orchids, and the auspicious

lingzhi fungus serves as the *jinbaori*'s lining. The damask's pattern, in contrast with that of the velvet, is asymmetrical and features multiple orientations, as is common in East Asian textiles. The two fabrics demonstrate the versatility of China's textile production and the enthusiasm for these products among the Japanese elite.

Like many treasured garments, this *jinbaori* has undergone significant changes. The tassel and family crest on the back are probably eighteenth-century additions, as is the metal button on the front that echoes the pattern of the family crest.[8] Both the trim around the jacket's edges[9] and the lapel cloth—a Japanese woven textile with a gold pattern of plum blossoms, auspicious objects, and hexagonal basketry—were probably also added at that time.   JD

1. This textile was previously published by Yoshida, "Metoroporitan bijutsukan shūzō no chaji sōka mon'yō birōdo jinbaori," pp. 40–49. Another *jinbaori* made from Chinese velvet—with similar technical details and a European-style pattern— is preserved in the Sendai City Museum, Japan. It formerly belonged to Yamaoka Shigenaga (1544–1626), who served the important Date clan, and is thought to have been given him by Tokugawa Ieyasu (1543–1616), the first shogun of the Edo period. See *Bushō no yosooi: Sendai-shi Hakubutsukan kaikan sanjisshūnen kinen*, p. 73.
2. East Asian textile patterns intended for clothing were frequently designed to have a dual orientation, allowing them to appear right side up on both the front and back of garments, which were constructed without a shoulder seam (as was this *jinbaori*).

3. In the Metropolitan Museum, see a possibly Spanish sixteenth-century silk and linen double cloth (acc. no. 36.90.1376). In addition, a variant of the pattern appears in an extravagant silk-and-gold ecclesiastical vestment of the late sixteenth century in the Sagrestia Capitolare del Duomo, Milan. See also the dress in a circa 1586 portrait of the daughter of Philip II of Spain, the infanta Isabella Clara Eugenia, by Alfonso Sánchez Coello (Museo del Prado, Madrid). Both the vestment and the portrait are illustrated in Buss, *Seta oro Incarnadino,* pp. 76–78.

4. For ceramics, see a classic example in the British Museum, London (no. PDF.680), that can be dated by its inscription to 1496. For textiles, see a sutra cover (acc. no. 2011.221.8) in the Metropolitan Museum.

5. The velvet's structure most resembles one diagrammed in Burnham, *Chinese Velvets,* p. 45, fig. 7, except that the present example has cut pile, rather than uncut loops. The foundation weave, also common among Chinese velvets, is a six-end irregular satin.

6. Ibid., pp. 9–16.

7. Yoshida, "Chūgoku ni okeru berubetto no keisei," pp. 35–47.

8. The technique of the metal button is typical of the eighteenth century, according to Morihiro Ogawa of the Arms and Armor Department, Metropolitan Museum. Personal communication, April 10, 2012. On the back of the surcoat, a band across the shoulders that is slightly less faded than the rest of the velvet may signal a previous placement of insignia or crest.

9. The trim around the outside edges contrasts with that around the front fastener, which is probably earlier in date.

32. COMPASS CLOAK

Portugal, second half of the 16th century

Textile: China, 16th century

Velvet, cut and voided, silk, with silk satin lining and metallic trim

Diam. 32 in. (81.3 cm)

The Metropolitan Museum of Art, New York,

Gift of J. Pierpont Morgan, 1906   06.941

Men's cloaks of different styles abounded in sixteenth-century Europe. According to Philip Stubbes's *Anatomie of Abuses* (1583), "They have clokes . . . of dyverse and sundry colors, white, red, tawnie, black, greene, yellowe, russet, purple, violet, and infinite other colors: some of cloth, silk, velvet, taffetie and such like, wherof some be of the Spanish, French and Dutch fashion."[1] This particular style of cape was called a compass cloak because of its circular shape. The term also described the mariner's directional tool that hastened the dissemination of textiles through global trade.[2] The value of such a versatile garment as the cloak was determined by the quality of the textiles and ornament used in its construction; the Metropolitan's example was made from prized cut silk velvet, lined with a rich red silk satin and trimmed with metallic bouclé. Ideal for kinetic display, the circular shape would have revealed dramatic spans of opulent velvet and flashes of the red lining with any sweeping gesture.

Several characteristics identify this velvet as typical of Chinese manufacture: markings on the selvage; the right-handed twist of the thread; and the gold thread made in the Chinese style with gilded paper wound on a core of orange silk.[3] In addition to its

popularity in Europe, such a textile would also have been prized in Japan (see cat. 31 for a discussion of the use of Chinese velvet on a Japanese *jinbaori*).

In the alternating diaper pattern of the cut velvet, the diamond shapes are each made up of four identical pommel-scroll motifs, so called because of their resemblance to the pommel of a Chinese sword. The pommel-scroll motif was a popular one, frequently applied to the kinds of luxury products that were commonly presented as diplomatic gifts, like lacquer boxes and trays.[4] The silk velvet of this compass cloak may well have been such a diplomatic gift that was taken home to Portugal to be made and flaunted in a popular contemporary style.   KS

1. As quoted in Arnold, *Patterns of Fashion,* p. 35.

2. Mott, "Navigation Techniques," in *The Oxford Companion to World Exploration.*

3. Notes from the object file, The Costume Institute, Metropolitan Museum.

4. One such example of the motif, on the lid of a small Chinese lacquer box of the late thirteenth–fourteenth century, is in the Metropolitan Museum, acc. no. 29.100.713.

33. SARASA WITH FIGURES, BIRDS, AND FANTASTIC ANIMALS

India (Coromandel Coast), for the Japanese market,
late 17th–early 18th century
Cotton, painted resist and mordant, dyed
27 ½ x 13 ¾ in. (69.9 x 34.9 cm)
The Metropolitan Museum of Art, New York,
Purchase, Friends of Asian Art Gifts, 2010   2010.56

On this extremely rare example of *sarasa*—Indian painted cotton produced for the Japanese market—the Indian artists responsible created a vision of Oriental fantasy. The hybridity achieved by juxtaposing imagined Oriental figure types, birds, and creatures in a forested and flowering landscape setting is unmatched in this genre of painted textiles. The figures are highly animated in their postures and are of stocky build, with unusually large eyes. They wear short waistcloths, reminiscent of drawn-up *lungi*, and are barefoot; some, more fully robed, ride fantastic beasts. In each repeat of the pattern, two figures carry a palanquin; another, standing near a small temple with a *makara*-spouted fountain, holds an umbrella canopy. Parrots and peacocks with curiously long beaks recur throughout the scene. All the figures are set against a dark ground, a treatment that evokes Chinese lacquer screens of the late seventeenth century, the so-called Coromandel screens in vogue in European stately homes. It is likely that this design was striving to emulate that effect. Its overtly Oriental flavor can be understood to represent an Indian interpretation of this type of chinoiserie—Chinese goods manufactured to reflect a Western spin on a Chinese style produced for European consumption. Here the style was conceived to appeal to Japanese taste.

This textile fragment has no exact matches and few strong analogies in published Japanese collections, the closest being a far less expressive figurative design in the Hikone Castle collection of the Ii family, a design featured in the *Sarasa benran* of 1781.[1] Similarly fantastic animals in landscape appear on a gilded painted cotton preserved in the Kyoto National Museum, though it is more refined and altogether more naturalistic in its approach.[2] And the border of a late seventeenth-century Chinese screen in the Ashmolean Museum, Oxford, is decorated with equally fantastic animals, mushroomlike foliage, and *ruyi*-shaped cloud formations.[3]

The repeat pattern appears to have been applied to the cotton fabric as a block-printed mordant, while variations in coloration make it clear that the resist-dyed and painted highlights were

33, detail

applied by hand. The textile was most likely produced in the southern Indian region of Tamil Nadu, an area linked to the production of narrative cloths, including the export *Ramayana* cloths and a genre of secular Hindu narrative textiles.[4] It is to these traditions that this rare piece of *sarasa* most closely relates.   JG

1. Hikone collection; Ogasawara, *Hikone sarasa*, p. 30, pl. 64.
2. Guy, *Woven Cargoes*, p. 173, fig. 228.
3. I am grateful to Sylvia Houghteling for alerting me to this screen; Ashmolean Museum of Art and Archaeology, Oxford (no. EAX.5331).
4. For an overview of the pictorial cloth, see Shah, *Masters of the Cloth*, no. 18; for related narrative painted textiles, see Guy, "Rama, Rajas and Courtesans: Indian Figurative Textiles in Indonesia," pp. 40–57; and Guy, "A Ruler and His Courtesans Celebrating Vasantotsava," pp. 162–73.

34. SARASA WITH SMALL ROSETTES

India (Coromandel Coast), for the Japanese market,
18th century
Cotton, painted resist and mordant, dyed
86 ⅛ x 13 ¾ in. (218.8 x 34.9 cm)
The Metropolitan Museum of Art, New York,
Purchase, Friends of Asian Art Gifts, 2010 2010.57

The exceptional length of this cloth, more than seven feet, suggests
that it may have served as part of a waistband (*obi*). It retains
one selvage; the other has been cut. Indian *sarasa* was particularly
popular in the Edo period (1615 – 1868) for *obi* and for the lining
of robes (*kosode*). For an untailored length of Indian cloth to
survive in Japan is rare, since most were cut up to make cloth
wrappers for valued objects or as swatches for collectors' sample
books, as witnessed by a fragment of a similar fabric, with red
ground, preserved in a *meibutsugire* album in a private collection
in Kyoto and another exhibited by the Nezu Museum, Tokyo.[1]

This cloth has a repeating pattern of regularly spaced rosettes
and roundels, interspersed with smaller floral elements, on a blue
ground. The design was undoubtedly made in India following supplied Japanese patterns or samples. Such floral roundel motifs
evoke Japanese Buddhist iconography—the lotus and the wheel—
as well as traditional motifs such as the chrysanthemum. The design
appears in the *sarasa* design manuals in vogue in late eighteenth-
century Edo and Kyoto, the *Sarasa benran* (1778 and later editions) and the *Sarasa zufu* (1785). These woodblock-printed
manuals, with the designs annotated with color advice when copying these patterns onto cloth, confirm that all these designs were
in wide circulation in later eighteenth-century Japan. JG

1. Guy, *Woven Cargoes*, p. 172, fig. 225; *Kowatari sarasa to wasarasa*, no. 170-10.

34, detail

35. PALAMPORE

India (Coromandel Coast, probably Pulicat or Nagapattinam),
for the Dutch market, first quarter of the 18th century
Cotton, drawn resist and painted mordant, dyed
112 x 53 ½ in. (284.5 x 136 cm)
The Cleveland Museum of Art, John L. Severance Fund, 2003.43

This Japanese-style chintz produced in India was probably made for the Dutch market, where from the late seventeenth century on there was burgeoning interest in chinoiserie in its various guises. Here the designers have adapted an array of Japanese motifs in a style evocative of Japanese taste, integrating them into a schema judged appealing to Dutch tastes of the early eighteenth century. The desire to emulate Japanese effects is seen in the speckled pattern on the red ground, likely an attempt to copy Japanese resist-dyeing methods, such as the *bingata* technique practiced in Okinawa, Ryukyu Islands.[1] The center field, with its light and bright motifs, is set against a contrasting dark red ground, in the manner of fashionable Coromandel screens. A floral meander border typical of those found on red-ground palampores of the period has been stitched to the edges. This richly detailed border, with finely rendered resist- and reserve-dyeing, is closely related to designs in vogue in the Netherlands in the last quarter of the seventeenth century, and as represented on a number of dated tombstones at the Dutch East India Company (Verenigde Oost-Indische Compagnie, or VOC) cemeteries, most notably at Pulicat, a major center of high-quality chintz production on the southern Coromandel Coast, and a likely source for this textile.[2]

Dominated by red, purple, brown, and green on a saturated red ground, the pattern has three units, repeated at stepped intervals over multiple registers: a pine tree with waterbirds, birds nesting in reeds at a pond, and a rocky outcropping (detail). While the rendering of each is distinctly Japanese in style, the dramatic composition and unexpected use of the diagonal reflect the recent innovations in European design of the so-called bizarre silk style of 1705–10.

Only one other version of this composition has survived; in the collection of a merchant's guild in Kyoto, it was used until recently to decorate the guild's float (*hoko*) at the annual Gion district festival, held every year in July.[3] It also has a palampore-style floral meander border added on all four sides, suggesting that these borders are original; certainly in both instances the colorways are a perfect match. The two cloths may be accepted as contemporary and probably share a common history as products of the VOC, commissioned to test the markets in the Netherlands and, it would seem, Japan. Two related examples are known: they share the motifs of the rocky landscape with pine trees and aquatic birds but follow a composition inspired by Indian carpets, with a central roundel and corner arches. They further differ in having white rather than red grounds and integrated borders that emulate Coromandel screen designs.[4]

As exhibited, this cloth represents half of the original textile, the other half being in the Cooper-Hewitt, National Design Museum, New York;[5] complete, it would have constituted a spectacular hanging, measuring in excess of nine by eight feet.   JG

1. Irwin and Brett, *Origins of Chintz*, p. 105.
2. For a tombstone dated 1684, see Guy, *Woven Cargoes*, pl. 140.
3. Collection Minami-Kannonyama Festival Preservation Society, Kyoto, published in ibid., pl. 232; also Ogasawara, *Sarasa*, pp. 154–55. A Portuguese Jesuit provides the first eyewitness description of the festival in 1561; Guy, *Woven Cargoes*, p. 174.
4. Royal Ontario Museum, Toronto (no. ROM 963.13), published in Irwin and Brett, *Origins of Chintz*, p. 105, no. 90, pl. 86.
5. Published in ibid., p. 103, fig. 53; Beer, *Trade Goods*, pp. 74–77, no. 11.

35, detail

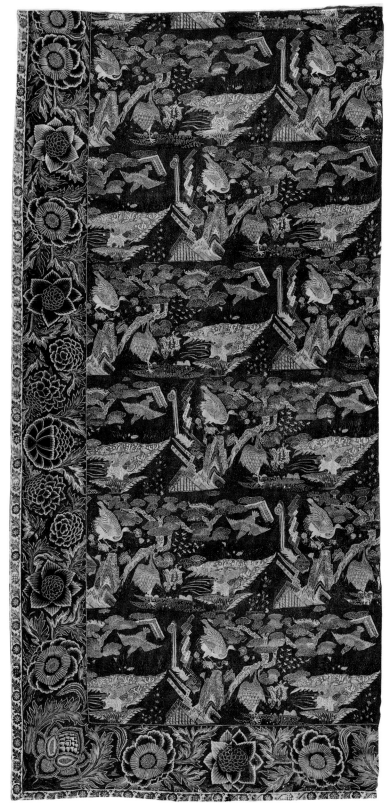

35

Hanging with palampore-style borders, a reconstruction from two halves, now in the Cleveland Museum of Art (cat. 35, left) and the Cooper-Hewitt, National Design Museum, New York (1956-146.1, right)

36. QUILT OR CARPET

India (Coromandel Coast), for the European market,
first quarter of the 18th century
Cotton, drawn and painted resist and mordant, dyed,
overpainted, with silk lining and cotton filling
112 ⅝ x 75 ⁹⁄₁₆ in. (286 x 192 cm)
The Metropolitan Museum of Art, New York,
Purchase, Friends of Asian Art Gifts, 2012 2012.165

Directly modeled on European designs of the early eighteenth century, this rare and important Indian chintz was lined with green Chinese silk and quilted sometime later that century, perhaps in a European enclave in Asia, and subsequently traded to Japan, where it was preserved, it appears, in tea ceremony collections.[1] When tea ceremony first emerged in Japan in the sixteenth century it was closely linked with the ruling martial elite, but by the eighteenth century a second school—*sencha*—had developed that was patronized by middle-class merchants and literati. Indian painted cloth, so-called *kowatari sarasa*, was widely favored specifically for *sencha*-style tea ceremony use. This quilted *sarasa* in all probability served as a tea ceremony carpet (*tutsumigire*), joining such other *sarasa* accoutrements as the tea bowl pouch (*shihuku*) and presentation mats (*fukusa*).

Yet the unequivocally European nature of the chintz design argues for its being produced with the intention of supplying clients in the Netherlands, France, or England. The pattern blends bold and elaborate strapwork and cartouche motifs of French derivation with a resist-painted infill decoration of flowers, leaves, and red berries typical of Indian chintz production of the period. The strapwork and cartouches, here in a vibrant ensemble of red, yellow, blue, and pink on a white ground, can most readily be traced to later seventeenth-century French designers, notably Jean Berain (1638–1711), whose creations are known to have been emulated in chintz,[2] and more immediately to Daniel Marot (1661–1752). This ornate Rococo decorative style was popularized in Holland and England by Marot, who as a French Huguenot immigrant to the Netherlands trained in his native country's fashion was quickly patronized by the Dutch elite, led by Stadtholder William III of Orange.[3] Marot specialized in all manner of interior design, particularly modeled plasterwork, as well as in the creation of formal gardens. His designs became the standard of the day and were widely disseminated through editions of engravings published as early as 1703, ensuring Marot's widespread influence.[4] It is highly probable that the patterns for this painted Indian cotton were adapted from designs by Marot (fig. 130) and that the textile was commissioned by a Dutch East India Company merchant active on the Coromandel Coast in the early eighteenth century. Major centers of the company's activity included Masulipatam and Pulicat, both important ports for the textile trade supplying Europe.

Evidence suggests that this chintz never reached its intended market in Europe. Probably soon after its manufacture, it was made into a quilt. The quilting—executed in an early eighteenth-century Baroque manner similar to that seen on Dutch quilts—incorporates pineapples, cornucopias, and asymmetrical floral motifs. However, if it had been converted into a bed quilt in Europe, it would undoubtedly have remained there. A more likely scenario is that it was tailored in a European household in Asia, probably Batavia (present-day Jakarta), the Dutch East India Company's headquarters for all of its Asian trading operations. Ships regularly linked India and Japan via Batavia, and this quilt may have spent some time in use there before being sent for sale to Japan, where it appears to have assumed a new role as a floor covering for a tea ceremony room.[5]   JG

1. It came from a Kansai-area dealer who purchased it at closed auction, supplied by a dealer specializing in tea ceremony equipment.
2. Brett, "A French Source of Indian Chintz Design," pp. 43–52.
3. William III married Mary Stuart, thereby assuming the English throne in 1688. For information on Daniel Marot, I am indebted to Ebeltje Hartkamp-Jonxis, formerly curator of textiles, Rijksmuseum, Amsterdam.
4. Daniel Marot, *Nouveaux* [sic] *livre d'ornements propres pour faire en broderie et petit point* (Amsterdam, 1703), and *Oeuvres du Sr. D. Marot, architecte de Guillaume III, roy de la Grande Bretagne: Contenant plusieurs, pensées utilles aux architectes, peintres, sculpteurs, orfeures, jardiniers et autres* (Amsterdam, 1712).
5. When purchased at auction in Japan in 2011, the quilt had an outer lining of dark brown cotton intended to protect the silk lining. The cotton lining had largely disintegrated from the corrosive effects of the iron dyes used and was removed by the dealer (personal communication from the vendor, 2012).

Fig. 130. Daniel Marot. Design
for a formal garden. Engraving.
From *Oeuvres du Sr. D. Marot,
architecte de Guillaume III, roy
de la Grande Bretagne. . . .*
Amsterdam, 1712.

37. PALAMPORE

India (Coromandel Coast), for the Sri Lankan market,
first quarter of the 18th century
Cotton, painted resist and mordant, dyed
72 x 44 ⁹/₁₆ in. (183 x 113 cm)
The Metropolitan Museum of Art, New York,
Purchase, Fernando Family Trust Gift, in honor of
Dr. Quintus and Mrs. Wimala Fernando, 2010 2010.337

Palampores were a regular feature of the eighteenth-century chintz
trade to Europe, where they were much favored as bedcoverings,
though as early as 1684 English East India Company records also
described them as appropriate "for covering of Cupboards and
Tables."[1] They were often made in pairs, suggesting that they functioned as curtains or wall hangings as well. Their characteristic
design is that of a large, flowering, and fruit-bearing serpentine
tree emerging from a hillock with stylized peaks or rocks, often
entwined with vines and populated with birds and insects. In addition to those made for the Dutch and English markets, a class of
smaller-format palampores were made expressly for the intra-
Asian trade. This robustly painted version, in shades of red, blue,
and maroon, came from Sri Lanka and is among the finest of a
type formerly known only from Indonesia. The heavy, extravagant floral motifs and dentate foliage identify it with textiles from
the early eighteenth century.[2] Such designs are most closely
associated with fabric made for sale in Europe, and it is likely
that these Asian-market palampores were intended for first use
by the European communities in Batavia and Colombo and by
families of mixed European and Asian descent who wished to
emulate a European lifestyle.

The reduced format of the Asian-market palampore adds
strength to its composition, the oversize, exotic, and sometimes
fanciful blooms bursting forth with an intense energy. The white
ground seen here serves as a dramatic counterpoint to the chromat-
ically rich tree, and the broad red border is enlivened by a complex floral-sprig meander pattern edged in an undulating blue.
A guard stripe at the edge of the center field has a tiny repeating
floral pattern. Individual blooms are rendered in variegated shades,
each representing a separate step in the dyeing process. Such complex painting techniques ensured that these cloths were among the
most beautiful and most expensive of the period. A closely related
palampore, differing only in its floral-infill detailing and in the rendering of the rock formations, came from Sumatra; another, from
Sri Lanka, has more recently been published.[3] These disparate
sources demonstrate the interconnectedness of the Dutch East India
Company's South India–Sri Lanka–Indonesia textile trade. Their
designs, however, reflect an older and more complex intersection
of sources that produced the hybrid blend of Persian, European,
Chinese, and Indian elements seen here.   JG

1. Irwin, "Indian Textile Trade in the Seventeenth Century: I. Western India," p. 29.
2. One such example is in the Victoria and Albert Museum, London (no. IS.182-
1965). See also Musée Historique des Tissus, Lyon (no. 1628), published in Irwin
and Brett, *Origins of Chintz*, p. 69, fig. 30.
3. For Sumatra, see Guy, *Woven Cargoes*, pp. 108–9, no. 143, now TAPI Collection, Surat (no. 99.1949); for Sri Lanka, see Cohen, "The Unusual Textile Trade,"
p. 76, fig. 22.

38. SKIRT CLOTH (TUPPOTIYA)

India (Coromandel Coast), for the Sri Lankan market,
late 18th century
Cotton, painted resist and mordant, dyed
11 ft. 5 in. x 40 ½ in. (348 x 102.9 cm)
The Metropolitan Museum of Art, New York,
Purchase, Fernando Family Trust Gift, in honor of
Dr. Quintus and Mrs. Wimala Fernando, 2010 2010.340

In the second half of the eighteenth century the southern
Coromandel Coast emerged as the premier center for the production of export-grade painted-cotton textiles. A significant
part of this trade was to neighboring Sri Lanka; it clearly
extended beyond the expatriate Tamil communities there and
seems also to have been favored among the Sinhalese elite.
Many of the painted-and-printed cloths in Sri Lanka, the earliest documented of which was worn by King Wimala Dharma
Suriya in 1602 (fig. 15), share design features with examples
recorded in the western Indonesian–Malay trade. The cut edges
at each end of this long cloth indicate that it was manufactured
as one of a repeating pattern. Its hand-painted, mordant- and
resist-dyed center field of exotic flowers on a white ground is a
design more frequently seen in Indian textiles created for the
European market, while its floral end borders edged with serrated
(*tumpal*) projections are typical of Nagapattinam and Saint
Thome cloths produced for the Malay trade. This, then, is a
fine example of the eclecticism of Sri Lankan taste.

The cloth probably served in Sri Lanka as a *tuppotiya*, a long,
rectangular skirt cloth often secured with a sash or belt. Two such
cloths are depicted in a watercolor of 1772 recording the reception of a Sinhalese court delegation from Kandy at the Dutch East
India Company factory in Colombo (fig. 23). One is worn
"drawn short," or secured with a waist sash, by a local person
of rank (second from left) who was likely a Sinhalese employee

of the company, perhaps as a negotiator
with the Kandyian court (detail); the second
is worn fully extended by a female servant
carrying a drink tray. In both instances,
the waist skirt has a floral-repeat ground
and *tumpal* end border displayed at the
front. A closely related cloth is depicted in
a miniature painting, also probably from
Colombo, attributable to the 1770s (fig. 22).
Examples of this design, though rarely with

Fig. 23, detail

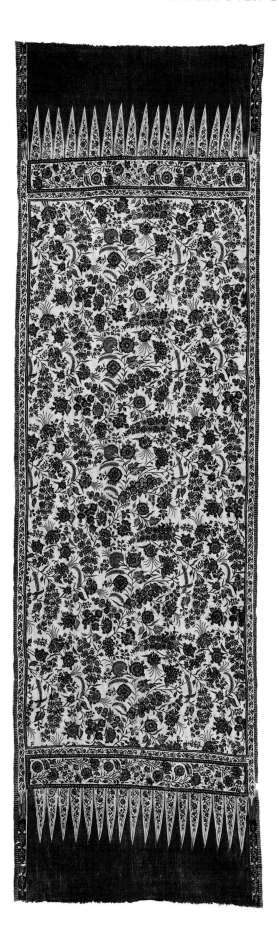

Fig. 131. Caraco and Petticoat. Tailoring: England, ca. 1770–80. Textile: India, Coromandel Coast, ca. 1770. Cotton, painted resist and mordant, dyed. Victoria and Albert Museum, London (T.229&A-1927)

so Europeanized a treatment of the floral sprays, are known from Sumatra, and several are preserved in historical Japanese collections. Variants of these patterns are also illustrated in the Japanese manual of *sarasa* designs, the *Sarasa benran* (1778), confirming their circulation as far as Japan, a legacy no doubt of the Dutch East India Company's Batavia–Japan trade.   JG

39. DRESS FABRIC

India (probably Gujarat), mid- to late 18th century
Cotton, embroidered with silk
41 x 34 in. (104.1 x 86.4 cm)
The Metropolitan Museum of Art, New York,
Rogers Fund, 1970 1970.185.2

Executed in a minute chain stitch, pretty red and blue flowers cover this panel of fabric in a lively, rhythmic pattern. The cloth was probably made in Gujarat, India's main source for embroidery, especially yardage of multicolor work for export to Europe. Fabrics of this style were produced elsewhere in India in dyed cotton, and in China in painted silk, and were most often used to make dresses (fig. 131). The similarity in the designs made in all three textile centers demonstrates a reliance on the same source

patterns, which were sent from Europe for foreign textile producers to work from.

The beauty of this fabric lies in the fact that the embroidered design is executed in such tiny stitches and in such flowing lines as to appear painted. Gujarat supplied embroideries of many styles through the 1800s, but to create the patterns required by changing contemporary women's fashion, embroiderers there gradually changed the methods by which they worked. While all Gujarati embroidery of the sixteenth, seventeenth, and early to mid-eighteenth centuries was done in chain stitch, in the late eighteenth or early nineteenth century embroiderers adopted the satin stitch, as it was better suited to the fine designs they were being asked to make.[1]

An allover floral pattern of this kind was fashionable from the mid- to late eighteenth century; later dresses incorporated panels of embroidery only around cuffs, hems, and on plackets (cat. 76).   MS

1. Crill, *Indian Embroidery,* p. 8.

40. FLOOR COVERING OR HANGING (PHA KIAO)
India (Coromandel Coast), for the Thai market, 18th century
Cotton, painted resist and mordant, dyed
66 ½ x 32 ½ in. (168.9 x 82.5 cm)
The Metropolitan Museum of Art, New York,
Gift of Mrs. Huntington Norton, 1944 44.71.2

High-grade painted-cotton textiles expressly commissioned for the Siamese court constitute a specialized category of the Indian chintz trade. These fabrics are characterized by designs that closely follow Thai aesthetics—densely rendered decorative detail typically arranged in trellislike lattice patterns that repeat across a center field. Repeated here against an overall green field, figures of the Hindu deity Brahma emanate from aubergine-ground cartouches with flame borders set within a trellis pattern composed of heavenly nymphs (*apsaras*) and four-petaled rosettes of the sandal flower. The rosette recurs as part of a border motif, alternating with cartouches containing a mythical elephant-headed lion (*gajasimha*) and set against a red ground with yellow edging. The four even borders of the textile indicate that it was intended for decor, not dress.

Brahma assumed a distinctive place in Thai Buddhist cosmology, and Brahamical ritual was integral to the performance of the duties of kingship in Thai society. The presence of Brahma as the central motif of this cloth confirms that it was commissioned for court use in the early Rattanakosin period, probably during the reign of Rama I (1782–1809) or Rama II (r. 1809–24). In addition to Brahma and the *apsaras* featured here, other Hindu motifs—such as Indra on the seven-headed white elephant Erawan, celestial worshippers (*thepanom*), *kinnari* (half-bird, half-woman beauties who occupy a pleasure realm of Buddhist heaven), the eagle Garuda, and the serpent nagas—served as emblems associated with royal use. Under court sumptuary laws their display was restricted to members of the nobility to whom the king gave them, conferring rank and favor. At the court of Ayutthaya in 1687–88, Simon de La Loubère, the French ambassador to Siam, observed that "pagnes [skirt cloths] of distinct beauty . . . the very fine ones of painted cloth, are permitted only to those to whom the Prince presents them."[1] Dress at the highly regulated Siamese court remained of critical importance as a means of demarcating rank, and the gifting of textiles such as this was a key component of the patronage system.

This *pha kiao* typifies the finest painted-cotton cloths commissioned during the late Ayutthaya–early Bangkok period. It is distinguished by its filigree-like attention to decorative detail, achieved by a series of repeat resist-dyeing processes that build up its polychrome complexity. A mural program attributable to an early eighteenth-century renovation in the ordination hall (*ubosot*) of Wat Yai Suwannaram at Phetchaburi depicts contemporary designs featuring comparable Hindu motifs, and a rare manuscript edition of the Buddhist cosmology treatise *Traiphum*, dated 1776, shows Indra seated on a throne covered with a trellis-patterned textile of this type.[2] The appearance of English United East India Company (UEIC) trading stamps on a number of similar cloths further secures an eighteenth-century dating.[3]   JG

40, detail

1. The La Loubère account was published in 1691; Loubère, *The Kingdom of Siam*, pp. 26–27.
2. Guy, *Woven Cargoes*, pls. 162, 182.
3. Ibid., pls. 177–79, 183.

41. SOLDIER'S JACKET (SU'A SENAKUT)

India (Coromandel Coast), for the Thai market, 18th century
Cotton, drawn resist, painted mordant, dyed
Length 27 ¼ in. (69.2 cm)
Royal Ontario Museum, Toronto, 1983.155.1

This garment is a rare survivor of the type of tunic worn by members of the royal guard to the king of Siam. Here the garment pattern has been carefully painted onto uncut cloth by the Indian dyers so that it could be tailored as required in Thailand. A blue gusset beneath the arms and blue edging on the sleeves allowed for customizing the tailored size as required; only the collar is separately tailored and joined. A Chinese-style cloud collar frames the design, beneath which is the fearful face of a grotesque demon with bulging eyes edged in blue and red, and fangs clasping a decorative band that encircles the entire tunic. The same face is seen in profile on each shoulder, jaws extended wide. This Thai deity, most often titled Kiartimuk, is derived from the Indian planetary deity Rahu, the bringer of eclipses ("seizer of the sun and moon"), fused with Chinese guardian imagery (fig. 132). Such blending of extraneous traditions is characteristic of later Thai art. A complex web of interlocking designs—fish-scale and wicker-basket patterns, perhaps both alluding to forms of rattan armor—infill the remainder of the garment.

That these tunics[1] were intended for the royal guard is clear from a representation of similarly attired soldiers, armed with long, sheathed swords and lances, parading as the escort at a royal funeral. This scene was part of a now-lost suite of murals at Wat Yom, Ayutthaya, painted in 1681 during the reign of Phra Narai, that were recorded in an 1897 manuscript, now preserved in the National Library, Bangkok.[2]   JG

1. Two fragmentary examples are preserved in the National Museum Collection, Bangkok.
2. Guy, *Woven Cargoes*, pl. 190.

Fig. 132. Planetary deity Kiartimuk eating the moon. Painting from a manuscript edition of Thai Buddhist texts, *Pritsana Tham Thai*. National Library, Bangkok

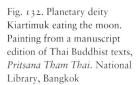

42. PATOLU WITH ELEPHANT DESIGN
India (Gujarat), for the Indonesian market, late 18th century
Silk double-ikat, resist-dyed
43 in. x 15 ft. 2 in. (109.2 x 462.3 cm)
The Metropolitan Museum of Art, New York, Purchase,
Friends of Asian Art Gifts, 2012   2012.164

A silk textile whose design is produced by pre-dyeing the patterns into both the warp and weft threads so that the intended composition is revealed when the two are combined on the loom, the patolu has traditionally been an expensive item of dress in Gujarat, where it is favored for use as a wedding sari and as a ceremonial textile for special occasions. They are characterized by designs of predominantly floral and basket-weave patterns, densely resist-dyed and tightly woven. At some point in the history of their development (records of their production first appear in the later sixteenth century) another class of patolu began to be produced expressly for the Southeast Asian markets. These generally exhibit a less dense—hence less expensive—ikat patterning and a looser weave structure, suggesting that they were produced for a less discriminating clientele.[1]

The design of this large silk cloth is devoted to two pairs of confronting elephants, each animal decked out with a howdah in which a crowned dignitary rides accompanied by an attendant holding a fly whisk and a driver (mahout) with a goad. Standard-bearers,

42, detail

soldiers with lances, and soldiers on horses and camels accompany the royal parade. Large palanquin blankets, elaborately decorated in patolu-related motifs, adorn the elephants. Such patterns are well documented in southern India, as witnessed in an early seventeenth-century mural painting (fig. 19).[2] The presence of tigers suggests that a royal hunt is in progress. It is a majestic textile, the design well suited to serving as a prestige item for display rather than for dress. The paired-elephant motif reflects the association of elephants with martial power, widely held in eastern Indonesia, where tusks were imported as a status symbol by clan leaders.

Silk does not stand up to the rigors of a tropical environment as well as heavier-gauge cotton does, and few patola appear to date before the later eighteenth century. The majority of known examples, such as those in Javanese *kraton* (palace) collections, typically date to the nineteenth or early twentieth century. Popular among these is a variant design depicting elephants and tigers that is closely associated with court use in Java. A small number of elephant-design patola have been recovered from the eastern islands of Indonesia, where they played an important role in the Dutch effort to secure trading privileges in the Maluku spice trade. Dutch East India Company records from the seventeenth century and later make it clear that patola were restricted in their distribution, limited to use as high-prestige gifts to local rulers. Dutch colonial-period collections confirm this, recording the islands of eastern Indonesia as the principal source, where they were preserved in the clan houses of island communities. The most prestigious of all the patola, and arguably among the earliest, is the double-elephant design seen here.   JG

1. Bühler, "Patola Influences in Southeast Asia," pp. 4–46; Bühler and Fischer, *The Patola of Gujarat.*
2. For evidence of patola in interregional trade within India, see Guy, "Cloth for the Gods: The Patola Trade to Kerala," pp. 27–37.

43. LENGTH OF BIZARRE SILK

France or Italy, 1700–1710
Silk satin, brocaded, silk and metal-wrapped thread
97 x 43 in. (246.4 x 109.2 cm)
The Metropolitan Museum of Art, New York,
Rogers Fund, 1964 64.35.1

The term "bizarre silk" was popularized with the publication of Vilhelm Slomann's *Bizarre Designs in Silks* (1953). Slomann's theory that these woven silks were designed, and in some cases produced, in India was quickly refuted, but the term has stuck.[1] The precise origin for this distinctive style of silk produced in Europe between about 1690 and 1720 has not been established; a number of cultures clearly contributed to the creation of these patterns. Certain relationships have been drawn: for example, an integration of Japanese design concepts such as the abstraction of motifs and a discrepancy of scale has been suggested as a primary influence.[2] In the panel shown here, the influence of Ottoman sixteenth- and seventeenth-century design is apparent in the meandering pattern and the layering of motifs, as well as in their large scale (fig. 133). Like many European bizarre silks, the motifs in this panel have become so stylized that they defy identification.

The high quality of this particular example and others of the type suggests that these textiles were made in well-established European weaving centers, such as Lyon or Tours in France, in Venice, or in other Italian or Spanish textile-producing cities. A small number of them have been associated with the Spitalfields weaving center (now in the East End of London) on the basis of the extant design drawings by several early eighteenth-century English designers.[3] The Dutch are known to have had a significant silk-weaving industry as well (cat. 65), and some Dutch examples of bizarre silk from the early eighteenth century have been identified.[4]

There are few complete garments surviving from the turn of the eighteenth century, but a rare unaltered bizarre silk mantua is at the Metropolitan Museum.[5] Mantuas of this period were relatively unstructured women's gowns that took most of their shape from draping and pinning on the body. The expanse of fabric from the shoulder to the train created an ideal showcase for such luxurious textiles with large patterns. Very few bizarre silks seem to have been used for interior decoration, though vegetal motifs similar to those seen on the dress silks found their way to embroidered furnishings (cat. 84). MW

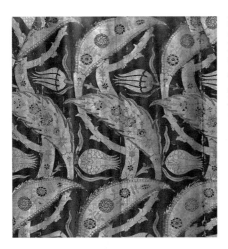

Fig. 133. Detail of the textile of a child's caftan. Ottoman Empire (Turkey), third quarter of the 16th century. Silk and metal-wrapped thread *kemha* weave. The Textile Museum, Washington, D.C. (OC1 68A)

1. Slomann, *Bizarre Designs in Silks,* pp. vii–ix. See also the *Burlington Magazine* review, rebuttal, and response in Irwin, Review of *Bizarre Designs in Silks,* pp. 153–54, and Slomann and Irwin, "Letter: *Bizarre Designs in Silks,*" pp. 322, 324–25.

For the largest single collection of these silks to be published recently, see Ackermann et al., *Seidengewebe des 18. Jahrhunderts.* A panel of the same design as catalogue number 43 is in the Museum of Fine Arts, Boston (no. 1977.179).
2. See Miller, "Europe Looks East," pp. 155–73, 211–24.
3. For a discussion of these rare early silk designs and the English industry, particularly the work of James Leman, see Natalie Rothstein, *Silk Designs of the Eighteenth Century,* esp. pp. 37–40, 65–78.
4. See Colenbrander and Browne, "Indiennes: *Chinoiserie* Silks Woven in Amsterdam," pp. 131–33, figs. 70–72.
5. Mantua and matching petticoat, British (French textile), ca. 1708; silk, metal thread (acc. no. 1991.6.1a,b). See Majer, "Costume Institute; Mantua and Petticoat," p. 54.

44A. LENGTH OF COTTON

India (Coromandel Coast), 1710–50
Cotton, painted resist and mordant, dyed
12 ft. 9 in. x 46 in. (388.6 x 116.8 cm)
The Metropolitan Museum of Art, New York,
Purchase, Rogers Fund, and Gerald G. Stiebel and
Werwaiss Family Charitable Trust Gifts, 2005 2005.166

44B. LENGTH OF SILK

China, 1710–20
Silk satin, brocaded, gilt- and silvered-paper-wrapped thread
41 x 21 ¾ in. (104.1 x 55.2 cm)
Museum of Fine Arts, Boston,
Helen and Alice Colburn Fund, 2009.4628

In the eighteenth century European silk designs spawned imitations and interpretations in India and China. These two examples, an Indian chintz and a Chinese woven silk, are among a relatively small group of Eastern textiles that were based on European bizarre silks of the early eighteenth century (for other examples of European-style silks woven in China, see cat. 62 and fig. 91).

As a group, bizarre silks present a mélange of motifs from around the globe. The two textiles shown here allude to designs that depict fantastic flora together with a striped or columnar background—elements that appeared in European silks periodically from the late seventeenth century to about 1720. Early English silk design drawings in the Victoria and Albert Museum, London, provide dated examples of such motifs, not only the juxtaposition of stripes and highly stylized plant forms, but also the integration of architectural fragments or features into the design, as seen in this Chinese silk.[1]

Indian chintzes and Chinese silks were firmly established in western European dress and furnishing fashion vocabulary by the early eighteenth century. Fine Indian chintzes with precisely drawn patterns based on European silk designs were clearly intended for consumers in the West (cat. 47B), but variations were also made for markets in the East (fig. 20). A chintz in the TAPI Collection, Surat, made for the Dutch Indonesian or Sri Lankan market, is extraordinary for its imitation of a damask background.[2] Generally, the painted cottons made for Eastern markets are characterized by a more limited palette and looser style of drawing than those intended specifically for export to western Europe. However, catalogue number 44A, like a Dutch *wentke* and a chasuble made of chintz (cats. 49, 70), seems to occupy a middle ground between the cottons known to have been intended for Europeans and the cottons firmly associated with the Eastern market. Like the TAPI Collection example, this length of Indian chintz may have been produced for the Dutch traders in Indonesia; equally, it could have found its way to western Europe.

The Chinese silk was probably meant for export to the West and is therefore dated to the period when this style of silk was made in Europe. Not only is it of a European-style design, it is also the same width as most European dress silks of the eighteenth century, unlike many other Chinese export silks, which were of a wider loom width (see cat. 121). A European monochrome damask of a very similar pattern is in the collection of the Abegg-Stiftung, Riggisberg, Switzerland.[3] It is possible that this type of silk was made in a conscious attempt to fool European customs officials or consumers, or both, in the wake of bans on the importation of Asian silk fabrics that were passed in England and France at the turn of the eighteenth century.   MW

1. One example in the Victoria and Albert Museum is a design by James Leman, dated 1711 (no. E.1861:32-1991; see Rothstein, *Silk Designs of the Eighteenth Century,* pl. 31 [VS26] and p. 105), and another is a design by Joseph Dandridge, dated 1719 (no. E.4452-1909).
2. See Barnes, Cohen, and Crill, *Trade, Temple and Court,* pp. 82–83.
3. See Ackermann et al., *Seidengewebe des 18. Jahrhunderts,* pp. 235–36, no. 126, called English or Italian.

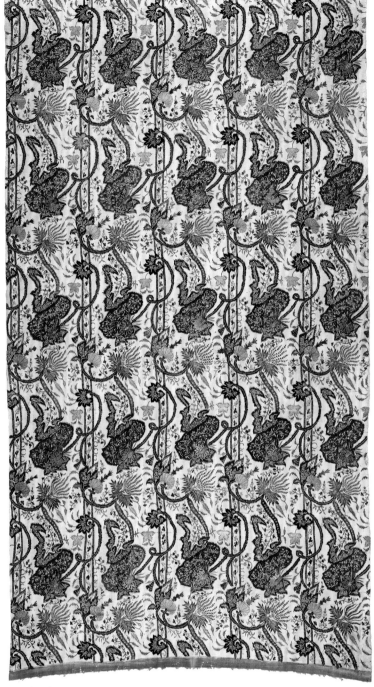

44A, detail

44B

45. DRESS (ROBE À LA FRANÇAISE)

France, ca. 1770
Textile: China, for the European market, 1710–20
Silk damask
Length 60 in. (152.4 cm)
The Metropolitan Museum of Art, New York,
Costume Institute Benefit Fund, 1999 1999.41a,b

During the first quarter of the eighteenth century, a vogue for silks woven with wild, abstract shapes in large repeats swept through Europe. Named "bizarre" by twentieth-century textile historians, these striking but short-lived silk designs mark the intersection of the Baroque and Rococo periods (cat. 43).[1] As emphatically as they developed, the strange and luxurious silks disappeared into a century-long taste for naturalistic imagery that incorporated identifiable botanical and architectural forms evolving in subject and delicacy.[2]

Until bizarre textile designs by European artists like James Leman (1688–1745) were discovered, the regional attribution of the bizarre style was hotly debated.[3] The design vocabulary of the style, with its ragged shapes and swooping lines, led to its attribution by some early scholars to Indian weavers.[4] Most surviving examples of bizarre silk, heavily brocaded with glittering metallic or polychrome silk threads, are now known to have been woven on European drawlooms.

The white damask of this *robe à la française*, however, bears characteristics of Chinese manufacture, including a soft hand, a loom width of more than twenty-eight inches, and an orange-striped selvage. By the early eighteenth century, Chinese silk weavers deftly manufactured designs that suited the tastes of the Western market.[5] The resulting imagery frequently blended Western and Eastern design motifs in a fantastic amalgamation, which, like all bizarre silks, bore little resemblance to the traditional aesthetics of either culture. In this silk the design comes full circle through the Chinese execution of a European design that was originally influenced by Chinese, Indian, and Persian decorative-arts motifs.

This damask was woven in the 1710s, when bizarre silks were briefly popular. It probably survived uncut in a European household into the 1770s because of the lasting monetary and aesthetic value of imported Chinese silk. Then it was made into a highly fashionable *robe à la française* adorned with elbow-length sleeves trimmed with tiered self-fabric ruffles, back pleats that fall from the neckline and are controlled at the waist, and a hip-enhancing pannier understructure. While the polychromatic brocades most typically associated with bizarre silks would have been rejected as gauche by a fashionable 1770s consumer, this shimmering

monochrome damask satisfied both the passing Rococo prefer-ence for delicately rendered chinoiserie and the burgeoning Neoclassical taste for white.   KS

1. Slomann, *Bizarre Designs in Silks*, pp. 5, 7.
2. Rothstein, *Silk Designs of the Eighteenth Century*, p. 37.
3. Thornton, *Baroque and Rococo Silks*, pp. 95–101.
4. Slomann, *Bizarre Designs in Silks*, pp. 26–34.
5. Martin, "Europe 1700–1900; Open Robe and Petticoat," p. 35.

46. BANYAN PANEL

India (Coromandel Coast), for the European market,
mid-18th century
Cotton, drawn and painted resist and mordant, dyed
53 ⅞ x 39 ½ in. (136.7 x 100.3 cm)
The Metropolitan Museum of Art, New York,
Gift of Mrs. William Sloane Coffin, 1975   1975.212.1

This Indian chintz was almost certainly part of a man's banyan (or morning gown), as a complete banyan with a nearly identical chintz pattern exists in France. It has been suggested that this banyan was made for the Dutch market, perhaps owing to its purple-speckled background pattern, which would be unusual in a textile intended for the French.[1] Indian painted cottons with dark backgrounds are generally assumed to have been made for export to the Netherlands. The English stated a preference for white backgrounds as early as the 1640s.[2] Another piece of Indian chintz with a similarly speckled background is in the Rijksmuseum, Amsterdam. Part of a group that came from the collection of a Frisian family, it is marked with the Dutch East India Company stamp and is dated to the early 1780s.[3] The present example is probably earlier in date—the symmetrical composition, mean-dering vine, and larger flowers all correspond to European silk designs of 1740–60. The pattern offers a charming combination of the fantasy flora associated with Indian chintz painters and flowers drawn in a more naturalistic European style, such as the pairs of variegated tulips in the center of the panel.

While chintz yardage and coordinating borders were pro-duced for garments (cat. 51A) and furnishings, the border design on the bottom edge of this chintz was painted on the same piece of cotton, creating a trim integral to the rest of the banyan. Several other banyans in the Rijksmuseum are made of chintz with the same type of borders. These fabrics may have been inspired by the practice of European women who adapted furnishing chintzes (palampores or hangings) for use in garments in the later seven-teenth century. According to one observer in 1719, "the ladies converted their Carpets and quilts into Gowns and Petticoats and made broad and uncouth Bordures of the former serve instead of the rich Laces and Embroideries they were used to wear."[4]   MW

1. See Jacqué and Nicolas, *Féerie indienne*, pp. 158–59, for a banyan in the Musée de l'Impression sur Étoffes, Mulhouse (no. 993.7.17), dated ca. 1750.
2. See Irwin, "Origins of the 'Oriental Style' in English Decorative Art," p. 109.
3. See Hartkamp-Jonxis, *Sitsen uit India/Indian Chintzes*, p. 64, no. 26.
4. [Defoe], *A Brief State of the Question*, p. 11, quoted in Irwin and Brett, *Origins of Chintz*, p. 33, and Hartkamp-Jonxis, *Sitsen uit India/Indian Chintzes*, p. 78.

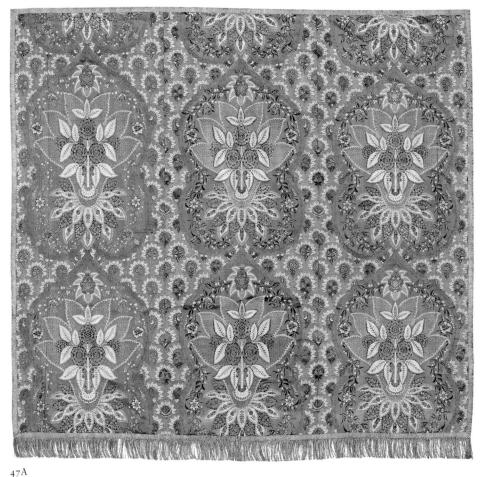

47A

47B

47A. PANEL OF LACE-PATTERNED SILK
France, 1720s
Lampas, silk and metal thread
58 ¾ x 62 in. (149.2 x 157.5 cm)
The Metropolitan Museum of Art, New York,
Gift of Alan L. Wolfe, 1961   61.80.2

47B. PANEL OF CHINTZ
India (Coromandel Coast), for the European market,
second quarter of the 18th century
Cotton, drawn and painted resist and mordant, dyed, with
applied gold leaf
26 x 19 in. (66 x 48.3 cm)
The Metropolitan Museum of Art, New York,
Gift of The United Piece Dye Works, 1936   36.90.121

In *Le dessinateur, pour les fabriques d'etoffes d'or, d'argent et de soie,* a manual for the silk designer published in 1765, one of the textile terms included is *persienne*. It is described as a weave structure with characteristics that correspond to those of many so-called lace-pattern silks of the 1720s. The principal feature of this fabric was, according to the author, Antoine Nicolas Joubert de l'Hiberderie, the juxtaposition of two contrasting foundation weaves—a dark or boldly colored satin weave and a white plain weave—that were augmented by brocading in additional colors of silk and possibly one or more metallic threads.[1] It is unclear in *Le dessinateur* whether persienne was a purely technical term or whether it also described a style. In addition to the technical definition given in the 1765 publication, evidence that persienne referred to a style as well as a structure is provided by labels inscribed on the drawings of such designs dating between 1723 and 1730.[2]

The serrated leaves and rather stiff drawing of the flowers on the present silk piece reflect both Ottoman and Indo-Persian floral designs. In its weave, the silk adheres to the technical definition of a persienne, while suggesting a debt to the art and architecture of the Islamic world in its use of the mihrab-shaped compartments that frame the central plant motif. So, while this distinctive type of silk, made in the weaving centers of France, England, and the Netherlands, is now referred to as "lace patterned" owing to its lacy ribbonlike motifs, the eighteenth-century term might serve just as well.

This type of vibrantly colored floral silk was used in both men's and women's fashions, including a number of men's banyans. That this textile was a product of European looms did not diminish the exotic properties that made it appropriate for leisure wear, just as the so-called bizarre silks were in earlier decades (cat. 43).

These European silks also spawned Indian chintz designs that were created both for the European market, like the panel shown here (cat. 47B), and for sale closer to the Indian subcontinent, such as the long cloth made for the Indonesian market (cat. 48). The subdued monochrome palette of this chintz may have meant that it was intended for mourning wear, the colors of which gradually shifted from black to increasingly lighter shades of blue and the eventual addition of red during the period of observance.[3] European fashions in silk design changed rapidly, so it is probably safe to assume that any chintzes made to imitate popular Western patterns were produced fairly quickly so as not to be outdated before they arrived in Europe. However, these patterns might have had a longer life span in markets in the East. MW

1. See Leclercq, "From Threads to Pattern Composition, Technique, and Aesthetics," pp. 139–54, 211–24.
2. Ibid., p. 139 n. 2.
3. See Gittinger, *Master Dyers to the World*, pp. 176–77, and fig. 150, a mourning *wentke* in blue and black in the Fries Museum, Leeuwarden, Netherlands (no. 1957-400). See also Hartkamp-Jonxis, *Sitsen uit India/Indian Chintzes*, pp. 84–85, a mourning *wentke* in blue with silver accents; and Crill, *Chintz: Indian Textiles for the West*, p. 103, no. 55, a *wentke* in black on white, also for mourning.

48. LONG CLOTH

India (Coromandel Coast), for the Indonesian market, ca. 1720s
Cotton, painted mordant, dyed
9 ft. 11 ¾ in. x 41 ½ in. (304.2 x 105.4 cm)
The Metropolitan Museum of Art, New York,
Purchase, Friends of Asian Art Gifts,
in honor of James C. Y. Watt,
2011 2011.44

Produced in the southern region of the Coromandel Coast, this painted cotton was modeled on lace-patterned woven silks in vogue in Europe, especially in France and England, in the early eighteenth century. Applied by brush, two different hues of madder-red dye were used to create a two-color effect. The design consists of a symmetrical repeat of an extravagant flowering form, associated with the pineapple plant, issuing from a vase. The presence of dentate acanthus leaves seems to derive from a misunderstanding of the nature of the pineapple plant, which has broad, sharp leaves projecting from beneath the fruit; here, these are

Fig. 134. *Ananas*. Engraving. Published by Johan Nieuhof, Amsterdam, 1665

depicted as the more familiar Neoclassical acanthus leaf. Other elements of the design consist of sprigs of flowers and hanging creepers, which are wedded into a complex composition of exotic plant forms.

Both selvages are complete. The textile was made as a long cloth, with the painted pattern repeated at regular intervals; the cut edges are untailored. The prototype is readily identified in Lyon (cat. 47A) and Spitalfields (London) silks of about 1700 and is related to the bizarre silks of the period in its adventurous uses of unfamiliar shapes, though it is dominated by an unrelenting frontal symmetry, unlike the bizarre style, which favors asymmetry and the use of the diagonal (cat. 43).[1] The exotic pineapple plant attracted the attention of seventeenth-century European students of Asian botany, such as the Polish Jesuit Michael Boym and the Dutch traveler Johan Nieuhof, whose *Flora Sinensis* (1656) and *Het Gezantschap der Neerlandtsche Oost-Indische Compagnie* (an account of the Dutch East India Company in China, 1665), respectively, provided early and realistic renderings (fig. 134).[2] This motif was quickly absorbed into the emerging chinoiserie style of early eighteenth-century Europe.

On the reverse of one cut end of this cloth is a maker's inscription in Telugu script, painted in mordant. Telugu, the language of the southern Indian state of Andhra Pradesh, was widely used on painted textiles both in its home territories and in the neighboring state of Tamil Nadu. Many Telugu-speaking *kalamkari* cloth painters migrated there following the shift of the textile industry's commercial center to the southern Coromandel Coast, as the English gradually displaced the Dutch as the premier textile traders in the course of the eighteenth century. This process began with the loss of Pulicat, the Dutch company headquarters on the Coromandel Coast, in 1690 and culminated with the surrender of Nagapattinam in 1784.

This long cloth is a rare survivor of a European-inspired textile produced as a somewhat rustic version of the parent design, intended for use in Indonesia. Both European and mixed-descent clients would have enjoyed such "fashionable" items. That a few examples have survived from rural settings in Indonesia—Sumatra and Sulawesi are likely sources—indicates that they also found their way into the collections of local rulers. The wealthy courts of Ternate and Tidore, the epicenters of the Maluku Islands clove trade, are two further candidates (fig. 14).[3] Because such cloths were assigned heirloom status (*pustaka*) and their use reserved for clan ceremonials only, they have survived well the rigors of a tropical environment.   JG

1. Rothstein, *Silk Designs of the Eighteenth Century in . . . the Victoria and Albert Museum*, p. 37.
2. Chang, "The Pineapple Images by Michael Boym," pp. 79–140; I am grateful to Mei Rado for alerting me to this reference.
3. A closely related example, also from Indonesia, is published in Guy, *Woven Cargoes*, pl. 134; a more refined and later version is preserved in the Tokugawa family collection, Nagoya, and published in *Sarasa no sekai ten*, no. 69.

49. COAT (WENTKE)

Netherlands, mid-18th century
Textile: India (Coromandel Coast), 1725–50
Cotton, drawn and painted resist and mordant, dyed
Length 52 3/8 in. (133 cm)
The Metropolitan Museum of Art, New York,
Purchase, Isabel Shults Fund, 2012   2012.561

A lightweight open coat worn by women in Hindeloopen, in the northern Dutch region of Friesland, from the seventeenth into the nineteenth century, the *wentke* was a garment reserved for special occasions and holidays.[1] Beginning in the mid-eighteenth century they were usually made of Indian chintz, often with quite bold patterns. Contrary to the mainstream practice of confining chintz to informal or private occasions, regional practice in Friesland elevated the exotic fabric to a more formal status. Edged with a coordinating Dutch-woven trimming of linen and wool at the neckline, front opening, and sleeves, and then topstitched to emphasize the seam lines, this coat would have been part of a colorful ensemble that often included other Indian cotton textiles in checked patterns (fig. 135).[2]

This brilliantly hued chintz retains some of its glazed finish, which is rare. However, chintz garments were plentiful and valuable enough to warrant the existence of professionals who specialized in laundering them: the *Amsterdamsche Courant* printed advertisements during the mid-eighteenth century for services that included reglazing the cotton and even touching up faded colors.[3] This style of chintz, with diaper-pattern and ribbonlike motifs

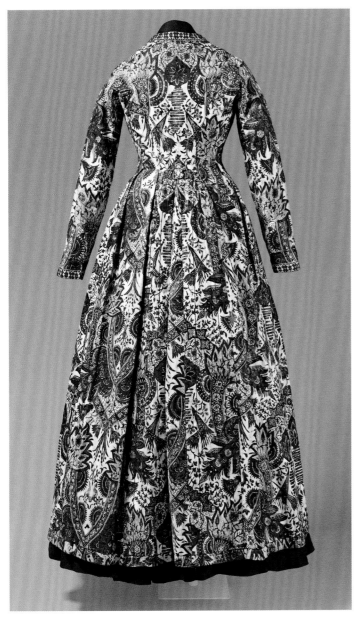

taken from European lace-patterned woven silks (cat. 47A), has survived in the largest numbers in garments associated with the Dutch market.

The chintz of this *wentke* is similar to one used in a chasuble in the Metropolitan Museum's collection (cat. 70), yet the dense design has been rearranged in both cases to form a new pattern. On the chasuble, one portion of the pattern appears on the back (the most visible side of the chasuble during the mass), while the remainder is displayed on the front. The careful rearrangement of the *wentke* chintz has rendered the fabric's original design all but illegible, creating a new sense of symmetry balanced with liveliness.   MW

1. Hartkamp-Jonxis, *Sitsen uit India/Indian Chintzes*, p. 84.
2. This woven tape was used here and on other chintz garments made for Hindeloopen and Marken; see Krohn and Miller, eds., *Dutch New York between East and West*, pp. 272–73, for two children's garments that use a similar woven tape; see also the *wentke* in Hartkamp-Jonxis, *Sitsen uit India/Indian Chintzes*, p. 84, and a red and white example in the Fries Museum, Leeuwarden, in Gorguet Ballesteros et al., *Modes en miroir*, pp. 174, 225, no. 161; the red and white combination was apparently typical for brides, see Arnolli, *Mode in Friesland*, p. 33.
3. Hartkamp-Jonxis, *Sitsen uit India/Indian Chintzes*, p. 33 and n. 1.

50. JACKET (CARACO)

Netherlands, second half of the 18th century
Textile: India, second half of the 18th century
Cotton, printed and painted resist and mordant, dyed
Length 26 in. (66 cm)
The Metropolitan Museum of Art, New York,
Purchase, Gifts from various donors, 2000 2000.251

A short, jacket-style bodice, the caraco began as a working-class garment, typically worn over a woman's short petticoat. Like the printed cottons that moved from domestic spaces into public ones, however, a version of the caraco was soon adopted as fashionable day wear. An illustration of a caraco-wearing "newly chic cook in Paris" appeared in the *Galerie des Modes* in 1778,[1] demonstrating the late eighteenth-century leisure class's interest in appropriating elements of popular dress in their pursuit of the emerging vogue for the simple life promoted by Rousseau and Locke. The fashion publication's intended audience was more likely the cook's employer than her peers.

The basic silhouette of this jacket echoes the long, uninterrupted seams of the *wentke*, a full-length cotton gown of Indian chintz (cat. 49). Here the seam placement of the *wentke* is applied to the Continental caraco style with fitted elbow-length sleeves, deep décolletage, and a full peplum, all hallmarks of 1770s French fashion. In the late eighteenth century the rise of illustrated publications like *Galerie des Modes* encouraged the dispersal of styles set by French fashion leaders. This caraco demonstrates the spread-

Fig. 135. Colored engraving depicting an unmarried woman from Hindeloopen. J. Grabner, *Brieven over de vereenigde Nederlanden* (Letters on the United Netherlands), Haarlem, 1792

ing taste for printed and painted cotton into the fashionable world addressed by these publications.[2]

Through clever merchandising by the Dutch East India Company, a taste for large-scale floral cotton prints was cultivated in the West.[3] Indian painted cottons were valued for the brilliance of their vivid colorfast dyes. European manufacturers quickly adapted to the vogue for flat layers of vibrant color, incorporating the successful motifs of woven designs into bright printed cottons. Naturalistic depictions of blooming and budding roses on thorny stems such as the ones seen here were popular in French silk-brocade meanders in the mid-eighteenth century. A European origin and an approximate date for the rose motif of this fabric have been confirmed by the exciting discovery of a nearly identical cotton print cut from the bolt with the name of the French maker and the date, 1766, marked visibly on the selvage (fig. 136).

Painted cottons remained popular in the Dutch market long after the decline of the Dutch monopoly of the textile trade in Asia. The cotton used in this example was probably painted in India for the Dutch market following the same design used for the French print. The lasting value of the textile may explain the resourceful construction of this example. Godets hidden in the seams of this caraco both accommodate the hips and hide the economical piecing of small scraps of the rose print. Larger pieces are used in the body of the garment to display the print to its best advantage.   KS

1. Blum, ed., *Eighteenth-Century French Fashion Plates*, p. 5.
2. Ribeiro, *Dress in Eighteenth-Century Europe*, pp. 85, 232.
3. Berg, *Luxury and Pleasure in Eighteenth-Century Britain*, p. 71.

50

Fig. 136. Cotton floral print. J. R. Wetter. France (Orange), 1765–75. The Metropolitan Museum of Art, New York, Gift of William Sloane Coffin, 1926 (26.265.50)

51A. MAN'S MORNING GOWN (BANYAN)
France, 1770–90
Textile: India, mid-18th century
Cotton, printed and painted resist and mordant, dyed,
with applied gold leaf, silk lining
The Cleveland Museum of Art, Gift of The Textile Arts Club,
1936.443

In the eighteenth century the term *banyan* was alternately applied
to any Gujarati Hindu trader from western India, to any practic-
ing Hindu from western India, and, eventually, to the loose-fitting,
long-sleeved overgarment associated with that population.[1]

51B. WAISTCOAT
France, 1770–90
Textile: India, mid-18th century
Cotton, printed and painted resist and mordant, dyed,
with applied gold leaf, silk lining
The Metropolitan Museum of Art, New York,
Rogers Fund, 1935 35.142

Edward Long referred to the banyan in his 1774 *History of
Jamaica* as "the dress of the mandarins at the courts of China and
Japan, of the nobility and gentry at Indostan and Persia" and
recommended it as a "luxuriously delightful" sartorial alternative

51B

to the "tyranny" of customary European attire in hot climates.[2] Long's attribution of the banyan to four separate Eastern nations relieved it of any regional specificity.

Produced in India for the French market, the palampore-inspired print of this banyan and matching waistcoat blends an ordered midcentury French meander with the fanciful foliate forms traditionally associated with Indian artistry. The labor-intensive gilding and application of painted and printed flowers elevate a modest cotton tabby to an exotic luxury fabric, perfectly suited for the attitude of refined negligence demanded of a *déshabillé* (or "undress") garment like this, intended for private encounters. The glittering gold leaf, meant to make a brilliant impression in candlelit interiors, was a popular effect often achieved in more formal garments through the woven or embroidered application of metal threads and ornaments. Here it serves not only to highlight the floral details but also to provide a vermicular ground pattern filling the interstitial space of the border. Gold leaf was usually fixed to Indian cottons by an aqueous gum that was painted, in this case very generously, on to the chintz.

The earliest banyans were kimono-like: voluminous and simply constructed along the straight lines of uncut cloth (cat. 98).

By the mid-eighteenth century a second style had developed that followed the cut of contemporary men's coats, with a tighter fit and set-in sleeves. More formal than the kimono-shaped banyan, this style was frequently worn with a matching waistcoat. The banyan shown here typifies a third style. A hybrid of the others, it is cut in one piece with the straight lines of the kimono, but is slim, with very narrow sleeves. It has been reunited with a matching waistcoat whose shorter length and low pocket placement help date the ensemble to the mid-1770s through the 1780s. These three informal menswear styles were alternately referred to as "banyans," "nightgowns," "morning gowns," and "India gowns."[3] The interchangeable application of these terms and the debate surrounding the qualities that distinguish each continue, a consequence of the European attitudes toward exoticism exemplified by Edward Long's early imprecision.[4]   KS

1. Swain, "Nightgown into Dressing Gown," p. 12.
2. Long, *The History of Jamaica*, p. 521.
3. Swain, "Nightgown into Dressing Gown," p. 10.
4. Cunningham, "Eighteenth Century Nightgowns," p. 2.

52. PALAMPORE

India (probably Coromandel Coast), for the European market,
ca. 1750
Cotton, painted resist and mordant, dyed
12 ft. 4 ½ in. x 8 ft. 10 ¾ in. (377.2 x 271.2 cm)
Winterthur Museum, Delaware,
Gift of Henry Francis du Pont, 1957.1290

Of the myriad types of Indian export textiles to arrive in Europe during the late seventeenth and eighteenth centuries, perhaps the most spectacular were the painted and dyed cotton bedcovers and hangings called palampores. The name derives from a Hindi word, *palang-pos*, meaning bedspread or coverlet.[1] These extraordinarily large cotton panels with their vividly colored, lifesize flowering trees must have amazed Europeans at first sight; many, like the present example, were made from a single piece of woven cotton fabric. Sometimes palampores and chintz quilts were made as pairs or sets, coordinating with floral chintz yardage that was also bought in large quantities to create ensembles of furniture covers, wall hangings, and curtains.[2] A rare example of such an ensemble survived in France at the Château Borély, Marseille, until the early twentieth century (fig. 137).

Although Tree of Life palampores would eventually appear throughout Europe and in the American colonies (cat. 118), they seem to have developed in part as a response to specific instructions from English clients. As early as 1643 English East India

Company (EIC) correspondence recorded a preference for white backgrounds and compositions that placed "the flowers and branch . . . in the middle of the quilt."[3] In 1669 a new English trend for "printing large branches for [the] Hanging of Romes [rooms]" was mentioned in EIC letters, where it was also noted that "we do believe . . . some of our Callicoes painted after that manner might vent [sell] well."[4] These detailed descriptions very likely refer to prototypes of the Tree of Life palampore we recognize today, though none of these mid-seventeenth-century hangings have survived. The documented intervention of the EIC, as well as a careful study of other potential sources of design from China, Persia, India, and England, led to the conclusion that "the flowering tree is neither an ancient inheritance nor wholly oriental, but the hybrid product of particular cultural cross-influences which prevailed under particular trading conditions in the seventeenth and eighteenth centuries."[5]

This superb example from the Winterthur Museum is notable for the quality of the painting.[6] The number of colors and refinement of detail, like the patterned petals of the large flower heads, are exceptional. Interestingly, the painter has reduced the tree itself to two slender, intertwined branches, wisely choosing to emphasize the lush blossoms over the tree trunks, avoiding a composition that can look heavy and ungainly. Similarly detailed flowers also appear on palampores generally dated to the first half of the eighteenth century.[7] The refinement of the composition and the presence of bouquets at each corner suggest a date closer to the middle of the 1700s. A set of chintz bed hangings made about 1774 for the English actor David Garrick and his wife Eva has similar bouquets tied with ribbons in each corner.[8] However, the larger flowers and more colorful palette indicate that the Winterthur palampore is significantly earlier in date. MW

1. Although the term is derived from a word for a bedcover, the Tree of Life compositions eventually found their way onto walls and were also used as curtains.
2. Irwin and Brett, *Origins of Chintz*, pp. 26–27.
3. Ibid., p. 18 n. 10.
4. Ibid., p. 18.
5. Ibid., p. 16.
6. According to Winterthur archives, John Irwin of the Victoria and Albert Museum, London, saw photographs of the palampore in 1984; he commented on its quality and suggested a date between 1690 and 1720, a date now thought to be too early. I am grateful to Rosemary Crill and Linda Eaton for their comments about the dating of this palampore.
7. See, for example, Crill, *Chintz: Indian Textiles for the West*, pp. 28, 38, 39, no. 6; Hartkamp-Jonxis, *Sitsen uit India/Indian Chintzes*, pp. 24–25 (no. BK-Br-327).
8. See Victoria and Albert Museum, London (no. 18-1906).

Fig. 137. Bedroom in Château Borély, Marseille. From G. P. Baker, *Calico Painting and Printing in the East Indies in the* XVIIth *and* XVIIIth *Centuries*, London: Edward Arnold, 1921

53. BEDCOVER

George Ormerod (active by 1719–died 1754)
England (Wallington, Surrey), dated 1752
Cotton, block printed and painted
105 x 99 in. (266.7 x 251.5 cm)
Philadelphia Museum of Art, Gift of A. S. W. Rosenbach
and Philip H. Rosenbach, 1951   1951-93-1

Inscription: TO JOHN VANDERMERSCH, ESQR. EAST-INDIA MERCHANT OF LONDON, AND TO REBECCA HIS VIRTUOUS SPOUSE, THIS IS DEDICATED BY THEIR MOST HUMBLE AND OBEDIENT SERVANT GEORGE ORMEROD, SENR. OF WALLINGTON, SURREY. ANNO DOMINI 1752.
ON VIRTUE. THE COMPANION OF ARTS AND MOTHER OF FAME NO CLOUD WHATS'EVER CAN / OBSCURE HER LIGHT. VIRTUE'S A GLOW-WORM, AND / WILL SHINE BY NIGHT.[1]

This bedcover is the earliest example of English calico printing that can be attributed to a specific manufacturer.[2] George Ormerod's masterpiece, it was produced using the block-printing technique in 1752, the same year that Mary Delany wrote of the discovery of colorfast copperplate printing on linen by Francis Nixon near Dublin.[3] The level of detail and the application of multiple colors belie the notion that European printed fabric designs were relatively crude before the use of copperplates. During the first half of the eighteenth century Ormerod ran a successful calico printing establishment, where he employed a number of apprentices and owned a full complement of the required equipment for textile printing.[4] He must have been a prominent member of this growing sector of the British textile industry: as early as 1719 he was a key participant in the petition against the proposed, and eventually successful, ban on printing cotton in Britain for domestic consumption, passed in 1719/20.[5] The area around Wallington, then in county Surrey, southeast of London, became a center of the new printing industry owing to its access to water for power and processing and its proximity to the fashionable consumer market in London, as well as local exporters.[6]

Ormerod's design for the present work is clearly modeled on the Indian armorial palampores being imported into Europe at the time through the various East India companies (fig. 78). The individual motifs are a combination of the classical and the exotic, including a Chinese or Mongol archer who appears in the border and the central field and may derive from Joachim Bouvet's *L'estat présent de la Chine en figures* of 1697. A prominent French Jesuit, and part of a group sent to China by Louis XIV, Bouvet (1656–1730) produced several volumes of writing and illustrations based on his travels.

In light of the debate regarding the consumption of printed cotton in England, it is perhaps ironic that Ormerod's tour de force of block printing not only imitates the painted-and-dyed textiles of India but also is dedicated to an English East India Company (EIC) merchant and his wife. John Vandermersch, a

Dutch emigrant, is known to have worked for the EIC during the years 1748–52. Perhaps this palampore was made or commissioned to mark his retirement from the company; the family coat of arms is repeated in the composition no fewer than thirteen times (detail). At least one other armorial textile was produced by Ormerod, in 1751, and dedicated to one Lord Edward Stanley, apparently Ormerod's landlord.[7] The production of two printed bedcovers of such ambition, dedicated to illustrious citizens, surely represents Ormerod's attempt to prove that English calico printers could produce large-scale, complex compositions on a par with the best of the products imported from India.   MW

1. "On Virtue" appears to be paraphrased from *Humane Prudence; or, The Art by Which a Man May Raise Himself and Fortune to Grandeur,* by William de Britaine; see the 6th edition published in London in 1693, p. 90. This volume was dedicated to Sir Edward Hungerford (1632–1711), a politician and merchant.
2. My thanks to Dilys Blum and the staff of the Costume and Textiles Department of the Philadelphia Museum of Art for generously sharing their research on this work.
3. Little, "Cotton Printing in Ireland in the Eighteenth Century," p. 15 n. 2, quotes a 1752 letter from Mrs. Delany to her sister: "Burke made me go with her to *Drumcondra,* half a mile off, to see a new manufactory that is set up there of printed linens done by copperplates, they are excessively pretty."
4. Maxted, *Exeter Working Papers in Book History,* http://bookhistory.blogspot.com/ (accessed April 10, 2012).
5. See Clayton and Oakes, "Early Calico Printers around London," pp. 135–39, for information on Ormerod's career and the early history of printing in this area.
6. Other towns in the vicinity include Merton, where William Morris set up the Merton Abbey textile printing works in 1881, with access to the river Wandle, the name he gave to one of his most famous patterns.
7. The present whereabouts of this piece is unknown, but a photograph of it is preserved in the files of the Philadelphia Museum of Art.

54. BEDCOVER
John D. Hewson (1745–1821)
Philadelphia, 1780–1800
Cotton, block printed and painted
106 ¼ x 103 ¼ in. (269.9 x 262.3 cm)
Winterthur Museum, Delaware, Museum Purchase, 1963.0048

Inscription (in ink): F.M.

When famed Philadelphia textile printer John Hewson wrote his Last Will and Testament on May 2, 1820, he very carefully divided up his possessions among his nine children.[1] His son John was bequeathed all the equipment necessary to carry on the printing business, while his married daughters were given furniture and household items, including a few very special textiles. Among the textiles were an "India Chintz bed quilt," an "India bedspread," and "One full Chintz bed spread of my own printing." This last piece, which descended through Hewson's family, is now in the Philadelphia Museum of Art and is almost identical to the work illustrated here.[2]

53, detail

54

Hewson clearly valued Indian palampores, since he specifically lists two in his will.[3] Although this bedspread is derived from such Indian prototypes, it is not inspired by the more familiar central flowering Tree of Life palampores (cat. 37). Instead, it imitates a type with a smaller central motif, sometimes a coat of arms, a vase, or a cornucopia of flowers (fig. 138). This style of palampore, from the southern region of the Coromandel Coast, is believed to have been influenced by the designs of both Persian and Indian knotted carpets, in which the field motifs emanate from inward-facing cartouches at each of the four corners, and the entire central area is surrounded by a wide floral border. In addition to the overall layout, the symmetrically branched flowers and exotic bird-on-tree motifs can be associated with Persian and northern Indian textile traditions as well.[4]

Palampores were imported into Philadelphia in large numbers after 1784, when the first American ships began to trade directly with India.[5] An advertisement that Hewson ran in 1790 seems to imply that he planned to compete with these Indian products, perhaps by selling bedspreads like the present example: "A favourable opportunity now presents itself for carrying on the Business

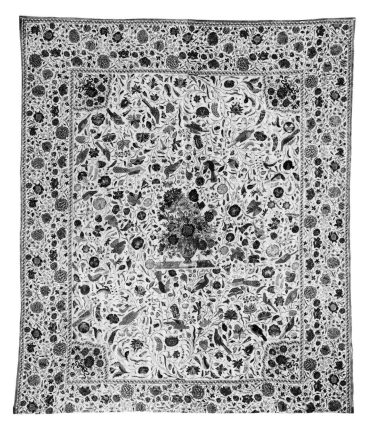

Fig. 138. Palampore. India (Coromandel Coast), 1720–50. Cotton, painted resist and mordant, dyed. Victoria and Albert Museum, London (IS.46-1956)

of Calico Printing in this country extensively, and with great advantage, particularly to those concerned in the East India trade, who have it in their power to reap many and great benefits that are peculiar to those only. Any person or persons, willing to enter into the abovementioned branch of business in an extensive manner, may have further information on the subject by applying to John Hewson & Co."[6]

If Hewson indeed intended to have his textiles compete with fashionable Indian fabrics, it would explain why he composed the overall design of his bedspreads to look as much as possible like a type of Indian palampore that could be made with the limited printing blocks he had at his disposal. He could not have produced Tree of Life palampores without far greater painting and printing skills. Today, only three of Hewson's complete bedspreads are known, rare survivals of the early efforts of one American textile printer to compete in the global market.   AP

1. For more on John Hewson, see Eaton, *Quilts in a Material World,* pp. 92–98; Gillingham, "Calico and Linen Printing in Philadelphia," pp. 97–110, pls. 1–2; Pettit, *America's Printed and Painted Fabrics,* pp. 161–72; Wulfert, "The Man of Many Vases: John Hewson, Calico Printer," pp. 58–69; and Hewson's will in Hewson Family Papers, 1767–1839, Joseph Downs Collection of Manuscripts and Printed Ephemera, Col. 203, The Winterthur Library, Winterthur, Delaware.

2. Philadelphia Museum of Art (no. 1930-100-1). The Winterthur bedspread has a history of descent in the family of John McAllister, a harness, whip, and cane manufacturer, who came to New York from Glasgow in 1775 and moved to Philadelphia in about 1780. It is marked with the initials "F.M.," probably for his second wife, Frances Wardale Lieber McAllister, whom he married in 1783.
3. The item that Hewson described as his "largest India Chintz bed quilt" was also given by his descendants to the Philadelphia Museum of Art (no. 1934-16-2a). Ironically, it is not actually Indian at all—it is a *mezzaro,* a traditional Italian head shawl large enough to cover an entire dress that was printed with a pattern based on Tree of Life palampores. Although the *mezzaro* is a centuries-old garment type, those with Tree of Life designs were popular products made by printers in the Genoa area from the late eighteenth through mid-nineteenth century.
4. There are certain aspects of the bedcover that also reference European design. The classical vase at its center, which appears in many of Hewson's textiles, was copied from a French wallpaper design; see Wulfert, "John Hewson and the French Connection," pp. 78–85. The dense, repeating floral border is similar to those on English and French shawls and handkerchiefs of the period.
5. See, for example, Thomas Mackie and Co.'s advertisement that lists "East-India palampores" among its various available bedcoverings for sale in 1785, soon after direct trade began. *Pennsylvania Packet,* no. 2108, November 7, 1785, p. 4.
6. *Pennsylvania Packet,* no. 3484, April 1, 1790, p. 4.

55. CHAIR SEAT COVER

India (possibly western), for the European market,
second quarter of the 18th century
Cotton, painted resist and mordant, dyed, with overpainting
18 ½ x 23 ¼ in. (47 x 59.1 cm)
The Metropolitan Museum of Art, New York,
Rogers Fund, 1927 27.195.1

While the intended use of some Indian chintzes is difficult to determine, there can be no doubt that this panel was made to cover a European-style chair seat, although it was never used. The design's overall shape indicates that it was created specifically for an English chair dating between about 1720 and 1740.[1] In comparison with the number of extant furniture frames from the eighteenth century, relatively few pieces of intact upholstery from that period have survived. We know that contemporary upholstery fabric—whether woven silk or wool, embroidery, or painted and dyed cotton, like the present example—was often ordered before the frame itself, which was then made to accommodate the textile. The fragility of this fine cotton fabric makes this survival all the more remarkable; had it been used, the seat cover would not be in such pristine condition. Parts of two related curtains also exist,[2] and the three pieces were likely from one matching suite of furnishing chintz. This suite was perhaps made specifically for an English East India Company employee, who could have potentially circumvented the official prohibition on Indian cotton imports into Great Britain in force between 1721 and 1774, although none of the extant pieces has a company mark to confirm this attribution.

More naturalistically drawn than in most Indian chintzes, the flowers can readily be identified as varieties common to European gardens of the time—roses, carnations, and hyacinths, among

55

similar to those found on other Indian cottons. We have further proof here of the Indian cotton painters' ability to adapt their considerable talents to specific tastes.   MW

1. Thank you to Nancy C. Britton, Conservator, Department of Objects Conservation at the Metropolitan Museum, for confirming the date range and for her identification of the shape as intended specifically for an English chair of this period.
2. The two curtains are in the Cooper-Hewitt, National Design Museum, New York (no. 1968-79-2), and the Royal Ontario Museum, Toronto (no. 934.4.25); see Irwin and Brett, *Origins of Chintz*, pp. 90–91, pl. 58.
3. Ibid., p. 90, catalogue entry for the matching curtain in the Royal Ontario Museum; the curtain also displays variegated tulips, which do not appear on the seat cover.

56. FLEURS TROPICALES ET PALMIERS (TROPICAL FLOWERS AND PALM TREES)
Oberkampf Manufactory (active 1760–1843)
France, ca. 1787
Cotton, block printed
108 x 35 ½ in. (274.3 x 90.2 cm)
The Metropolitan Museum of Art, New York,
Rogers Fund, 1937 37.170

others.[3] The seat cover design can be compared with European embroidered upholstery of the period, particularly English pieces made of wool and silk tent stitch on canvas; some of these embroideries also depict exotic-looking goods along with the flowers, such as a blue-and-white ceramic vase that contains the bouquet on an English chair upholstery dated 1739 (fig. 139).

The composition of this painted-and-dyed cotton chair seat is, in fact, a domesticated variation of the Tree of Life palampore—with the tree minimized. A room furnished with a suite of this Indian chintz design would have had a look very different from that of a room furnished with grand Tree of Life hangings (cat. 52): the exotic forest has been transformed into a garden of familiar flowers, with borders that contain fantasy flora and leaves

The Oberkampf manufactory at Jouy-en-Josas was located just two and a half miles from Versailles and about twelve miles south of Paris. Owner Christophe-Philippe Oberkampf (1738–1815) established the factory in close proximity to the center of the fashionable world and initially printed textiles only on special commission. One illustrious client took pleasure in the fact that an imitation Indian chintz made at the Jouy manufactory fooled his fellow courtiers, and he boasted of his triumph at the salon of the duchess de Choiseul in 1776.[1]

Though the Jouy manufactory started on a small scale, it became one of the most successful textile-printing enterprises in Europe, and to this day the phrase "toile de Jouy" is used to describe printed cottons with figural patterns. Determined to make the best possible products, Oberkampf himself was closely involved in procuring the necessary raw materials—from dyes and mordants to the foundation fabrics on which to print. The ideal fabric was made of evenly spun cotton warps and wefts, resulting in a smooth surface. When Oberkampf found that the cotton and linen textiles produced by French weavers were inconsistent in quality, he did not hesitate to purchase Indian cotton cloth from the French Compagnie des Indes Orientales or the English East India Company. In 1773 he made his first trip to London to visit local calico printers, whose work he considered technically superior, and to purchase an entire year's supply of Indian cotton cloth.[2] The pattern seen here was very likely printed on Indian yardage: the width of the printed design is narrower than the foundation fabric, indicating that it was not drawn for

Fig. 139. Chair cover (detail). England, dated 1739. Linen, embroidered with wool and silk. The Metropolitan Museum of Art, New York, Bequest of Irwin Untermyer, 1973 (1974.28.204a,b)

this particular cotton, which is wider than those woven in Europe at this date.

A drawing for a portion of this textile survives in the Musée de la Toile de Jouy, Jouy-en-Josas, and it includes alternative motifs hidden under flaps of paper adhered to the drawing.[3] While the identity of the designer is unknown, the lush, fantastic flower heads and bold, curling leaves are clearly modeled on variations of Indian Tree of Life palampores.[4] Despite the large pattern repeat of nearly fifty inches, which might indicate that it was to be used as a furnishing fabric, this textile was most likely intended to be made into an article of clothing such as a banyan; several extant European garments from the second half of the eighteenth century (cat. 51A) are made from the same type of Indian chintz yardage that this design imitates.   MW

1. This was reported to Oberkampf in a letter from one of his business partners, the socially well-connected Joseph-Alexandre Sarassin de Maraise; see Chapman and Chassagne, *European Textile Printers in the Eighteenth Century*, p. 147.
2. For a discussion of Oberkampf's search for cotton fabrics that met his standards, see Brédif, *Toiles de Jouy*, pp. 30, 65–67.
3. Musée de la Toile de Jouy, Jouy-en-Josas (no. 986.36.3); other extant examples of this textile include one in the Musée de l'Impression sur Étoffes, Mulhouse (no. 981.52.1), and one in the Royal Ontario Museum, Toronto (no. 934.4.182).
4. A similar Oberkampf design (a border design called *Bordure de Fleurs Exotiques*) of the same date as the present example is closely related to a palampore in the Victoria and Albert Museum, London (no. IS.182-1965); see Brédif, *Toiles de Jouy*, pp. 12, 106. A book of design drawings from the Oberkampf manufactory, based on Indian textiles, survives in the Musée de la Mode et du Textile, Paris; see ibid., pp. 106, 142 n. 20.

57. TEXTILE WITH PHEASANTS AND EXOTIC FLOWERS
Attributed to Talwin and Foster, Bromley Hall, Middlesex
(active ca. 1763–83)
England, 1765–75
Fustian, copperplate printed
96 x 31 in. (218.4 x 78.7 cm)
The Metropolitan Museum of Art, New York,
Rogers Fund, 1970 1970.237.3

The textile printing works at Bromley Hall, Middlesex, England, was one of the larger early manufactories set up in the environs of greater London. Calico printers had been on the site since the 1740s, when the manufactory was operated by a Quaker family named Ollive that had reputedly been in the business since the late seventeenth century. This piece was probably produced when the business was run by the Talwin and Foster families, between about 1763 and 1783. The factory continued to operate until 1823 under the name Foster & Co.[1]

A Bromley Hall pattern book of 144 copperplate designs printed on paper is preserved in the Victoria and Albert Museum, London, and contains patterns dating from about 1760 to 1800.[2]

57

Though the design for the present fabric is not included in this book, there are a number of similar patterns incorporating birds and large flowers, and such finely drawn avian patterns appear to have been one of the factory's specialties. The image of a meandering branch supporting long-tailed pheasants is an energetic mixture of European textile design and the exoticism of bold, fantastic flowers. The foliage recalls the multiflowering trees of Indian palampores, especially the giant curling leaf on the right side, which draws from the Chinese-inspired motifs that appear in the Indian chintzes. The long-tailed pheasants bear a resemblance to those in the Chinese garden scene attributed to John Munns (cat. 89), who along with the Bromley Hall designer must have taken advantage of the many prints and pattern books available in the eighteenth century, such as *The Ladies Amusement: Or, The Whole Art of Japanning Made Easy* (first edition, 1760) and *A New Book of Birds* (1765), both published by Robert Sayer in London.

English calico printers excelled at these large-scale monochrome designs produced by the copperplate printing technique developed in Drumconda, Ireland, in the early 1750s. Their advantage over Continental competitors during the first decade that the technique was in use lessened as the secret quickly spread. Nonetheless, the French, Swiss, and Dutch printers never attempted expansive patterns of this kind or scenic landscapes like those of John Munns or Robert Jones at Old Ford.   MW

1. For a short history of Bromley Hall, see *Catalogue of a Loan Exhibition of English Chintz*, p. 22.
2. Victoria and Albert Museum, London (no. E.458–1955).

58. DRESS (ROBE À LA FRANÇAISE)
France, 1750–75
Cotton, block printed
Length 58 in. (147.3 cm)
The Metropolitan Museum of Art, New York, Purchase,
Irene Lewisohn Bequest, 1964 C.I.64.32.3a, b

China's strict diplomatic and trade regulations encouraged the European inclination to view the East through a veil of mystery and fantasy. Filtering Chinese art and culture through the lens of Western taste, European artists built fantastic tableaux of frivolity in an imaginary land called "Cathay." Ironically, the Chinese were themselves trying to produce fabrics that appealed to European tastes rather than export their more traditional designs.[1] The imaginary flowering branches that meander across the creamy surface of this informal cotton gown exemplify the spirit of Orientalist fantasy and its perfect adaptation to Rococo taste in French fashion.

novelty. Printed cottons like this one fed the accelerated fashion cycle with inexpensive, bright, and novel fodder. The *robe à la française* began its life as a negligee garment, and, like the men's clothing made from cotton textiles from the East (cat. 51A, B), women wore the style in informal moments and intimate spaces. Exotic chinoiserie flowers printed on cotton, self-fabric trimmings, and the front-closing false bodice—a comfortable alternative to the stifling stomacher—date this gown to the mid- to late 1760s and represent the height of Rococo gaiety for the once *déshabillé* fashion. Later in the century, the bodice tightened around the waist and bust, the skirt grew to accommodate massive panniers, and both were executed in increasingly formal and expensive textiles and trimming, resulting in the codification of the *robe à la française* as the most formal silhouette of the period.[2]   KS

1. Jacobson, *Chinoiserie*, pp. 19–20.
2. Ribeiro, *Dress in Eighteenth-Century Europe*, p. 184.

59. WALL PANEL WITH GARDEN URNS

China, for the European market, late 18th century
Silk taffeta, painted and printed
78 x 43 in. (198.1 x 109.2 cm)
The Metropolitan Museum of Art, New York,
Rogers Fund, 1980 1980.120

The Chinese produced both painted wallpaper and painted silk wall hangings for export during the eighteenth century, and the workshops that made these wall coverings may have used the same patterns for both techniques. Silk wall coverings accounted for a very small percentage of the textiles exported from China to the West.[1] Along with the painted papers, however, their influence on the perception of chinoiserie in Europe is probably disproportionate to the actual number produced, as these wall coverings became closely associated with the invention of the "Chinese room," an essential feature of European country houses and retreats.[2]

Painted pictorial wall decorations were entirely new products developed specifically for the European export market. Nothing like them were used in domestic Chinese interior decoration. The antecedent may have been the Chinese practice, noted by early travelers, of using monochrome paper coverings on their interior walls to create the effect of a uniformly white wall, without other decoration.[3] Painted silk may have been used as a substitute for paper in the eighteenth century, as suppliers had a difficult time manufacturing enough paper to meet the requirements of European clients. In 1759 one such customer, Emily Lennox (1731–1814), great-granddaughter of Charles II of England and wife of James Fitzgerald, Earl of Kildare (1722–1773), commissioned

A quintessentially eighteenth-century conception of Oriental life was established in small vignettes by Antoine Watteau and François Boucher, who illustrated scenes of feathery flora, tiered bells, pagodas, and parasols in the swooping lines of the Rococo style. Applying this tradition of appropriation to the decorative arts in the 1750s and 1760s, Jean Pillement was perhaps the most influential textile designer to merge Rococo and Orientalist fantasies through his depictions of an imaginary world with exotic flowering plants such as those seen here. His images were made available for the design of textiles and decorative arts in publications like *A New Book of Chinese Ornament*, published in 1755.

As the eighteenth century progressed, the pace of fashion innovation quickened. Informal dress gained status and visibility through illustrated publications such as the *Galerie des Modes*. Fashionable women appropriated elements of intimate and working-class dress into their wardrobes in a relentless pursuit of

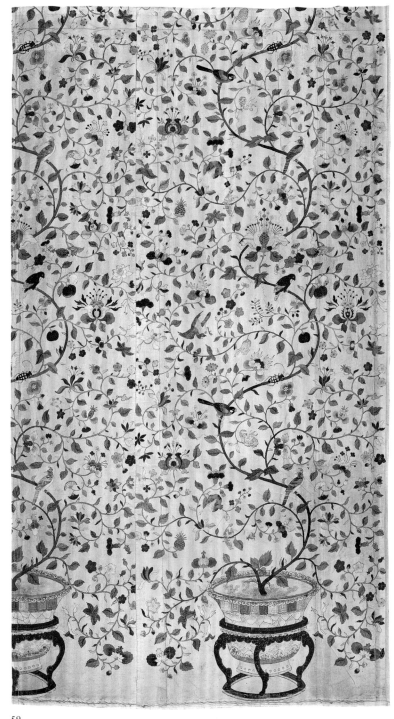

59

Paper hangings depicting garden scenes with flowering trees that grow from large Chinese vessels resting on decorative stands are preserved in several German and English collections.[5] This painted silk also appears to be influenced by Indian chintz palampores, with their delicate meandering branches bearing a variety of fruits and flowers and populated by assorted small birds and insects. Here the regular meander and the delicacy of the design are closer to the dress silks of the later eighteenth century than to the more regimented garden scenes of the wallpapers.[6] It is a charming hybrid of the Chinese and Indian motifs that continued to be popular into the late eighteenth century.   MW

1. See Jolly, "Painted Silks from China," p. 167. This type of export textile may have begun as a luxury good acquired by private individuals in the trade, then presumably made on a commercial scale once they had achieved a certain degree of popularity.
2. Clunas et al., *Chinese Export Art and Design*, p. 114; Jolly, "Painted Silks from China," p. 167.
3. Clunas et al., *Chinese Export Art and Design*, p. 112.
4. Tillyard, *Aristocrats*, pp. 154–55.
5. See Wappenschmidt, *Chinesische Tapeten für Europa*, pl. 10, figs. 89–91.
6. My thanks to Anna Jolly for her comments on this painted silk.

Peter Paul Rubens (Flemish, Siegen 1577–1640 Antwerp)
60. PORTRAIT OF JESUIT NICOLAS TRIGAULT IN CHINESE COSTUME
1617
Black, red, and white chalk, blue pastel, and pen and brown ink
on light brown laid paper
17 9/16 x 9 3/4 in. (44.6 x 24.8 cm)
The Metropolitan Museum of Art, New York,
Purchase, Carl Selden Trust, several members of
The Chairman's Council, Gail and Parker Gilbert, and
Lila Acheson Wallace Gifts,
1999 1999.222

Nicolas Trigault (1577–1628), depicted here in a Chinese-style robe of luminous silk, was part of the Jesuit mission to China from 1610 until his death. Rubens made this drawing in 1617 while Trigault was back in Europe on a fund-raising and recruitment tour. Judging from the Latin notations the artist made on this drawing, he probably considered it a costume study, and it is one among several drawings of Jesuit missionaries he completed about this time.[1] Trigault's famous predecessor in China, Matteo Ricci (1552–1610), had initiated the Jesuits' adoption of garments resembling Chinese scholars' dress in an attempt to win the social support and political protection of the elite—scholars and officeholders.

Jesuits and other missionaries were drawn to the Portuguese trading outpost of Macau, founded in 1557, in the hope that they

her husband to buy her 150 yards of painted taffeta for bedroom furnishings while he was in London. Although the acquisition of this amount in a single pattern was said to be impossible, he finally succeeded, and according to Emily the painted "Indian" silk was only slightly more expensive than a silk damask available in Dublin, and infinitely more attractive.[4]

their heads and faces. A subsequent shift away from Buddhist dress occurred in the mid-1590s, largely at the behest of Ricci, whose thorough knowledge of Chinese culture and association with Chinese scholars had revealed the Confucian elite's disparagement of Buddhist clergy, whom they considered outsiders. When the Jesuits abandoned Buddhist dress about 1594, they grew their hair and beards in keeping with mainstream Chinese custom and wore silk robes when visiting important Chinese men.[3]

Ever sensitive to Chinese cultural markers such as dress, Ricci based his own formal silk visiting robe, which he first wore publicly in 1595, on local scholars' garments.[4] While no portraits of Ricci in his robe have survived, the costume worn by Trigault in Rubens's drawing echoes Ricci's description of its long, wide sleeves and contrasting wide border at the hem, wrists, and neck.[5] That description also matches an illustration of a *lan shan* robe in the late Ming encyclopedia *Sancai tuhui*, where it is noted that the robe is for an educated man.[6]

Elite Chinese men always covered their heads, and the Jesuits did likewise, even in the celebration of mass.[7] A hat comparable to the one Trigault wears in this drawing appears in a Chinese literati group portrait commemorating a gathering of 1635.[8]　JD

1. Logan and Brockey, "Nicolas Trigault, SJ: A Portrait by Peter Paul Rubens," p. 159; a translation of his comments is included on p. 157.
2. See Brockey, *Journey to the East,* esp. pp. 1–21. The book traces the history of Jesuit activity in China, incorporating previously neglected Portuguese-language evidence while also considering both recent Chinese-language studies and more traditional Jesuit accounts.
3. Peterson, "What to Wear?," p. 412.
4. Ibid., p. 414.
5. Ibid.
6. Wang and Wang, *Sancai tuhui*, vol. 2, p. 1535; absent from Ricci's description and from the Ming encyclopedia is the sash seen in the drawing of Trigault.
7. During Trigault's trip to Europe, on January 15, 1615, the Jesuits requested—and on March 26, 1615, received—permission from Rome to wear a headpiece even while celebrating mass. Shortly thereafter, a headpiece was designed for precisely that purpose (see Dunne, *Generation of Giants*, pp. 164–65).
8. The group portrait was painted by one of the participants, Xiang Shengmo (1597–1658), in cooperation with a professional portrait painter; see Robert D. Mowry in Li and Watt, *The Chinese Scholar's Studio*, pp. 66–67, 144, 201, no. 1. Each of the participants wears a different type of headgear; one similar to Trigault's is worn by the artist.

61. TEMPLE HANGING WITH A HINDU DEVOTEE

India (Tamil Nadu), for the Sri Lankan market,
late 17th–first quarter of the 18th century
Cotton, painted mordant and iron, dyed
42 7/8 x 61 in. (109 x 155 cm)
Collection of Karun Thakar, London

This is a masterwork of *kalamkari* cloth painting—not for its dyeing complexity (it is a relatively simple two-stage process), but rather for the sensitivity of the painted line, the sophisticated

would ultimately be permitted to enter China. In 1579 the Jesuits began studying Chinese and adopting the customs and dress of the country as part of a new evangelizing strategy authorized by Alessandro Valignano (1539–1606), head of all Jesuit activities in Asia. This helped smooth Jesuit entry beyond Macau onto Chinese soil in 1582, but results were mixed, and the mission ultimately failed. Although some Jesuits served at the imperial court, especially in scientific capacities, they made few converts among the Chinese elite; nevertheless, by 1700 about 200,000 Chinese had become Christians. In 1724 the Yongzheng emperor banned Christianity; Jesuit buildings were seized and missionaries expelled.[2]

When the Jesuits switched from European clerical garb to vestments of the established Chinese religion of Buddhism in the early 1580s, they also followed Buddhist tradition and shaved

61, detail

integration of the figure into a foliate landscape, and for the artist's skill in capturing the devotional sentiment of the subject.[1] It depicts a Shiva devotee (*bhakta*) gathering flowers, probably oleander (*Nerium oleander*, Tamil, *arali*), a blossom much favored in the worship of Shiva.[2] His allegiance to Shiva is indicated by the sectarian *tilaka* mark on his forehead, repeated on his shoulders and chest, and in the *rudraksha* beads—sacred to Shiva—that he wears. The worshipper is festooned with jewelry and garlands and wears a skirt cloth (*lungi*) with a finely detailed border. A small bag that hangs from his wrist holds the wildflowers he is collecting to offer to Shiva; they will adorn a *linga*, his aniconic representation, or will garland a processional icon.

Although this is the only known version of the subject, others must once have existed, as witnessed by a late eighteenth-century Japanese woodblock edition of Indian designs popular in Japan. In the print representing this theme (fig. 140), an ascetic (*rishi*) with uncut matted dreadlocks (*jata*) gathers fallen flowers. The sensitivity of the painting in the hanging has few parallels in other Nayaka-period works of seventeenth- and eighteenth-century south India. Murals at the Shiva temple of Narumbunatha at Tiruppudaimarudur, Tamil Nadu, commissioned by a branch of the Vijayanagar royal household, probably in the first half of the seventeenth century, come closest in quality (fig. 18).

While unquestionably produced in one of the great cloth-painting centers of south India, this hanging, by virtue of its religious subject matter and its provenance, was intended to be traded to Sri Lanka.[3] The presence of a large Tamil-speaking Hindu minority in Sri Lanka, a legacy of the Chola invasions of the eleventh century, together with the island's Sinhalese Buddhist ruling elite, generated a demand for imported Indian textiles.[4] Large pictorial temple cloths, displayed during religious festivals for both their narrative and decorative effects, were evidently a part of the south Indian–Sri Lankan trade.[5]   JG

1. Guy, "Choice Varied Flowers," pp. 78–81.
2. I am grateful to Dr. Helmut Neumann for this identification.
3. It was collected in Sri Lanka in the 1990s, very likely from a temple source.
4. Cohen, "The Unusual Textile Trade between India and Sri Lanka," pp. 56–80, and Guy, "A Ruler and His Courtesans Celebrate Vasantotsava," pp. 162–75.
5. Analogous are the so-called *Ramayana* cloths from Tamil Nadu that have been found exclusively in Indonesia; see Guy, "Rama, Rajas and Courtesans: Indian Figurative Textiles in Indonesia," pp. 40–57.

Fig. 140. Page from a woodblock-printed manual, *Sarasa benran*, depicting a Hindu ascetic (*rishi*) gathering flowers. Published Edo (Tokyo), 1778. The Metropolitan Museum of Art, New York, Lent by Paul T. and Betty M. Nomura (L.1993.9.29)

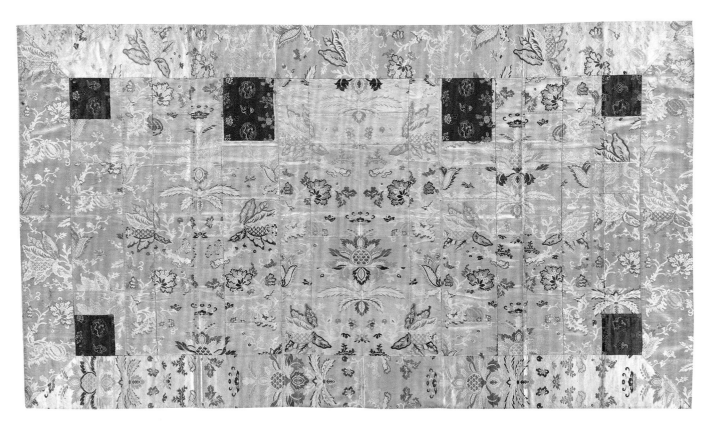

62. BUDDHIST VESTMENT (KESA)

Japan, 18th century

Main textile: China, for the European market, first half of the
18th century; lampas, silk

Squares: China, ca. 1738; silk satin, brocaded,
silk and gilt-paper-wrapped thread

46 x 83 in. (116.8 x 210.8 cm)

The Metropolitan Museum of Art, New York, Purchase,
Joseph Pulitzer Bequest, 1919 19.93.111

Surprisingly European in flavor, this Japanese Buddhist vestment
(*kesa*) was made from Chinese cloth intended for the European
market. While the European-style patterning of the cloth is unexpected, the use in Japanese *kesa* of textiles imported from China
is in keeping with a centuries-old tradition.[1] The present work
reflects not only that tradition but also a taste for the exotic among
the Japanese, including the Buddhist clergy.

Like Buddhist vestments of other cultures, the Japanese *kesa*
is a patchwork made in a particular configuration. This one consists of a border surrounding seven vertical columns, a vertical
and horizontal internal framework separating and segmenting
the columns, and contrasting squares in the corners and flanking
the central column; it was constructed for minimal interruption
of the main textile's design. As usual in examples of this type, the
central column is the widest and provides the greatest unbroken
expanse of the main textile's design.

This particular textile most resembles European lace-patterned
woven silks, but with variations. Like those silks (cat. 47A), the
floral design here is symmetrical and in mirror image, but, lack-
ing the dense, lacelike patterns of European examples, the
ground is more open. Even so, the design is rather awkward,
and other European-style Chinese textiles made for the West,
whether naturalistic or "exotic" and "bizarre" (cat. 44), are
more successful.[2] The awkwardness of this pattern may have led
to its preservation in Japan rather than in its intended market of
Europe. Or, its use as a vestment in Japan may have improved its
chances for survival; in Europe it would have been the fabric for
a fashionable dress and therefore more likely to be short-lived.

The six red squares of the *kesa* are made of a more conventional Chinese textile. These squares—with their dragon roundels,
clouds, and flowers—closely resemble a piece in the Metropolitan
Museum's collection from the tomb of Guoqin Wang, a Chinese
prince who died in 1738.[3] JD

1. Buddhism reached Japan from the Asian continent. A recent landmark exhibition explored the interrelationship of Japanese clerics, their continental (largely
Chinese) teachers, and *kesa* of the eighth through fifteenth century that were
treasured in Japan for having been transmitted from China. See Yamakawa and
Bethe, *Kōsō to kesa*.
2. Jolly, "Une soierie chinoise d'après un dessin anglais du XVIIIe siècle," pp. 75–83.
3. Metropolitan Museum, acc. no. 51.83.6.

63. COPE COLLAR

Russia (probably Moscow), 17th century
Silk satin, embroidered with metal-wrapped thread
13 ¼ x 32 ¼ in. (33.5 x 82 cm)
The Metropolitan Museum of Art, New York,
Rogers Fund, 1917 17.157

Ottoman silks, whether produced for the luxury market or spe-cifically for the Church with Christian motifs, were made into religious vestments in many parts of Europe. In Russia these vest-ments were often embellished with locally made embroidered cuffs and collars.[1] The Russian embroideries were typically com-pleted in gold and silver metal-wrapped thread on a ground of black or crimson velvet, and often in a style closely related to the Ottoman textiles to which they were attached, including the characteristic motifs of carnations, tulips, and pomegranates flow-ering from scrolling vines. Other Russian embroideries, however, have entirely unrelated geometric ornament incorporating pearls and silver-gilt plaques.[2]

This collar has been detached from the cope that it once adorned. In the Russian Orthodox Church the cope took a slightly different form from the semicircular vestments used in western Europe (cats. 64, 65). With an attached collar of this kind, the Russian style of cope would have been donned by placing the head through the collar, and the plackets on the front of the garment would have stayed in place next to each other without the need for a fastening device such as a morse. This construction also obviated the inclusion of the orphrey, the embroidered band located along the straight edge of a Western-style cope.

The ground of this collar is a red silk satin rather than a velvet. It has been embroidered with a gold tulip-bearing vine that forms a trellis enclosing serrated silver leaves with golden crosses. Additional touches of blue and green are found at the center of the tulips and leaves. Other vestments with Ottoman-style embroi-dery include a dalmatic in the collection of the Kremlin Armory Museum, Moscow, and several copes in the State Hermitage Museum, St. Petersburg.[3] MS

1. Walter B. Denny is responsible for the new identification of this hood, previously considered Armenian, eighteenth century. See Denny in Denny and Krody, *The Sultan's Garden*, pp. 170–71, no. 53 (but there the ground is incorrectly identified as velvet).
2. For several examples, see Atasoy, Denny, Mackie, and Tezcan, *Ipek*, pp. 249–50.
3. For the Kremlin Armory Museum dalmatic, see Levykin et al., *The Tsars and the East*, pp. 12, 122–23, 134, no. 62, and Atasoy and Uluç, *Impressions of Ottoman Culture in Europe*, p. 92. For the State Hermitage Museum copes, see the latter publication, pp. 80, 89, 92.

64. COPE

Iran (?), 18th century
Textile: Iran, first half of the 17th century
Velvet, cut, voided, and brocaded, silk and metal-wrapped thread, cotton lining
Orphrey: Silk, embroidered with silk and metal-wrapped thread, engraved metal fittings
44 ½ x 103 in. (113 x 261.6 cm)
The Metropolitan Museum of Art, New York,
Rogers Fund, 1914 14.67

This cope has been fashioned from cut-and-voided silk velvet dating to the first part of the seventeenth century, a product of Safavid looms. Its rows of flowering plants, made from raised, multicolor pile, were once surrounded by a ground of yellow silk wrapped in strips of silver-gilt metal, the contrasting textures and coloration combining for a luxurious effect.[1]

The fabric was made into items of clothing that eventually found their way into the collection of an Armenian church, where they were reconfigured as vestments for ceremonial use with the seams of the earlier coats or robes still visible. In addition to this cope, a second cope was made of the same fabric and would have been worn during ceremonies in which several clergy wearing matching vestments officiated.[2]

It is not clear when the embroidered band, or orphrey, on the straight end of the cope was attached to it. Armenian copes do not typically have this element; instead, a stole (Greek *epitra-chelion*, Armenian *p'orurar*) performing the same decorative function is worn separately.[3] The inexpert handling of this addi-tion is revealed in the inscriptions that identify the figures embroi-dered on the orphrey. While the inscriptions for "St. Nerses Patriarch," "St. Nicholas Patriarch," and "St. Sahak Patriarch" are placed next to the corresponding images of these bishops, the inscription for the fourth bishop has been cut off. That for Mary has been placed below two of the crosses, with half of the inscrip-tion ("Virgin Mary") on one side of the cope and half ("Mother of God") on the opposite side.[4] The stole probably belonged to an archbishop, as indicated by the inclusion on it of four bishop-saints and four crosses, the hierarchy of the Church mirrored in

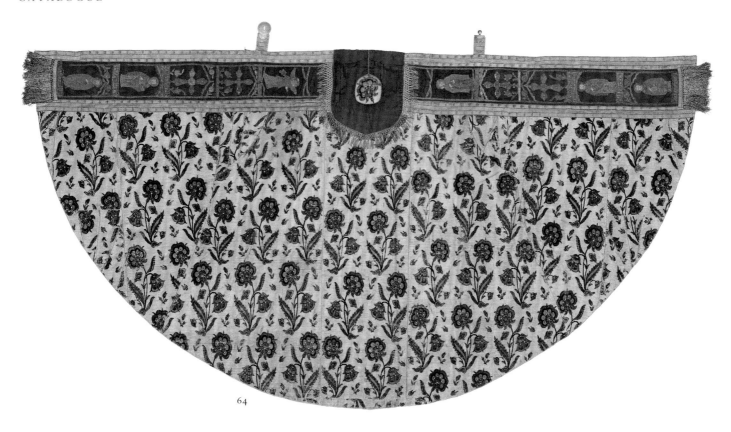

64

the number of such symbols each official could wear on his vest-ments.[5] As Armenian communities were found throughout Safavid lands, notably in the capital of Isfahan, it is unclear whether the original velvet textile was ever traded abroad. The cope fits into the story of trade, however, as the Armenian community played a crucial role in the conveyance of silk from the Safavid Empire to European markets. MS

1. See technical observations by Daniel Walker in Ekhtiar, Soucek, Canby, and Haidar, eds., *Masterpieces . . . of Islamic Art in The Metropolitan Museum of Art*, pp. 251–53, no. 175. Other fragments of the same velvet textile are in the David Collection, Copenhagen (Folsach and Bernsted, *Woven Treasures*, p. 113) and the Textile Museum, Washington, D.C. (Bier et al., *Woven from the Soul, Spun from the Heart*, pp. 172–73).
2. The last known whereabouts of the second cope were recorded in 1910, when it was in the collection of Dr. Roden of Frankfurt (see Sarre and Martin, eds., *Die Ausstellung von Meisterwerken muhammedanischer Kunst in München*, vol. 3, pl. 202).
3. See the copes illustrated in Marchese and Breu, *Splendor and Pageantry*, pp. 152–53 and 154–55. For the use and form of the cope in the Armenian Church, see Muyldermans, "Le costume liturgique arménien," pp. 285–86.
4. The embroidered figures were previously identified as the Virgin Mary, the arch-angel Gabriel, and Saints Athanasius, Gregory of Nazianzen, Basil the Great, and John Chrysostom (as in M[orris], "An Early Seventeenth-Century Cope," pp. 147–48); and then, correctly, as the Virgin Mary, Nicholas of Myra, Nerses I, and Sahak I (Armenian inscriptions as read by Amy Landau, cited by Daniel Walker in Ekhtiar, Soucek, Canby, and Haidar, eds., *Masterpieces . . . of Islamic Art in The Metropolitan Museum of Art*, pp. 251–53, no. 175). V. Rev. M. Daniel Findikyan, Dean and Professor of Liturgical Studies, St. Nersess Armenian Seminary, New Rochelle, New York, re-read the inscriptions for me and noted that the orphrey had been cut and incorrectly attached to this cope.
5. Muyldermans, "Le costume liturgique arménien," pp. 286–87.

65. COPE

Main textile: Netherlands, 1720s; silk satin, brocaded, silk and metal-wrapped thread
Hood textile: Italy, mid-17th century; cloth-of-gold, brocaded, silk and metal-wrapped thread
57 ½ x 119 in. (146.1 x 302.3 cm)
The Metropolitan Museum of Art, New York, Rogers Fund, 1976 1976.12

Until recently, products of the Dutch silk-weaving industry have been difficult to identify. The duc de Richelieu (Louis-François-Armand de Vignerod du Plessis, 1696–1788) collected hundreds of European textile samples between 1720 and 1736 in an attempt to document local and regional production; included in this col-lection are several woven silks from the Netherlands labeled "Indiennes." This nomenclature and certain characteristics of the group have been confirmed by recent archival research in Amsterdam.[1] These fabrics have a width of about 30 ½ inches (78 centimeters) and feature distinctively playful patterns with exotic elements, mostly interpretations of Chinese motifs.[2]

Dutch silk indiennes were certainly intended for fashionable women's dress, as is evident from a particularly spectacular example of Dutch silk weaving (cat. 82). The Dutch were export-ing silk textiles to England, France, and Portugal (and probably indirectly to North America through the British trade) by at least the early eighteenth century. In 1707 an Amsterdam silk manu-

65

facturer was called upon to testify to the origin of several Dutch silks after such goods were stopped by English customs on their way into London because they were thought to be from India.[3] Both England and France banned the import of Asian silks around the turn of the eighteenth century as protectionist measures in favor of their own silk-weaving industries.[4] Whether the Dutch silk indiennes of the 1720s to 1750s were still confused with Asian silks is not certain; to the modern eye, they are clearly examples of European chinoiserie.

This particular pattern shows a compact walled garden with tiny pagodas flanked by oversize Chinese-style vases holding large flowers (detail). In his 1769 memoirs Jacques-Charles Dutillieu

(1718–1782), a French silk designer and manufacturer, dismissed the quality of Dutch silk designs, saying they were either bad copies of French patterns or designs taken from textiles from the "Indes Orientales" appropriated with a rather unrefined taste.[5] While his comments are clearly untrue of this charming design, they confirm the competitive nature of the silk industries within western Europe.

65, detail

Although the use of fashionable textiles for ecclesiastical vestments certainly predates the eighteenth century, based on surviving vestments this practice appears to have accelerated after 1700. Eighteenth-century vestments made of dress silks are often attributed to France; the use here of the older Italian woven silk as the hood of this cope is an unusual variation on the practice.   MW

1. Weigert, *Textiles en Europe sous Louis XV*. The textiles were collected and arranged in eight volumes that were part of the duke's extensive library; they were sold at the auction of his estate in 1788 in a lot totaling fifty-two volumes under the heading "Records of Our Times." See Folliot, Regnault-Delalande, Julliot, and Quillau, *Catalogue de . . . le cabinet de feu M. le duc de Richelieu. . . .* The term *indiennes* was more commonly used in France to refer to European imitations of Indian cotton textiles, but rather confusingly the Richelieu volumes also employ the word to refer to the printed cottons being made at Marseilles and Genoa.

The Amsterdam silk-weaving industry and its products have most recently been documented by Sjoujke Colenbrander in *When Weaving Flourished: The Silk Industry in Amsterdam and Haarlem, 1585–1750*.

2. See Colenbrander, "Dutch Silks, Narrow or . . . ?," pp. 59–65, and Colenbrander and Browne, "Indiennes: *Chinoiserie* Silks Woven in Amsterdam," pp. 127–38, 211–24, for a discussion of the width of these silks.

3. Colenbrander and Browne, "Indiennes: *Chinoiserie* Silks Woven in Amsterdam," p. 128.

4. Ibid., pp. 128–29; England passed a ban in 1699 and France in 1702; the latest known archival mention of a Dutch indienne is from 1754, ibid., p. 128.

5. Rothstein, "Dutch Silks—An Important but Forgotten Industry," p. 156 and n. 24; for the life and work of Dutillieu, see Miller, "Manufactures and the Man," pp. 19–40.

66. LENTEN CURTAIN
Peru (Chachapoyas), before 1775
Cotton, painted resist and dye
93 ½ x 89 in. (237.5 x 226.1 cm)
American Museum of Natural History, New York, 40.1/2291

Lenten curtains have long been used in churches during the holy period that begins with Lent and leads up to the Crucifixion and

the celebration of Easter, the high point of the liturgical calendar. Such curtains were hung between the chancel and nave of the church, screening the visual riches of the high altar from the congregation during mass and creating a setting more consistent with the penitential journey of the faithful during the season of Christ's suffering and death. Frequently made of sheer cloth, the curtains are also referred to as veils. In Europe, they are usually white, somewhat sheer, and plain. In the Andes, and particularly in the northern highlands around the area of Chachapoyas, a type of Lenten curtain was constructed of local cotton cloth and traditional dyes.

The Instruments of the Passion, symbolizing Christ's suffering during the events leading up to his Crucifixion, are rendered with tender devotion and charming detail. The crucified Christ with two Marys in attendance—his mother and Mary Magdalene—is depicted here by Andean artisans who bring to the enterprise their distinctive hand. Added to the traditional checklist of Christian attributes, this version contains some local features that include the lace edging on the women's garments, native baskets and tools, images of the sun and the moon in the upper corners, and other design elements drawn from regional weaving traditions. Two Jesuit priests atop ladders peer down on the scene, awaiting their role—perhaps a revisionist view of history proposed by the Order—as the overseers of the descent of the body of the dead Christ from the Cross.[1]

A primary justification for the Spanish colonial enterprise in the Americas was the conversion of native populations to Christianity. Local churches were built, with congregations of devoted followers producing both architecture and furnishings. The Jesuits especially encouraged native artists to participate in decorating these churches, and the curtain here is one such contribution. Composed of locally produced handspun cotton cloth, it was woven in the narrow lengths characteristic of the area and then stitched together to form a hanging.[2] The painted scenes were created directly on the cloth using natural textile dyes and paste resist-dyeing techniques. This resist technique—similar to that used in India, but with very different results—is most evident along the ribbonlike zigzag designs at the borders. Various colors have been used, including several pale shades of cream, pink, and gray, as well as the stronger hues from tannin browns and indigo blues. Although this dyeing process has a long history in the Precolumbian world, here it appears in an entirely new colonial context.   EP

1. On the role of the Jesuits in establishing the visual program for these curtains, see Keleman, "Lenten Curtains from Colonial Peru," pp. 8–10.
2. The curtain is composed of three panels of selvage-to-selvage widths of 29 ½ inches, 29 ½ inches, and 29 inches from left to right. The cotton yarns in both warp and weft are Z-spun singles, woven in plain weave.

67. TORAH ARK CURTAIN (PAROKHET)
Northern Italy, after 1685–86
Silk satin and linen, embroidered with silk and metal-wrapped thread, metallic braid, silk and metallic fringe
76¾ x 57½ in. (194.9 x 146.1 cm)
The Jewish Museum, New York, Purchase: Eva and Morris Feld Judaica Acquisitions Fund, 1981-319

Inscription (translated from Hebrew): IN HONOR OF THE LORD / THE DONATION OF / SIGNORA SARAH / THE WIFE OF . . . JOSEPH JOSHUA / LAID TO REST [IN] THE YEAR [5]446 (1685–86) . . . / "THE TEACHING OF THE LORD IS PERFECT, RENEWING LIFE; THE DECREES OF THE LORD" (PS. 19:8) W[ILL BE FOR A] B[LESSING] A[MEN].

Meant to cover the opening of the ark in which Torah scrolls were stored, this glorious embroidered curtain was donated to a now unknown Italian synagogue in memory of Joseph Joshua by his wife, Sarah. It has long been common practice to donate textiles to beautify synagogues, often in commemoration of life passages or religious events. In the early modern period in Europe, valuable silk textiles were often reused—pieced together and further embellished to suit a new purpose. Many of the textiles employed to make ceremonial coverings for the ark, reader's desk, and Torah scrolls themselves were first made into nonsacred items, such as dresses. In the case of this curtain, the scrolling floral side borders, stitched in an embroidery style that conforms to late sixteenth-century practice, appear to have been used before, perhaps as bor-

Fig. 141. Palampore. India (Coromandel Coast), for the English market, 1730–40. Cotton, drawn and painted resist and mordant, dyed, with overpainting. Royal Ontario Museum, Toronto (934.4.16)

ders for a larger set of curtains or bed valances; at a somewhat later date, they were cut down and attached to the central field of cream-colored silk satin that is embroidered with the Hebrew inscription and five bouquets of roses, tulips, and carnations.[1]

The overall design of this curtain resembles other embroidered Italian textiles of the period.[2] But that design has international roots. Perhaps referencing the type of Indian *kalamkari* used as light floor coverings, the curtain's overall layout features a central element with four inward-facing designs, one at each corner, the whole surrounded by a scrolling border. Such *kalamkaris* were originally made for Muslim areas of India and the Middle East, but by the early eighteenth century, a version based in part on European design sources had become popular in the West (fig. 141).[3] On this curtain, East and West also meet in the formal, symmetrically presented bouquets inspired by floral decoration on Ottoman textiles; however, the flowers are tied with distinctly European bowknots.

Traditionally involved in the textile trade, the Jewish people of Europe were also known for their skills as weavers and embroi-

derers.[4] Exiled from Spain in 1492, when they were given the choice to either convert to Catholicism or die, many Jews made their way to Italy. Italian Jewish traders retained good connections with Levantine Jews as well as trading partnerships with the Ottoman Turks and thus had access to textile goods from India and the Middle East. As they settled in Italy, Jews encountered fear and prejudice and were soon forced into ghettos within the Italian cities, where they were told that they could work only as doctors, pawnbrokers, or traders of secondhand goods—the latter occupation bringing into their possession fine textiles that could be turned into magnificent synagogue decorations.   AP

1. An embroidered Italian Torah cover in the Sotheby's sale catalogue *A Treasured Legacy . . . Steinhardt Judaica Collection*, lot 78, has many similarities to this Torah ark curtain, including a central bouquet of flowers tied with a bowknot, and may have originally been part of an ensemble with the curtain.
2. See Metropolitan Museum, acc. nos. 69.67 and 1973.177, as well as several ceremonial textiles in the Steinhardt Collection catalogue (see note 1 above).
3. For more on these *kalamkaris* for the European market based in part on European print sources, see Irwin and Brett, *Origins of Chintz*, pp. 98–99.
4. Liscia Bemporad, "Jewish Ceremonial Art in the Era of the Ghettos," p. 124.

68. COPE WITH HOOD
Mexico, ca. 1730
Silk satin, embroidered with silk and metal-wrapped thread,
metallic braid
Cope: length 53 in. (134.6 cm)
Hood: length 30 in. (76.2 cm)
Los Angeles County Museum of Art, Costume Council Fund,
M.85.96.7a-b

Among the most refined and resplendent artworks produced in
New Spain, embroideries created for the Church were made
entirely of luxurious silk and gold threads. They demonstrate not
only the presence in Mexico of highly skilled artisans—including
guild embroiderers originally trained by Spanish masters and
who had access to these materials—but also the enormous
wealth and resources the Church invested in their commission.
Vestments were produced as sets; the cope and hood here
are part of a set that includes chasuble, dalmatic, and stole, as
well as lectern covers and a hanging.[1] Perhaps the most famous
set of Mexican vestments is that from the Metropolitan Cathedral in Mexico City, produced by Marcus Maestre, a master

embroiderer from Seville.[2] The maker of this set, however, is
not known.

Designed in an opulent European Baroque style, the cope's
large-scale floral motifs, fruits, and cherubs are elaborately
embroidered with polychrome Chinese silk threads on an ivory
silk ground. Every surface is covered with silk embroidery in a
rich assortment of stitches and patterns (detail). Following
Spanish and Italian techniques, the raised surfaces of metallic

68, detail

embroidery provide additional variety and dimension. The hood, with its heavy European silk and silver tassel, attaches to the back of the garment with gold hooks and latches. It is embroidered with the image of a tower with palms at its base, presented by two cherublike figures and surrounded by a ring of flowers that seem to be either lilies or gladioli (also referred to as sword lilies), symbols of the Virgin Mary.[3] The tower, a common symbol of the Virgin's purity, relates to the Laurentian litanies that were part of Marian devotion celebrated throughout the Hispanic world since the late sixteenth century.[4] With its Christian imagery, Baroque florals and cartouches, and construction methods and materials of both European and Asian origin, this splendid cope embodies the refinement of the Mexican embroiderer's art. EP

1. See Butler, ed., *Los Angeles County Museum of Art*, pp. 140–41.
2. See Virginia Armella de Aspe in Paz et al., *Mexico: Splendors of Thirty Centuries*, pp. 383–85, no. 162; Dilys Blum in Rishel et al., *The Arts in Latin America, 1492–1820*, pp. 170–73, nos. 11-6–11-10.
3. Taylor, *Our Lady of Guadalupe and Friends*.
4. The tower motif also refers to the Virgin of Loreto, whose shrine was built in Mexico City by the Jesuits. Its completion in the early eighteenth century was perhaps the motive for commissioning the set of vestments now in the Los Angeles County Museum of Art. Luisa Elena Alcalá, Universidad Autónoma de Madrid, presented a lecture on December 2, 2011, on the building of this shrine: "Material Choices: Representing the Virgin's Domesticity in Colonial Mexico." I thank Luis Eduardo Wuffarden for providing insight into the significance of the Marian imagery here (personal communication, August 8, 2012).

69. CHASUBLE

Europe (southern Germany or Austria?), 17th century
Textile: Turkey, 17th century
Lampas, silk, metal-wrapped thread, with metallic braid
46 x 27 ½ in. (116.8 x 69.9 cm)
The Metropolitan Museum of Art, New York,
Gift of J. Pierpont Morgan, 1906 06.1210

The design of the textile used to create this chasuble is a variation on the ogival pattern found on many Turkish silks. One ogival trellis is created by chevron-striped bands that connect large, leafy palmettes with pomegranates at the center. This intersects with another trellis created by serrated *saz* leaves whose stems are bound by a semicircular motif.[1]

While silks of this kind were made to satisfy fashionable tastes in Turkey, they were also exported abroad. The presence of many similar silk ecclesiastical garments in church treasuries is due in part to policies like those in effect in Venice, where ambassadors were required by law to surrender to the state any items presented to them while serving at foreign courts. Often the robes of honor the ambassadors received at the Eastern courts to which they were posted were hopelessly unfashionable at home and so were relinquished without protest. Offered at public auction, these items, if not sold, were donated to churches, where the textiles were repurposed for vestments.[2]

Unlike an eighteenth-century cope from Safavid Iran (cat. 64), this chasuble reveals no traces of the original garment from which it might have been made. Seams on the back and front correspond to the three panels created by the application of gold braid, and in each instance, the pattern has been carefully matched across the seam. The style of the chasuble, with a cross on the back and a V-shaped double orphrey band at the neck, suggests that it was made in southern Germany or Austria.[3] MS

1. A similar textile serves as the central band on the back of a chasuble in Skokloster Church, Stockholm (see Atasoy, Denny, Mackie, and Tezcan, *Ipek*, p. 262).
2. Monnas, "Textiles and Diplomacy: Ottoman Silks," forthcoming.
3. Johnstone, *High Fashion in the Church*, pp. 141–46.

70. CHASUBLE
Central Europe, 18th century
Textile: India (Coromandel Coast), second quarter
of the 18th century
Cotton, drawn and painted resist and mordant, dyed, silk trim
47 ½ x 28 ½ in. (120.7 x 72.4 cm)
The Metropolitan Museum of Art, New York,
Gift of Mrs. William Sloane Coffin, 1975   1975.212.5

This chasuble is constructed from a most unusual textile, from
which two distinct designs were taken to create the front and back
of the vestment. The back of the garment, shown here, was made
from a portion of the fabric with a pattern of repeating mound-
shaped motifs enclosed in an ogival frame linked by floral sprays;
the front uses a pattern of red diamond-shaped motifs resting
on a blue band, which once appeared on each side of the repeating-
mound pattern.

A departure from most of the dyed cloths made for export
on India's Coromandel Coast, this textile finds its closest visual
parallel in a group of European brocaded silks now referred to
as "lace-patterned." These eighteenth-century textiles are characterized by the use of large-scale motifs, especially streamers and
floral sprays, which are set against delicate, lacelike diaper patterning and floral vines. Although these silks were related to contemporary eighteenth-century fashions in lace, at the time they may
have been known as "persiennes" and were seen as having an
exotic Eastern flair (cat. 47A).

The relationship between this cloth and its European prototype is less direct than that of other Indian dyed cloths modeled
after the so-called lace-patterned silks, samples of which must
have been taken to India for the textile dyers to copy (cat. 47B).
Both this fabric and a very similar one used to make a Dutch
wentke recently acquired by the Metropolitan (cat. 49) have
diamond-shaped motifs and ogival frames linked by floral
sprays, showing a reliance on the same European textile source.
The prototype may have been Italian, as these fabrics reveal
intriguing resemblances to Italian examples from the first quarter
of the eighteenth century, which have comparably robust designs.[1]

The style of the chasuble—combining aspects of Austrian
and southern German fashions of the mid-eighteenth century—
suggests that the fabric was traded to central Europe.   MS

1. See, for example, Metropolitan Museum, acc. no. 52.1.3.

71. CHASUBLE
Portugal, early 18th century
Silk satin, brocaded with chenille and silk
Orphrey: Silk satin, embroidered with silk
and metal-wrapped thread
48 x 29 in. (121.9 x 73.7 cm)
The Metropolitan Museum of Art, New York,
Rogers Fund, 1942 42.97

Constructed from two different fabrics, this chasuble was probably made and used in Portugal in a Jesuit context. The body of the garment is a Portuguese white silk of the late seventeenth–early eighteenth century brocaded with polychrome silk and chenille yarns. The bright white satin ground of the center panels at front and back are embroidered with silk and silver threads; the materials of this center panel, including the satin ground fabric, are likely from Asia.[1] Narrow metallic woven bands, or galloons, outline the panels and neckline.[2]

A variety of images—including fanciful fountains, unicorns amid cypress trees, spotted leopards, peacocks with tails in full display, and several figures including Hercules and the haloed Christ Child—have been scattered by the weaver throughout the largely secular brocade of the side panels.[3] In contrast, the subject matter of the embroidered center panels is entirely Christian. On the front panel are the embroidered initials *IHS*, the Latin anagram for Jesus Christ used by the Jesuits, while the back panel bears a superimposed *A* and *M* for "Ave Maria" (or Hail Mary), the archangel Gabriel's salutation to the Virgin as reported in Luke 1:28. Above the two letters is a crown, and the entire image is surrounded by lilies. An embroidered inscription, QUI PASCITU INTER LILIA, a phrase from the Song of Songs (6:3) that translates as "He who feedeth among the lilies," surrounds a silver Paschal Lamb (representing the Lamb of God). Other Christian symbols in the panels include the Pelican in Her Piety, a flowering rose, and a silver pomegranate. The many references to the Virgin in the imagery suggest that this chasuble was used in a convent or in a Jesuit church dedicated to Marian devotion.[4]

This elaborate embroidery, with its variety of silk and metallic threads, shares traits and materials from both Portugal and Asia. The multicolor bands that represent the pelican, for example, are typical of Philippine embroidery (detail), yet the bright yellow dye is weld, a European dyestuff.[5] The flatness of the needlework and its limited palette, as well as the detailed rendering of the individual feathers at the tips of the birds' wings, are features that may be more Asian than European. A Peruvian example, based on an Asian model, also depicts bird feathers in this way.[6] It may be that the embroidery took place in Portugal,

71, detail

with artisans also following the Asian model, using a composite of Asian and Portuguese materials.   EP

1. The brocade, a five-harness silk on a white satin ground with weft float patterning, includes a number of different colors and types of yarns. Some are unspun silk, others are plied two-color (black and white), and still others are chenille yarns with a pile. The two center panels are a white satin seven-harness ground fabric with warp and weft yarns bearing no twist, which likely was imported from China. The embroidery for the silk is satin stitch, with couching stitches to hold the metallic yarns that outline the designs. The embroidery is sparse, revealing the white background throughout.

2. The tape is composed of weft-faced plain weave with silk warp and silk wrapped with metal-sheet weft.

3. This imagery is related to that in a more narrative panel with a large fountain as its central motif (Metropolitan Museum, acc. no. 35.30). Adele Weibel has identified this type of fabric as either Portuguese or from Extremadura in Spain and believes that a group of related textiles with fountains and chenille threads was produced by the same (unknown) master weaver; see Weibel, *Two Thousand Years of Textiles*, pp. 151–52, nos. 272 and 276. Another example can be found in the Textile Museum of Terrassa, Spain (no. 20926).

4. Letter from Ann Plogsterth to Alice Zrebiec, December 6, 1979, curatorial files, European Sculpture and Decorative Arts, Metropolitan Museum.

5. Dye analysis conducted in 2012 by Nobuko Shibayama in the Department of Scientific Research, Metropolitan Museum, using High Performance Liquid Chromatography (HPLC) confirmed the European dye source.

6. See Elena Phipps in Phipps et al., *Colonial Andes*, pp. 252–54, no. 76.

72. CHASUBLE

China, for the European market (possibly Spain),
mid-18th century
Silk satin, embroidered with silk
48 x 32 in. (121.9 x 81.3 cm)
The Metropolitan Museum of Art, New York, Gift of Nobuko
Kajitani, in honor of Nancy Haller, 1998 1998.368

This deep red satin chasuble was embroidered in China. Its slender, A-line shape was common in chasubles of eighteenth-century Spain, where it may have been used.[1]

The focal point of the embroidered design is the roundel with a double-headed eagle at the center of the vestment's front and back. Although the double-headed eagle surmounted by a crown was a symbol of the Habsburg monarchy, here it is purely decorative and tinged with an auspicious Chinese flavor.[2] Instead of grasping arrows in their talons, as they would in the Habsburg motif, the birds dangle flowering and leafy stems from their beaks. In Chinese textiles auspicious birds frequently hold symbolic flora: a rank badge in the Metropolitan Museum's collection features a crane that grips a branch bearing both a peach and a peach blossom.[3]

The front and back of the chasuble are each divided into three vertical sections, separated by narrow embroidered floral trim that also borders the neck and edges.[4] The central section consists of a series of vertically aligned roundels, floral rosettes, and geomet-

rically decorated vessels resting on stands amid a simple ogival pattern of flowering vines. On each of the two side sections, a graceful design of delicately curving leafy stems emerges from a multicolored cornucopia, a long-standing European motif. Cornucopias are included in at least two other eighteenth-century chasubles embroidered in China, one now in the Metropolitan and the other in the Museo Nacional del Virreinato, Tepotzotlán, Mexico, and formerly in the Catedral de Mexico—a reminder that there were markets besides Europe for chasubles embroidered in China.[5]

The scrolling pattern of the side panels is punctuated with large flowers, some of which include elements from Chinese decorative arts and others that are unusual from a Chinese perspective—even quite fantastic. The large flowers close to the cornucopias on the front of the garment and flanking the eagle roundel on the back are rather unrefined in technique, featuring dots on their radiating petals and a bold red, white, yellow, and blue coloration that lacks the more subtle shades of light red seen in the smaller flowers nearby, a customary coloration in Chinese embroidery. As dotted petals are fairly common in Indian floral textiles of the eighteenth century but unusual in Chinese examples, these bold flowers and other similarly distinctive blooms may reflect the Chinese embroiderer's attempt to mimic the Indian floral patterns that were so popular in international trade.   JD

1. Johnstone, *High Fashion in the Church*, p. 109.
2. Some examples of purely decorative double-headed eagles are found in Portuguese collections. See, for example, the detail of an eighteenth-century *colcha* in Pacheco Ferreira, *As alfaias bordadas sinoportuguesas*, p. 158, fig. 108.
3. Metropolitan Museum, acc. no. 36.65.10. Doubly auspicious, the crane represents the highest rank for a civil official, and both crane and peach are associated with longevity.
4. Another chasuble, embroidered in China and now in the Metropolitan Museum's collection (acc. no. 61.227), also has a tripartite division and a similar embroidered trim.
5. For the Metropolitan's example, see note 4 above; for the chasuble in Mexico, see Mayer et al., *Raiment for the Lord's Service*, pp. 274–75, no. 140.

73. CHASUBLE

Italy (probably Venice), mid-17th century
Plain-weave silk, brocaded
47 x 30½ in. (119.4 x 77.5 cm)
The Metropolitan Museum of Art, New York,
Gift of Dr. Richard J. Cross, William R. Cross Jr.
and Dr. Thomas N. Cross, in memory of their mother,
Mrs. William Redmond Cross, 1981   1981.85.3

Ecclesiastical vestments made of precious silk textiles imported from the Middle and Far East are documented in Europe by the Middle Ages. Vestments were normally made of a luxurious fabric, whether imported from afar or made closer to home. The silk of this chasuble exemplifies the conspicuous adaptation by European weavers of a design inspired by foreign sources. The colorful, stylized tulips and carnations arranged stiffly in rows of alternating diagonals are a nod to the more elegantly stylized floral silks of Safavid Iran (cat. 64).[1] Patterns of this type, with unconnected floral motifs, appear in Italian silks of the first half of the seventeenth century and signal a transition from earlier woven silk and velvet patterns that employed a continuous ogival framework (cats. 4, 5).[2] This particular design is augmented by the presence of a small floral motif between each of the larger ones, as well as the use of many different and apparently randomly arranged brocading colors for the flowers. The polychrome brocading threads are arranged to avoid any obvious pattern, which is characteristic of Safavid velvet weaving and has the effect of making a small pattern appear less repetitive and more complex.[3]

It has been suggested that this chasuble was made for a private chapel.[4] The coat of arms on its back has been tentatively identified with the Gradenigo family of Venice, which lends further support to an Italian origin for the textile. It was perhaps more acceptable to use an unusual or foreign-looking fabric for worship in a semiprivate setting, not unlike the European custom in the secular realm of reserving exotic textiles for informal dress and use in private spaces.   MW

1. For an analysis of the design and weave structure, see Watt, "Exploring Pattern in Woven Design," pp. 446–55, where the flowers were identified as tulips, daisies, violets, and strawberry plants. I would now identify the daisy as a carnation, and the violet as an iris or pansy.
2. For a selection of vestments made from European silks of this type, see Johnstone, *High Fashion in the Church*, p. 87.
3. Bier and Bencard, *The Persian Velvets at Rosenborg*, quoted in Watt, "Exploring Pattern in Woven Design," p. 451.
4. Walker et al., *Life and the Arts in the Baroque Palaces of Rome*, p. 249.

74A

74A. CURTAIN
India (Gujarat), late 17th century
Cotton, embroidered with silk
104 ¾ x 102 ⁹⁄₁₆ in. (266 x 260.5 cm)
Museum of Fine Arts, Boston, Samuel Putnam Avery Fund
and Gift of Mrs. Samuel Cabot, 53.2202

74B. CURTAIN FRAGMENT
England or Scotland, late 17th century
Fustian, embroidered with wool
55 ⅛ x 26 in. (140 x 66 cm)
Museum of Fine Arts, Boston,
The Elizabeth Day McCormick Collection, 53.172

74B

These two embroideries, one Indian and one British, are part of an extraordinary group of related furnishing textiles. The Indian curtain (cat. 74A) is one of a group sold in 1953 after the death of Lady Catherine Ashburnham (1890–1953), the last resident of Ashburnham Place, Sussex, a site occupied by her family for almost a thousand years.[1] The Ashburnham textiles are decorated with lively pastoral scenes along the lower border, with tall slender trees that grow from the rocky ground, sprouting bold flowers around which birds and insects fly. What makes this entire group unique is the fact that the pattern appears in both the embroidered curtains as well as the painted-and-dyed chintz curtains that were found at Ashburnham Place (fig. 142). The survival of two coordinating Indian embroidered panels—possibly bedcovers—with a central phoenix motif suggests that there were at least two sets of bed furnishings, although it is not clear whether the sets were originally intended to be grouped by technique (for comparably arranged creatures on Chinese embroideries, see cats. 26, 28).[2]

Taken together, these textiles present compelling evidence for the correspondence between European designs and the products of Indian cotton painting and embroidery workshops. It has been suggested that the entire set had a single European (probably British) prototype and that the Indian embroideries were based on the Indian painted chintzes that were produced first.[3] Although no patterns, or "musters," as they were called in the seventeenth century, have survived, this theory appears entirely plausible, particularly when we consider the culturally diverse

range of motifs present in these designs. The Chinese-inspired motif of perforated garden rocks anchors the landscape. The bold foliage and lively hunt scene reference European tapestries and embroideries, while the Anglo-Indian multiflowering tree that dominates the hangings would become the model for chintz and embroidered palampores of the eighteenth century (see cats. 37,

Fig. 142. Curtain. India (probably Gujarat), late 17th century. Cotton, painted resist and mordant, dyed. Museum of Fine Arts, Boston, Samuel Putnam Avery Fund and Gift of Mrs. Samuel Cabot (53.2201)

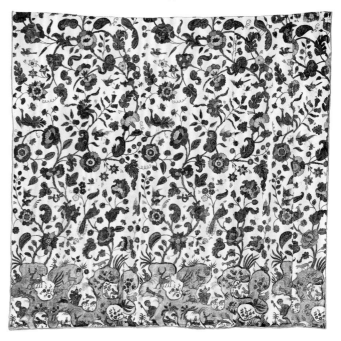

52, 75, 118). This pastiche of motifs, typical of European chinoiserie, was applied to fabrics that conform to the shapes and dimensions required for European bedchamber furnishings (fig. 137, cat. 52).

Whether the Ashburnham family was the original owner of the Indian-made furnishings has not been established, though the family had a taste for exotic goods. The first Earl of Ashburnham (John Ashburnham, 1687–1737) had a set of Chinese porcelain decorated with his coat of arms that survived in the house until 1953, as did several Asian export wallpapers, lacquer screens, and cabinets.[4]

The fragment of wool embroidery on fustian (cat. 74B) is one of three surviving British-made pieces with the same design as the Indian textiles. Two curtains also survive in Scottish collections, and all three pieces came from Cullen House, Banffshire, undoubtedly part of a single suite of furnishings.[5] While based on the same source,[6] the British embroidery fragment and the related curtains were almost certainly never part of the Ashburnham set. Technically these display an even closer relation to English seventeenth-century embroidery in the use of the dense cluster of knots forming the landscape, the shading of the hillocks, and the lively hunt scene—features typically found on works of the second half of the seventeenth century.   MW

1. For a history of Ashburnham Place and its occupants, see Hussey, "Ashburnham . . . ," in three parts. Sotheby's sold the contents of Ashburnham Place on June 24 and 26, and July 7–9, 15, 1953; these Indian furnishing textiles appeared in lots 476–86, in a section of the catalogue titled "Early Indian Embroideries and Chintzes, Etc." The chintz and embroidered panels from the sale are now divided among five museums: the Victoria and Albert Museum, London (chintz no. IS.156-1953, embroidery nos. IS.152-1953 through IS.155-1953); Cooper-Hewitt, National Design Museum, New York (chintz no. 1953-123-1, embroidered bedcover or palampore no. 1953-123-2); Museum of Fine Arts, Boston (chintz nos. 53.2201 and 54.28, embroidery no. 53.2202 [cat. 74A]), Calico Museum of Textiles, Ahmedabad, India (chintz no. 324, embroidery nos. 323, 325), and Metropolitan Museum (embroidery no. 54.21). Closely related pieces are also found in the Royal Ontario Museum, Toronto (embroidered bedcover or palampore, no. 978.33.1.1), and the Österreichisches Museum für angewandte Kunst/Gegenwartskunst, Vienna (chintz nos. H 1504 and T 9073).
2. For the bedcovers or palampores, see Beer, *Trade Goods*, pp. 57–58, no. 2; and Vollmer and Krasuski, "Preserving the Past: An Indian Embroidered Coverlet," pp. 24–31.
3. Irwin, "The Commercial Embroidery of Gujerat [*sic*] in the Seventeenth Century," pp. 51–57; Irwin and Brett, *Origins of Chintz*, p. 67.
4. Hussey, "Ashburnham Place, Sussex—II," pp. 1248, 1250.
5. For the curtains, see Swain, *Scottish Embroidery, Medieval to Modern*, pp. 54–59, and Arthur, *Embroidery 1600–1700 at the Burrell Collection*, p. 42, fig. 23.
6. Liz Arthur has identified the parrot motif in the British curtains as derived from Thomas Johnson's *Animalium quadrupedum . . . /A Booke of Beast [sic], Birds, Flowers, Fruits, Flies and Wormes* (1630); see Arthur, *Embroidery 1600–1700 at the Burrell Collection*, p. 42, fig. 23.

75. PALAMPORE

India (Coromandel Coast), for the European market,
mid-18th century
Cotton, embroidered with silk
11 ft. 1 in. x 8 ft. 6 in. (3.38 x 2.59 m)
Museum of Fine Arts, Boston,
Gift of Mrs. Frank Clark, 1957 57.168

Extraordinarily detailed, this embroidered palampore was chain stitched in silk on a cotton twill ground to imitate a painted palampore as precisely as possible, even to using white silk stitches within the flowers to simulate the tiny reserve patterns common to painted examples. Instead of springing from the more usual hilly mound, the tree on this piece grows out of a formation that is an interpretation of a Chinese scholar's rock, highlighting the easy overlapping of Chinese, Indian, and European motifs in eighteenth-century "exotic" textiles.[1] The flowers on the tree are a blend of European and Asian types; of particular note is the large pineapple, a New World fruit, that hangs from a branch at the upper right.

Patterns were available to the artisans who made both painted and embroidered palampores, and those patterns could be used interchangeably. In this piece, the central area of the embroidery with the rock and about two-thirds of the tree is almost identical to a painted example in the Victoria and Albert Museum, London (fig. 143). Although that palampore has a very different, wide swag border painted around the tree, both have identical narrow outside borders. The embroidered palampore is quite a bit larger than its painted relation, which explains why the branches of tree on the embroidery had to be extended and populated with somewhat more awkward flowers and leaves. Note that several of the floral elements on the lower part of the tree were repeated to fill the space: for example, the tulip and leaf from the lower left also appear at the upper left.

It is hard to precisely date this piece, which descended in the Dix family of Boston. Family history relates that it was first owned by Dorothy Lynde Dix (1746–1837), who married apothecary Elijah Dix (1747–1809) of Worcester, Massachusetts, in 1771. Elijah was no ordinary small-town druggist; throughout his life he also bought and sold real estate, owned vessels that plied the West Indies trade (the source of the various dyestuffs he sold in his shop), and in the late 1790s advertised that he had brigs setting sail for Amsterdam and Hamburg. He even seemed to have a stake in a "Calico Printing Manufactory" in Newton Falls, Massachusetts, which he advertised for sale in 1799.[2] In 1795 the Dixes moved from Worcester to a mansion in Boston, where Dorothy lived until her death. The first bequest of her will, to her

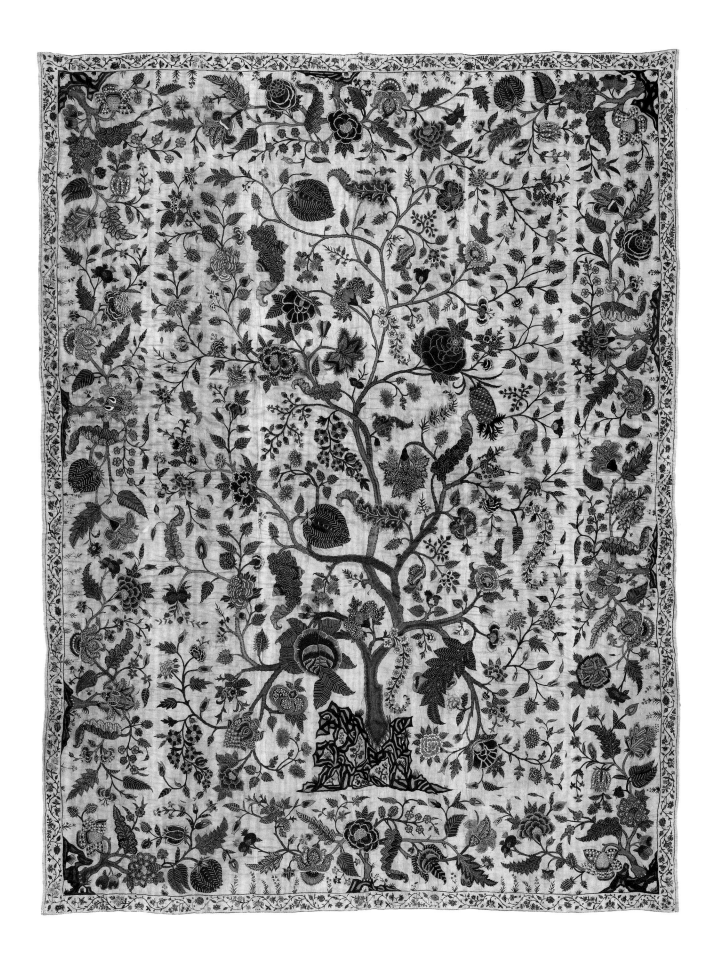

Fig. 143. Palampore. India (Coromandel Coast), ca. 1724–50.
Cotton, painted resist and mordant, dyed. Victoria and Albert
Museum, London; Given by G. P. Baker (IS.136-1950)

daughter, Mary Harris, was of her "worked counterpane."[3] This
treasured embroidery was handed down through five generations
in miraculously good condition before it was donated to the
Museum of Fine Arts, Boston, in 1957.   AP

1. For more on the blending of cultures in palampores, see Irwin, "Origins of the
'Oriental Style' in English Decorative Art," pp. 106–14.
2. In an advertisement in the *Massachusetts Spy, Or, The Worcester Gazette* (22,
no. 1090, February 20, 1794, p. 4), Dix announced the sale of "Drugs and Medicines, fresh imported . . . Die [*sic*] Stuffs, and West India Goods, as usual." In
1797 he advertised freight or passage on the brig *Ruthy* sailing for Amsterdam, and
the following year he sent out the brig *Minerva*; see *Massachusetts Mercury* 9,
no. 50, June 23, 1797, p. 3, and *Columbian Centinel* 29, no. 37, July 11, 1798,
p. 3. The calico printworks, which included all variety of tools and "patterns for
Calicoes, Copperplates, Shawls, and Handkerchiefs. . . . The prints are well executed, by an experienced print cutter, from Europe," was described in fascinating
detail in a notice in the *Massachusetts Mercury* 13, no. 49, June 18, 1799, p. 3.
3. Suffolk County, Massachusetts, Probate #31557 Will of Dorothy Dix, May 29,
1837 (date probated), Judicial Archives, Boston.

76. DRESS AND FICHU

Probably assembled and embroidered in England, ca. 1798
Textile: India, late 18th century
Cotton, embroidered with silk
Length 71 ¼ in. (181 cm)
The Metropolitan Museum of Art, New York, Purchase,
Irene Lewisohn and Alice L. Crowley Bequests, 1992
1992.119.1a–c

Thought to have been owned by Catharine Beekman (1762–1839),
third wife of New Jersey Supreme Court Justice Elisha Boudinot
and daughter of textile importer and dry-goods merchant James
Beekman, this embroidered cotton gown beautifully demonstrates
the participation of the American upper classes in the international luxury market (see the essay by Amelia Peck on East
India Company textiles for the North American market in this
publication). Catharine's father, descendant of a Dutchman who
settled in New York in the mid-seventeenth century, and his wife,
Jane Keteltas Beekman, were important members of New York's
social elite. Decades after attending George Washington's first
inaugural ball in New York in 1789, Jane Beekman was described
by a Colonel Stone to Rufus Wilmot Griswold as "among the
most distinguished women at the ball," all "'dressed with con-
summate taste and elegance.'"[1]

This open robe and underdress are cut in a fashionable silhouette of the late 1790s, constructed from fine Indian cotton
mull, embroidered with silk floss, and accompanied by a matching fichu, or scarf.[2] An elegant ensemble, it was probably
imported from Europe to satisfy the sartorial needs of a sophisticated consumer. A soft columnar form of gossamer mull, which
only hints at the contours of the body beneath, replaces the structured edifice of waist-cinching, hip-enhancing armature and
crisp silk of the early and mid-eighteenth century. Frequently
attributed to the late eighteenth-century interest in Neoclassical
imagery, the narrow silhouette also reflects the long-standing
influence of foreign trade on European taste. Early trade with
India introduced to ancient Rome a cotton textile so fine that
writers of the period described it as "woven air."[3] The muslin
was too precious a commodity to cut and so was draped and
pleated on the body into the unfitted forms said to inspire the
Neoclassical silhouette. Indian miniatures made for export introduced the eighteenth-century consumer to the same draped and
pleated treatment of the ethereal cloth (fig. 144). As the taste for
cottons in Europe shifted from inexpensive and cheerfully patterned textiles to fabrics attuned to the new desire for elegant
simplicity, fine Bengali muslins replaced the Gujarati printed
cottons as the primary textile import from India.[4]

In the 1780s white became the preferred color for fashionable women.[5] White silks and muslins like this were often embroidered with tambour work, a chainlike stitch made with a tiny hook developed in India and by midcentury adopted in Europe by both amateur and professional embroiderers. The polychromatic silk floss embroidery adorning this gown incorporates a number of stitch styles, including tambour work, into a border of flowers and decorative elements. The vermicular stems and looping daisy forms suggest the influence of northern India in style and technique, but both dress and embroidery were probably created in Europe.[6] Identifiable pansies, roses, carnations, wheat, ribbons, and bows reflect a European sensibility in the representational execution of popular English motifs. The meander of chains, vines, and swags synthesizes Eastern influences with an orderly Neoclassical arrangement along the border and hem of a fashionable European silhouette.   KS

1. Griswold, *The Republican Court*, pp. 155–56, illus. facing p. 155.
2. Golthorpe, "Europe 1700–1900; Open Robe with Underskirt and Fichu," p. 37.
3. Guy and Swallow, eds., *Arts of India, 1550–1900*, p. 22.
4. Berg, *Luxury and Pleasure in Eighteenth-Century Britain*, p. 62.
5. Ribeiro, *Dress in Eighteenth-Century Europe*, p. 234.
6. Campbell, "Embroidered Bodices," p. 61.

Fig. 144. *A Lady of William Fullerton's Household Seated on European Chair, Smoking a "Huqqa."* Murshidabad, India, ca. 1760–64. Gouache. Victoria and Albert Museum, London (D.1181-1903)

77. WAISTCOAT

England, second quarter of the 18th century
Linen, embroidered with silk and metal-wrapped thread
Length 40 in. (101.6 cm)
The Metropolitan Museum of Art, New York,
Rogers Fund, 1945 45.49

The plain white linen of this sleeved waistcoat, the requisite layer
between a gentleman's shirt and jacket, achieves the glamour of
early eighteenth-century luxury through the exotic flowers and
vines embroidered in polychrome silk and metallic thread over a
dense geometric filling pattern of flat quilting. A length of the
linen was embroidered and quilted *à la disposition* in the shape
of the pattern pieces that would be cut out and sewn together.
The continuation of both the quilted and the embroidered designs
around the back of the waistcoat and along the back vent is
unusual for a garment typically seen only through the opening of
a jacket. Likely the wearer intended to display this fine waistcoat

by removing his jacket in familiar company. The long sleeves,
straight cut, buttoned front, and fullness at the sides date this
waistcoat to early in the second quarter of the eighteenth century,
before the fashion for an increasingly slim cut of the outer jacket
eliminated the sleeves and the full skirt seen in this example.

The climbing vines embroidered in brilliant hues along the
borders of this waistcoat recall the vivid and exotic flowers of the
popular Tree of Life motif. This motif, long associated with
palampores imported from India beginning in the seventeenth
century, may in fact have its roots in European interpretations
of Chinese imports from the sixteenth century. It has been
argued, for example, that the Tree of Life form on palampores
bears closer resemblance to the painted wall hangings popular
in Elizabethan chinoiserie interiors than to the ancient Tree of
Life of Persian origin. European interpretations of Chinese motifs
made their way to India through the sample patterns sent to
Indian cotton painters and embroiderers by directors of the East
India companies.[1] On the floriated vines climbing our waistcoat,
the vibrant colors and denticulate edges of the petals and leaves
support an argument that the Indian interpretation of English
pattern sources in bright mordanted dyes indelibly altered the
images, rendering their possible Chinese origins unrecognizable.

The waistcoat's flat quilting offers evidence of more direct
Indian influence. Although the repeating geometric forms derive
from traditional English quilting patterns, the yellow thread on
an ivory substrate recalls the Indo-Portuguese quilts made in
Bengal in the seventeenth century (cat. 6). The popular application of flat or false quilting as a decorative feature on eighteenth-
century Western textiles has been attributed to Indian, Chinese,
and Persian embroidered imports.[2] Perhaps like the Chinese
roots of the Tree of Life motif, quilted patterns became so
inextricably associated with the domestic interiors of English
and American households that their Eastern origins are barely
distinguishable.   KS

1. Irwin, "Origins of the 'Oriental Style' in English Decorative Art," pp. 109–10.
2. Synge, *Art of Embroidery*, p. 184.

78. JACKET (CASAQUIN AND PETTICOAT)

Italy (probably Venice), ca. 1725–40
Linen, embroidered with wool
Jacket: length 32 ¾ in. (83.2 cm)
Petticoat: length 37 ½ in. (95.3 cm)
The Metropolitan Museum of Art, New York,
Purchase, Irene Lewisohn Bequest, 1993 1993.17a,b

This informal dress of simple linen is transformed by the fanciful embroidery in colorful wool thread that runs down its bodice and around the edges of the sleeves and forms a deep band around its skirt. The embroidery depicts exotic figures amid a profusion of exuberant flowers, fruits, birds, and pagodas that recall the dancing figures populating grotesques in the style of French designer Jean Berain (1640–1711).[1] The animated postures of the figures also correspond with those of mid-eighteenth-century Meissen porcelain groups representing the Four Continents. Personifications of the continents were a popular motif for a variety of decorative arts.[2] The dark and tawny skin tones of these embroidered figures, however, suggest that instead of an allegorical allusion they signify a general state of exoticism. Similarly, the pagodas specify an exotic locale, unlike the effect of a landscape of crumbling grottoes or Roman arches. The pagoda may have been recognized as an architectural symbol of the East from as early as 1665, when Johan Nieuhof, steward to the Dutch ambassador to China, published his illustrated catalogue of observations on Beijing (Peking) (see cat. 82).[3]

The large floral imagery articulated with shading as well as the architectural structures embedded in the fantastical landscape of oversize plants and animals is consistent with 1730s woven silks and embroidery designs (detail). However, crewel-work (bright embroidery in wool on a linen ground) was typically associated with domestic furnishings and fashion accessories and is rarely found on full ensembles.

The combination of *casaquin*, or jacket-bodice, and petticoat was popularized during the first quarter of the eighteenth century when the rigorous formality of the court of Louis XIV began to give way to the less restrictive elegance of negligée style.[4] It exemplifies the tendency among the fashionable elite of the time to incorporate working-class styles such as the *casaquin* and informal garments into their sartorial vocabulary. The striking character of the crewel embroidery on this *casaquin* and petticoat may indicate that they were meant to be worn to a masquerade, a social event in which the exotic and idiosyncratic reigned supreme.[5] KS

78, detail

1. Majer, "Europe 1700–1900; Casaquin and Petticoat," p. 38; a tapestry containing figures in the grotesques style of Berain is in the Metropolitan Museum, acc. no. 1977.431.2.

2. See Backlin, *The Four Continents, from the Collection of James Hazen Hyde.*
3. Nieuhof et al., *An Embassy from the East-India Company of the United Provinces to the Grand Tartar Cham, Emperor of China,* p. 195.
4. Boucher and Deslandres, *20,000 Years of Fashion,* p. 303.
5. See Ribeiro, "The Dress Worn at Masquerades in England," pp. 217–30.

79. PETTICOAT PANEL (ONE OF TWO)

England, 1690–1710
Linen, embroidered with silk
35 ½ x 52 ¾ in. (90.2 x 134 cm)
The Metropolitan Museum of Art, New York, Purchase,
Friends of European Sculpture and Decorative Arts Gifts,
2011 2011.413

By the late seventeenth century, the appeal of Far Eastern goods and motifs had reached most levels of English society. Those who could not afford a cabinet mounted with imported Asian lacquer panels or a suite of tapestries like those produced by John Vanderbank (cat. 85) could still satisfy their taste by wearing a petticoat or other fashionable accessory decorated with exotic motifs.

In 1688 John Stalker and George Parker published *A Treatise of Japanning and Varnishing*, which includes twenty-four copperplate designs that could be used to decorate a variety of objects (fig. 145). This book also gives detailed instructions on how to create imitation lacquer, or japanning, on various household objects. The text shows a lack of specificity regarding culture and geography that was typical of the period. For example, in their preface, the authors sing the praises of Japan and its architecture,

Fig. 145. A selection of toilet table accessories. Engraving. From John Stalker and George Parker, *A Treatise of Japanning and Varnishing. . .* , London, 1688, plate 4. The Metropolitan Museum of Art, New York, Harris Brisbane Dick Fund, 1932 (32.80.2)

but in the instructions the reader is advised "that if you would exactly imitate and copie [*sic*] out the Japan [design for imitation lacquer]" one should look to "the true Indian work" where they "never crowd up their ground with many Figures, Houses, or Trees, but allow great space to little work."[1]

There are extant English mirrors that retain their original "Japanned" frames, as well as American furniture decorated with motifs from works like *A Treatise of Japanning and Varnishing*.[2] However, such books inspired more than just imitation lacquer on furniture. This embroidered panel and its mate are among a number of English examples from the late seventeenth and early eighteenth centuries that are stitched with similar exotic designs. A small quilt in the Metropolitan Museum and two panels in the Museum of Fine Arts, Boston, are all embroidered with the motifs of the woman carrying a fan with an attendant who shades her with a parasol, and tiny pavilions dwarfed by oversize foliage.[3] One of the panels in Boston bears the rare signature of a professional pattern draftsman, one John Stilwell who had a shop near Covent Garden, London. Stilwell would have drawn his designs directly on fabric that was then embroidered; for inspiration he probably relied on publications such as *A Treatise of Japanning and Varnishing*. MW

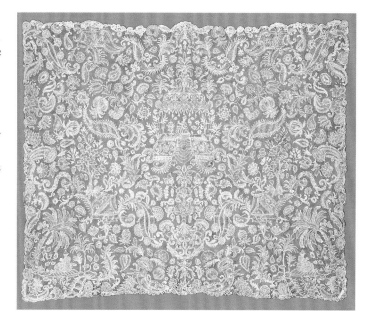

1. Stalker and Parker, *A Treatise of Japanning and Varnishing . . . 1688*, pp. xv, 40.
2. See, for example, a Connecticut chest of drawers, dated 1735–50, in the Metropolitan Museum, acc. no. 45.78.3; Safford, *American Furniture in The Metropolitan Museum of Art*, vol. 1, *Early Colonial Period*, pp. 275–78, no. 112.
3. See Metropolitan Museum, acc. no. 40.25, and Museum of Fine Arts, Boston (nos. 43.259 and 1995.5). The latter (1995.5) is inscribed in ink on the fabric: *John Stilwell Drawear at Ye Flaming Soord* [sword] *Rusill Street Covint Garden Remoove at Quartear-Day 2 ye* [3?] *Pidgins in halfe moone sreet.*

80. LACE COVER

Belgium (Brussels), 1730–50
Bobbin lace, linen
27 x 33 ½ in. (68.6 x 85.1 cm)
The Metropolitan Museum of Art, New York,
Gift of Mrs. Albert Blum, 1953 53.162.45

Lace played an especially important role in dress and interior decoration in eighteenth-century Europe. The finest handmade work was very expensive owing to the labor-intensive nature of its production. Lace design for fashionable dress was closely associated with that of other textiles, particularly the silks and velvets with which the finished product would be worn. Figural patterns are less common than floral ones, but many laces combined small figural scenes within an overall floral arrangement, as seen here in this lively example depicting people in Chinese dress taking tea. The scenes, typical of European chinoiserie, have little to do with the actual lives and appearances of Chinese people. Rather, they reflect a romanticized notion of the East as a place of pleasure, where one might relax in a garden, wearing capacious garments while sipping tea.

There was no shortage of visual sources from which a lace designer might draw this type of scene. It has been suggested that similar laces were inspired by early eighteenth-century editions of the tapestry series known as the Story of the Emperor of China.[1] Indeed, the seated figure at the center of this panel is a simplified version of the Chinese emperor in his fantastic pavilion, an oriental carpet spread before his feet (fig. 85). This popular series of tapestries was produced so many times during the early eighteenth century that by 1732 the cartoons at the Beauvais manufactory were almost completely worn out.[2]

Lace with obvious exotic motifs was relatively unusual; a spectacular example dates from 1744, when the provinces of the Austrian Netherlands gave the Austrian empress Maria Theresa an entire dress of bobbin lace decorated with feathery palm trees and exotic fruits. The empress was evidently so fond of this dress that she was painted wearing it not once, but twice.[3] MW

1. See Wardle, *75 x Lace*, pp. 55–56, no. 36, who discusses a needle lace flounce in the Rijksmuseum collection, Amsterdam, that has similar seated Chinese figures.
2. Standen, *European Post-Medieval Tapestries*, vol. 2, p. 464; for a discussion of the various design sources, see Standen, "The Story of the Emperor of China," pp. 103–17.
3. See Levey, *Lace: A History*, p. 71, fig. 329, and dust-jacket front; the portraits are by Martin van Meytens II (1695–1770) and an unknown artist.

81. PETTICOAT PANEL

India (Coromandel Coast), for the Dutch market,
third quarter of the 18th century
Cotton, painted resist and mordant, dyed
33 ⅝ x 67 ½ in. (85.4 x 171.5 cm)
The Metropolitan Museum of Art, New York, Purchase, Friends
of European Sculpture and Decorative Arts Gifts, 1992 1992.82

Like the *wentke* (cat. 49), petticoat panels made from this particular style of chintz are known to have been popular in the
Dutch province of Friesland in the mid- to late eighteenth century.
This panel was clearly made for use in a specific European market, but, like many chintzes, it is a hybrid of western European
and Indian styles. The scenes depicted on it may reflect the lives
of wealthy Dutch East India Company employees living in the
East. In the middle register, socializing groups of figures wear
European-style dress made of boldly patterned fabrics that appear
to be Indian painted cotton. Most notable are the women's petticoats fashioned of horizontal bands of differently patterned
textiles. In the lower border, military men on horseback brandish
sabers, and others on foot play musical instruments (for soldiers
in similar uniforms, see cat. 105). The central figure of this procession, clearly a man of importance, rides in an open carriage
decorated with multiple patterns. Both the stepped horizon on
which the socializing figures rest and the procession are related

Fig. 146. Petticoat. India (Coromandel Coast), ca. 1750. Cotton, painted and
dyed. Victoria and Albert Museum, London, Given by G. P. Baker (IS.13-1950)

to the painted-cotton hangings that were produced for the local Indian and Persian markets.

Petticoats decorated with wide decorative borders near the hemline such as this were fashionable in western Europe from about the 1730s through the middle of the century, and a number of European woven silk and embroidered examples survive.[1] Petticoats made for the provincial Frisian market, however, are thought to be of a slightly later date.[2] Unlike the panel shown here, some of the extant chintz examples adhere quite closely to European-style floral patterns and may have been made to appeal to a broader market than just Friesland. Others display an even more exotic flavor than the Metropolitan's panel, such as figure 146, in which the human figures are dwarfed by the grand flamelike arches over them, which allude to Thai architecture.[3]   MW

1. See, for example, an Italian embroidered version with chinoiserie motifs in Takeda et al., *Fashioning Fashion: European Dress in Detail*, p. 140; the Metropolitan Museum has a British embroidered version with Indian-inspired flowers, acc. no. 61.172, and a French woven version, acc. no. C.I.63.33.1.
2. See [Hartkamp-]Jonxis, "Some Coromandel Chintzes," pp. 37–57, for a discussion of this group of petticoat panels dated on the basis of European fashions; Hartkamp-Jonxis expressed a revised, later dating for this group in a letter of August 8, 1992 (department archives, European Sculpture and Decorative Arts, Metropolitan Museum).
3. The Victoria and Albert Museum example illustrated here is nearly identical to one in the Historisch Museum, Rotterdam (no. 23-1-1914); see Hartkamp-Jonxis, *Sits: Oost-west relaties in textiel*, pp. 208–9, no. 150.

82. DRESS (ROBE À LA FRANÇAISE)

France, ca. 1735; dress restyled ca. 1770
Textile: Dutch, ca. 1730
Silk satin, brocaded, silk and metal-wrapped thread
Length 63 in. (160 cm)
Museum of Fine Arts, Boston,
The Elizabeth Day McCormick Collection, 43.1871a–c

The polychrome silk-and-gilt brocaded satin that makes up this *robe à la française* has been attributed to Dutch production during the 1730s. With a pattern of lighthearted and exotic subject matter, this textile was a fashionable novelty in its time and would have been especially appropriate for the voluminous, loose sacque gowns then in vogue. The dress was remade into this more form-fitting style about 1770, when cotton was rapidly replacing even lightweight silks as the favored textile for informal dress, and the *robe à la française* was increasingly confined to formal occasions (see also cat. 58).[1] This example is cut with the very wide, flat panniers, pleated or "Watteau" back, square neck, V-front waistline, and fitted sleeves trimmed with tiered ruffles that characterized formal dress in 1770.

Brocades and damasks with large repeats of architectural motifs, genre scenes, and landscapes of heavily shaded three-dimensional flowers were popular for dress fabrics in the 1730s. In this example, rocky islands bloom with exotic oversize flora, and fanciful boats carry Asian characters. The images, though invented, demonstrate a familiarity with Chinese motifs. The restyling of this 1730s textile for a fashionable gown in the 1770s illustrates the enduring appeal of chinoiserie motifs throughout the eighteenth century. Not exclusive to silk design, Chinese figures were depicted at work and play on European printed cottons as they entered the fashionable market. Indeed, one of the first vignettes attributed to Christophe-Philippe Oberkampf's textile printing factory in Jouy-en-Josas was "Le chinois à la brouette," or "Chinaman with a Barrow" (1760).[2] In 1770 Oberkampf adopted a copperplate-printing technique that enabled the printers to achieve a subtlety in shading and design similar to that attained by weavers in the 1730s.[3] The arrangement of floating vignettes of chinoiserie fantasy on Oberkampf's cottons bear a striking similarity to the enchanting islands arranged on this 1730s silk.

In 1665 Johan Nieuhof, steward to the Dutch ambassador, published illustrations of an otherwise largely unsuccessful embassy to China.[4] Although the embassy failed to establish a free trade agreement with China, Nieuhof recorded images and descriptions during the mission that captured the imagination of all of Europe. Nieuhof's publication, *An Embassy from the East-India Company of the United Provinces to the Grand Tartar Cham, Emperor of China*, proved popular enough to be published in Latin, French, and English.[5] The influence of Nieuhof's book can be seen in this gown's brocade, with its prominent representation of an evergreen tree that corresponds to illustrations in his chapter 15, "Of Roots, Herbs, Flowers, Reeds, Trees, and Fruits."[6] As ships provided a crucial link between Europe and the unknown world of the exotic "other," it is no surprise that images of boating and fishing figure prominently in the fabric. The maritime world remained a popular subject for Rococo interpretations of chinoiserie by François Boucher, Jean Pillement, and other eighteenth-century European artists.   KS

1. Ribeiro, *Dress in Eighteenth-Century Europe*, pp. 33, 184.
2. Riffel and Rouart, *Toile de Jouy*, p. 165.
3. Ibid., p. 27.
4. The commercial missions of the East India companies were assigned charters by their native governing bodies authorizing them to form colonial constitutions and international trade agreements. Representatives of both government and private corporations traveled and worked together on these great commercial and ambassadorial missions.
5. Jacobson, *Chinoiserie*, p. 19.
6. Nieuhof et al., *An Embassy from the East-India Company of the United Provinces to the Grand Tartar Cham, Emperor of China*, p. 213.

83. DRESS (ROBE À LA FRANÇAISE)

Netherlands or Germany, ca. 1740s
Silk moiré, painted
Length 58 in. (147.3 cm)
The Metropolitan Museum of Art, New York,
Harris Brisbane Dick Fund, 1995   1995.235a, b

Oriental objects and images entering Europe in the eighteenth century were eagerly appropriated into an environment in which fashion theatrically incorporated cultural fantasies. The large-scale floral motifs on this *robe à la française* seem barely contained by the passementerie lattice of crocheted netting on which climb polychrome silk fly-fringe flowers. Billowing with the style's characteristically full back pleats over a corseted waist and broad pannier, the flowered silk transforms its wearer into an exotic floating garden.

Truly an inventive fancy, the painted application and dramatic execution of the flowers on this textile hint at an Asian source, but technical analysis has placed the fabric's likely area of manufacture in either the Netherlands or Germany. In response to demand for the textiles of India and China, factories were established in England, France, Holland, and Flanders to produce "indiennes," domestic cloth painted and printed after Asian styles made for export.[1] In 1681 an order from the English Court of Directors outlined the urgency for novelty in the market: "Now this for a constant and generall Rule, that in all flowered Silks you change ye fashion and flower as much as you can every yeare, for English Ladies and they say ye French and other Europeans give twice as much for a new thing not seen in Europe before, though worse, than they will give for a better Silk for the same fashion worn ye former yeare."[2]

Painted dress silks of the period were most commonly imported from China, but this silk has a European-style selvage with no contrasting color or temple holes (minor selvage imperfections) and is only nineteen and a half inches wide, a common width for a European loom. The paint, applied with the loose viscosity of watercolor directly on to the silk, has a chemical structure that is inconsistent with what was used on Chinese silks; that paint typically rests above the fibers on a thick lead-pigment base.[3] In addition, the colors on this silk were painted in layers to create a flat shaded effect on the swooping vines laden with lush and jagged blooms and berries, reminiscent of the much-favored Indian cotton palampores. The red-toned palette of the palampores, however, was replaced here with a cooler one, to suit contemporary taste, heavily reliant on the German discovery of Prussian blue.[4]   KS

83

1. Paulocik, "Investigating a Unique 18th-Century Painted Silk Costume," p. 41.
2. Jörg, "Chinese Export Silks for the Dutch in the 18th Century," p. 8.
3. Paulocik, "Investigating a Unique 18th-Century Painted Silk Costume," p. 42.
4. Martin, "Unraveling the Material History of Painted Silk Textiles through Micro-Analysis," p. 50.

84A, B. PAIR OF SIDE CURTAINS FOR A BED

Probably France, early 18th century
Linen, embroidered with wool and silk
A (53.32.1): 11 ft. 2 in. x 34 in. (340.4 x 86.4 cm)
B (53.32.2): 11 ft. 5 in. x 34 in. (348 x 86.4 cm)
The Metropolitan Museum of Art, New York,
Gift of Irwin Untermyer, 1953   53.32.1a–c, .2a–c

This pair of embroidered curtains with chinoiserie designs would have decorated the sides of a European state bed of the late seventeenth to early eighteenth century. Originally, these curtains may have been part of a larger suite of furnishings for the decoration of an entire bedroom—a canapé (settee) now in the private rooms of Madame de Maintenon at Fontainebleau has very similar embroidered designs.[1] The complete set of bed hangings probably included matching upper valances for the tester, lower valances for the frame supporting the mattresses, and a coordinating bedcover and headcloth, like the set of French bedroom furnishings now in the Metropolitan Museum (fig. 147).

Oversize fanciful flora, a design element familiar from the so-called bizarre silks, are joined in these curtains by human figures dressed in vaguely Chinese garments, imaginary Asian winged dragons, and pairs of long-tailed birds. Early chinoiserie-style furnishings, made in sturdy tent and cross stitches on canvas, were used over a wide geographic area in northern Europe during the first half of the eighteenth century, and a good number have survived.[2] The Metropolitan's side curtains, with their yellow background, are most likely French, as extant examples of the yellow or pale backgrounds are associated with production or use in France. To date, no documentation regarding the commission or production for these various suites of furnishings has been discovered, though we know that another such group was probably ordered from Paris in 1721 for Favorite Palace in Ludwigsburg, Germany, the summer residence of Sybilla Augusta, margravine of Baden-Baden (1675–1733).[3]

Most of these embroideries, however, were worked on a dark background, either blue or black, and are therefore more closely connected with the aesthetic of English tapestries from the likes of John Vanderbank, with their reference to the dark backgrounds of Asian lacquer screens (cat. 85). No design drawings or sources have been identified for these embroideries, which, like the Vanderbank tapestries, are decorative pastiches probably taking inspiration from the same variety of sources employed by contemporary tapestry designers, including imported fabrics and their European counterparts, the bizarre silks.[4]

Fig. 147. Bed with embroidered side curtains, upper and lower valances depicting scenes from Ovid and Aesop's Fables. France, early 18th century. The Metropolitan Museum of Art, New York, Gift of Irwin Untermyer, 1953 (53.2.1–8)

A feature of Chinese art that confounded and intrigued European observers is very much present in these embroideries. Writers from the late seventeenth and well into the eighteenth century remarked on the asymmetry that was prevalent in Chinese design and architecture, as opposed to the preference for symmetry and pleasing proportion in Western taste.[5] These early chinoiserie embroideries embody the attempt to capture the "beautiful disorder" that Europeans found so irresistible.   MW

1. See Véron-Denise, "Un mobilier à décor brodé de 'chinoiseries' au château de Fontainebleau," pp. 63–71; this suite, which is not original to the palace, is composed of several slightly different patterns; it was assembled in the nineteenth century from eighteenth-century elements.
2. For example, a set of chairs at Scone Palace, Scotland; wall hangings at Favorite Palace, Ludwigsburg, Germany; and other items in public collections in France, the United Kingdom, and America.
3. Grimm, "Favorite, a Rare Palace Exuding the Spirit of an Age when *Chinoiserie* Reigned Supreme," p. 83.
4. For a discussion of some of the possible sources, and the essentially decorative nature of these embroideries, probably designed by an unknown "artist ornemaniste," see Véron-Denise, "Un mobilier à décor brodé de 'chinoiseries' au château de Fontainebleau," p. 60.
5. For the comments of Europeans on the disorder and asymmetry of Chinese art and architecture, see Standen, "Embroideries in the French and Chinese Taste," p. 147, and Mitchell, "The Influence of *Tartary* and the Indies," p. 30.

85. THE TOILET OF THE PRINCESS

Attributed to John Vanderbank (active ca. 1680–1717),
Great Wardrobe tapestry workshop, London, 1690–1715
Tapestry weave, wool and silk
10 ft. x 12 ft. 10 in. (305 x 391 cm)
The Metropolitan Museum of Art, New York,
Gift of Mrs. George F. Baker, 1953   53.165.2

During his tenure as governor of the Dutch-controlled area of Brazil, Johan Maurits (1604–1679) commissioned two artists in his service to record the area's wildlife and inhabitants. The resulting works were translated into tapestries for him by 1678; he found them so impressively lifelike that he wrote, "it would be possible, by the tapestries, to see Brazil without crossing the ocean."[1] In contrast, the first English tapestries depicting exotic and foreign scenes were inventive compilations of motifs from the Far East. John Vanderbank, weaver in London, is recorded as having supplied nine pieces in the "Indian Manner" for the decoration of Kensington Palace in the 1690s.[2] These tapestries are thought to have been of the same type as the present hanging, and if this theory is correct, they would have complemented the vast collection of Asian porcelain and Dutch Delft ceramics of Queen Mary II (1662–1694). A print by Daniel Marot the Elder suggests the appearance of such a collection juxtaposed with wall decoration of either Asian lacquer panels or some European imitation.[3]

The Toilet of the Princess is one of two Indo-Chinese tapestry scenes in the Metropolitan Museum's collection. As many as fifty variations on these compositions of exotic characters on little islands floating on plain backgrounds were made in England, attesting to their popularity.[4] These tapestries were made in sets of varying dimensions and numbers of panels, depending on the room for which they were intended. Placing scattered vignettes against a dark background was a concept clearly inspired by the lacquer panels that were being imported to Europe from Japan and China. The diarist John Evelyn mentioned seeing an inventive use of lacquer panels in 1682, writing, "in the hall are contrivances of Japan Skreens, instead of wainscot; . . . The landskips of the skreens represent the manner of living, and country of the Chinese."[5] Individual motifs and groupings on the tapestries are an imaginative combination of Chinese and Indian scenes that derived from a variety of sources, including illustrations from the works of such European travelers and artists as the Danish Melchior Lorck (1526–after 1588) and the Dutch Arnold Montanus (1625?–1683).[6] The designer of the tapestries attributed to Vanderbank has not been discovered.

The original owner of this tapestry is not known. However, Elihu Yale (1649–1721) had four tapestries in this style, two

85

with designs very close to those in the Metropolitan Museum.[7] Yale was born in Boston, but his family moved back to England when he was a child. He served the East India Company from 1670 to 1692 and remained in Madras, India, until 1699, looking after his lucrative personal business interests there. Yale was governor of Fort St. George in Madras from 1687 to 1692. According to an English visitor to Madras in 1675, the English governors lived in great splendor with numerous attendants, thus Yale may have been attracted to these charming tapestries as a reminder of his lifestyle during his tenure in India.[8] Though he never returned to North America, Elihu Yale agreed to support a newly established college in New Haven by sending 417 books as well as bales of cloth to be sold, which brought in 562 British pounds.[9] The founders were so grateful for this windfall that in 1718 they renamed the school Yale College.   MW

1. See Campbell et al., *Tapestry in the Baroque: Threads of Splendor*, pp. 390–96, no. 48, this pp. 390–92. The original weavings are lost, but later sets survive.
2. See Standen, "English Tapestries 'After the Indian Manner,'" pp. 119–42, and Standen, *European Post-Medieval Tapestries*, vol. 2, pp. 717–25, no. 127. The tapestries made for Kensington Palace are recorded in the 1697 inventory, but they may not have survived to the present, as they have not been identified.
3. *Chimney-Piece with Various Porcelain Vases*, etching from *Oeuvres du Sr. D. Marot*, Daniel Marot (French, 1661–1752), published by Pierre Husson, 1703, Metropolitan Museum, acc. no. 30.4[43]. The medium of the wall panel in this print has been debated; Standen ("English Tapestries 'After the Indian Manner,'" pp. 137–38) noted that "it is always considered to be a leaf of a Coromandel screen, but it is not impossible that it represents a Vanderbank tapestry, perhaps even one in Kensington Palace." It is also possible that this represents a painted panel.
4. Ibid., p. 119. Very few of these tapestries are actually signed by Vanderbank, and other English producers made similar tapestries. My thanks to Elizabeth Cleland for her comments on this subject.
5. Quoted in ibid., p. 127.
6. Ibid., pp. 128–37.
7. *The Concert* (no. 1926.30), *The Toilet of the Princess* (no. 1926.31), *The Promenade* (no. 1926.32), and *The Palanquin* (no. 1932.130), Yale University Art Gallery, New Haven. None of the Yale tapestries are signed by Vanderbank.
8. See N[agel], "An Elihu Yale Tapestry," p. 143.
9. The cloth included calico, worsted (wool), poplin, and muslin to be sold, and some black silk crepe to make tutors' gowns; see Bishop, "Campus Honors Man Who Gave Yale Its Name."

86A, B. TWO PANELS FROM A TABLE CARPET SHOWING THE FOUR CONTINENTS, THE SEASONS, AND FOUR PLANETS

England, between 1662 and 1680
Linen and silk satin, embroidered with silk and wool,
passementerie of silk thread, silk-wrapped parchment, and metal
A (64.101.1347): 40 ½ x 94 ½ in. (102.9 x 240 cm)
B (64.101.1348): 41 ¾ x 95 ½ in. (106 x 242.6 cm)
The Metropolitan Museum of Art, New York,
Gift of Irwin Untermyer, 1964 64.101.1347, 1348

Personifications of the Four Continents, with symbolic animals and natural resources characteristic of each region, appeared in western European arts beginning in the sixteenth century. This imagery was frequently employed to confer honor and authority on a specific European ruler. The continents were most often represented by individual females rather than couples as seen here, and Europe was usually distinguished by her costume or a crown as superior to the others. In this instance, the couple representing Europe in the lower right of catalogue number 86B closely resembles contemporary images of King Charles II of England (r. 1660–85) and his Portuguese wife, Catherine of Braganza (1638–1705); in keeping with the tradition of presenting Europe as ruler over the others, they wear crowns and carry scepters.[1] The figures for Asia, Europe's closest neighbor and trading partner (presented to the left of the Europeans), are second in splendor to the Stuart monarchs and have the same number of attendants in their retinue. Africa and America occupy the same positions in the lower center of catalogue number 86A and display no discernible trappings of royalty.

Imagery in seventeenth-century English embroideries was highly dependent on published print sources, usually Continental imports or English adaptations of these Continental works. The seventeenth century saw a huge increase in the production and consumption of printed materials, from early newspapers to decorative prints, and London printsellers kept popular works in their inventories for decades.[2] In these two panels the continents and the planets can be traced to diverse sources.[3] Printers of decorative world maps also made creative use of contemporary images, and, not surprisingly, similar personifications of the continents were deemed suitable to decorate the corners of examples printed in London (fig. 148). As with contemporary embroidery compositions, successful motifs like the couples representing the continents were used repeatedly for many years.

These two embroidered panels were once probably part of a decorative table cover or carpet. The presence of table carpets in Europe is well documented in paintings and inventories of the

sixteenth and seventeenth centuries. The practice began as early as the thirteenth century with the importation from the Middle East of pile carpets that were too precious to use as floor coverings.[4] These were then imitated in various techniques, including needlework, by European craftsmen.[5] A square table carpet would have been an appropriate furnishing in a private library or study, where carpets or other fabrics decorated plain wood tables. Alternatively, these two panels may be the ends of a much longer, rectangular cover for a dining table. If that were the case, we cannot be certain how much is missing from the center.[6] What can be inferred from the combination of imagery on these panels is the owner's enthusiasm for the restored Stuart monarchy and his or her sanguine view of England's geopolitical standing during the later seventeenth century.   MW

1. Another image of the Stuart monarchs at the center of the world appears in an elaborately beaded basket in the Metropolitan Museum's collection, acc. no. 39.13.1; see Morrall and Watt, eds., *English Embroidery from The Metropolitan Museum of Art*, pp. 134–36.
2. See Griffiths, *The Print in Stuart Britain*, for a history of the production and consumption of printed material in seventeenth-century Britain.
3. See Hackenbroch, *English and Other Needlework, Tapestries and Textiles in the Irwin Untermyer Collection*, pp. xlii–xlv, 43, pls. 92–93. Hackenbroch attributed the prints of the Four Continents to Gilles Rousslet after Charles

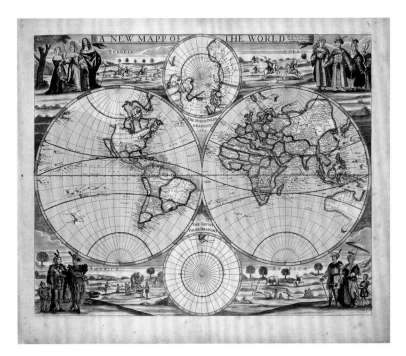

Fig. 148. *A New Mapp of the World*, after Robert Greene, ca. 1676. From *The Sea-atlas: Containing an Hydrographical Description of Most of the Sea-coasts of the Known Parts of the World*. Published by Samuel Thornton, London, ca. 1702–7. New York Public Library, Map Division (02-295)

86A

86B

Le Brun (1619–1690), but they are almost certainly after prints published by
Frederik de Wit (d. 1706), a printseller active in Amsterdam in the second half
of the seventeenth century who also produced maps; the Planets are probably
after Maarten van Heemskerck (1498–1574). Although Hackenbroch did not
identify sources for the Four Seasons, personifications of the seasons were popular
in seventeenth-century Britain. See Griffiths, *The Print in Stuart Britain*,
pp. 110–15.

4. For a concise history of the use of imported Eastern carpets as table coverings
in Europe, see Mills, "The Coming of the Carpet to the West," pp. 10–23.
5. One of the best-known English examples is the early seventeenth-century Brad-
ford table carpet in the Victoria and Albert Museum, London (no. T.134-1928).
6. I am grateful to Annabel Westman, Executive Director of the Attingham Trust,
London, and Cristina Carr, Conservator, Department of Textile Conservation at
the Metropolitan Museum, for their comments.

87A. PICTORIAL CARPET
Iran, Safavid period (1501–1722), 17th century
Silk (warp, weft, and pile),
metal-wrapped thread, brocaded
91 ½ x 68 in. (232.4 x 172.7 cm)
The Metropolitan Museum of Art, New York,
Gift of C. Ruxton Love Jr., 1967 67.2.2

87B. MIRROR WITH JAEL AND BARAK
England, 1672
Satin, embroidered with silk and metal-wrapped thread, beads,
purl, mica, seed pearls; wood frame, celluloid imitation
tortoiseshell, mirror glass, silk plush
28 ¾ x 23 ¾ in. (73 x 60.3 cm)
The Metropolitan Museum of Art, New York, Purchase,
Mrs. Thomas J. Watson Gift, 1939 39.13.2a

This extremely fine silk carpet (cat. 87A), with approximately 1,025 knots per square inch, is exceptional in subject matter, palette, and execution. Its unusual features have confounded scholars, who have proposed dates ranging from the sixteenth to the nineteenth century, places of origin from Iran to India and Istanbul, and sources of inspiration from English and Flemish tapestry. Recently, however, the attribution of the carpet has been restored to seventeenth-century Iran, the identification with which it had entered the Metropolitan Museum in the 1960s.[1]

The context for this carpet's production thus emerges as the cosmopolitan world of Safavid Iran, which in the 1600s was expanding its diplomatic and commercial contacts with Europe. As a result, prints, paintings, and books presented as gifts by European emissaries circulated at the court, and Iranian artists started to experiment with elements of European art such as modeling, perspective, and Christian subject matter.[2]

It appears that the designer of this carpet was similarly inspired by a European source, though perhaps a book rather than the tapestries usually suggested. John Gerarde's 1597 *The Herball or Generall Historie of Plantes*, expanded, reprinted, and widely available in the seventeenth century, has a title page with a layout comparable to the carpet's, with a central field bordered by several rectangular panels and figures in arched niches (fig. 149). Several other features are common to both title page and carpet, including the figures of Pomona, the Roman goddess of fruitful abundance (shown on the carpet holding apples, one variation of her iconography), and her husband Vertumnus, god of seasons and change (sometimes depicted with a dog), as well as vases filled with towering arrangements of flowers. Similar vases also appear in English embroideries of the period.[3]

While Gerarde's *Herball* was not the exact source for the carpet, several seventeenth-century books on botany that include Roman goddesses such as Pomona and Ceres and vases holding flowers were almost certainly available in Iran. We know that Nicholas Wilford, an envoy of Charles I of England (r. 1625–49), took with him to Iran "A Booke of flowers stampd" and had been instructed by the king to deliver portraits of the English royal family in order to win the favor of the Safavid shah.[4] The carpet's designer must have copied one half of a title page, reversed it to create the other half of the pattern, and then filled the center of his composition with a European-inspired landscape.[5]

The adaptation of design and imagery from title pages, biblical illustrations, and allegorical prints was also common practice among embroiderers in Europe, particularly in the small workshops around seventeenth-century London. English domestic furnishings from this period are frequently decorated with combinations of biblical narratives and mythological figures, and this mirror frame (cat. 87B) has such a combination of imagery.[6] In keeping with the tradition of using exemplary biblical characters and narratives as didactic tools within a secular domestic setting,[7] the figures flanking the glass are Jael, a heroine who craftily slew one of the Israelites' enemies, and Barak, the Jewish general who triumphed thanks in part to her intervention (the story comes from chapter four of Judges). An allegorical group of Charity with three children surmounts the mirror. The embroidered figures are arranged around the mirror, much in the way that figures are arranged around the center of a book's title page.

In the corners, however, where one often finds the lion and the leopard from the English royal coat of arms, we find instead four animals that almost certainly signify the Four Continents. In the lower corners are the stag, associated with Europe, and the camel, associated with Asia—typical iconography that was developed in the sixteenth century (cat. 86A, B). Here the creatures that represent Africa and the Americas are mythological: the griffin, with its lion's body, most likely represents Africa, and the basilisk, which is part reptile, probably personifies the Americas, though the symbols for these two continents were not always used consistently.[8] Reference to the wider world begins to appear in English secular embroidery during the second half of the seventeenth century, as the nation expanded and strengthened trade relations with the East.   MS and MW

1. For the original attribution, see Martin, *A History of Oriental Carpets before 1800*, p. 68. For the recent confirmation of this attribution, see Daniel Walker in Ekhtiar, Soucek, Canby, and Haidar, eds., *Masterpieces . . . of Islamic Art in The Metropolitan Museum of Art,* p. 269, no. 188.
2. For an identification of some of the European works known to have been in Iran, see Sims, "The European Print Sources of Paintings by the Seventeenth-Century

87A

Persian Painter, Muhammad Zaman ibn Haji Yusuf of Qum," pp. 73–83, figs. 75–85; and Ferrier, "Charles I and the Antiquities of Persia," pp. 51–56.
3. See, for example, Metropolitan Museum, acc. no. 64.101.1298.
4. Ferrier, "Charles I and the Antiquities of Persia," pp. 51, 55.
5. Similar landscapes appear in other Safavid works, such as on a lacquered pen box signed by the artist Hajji Muhammad, Metropolitan Museum, acc. no. 2000.491a, b.
6. See Geuter, "Embroidered Biblical Narratives and Their Social Context," pp. 56–77, for more on the practice of domestic decoration with embroidered biblical figures; in the same catalogue, Morrall and Watt, eds., *English Embroidery from The Metropolitan Museum of Art*, see pp. 216–21, no. 56, for this mirror frame.
7. See Morrall and Watt, eds., *English Embroidery from The Metropolitan Museum of Art*, for this practice in embroidery; see also Wells-Cole, *Art and Decoration in Elizabethan and Jacobean England*, for the use of Continental prints in other secular decoration.
8. This iconography also appears on a beaded basket in the Metropolitan Museum's collection, acc. no. 39.13.1; see Morrall and Watt, eds., *English Embroidery from The Metropolitan Museum of Art*, pp. 134–36.

87B

Fig 149. Title page of John Gerarde (English, 1545–1611/12), *The Herball or Generall Historie of Plantes*. London, 1597.

88. LA FOIRE DU CAIRE (THE CAIRO FAIR)

Attributed to Petitpierre et Cie

France (probably Nantes), 1785–90

Cotton, copperplate printed

86 x 37 in. (218.4 x 94 cm)

The Metropolitan Museum of Art, New York,

Gift of Mrs. William Sloane Coffin, 1975 1975.212.10a

La caravane du Caire, an opera-ballet composed by André-Ernest-Modeste Grétry (1741–1813) with a libretto by Étienne Morel de Chédeville (1751–1814), was first performed at Fontainebleau on October 30, 1783.[1] The French elite so adored the exotic and dynamic work that it was performed more than five hundred times in Paris before 1829. The opera was one of the many manifestations of the French fascination with the Ottoman Empire (Egypt was then part of the empire, making Cairo a legitimate site for the story). During the second half of the eighteenth century, operatic themes of intrigue and romance based on characters and tales from the Middle East gained favor over the traditional ones taken from antiquity and classical mythology.[2] The seraglio, or harem, so intriguing to Europeans, inevitably made an appearance in these stage productions. In *La caravane du Caire*, the plot is driven by the fate of a pair of lovers—Saint-Phar, a Frenchman, and Zélime, the daughter of an East Indian ruler—who meet as captive slaves. Zélime's rescue from the harem and her reunion with her lover provide the requisite happy ending.

The opera, which dealt nominally with the subject of slavery, was commemorated on at least three variations of French toile (for another treatment of the subject of slavery, see cat. 107B).[3] Dubbed "the Cairo fair" or market, this piece of fabric contains one vignette showing a grand domed pavilion, which houses various wares for sale. Another vignette printed on the fabric shows the pasha reclining on cushions in an open tent and admiring a

88

woman of the harem, presumably Zélime. This type of tent, which resembles an oversize version of the French daybed known as a *lit à la Turque,* is identified as Turkish by the small crescent motifs above the draped and tasseled curtains. The composition is reminiscent of the representation of Asia in the Beauvais tapestry series of the Four Continents (cat. 102D) and in Amédée van Loo's designs for Turkish-themed tapestries.[4] While neither the designer nor the exact source of the design for the *La foire du Caire* is known, the vignette is typical of contemporary European representations of the luxurious life of a benevolent sultan and his seraglio.   MW

1. For a synopsis and brief history of the opera, see Charlton, "Caravane du Caire, La."
2. See Meyer, "*Turquerie* and Eighteenth-Century Music," pp. 474–88, for a summary of this phenomenon.
3. Two other textiles inspired by the opera are in the Metropolitan Museum, acc. nos. 26.233.24, a contemporary printed textile, and 31.130.7, a nineteenth-century adaptation.
4. See Stein, "Amédée Van Loo's *Costume turc,*" pp. 428–30, esp. p. 429, fig. 15.

89. CURTAIN FROM A SET OF FURNISHINGS

Attributed to John Munns (active ca. 1769–84)
England (probably Crayford, Kent), ca. 1770
Cotton, copperplate printed
83 ¾ x 58 ½ in. (212.7 x 148.6 cm)
Philadelphia Museum of Art: Gift of Mrs. Horace Wells Sellers
in memory of her husband, 1935 1935-38-5a

The garden design on this chinoiserie-style cotton is attributed to John Munns, an English calico printer who established himself in the business after first working as a gunpowder manufacturer.[1] The crisp, detailed printing demonstrates that Munns's workshop was capable of producing high-quality copperplate prints on fabric. Munns's reputation must have spread, for his was one of the English manufactories visited in 1774 by Christophe-Philippe Oberkampf, owner of the successful printworks at Jouy-en-Josas, France.[2] Indeed, there is a paper impression from a copperplate of another Chinese-inspired garden design by Munns in the Musée de l'Impression sur Étoffes, Mulhouse, further evidence of French interest in English products and technology.[3]

   The curtain is one of eleven surviving pieces from a set of furnishings, probably for a bedroom. The other pieces include valances (for a bed tester) and chair-seat covers. This set may have been purchased by ancestors of the donors; the Sellers family has been in the Philadelphia area since the eighteenth century.[4] Benjamin Franklin, in a letter to his wife written from London in February 1758, described his purchase of a large quantity of fabric for a similar suite of furnishings as well as some dress fabric: "There are also 56 Yards of Cotton, printed curiously from Copper Plates, a new invention, to make Bed & Window Curtains; and 7 yards Chair bottoms, printed in the same Way, very Neat. . . . Also 7 yards of printed Cotton, blue Ground, to make you a gown."[5] The dress fabric seems not to have been a copperplate print, since it was on a blue background, and as far as we know, the new copperplate designs were printed exclusively on plain white backgrounds.

The concept for Munns's Chinese garden fabric may have been inspired by the towering pagoda at Kew Gardens, designed by Sir William Chambers (1722–1796) between 1757 and 1763. Chambers then published his work in *Plans, Elevations, Sections, and Perspective Views of the Gardens and Buildings at Kew in Surrey . . .* (1763), and fragments of a copperplate-printed cotton in the Victoria and Albert Museum, London, include a view of the pagoda from this book.[6] The pagoda in Munns's copperplate print is closer to the single-story structures illustrated in plates 42, 49, 53, 60, and 103 of *A New Book of Chinese Designs* (1754) by Matthew Darly (ca. 1720–1778). In addition, a willow tree and fence in plate 81 of Darly's book are very similar to those near the little bridge in Munns's pattern (fig. 150). Darly's plates were probably intended for use by professional craftsmen, but they were adapted and republished in a popular compilation of 1760 called *The Ladies Amusement: Or, The Whole Art of Japanning Made Easy.*   MW

1. *Catalogue of a Loan Exhibition of English Chintz*, p. 25.
2. Chapman and Chassagne, *European Textile Printers in the Eighteenth Century*, p. 156.
3. See Callahan, "A Quilt and Its Pieces," p. 127, fig. 36; and Montgomery, *Printed Textiles: English and American Cottons and Linens*, p. 238. A total of thirty-two paper impressions by John Munns are preserved in the museum in Mulhouse.
4. I thank Philadelphia Museum of Art staff members Dilys Blum and Laura Camerlengo of the Costume and Textiles Department for sharing their research into the genealogy of the donor family.
5. Quoted in Montgomery, *Printed Textiles: English and American Cottons and Linens*, p. 29, from a letter in the American Philosophical Society, Philadelphia.
6. Victoria and Albert Museum, London (nos. 492-1894, 827-1894, and 1615A&B-1899), made by Collins, Woolmers, in 1766.

89, detail

Fig. 150. *Varied Rails*. Etching and engraving. Plate 81 of Matthew Darly, *A New Book of Chinese Designs*. . . . Published by Kimball & Donnell, 1754. The Metropolitan Museum of Art, New York, Harris Brisbane Dick Fund, 1931 (31.88)

90. SALTCELLAR
Edo peoples, court of Benin, Nigeria, ca. 1525–1600
Ivory
Height 7 1/8 in. (18.1 cm)
The Metropolitan Museum of Art, New York,
Louis V. Bell and Rogers Funds, 1972 1972.63a, b

This work belongs to a corpus of some two hundred Afro-Portuguese ivory artifacts that are the earliest creations from Africa to enter European collections beginning in the late fifteenth century. The carvers, active in Sierra Leone and southwestern Nigeria at the court of Benin, were engaged by Portuguese merchants who established trading partnerships along the coast of West Africa. European spoons, forks, horns, and saltcellars were reinterpreted to embrace local motifs and aesthetic sensibilities. The resulting African creations, such as this example, represent a distinctive hybrid of European and African decorative arts and iconography. Acquired as exotic mementos and presentation pieces for persons of distinction, many of these found their way into royal *cabinets de curiosités*.

It has been proposed that this work and at least fifteen other closely related saltcellars were commissioned by a Portuguese

official who was based in the region of the kingdom of Benin over a period of several years.[1] Direct contact between emissaries of King João II of Portugal (r. 1481–95) and Benin was established in 1486.[2] Benin emerged as a regional power as a result of the trading partnership that developed between its king and Portugal; in addition to ivory, pepper was a precious commodity in early trade. Over time, slaves, stone beads, and locally woven textiles were acquired at Benin by the Portuguese. These goods were exchanged for gold obtained at Elmina, situated farther up the coast in present-day Ghana. The Portuguese in turn provided the king of Benin with brass and copper, cowrie shells, coral and glass beads, and European and Indian textiles.[3] They also came to serve as mercenaries in the Benin army and sought unsuccessfully to convert Benin's leadership to Christianity.

Stylistically the works produced by artists at the Benin court emphasize exacting representations of physiognomy, dress, and regalia of both local and foreign subjects. In that hierarchical center, apparel was an important sign of rank and status. The degree of attention given to details of dress of the exotic outsiders captured in this work created for export, however, surpasses that of contemporary plaques cast in brass that were commissioned by the king of Benin for the exterior of his palace.[4] This saltcellar is made up of two halves of a sphere that meet about the midline of the figures and, at the level of their heads, another hemispherical chamber that is missing its lid. The figures of four Portuguese men gripping weapons ring the perimeter: two face frontally, wearing pectoral crosses, brigandines (fabric jackets to which metal plates are fixed with rivets), decorated stockings, shoes, and high-crowned feathered hats; alternating with them, two figures in three-quarter stance wear keys at their belts and are dressed in jerkins, plain stockings, shoes, and caps.[5]   AL

1. Bassani, Fagg, and Mark, *Africa and the Renaissance: Art in Ivory*, p. 166.
2. Ezra, *Royal Art of Benin*, p. 12.
3. Ibid.
4. Ibid., pp. 128, 143–45.
5. Bassani, Fagg, and Mark, *Africa and the Renaissance: Art in Ivory*, p. 161.

91A

91B

91A. YOUNG MAN IN PORTUGUESE DRESS

Iran, Safavid period (1501–1722), mid-17th century
Ink, opaque watercolor, and gold on paper
Painting 7 x 3 ⅞ in. (17.8 x 10 cm),
page 12 ¼ x 7 ¼ in. (31.1 x 18.4 cm)
The Metropolitan Museum of Art, New York,
Rogers Fund, 1955 55.121.23

Attributed to Mukunda

91B. ALEXANDER IS LOWERED INTO THE SEA

Folio from a *Khamsa* (Quintet) of Amir Khusrau Dihlavi
India, Mughal period (1526–1858), 1597–98
Ink, opaque watercolor, gold on paper
9 ⅜ x 6 ¼ in. (23.8 x 15.9 cm)
The Metropolitan Museum of Art, New York,
Gift of Alexander Smith Cochran, 1913 13.228.27

In Iran and India, the Portuguese had fairly autonomous colonies from which their commercial activities operated, which gave them an advantage over the trading concerns of other European countries. In Iran, their base was the Persian Gulf island of Hormuz, from which Indian Ocean trade was launched; in India, it was Goa, a major port on the subcontinent's west coast. The Portuguese presence in these regions is reflected in the two paintings shown here, one a study of a young man in Portuguese-style cloth-

ing, the other an illustration in which several protagonists are depicted as Portuguese.

European figures generally appear in two modes in Safavid-period painting from Iran, either in erotic scenes or in gently mocking portraits. The former became popular in the mid-seventeenth century and show men in European dress making love to women whose dress and accessories mark them as prostitutes. The latter are part of a larger group of paintings inspired by the artist Riza, who made several portraits of foreigners between the years 1625 and 1630.[1] Paintings by Riza and other artists in his circle captured what they saw as the most characteristic aspects of European dress and behavior. Foreigners are shown wearing hats with squared crowns and wide brims, buttoned tunics with white collars and cuffs, and voluminous pants tucked into tall leather boots; they engage in what was considered a highly odd activity, doting on their pet dogs. This painting of a young man (cat. 91A) does not fall easily into either category. His facial features are those of the beautiful Iranian court youths commonly depicted in the seventeenth century, unlike the broader features used to denote European ethnicity. The habit of dressing in exotic costume was not as widespread in Iran as it was in Europe, but this portrait may record a passing trend.

In Mughal India, the Portuguese were accorded more respect than they were in Iran. Jesuit priests were called to the court of the emperor Akbar (r. 1556–1605) for serious discussions of their religious beliefs, and the establishment of the colony at Goa allowed for extended cultural exchanges with the Mughal and other regional courts. *Alexander Is Lowered into the Sea* (cat. 91B) was painted to illustrate a luxury copy of a poem by the Indian poet Amir Khusrau Dihlavi (1253–1325), of which part concerns the life of Alexander the Great. The Macedonian conqueror is shown being lowered in a glass diving bell into the sea, where he spent one hundred days as a test of his faith.

All of the figures in this painting wear dress incongruous to the fourth-century B.C. setting for the story, but while those in Indian dress come from the sixteenth-century milieu in which the painting was made, the appearance of men in Portuguese dress is surprising. It has been suggested that, in Mughal minds, the strong connection between Europeans and shipping prowess explains their inclusion here and in other paintings that feature boats; indeed, most ships that appear in Mughal paintings have European crews.[2] In the late 1590s the main European power in India was Portugal, whose might was founded on her maritime strength.   MS

1. See the discussion in Canby, *The Rebellious Reformer*, pp. 174 and 176, fig. 9 and nos. 127 and 128.
2. Seyller, "Pearls of the Parrot of India," p. 90.

92A. HAREM SAMPLER

Laura Hyde (born 1787)
Franklin or Norwich, Connecticut, 1800
Linen, embroidered with silk
13 1/4 x 13 in. (33.7 x 33 cm)
The Metropolitan Museum of Art, New York,
Rogers Fund, 1944 44.113

Inscription: INDIA WITHIN / THE GANGES // LAURA HYDE / HER SAMPLER Æ / 13 JUNE 27 1800 // THE OUTPART OF / THE KAYS HAREM / THE BRITISH EMBAS / SADORS LADY AC / COMPANIED BY A / GRECIAN LADY VISETS [*sic*] / THE KAYS LADY AT THE HAREM // BAY OF BENGAL

92B. FRONTISPIECE: "LADY MARY WORTLEY MONTAGU 1720"

From *The Works of the Right Honourable Lady Mary Wortley Montagu: Including Her Correspondence, Poems, and Essays*, edited by James Dallaway, 5 vols. (Richard Phillips, London, 1803)
Printed book with engraved frontispiece illustration
6 5/8 x 3 5/8 in. (16.8 x 9.2 cm)
General Research Division, The New York Public Library,
Astor, Lenox and Tilden Foundations

Inscription (around edge of engraving): SIR GODFREY KNELLER PINX. FREEMAN SCULPT

In 1800 thirteen-year-old Laura Hyde made the rather surprising choice to embroider a scene of a Turkish harem onto her needlework sampler. Hers is one of a small group of samplers made by girls from the neighboring towns of Franklin and Norwich, Connecticut. The related samplers all have similar layouts showing a variety of compartmentalized scenes and motifs, and some include large sailing ships and views of foreign lands, such as Laura's scenes of "India Within the Ganges" and the "Bay of Bengal."[1] While these views may have derived from prints or illustrated books, common sources of inspiration for teachers and students of needlework, Laura's scene of the harem is unique, not based on any known print.[2] It illustrates letter 33 in the published correspondence of Lady Mary Wortley Montagu (1689–1762), one that she wrote to her sister the Countess of Mar, from Adrianople, Turkey. In it she describes her visit to the harem of the "*kayha*'s lady," the "gloriously beautiful" Fatima.[3] In Laura's embroidery the scene unfolds as described: Lady Mary and "the Greek lady" (her interpreter), under a large umbrella, are escorted into the tent of the harem. There they walk "between two ranks of beautiful young girls" to "a sofa, raised three steps, and covered with

92A

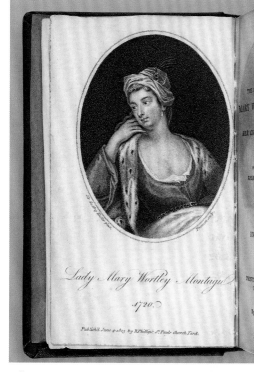

92B

fine Persian carpets," where they meet Fatima and her two young daughters.

Lady Mary traveled to Turkey in 1716, when her husband, Edward Wortley Montagu, was appointed English ambassador. Although they were in Turkey for only a year, she enjoyed her travels and admired much of what she saw. She kept copies of the letters describing her experiences that she sent to family and friends. In the 1720s she edited the letters, and though they were circulated in manuscript form, they were not published until 1763, the year after her death. *The Turkish Embassy Letters*, as they are known, were widely read and may have been influential in bringing greater European acceptance of Turkish arts and culture. But almost immediately upon her return, Lady Mary popularized the taste for wearing exotic "Eastern" costumes in portraits and to masquerades; she posed for several portraits wearing Turkish dress she had brought home from her travels, such as the garments seen here in the portrait frontispiece of her writings after a 1720 painting by Sir Godfrey Kneller (see also cat. 100 and fig. 82).

Why did scenes of Turkey and India appeal to young Laura Hyde as subjects for embroidery? One of the ships in her rendition of the Bay of Bengal flies an American flag. The sampler was made not long after the commencement of direct American trade with India in 1784, and Norwich, a shipping town north of New London on the Thames River, likely benefited from this connection. This schoolgirl's sampler reminds us that trade facilitated the new United States' arrival on the world stage. In addition, the turn of the nineteenth century saw a greater emphasis on the intellectual education of girls, and who could have been a better role model for a young woman than the glamorous, literate, and adventurous Lady Mary? AP

1. A sampler similar to Laura's was made in 1803 by Anna Huntington, another Franklin girl. At the bottom left, instead of the "Bay of Bengal," Anna showed a view of "Jerusalem," and on the bottom right, instead of the harem, she illustrated a river filled with sailing ships labeled "The Levant." Some of the ships are identical to those in Laura's "Bay of Bengal." See Krueger, *New England Samplers to 1840,* fig. 64.

2. At the time these samplers were made, the bookstore of printer John Trumbull (1752–1802) was in Norwich. He advertised an extensive range of schoolbooks, maps, and prints that would have been available to local teachers. See advertisement, *Norwich Packet* 24, no. 1242, January 2, 1798, p. 4, and advertisement, *Norwich Packet* 28, no. 1440, October 20, 1801, p. 1.

3. The *kayha* (abbreviated "kay" by Laura Hyde) was the steward of the grand vizier's establishment, a job that clearly brought him enough wealth and position to have a harem of his own.

93A

93B

**93A. PANEL WITH ROSEBUSH, BIRDS,
AND DEER PATTERN**

Iran, late 17th–early 18th century
Compound twill, brocaded, silk and metal-wrapped thread
44 ⅝ x 27 ¾ in. (113.3 x 70.5 cm)
The Metropolitan Museum of Art, New York,
Anonymous Gift, 1949 49.32.99

**93B. PANEL WITH BIRDS AMID
FLOWERING VINES**

Iran, first half of the 17th century
Compound plain weave, silk and metal-wrapped thread
31 ½ x 62 ³⁄₁₆ in. (80 x 158 cm)
Museum of Fine Arts, Boston, Gift of Philip Lehman in memory
of his wife Carrie L. Lehman, 1938 38.1055

Even though raw silk, rather than finished textiles, was the main commodity exported from Iran, the country's luxury textiles circulated abroad as part of the diplomatic exchanges that took place to facilitate this trade. Gifts sent from the Safavid shahs to their foreign counterparts were composed primarily of textiles, either bolts of cloth or finished garments. In this way, high-quality Safavid fabrics of the types illustrated here, as well as velvets (cat. 64), passed through royal treasuries in Europe and into the collections of churches and court aristocrats, sometimes influencing local fashion and design.

The first panel (cat. 93A), of which additional fragments are known,[1] represents the best of Safavid production and exemplifies the type of luxury fabric offered as a royal gift. In its Iranian context, the pattern of rosebushes, birds, and deer is one that appears frequently between the seventeenth and nineteenth centuries, created in many types of weave structures.[2] This particular piece was made in a samite weave, a weft-faced compound weave in which the passes are bound in twill. What appear to the modern eye to be very bold patterns were fashionable in the mid-seventeenth century for clothing, and it was common to wear garments of contrasting figural designs layered over one another.

The second textile (cat. 93B) also displays a design of birds and flowers. In this case, rather than being arranged in discrete motifs that repeat across the field, the flowering vines create an allover trellis pattern in which parakeets and nightingales perch among blossoms of roses, lilies, carnations, and irises. The pattern is created in the common seventeenth-century technique of *taqueté*, a weft-faced compound weave in which the weft is bound in tabby. The metallic ground of the fabric is woven with flat strips of gilt silver wrapped around a yellow silk core that enhances the golden color of the metal. Comparatively stiff textiles like this were used for furnishings such as curtains and door hangings, or for more tailored garments such as robes with straight, flaring hips that were worn as the outermost layer of clothing.[3]

Textiles of this type were presented to the Habsburg rulers of Spain and Portugal and can also be found in royal treasuries in Russia, Denmark, and Sweden. In Europe these fabrics were used to furnish palaces, to create garments presented to courtiers, and, in some cases, to serve as gifts to other heads of state. In an instance of re-gifting, albeit on a very high level, Tsar Alexis I Mikhaylovich (r. 1645–76) sent a Persian robe that he had received from a Safavid delegation to Queen Christina of Sweden (r. 1632–54), possibly on the occasion of her accession to the throne (see fig. 74). It remains in the Swedish royal collection.[4] MS

1. These are in the Textile Museum, Washington, D.C. (no. 3.141), the Nelson-Atkins Museum of Art, Kansas City, Mo. (no. 31-126/41 C), and the Yale University Art Gallery, New Haven, Conn. (no. 1937.4871). Many other similar textiles are known, including one in the David Collection, Copenhagen (no. 33/1992).
2. Mary Anderson McWilliams in Bier et al., *Woven from the Soul, Spun from the Heart*, pp. 176–77, no. 20.
3. See the discussion by McWilliams in ibid., pp. 172–73, no. 18.
4. The robe, dated about 1630, is made of velvet with a metal ground. It was likely from the 1639 embassy en route to visit the duke of Holstein. Published in Geijer, *Oriental Textiles in Sweden*, p. 103 and pl. 15; and Walton, "Diplomatic and Ambassadorial Gifts of the Sixteenth and Seventeenth Centuries," pp. 78, 86–87.

94. PANEL WITH FLORAL MEDALLIONS IN A DECORATED LATTICE

Turkey, late 16th century
Lampas, silk and metal-wrapped thread,
with later silk lining and cotton fringe
46 x 26 ¼ in. (116.8 x 66.7 cm)
Philadelphia Museum of Art, Purchased with Museum funds,
1876 1876-1174c

94, detail

In this length of fabric, gold ogival medallions contained within an ogival lattice are arranged in staggered horizontal rows. The medallions are decorated with red, white, and blue flowers, which include the typically Ottoman tulips, carnations, and narcissi. The gold lattice is articulated with a band outlined in blue and filled with a red checkerboard pattern.

This type of textile is known in Turkish as *kemha*, meaning it was woven in a lampas structure, that is, the red areas were woven in satin weave, while the gold, blue, and white areas were woven in twill. To create the areas of gold, a thin strip of gilt-silver foil was wrapped around a silk thread; in some areas, the metal has tarnished or worn away, leaving the yellow silk core visible. A hexagonal stamp on the reverse of the fabric, still undeciphered, may be that of the *damga emini*, or stamping official, who was charged with inspecting finished bolts of silk. Those that met the government-set standards were marked with his stamp, permitting their sale.

Within the Ottoman realms, large-pattern silks were popular for clothing made for the sultans and the elites who served at his court. These silks are characterized by the arrangement of motifs along undulating vines, in staggered or aligned rows, or within ogival lattices. On these textiles, dark blacks, reds, and purples contrast with light yellows, greens, and blues and are complemented by rich silver- and gilt-metal-wrapped threads. These patterns and palette were applied to a variety of media, including glazed tiles and carpets, and were used on fabrics of all levels of production, from court to bazaar. What marked the best textiles from those for cheaper markets was the warp density, the quality of the silk and dyestuffs, and the silver content of the metal-wrapped threads.[1]

Throughout the fifteenth century, as Ottoman conquests brought important land and sea routes under the control of the sultan, the networks of commerce by which Ottoman wares could reach external markets were expanded, and Ottoman silks found new buyers, especially in eastern Europe. This textile must certainly have passed to a European owner, who added the multicolor fringe and green lining now attached to it.   MS

1. As revealed through a 1502 judicial inquiry discussed in Atasoy, Denny, Mackie, and Tezcan, *Ipek*, pp. 162–64.

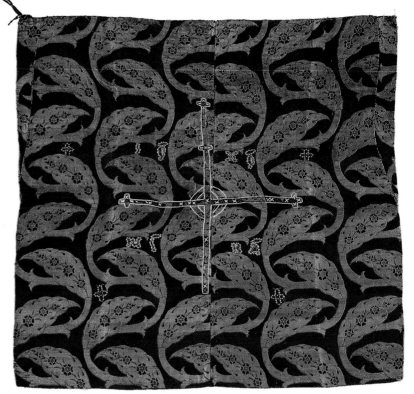

95. CHALICE COVER
Russia, 17th century
Textile: Turkey, second half of the 16th century
Lampas, silk and metal-wrapped thread,
later embroidered with pearls
21 ⅝ x 23 ¼ in. (54.5 x 59 cm)
Los Angeles County Museum of Art,
Gift of Miss Bella Mabury, M.39.2.478

Representing another major stylistic group within the corpus of Ottoman silks, this textile bears a design of leaves growing from a sinuous vine. The rhythmic arrangement of the motif is thought to derive from fourteenth-century Chinese brocaded silks with undulating vines (fig. 151), but by the sixteenth century the pattern had been modified according to local tastes, and this example is executed in a distinctively Ottoman manner. The leaves have the serrated profile that is a hallmark of the *saz* design style, and they are filled with the stencil-like floral sprays found on many Ottoman textiles. The fabric's structure is *kemha*, a lampas combining twill and satin weaves.

In the Ottoman world, the wavy-vine pattern was most popular between the mid-sixteenth and the early seventeenth century and came to be applied to works in many materials, including the ceramic tiles so commonly employed to decorate architectural interiors.[1]

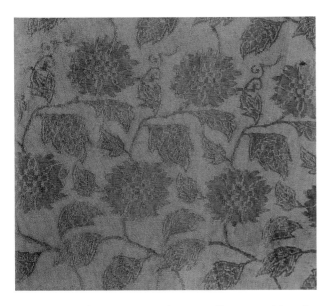

Fig. 151. Silk textile with a design of peony scrolls. Excavated from the tomb of Qian Yu, Wuxi, Jiangsu. Dated 1320. Wuxi Museum, China

Aside from their use in the Ottoman realms, silks like this traveled throughout Europe via commercial and diplomatic routes. They made an impression in Russia particularly, becoming very fashionable for a period in the seventeenth century. At formal events, *boyars* and *okolnichy* (the aristocrats closest in rank to the ruling princes) wore only clothing made of richly brocaded Turkish textiles.[2]

Similarly, many churches in Russia owned vestments and paraphernalia made of Ottoman silks. The square textile shown here appears to have been pieced from several fragments or adapted from a garment whose seams are still visible. It was embellished with pearl embroidery of a kind found on many Turkish textiles used in Russian churches and was fashioned into a cover to protect the chalice of Eucharistic wine during the Communion service.[3] MS

1. See, for example, a tile panel with a comparable design in the Metropolitan Museum, acc. no. 22.185.13a–f.
2. Zagorodnyaya, "Russian Foreign Relations and Diplomacy," pp. 20–41, esp. p. 27.
3. For examples of Ottoman textiles embroidered and used in Russian churches, see Atasoy, Denny, Mackie, and Tezcan, *Ipek*, pp. 249–50.

96. MAN'S MORNING GOWN (JAPONSCHE ROCK)

Japan, for the Dutch trade, ca. 1725–75
Silk, resist-dyed and painted, silk lining and filling
Length 68⅞ in. (175 cm)
Centraal Museum, Utrecht, The Netherlands, 8141

As of 1641, the Dutch were granted a highly profitable privilege: they became the only European power permitted by the shogunate to trade with Japan. This men's silk morning gown (called *japonsche rock* in Dutch) was made in Japan especially for that trade.[1] It represents an eighteenth-century continuation of Dutch traders' practice of acquiring Japanese robes for shipment to high officials of the Dutch East India Company (Verenigde Oost-Indische Compagnie, or VOC) in the Netherlands.

Dutch traders received *japonsche rocken* during their annual audience with the shogun to renew the trade agreement. Engelbert Kaempfer, a German doctor who accompanied the group of traders from the VOC's compound near Nagasaki to Edo (Tokyo) in 1691–92, provided firsthand observations describing how the Dutch were given robes at various phases of the journey by officials ranging from local magistrates to the shogun himself. At that time the shogun's formal gift consisted of thirty robes; those were considered the most desirable because of both the donor and the robes' high quality.[2]

Judging from four similar robes in museum collections[3] and from a list of *rocken* sold at auction in 1765,[4] the present example—made of silk with pictorial patterns—is typical of robes the Dutch received in the eighteenth century. The fashionable patterns and techniques used in this fabric show that the Japanese were clearly not passing off inferior merchandise to the Dutch. This gown's yellow kerria roses (*yamabuki*) were associated poetically with flowing water (suggested by its blue background), as in this poem by Fujiwara no Shunzei (1114–1204) about the Tamagawa (Jewel River) at Ide, south of Kyoto: "As I stop my horse to give him water, / *yamabuki* flowers drop their dew / Into the stream of Tamagawa at Ide."[5] The poem was one of many alluding to six specific rivers named Tamagawa, and about 1700 these rivers and their associated poems became a unified theme in Japanese literary arts.[6] Coincidentally, the Dutch traders probably traveled near the Tamagawa at Ide on their trip between Nagasaki and Edo.

Among the flowering branches are auspicious drawstring bags for valuables. The bags' top edges and some of the *yamabuki* blossoms feature a paste resist-dyed spotted pattern that mimics *kanoko shibori*, or spotted tied resist-dyeing; both pattern and technique are consistent with Japanese textiles of the first half of

96

the eighteenth century (fig. 152). Wider than the usual Japanese silk, the fabric of the gown may have been imported from China; the cloth may also have been intended for a *yogi*, a kimono-shaped coverlet.[7]

In this example and two of the others, the patterns evoke male literary characters; perhaps the Japanese were considering the intended recipients when the garments were made.[8] In form, the *japonsche rocken* resemble the Japanese kimono in having been constructed without shoulder seams. Instead, the body pieces of both styles consist of two long pieces of cloth, the right and left sides of the garment, which extend unbroken over the shoulders; however, the sleeves of the *rocken* were joined to the body in a manner typical of Western dress rather than of a kimono.   JD

1. The dressing gown has been published in Akveld and Jacobs, eds., *De kleurrijke wereld van de VOC*, p. 46; Brand and Teunissen, eds., *Global Fashion/Local Tradition*, p. 189.
2. Kaempfer, *Kaempfer's Japan*, esp. pp. 368, 411.
3. Four similar *japonsche rocken* are known to this author. Two are preserved in the Gemeentemuseum, The Hague (no. K 77-x-1987 [on permanent loan from Museum De Lakenhal, Leiden] and no. K 492-1892) and have been exhibited in various venues (Kyoto, Paris, Tokyo, among others) of an international traveling exhibition organized by the Kyoto Costume Institute: *Mōdo no japonisumu: Kimono kara umareta yutori no bi*, pp. 53–54, 145; *Japonisme et mode*, pp. 187–88; and *Mōdo no japonisumu*, pp. 35–37. A third example, unpublished, is in the Huis Van Gijn, Dordrecht (no. 2810). A fourth candidate is in the Gotha Sammlung Völkerkunde (Eth. 18T); see Bräutigam and Morper, *Über den ziehenden Wolken der Fuji*, p. 167, no. 220. Detailed information about the provenance of the five dressing gowns is so far not available. The present piece

Fig. 152. Design no. 195. Yamanobe Tomoyuki and Ueno Saeko, *Kosode moyō hinagatabon shūsei* (Compendium of kimono design pattern books), vols. [17–27], facsimile of *Nishikawa yu momiji* (Evening maple leaves of west river [Kyoto, 1718]), Tokyo: Gakushū kenkyūsha, 1974

was given to the Centraal Museum, Utrecht, by a Dutch noble family in 1937, according to Ninke Bloemberg, Curator, Fashion and Costumes, Centraal Museum, email message to the author, February 15, 2012.

4. VOC records are cited in support of this list. See Lubberhuizen-van Gelder, "Japonsche Rocken," pp. 137–52, esp. pp. 144–45.

5. Murase et al., *Jewel Rivers*, pp. 156, 159 n. 11, as amended by Murase, email message to the author, January 30, 2013.

6. Ibid., p. 156.

7. Miller, "Europe Looks East," p. 163. Miller mentions that Professor Iwao Nagasaki commented in 2003 that the Dutch in Japan wore *yogi* coverlets.

8. The example on loan to the Gemeentemuseum from the Museum De Lakenhal (see note 3 above) has a pattern of conch shells, frequently linked to the hero Benkei; the other robe in the Gemeentemuseum features several *tori kabuto*, headgear for a court dance, amid maple leaves, suggesting Prince Genji's dance in chapter 7 of *The Tale of Genji*; the present dressing gown, in its association with Shunzei's poem, evokes a male traveler on horseback.

97. MAN'S MORNING GOWN (BANYAN OR ROCK)
India (Coromandel Coast), for the Dutch market,
early 18th century
Cotton, painted resist and mordant, dyed
51 ⅛ x 74 ¾ in. (130 x 190 cm)
Royal Ontario Museum, Toronto, 959.112

The Dutch term *rocken* (gowns) best identifies this class of Indian export textile for the Dutch market, although *banyan*— a word used in the late seventeenth- and eighteenth-century English textile trade for an Indian-made loose-fitting gown for relaxed wear—has wider currency.[1] Tailored from Indian chintz

Fig. 153. Kimono with Three Friends design, symbolizing the noble virtues of good character. Japan, late 17th century. Silk, tie-dyed and embroidered. Royal Ontario Museum, Toronto (949.49)

that has been painted to a pattern anticipating the intended garment, this gown consciously imitates a Japanese kimono decorated with the Three Friends theme (fig. 153), here expressed as a pine tree and prunus blossom on a red ground. Unlike most garments tailored from chintz to European requirements, which were cut from lengths of repeat-patterned cotton, this gown was patterned expressly to produce a *rock*: selvages and cut edges were assembled before dyeing.[2] The floral borders of the sleeves and front opening are integral to the fabric, not tailored; only the collar has been worked separately, from excess fabric resulting from the reduction to the drop of the sleeves to reflect shifting fashion, probably in the third quarter of the eighteenth century.[3]

In the late seventeenth century the wearing of a man's Oriental-style morning gown became de rigueur in Europe. Such was its popularity that special regulations were proclaimed to dissuade men from wearing them to church.[4] This curious style innovation was the direct result of the Dutch trading companies' annual petitioning of the Japanese shogun at Edo for trading privileges. As part of the associated gift exchange, large numbers of padded silk kimonos were received by the Chief Merchant; in 1692, for example, one hundred twenty-three gift gowns

(*schenkagierocken*) were inventoried as a result of one such royal audience.[5] Each year these gowns, which the Dutch called *japonsche rocken*, were duly dispatched to Batavia for export to Amsterdam, where they proved immediately popular, both for their exoticism and for their comfort (see cat. 96). Such was the demand for them that it was decided to commission painted-cotton versions from the Coromandel Coast. In 1688 the Dutch East India Company commissioner-general at Fort Geldria, Pulicat, Hendrick A. van Rheede, made a pioneering study of chintz production, the first detailed and accurate description of this manufacturing process.[6] A year later van Rheede advised that he was sending from Pulicat six Indian chintz gowns in the Japanese style and that he could supply one thousand next year if so requested.[7] The popularization of the chintz version of the original silk gown, still named *japonsche rock*, had begun in earnest, and persisted throughout the eighteenth century.[8] It remained the gentleman's preferred literati attire, so much so that many elected to have their portrait painted wearing this favorite gown (cat. 99).   JG

1. The term *banyan* was adapted from the Hindi word for trader, denoting their distinctive mode of dress.
2. This rarely occurs; another notable example is a Siamese soldier's jacket in this publication (cat. 41).
3. Irwin and Brett, *Origins of Chintz*, p. 108, no. 102, pl. 96.
4. As early as 1672, English East India Company officers and soldiers serving in India were ordered to wear only "English apparel" on the Sabbath; Yule and Burnell, *Hobson-Jobson: Being a Glossary of Anglo-Indian Colloquial Words and Phrases*, p. 65.
5. Breukink-Peeze, "Japanese Robes: A Craze," p. 54.
6. Dutch East India Company Records, December 1, 1688, translated by Laarhoven in Guy, *Woven Cargoes*, pp. 34–36. This preceded by some fifty years the French description by M. de Beaulieu in 1734.
7. Breukink-Peeze, "Japanese Robes: A Craze," p. 56.
8. Gorguet Ballesteros et al., *Modes en miroir*, pp. 92, 96, 223, no. 124.

98. MAN'S MORNING GOWN (BANYAN)

England, 1735–40
Silk
Length 59 ⅝ in. (151.4 cm)
The Metropolitan Museum of Art, New York, Purchase,
Irene Lewisohn Bequest, 1981 1981.208.2

In the early eighteenth century, masculine displays of luxury in public were conveyed through the graceful management of stiffly tailored suits of fine cloth and heavy ornamentation. In private, however, sartorial luxury was found in the ease and comfort of unstructured attire. For men, the most popular garment for these informal settings was the banyan.

The earliest and most commonly depicted banyan silhouette was a kimono-shaped garment like this example in brown silk faille. A relaxed fit and lightweight textile provided welcome reprieve from the unforgivingly slim silhouette of conventional eighteenth-century formal jackets.[1] Although the shape of this banyan reflects Japanese influence, the narrow width of the fabric (fewer than sixteen inches) and the faille weave indicate European manufacture.

This silhouette may have originated in a Dutch adaptation of the Japanese kimono (cat. 96). Like the one shown here, the silk kimono-style banyan was frequently made in a muted monochrome fabric, offering a respite from the elaborate ornamentation as well as the rigid construction of formal dress. Veering away from the bright colors of the *japonsche rocken*, this impeccably made, fully lined banyan anticipates the modern standard for luxury in menswear—a taste for subtle sophistication that emerged at the end of the eighteenth century.

The banyan was popular for private portraits from as early as the mid-seventeenth century, when such undress communicated elite worldliness without displaying more ostentatious fashions that were often criticized as effeminate;[2] the garment's apparent exoticism existed outside the judgment of prevailing gender norms. When the banyan left the intimate precincts of the domestic interior, it carried with it an aura of exclusive fraternity. Contemporary descriptions of banyans worn in public, both critical and kind, placed it most frequently in the secluded haunts of masculine culture. In 1711, for example, the English writer and politician Joseph Addison observed law students wearing "Night-gowns"; in 1713 it was mentioned in *The Guardian* that men in banyans were seen at the Pump in Bath; and in 1772 it was noted that they were worn by men in gambling houses.[3] When depicted in prints and paintings of mixed company in public, the banyan most often identified its wearer as a merchant, somebody with access to the peripatetic network of traders, trav-elers, and commercial ambassadors. With one foot in the shop and one foot on the cargo ship, merchants claimed a worldly sophistication by donning a garment evocative of international provenance (cat. 99). KS

1. Ribeiro, *Dress in Eighteenth-Century Europe*, p. 20.
2. Kettering, "Gentlemen in Satin," p. 46.
3. Cunningham, "Eighteenth-Century Nightgowns," pp. 5–6.

John Singleton Copley (1738–1815)
99. JOSEPH SHERBURNE (1710–1779)
Boston, ca. 1767
Oil on canvas
50 x 40 in. (127 x 101.6 cm)
The Metropolitan Museum of Art, New York,
Amelia B. Lazarus Fund, 1923 23.143

John Singleton Copley, North America's best portraitist of the
eighteenth century, painted most of his male sitters in traditional
three-piece suits consisting of a long-sleeved coat and matching
knee breeches, with either a contrasting or a matching waistcoat,
in fabrics ranging from the finest silk velvet to stout wool. But a
few, including Joseph Sherburne, chose to have themselves painted
in a type of informal "undress," wearing voluminous morning
gowns, or banyans, with turbanlike hats on their heads instead of
wigs. (For more on the use of the banyan in the West, see cats. 96–
98). At the time of Sherburne's portrait, this fashion of scholars,
scientists, artists, and writers to sit for their likenesses in banyans

was already a century old. Indeed, being portrayed in a banyan
had unmistakable cultural connotations of gentility, creativity,
and intellectual pursuits.[1]

Joseph Sherburne was a wealthy Boston merchant, age
fifty-seven at the time this portrait was painted. He was the
son of a merchant of the same name from Portsmouth, New
Hampshire; his father had spent his early life as a mariner and
shipmaster. Joseph left New Hampshire for Boston and opened
a successful hardware business, which sold "all sorts of Iron-
mongery, Braziery and Pewter Ware, also Ships Chandlery
Ware, by Wholesale or Retail. . . ."[2] In addition to his business,
he invested in real estate. While Sherburne was known to be a
charitable gentleman involved with good causes in Boston,[3]
there is no particular evidence that he had intellectual pursuits.
In this portrait, it seems as though the merchant's wealth was
the message, and the abundance of expensive imported English
silk damask around him was an effective vehicle. Sherburne
supports his slightly reclining torso with arms resting casually
on the silk-covered table to his right and the chair back on his
left, a man who is clearly at ease in the world. His informal
dress accentuates his comfort in his sphere.

During the late 1760s Copley depicted several Boston gentlemen, including himself, in banyans.[4] Although these garments
were certainly for sale and in use in Boston at the time, it is not
known whether the gown we see on Sherburne was his own or a
studio prop. The image of Sherburne completely fitted out in
exotic fashion, that is, wigless, with a shaved head and turban,
however, was not the way he was originally depicted. Recent
digital X-radiographs of the canvas reveal that he was painted
with his own longish hair; sometime after the portrait was finished,
he must have asked Copley to paint over his hair and add a turban to complete the look. Copley made two attempts at this, for
the pentimento of the first try can still be seen to the right above
Sherburne's head.   AP

1. Fortune, "'Studious Men are Always Painted in Gowns,'" pp. 27–40.
2. *Boston Evening-Post,* no. 426, October 3, 1743, p. 2.
3. Sherburne was an "Overseer of the Poor" for the city of Boston, and in 1748 he
donated £50 to promote domestic linen manufacture. Sherburne, *Some Descendants
of Henry and John Sherburne of Portsmouth, N.H.,* pp. 10–11.
4. Copley's 1769 pastel self-portrait is at the Winterthur Museum, Delaware. See
Rebora et al., *John Singleton Copley in America,* p. 36, fig. 25. He also made a
miniature version in watercolor on ivory that is in the collection of the Metropolitan Museum, acc. no. 2006.235.32. For more on Copley and his portraits of
gentlemen in banyans, see Barratt, "Oriental Undress and the Artist," pp. 18–31.

100A

100B

Workshop of Sir Joshua Reynolds
**100A. MRS. GEORGE BALDWIN
(JANE MALTASS, 1763 – 1839)**
London, 1782 or later
Oil on canvas
36 ⅛ x 29 ⅛ in. (91.8 x 74 cm)
The Metropolitan Museum of Art, New York,
Gift of William T. Blodgett and his sister Eleanor Blodgett,
in memory of their father, William T. Blodgett, one of the
founders of the Museum, 1906 06.1241

Sir Joshua Reynolds (1723 – 1792)
**100B. MRS. HORTON, LATER VICOUNTESS MAYNARD
(DIED 1814/15)**
London, ca. 1770
Oil on canvas
36 ¼ x 28 in. (92.1 x 71.1 cm)
The Metropolitan Museum of Art, New York,
Fletcher Fund, 1945 45.59.3

After Lady Mary Wortley Montagu returned to London from Turkey in 1719 (see cat. 92 and fig. 82), she sat for several portraits in the Turkish dress she had worn while abroad. She was a force within British society and so was influential in popularizing the fashion for interpretations of women's dress from the Levant, all of which was labeled "Turkish" no matter what its actual source.[1] By the mid-eighteenth century, it was de rigueur for ladies to pose for portraits in variations of *turquerie*. An image of a woman in this loosely cut style instead of the rigidly corseted dresses of the day identified her as alluring and sophisticated (although perhaps a bit indecorous). This taste paralleled one for depicting women in artistically draped "Classical" dress; both styles were perceived as being timeless, since a viewer could not find the sitter old and out-of-date as contemporary fashions changed. Turkish dress was also worn to the popular masquerade parties of the time.[2]

The two ladies seen here, both painted by Sir Joshua Reynolds, the preeminent British portrait painter of his day, were not simply upper-class women playing at being exotic. Each was something of an outsider to conventional London society, with a personal history that may have influenced her choice of costume worn for her portrait.

Jane Maltass was a daughter of William Maltass, an English merchant for the Levant Company. She was born in Smyrna,

Turkey, in 1763, and lived there until her marriage at age sixteen to George Baldwin (1744–1826). Baldwin was almost twenty years her senior and had spent the previous decade setting up a trade network between India and Egypt through the Red Sea.[3] The newlyweds left Smyrna for Europe in 1780, and upon arrival in London the beautiful Jane made quite a stir. She was painted by Richard Cosway as well as by Joshua Reynolds (the full-length portrait by him is now at Compton Verney House, Warwickshire); Reynolds's workshop made this bust-length copy. She sat for Reynolds in her own home, which, if the interior he painted is true to life, was apparently decorated in Eastern style. However, it is also possible that Reynolds made up the low divan on which she is seated, since this type of soft lounging furniture would be recognizably "Turkish" to a contemporary viewer and would reinforce her exotic air. While her costume is assumed to be "fancy dress," it is possible that parts of it were authentically Turkish. It was certainly clothing she owned, not studio dress or a figment of Reynolds's imagination, since it is known that she also wore this outfit to a ball given by King George III.[4]

Anne (or Nancy) Parsons, daughter of a Bond Street tailor, made her way into elite society by attaching herself to a succession of well-to-do men. The first was a Mr. Horton (or Houghton), a West Indian slave trader, to whom she may or may not have been married. She accompanied him to Jamaica but by 1763 was back in London, where she had liaisons with several members of the nobility before marrying Sir Charles Maynard, second viscount and fifth baronet, in 1776.

Mrs. Horton sat for George Willison wearing Turkish dress about the same time she sat for Reynolds.[5] Here, her costume is a more restrained version of the exotic, conveyed mainly by the long, narrow Indian Kashmir shawl that she wrapped around the silk turban on her head and attached at the front with pearl pins. The ends of the shawl cross behind her neck, then drape over her shoulders and tie at her waist in imitation of the ornate sashes worn by Indian men.   AP

1. In addition to Lady Mary's influence, the eighteenth-century taste for *turquerie* also owed its start to the 1714 publication of engravings of Ottoman life after paintings by Jean Baptiste Vanmour, titled *Recueil de cent estampes représentant différentes nations du Levant.*
2. Ribeiro, "The Dress Worn at Masquerades in England, 1730 to 1790."
3. Mew and Manley, "Baldwin, George (1744–1826)," in *Oxford Dictionary of National Biography.*
4. Ribeiro, "The Dress Worn at Masquerades in England, 1730 to 1790," p. 232.
5. The Willison portrait is at the Yale Center for British Art, New Haven, Paul Mellon Collection (B1981.25.681).

101A. SASH

Iran (possibly Kashan), 17th century
Compound plain weave, brocaded,
silk and metal-wrapped thread
13 ft. 8 in. x 24 ½ in. (416.5 x 62 cm)
The Metropolitan Museum of Art, New York,
Gift of George D. Pratt, 1933   33.80.18

101B. SASH

Madjarski Manufactory,
Poland (Słuck), 1767–80
Compound plain weave, silk and metal-wrapped thread
with metallic fringe
11 ft. 8 in. x 14 in. (355.6 x 35.6 cm) without fringe
The Metropolitan Museum of Art, New York,
Anonymous Gift, 1949   49.32.48

Inscription (in two corners on one end panel): SŁUCK

101C. SHAWL

Probably Nadezhda Merlina manufactory
Russia (probably Nizhny Novgorod province),
early 19th century
Tapestry and twill weave, goat fiber
95 x 23 ¾ in. (241.3 x 60.3 cm)
The Metropolitan Museum of Art, New York,
Rogers Fund, 1965   65.91.1

A study of paintings from Iran indicates that in the early sixteenth century the typical waist girdle was a leather strap with metal plaques, which then gave way to a narrow textile band with gold fasteners.[1] By the seventeenth century, a long and wide sash wrapped and knotted around the waist was customary.[2] These sashes had a central field of narrow stripes with decorative panels of flowering plants at either end; they were tied so that these floral panels were visible.

The sash was an indispensable accessory and a tool for projecting the status of the wearer. Thomas Herbert, part of an English embassy to Iran in the late 1620s, remarked on both the length of these sashes and the meaningful variation in their materials: "Their waists are girt with fine towels [a plain fabric band worn under the sash] of silk and gold about 8 yards long; those and the sashes distinguish the quality of those that wear them; dukes and other of the noble sort have them woven with gold, merchants and *qezelbash* with silver; of silk and wool those of inferior rank."[3] By this measure, the Iranian sash illustrated here (cat. 101A), with its gold ground extending the whole of its

101A

101B

101C

almost fourteen-foot length, must have been worn by a rich and important personage.[4] A further mark of its quality is the fact that the back of the sash is well finished.

Similar sashes were also worn in the Ottoman and Mughal realms on either side of the Safavid cultural sphere. By the late seventeenth century this fashion had spread to parts of eastern Europe such as Poland and Russia, where textiles imported from Iran and Turkey had become status symbols worn by courtiers.

Persian sashes became a requisite part of the wardrobe for noblemen of the Polish-Lithuanian Commonwealth, at the crossroads between the Ottoman Empire, the Russian Empire, and the European Holy Roman Empire. The aristocracy's entire style of dress was influenced by fashions from the Safavid and Ottoman courts, but the sash retained its popularity long after other features became more Westernized. By the eighteenth century the demand for silk sashes, or *kontusz* (and thus known as *kontusz* sashes) worn over an outer coat, became so great in Poland that domestic manufactories, called *persiarnie*, were established.[5] One of the finest eighteenth-century producers was the establishment founded in the city of Słuck, east of Warsaw, by an Armenian named Jan Madjarski and his son Leo (cat. 101B).[6] The Madjarskis clearly took great pride in their work and "signed" their sashes with woven inscriptions on the end panels, where they were certain to be seen. These sashes were normally worn folded in half lengthwise and then wound around the waist. An innovation introduced by the Polish manufacturers was the production of a two-color, double-sided main field that enabled the wearer to extend his wardrobe by folding and tying his sash up to four different ways.[7]

From the mid-seventeenth century European observers used the word *shawl*, derived from the Persian *shāl*, to describe the oblong textiles woven of very fine wool that were used by Iranian men as waist sashes and by Indian men as shoulder coverings. By the late eighteenth century the white "Kashmir" shawls with colorful pinecone or paisley motifs at each end became the de rigueur fashion accessory for European women (for an unusual and creative use of a shawl as headgear, see cat. 100B). An early reference to shawls imported to England from the Kashmir region appears in 1767, in the correspondence of British author Laurence Sterne.[8] French Empress Josephine is often credited with popularizing the trend at the turn of the nineteenth century and is said to have owned more than fifty expensive imported shawls.

During the early nineteenth century Kashmiri shawl makers began to replace the plain white field of these textiles with bold colors or stripes. At the same time, Europeans started weaving shawls in an attempt to meet the increased demand for the fashionable accessories. Traditional Kashmir shawls were patterned using a twill tapestry technique, which was extremely time-consuming. Driven to make shawls more quickly, European makers normally employed faster weaving techniques, but a few Russian makers retained the tapestry method.[9] Several of the Russian workshops were run by female members of the landed gentry, who took advantage of the inexpensive serf labor available to them to produce these amazingly fine textiles (cat. 101C).[10] In this case, the flowers in the pinecone shapes at each end of the shawl can be identified as European species such as poppies, roses, and cornflowers; there even appears to be a type of tuber vegetable anchoring the individual motifs. The vivid stripes of this shawl may have been inspired in part by the colorful men's sashes being produced in Poland, Russia, and France, which themselves had been inspired by Iranian and Indian precursors.   MS and MW

1. Goetz, "The History of Persian Costume," p. 2247.
2. Scarce, "Vesture and Dress: Fashion, Function, and Impact," pp. 36, 42.
3. Herbert, *Travels in Persia, 1627–1629*, p. 232.
4. Sir Jean Chardin, writing in the 1660s, noted the large costs incurred by courtiers to maintain their wardrobes. Quoted in Floor, "Economy and Society: Fibers, Fabrics, Factories," p. 22.
5. Poskrobko-Strzęciwilk, "Polish Kontusz Sashes in the Collection of The Metropolitan Museum of Art," pp. 19, 23. I am grateful to Ms. Poskrobko-Strzęciwilk for her generosity in sharing her time to discuss this research.
6. Ibid., p. 24.
7. Ibid., p. 32.
8. See Irwin, *The Kashmir Shawl*, p. 19.
9. Catalogue number 101C is composed of twill-woven solid-color stripes and tapestry-woven patterned areas; these components were woven separately and then skillfully joined.
10. The two most prominent female-owned manufactories in Russia were those of Nadezhda Merlina (active in Nizhny Novgorod, 1806–34) and Vera Andreevna Eliseeva; see Cooper, "Luxury Textiles from Feudal Workshops: 19th Century Russian Tapestry-Woven Shawls," pp. 224–35. For a shawl signed by the Merlina workshop (very similar to cat. 101C), see Metropolitan Museum, acc. no. 1972.175.

102A – D. SUITE OF TAPESTRIES DEPICTING THE FOUR CONTINENTS

Designed by Jean-Jacques-François Le Barbier (1738–1826)
Royal Manufactory, Beauvais, workshop of de Menou
(active 1780–93)
France (Beauvais), designed ca. 1786, woven 1790–91
Tapestry weave, wool and silk
America, Europe, and Africa 12 ft. x 15 ft. (365.8 x 457.2 cm);
Asia 12 ft. x 16 ft. 6 in. (365.8 x 503 cm)
The Metropolitan Museum of Art, New York, Purchase,
Mr. and Mrs. Claus von Bülow Gift, 1978 1978.404.1
(America), 1978.404.2 (Europe), 1978.404.3 (Africa),
and 1978.404.4 (Asia)

This suite of four tapestries and its coordinating upholstery (cat. 103A–F) were commissioned from the Beauvais manufactory in 1786 and woven between 1790 and 1791.[1] As has been noted, "The attractive and not impossible suggestion that the set was intended to be a gift from King Louis XVI to George Washington was made by the first scholar to publish the work . . . but it is not supported by any contemporary evidence."[2] Regardless of whether the suite was intended as a gift to President Washington,

the French Revolution intervened, and it is perhaps miraculous that the tapestries were woven at all. By the time they were complete, the French king was in no position to bestow diplomatic gifts on anyone.

It is the representation of America as a rather demure-looking young woman that sets this iconographic scheme apart from other groupings of the Four Continents. In the Beauvais tapestry set, America has evolved from the scantily clad, spear-toting, armadillo-riding, cannibalistic warrior princess seen in sixteenth-century representations to the woman dependent on the protection of the female personifications of Liberty and Minerva (whose shield carries the fleur-de-lis of France).[3] In addition to this representational shift, the Indian princess who had originally stood for the entire Western Hemisphere here represents only the United States. The concept for this view of America defended by France in the guise of Minerva was suggested by none other than Benjamin Franklin, and a medal based on his suggestion was designed by Augustin Dupré and struck in France in 1782.[4]

The production of these tapestries is thus a vivid example of the Gallic enthusiasm for the American colonists' struggle for independence from Great Britain, France's longtime foe, which existed at the highest levels of society. This was not the first American subject for the designer of the series, Jean-Jacques-François Le Barbier (an official *peintre du Roi* by 1780). In 1782 his illustration of the first Continental Congress appeared as the frontispiece in *Essais historiques et politiques sur les Anglo-Américains* (Brussels, 1781–82), just one of several publications on the subject of the American cause that appeared in the early 1780s.[5]

Of course, the French expressed their enthusiasm for the American struggle against the British with more than works of art and propaganda. They supported the Continental Army with money, supplies, and soldiers, including the wealthy marquis de Lafayette (1757–1834), whose fervor for the cause was so great that he sailed to America disguised as a woman to escape detection.   MW

1. For a complete account of the tapestry suite, see Standen, *European Post-Medieval Tapestries,* vol. 2, pp. 572–605; and Standen, "Jean-Jacques-François Le Barbier and Two Revolutions," pp. 258–65.
2. Standen, "Jean-Jacques-François Le Barbier and Two Revolutions," p. 273 n. 16. The earliest scholarly publication referred to by Standen is Doniol, *Histoire de la participation de la France à l'établissement des États-Unis d'Amérique*; see Standen, *European Post-Medieval Tapestries,* vol. 2, p. 573.
3. For a selection of sixteenth- and seventeenth-century representations of America in prints and drawings, see Honour, *The European Vision of America*, pp. 114–23.
4. Standen, "Jean-Jacques-François Le Barbier and Two Revolutions," pp. 261, 262, fig. 11; the Metropolitan Museum has two examples of this medal, acc. nos. 07.251.23 and 36.110.41. This was one of a number of medals depicting American Revolutionary War subjects designed by Dupré.
5. Standen, "Jean-Jacques-François Le Barbier and Two Revolutions," p. 255.

102A America

102B Europe

102C Africa

102D Asia

103A – F. FURNITURE DEPICTING THE FOUR CONTINENTS (TWO SETTEES AND FOUR ARMCHAIRS)

Tapestry designed by Jean-Jacques-François Le Barbier
(1738–1826); Royal Manufactory, Beauvais,
workshop of de Menou (active 1780–93);
Textile: France (Beauvais), designed ca. 1786,
woven 1790–91
Tapestry weave, wool and silk on gilt wood frames
Furniture frames: probably France, probably second
half of the 19th century,
Settees each 42 ¼ x 75 ⅜ x 28 in. (107.3 x 191.5 x 71.1 cm)
Armchairs each 37 ¾ x 27 x 24 in. (95.9 x 68.6 x 61 cm)

The Metropolitan Museum of Art, New York, Purchase,
Mr. and Mrs. Claus von Bülow Gift, 1978 1978.404.5a–c
(settee with Europe and America), .6a–c
(settee with Asia and Africa), .8a–c (armchair with America),
.10a–c (armchair with Europe), .13a–c (armchair with Africa),
.18a–c (armchair with Asia)

Tapestry-woven upholstery for two settees and twelve armchairs
was commissioned at the same time as the wall hangings depicting
the Four Continents (cat. 102A–D).[1] The Four Continents was
one of two suites—each including four wall tapestries and coordinating seating furniture—that were ordered from Beauvais in

103A Europe

103B America

103C Africa

103D Asia

103E Europe and America

103F Africa and Asia

1786; the subject of the other suite was to be a series illustrating the arts, sciences, agriculture, and commerce. An earlier suite of tapestry furniture covers depicting the continents was produced at the Royal Manufactory of Gobelins in 1748, and the arrangement of the motifs in Le Barbier's covers is similar: personifications of the continents are set against a landscape on the seat backs, and native animals populate the seat covers.[2] This subject in tapestry aligns with the contemporary popularity of the Four Continents in eighteenth-century European art: everything from porcelain table decorations and tablewares to dinner napkins and ceiling frescoes incorporated personifications of the continents (cat. 86).

The settee showing America and Europe emphasizes the close relationship between France and the new United States, which France promoted so forcefully in the tapestry depicting America. The figure of France occupies the center of the sofa back, and America is seated off to the left. In this composition, France is "introducing the new nation to Europe across Neptune's domain, the Atlantic; France's discarded armor lies at her feet, as the war has been won, and Victory crowns her."[3] The armchairs repeat the female personifications of each continent, attended by male figures and some of the fauna typically associated with each. There are three variations on each of the four continents, and, although they are all slightly different, the iconographic program is consistent.

It appears that this upholstery was not affixed to furniture frames until sometime after 1852, decades after its production.[4] Usually, a client commissioned or purchased high-quality tapestry upholstery before furniture frames were made to accommodate the weavings. This type of upholstery was quite popular in the late eighteenth century, and the Beauvais manufactory made many such sets.[5] However, the combination of matching wall hangings and seating furniture was more unusual, and clearly more expensive. A suite of furnishings would have been reserved for a formal room, such as a salon or drawing room.   MW

1. See Standen, *European Post-Medieval Tapestries*, vol. 2, pp. 572–73.
2. Ibid., p. 573; the Gobelins tapestry upholstery depicted the continents as merchants on the sofa backs. Some of Le Barbier's designs for the upholstery survive; none of the cartoons for the wall tapestries exist today. See ibid., pp. 572, 588–603, figs. 67–74, all in the Mobilier National, Paris.
3. Ibid., p. 591.
4. Ibid., p. 573, from the sale listing of May 18, 1852, hôtel of the duc de Richlieu; no furniture frames were mentioned, nor was the ownership indicated.
5. Kisluk-Grosheide, "Peregrinations of a *Lit à la Duchesse en Impériale* by George Jacob," p. 144, and personal communication.

104. BEDCOVER OR HANGING

India (Gujarat), for the Portuguese market, 17th century
Silk satin, embroidered with silk
8 ft. 8 in. x 79 ½ in. (264 x 202 cm)
Museum of Fine Arts, Boston,
The Elizabeth Day McCormick Collection, 50.3224

A harrowing scene unfolds in this striking embroidery. Rival groups of infantrymen, amassed under a forest of lethal spears, and sword-brandishing cavalrymen face off in a great battle. Within the field dividing the four military companies, cannons expel gray drafts of gunpowder, as dead soldiers lie among the severed heads and limbs scattered along the front lines. Some of the flags bear the red cross, emblem of the Portuguese Military Order of Christ, and some display a crescent shape. Other flags, such as the striped examples, have yet to be identified, but the double-headed crowned eagle in the lower left corner of the border, symbolizing the Habsburg Empire, indicates that this cover may have been made as a celebratory record of a Portuguese military victory. As such, this Indian textile embodies an intriguing duality, as it is both a luxury trade object, likely commissioned to beautify the home of a Portuguese client, and a vivid illustration of the brutality that facilitated the growth of global trade networks.

The Portuguese discovery of a direct sea route to India in 1498 led to numerous military conflicts, on land and sea, with powerful empires such as the Ottomans and Safavids—each seeking to assert its dominance over the lucrative maritime trade between Europe and the East. Until the seventeenth century the Portuguese dominated their rivals in the open ocean, but on land the insufficient military presence in their littoral

104, detail

network of forts made them susceptible to attack. By the early seventeenth century Portugal's rivals also included the British, the French, and the Dutch, who began to successfully challenge Lusitanian authority. This embroidery and its triumphant battle scene may therefore commemorate either a recent victory or one achieved several decades earlier, when the Portuguese Empire had reached the pinnacle of its power.

While its violent subject matter makes this cover unique, it is related to a group of Gujarati textiles made for the Portuguese market, with blue silk foundation fabrics that are embroidered with colorful silks in chain stitch. One such piece, also in the Museum of Fine Arts, Boston (no. 1998.58), is representative of this group, which often features the Five Senses, personified as beautiful women in European dress, surrounded by a whimsical mix of Persian, Indian, and European motifs.[1]   AB

1. For an analysis of another bedcover featuring the theme of the Five Senses, see Blum, "Indo-Portuguese Bedcover, Late Seventeenth Century," pp. 8–10. Blum notes that the composition of the cover (no. 1988-7-4) is based on that of Persian and Indian carpets. Other, similar works are in the collections of the Art Institute of Chicago (no. 1982.18) and the Museo Nazionale del Bargello, Florence (no. C2255).

105. HANGING DEPICTING A EUROPEAN CONFLICT IN SOUTH INDIA, PROBABLY THE SIEGE OF PONDICHERRY, 1760–61

India (Coromandel Coast), for the English market, after 1761
Cotton, drawn and painted resist and mordant, dyed
115 x 103 ½ in. (292 x 263 cm)
Courtesy of Titi Halle

This tableau of an unidentified battle is the most spectacular, complex, and complete surviving example of a rare genre—chintz paintings of historical events.[1] The formulaic composition and figure types mirror European compositional conventions of later seventeenth- and eighteenth-century battle scenes (fig. 154).[2] The events depicted represent the stages of a single, certainly specific, campaign between the armies of the English and French East India companies, which were engaged in fierce competition to secure control of the Indian textile trade throughout much of the eighteenth century. On the reverse of the cloth is the stamp of the United East India Company, confirming that the painting was an English commission; the chop design is characteristic of those in use in the second half of the eighteenth century.[3] That this work was commissioned to celebrate a victory on the part of the English seems clear, and visual evidence strongly suggests that the painting's subject is the siege and capture of French Pondicherry by the forces of the English East India Company in 1760–61.[4] An English commander—presumably Lieutenant-General Sir Eyre

Coote (1726–1783)—appears in a sequence of scenes in a narrative played out over six registers, variously depicted on horseback or in a carriage, supervising stages of the battle.[5]

The English forces, comprising the European Regiment of Madras, sepoys (Indian troops in English service), and allied local soldiers, march under not only the Union flag but also an array of local standards. Indian regiments appear to be distinguished by dress—the Muslims in long gowns and with bushy beards, the Hindus in skirt cloths (*lungi*), indicative of the complex web of alliances forged by the European trading companies with local rulers. At lower right, the Union flag flies over a fort tower decorated with the lion and unicorn crest; this register likely depicts—according to the identification proposed—the departure of the English commander and his troops from Fort St. George, Madras (Chennai). Although the opposing land forces are curiously unidentified, two European ships (at the center of the naval battle depicted in the upper register) appear to display, much reduced and simplified, the triple fleur-de-lis and crown in circle, the insignia of the French East India Company flag from 1756 (detail).

Pondicherry, in the heart of a major textile-producing region on the southern Coromandel Coast of India, was the headquarters of the French East India Company. After decades of conflict over contested territorial and trading interests, and an official state of war declared in Europe in 1756 (marking the beginning of the Seven Years' War), the English company laid siege to Pondicherry in September 1760, and succeeded in forcing a French surrender in January 1761. Dress conventions support this dating: the styling of the commander's narrow coat, flared below the waist, the campaign wig, and the black, broad-brimmed hat, possibly a tricorn,

Fig. 154. Romeyn de Hooghe (Dutch, 1645–1708). *The Conquest of the Sultanate of Macassar,* 1670. Engraving heightened with watercolor and gold. Van Stolk Atlas, Rotterdam (no. 2391)

105, detail showing the regimental flag of the Compaignie des Indes Orientales (French East India Company) flying from the sterns of the French ships

conform to early to mid-eighteenth-century conventions of uniform dress.[6] Likewise, the Indian sepoys are not yet in regimental uniform, which had become standard attire by the 1770s.[7]

This remarkable document of eighteenth-century South Indian history was likely commissioned by the directors of the East India Company at Fort St. George, perhaps for display in their boardroom, to celebrate their 1761 victory over the French. The celebration, however, was short-lived: much to the consternation of the company, Pondicherry was restored to the French under the Treaty of Paris in 1763.[8] We may thus provisionally date this painting to the years 1761–63. JG

1. Only one other chintz depicting European forces engaged in battle in India is known to this writer; it is in a private collection in Portugal. I am grateful to Sir Christopher Bayly, William Dalrymple, Pip Dodd, M. Gobalakichenane, Titi Halle, Sanjay Subramanyan, Robert Travers, and curatorial colleagues on the *Interwoven Globe* team for fruitful discussions on this painting.
2. Such pictorial devices were already present in chintz painting a century earlier; see the equestrian rider depicted in a chintz in the Metropolitan Museum, acc. no. 20.79.
3. Irwin and Brett, *Origins of Chintz*, compare numbers 151, 154, 155.
4. The surrender of Pondicherry by the French effectively ended that country's territorial interests in India, although in 1763 Pondicherry was returned to France as a trading station by the Treaty of Paris; see Baugh, *The Global Seven Years War, 1754–1763*, p. 482.
5. Lieutenant-General Sir Eyre Coote was a fellow officer with Robert Clive at the battle of Plassey in 1757 and commanded the English victory over the French at the battle of Wandiwash in 1760. At both Wandiwash and Pondicherry, Coote's adversary was the French commander, the comte de Lally.
6. I am grateful to Kristen Stewart for her insightful guidance on the dating of eighteenth-century dress.
7. My thanks to Pip Dobb, National Army Museum, Chelsea, for this observation.
8. In 1778 England and France were again at war following France's support of the American War of Independence, and English forces again captured Pondicherry, destroying the city and its fortifications.

106. QUILT

Probably England, ca. 1785–90
Cotton, copperplate printed, with cotton filling
92 x 77½ in. (233.7 x 196.9 cm)
The Metropolitan Museum of Art, New York,
Gift of Ellen H. Getman, in memory of her husband,
Frederick Hutton Getman, 1945 45.145

The scenes printed on the cottons making up the front and back of this quilt speak to the social, cultural, and economic impact of Europe's contact with distant peoples. The front, copperplate printed with blue floral vines on a white ground, offers a refined vision of exotic flora, inspired by designs on Chinese export goods.[1] The scenes on the back, copperplate printed in red, reveal the power of images in the construction of history and testify to the role textiles played as effective vehicles for the propagation of a nation's public image.[2] On February 14, 1779, at Kealakekua Bay in the Sandwich (now the Hawaiian) Islands, Captain James Cook was killed during a confrontation with local inhabitants. His well-publicized death catapulted Cook from famous British naval captain to mythologized hero—and martyr to the cause of Europe's inexorable expansion across the globe.

On Cook's third and final voyage to the Pacific aboard the HMS *Resolution*, he was accompanied by John Webber (1751–1793), the expedition's official artist. Many of the subsequent paintings and engravings of Cook's last voyage were based on Webber's in situ drawings, as well as on widely published descriptions. The first two scenes on the back of this quilt depict a lush, thriving place inhabited by peaceful islanders who offer gifts to the captain and his men as local priests escort them ashore. Juxtaposed to these serene images, a third scene shows a mob of rioting, armed Hawaiians surrounding the body of the lifeless captain (detail). In the print, one Hawaiian raises a knife above Cook, a reminder that, according to sailors' accounts, Cook's body was dismembered and the parts distributed among high-ranking chiefs on the island, following local custom in the death of an important figure. The *Resolution*'s officers managed to recover some of Cook's remains, which they eventually buried at sea in Kealakekua Bay. The death scene depicted on this quilt differs from the most popular versions of the infamous event, including Webber's much-copied version that presents Cook in a heroic stance between his men and the Hawaiians in an attempt to quell the violent confrontation. Yet here Cook is utterly vulnerable to the menacing Hawaiians, perhaps signaling the artist's attempt—however unnerving for Cook's admirers—to promote his grisly demise.

The Cook-themed cotton played a part in the process of constructing, memorializing, and circulating the image of an icon

106, front

106, back

who personified Britain's aspirations of maritime dominance. Other textiles played a different but still key role in the interactions between the British and native peoples in such places as the Pacific Islands and North America. European-made red wool, for example, was a popular trade item (see cats. 30, 110), and indigenous cloth served as an important category of gift bestowed upon prominent foreigners like Cook.   AB

1. See Peck with Schaffner, *American Quilts and Coverlets in The Metropolitan Museum of Art,* pp. 126–27, no. 50, for further discussion of this quilt, which belonged to a New York family but was likely created in England. The source of the design of the undulating flora on the front has been identified in a collection of paper impressions from the Bromley Hall printworks, now in the collection of the Victoria and Albert Museum, London. The inscription on the related impression contains the last names of the two men who ran the firm from 1785 to 1790— Joseph Talwin and Joseph Foster. The copperplate engravers at Bromley Hall were likely inspired by the elegant designs of Frenchman Jean Pillement, whose publications such as *Oeuvres de fleurs, ornements, cartouches, figures et sujets chinois* (1771) helped fuel the popularity for the chinoiserie style.
2. For a discussion of the visual imagery surrounding Cook's death and the general construction of his reputation, see Smith, *Imagining the Pacific in the Wake of the Cook Voyages,* pp. 225–40.

106, detail

107A. TRIUMFA ESPAÑA EN LAS AMERICAS (THE TRIUMPH OF SPAIN IN THE AMERICAS)

Spain, late 18th century

Cotton, block printed

15 ¾ x 29 ⅝ in. (40 x 75.2 cm)

The Metropolitan Museum of Art, New York,

Gift of Estate of James Hazen Hyde, 1959 59.208.89

Inscription: TRIVMFA ESPAÑA EN LAS AMERICAS

107B. TRAITE DES NÈGRES (THE SLAVE TRADE)

Frédéric Étienne Joseph Feldtrappe (1786–1849)

France (Alsace), early 19th century

Cotton, roller printed

101 x 33 in. (256.5 x 83.8 cm)

The Metropolitan Museum of Art, New York,

Rogers Fund, 1926 26.189.2

Inscription: FELDTRAPPE

107A, detail

Both of these printed fabrics demonstrate the potential for textiles to serve as platforms for political and social declarations. Of probable Spanish origin, *Triumfa España en las Americas* depicts "America" as a Native American female upon a litter supported by two young men among stylized flora. Europeans began personifying the Americas as an exotic native woman in the sixteenth century, but the inclusion of the legend "Triumfa España en las Americas" suggests that the design's authors were attempting to communicate something more explicit than the portrayal of the colonial Americas as a noble (but still inferior) savage. For most of the eighteenth century, Spanish rule in the Americas was marked by intense civil conflict across an exceptionally broad spectrum of colonial society, largely in response to the waves of colonial administrative reforms effected by the Bourbon rulers in Spain.[1] The Andean region alone witnessed more than one hundred insurrections between the 1730s and the Great Andean Rebellion of 1780–81 in Peru and Bolivia. Only months later, Spanish officials contended with another major uprising led by *mestizos* (persons of mixed descent) in the Revolt of the Comuneros (1781–82) in present-day Colombia and Venezuela. Given the violent resistance and general resentment festering in the Americas, it would not be surprising if the creator of this panel viewed it as an expression of affirmation for Spanish loyalists.

While *Triumfa España* artfully promotes European imperialism in the Americas as both universally accepted and enduring, *Traite des Nègres* represents an attempt to undermine that authority. Frédéric Feldtrappe designed *Traite* in France in the

107B, detail

early nineteenth century. Of the four narrative scenes he included in the textile, two reference earlier paintings by English artist George Morland (1763–1804), *The Slave Trade* (1788) and its companion, *European Ship Wrecked on the Coast of Africa* (1790), eventually dubbed *African Hospitality*. The works contrast the brutality of Europeans toward Africans (*The Slave Trade*) with the kindness of Africans who minister to a shipwrecked European family (*African Hospitality*). Among the earliest visual indictments of the slave trade, Morland's paintings gained wide exposure after being published in 1791 as mezzotints by the well-known engraver John Raphael Smith, who took advantage of the rising antislavery fervor brewing in Britain in the 1780s and early 1790s. These scenes also appeared in France, printed by chez Depeuille of Paris in 1794. The other two scenes on this textile, *Habitation des Nègres* and *Arrivée des Européens en Afrique*, both from 1795, were based on engravings by Nicolas Colibert. *Habitation* shows a happy, intact African family enjoying the paradisiacal setting. In *Arrivée* the appearance of Europeans in Africa, laden with exchange goods, ominously foreshadows the horrors of the traffic in human beings.

That Feldtrappe tapped English visual precedents that predated his textile by several decades is not surprising, given the history and character of the French abolitionist movement and its relationship to its counterpart across the English Channel. The small, elite group that made up the Société des Amis des Noirs, founded in 1788, was heavily influenced by the London Society for the Abolition of the Slave Trade, established the previous year.[2]

In particular, the Amis adopted the English abolitionist tactic of condemning the trafficking of enslaved persons rather than the entire institution of slavery. Ostensibly this approach allowed antislavery supporters to condemn the trade without appearing to threaten the colonial economies, which could not be maintained without slavery. For many in the Amis, the end of the trade would (theoretically) mark the beginning of the end of slavery, which would gradually decline for the want of a supply of forced labor. Feldtrappe's design reflects the perpetuation of this strategy that allowed observers of such images to curse the slave trader while taking their coffee with sugar, wearing indigo-dyed textiles, and decorating their homes with mahogany furniture—all products of the French-held islands in the colonial West Indies.

Images promoting the innate goodness or childlike nature of Africans had been a common trope in Western art during the early modern period, but news of the violence that occurred during the uprising of slaves, free blacks, and mulattoes in Saint-Domingue (present-day Haiti) would thereafter complicate this image. While the French state censored much of the news of the revolt, images circulated. Some abolitionists argued that reported violence against whites, which appeared in a few depictions of the Haitian Revolution (1791–1804), was the consequence of centuries of European cruelty (fig. 155).

Feldtrappe produced his textile during a moment of intense debate in France over the viability and morality of the slave trade, which was definitively abolished by the Second Republic in 1848. He drew from older antislavery images, illustrating the cultural currency they acquired over the long fight to end slavery and suggesting the challenges of representing slavery for abolitionists living in the aftermath of the French and Haitian revolutions.   AB

1. Intended to stimulate manufacturing and improve government efficiency, the Bourbon Reforms (*Reformas Borbónicas*) consisted of political and economic legislation introduced by the Spanish Crown during the eighteenth century. The reforms were also intended to limit the power of the Creoles living in the Americas and restore it to Spain. For more information on the reforms and their effects on the Americas, see Barbier, "The Culmination of the Bourbon Reforms," pp. 51–68. 2. The formal successor organizations of the Amis were the Amis des Noirs et des Colonies (1796–99) and the Société de la Morale Chrétienne (1821–60/1). For a detailed discussion of the French antislavery movement, see Jennings, *French Anti-Slavery*.

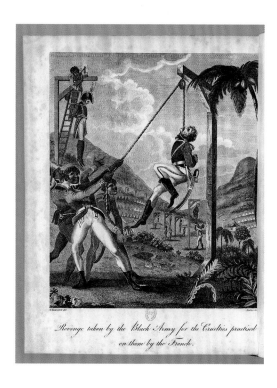

Fig. 155. J. Barlow. *Revenge Taken by the Black Army*. Engraving after the author, in Marcus Rainsford, *An Historical Account of the Black Empire of Hayti*, London, 1805

108. TEXTILE SAMPLE BOOK

England, 1771

Paper, cloth binding, with attached samples
of fustian

9 x 5 ¼ x 2 ¾ in. (22.9 x 13.3 x 7 cm)

The Metropolitan Museum of Art, New York,

Rogers Fund, 1918   156.4 T31

Inscription: BENJAMIN & JOHN BOWER / MANCHESTER. /APRIL 1ST
1771 / THE BRIGANTINE HAVANNAH / CAPT. NICHOLSON

108, title page

England's exports of domestically produced cotton products
expanded considerably over the course of the eighteenth century,
a result of the desire to compete with popular Indian-made cottons.[1] Though Indian cottons had been imported into Britain
earlier by the Portuguese, they entered London via the English
East India Company in the early seventeenth century, beginning
with approximately 5,000 pieces in 1613.[2] By midcentury, in
1661, the company had imported 253,000 pieces, and by 1694
1,400,000.[3] To protect the supremacy of the English home textile
industries, Parliament began restricting the importation of Indian
cottons as early as 1701, while allowing them to be reexported to
the British colonies and West Africa.

British textile manufacturers, many of whom were clustered
in the Lancashire region, sought to supplant the Indian-textile
reexport trade, then centered in London, with their own British-
made products. By the third quarter of the eighteenth century,
locally manufactured textiles could finally compete with Indian
reexports, and innovative marketing techniques, including the
use of sample books, played a vital role in their success. The
Manchester cotton firm of Benjamin & John Bower sent samples
and sales agents to colonial cities around the Atlantic World to
create and maintain crucial business networks.

The Bower sample book, which traveled with Captain
Nicholson to New York City via Liverpool and Dublin on the
brigantine *Havannah* in 1771, contains five hundred swatches of
ordinary cloth that would have been worn by sailors, artisans,
and enslaved persons or used as decorative furnishings.[4] Advertisements, inventories, shipping lists, and other documentary
evidence from the period reflect the ever-increasing focus on variety and consumer choice that signified sophistication, refinement, and membership in a global network of commerce (see
the essay by Amelia Peck on East India Company textiles for the
North American market in this publication).

That 40 percent of the swatches in the Bower book are colorful checks (see page at right) and stripes is not surprising, given
the predominance of this category of textile in the export market.[5]
While the diversification in European cotton textile design that

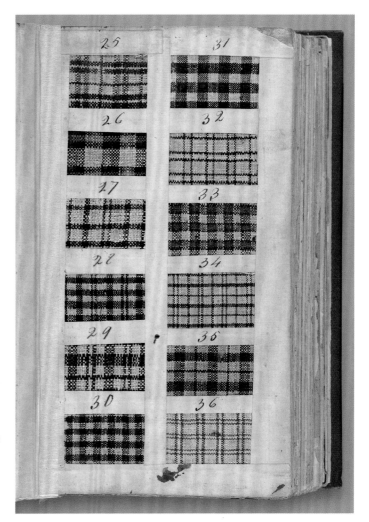

108, page of checked fabrics

began to expand midcentury has often been attributed to the desire for novelty on the part of British consumers, the role of West African demand for variety in textile design was crucial. Cloth constituted Europe's largest category of export to Africa, and the varieties represented in this book served as currency, exchanged for enslaved African men, women, and children.[6] So popular were these types of cottons in Africa that they were known as "Guinea cloths," after the coastal region of West Africa.

In March 1765 the Merchants of Liverpool Trading sent a memorandum to His Majesty's Treasury reporting on the products exported to Africa, including "checks & other goods made at Manchester in imitation of East India Goods, when the latter are at high prices, or not to be got, but some they cannot imitate & their imitation of many kinds is but indifferent. [The] trade on the coast of Africa differs from the trade in civiliz'd Nations, & is carried on chiefly by Barter . . . they must either have proper assortments of goods, or not adventure to those parts."[7] African traders knew that African consumers preferred the finer all-cotton fabrics from India over the linen/cotton mixtures prevalent in Europe; highly discerning, they regularly rejected items they deemed inferior or unsalable and influenced the way in which European textiles were designed, produced, and marketed.[8] The dominance of this mixed cotton-and-linen cloth in the Bower sample book reflects the technological limitations that persisted in England until the last decades of the eighteenth century, when manufacturers finally mastered the production of fine cotton threads strong enough to function as a fabric's warp.[9] AB

1. Wadsworth and Mann, *The Cotton Trade and Industrial Lancashire.*
2. Inikori, "Slavery and the Revolution in Cotton Textile Production in England," p. 349.
3. Ibid., p. 350.
4. "According to the *New York Gazette* or *Weekly Post Boy*, the Brigantine *Havannah* was cleared to Dublin and Liverpool on 31 December 1770, and the following 1 July 1771 she was cleared outward for Lisbon. On both occasions John Hamilton is listed as her captain." Burbidge, "The Bower Textile Sample Book," p. 221. Very little is known about the Bower textile firm; Burbidge states that Benjamin Bower, born in 1731, was the son of the Manchester hatter Jeremiah Bower, and John may have been Benjamin's first cousin.
5. In 1750, for example, the total value of export cotton checks was £9,743, with £7,839 (80.5%) going to West Africa and £1,904 (19.5%) to New World plantations. Yet by 1769 the total value of export cotton checks was £142,302, with £97,972 (68.8%) going to West Africa and £40,597 (28.5%) to plantation societies. It should be noted that the overall value of cotton exports in 1750 was £19,667 and in 1769 £211,606, which reflects the strength of the check industry relative to total exports. See Wadsworth and Mann, *The Cotton Trade and Industrial Lancashire*, p. 146.
6. Thornton, *Africa and Africans in the Making of the Atlantic World*, p. 45.
7. Inikori, "Slavery and the Revolution in Cotton Textile Production in England," p. 361.
8. Adenaike, "West African Textiles, 1500–1800," p. 260; see also Kriger, *Cloth in West African History.*
9. For a detailed discussion of the technological development of the cotton industry in Britain, see Smith and Cothren, eds., *Cotton: Origin, History, Technology, and Production.*

Agostino Brunias (1728–1796)
109A. LINEN DAY, ROSEAU, DOMINICA — A MARKET SCENE
West Indies, ca. 1780
Oil on canvas
19 5/8 x 27 in. (49.8 x 68.6 cm)
Yale Center for British Art, Paul Mellon Collection, New Haven, Connecticut, B1981.25.76

109B. FREE WEST INDIAN DOMINICANS
West Indies, ca. 1770
Oil on canvas
12 1/2 x 9 3/4 in. (31.8 x 24.8 cm)
Yale Center for British Art, Paul Mellon Collection, New Haven, Connecticut, B1981.25.74

109C. A WEST INDIAN FLOWER GIRL AND TWO OTHER FREE WOMEN OF COLOR
West Indies, ca. 1769
Oil on canvas
12 1/2 x 9 3/4 in. (31.8 x 24.8 cm)
Yale Center for British Art, Paul Mellon Collection, New Haven, Connecticut, B1981.25.75

Agostino Brunias's paintings offer idealized visions of West Indian life, likely produced as souvenirs for absentee planters or advertisements to lure aspiring masters. While working in London, the Italian-born artist met Sir William Young, Commissioner and Receiver of land sales in the formerly French-controlled islands that included Dominica, St. Vincent, and Grenada. In 1764 Brunias accompanied Young to the West Indies, where the artist would spend most of the next three decades. His images portray the region's slave-based societies as sites of communal stability, refinement, exoticism, and diverse social ranks, all made legible by means of varying skin tones and the quality and quantity of personal attire. Despite their romanticization, Brunias's paintings offer intriguing portrayals of the West Indian material world. Textiles—key indicators of social status—are rendered in fine detail, and the types and styles of clothing represented correspond with many firsthand European accounts.

Numerous subtle social categories existed within West Indian society, in which dress played an important role in announcing (or constructing) one's identity. Well-to-do whites and free persons of color had access to the latest European modes. In the mid-1770s, the Scottish traveler Janet Schaw commented on Antigua's stylish set, who "have the fashions every six weeks from London" in St. John's "elegant shops."[1] It is no accident that in Brunias's

109A

Linen Day (cat. 109A) the most sophisticated woman, dressed in a delicate white muslin gown (detail), also happens to have the fairest skin. Mulattoes often used upscale European fashion as a means of positioning themselves above Africans and dark-skinned Creoles. The woman's brilliant white dress would likely have communicated her status not only as free, but also as a person of refinement who could afford to buy fine Indian muslin and to keep it bright white (suggesting her eschewal of physical labor). Unlike the central figure, several of the women do not have shoes or stays and let their shifts casually hang off their shoulders, indicators of inferior social status.

Even among enslaved persons there existed a social hierarchy articulated, in no small part, by clothing. In the background of Brunias's *A West Indian Flower Girl and Two Other Free Women of Color* (cat. 109C) an enslaved man pushing a barrel wears nothing but breeches, while a boy seated in a doorway in the foreground is dressed in a white shirt and breeches, suggesting that he may be a house slave. Those who worked in a planter's house

had better clothing than artisans or field and mill workers, though some possessed at least a few items they reserved for market days or special occasions. Plantation owners, in theory, annually distributed cloth, often a durable but prickly fabric like osnaburg (unbleached linen or hemp), and some provided small amounts of inexpensive cottons, especially the popular checked and striped varieties.[2] Slaves sometimes received new or used clothing (or money for cloth), but clothing, like food, could also be withheld or taken away as a form of punishment.

Weekly markets throughout the Caribbean were dynamic sites of economic and social exchange where textiles could be acquired. *Linen Day* highlights this important sphere of intra-island economies, wherein enslaved persons could participate in the global trade networks. A St. Vincent landowner's wife, A. C. Carmichael, noted that the slaves' "showy" handkerchiefs were "of British manufacture, but many [were] costly silk ones from Martinique,—while others wear them of India muslin."[3] Brunias's depiction in *Linen Day* of two women selling imported European

109B

109C

and possibly Indian textiles corresponds to contemporary descriptions of women who were often the vendors of cloth in the markets.

Access to these textiles offered Creoles and Africans in the West Indies opportunities for self-fashioning. They adopted European fashions into which they integrated African modes such as the head wrap, resulting in a distinctive Creole look. In *Free West Indian Dominicans* (cat. 109B) a stylish trio demonstrates this trend as they sport fine European attire, including hats, which were often worn on top of elaborate head wraps. In *Linen Day* Brunias depicts many head wraps fixed in individual configurations that could convey different messages comprehensible only to those fluent in the local sartorial language.[4]   AB

1. Schaw, *Journal of a Lady of Quality*, p. 115.
2. McDonald, *The Economy and Material Culture of Slaves*.
3. Carmichael, *Five Years in Trinidad and St. Vincent*, vol. 1, p. 146.
4. For a discussion of different types of head wraps and their meaning, see Buckridge, *The Language of Dress*, pp. 86–96.

109A, detail

110. MAN'S HEADDRESS (PART OF CHIEF'S COSTUME)

Malecite tribe, New Brunswick, Canada,
mid- to late 18th century
Wool broadcloth, silk ribbon, embroidered with
metal-wrapped thread, glass beads
Height 24 in. (62 cm)
New Brunswick Museum, St. John, New Brunswick, Canada,
Purchased with the assistance of a Movable Cultural Property
grant accorded by the Department of Canadian Heritage
under the terms of the Cultural Property Export
and Import Act, 1983 1983.47.2.3

110, front

Textiles represented the principal trade item between Europeans and Native Americans and served as essential tools of the French, English, and eventually Americans who vigorously sought to dominate the lucrative fur trade. This headdress was part of a Malecite chief's costume that included a cloak, breechclout (a type of loincloth), leggings, and sashes. Like many of the costume components, the headdress is made of red-dyed English "stroud"—named after the eponymous Gloucester river region where such wool was manufactured—and other European-made items including yellow silk ribbon, gold thread, and blue and white glass beads (of possible Venetian origin). The variety of trade materials demonstrates the involvement of North American tribes in global trade owing to their control of the fur supply so coveted by Europeans. Certain aspects of the headdress's design reveal inventive aesthetic decisions that developed with the incorporation of such trade goods. For example, white marks along the flare of the hood indicate where clamps held the fabric during the dyeing process; rather than hiding them, the maker has integrated the marks into the design.

The Malecites, like other tribes, were keenly aware of the mercantile competition between the Europeans. They deftly negotiated for goods and pitted the foreigners against one another to gain advantage. The letters of frustrated traders reveal that Native Americans readily rejected anything that did not meet their requirements. In response, European manufacturers repeatedly modified their items to suit those who had convinced both the French and English that their rival's goods were superior. By the late seventeenth century, England's Hudson's Bay Company (HBC) merchants sometimes secretly copied, bought, or imported French blankets because the tribes claimed to prefer them, while the French purchased cloth from the HBC or manufactured imitations of British textiles.[1] The specificity of their complaints reveals that Native American traders proved to be excellent judges of quality and could often identify a French-made blanket that was being advertised as English and vice versa.

In addition to the fur trade, cloth and articles of clothing also served as essential currencies for other commodities, including land. A printed cotton from the late eighteenth century depicts a famous rendering of William Penn and fellow English traders offering a bolt of bright white cloth to the Delaware Indians in exchange for the land that now comprises Philadelphia and its environs (fig. 156). Though the scene is fictitious, Penn did in fact trade cloth with local tribes as he attempted to gain control of Native American lands in the mid-Atlantic region. The bolt of cloth may represent all trade goods, and if so, it is telling that a textile—rather than a weapon, cask of alcohol, or hogshead of tobacco—was chosen to stand in for all such commodities. And, as one scholar has remarked: "The bolt of cloth, simultaneously a payment, a gift, a commodity, and a promise of peace, masks under the guise of trade, an act of conquest."[2] AB

1. The HBC, chartered in 1670, monopolized British fur trade and set up trading forts along the coasts of the Hudson and James Bays, where major rivers connected them with the Canadian interior. See Ray, "Indians as Consumers in the Eighteenth Century," pp. 320–43.
2. Tobin, *Picturing Imperial Power*, p. 63.

110, back

Fig. 156. *Penn's Treaty with the Indians*. England, ca. 1788. Cotton, copperplate printed. The Metropolitan Museum of Art, New York, Bequest of Charles Allen Munn, 1924 (24.109.105)

Ralph Earl (1751–1801)
111. ELIJAH BOARDMAN (1760–1823)
New Milford, Connecticut, 1789
Oil on canvas
83 x 51 in. (210.8 x 129.5 cm)
The Metropolitan Museum of Art, New York,
Bequest of Susan W. Tyler, 1979 1979.395

In this extraordinary American portrait, shopkeeper Elijah Board-man proudly displays his stock of textiles.[1] A year before the pic-ture was painted, he and his partner, brother Daniel, advertised that "At their Store in New-Milford, [they] Have for Sale a very large and general Assortment of European, East & West-India Goods."[2] They ran a general dry-goods store, so, in addition to the luxurious imported textiles that Elijah clearly wanted his business to be known for, the store sold such mundane products as local foodstuffs, frying pans, and bar iron. They also supplied New Milford residents with rum, sugar, molasses, and indigo from the West Indies, as well as Chinese tea and pepper from South-east Asia. It is likely that all of the fabrics they sold were imported, since there was only the most rudimentary, small-scale production of linen and woolen textiles in the United States at this time.

In at least one of the advertisements, the Boardmans enumer-ated the textiles they had on hand. From England, they had woolens of many types, such as "Superfine Broad-Cloth" in an assortment of colors, baize, and callimancoes. They stocked silk "taffety" (taffeta) and satin, and "striped, spotted, and plain Silk Gauzes," as well as "black and figur'd Ribbands." Cotton "Calicoes & Chintz," either English or Indian-made, were also available. They listed fabrics together that were undoubtedly Indian—yardage of cotton muslin grouped with "bandano, [and] romal . . . silk Handkerchiefs."[3]

In the painting some of these advertised fabrics are immedi-ately recognizable. On the topmost shelf, partially obscured by the doorframe, are the spools of silk ribbon. The shelf below holds a selection of narrow-width plain and patterned fabrics, including a brown small-patterned cotton calico and a red-spotted bolt that is probably tie-dyed Indian bandanna fabric, perhaps not as yet cut up into individual handkerchiefs.[4] The next shelf is topped by three fine fabrics with white-on-white patterns—likely the type of "striped, spotted, and plain Silk Gauzes" adver-tised. Under them are bolts of what appear to be green and pink silk taffeta, and then a bolt of fancy brown-, white-, and gold-figured silk stripe. Beneath the stripe is a floral trail-patterned fab-ric that could be a silk but is more likely a printed cotton chintz. White-ground floral chintz, Indian or English, was very popular for dresses and banyans in this country (cats. 112, 113). Under

that is what looks like a gold-colored satin. The lowest shelf is given over to woolens, possibly the "Superfine Broad-Cloth" that topped the Boardmans' ad. The lowest bolt hangs open to display what is likely an English excise tax mark, assuring the viewer of the origins and assumed high quality of the imported goods.   AP

1. For more about this painting and Ralph Earl, its artist, see Kornhauser et al., *Ralph Earl: The Face of the Young Republic*, pp. 154–55.
2. *Connecticut Courant*, no. 1209, March 24, 1788, p. 4.
3. *Connecticut Journal*, no. 746, February 14, 1782, p. 1.
4. Identified in Bean, "The Indian Origins of the Bandanna," pp. 832–39.

112. DRESS (ROBE À L'ANGLAISE)

America, 1785–95
Textile: India, second half of the 18th century
Cotton, painted mordant, dyed, baleen
Length 54 in. (137.2 cm)
Brooklyn Museum Costume Collection at The Metropolitan
Museum of Art, Gift of the Brooklyn Museum, 2009;
A. Augustus Healy Fund, 1934 2009.300.647

The apparent regularity of the meandering line and repeating floral motif on the fabric of this dress suggests that the cotton was block-printed in England, where calico printing was common by the late eighteenth century. Subtle differences in each leaf and flower, however, prove that the vines on this American-made dress were meticulously hand-painted, pointing to the fabric's Indian origins. The broad width of the yardage, forty-four inches, also points to Indian manufacture. Notwithstanding early technological advancements in European printing centers in France and England, the exoticism and affordability of Indian painted and printed cottons encouraged their popularity, especially in the newly established United States.

An Anglomaniacal impulse drove the international vogue for the *robe à l'anglaise*, which, by the 1780s, closed neatly down the front of the bodice without the added fuss of a stomacher.[1] Anti-British feeling shortly after the Revolutionary War did not prevent Americans from following this close-bodied style, which by the last quarter of the century was as easily associated with the French as with the British.[2] Baleen, or whalebone (an American product over which the British had lost control during the war), is sewn into the back bodice seams to reinforce the fashionable posture.[3]

The Treaty of Paris (1783) signaled the end of the Revolution and allowed North Americans to further indulge their desire for fashionable foreign textiles. This textile may have come to the United States through American merchants trading with English East India Company agents, no longer limited by the Navigation

Acts, oppressive taxes, and trade restrictions, or, after 1783, through direct trade with India: the young country took up commerce with China and India with alacrity after gaining independence from Britain.[4] A bolt of flowered cloth in the 1789 portrait of Elijah Boardman (cat. 111) bears a striking similarity to the pattern in this dress. The textile in the painting could be either painted Indian cotton, like this gown, or one of the many English cotton block prints of similar design.   KS

1. Ribeiro, *Dress in Eighteenth-Century Europe*, p. 185.
2. Ribeiro, *The Art of Dress*, p. 66.
3. Tower, *A History of the American Whale Fishery*, pp. 45–46.
4. Warwick, Pitz, and Wyckoff, *Early American Dress*, p. 212.

Prince Demah Barnes
113. WILLIAM DUGUID (BORN 1747?)
Boston, 1773
Oil on canvas
20¾ x 15¾ in. (52.7 x 40 cm)
The Metropolitan Museum of Art, New York,
Friends of the American Wing Fund, 2010 2010.105

Inscription (on stretcher): WD ÆTATIS SUI 26 1773 / PRINCE DEMAH BARNES ~~SCULPT~~ PINXIT FEBRY 1773

William Duguid, a Scottish immigrant textile importer in Boston, is the subject of this engaging portrait. Newspaper advertisements record that Duguid was active in the Boston textile trade between 1769 and 1772, although his career may have extended beyond those years. His identity is known through family history and is substantiated by his initials and age noted in the inscription painted on the stretcher of the canvas by the elusive artist Prince Demah Barnes. Duguid's straightforward gaze, the half smile that plays about his lips, and the fact that he is wearing "at-home" dress add to the intimate nature of this portrait, which may once have been paired with one of his wife. The silver and garnet heart-shaped pin that closes the neck of his ruffled shirt came down in the family as well (fig. 157,), a treasured token of love.

Part of the painting's appeal comes from the floral pattern on the softly draped banyan that Duguid is wearing (for more on banyans, see cats. 96–99). It appears to be made from a printed cotton of either Indian or European manufacture (cat. 112). Duguid's choice of dress could be interpreted as his proudly showing off his textile wares, but Boston newspaper records suggest that he specialized in importing woolen goods. He is first noted as receiving "2 bales Woolens" listed on the cargo manifest of the *Nancy*, which arrived in Boston from Glasgow on October 10, 1769.[1] In May and June 1772 "William Duguid and Com-

pany" posted several advertisements announcing that there were for sale in his shop on Treat's Wharf "A Very neat Assortment of Spring and Summer Goods Received in the last Ships from London and Glasgow" that were "Of a much better Quality than generally Imported."[2] In June 1772 he also advertised having for sale "Some extremely good Broad Cloths."[3]

Duguid, born in Aberdeen, maintained contact with his Scottish homeland through his importing business, and his heritage is attested to by one of the books proudly displayed in the Chippendale-style desk and bookcase behind him, William Robertson's *History of Scotland* (1759). Also in the bookcase are collections of plays by Shakespeare and William Congreve, in keeping

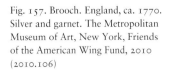

Fig. 157. Brooch. England, ca. 1770. Silver and garnet. The Metropolitan Museum of Art, New York, Friends of the American Wing Fund, 2010 (2010.106)

114

Fig. 158. John Eddy's sleeved waistcoat. Possibly made by Elizabeth Brainerd Eddy, East Middletown (now East Hampton), Connecticut, ca. 1758–60. Linen, embroidered with wool. Connecticut Historical Society, Hartford, Gift of Mrs. Lavinia K. Walsh (1978.104.0)

with the tradition that a sitter's depiction in a banyan indicated his interest in the life of the mind.

It is not known when Duguid arrived in Boston, and after 1772 he disappears from published records. The last time his name appears is in an advertisement in which he is listed as a shipping agent for those wanting to book freight or passage on the ship *John* sailing from Boston to Glasgow in November 1772.[4] His daughter Mary, born in 1771/72, eventually settled in Gorham, Maine, and the portrait of her father descended in the family through five generations of Maine residents before it came to the Metropolitan Museum.   AP

1. Shipping News, *Boston Chronicle* 3, no. 7, February 12–15, 1770, p. 56.
2. Advertisement, *Boston Post-Boy*, no. 769, May 18, 1772, p. 3.
3. Advertisement, *Boston Post-Boy*, no. 772, June 8, 1772, p. 3. Broadcloth is a plain-weave English woolen cloth woven on wide looms of 54 to 63 inches.
4. Advertisement, *Boston News-Letter*, no. 3606, November 12, 1772, p. 4.

114. DRESS FOR A YOUNG BOY

New England, 1755–65
Linen, embroidered with wool
Length 27 ½ in. (69.9 cm)
The Metropolitan Museum of Art, New York,
Rogers Fund, 1954 54.124

From as early as the sixteenth century in western Europe, domestic interiors and intimate accessories were decorated with colorful abstract floral and figural forms inspired by Indian and Chinese designs.[1] This decorative strategy continued into the eighteenth century, when Americans followed suit using crewelwork to ornament domestic spaces and dress, including coverlets, bed hangings, headcloths, petticoats, and, sometimes, children's clothing.[2] On this boy's frock, familiar motifs of carnations, tulips, roses, thistles, grapevines, and strawberry plants bloom alongside exotic feathery fruit trees, abstract acanthus leaves, and fantastic floral forms. The embroidery demonstrates colonial American adaptation of European designs, which in turn were appropriated from designs acquired from trade with the East.

Connecticut is unique among American colonies in that crewelwork-embellished dresses are often found among the array of embroidered pieces; in other American colonies, extant examples of embroidery in wool typically include only ornamented interior furnishings and accessories.[3] The crewelwork on this boy's dress reflects a style identified with work done by women in the Connecticut River valley. The stitches employed are commonly associated with all New England embroidery: the flat stitch and the laid couching stitch, or economy stitch.[4]

Both techniques use long stitches on the right side of the fabric and short anchoring stitches on the back, allowing the embroiderer to achieve the most colorful effects possible without wasting thread that was difficult to spin and dye and expensive to purchase. Another crewel-embroidered garment made for a small boy is known to come from the Connecticut River valley: a sleeved waistcoat (fig. 158) probably worked by his mother, Elizabeth Brainerd Eddy, in East Middletown (now East Hampton), Connecticut.[5] It was cut with the flared skirts and large pocket flaps fashionable for adult men during 1758–60, when John Eddy was between three and five years old.

Attitudes about childhood shifted dramatically in the late seventeenth and early eighteenth centuries, when philosophers John Locke and Jean-Jacques Rousseau presented children as unique beings whose development could be improved or disrupted by careful or negligent parenting. Recognizing the importance of dress, Locke prescribed sartorial solutions for healthy children that facilitated range of movement and exposure to the elements: "Let nature have scope to fashion the body, as she thinks best."[6] Although this boy's frock predates the high-waisted shift and skeleton suit that accommodated "the limbs of a growing child," as Rousseau recommended,[7] the plain-weave linen from which it was made was, for a child, a comfortable alternative to the stiff silks often used for more formal interpretations of the same silhouette for boys.[8] Rousseau wrote that he had "not chosen [his] European pupil in order to make an Asiatic of him," but the "short skirts" and then the "loose dress" he recommended for children bear closer resemblance to Indian and Chinese menswear styles than the European ones after which young Western boys' clothing had always been modeled.[9] KS

1. For a discussion of Asian-inspired floral hangings in Elizabethan interiors, see Irwin, "Origins of the 'Oriental Style' in English Decorative Art," p. 110.
2. Synge, *Art of Embroidery: History of Style and Technique*, p. 165.
3. Rowe, "Crewel Embroidered Bed Hangings in Old and New England," p. 136.
4. Ibid., pp. 119–20, fig. 15.
5. Schoelwer et al., *Connecticut Needlework*, p. 62.
6. Locke, "Some Thoughts Concerning Education," section 11, p. 18.
7. Rousseau, *Rousseau's Émile; or, Treatise on Education*, p. 90.
8. Warwick, Pitz, and Wyckoff, *Early American Dress: The Colonial and Revolutionary Periods*, p. 239.
9. Rousseau, *Rousseau's Émile; or, Treatise on Education*, p. 91.

115. COVERLET
Ruth Culver Coleman
Sag Harbor, New York, ca. 1760–80
Linen, embroidered with wool
80¾ x 95⅝ in. (205.1 x 242.9 cm)
The Metropolitan Museum of Art, New York,
Sansbury-Mills Fund, 1961 61.48.1

This exceptional coverlet persuasively demonstrates that eighteenth-century American women happily decorated their homes with fashionable patterns adopted from faraway lands, whether or not they were aware of the ultimate source of their designs. The embroidered flowers and plants seen here are undeniably exotic in nature, especially the sinuous blooms in shades of blue that appear in the border. Some motifs have several types of flowers emanating from a single stem, as is common in earlier textiles from India, Iran, and Turkey. While it is unlikely that its maker, Ruth Culver Coleman, living in a remote rural community on the far eastern end of Long Island, would have had direct knowledge of Persian or Ottoman textiles, imported Indian and European printed cottons were available in America, and active shipping between Sag Harbor and New York City meant they could have been readily acquired.

A tantalizing (although perhaps completely erroneous) clue about the origin of the designs for the floral motifs is found in the 1909 catalogue of the Hudson-Fulton Exhibition, when the coverlet was first shown at the Metropolitan Museum. It was lent by its owner at the time, Miss Anna Mulford, the great-granddaughter of its maker. The caption in the exhibition catalogue stated: "Embroidery. Homespun white linen with elaborate design of flowers and leaves embroidered in crewel work. Designs copied from a piece of French printed cotton in the possession of the owner."[1]

Could the designs on the bedcover have been copied from a French cotton fabric? Or did they have a different source? The only French textiles that could have inspired the flowers in the bedcover are brightly colored printed cottons called indiennes, which began to be made about 1785 and adapted motifs from seventeenth- and eighteenth-century Indian printed palampores and chintzes (cat. 56).

The precise year that the coverlet was made is difficult to know, since it is not signed or dated, but a date after 1785 seems unlikely. In overall design and its use of individual floral bouquets it is similar to other documented New England examples from the third quarter of the eighteenth century.[2] If we accept a date before the era of French indiennes, perhaps Coleman was inspired by a piece of earlier Indian printed cotton, mistakenly identified

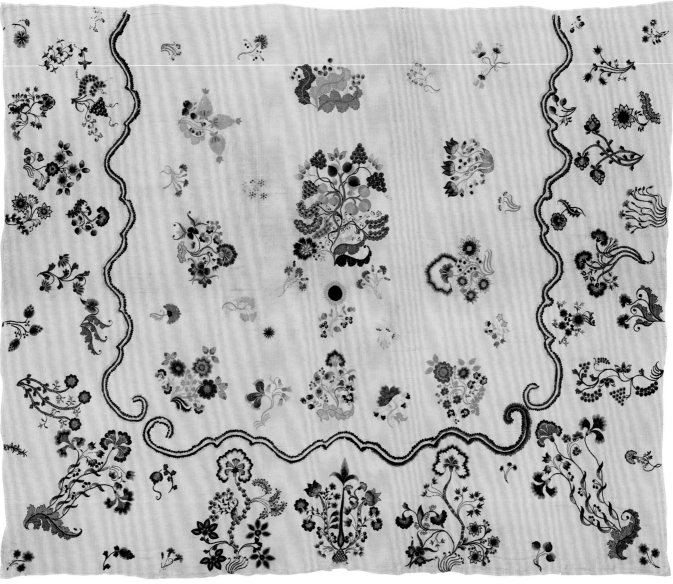

115

in 1909 as French. Then again, the coverlet's connection with the piece of fabric may have been purely family mythology. The supposedly French fabric did not enter the Museum's collection with the coverlet when it was purchased in 1961, so the question must remain unanswered. However, American embroidered coverlets and bed hangings of the eighteenth century do generally trace their designs to simplified interpretations of earlier English examples, and those English embroideries were originally influenced by imported Indian and Asian textiles. No matter the exact source, the artistic Coleman created her swirling flowers in a relatively

common American fashion of the time, in all likelihood without ever knowing about their precursors from the other side of the world.   AP

1. Kent and Levy, *The Hudson-Fulton Celebration*, p. 158, no. 592. This exhibition was held as part of a larger celebration of the three hundredth anniversary of Henry Hudson's discovery of the river that now bears his name and the one hundredth anniversary of Robert Fulton's first steamboat.
2. See Peck with Schaffner, *American Quilts and Coverlets in The Metropolitan Museum of Art*, pp. 190–201, and Rowe, "Crewel Embroidered Bed Hangings in Old and New England," pp. 102–64, cover ill.

116. BLUE-RESIST PANEL

Probably India, for the American market, mid-18th century
Cotton, painted and block-printed resist, dyed
78 ¼ x 59 ⅝ in. (198.6 x 151.4 cm)
The Metropolitan Museum of Art, New York,
Rogers Fund, 1940 40.128

Determining the country of origin of this type of resist-painted and printed and indigo-dyed furnishing fabric has frustrated several generations of American textile historians. It is found in abundance in museums with major American textile collections, most often acquired between the 1920s and 1960s.[1] It entered those collections as examples of rare, early American-made fabric, often with family histories that attested to early ownership in New York's Hudson River valley or Long Island, or occasionally coastal Connecticut.

Blue-resist has been the subject of conferences, book chapters, and numerous articles.[2] The printing and dyeing process that made the characteristically large-scale patterns has been puzzled out, but where that process took place has been debated. Part of the mystery is that while English manufacturers were the source of many of the textiles imported to North America in the eighteenth century, blue-resist fabric like this is not found in England. So far the only evidence of it found there are some hand-painted paper swatches in a sample book likely copied after pieces of the actual fabric and the lining fabric of an embroidered stomacher.[3] Yet, after years of study most scholars came to the conclusion that since there was little documentary evidence of mid-eighteenth-century American textile printing, this fabric had to have been made in England.[4] This theory was seemingly backed up by a single piece of blue-resist in the collection of the Albany Institute of History and Art that bears an English excise tax stamp. That stamp (fig. 159) was seen as proof of English manufacture. However, in addition to the letter- and number-coded horizontal "frame mark," the piece has the mark of a crown with the intertwined initials of the monarch and the word "Callicoe" beneath. The British Textiles Tax Act of 1774 specifically called for different stamps for all-cotton printed calicoes made in Britain as opposed to those of foreign manufacture, stating: "each Piece of the [British] Stuffs, when printed . . . shall be stamped at each End with a Stamp and instead of the word Callico, which stands for Foreign Callicoes, each Piece shall be marked with the words British Manufactory." Therefore, the word "Callicoe" on the stamp on the Albany piece shows it was made someplace other than in Britain.[5]

Resist-dyeing with indigo was common in India at least as early as the thirteenth century. It is likely that these early and mid-eighteenth-century blue-resist textiles—with their loosely spun all-cotton base fabric that was certainly woven in India (since the English did not perfect weaving pure cottons until the 1770s)—were also printed in India, commissioned by the English East India Company specifically for the American market. When this textile was made there was a ban on importing Indian calicoes into England, but not to the North American colonies. The large-scale patterns, mostly of oversize flowering vines and birds, bear a resemblance to other Indian goods based on European designs commissioned by the East India Company. These decorative yet crudely printed goods would not likely have been appreciated in refined European markets. In America, however, as bed hangings, quilts, and curtains, they brightened up the homes of many colonists.   AP

1. There are probably more than one hundred pieces of blue-resist in many different patterns extant in American museums and historic houses. About fifty pieces are in the collection of the Winterthur Museum, Delaware, alone, and fifteen in the Metropolitan Museum. The fact that so much of the fabric survived to end up in museum collections is worth further investigation.
2. Blue-resist was the subject of a "Field Day" at the Cooper Union, New York City, on May 17, 1956, attended by the leading textile historians of the time. This led to a deeper investigation of the fabric by Florence Montgomery in her seminal book *Printed Textiles* (1970) and an entire book on the subject by Florence H. Pettit called *America's Indigo Blues* (1974). More recently, Mary E. Gale and Margaret T. Ordoñez have published two informative articles on its use and the techniques of its manufacture: "Eighteenth-Century Indigo Resist Fabrics" and "Indigo-Resist Prints from Eighteenth-Century America."
3. The paper patterns are in Baker Tuckers Pattern Book 2 (G.P. & J. Baker Limited, Bucks, U.K.); see Gale and Ordoñez, "Eighteenth-Century Indigo Resist Fabrics," pp. 165–69. The only actual textile known in England at this time is the blue-resist lining of a white satin stomacher, ca. 1700, embroidered with pelicans and unicorns in silk and metallic threads, in the collection of Platt Hall in Manchester (no. 1953.325). The lining is assumed to be original, which would mean that blue-resist fabric was produced considerably earlier than has been thought.
4. The resist-dyeing technique was used in England and other European countries in the eighteenth century, but none of the European fabrics are as boldly patterned or as loosely printed as the type discussed here.
5. See Dagnall, *The Marking of Textiles for Excise and Customs Duty*, pp. 15–18, 21–24. The code on the Albany fabric's frame mark dates it to 1766 (the number 54 added to 1712, the first year that duties were imposed on cloth and the marking system began). Though this fabric's mark predates the 1774 Tax Act, I have made the assumption that the printing of the word "Callicoe" to identify non-English printed cottons for tax purposes was already in place before it was noted in the 1774 act.

Fig. 159. Blue-resist fabric with English excise tax stamp. Albany Institute of History and Art, New York (1948.31.113)

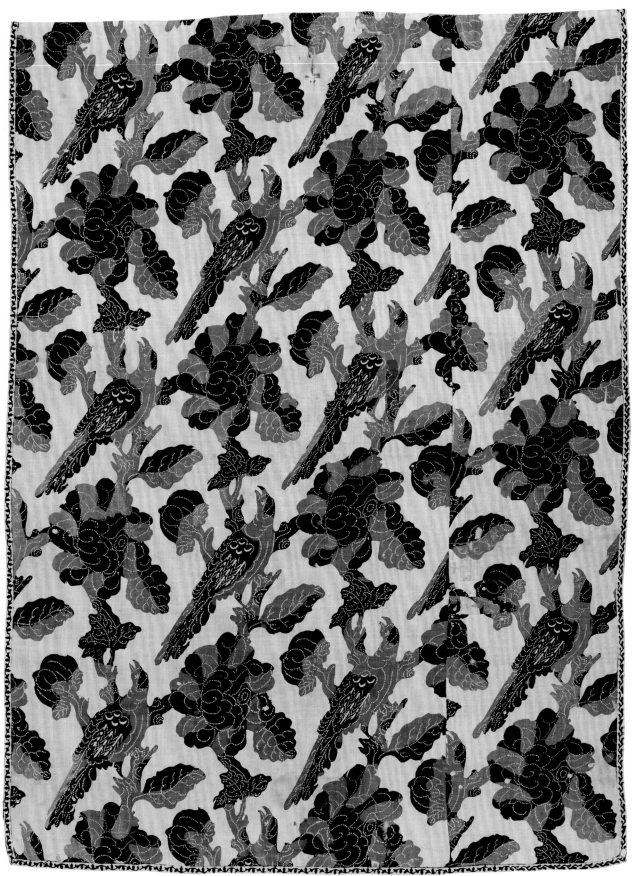

117. DRESS (ROBE À LA POLONAISE)

France, probably for the American market, 1780–85
Textile: China, late 18th century
Silk, painted
Length 50 in. (127 cm)
The Metropolitan Museum of Art, New York, Gift of heirs of
Emily Kearny Rodgers Cowenhoven, 1970 1970.87a, b

This *robe à la polonaise* of imported Chinese painted silk demonstrates that North Americans acquired luxurious Eastern textiles that could be sent to French dressmakers and incorporated into fashionable Western silhouettes. The polonaise style consists of a fitted bodice with a long, open overskirt cleverly looped into three swags over a short petticoat. Though the style was originally introduced among the fashionable bourgeoisie of Paris, this interpretation, with its close-fitting bodice, efficiently trained overskirt, and minimal trim, gives evidence of an American sensibility for fit and simplicity.[1] The polonaise was extremely popular in the young United States after the Revolution, reflecting, as it did, the burgeoning American interest in all things French without abandoning the familiar pragmatism of the English walking dress.[2]

The rounded neckline, elbow-length sleeves, simple cuffs, and separate overskirt pleated into the bodice all date this dress to the early 1780s. Ownership of the dress has traditionally been attributed to one of the wives of Jonathan Belcher, the British governor of New Jersey from 1747 to 1757.[3] It is more likely that the dress was worn by a descendant of the family. The governor's first and second wives had both died by 1780 and so could not have worn this late-century style. Additionally, trade restrictions during the war limited access to imported goods. It seems likely, then, that this fashionable French polonaise of Chinese silk arrived after the end of the American Revolutionary War.

Painted silk textiles like the one used to create this dress were produced exclusively for export, since Chinese consumers had no interest in this quick and relatively inexpensive approach to decorating silk. The painting techniques and popular motifs seen on this dress and similar furnishing fabrics suggest a Chinese response to the European interest in painted cottons from India rather than an extension of the traditional Chinese art of painting on silk. This bright yellow silk in particular features individual flowering plant forms with the characteristic drooping bud associated with traditional Indian plant iconography.

Though in demand for their novelty and low production cost relative to comparable woven designs, many of these whimsical Chinese silks were bought and never used, resulting in a surprising quantity of uncut yardage still extant. The European bed hangings and dresses for which these painted silks were popular required

more yardage of painted silk than was commonly produced in one motif by Chinese suppliers.[4] The limited availability of Chinese painted silks in usable quantities increased the demand for their novel appeal, especially valued by the American market.   KS

1. Ribeiro, *The Art of Dress,* p. 66.
2. Warwick, Pitz, and Wyckoff, *Early American Dress: The Colonial and Revolutionary Periods,* pp. 179–80.
3. Druesedow, "In Style: Celebrating Fifty Years of the Costume Institute," p. 15.
4. Wilson, "Chinese Painted Silks for Export in the Victoria and Albert Museum," p. 30.

118. PALAMPORE

India (Coromandel Coast), for the European market, ca. 1765
Cotton, painted resist and mordant, dyed, with overpainting
112 ¼ x 88 ½ in. (285.1 x 224.8 cm)
Historic Cherry Hill, 3306

Appearing almost as fresh as it must have on the day it arrived in Albany, New York, this palampore was found in the 1960s among other eighteenth-century fabrics in a trunk in the garret of Cherry Hill, the Georgian home built there by Philip Van Rensselaer (1747–1798). Philip was a cousin of the more well-known Van Rensselaers, the Dutch patroons who once owned much of the land that today forms Albany and Rensselaer Counties in New York State.[1] He too was affluent and influential in his hometown of Albany, becoming a successful merchant after marrying Maria Sanders (1749–1830) in 1768. Maria's father, Robert (1705–1765), and paternal grandfather, Barent (1678–1757), were long-established merchants of Albany and nearby Schenectady, New York, who bought and sold all manner of goods, including textiles. Her uncle John (1714–1782) was also a merchant, centered in Schenectady. Their account books reveal the family's close relationships with London and Amsterdam merchants, through whom they ordered items for sale and for their own use.[2] Philip Van Rensselaer took over his recently deceased father-in-law's business when he married Maria.

The imagery on the Cherry Hill palampore is particularly intriguing. Most palampores focus on the abundant flowers of the central tree, each usually a different variety. Sometimes small animals cluster on the mound at the tree base, and birds and butterflies fly among its branches. Like the others, this palampore has a myriad of gloriously unrealistic flowers, including several that resemble heads of palm trees, and a lush floral border. But this is one of only a few that feature small humans at the base.[3] Five couples in European dress relax among the rockery under the tree. Other people, seemingly unclothed, climb the tree's trunk to gather its fruit. The people are joined by several types of birds

and beasts, each with a mate, including a pair of toothy, crowned lions (detail).

It is tempting to make a few assumptions about this palampore based on its iconography, although ultimately they cannot be proved. Perhaps it was a wedding present, given to Philip and Maria to celebrate their marriage in 1768. All the people, animals, and birds are paired two by two and could be intended as a nuptial message. In addition, the small person in the tree throwing down fruit to the pair below is a traditional symbol of fertility, dating back to illuminated manuscripts of the Middle Ages.

It is likely this palampore was originally intended for the Dutch market and came to Albany through Amsterdam.[4] The drawing of the human couples strongly resembles that on another Indian chintz known to be for the Dutch market (cat. 81). Certainly, Albany was primarily a Dutch town in the eighteenth century, and we know that the bride's family imported goods from Amsterdam. Finally, the two unusual grinning, crowned lions seem to have been copied from the smiling lions on the Dutch silver ducaton coin. Between 1728 and 1751 the ducaton was minted bearing the Dutch East India Company monogram and was used by the company for trade in the East.[5]   AP

1. The original Van Rensselaer Manor encompassed more than one million acres, with Albany as the family's central headquarters.
2. Sanders Family Papers, 1711–1833, New-York Historical Society.
3. Another palampore in this design is in the collection of the Royal Ontario Museum, Toronto (no. 934.4.11).
4. The palampore is stamped on the back with a multipronged design within a circle, the function or meaning of which is not known. It does not bear the mark of either the English or the Dutch East India Company.
5. For the history of the ducaton, and images, see: "Silver Riders (Ducatons)," in *World of Coins;* http://www.worldofcoins.eu/forum/index.php?topic=7994.0.

118, detail

119. COVERLET

Attributed to Sarah Furman Warner Williams (1764–1848)

New York City, ca. 1803

Linen and cotton, embroidered with silk

103 ¼ x 90 ½ in. (262.3 x 229.9 cm)

The Metropolitan Museum of Art, New York,

Gift of Catherine E. Cotheal, 1938   38.59

This engaging appliquéd coverlet, the layout of which is based on a Tree of Life palampore design, was likely made as a gift celebrating the 1803 marriage of a young New York City woman named Phebe Berrian Warner (1786–1844) to Henry Cotheal (1779–1849). It is thought to have been made by her first cousin, Sarah Furman Warner Williams, an extremely talented quiltmaker.[1]

The lives of both the quiltmaker and the quilt owner are marked by numerous connections with shipping and trade. The maker, Sarah, was the stepdaughter of George Warner (died 1825), who came to New York from England at a young age and became wealthy by making ships' sails and rigging in a business he started with his brother Richard. Sarah married Azarias Williams (1765–1849), who at the time of their marriage in 1787 was a merchant, but he eventually made his fortune in New England real estate. Phebe Berrian Warner married Henry Cotheal, another merchant who was actively involved in shipping for his entire career. At first his interests were local, and he traded in basic foodstuffs. As of 1817, however, he went into business with his brother David, and together they invested in brigs and schooners that traded up and down the East Coast. In the 1820s they held interest in ships that brought tobacco from Kentucky and cotton from New Orleans and in others that made the trip to the West Indies, bringing back, among other things, hundreds of coconuts and tons of fustic, a bright yellow fabric dye.[2] When the brothers were listed in a book about wealthy New York citizens in 1845, they were said to be "Importers of Horns, Hides, Indigo, &c. from the West Indies."[3]

There is no question that Sarah Furman Warner Williams would have been familiar with the palampore design on which she modeled the coverlet. The large central urn filled with flowering vines mimics the painted Indian Trees of Life, complete with the oversize, brightly plumed birds staring down from the branches. The domesticated animals in the shepherd's care below the urn parallel similar groupings of wild beasts often seen among the rocky hills at the base of Indian examples (cat. 118). In the period between 1785 and 1825, after the opening of direct trade between India and the United States, palampores seem to have been the height of fashion and are frequently mentioned in newspaper advertisements as being for sale by vendors in New York City.

Other Indian fabrics were also coming to New York in quantity, but, interestingly enough, none of the many fabrics that Sarah appliquéd onto her American "palampore" can be definitely identified as Indian; for the most part they appear to be of English manufacture.   AP

1. Other quilts or portions of quilts attributed to Sarah Furman Warner Williams can be found at the Winterthur Museum, Delaware (nos. 59.1496 and 59.1497), and in a private collection; one, formerly in the collection of the Henry Ford Museum, was burned in a fire in 1970. For more on the present quilt, see Peck with Schaffner, *American Quilts and Coverlets*, pp. 16–19.
2. Advertisement, *New-York Gazette* 31, no. 13068, January 17, 1821, p. 4.
3. [Beach], *Wealth and Biography of the Wealthy Citizens of New York City*, p. 7.

120. CHINESE PALAMPORE

China (Guangzhou, formerly Canton), for the European or

American market, 1750–1800

Silk satin, embroidered with silk

108 x 90 in. (274.3 x 228.6 cm)

The Metropolitan Museum of Art, New York,

Gift of Louise Housman, 1947   47.63

Among his groundbreaking work on Indian textiles, John Irwin (1917–1997), the longtime Keeper of the Indian Department at the Victoria and Albert Museum, London, investigated the source of the flowering Tree of Life pattern that decorated Indian chintz palampores beginning in the late seventeenth century. In an extremely convincing 1955 article published in the *Burlington Magazine*, Irwin argued that the large flowering trees on palampores were not an Indian design tradition but were the result of product specifications requested by the British, who had begun to form a taste for chinoiserie (perhaps better thought of as exoticism) by the early seventeenth century, soon after the English East India Company (founded 1600) began to bring back wares from China and Japan.[1] But when the British imported Indian painted chintz bedcovers, many with "sad red grounds," they discovered English consumers were not very enthusiastic about them. Responding to market preferences, in 1643 the London directors of the English East India Company wrote explicit instructions to their factories in Surat, asking that "Those [quilts] which hereafter you shall send we desire may be with more white ground, and the flowers and branch to be in colours in the middle of the quilt as the painter pleases."[2] With this type of instruction, the Indian palampore evolved into the form we know today, and the central flowering tree on textiles became extremely popular, persisting as an internationally favored design into the early nineteenth century.

The Chinese embroidered coverlet seen here represents the closing of the trade circle of the central tree design, from China to

England to India, and finally back to China, where Cantonese craftspeople embroidered it in imitation of an Indian painted cotton palampore. It is one of four Chinese pieces with this tree-and-border design that are known: the Metropolitan's example and two others are embroidered with silk thread, primarily in satin stitch, and one is painted.[3] While there are slight variations among them, the basic design is the same, which points to the use of a pattern, perhaps even one traced from an Indian palampore.

Irwin dated the group of Chinese palampores, all four made of white satin, to the early eighteenth century. However, it seems possible that they were made quite a bit later, judging by the rather spindly, attenuated tree that is similar to the trees in Indian palampores made after 1750. Additionally, European and American Neoclassical fashions of the late eighteenth century would have favored pastel colors on a shiny white ground. When the Metropolitan Museum's coverlet was donated by Louise Housman in 1947, it was placed in the collection of the American Wing, indicating that it probably came to the Museum with a family history of early American ownership.[4] While it might have made its way here through Europe first, it is also possible that it came to the United States when the country began trading directly with China in 1784. Silk textiles from Canton were highly coveted by Americans (cat. 121). In 1808 the New York merchants Bleecker, Bibby and Co. offered for sale "an elegant assortment of Canton Goods." Among the typical Chinese products, they included a listing for "A few superb Palampours [sic]."[5] Perhaps they looked like this one.   AP

1. Irwin, "Origins of the 'Oriental Style' in English Decorative Art," pp. 106–14.
2. India Office Archives, Factory Records Miscellaneous, XII, folio 99, as quoted in Irwin, above, p. 109.
3. In addition to the present palampore (cat. 120), there is an embroidered version in the collection of Colonial Williamsburg, Virginia (no. 1964-455), and both embroidered (no. 914.7.17) and painted (no. 955.70) examples are owned by the Royal Ontario Museum, Toronto. For more on the two in the latter collection, see Brett, "Variants of the Flowering Tree Design, Part II," pp. 280–83.
4. The original correspondence with the donor that could shed a light on why the piece entered the American Wing collection has not been found. The other three were purchased by the various museums from antiques dealers in the mid-twentieth century.
5. Advertisement, *Mercantile Advertiser* (New York), no. 4936, June 10, 1808, p. 4.

121A. FURNISHING SILK

China (Guangzhou, formerly Canton),
for the American market, 1815
Silk damask
25 ½ x 29 ¾ in. (64.8 x 75.6 cm)
The Metropolitan Museum of Art, New York,
Gift of Miss M. E. Powel, 1925   25.84.4

121B. FURNISHING SILK

China (Guangzhou, formerly Canton),
for the American market, 1815
Silk damask
25 ¾ x 29 ½ in. (65.4 x 74.9 cm)
The Metropolitan Museum of Art, New York,
Gift of Lydia Bond Powel, 1967   67.261

Chinese silk damask has long been popular in America, as attested by the many silk gowns in historical collections with specific histories of ownership by eighteenth-century American women.[1] Surviving furnishing silks such as these fragments of curtain and upholstery fabric are rarer owing to light exposure and the rigors of everyday wear and tear. They are especially valuable because the original memorandum documenting when they were ordered, and for whom, also survives.

The Chinese silks that arrived in this country through most of the eighteenth century were first purchased at their source by the English East India Company and then imported through England by American merchants. However, that changed after the American Revolution ended with the Treaty of Paris on September 3, 1783. The first American ship to trade directly at Canton, the *Empress of China*, set sail from New York harbor on February 22, 1784. It was in large part funded by Robert Morris, merchant of Philadelphia.

During the late eighteenth century and into the nineteenth, Philadelphia merchants were very actively involved in the China trade. One of the leading firms of China-trade merchants was Willings and Francis. Thomas Willing Francis (1767–1815), nephew of Elizabeth Willing Powel (1742–1830), was a principal of the firm, and it is to him that she addressed her order in 1815.[2] She was in need of new silk fabric for curtains and furniture upholstery, to be purchased in Canton. Powel was a wealthy woman, so it is unlikely she chose Chinese-made fabric because it was often less expensive than European silk damask. Chinese export silks, imported directly by American ships, were the height of fashion for patriotic citizens of the new American republic.

For her tearoom Powel ordered "Two Hundred yards of bright yellow satin Silk Damask, of the quality and color of the

121A

121B

sample sent herewith. The pattern of flowers handsome and well-executed." She also asked for "Ninety yards of slight glossy yellow Persian" for curtain lining,[3] "Fifty yards of plain Silk fringe, four inches deep" in a yellow that exactly matched the damask, one hundred yards of yellow silk binding, three pounds of silk sewing thread that could also be made into curtain tassels if so desired, and seventy-five yards of silk cord. For her "dining parlour" she ordered much the same, but in "bright scarlet."[4] These two pieces were given to the Museum by Powel family descendants.

The yellow damask features a fairly common basket pattern that probably originated in France in the 1780s and would not be easily identifiable as Chinese if not for the Chinese characters evident on a surviving piece of matching fringe that have been translated with varying meanings by different scholars. They are all in agreement that in the inscription the silk is referred to as "precious square," or bolt. Yellow was a particularly favored color

for Chinese export silks (cat. 117). The scarlet damask, with the large lotus flower supporting the vase, looks more overtly Chinese. This design is related to several silks found in European collections dating from the late seventeenth to early eighteenth century that have been variously attributed to Italian, French, English, and Chinese weavers, showing the pervasiveness of certain designs in the global textile trade.[5] AP

1. See Rothstein, "Silks for the American Market," pp. 90–94.
2. Thomas Willing Francis was the son of Elizabeth Powel's sister Anne, who married Tench Francis. He died in Philadelphia in June 1815, just two months after the silks were ordered.
3. "Persian" was the name at this time for a thin, plain silk taffeta fabric generally used for both clothing and curtain linings.
4. "Memorandum March the 7th 1815 Of a list of Furniture to be sent for from Canton by Thomas W. Francis Esq. for the use of his friend Elizabeth Powel." Cadwalader Family Papers, Collection 1454, The Historical Society of Pennsylvania, Philadelphia.
5. Browne, "Silk Damask Bed Furnishings in the Early Eighteenth Century," pp. 47–58.

TEXTILE GLOSSARY
Compiled by Cynthia V. A. Schaffner

anacu Traditional Andean woman's wraparound dress.

annatto Yellow-to-orange-colored dyestuff made from the pulp surrounding the seeds of the tropical achiote tree, *Bixa orellana.*

baffeta Indian plain cotton cloth of varying quality ranging from coarse to fine; dyed red, blue, or black for the Southeast Asian market, kept white for the European market.

bandano Printed silk handkerchief produced in India.

banyan European-made loose-fitting man's morning gown, modeled on Eastern styles of dress.

bayeta Spanish woolen flannel or felted cloth.

block printing Method of producing a repeating pattern on the fabric surface by pressing a carved block of wood dipped in dye onto the cloth.

boxshale Indian piece goods from the Coromandel Coast; favored in Japan and Thailand (Siam).

brazilwood Tropical trees, particularly the Brazilian *Caesalpinia echinata,* which produce a brilliant red dye.

buckram Coarse plain-weave linen or cotton cloth produced in Europe.

calico Originally, plain white all-cotton yardage or patterned cotton with dye-fast hand-painting or printing from India; name taken from the port of Calicut (now Kozhikode), India.

Cambay cloth Checked fabric exported from Cambay (now Khambhat, Gujarat), India, and widely worn in Southeast Asia.

cambric Fine white linen plain-weave cloth produced in Europe.

chay Red dye extracted from the root of the low-growing plant *Oldenlandia umbellata* from the Coromandel Coast delta.

chelloes Rough, striped, or plaid Indian cotton cloth exported to England; used in America to clothe slaves and also reexported to the West Indies.

cheney Worsted or woolen furnishing material produced in England.

cherryderry Striped or checked woven Indian cloth of mixed silk and cotton.

China blue Printing process invented in England to overcome the problem of indigo oxidizing and becoming insoluble on the way from dye vat to cloth.

chintz Seventeenth-century term originally applied equally to multi-colored painted or printed cloths produced in India; the finest quality came from the Coromandel Coast, principally Masulipatam and Pulicat. Used in Europe and America for clothing and furnishings.

cochineal Brilliant red dye produced from the female of the insect species *Dactylopius coccus,* native to Mexico and South America.

cope Semicircular ecclesiastical vestment worn by Christian priests over the shoulders like a cloak; often enriched with embroidery and jewels.

copperplate printing Technique of printing on the surface of cotton or linen fabric using large etched copperplates; introduced first in Ireland in 1752 by Francis Nixon.

cotton Fiber from the seed hair of plants of the genus *Gossypium;* various cultivated species of cotton originated in India, the Americas, and Africa.

cumbi Fine tapestry-woven cloth used for Inca garments.

damask Monochrome patterned fabric, the design visible through the juxtaposition of the two faces of the weave structure presented on the same surface of the textile; originally produced in China but later woven throughout the world and from any fiber.

dimity White cotton cloth often textured with woven cords or ribs; originally imported from India and later manufactured in Great Britain, where some dimities were woven with stripes, checks, or flowers and made of cotton, linen and cotton, or linen and silk.

dōbuku Japanese term for a samurai man's outer garment worn over armor or other clothing.

donsu Japanese term for a damasklike fabric, frequently of two colors and imported from China; category of *meibutsugire.*

dupata Textile designed in two loom-widths of fabric, sewn together and worn as a head scarf or shawl by women in India.

East India goods Products originating in India, China, or Southeast Asia sold worldwide by the large European trading companies, such as the English East India Company and the Dutch East India Company.

embroidery Designs created on a fabric with contrasting threads, stitched with a needle; many types of stitches can be employed.

faille Tightly woven silk fabric with a slight rib.

fustian Plain-weave fabric with a linen warp and a cotton weft.

garlix Linen cloth first imported from Goerlitz, Silesia (Germany).

gingham Striped or checked cloth; in India sometimes woven of silk and cotton combined, but usually of all cotton.

gorgoron, grogram Ribbed silk fabric woven in China.

goshee English term for a silk-and-cotton fabric made in China.

Guinea cloth Checked or striped rough cotton cloth produced in large quantities on the Coromandel Coast and Gujarat for the African markets; used in America to clothe slaves and also reexported to the West Indies.

hamsa Block-printed textile design with a repeating pattern of an ancient Indian mythical-goose motif.

Holland cloth Finely woven linen made in Holland.

humhum (See *muslin.*)

ikat Term originating in Indonesia and now widely used to describe the process by which a pattern is resist-dyed on the warp and/or the weft before being woven; also, the resulting fabric.

Indianillas Printed-cotton textiles made in Mexico that replicated imported East Indian calicoes.

indigo Blue dye whose color compound, indigotin, is extracted from the leaf of the indigo-bearing plant *Indigofera tinctoria,* found in India, and *Indigofera suffruticosa,* found in Africa and the Americas. (See *woad.*)

jinbaori Japanese battle jacket, usually made of bold or luxurious, often imported, textiles.

kalamkari Hand-painted resist- and mordant-dyed cotton textiles produced on the Coromandel Coast and around Surat, India.

kemha Turkish term for a silk lampas textile with a satin-weave ground and a twill weave pattern, executed with supplementary wefts of silk and metallic thread.

kersey Twill-woven coarse woolen cloth produced in Kersey, England.

kesa Japanese term for a Buddhist priest's rectangular vestment, usually made from patchwork in a prescribed configuration.

kimono, *kosode* Long robe with wide sleeves worn with a broad sash as an outer garment by the Japanese; pre-Meiji period Japanese term for kimono is *kosode.*

kinran Japanese term for silks with patterns woven in gold thread, frequently imported from China; category of *meibutsugire.*

lampas Figured weave in which a pattern composed of weft floats held by a binding warp is added to a ground weave formed by a main warp and weft.

linen Cloth of many grades and weaves produced with threads spun from the fibers of the flax plant *Linum usitatissimum.*

liclla Traditional Andean woman's shoulder mantle or shawl.

Londres, Londrins Fulled or matted woolen cloth manufactured in France and used in the Levant trade.

long cloth Cotton cloth from the Coromandel Coast, usually measuring 37 yards in length.

loom Instrument that facilitates weaving by holding the warp yarns with some degree of tension, allowing the weaver to insert the weft yarns.

lungee, lungi Length of unstitched fabric worn as a waistcloth in southern India.

madder Mordant dye from the roots of plants in the Rubiaceae family that produces reds with an orange hue that may range from deep scarlet to purple.

meibutsugire Japanese term for valuable, often imported cloth used to wrap tea implements and vessels.

metallic or metal-wrapped thread Thin sheets of gold, silver, and gilt silver or copper used in textiles for weaving or embroidery either as flat strips on a substrate or wound around a core yarn; East Asian flat metallic threads have a substrate of paper not found in European examples.

mordant Substance that bonds certain dyes to cloth to render them colorfast.

moree Coromandel Coast cotton cloth of a superior quality favored for chintz painting.

mōru Japanese term for woven textiles thought to be from India; category of *meibutsugire*.

mullmull (See *muslin*.)

muslin Plain-weave undyed Indian cotton that came in many weights, *mullmull* being the lightest; coarser *humhum* was often used for toweling.

nankeen Chinese plain-weave cotton, usually of a naturally yellowish hue.

Norwich stuff General term for worsted wool fabric marketed at Norwich, England.

osnabrig Coarse unbleached linen made in Germany, Holland, and Belgium.

padusoy Heavy silk with a self-colored pattern; often brocaded.

palampore Large, usually hand-painted cotton bedcovering or hanging made in India for export markets; often decorated with Tree of Life designs and motifs culled from both East and West.

pechuga de paloma Iridescent fabric produced in the Andes of fine, highly twisted alpaca yarns woven with black in the warp and pink in the weft.

peelong English term for satins and gauzes made in China.

pencascoes, peniakoes, peniascoes Colored fabric, probably of mixed cotton and silk, usually striped; likely meant to clothe servants and slaves.

pencil blue Short-lived indigo hand-painting technique developed in Europe in the 1730s for the application of the blue dye directly on to the cloth; precursor to the more efficient *China blue* printing technique.

percallaes High-grade plain cotton cloth favored for chintz painting, produced primarily in Madras and Golconda.

perpetuana Durable wool fabric produced in England.

Persians Lustrous plain-weave silk, a variety of silk taffeta; lightweight and often used as a lining fabric.

persienne A type of lampas usually augmented with silk and metal-thread brocading.

pintado High-quality Indian painted cotton whose name comes from the Portuguese word for "spotted"; by 1680 the English used the terms *chintz, calico,* and *painted calico* instead.

pitcharies Colored Indian calicoes produced mainly for Indonesia.

plain weave Weave structure in which one weft thread passes under and over one warp thread, producing a balanced weave pattern.

poisee, powee English term for Chinese satin painted with floral motifs.

rebozo Mexican term for a long rectangular woven cloth worn by women around the shoulders or used as a head cover or baby carrier.

resist-dyeing Process of creating dyed designs using various techniques—such as applying wax or paste, tightly wrapping thread or cloth, or clamping with wooden blocks—to prevent the penetration of dye into the treated area.

rinzu Japanese term for lightweight monochrome patterned silk; imported from China in large quantities during the first half of the seventeenth century.

roller printing Technique for creating a continuous repeating design on textiles by feeding the fabric through a series of metal rollers.

romall, **rumal** Indian handkerchief made of cotton, silk, or a blend of the two fibers woven with stripes or plaids or printed.

Rouen (*Ruan*) cloth Lightweight woolen textile produced in Rouen, France, often with wool fleece from Spain; sent to the Americas by the Spanish.

salampore Plain and dyed cotton cloth made on the Coromandel and Malabar coasts of India and Sri Lanka.

sarasa High-grade finely painted and printed Indian cotton in demand in Southeast Asia and Japan.

satin Weave structure, based on a unit of five or more warps and an equal number of wefts, in which the binding points of the long floats are distributed in an unobtrusive manner, resulting in a smooth, lustrous sheen on one face and a dull reverse.

saya Japanese term for a damasklike monochrome silk textile characterized by a pattern in twill on a plain-weave ground; imported from China in the seventeenth century.

seersucker Indian striped fabric of cotton or mixed silk and cotton; the woven stripes run with the warp in pink, blue, gold, and other light colors.

selvage Tightly woven edge of a textile closed by weft loops, often distinguished by warp threads and/or a binding system different from the rest of the cloth.

seraser Turkish term for cloth of gold and silver woven in a *taqueté* structure; silk textile that combines a silk warp with wefts containing both silk and metal-wrapped threads.

shagreen Silk fabric with a pebbled surface often used for linings.

sickersoy Indian blended fabric of silk and cotton.

silk Long, lustrous, strong protein fiber produced from secretions of various caterpillar larvae including the cultivated Asian silkworm *Bombyx mori*.

suasey, soosey Striped or checked Indian fabric of silk or cotton and silk, popular in England and America.

taffeta Lustrous plain-weave silk in a multitude of colors woven in China, India, and Europe.

tappe, tapichindaes Garment made of inexpensive painted or woven cotton produced in India for the Indonesian market.

taqueté Compound-weave textile with both ground and pattern woven entirely in weft-faced complementary plain weave; sometimes enriched with supplementary wefts.

teapoy Indian fabric of silk and cotton.

tornesol Spanish word for a luxury silk produced in Europe, India, and Asia composed of two distinct colors, one used in the warp, the other in the weft, that when woven together create a shimmering effect; in English called "changeable" silk.

tumpal Elongated sawtooth or flamelike pattern found in the borders of Indian trade cloths for the Malay–Indonesian market.

Turkey Red Fine, bright red based on madder, first successfully dyed on cotton cloth in 1810.

tussah Silk with a naturally yellow-brownish sheen produced by the wild moth *Antheraea myllita*, common in Asia; also, silk from non–*Bombyx mori* silkworms.

twill weave Weave structure in which the weft threads pass over one and under two or more warp threads, producing a characteristic pattern of diagonal ribs.

vestment Ceremonial robe, including copes, chasubles, and dalmatics, worn by ecclesiastical officiates as an indication of their rank and appropriate to the rite being celebrated.

vicuña Silklike fiber from wild camelids (related to the domesticated llama and alpaca) native to the Andean highlands.

woad Blue dye derived from the low-growing European plant *Isatis tinctoria*, with leaves that contain the indigotin colorant that yields a blue dye; produces a color less intense than indigo.

worsted Lightweight cloth made of long-staple combed-wool yarn; name derived from the village of Worstead, England, a center of worsted weaving.

NOTES TO THE ESSAYS

Trade Textiles at the Metropolitan

1. For more on blue-resist textiles and the possible reattribution of their origins, see catalogue number 116 and the essay by Amelia Peck on East India Company goods in North America in this publication.

2. During the course of preparing the exhibition that this publication accompanies, one actual piece of blue-resist fabric was found in England, lining the back of a silk-embroidered dress stomacher in the collection of Platt Hall, Manchester (no. 1953.325). My thanks to Giorgio Riello of Warwick University, Coventry, for bringing it to my attention.

3. Blue-resist textiles are known to have been produced in France in the eighteenth century, but they are quite different in appearance from these, with smaller, more regimented patterns, and a ground fabric that is usually much heavier and coarser. See Metropolitan Museum, acc. nos. 1981.353.5–.8.

4. For just a few of the books and articles written on these puzzling fabrics, see Florence M. Montgomery, *Printed Textiles: English and American Cottons and Linens, 1700–1850* (New York: Viking Press, 1970), pp. 194–211; Florence H. Pettit, *America's Indigo Blues: Resist-Printed and Dyed Textiles of the Eighteenth Century* (New York: Hastings House, 1974); and Mary E[lizabeth] Gale and Margaret T. Ordoñez, "Eighteenth-Century Indigo Resist Fabrics: Their Use in Quilts and Bedhangings," *Uncoverings: The Research Papers of the American Quilt Study Group* 25 (2004), pp. 157–79.

5. Ebeltje Hartkamp-Jonxis, *Sitsen uit India/Indian Chintzes,* Aspecten van de verzameling beeldhouwkunst en kunstnijverheid 5 (Amsterdam: Rijksmuseum; Zwolle: Waanders Uitgevers, 1994), pp. 84–85.

6. The Meetinghouse Gallery, with its reproduction heavy timber-framed ceiling, was inspired by the Old Ship Meetinghouse in Hingham, Massachusetts, built in 1681, which was a place for religious and community meetings rather than the decorated domestic space now on display. The only remaining Puritan meetinghouse in America today, it was restored in the years just prior to the American Wing's opening in 1924. At the time of the restoration, the wood beams that supported the meetinghouse's roof were rediscovered after being hidden by a flat plaster ceiling installed in the eighteenth century. These beams were considered such an extraordinary survival that the Museum had a reproduction of the ceiling designed for the third floor of the American Wing, then under construction. The Meetinghouse Gallery is much smaller and of a shape entirely different from the actual meetinghouse, but the look of the beamed ceiling remains evocative.

7. These palampores (acc. nos. 28.78.1–.3) were on loan from textile manufacturer and collector Harry Wearne (1852–1929) when the American Wing opened in 1924. He gave them to the Museum in 1928. They seem to have hung in the Meetinghouse Gallery for decades, until 1956, when someone attempted to wash them: one (28.78.1), weakened by the years of exposure to dust and unfiltered light, fell apart, and the two others are in poor condition. Textiles are no longer shown in this gallery.

8. Recent notable textile exhibitions at the Metropolitan include "When Silk Was Gold: Central Asian and Chinese Textiles" (1997), "Candace Wheeler: The Art and Enterprise of American Design" (2001), "Tapestry in the Renaissance: Art and Magnificence" (2002), "The Colonial Andes: Tapestries and Silverwork, 1530–1830" (2004), and "Tapestry in the Baroque: Threads of Splendor" (2007).

9. "The textile collection at the Metropolitan Museum of Art, newly arranged, has in the last few days been visited by many designers seeking inspiration from fabrics to be seen there, old and new. . . . The museum has at the service of manufacturers and artisans a special study room, where duplicate specimens of textiles and small pieces may be handled. The specimens are mounted on heavy linen stretched on walnut frames of uniform size. Two thousand of these frames are placed in wall cases convenient to the tables. The designer may select what specimens he wishes. The material dates from prehistoric times to the present. [Textiles] can be seen in numerous examples, not only in the study collections but in the many thousands of specimens which are on public view. The talented designer may be stimulated to make many entirely new patterns through the beauty of these old models." Undated clipping from unknown newspaper, ca. 1910. Textile Study Room Files, MMA Archives. The original mission of the Metropolitan Museum, chartered in 1870, stated that in addition to "encouraging and developing the study of fine arts," the Museum would also aid in "the application of arts to manufacture and practical life." MMA website, "Museum Mission Statement," www.metropolitanmuseum.org.

10. Morris was one of the first two women with curatorial titles at the Metropolitan Museum. Gisela Richter (1882–1972) in the Department of Classical Art was also made an assistant curator in 1910. After eleven years as an assistant curator, Morris was made an associate curator in 1921; in 1929 she asked to be promoted to full curator. She had received an offer for a better-paying job from Arden Studios, a New York City gallery devoted to exhibitions of antique artworks meant to inspire modern designers. The administration gave her a raise of $500, bringing her salary to $6,000 per year, but refused to promote her. A few months later she resigned to go on an extended tour of the Far East. Though she never returned to the Museum, she continued as an active force in the textile world, including as a founder of "The Needle and Bobbin Club," among other projects. In 1925 Gisela Richter was the Museum's first woman to reach the position of full curator. Frances Morris Folder, MMA Archives, and also Joseph Breck, "Resignation of Miss Frances Morris," *The Metropolitan Museum of Art Bulletin* 24, no. 10 (October 1929), p. 266.

11. "Textile Study Room at the Metropolitan Museum of Art," *Posselt's Textile Journal,* August 1923, p. 36, clipping in Frances Morris Folder, MMA Archives.

12. Morris wrote about this issue in a draft to Joseph Breck (1885–1933), curator of the Department of Decorative Arts and her boss, who then included it in a letter to Museum president Robert de Forest about her collecting more eighteenth-century printed textiles for the Museum. Letter dated May 13, 1926; both the undated draft and letter, Frances Morris Folder, MMA Archives.

13. Letter from Frances Morris to William Sloane Coffin, May 11, 1926. Frances Morris Folder, MMA Archives. Coffin (1879–1933) was a director of a very successful family business, the W. & J. Sloane furniture and carpet store in New York City. He was elected to the Board of Trustees in 1921 and served the Museum as trustee, treasurer, first vice president, and finally president until his sudden death

in 1933. He collected textiles himself and was a lender to "Painted and Printed Fabrics."

14. The exhibition ran from May 16 through October 3, 1927, and there were 392 objects in the show. With a total of 40,378 visitors, it must have been quite popular, even by today's standards. Note in Exhibition File, MMA Archives.

15. Frances Morris, "Indian Textiles in the Exhibition of Painted and Printed Fabrics," *The Metropolitan Museum of Art Bulletin* 22, no. 6 (June 1927), pp. 170–72.

16. Harry Wearne lent six Indian textiles to the show. In 1926 Wearne designed and produced an extraordinary modern-day palampore that is in the Museum's collection, acc. no. 27.54.

17. Morris, "Indian Textiles in the Exhibition of Painted and Printed Fabrics," pp. 170–72. *Mezzari* are nineteenth-century Italian copies of palampores, and *indiennes* are French printed fabrics made in imitation of Indian painted textiles (see cat. 56).

18. Frances Morris, "Chinoiserie in Printed Fabrics," *The Metropolitan Museum of Art Bulletin* 22, no. 7 (July 1927), pp. 194–96.

19. *Painted and Printed Fabrics: The History of the Manufactory at Jouy and Other Ateliers in France, 1760–1815,* by Henri Clouzot, *Notes on the History of Cotton Printing, Especially in England and America,* by Frances Morris (New York: The Metropolitan Museum of Art, 1927). According to a note at the beginning of the book: "The Museum is indebted to the generosity of William Sloane Coffin for the privilege of publishing this translation of a manuscript by one of the leading authorities upon the subject of the history of printed cottons." The work was widely and favorably reviewed in publications ranging from *The Burlington Magazine* and *International Studio* to *Textile World* and *The Dry Goods News.* MMA Clippings File, Watson Library.

20. In addition to being one of the first noted scholars of American decorative arts, who published many books and articles that are still widely respected today, Downs had an artistic bent. Born in Massachusetts in 1895, he served in World War I and in 1921 graduated from the Boston Museum School, a fine-arts training school. He was awarded a fellowship upon graduation to travel abroad to continue his art studies. After his return, he worked at the Museum of Fine Arts, Boston, for two years, then spent two years in New York designing furniture, until 1925, when he was hired by the Philadelphia Museum of Art. He stayed there until 1932, when he came to the Metropolitan. Prior to the "China Trade" exhibition, he had written on Chippendale furniture, Pennsylvania German arts, and American pewter, among other topics.

21. Joseph Downs, "The China Trade and Its Influences," *The Metropolitan Museum of Art Bulletin* 36, no. 4 (April 1941), p. 86.

22. All of Downs's requests to other Museum departments are outlined in memos he wrote, including "Department of Renaissance and Modern Art: Objects Desired for Exhibition in E15," "Department of American Wing: Objects Desired for Exhibition in E15," and "Department of Near Eastern Art: Some Suggestions for Exhibition in D6." The show appeared in Gallery D6, which implies that the E15 requests were earlier in the planning process. American Wing Exhibition Files.

23. This was one of two very fine late seventeenth-century palampores bought by William Sloane Coffin while traveling abroad, which he purchased for the princely sum of $1,000 each and then sold to the Museum at his cost. This was more than Breck was used to spending on palampores. Unfortunately, they are both currently in very fragile condition and cannot be exhibited. Breck Correspondence Files, MMA Archives.

24. While not in the earlier exhibitions, a related group of textiles that were most likely collected by William Sloane Coffin, though not given to the Museum until 1975 by his widow, include a painted and printed Indian cotton chasuble (cat. 70), a panel of Indian banyan fabric (cat. 46), and the French printed "Caravan" fabric (cat. 88). One particular item has been a loan to both "Painted and Printed Fabrics" and "Interwoven Globe"; a banyan currently in the collection of the Royal Ontario Museum, Toronto (cat. 97), was borrowed by Morris from textile dealer Elinor Merrill for "Painted and Printed Fabrics."

25. Letter to Joseph Breck from Frances Morris, May 8, 1924. Breck Correspondence Files, MMA Archives.

26. Note to Frances Morris from Joseph Breck, May 13, 1929. Breck Correspondence Files, MMA Archives. While not every month was quite this active or involved such a preponderance of non-European textiles, a representative sampling of the textiles coming into the Museum in 1926 can be discerned from the accessions list for March of that year, which included "Pieces (86) of embroideries and brocades, Eastern European and North African, XVII–XVIII cent., Bequest of Richard B. Seager" and the purchase of "Carpets (3), Nabeshima, XVIII cent.; embroidered hangings (2) mounted with gilt-metal ornaments, abt. 1815; temple hangings (4) in blue silk and brocade with gilt-metal ornaments, XIX cent.,— Japanese; batik sarongs (2), Javanese, XVIII cent.; printed and painted hanging, Indian, XVIII cent.; pieces (2) of painted cotton, Indian, XIX (?) cent." "List of Accessions and Loans," *The Metropolitan Museum of Art Bulletin* 21, no. 3 (March 1926), p. 93.

27. Some of the extraordinary early purchases made using the Rogers Fund (and possibly picked out by Frances Morris) that are in this publication include a Peruvian wedding mantle (cat. 17), both a Turkish and an Italian velvet (cats. 4, 5), one of the sixteenth-century Chinese silks for the Portuguese market (cat. 15), an Indian painted chair seat for the European market (cat. 55), and a cope for an Armenian church made of recycled pieces of a Safavid velvet caftan (cat. 64).

28. It is interesting to contemplate why the Museum acquired all three of these without having a gallery in which to hang them where they would be properly contextualized. The Marquand provenance would certainly have been a persuasive reason to acquire at least one of them, since the Museum was the recipient of many important works from his collection. The three hangings were once part of a much larger set: Marquand had owned four, three others are known that are likely in private collections today, one is in the Musée des Beaux-Arts, Lyon, and it is likely that there were others that have since been lost. Perhaps the mind-set was like that used when collecting tapestries, assuming that possession of several works within the series would help with the understanding of the narrative, or, perhaps, as with many of the Museum's rarely seen tapestries that have been collected in sets, hope sprang eternal that new and appropriate galleries might one day be added to the Museum building. *The Abduction of Helen* (cat. 14) was actively sought for the collection; on loan here since 1966, it was gifted to the Museum in 1979.

For more on this group, see Edith Appleton Standen, *European Post-Medieval Tapestries and Related Hangings in The Metropolitan Museum of Art*, 2 vols. (New York: The Metropolitan Museum of Art, 1985), vol. 2, pp. 796–801. My thanks to Elizabeth Cleland, Associate Curator in the Department of European Sculpture and Decorative Arts, who is in charge of the Museum's postmedieval tapestry and needlework collection, for helping me think through the acquisition of these Chinese hangings.

29. After Morris left the Museum in 1929, several other notable textile scholars were put in charge of the Textile Study Room, including Frances Little (1931–42); Marion P. Bolles (1942–49); Edith Appleton Standen (1949–70); Jean Mailey, who joined the Metropolitan in 1958 as an assistant curator in the Far Eastern Art Department but eventually took over the Textile Study Room in 1970, where she remained until 1988; and Alice Zrebiec (1988–94). Zrebiec left the Museum in 1994 and today is the Avenir Foundation Curator of Textile Art at the Denver Art Museum.

30. Philippe de Montebello, "Director's Foreword: Antonio Ratti Textile Center," *The Metropolitan Museum of Art Bulletin*, n.s., 53, no. 3 [*Textiles in The Metropolitan Museum of Art*] (Winter 1995–96), p. 5.

31. Ibid., pp. 5–6.

32. Opened in 1988, The Henry R. Luce Center for the Study of American Art had the first digital catalogue in the Museum, containing all of the objects in the American Wing's collection.

"One Thing Leads to Another"

1. These commercial documents date predominantly from 1080 to 1160, with a few extending to 1240. They uniquely survive because they are written in Hebrew script, and synagogues, through their rabbinical courts, served as a place for the adjudication of disputes. For a study of the Geniza records, see S. D. Goitein, *A Mediterranean Society: The Jewish Communities of the Arab World as Portrayed in the Documents of the Cairo Geniza*, 6 vols. (Berkeley and Los Angeles: University of California Press, 1967–93), and S. D. Goitein and Mordechai Akiva Friedman, *India Traders of the Middle Ages: Documents from the Cairo Geniza, "India Book,"* Études sur le judaïsme médiéval 31 (Leiden: Brill, 2008).

2. Texts from the S. D. Goitein Laboratory for Geniza Research at Princeton, quoted in Goitein and Friedman, *India Traders of the Middle Ages*, pp. 141–42.

3. Ibid., p. xxi.

4. Ibid., pp. 15–20.

5. Ibn Battuta, *The Travels of Ibn Battuta, A.D. 1325–1354*, translated by H. A. R. Gibb et al., 5 vols., Works Issued by the Hakluyt Society, Second series 110, 117, 141, 178, 190 (London: Hakluyt Society, 1958–2000), esp. vol. 5.

6. For background to the Portuguese expansion in Asia, see Anthony Disney and Emily Booth, eds., *Vasco da Gama and the Linking of Europe and Asia* (Delhi and Oxford: Oxford University Press, 2000).

7. The Portuguese were the first Europeans to have a presence at the Siamese capital, with the first ambassador sent by Afonso de Albuquerque in 1511, during the siege of Melaka. Joachim de Campos, "Early Portuguese Accounts of Thailand," in *500 Years of*

Thai-Portuguese Relations: A Festschrift, edited by Michael Smithies (Bangkok: Siam Society, 2011), pp. 15–36.

8. Tomé Pires, *The Suma Oriental of Tomé Pires: An Account of the East, from the Red Sea to Japan, Written in Malacca and India in 1512–1515*, translated and edited by Armando Cortesão, 2 vols., Works Issued by the Hakluyt Society, Second series 89–90 (London: Hakluyt Society, 1944).

9. Late thirteenth-century Chinese sources are surprisingly helpful, as are those of Ibn Battuta and Marco Polo from the early fourteenth century, but following them there is a hiatus until the appearance of the first Portuguese accounts early in the sixteenth century. We have been able to fill some of the gaps in our knowledge of the later medieval Indian Ocean textile trade through the scientific dating of cloths.

10. Friedrich Hirth and W[illiam] W. Rockhill, *Chau Ju-kua: His Work on the Chinese and Arab Trade in the Twelfth and Thirteenth Centuries, entitled Chu-fan-chï* (Saint Petersburg: Imperial Academy of Sciences, 1911; reprint, Taipei: Ch'eng-Wen Pub., 1967), p. 218.

11. John Guy, *Woven Cargoes: Indian Textiles in the East* (London: Thames and Hudson, 1998), p. 155.

12. Ibn Battuta, *The Travels of Ibn Battuta*.

13. Ibid., vol. 4, pp. 882, 890. Battuta probably based his generalizations about China on his observations of Quanzhou, the southern port city known in Arabic as Zaitun; see John Guy, "Quanzhou, Cosmopolitan City of Faiths," in *The World of Khubilai Khan: Chinese Art in the Yuan Dynasty*, by James C. Y. Watt et al., exh. cat. (New York: The Metropolitan Museum of Art, 2010), pp. 158–78.

14. Duarte Barbosa, *The Book of Duarte Barbosa . . . 1518 A.D.*, edited by Mansel Longworth Dames, 2 vols., Works Issued by the Hakluyt Society, Second series 44, 49 (London: Hakluyt Society, 1918–21), vol. 2, p. 176.

15. Hirth and Rockhill, *Chau Ju-kua*, p. 20; J[ohanna] E. van Lohuizen-de Leeuw, "An Early 16th Century Link between Gujarat and Java," in *Essays Offered to G. H. Luce*, edited by Ba Shin et al., 2 vols. (Ascona: Artibus Asiae, 1966), vol. 2, pp. 89–93; Elizabeth Lambourn, "From Cambay to Samudera-Pasai and Gresik: The Export of Gujarati Grave Memorials to Sumatra and Java in the Fifteenth Century C.E.," *Indonesia and the Malay World* 31, no. 90 (July 2003), pp. 221–89; Jeremias van Vliet, translated by L. F. van Ravenswaay, "Description of the Kingdom of Siam," *Journal of the Siam Society* 7, pt. 1 (1910), p. 63, respectively.

16. Donald S. Whitcomb and Janet H. Johnston, *Quseir al-Qadim 1980: Preliminary Report*, American Research Center in Egypt 7 (Malibu: Undena Publications, 1982); G[illian] M. Vogelsang-Eastwood, *Resist Dyed Textiles from Quseir al-Qadim, Egypt* (Paris: A.E.D.T.A., 1990).

17. This study was pioneered by R. Pfister, *Les toiles imprimées de Fostat et l'Hindoustan* (Paris: Les Éditions d'Art et d'Histoire, 1938).

18. Barbosa, *The Book of Duarte Barbosa*, vol. 2, p. 56.

19. Pires, *Suma Oriental of Tomé Pires*, vol. 2, p. 269.

20. Ibid., vol. 1, p. 45.

21. Recent ethnographic observations of textiles in social settings suggest that these textiles were prized as communal heirloom property and preserved by the clan elders for rites of passage ceremonies. See, for example, C. H[etty] M. Nooy-Palm, "The Role of the Sacred

Cloths in the Mythology and Ritual of the Sa'dan Toraja of Sulawesi, Indonesia," in *Indonesian Textiles: Irene Emery Roundtable on Museum Textiles, 1979 Proceedings*, edited by Mattiebelle Gittinger (Washington, D.C.: The Textile Museum, 1980), pp. 81–95.

22. John Guy, "Rama, Rajas and Courtesans: Indian Figurative Textiles in Indonesia," in *The Secrets of Southeast Asian Textiles— Myth, Status and the Supernatural: The James H. W. Thompson Foundation Symposium Papers*, edited by Jane Puranananda (Bangkok: River Books, 2007), pp. 40–57.

23. Cleveland Museum of Art, illustrated in Mattiebelle Gittinger, *Master Dyers to the World: Technique and Trade in Early Indian Dyed Cotton Textiles*, exh. cat. (Washington, D.C.: The Textile Museum, 1982), pp. 46–47, nos. 31–32.

24. Elizabeth Lambourn, "Carving and Communities: Marble Carving for Muslim Patrons at Khambhāt and around the Indian Ocean Rim, Late Thirteenth–Mid-Fifteenth Centuries," *Ars Orientalis* 34 [*Communities and Commodities: Western India and the Indian Ocean Eleventh–Fifteenth Centuries*] (2004), pp. 99–133.

25. Guy, *Woven Cargoes*, pp. 42–45.

26. For the English, see K. N. Chaudhuri, *The Trading World of Asia and the English East India Company, 1660–1760* (Cambridge and New York: Cambridge University Press, 1978); for the Dutch, see J. R. Bruijn, F. S. Gaastra, and I. Schöffer, *Dutch-Asiatic Shipping in the 17th and 18th Centuries*, 3 vols., Rijks geschiedkundige publicatiën, Grote serie 165–67 (The Hague: Martinus Nijhoff, 1987); and for the French, Donald C. Wellington, *French East India Companies: A Historical Account and Record of Trade* (Lanham, Md.: Hamilton Books, 2006); in 1600 the French launched the first of several unsuccessful trading companies before that of 1664.

27. François Bernier, *Travels in the Mogul Empire, A.D. 1656–1668*, edited by Archibald Constable (London: Constable and Co., 1891), p. 439.

28. Niels Steensgaard, *The Asian Trade Revolution of the Seventeenth Century: The East India Companies and the Decline of the Caravan Trade* (Chicago: University of Chicago Press, 1974), p. 407.

29. Henry Middleton, *The Voyage of Sir Henry Middleton to the Moluccas, 1604–1606*, edited by William Foster, Works Issued by the Hakluyt Society, Second series 88 (London: Hakluyt Society, 1943), pp. 184–85. Both struggled to prosper in the face of aggressive competition from the Dutch. The VOC's creation of a rival and successor port city at Jakarta in 1619, which they renamed Batavia, marked the demise of English interests in Java for nearly two centuries.

30. Ibid., p. 185.

31. Clove is native to Ternate and Tidore, small islands of the Halmahera group; nutmeg and mace, its bark, were originally exclusive to the island of Banda. Magellan's expedition finally succeeded in reaching Maluku in November 1521 and purchased their prized cargo at Tidore, the first European venture to succeed in securing these spices at their source; see Antonio Pigafetta, *Magellan's Voyage: A Narrative Account of the First Circumnavigation*, translated by R. A. Skelton, 2 vols. (New Haven: Yale University Press, 1969), vol. 1, pp. 113–30.

32. Sir Francis Drake, cited in Leonard Y. Andaya, "Cultural State Formation in Eastern Indonesia," in *Southeast Asia in the Early Modern Era: Trade, Power, and Belief*, edited by Anthony Reid (Ithaca: Cornell University Press, 1993), p. 38.

33. The VOC controlled much of the Persian Gulf and Iran trade through their fort at Hormuz and are known to have been active in the commissioning of luxury textiles in Iran. I am indebted to Dr. Brigitt Borkopp for the suggested source of the designs depicted.

34. The VOC routinely gifted gold chains to local rulers in recognition of their alliance to the company. Others are recorded as having been in the regalia of the sultan of Ternate, a neighboring kingdom in Maluku; Kees Zandvliet et al., *The Dutch Encounter with Asia, 1600–1950*, exh. cat. (Amsterdam: Rijksmuseum; Zwolle: Waanders Uitgeverij, 2002), pp. 119–20.

35. Leonard Andaya, *The World of Maluku: Eastern Indonesia in the Early Modern Period* (Honolulu: University of Hawai'i Press, 1993), p. 171.

36. Ebeltje Hartkamp-Jonxis, personal communication, 2012; see also John Guy, "Choice Varied Flowers," *Hali*, no. 172 (Summer 2012), pp. 78–81.

37. The paintings, installed in the sacristy, served as part of the propaganda campaign in support of Francis Xavier's beatification; all of the paintings are illustrated in Vítor Serrão, *A lenda de São Francisco Xavier pelo pintor André Reinoso: Estudo histórico, estético e iconológico de um ciclo barroco existente na Sacristía da Igreja de São Roque*, Colecção património artístico da Santa Casa da Misericórdia de Lisboa 1 (Lisbon: Quetzal Editores; Santa Casa da Misericórdia de Lisboa, 2006).

38. *Inventory of the Church of the Conceição*, Lisbon, cited in Nuno Vassallo e Silva, *No caminho do Japão: Arte oriental nas colecções da Santa Casa da Misericórdia de Lisboa*, exh. cat. (Lisbon: Museu de São Roque, 1993), pp. 16–17.

39. Jan Huyghen van Linschoten, *The Voyage of John Huyghen van Linschoten to the East Indies from the Old English Translation of 1598*, edited by Arthur Coke Burnell and P. A. Tiele, 2 vols., Works Issued by the Hakluyt Society 70–71 (London: Hakluyt Society, 1885), vol. 1, p. 91.

40. Jean Deloche, *A Study in Nayaka-Period Social Life: Tiruppu-daimarudur Paintings and Carvings*, Collection Indologie 116 (Pondicherry: Institut Français de Pondichéry, École Française d'Extrême-Orient, 2011), p. 2, argues that, on the evidence of datable horse trappings depicted, the murals cannot be earlier than the first quarter of the seventeenth century.

41. Meera Abraham, *Two Medieval Merchant Guilds of South India* (New Delhi: Manohar Publications, 1988). I am indebted to Anna Seastrand for providing these photographs.

42. Published in Guy, *Woven Cargoes*, p. 26.

43. Illustrated in Deloche, *A Study in Nayaka-Period Social Life*, p. 14, fig. 18. During the late Vijayanagar period, west coast ports extended from Goa to Calicut; see T. V. Mahalingam, *Administration and Social Life under Vijayanagar*, pt. 2, *Social Life*, 2nd ed. (1940; Madras: University of Madras, 1975), pp. 152–56. The location of this mural, near Nagapattinam on the southeastern coast, suggests that ports on the Coromandel Coast assumed more importance for this trade in the early Nayaka period.

44. A *qalam* and its use are illustrated in Guy, *Woven Cargoes*, pp. 22–23.

45. Illustrated in John Guy et al., *L'escultura en els temples indis: L'art de la devoció*, exh. cat. (Barcelona: Fundació la Caixa, 2007), p. 231, no. 186.

46. Illustrated in C. Sivaramamurti, *South Indian Paintings* (New Delhi: National Museum, 1968), chap. 18.

47. A number of visitor accounts of this period, by the Italian Nicoli de Conti (1420), the Portuguese mercenary Domingo Paes (1520), and the horse trader Fernao Nuniz (1536–37), stress the importance of the Arab horse trade to the Vijayanagar kingdom, which the Portuguese came to dominate, supplying Arabian horses through the Indian west coast ports. See Mahalingam, *Administration and Social Life under Vijayanagar*, pp. 127, 134–35.

48. Nagapattinam rose to prominence as the Chola kingdom's premier port, and trade and diplomatic links with Southeast Asia and China were conducted from there; see John Guy, "Tamil Merchant Guilds and the Quanzhou Trade," in *The Emporium of the World: Maritime Quanzhou, 1000–1400*, edited by Angela Schottenhammer (Leiden: Brill, 2001), pp. 283–308.

49. As early as the 1590s van Linschoten extolled the virtues of finely painted cloths, floral and figurative, from both the northern and southern Coromandel Coast: "There is excellent faire linnen of Cotton made in Negapatan, Saint Thomas, and Musilepatan, of all colours, and woven with divers sorts of loome work [Dutch *looff-werck*, or flowers] and figures, verie fine and cunningly wrought, which is much worne in India, and better esteemed than silk . . . the best sort are named clothes of Sarasso." See Linschoten, *Voyage of John Huyghen van Linschoten*, vol. 1, p. 91.

50. The following examples give the flavor of the records: *baffetas* (*baftas*), "in fineness surpassing Holland cloth" (1611; Broach, western India); *boxshales*, piece-goods favored in Japan (1615); *chatars, chintes, chits,* chintz, "painted cloth called chits" (1626); *longcloth,* staple of Coromandel trade, average length 37 yards, plain and later painted, that from Masulipatam the "only sorte fitting for Europe" (1621); *morees,* staple Coromandel cloth of superior quality favored for chintz-painting, average length 9 yards, from Masulipatam early in seventeenth century, later Madras region; *palampore* (from Persian *palamposh*), bedcover, "Chintes of palamposh" (1614), hence English *palempore,* or chintz bedspread, which by late 1600s had extended in meaning to "calico paintings or palamposts for covering of Cupboards and Tables" (1684); *percallaes,* high-grade plain cotton favored for chintz-painting, mostly from Madras, average length 8 yards; *pitcharies,* colored calicoes mainly for Indonesia, seemingly plain-dyed not painted; *sarassa* (from Hindi *sarasa*), superior, high-grade painted cotton in demand in Southeast Asia and Japan, "the best sorte are named Sarasso" (1583; Linschoten); *salampores,* staple cotton cloth of Coromandel Coast, various grades of quality, large-volume exports to Europe from 1660s, average length 16 yards; *tappe, tapi-chindaes,* from Javanese *tapih* or skirt[cloth], flowered cloth; inexpensive painted cotton for Indonesian market. Extracted from the English East India records and contemporary commentaries, principally by John Irwin in "Indian Textile Trade in the Seventeenth Century: I. Western India," *Journal of Indian Textile History,* no. 1 (1955), pp. 25–30; "II. Coromandel Coast," no. 2 (1956), pp. 40–42; "IV. Foreign Influences," no. 4 (1959), pp. 57–64.

51. It is reported that such cloths were favored in Sumatra as floor spreads during wedding ceremonies; see Deepika Shah, *Masters of the Cloth: Indian Textiles Traded to Distant Shores, TAPI Collection,* exh. cat. (New Delhi: National Museum, 2005), p. 24. The antiquity of these practices is not known.

52. Lodewijk J. Wagenaar, "The Castle of Batavia . . . ," in *Dutch New York Between East and West: The World of Margrieta van Varick,* edited by Deborah L. Krohn and Peter N. Miller, exh. cat. (New York: Bard Graduate Center, 2009), p. 145, no. 8.

53. The late seventeenth-century designs of the French illustrator P. A. Ducerceau are one of many examples that can be cited.

54. Guy, *Woven Cargoes,* pl. 140.

55. R. K. de Silva and W. G. M. Beumer, *Illustrations and Views of Dutch Ceylon, 1602–1796: A Comprehensive Work of Pictorial Reference with Selected Eye-Witness Accounts* (London: Serendib Publications, 1988), pp. 339–47.

56. Here the term *Siam* is used for the historical political entity, *Thai* for the people. Historically, Thais have assigned a name for their state on the basis of the epicenter of power, hence the polities of Sukhothai and Ayutthaya were proclaimed as states, and recognized by others as such, receiving annual tribute. The earliest Western sources for Thailand, Portuguese commentaries of the early sixteenth century, refer to the region as Siam, a racial demarcator that over time won universal acceptance, including among Thais themselves. The title Siam persisted until 1939, when Thailand was adopted as the country's official title, reflecting the country's dominant ethnic identity and aspirations for a wider linguistic unification.

57. Peter Floris, *Peter Floris, His Voyage to the East Indies in the Globe 1611–1615,* edited by W. H. Moreland, Works Issued by the Hakluyt Society, Second series 74 (London: Hakluyt Society, 1934), p. 71.

58. Dhiravat na Pombejra, "Conflict and Commerce in the Gulf of Siam, c. 1629–1642: Using Dutch Documents to 'De-centre' Ayutthayan History," in *Southeast Asian Historiography, Unravelling the Myths: Essays in Honour of Barend Jan Terwiel,* edited by Volker Grabowsky (Bangkok: River Books, 2011), p. 156.

59. Pires, *Suma Oriental of Tomé Pires,* vol. 1, p. 108.

60. Ibid., p. 109.

61. Barbosa, *Book of Duarte Barbosa,* vol. 2, p. 164.

62. Middleton, *Voyage of Sir Henry Middleton to the Moluccas,* p. 184.

63. Heert Terpstra, *Vestiging van de nederlanders aan de kust van Koromandel* (Groningen: De Waal, 1911), quoted in Floris, *Peter Floris, His Voyage to the East Indies in the Globe,* p. 71 n. 6.

64. The first embassy was despatched by King Narai in December 1680, sailing initially to Batavia and eventually departing in August 1681, but was lost at sea with the sinking of the *Soleil d'Orient,* pride of the French East India Company, in November 1681. A second, smaller mission was sent in 1684 to trace the lost mission, embarking in January 1684 on an English vessel and stopping over in London before arriving in Paris; see also Dirk van der Cruysse, *Siam and the West, 1500–1700* (Chiang Mai: Silkworm Books, 2001), chap. 12.

65. Floris, *Peter Floris, His Voyage to the East Indies in the Globe,* pp. 73–74.

66. *Records of the Relations between Siam and Foreign Countries in the 17th Century,* 5 vols. (Bangkok: Council of the Vajiranāna National Library, 1915–21), vol. 2, pp. 36–38. The term *puttelaes* is a variant of *percallaes,* referring to high-grade painted-cotton cloths best produced in South India; see Irwin, "Indian Textile Trade in the Seventeenth Century: II. Coromandel Coast," p. 42.

67. *Muster,* a term adapted from the Portuguese *mostra*; see Henry Yule and Arthur Coke Burnell, *Hobson-Jobson: Being a Glossary of Anglo-Indian Colloquial Words and Phrases, and of Kindred Terms; Etymological, Historical, Geographical, and Discursive,* new ed. (1886; London: John Murray, 1903), p. 605.

68. Guy, *Woven Cargoes,* pp. 131–34.

69. Van Vliet, "Description of the Kingdom of Siam," p. 65.

70. William Methwold in W. H. Moreland, ed., *Relations of Golconda in the Early Seventeenth Century,* Works Issued by the Hakluyt Society, Second series 66 (London: Hakluyt Society, 1931), p. 39. Tenasserim was the hub of a major transshipment route connecting Ayutthaya to the Bay of Bengal; from there ships sailed regularly directly to the Coromandel Coast.

71. Celebrated in the historical novel *Siamese White* by Maurice Collis (1932).

The Iberian Globe

Unless otherwise indicated, all translations are by the author.

1. "Sábese la concession del Papa Alexandro; la division del mundo como una naranja." Letter of Alonso de Zuazo to Charles V, January 22, 1518, in Luis Torres de Mendoza, Joaquín Francisco Pacheco, and Francisco de Cárdenas y Espejo, eds., *Colección de documentos inéditos, relativos al descubrimiento, conquista y organización de las antiguas posesiones españolas de América y Oceanía, sacados de los archivos del reino y muy especialmente del de Indias,* 42 vols. (Madrid, 1864–84), vol. 1, p. 296, quoted in Emma Helen Blair and James Alexander Robertson, eds., *The Philippine Islands, 1493–1803: Explorations by Early Navigators, Descriptions . . . ,* 55 vols. (Cleveland: A. H. Clark Co., 1903–9), vol. 1, p. 156 n. 7. For a detailed description of the adjustments to this division through a series of papal bulls and treaties, see preface to vol. 1 of ibid., which also includes the text of the treaties.

2. See Sabine MacCormack, *Religion in the Andes: Vision and Imagination in Early Colonial Peru* (Princeton, N.J.: Princeton University Press, 1991).

3. Brazil was initially named "the Land of the Holy Cross" by Pedro Álvarez Cabral, whose voyage to Brazil in 1500 began the period of colonial engagement.

4. James Lockhart and Stuart B. Schwartz, *Early Latin America: A History of Colonial Spanish America and Brazil* (Cambridge and New York: Cambridge University Press, 1983), chap. 6, "Brazilian Beginnings," pp. 181–201.

5. Scenes of Tupi villages were depicted by Theodor de Bry in 1592 in a later version of accounts first published in 1557 by Hans Staden, a German who had been captured by tribesmen on Guanabara Bay and escaped. See John M. Monteiro, "The Crisis and Transformations of Invaded Societies: Coastal Brazil in the Sixteenth Century," in *The Cambridge History of the Native Peoples of the Americas,* vol. 3, *South America,* pt. 1, edited by Frank Salomon and Stuart B. Schwartz (Cambridge and New York: Cambridge University Press, 1999), pp. 973–1023. See also Sabine MacCormack, "Ethnography in South America: The First Two Hundred Years," in the same volume, pp. 98–187.

6. See also Jean Michel Massing in Jay A. Levenson et al., *Circa 1492: Art in the Age of Exploration,* exh. cat. (Washington, D.C.: National Gallery of Art; New Haven and London: Yale University Press, 1991), p. 574, no. 408.

7. *Tapirage*—in which frog poisons were applied to feather shafts in the living bird—was also documented in an eighteenth-century Jesuit treatise on medicine, *Coleção de várias receitas e segredos particulares da nossa companhia de Portugal, da Índia, de Macau e do Brasil: Compostas e experimentadas pelos melhores médicos e boticários mais celebres que tem havido nestas Partes; Aumentada com alguns índices e notícias muito curiosas as e necessárias para a boa direção e acerto contra as enfermidades* (Rome, 1766), and Cod. Opp. N.N. 17, Archivum Romanum Societatis Iesu, Rome. See Patrícia Albano Maia, "Práticas de cura no encontro de culturas: Jesuítas e a circulação de receitas médicas," in *Anais do XXVI Simpósio Nacional de História—ANPUH, São Paulo, julho 2011*; http://www.snh2011. anpuh.org /resources/anais/14/1300867080_ARQUIVO_ANPUH2011-Praticas decuranoencontrodeculturas.pdf. See also Amy J. Buono, "Winged Migrations: Tupinambá Featherwork and Its Ritual Performance from Brazil to Early Modern Europe," *Center: Record of Activities and Research Reports* [National Gallery of Art, Washington, D.C.] 27 (June 2006–June 2007), pp. 66–69.

8. "Matrícula de Tributos," fol. 23. Codex 35–52, Biblioteca Nacional de Antropología e Historia, Mexico City.

9. For examples of archaeological textiles from Precolumbian Mexico, see Alba Guadalupe Mastache, "El tejido en el México antiguo," *Arqueología mexicana* 19 [*Textiles del México de ayer y hoy*] (2005), pp. 20–31.

10. "Demás d'esto, me dió el dicho Mocteuma ropa de la suya, que era tal, que considerda ser toda de algodón y sin seda, en todo el mundo no se podía hacer ni tejer otra tal . . . había paramentso para camas, que hechos de seda no se podía comparar." Jan Bazant, "Evolución de la industria textil Poblana (1544–1845)," *Historia mexicana* 13, no. 4 (April–June 1964), p. 494. The article, as published in English and noted below, does not quite translate the quotation appropriately. Author has altered the translation accordingly, from the Spanish version. Jan Bazant, "Evolution of the Textile Industry of Puebla, 1544–1845," *Comparative Studies in Society and History* 7, no. 1 (October 1964), pp. 56–69 (quotation p. 66).

11. See Elena Phipps, "Garments and Identity in the Colonial Andes," in *The Colonial Andes: Tapestries and Silverwork, 1530–1830,* by Elena Phipps et al., exh. cat. (New York: The Metropolitan Museum of Art, 2004), pp. 16–39.

12. In 1568 in the region of Chucuito, Peru, one thousand garments—half of them finely woven Inca-style *cumbi* and the other half *ahuasca* (the Inca term for simple, coarse cloth)—were given to Spanish administrators. Silvio Arturo Zavala, *El servicio personal de los indios en el Perú: Extractos del siglo XVI–XVIII,* 3 vols. (Mexico City: El Colegio de México, 1978–80), vol. 1, p. 43.

13. Francisco de Toledo, "Instrucciones por los visitadores 1569–1579 Ciudad de los Reyes," in *Disposiciones gubernativas para el Virreinato del Perú, 1569–1574,* vol. 1, transcripts by María Justina Sarabia Viejo, edited by Guillermo Lohmann Villena, Publicaciones de la Escuela de Estudios Hispano-Americanos de la Universidad de Sevilla 320 (Seville: Escuela de Estudios Hispano-Americanos, 1986), p. 24.

14. For details on shipping quantities and the value of vicuña cloth to Spain, see John Fisher, "The Imperial Response to 'Free Trade': Spanish Imports from Spanish America, 1778–1796," *Journal of Latin American Studies* 17, pt. 1 (May 1985), pp. 35–78 (table 5, p. 53).

15. Another type of highly prized Aztec featherwork is seen in the feather mosaic pictures of Christian subjects produced in the workshops of Bernardino de Sahagún (1499–1590). These are described in detail in his "Historia general de las cosas de Nueva España," Mediceo Palatino 218–20, Biblioteca Medicea Laurenziana, Florence. See also a sixteenth-century Mexican triptych in the Metropolitan Museum, acc. no. 88.3.1.

16. Fisher, "The Imperial Response to 'Free Trade,'" pp. 35–78.

17. See Allyn A. Loosley, "The Puerto Bello Fairs," *The Hispanic American Historical Review* 13, no. 3 (August 1933), pp. 314–35.

18. Francisco López de Gómara, *Historia de las conquistas de Hernando Cortés*, edited by Carlos María de Bustamante, 2 vols. (Mexico City: Testamentaría de Ontiveros, 1826), vol. 1 [1553], chap. 103, pp. 230–31. For rabbit-hair and featherwork textiles, see Elena Phipps and Lucy Commoner, "Investigation of a Colonial Latin American Textile," in *Textile Narratives and Conversations: Proceedings of the 10th Biennial Symposium of the Textile Society of America, October 11–14, Toronto, Ontario*, edited by Carol Bier and Ann Svenson Perlman (CD-ROM format; Middleton, Del.: Textile Society of America, 2007), pp. 485–93; http://digitalcommons.unl.edu/tsaconf/358/.

19. " . . . que en el tiempo del ynga no había mercaderes en grueso como los hay entre los españoles sino eran los indios del tiangues que vendían unos a otros comidas solamente y que ropa no se compraba porque cada uno hacía la que había menester y las otras cosas eran de poca cantidad." From Iñigo Ortiz de Zúñiga in *Visita de la provincia de León de Huánuco en 1562*, edited by John V. Murra, 2 vols. (Huánuco, Peru: Universidad Nacional Hermilio Valdizán, Facultad de Letras y Educación, 1967–72), vol. 2, p. 29.

20. Martín de Murúa, *Historia general del Perú: Origen y descendencia de los Incas*, introduction by Manuel Ballesteros Gaibrois, 2 vols., Bibliotheca americana vetus (1611; Madrid, 1962–64), vol. 2, p. 507. See also Stanley J. Stein and Barbara H. Stein, *Silver, Trade, and War: Spain and America in the Making of Early Modern Europe* (Baltimore: The Johns Hopkins University Press, 2004).

21. William Lytle Schurz, *The Manila Galleon* (1939; New York: E. P. Dutton & Co., 1959), p. 365.

22. In his report on his voyage along the coast of Peru during 1712–14, Amédée-François Frézier noted that Callao, the main port for Lima, was closed to ships trading from the Far East, but several leagues south, at Pisco, warehouses were awaiting shipments of silks and exotic goods not only from the Far East but also from Mexico and Guatemala. Frézier, *Relation du voyage de la mer du Sud aux côtes du Chili, du Pérou et de Brésil, fait pendant les années 1712, 1713, et 1714* (Amsterdam: Chez Pierre Humbert, 1717), p. 179.

23. Fisher, "The Imperial Response to 'Free Trade,'" pp. 35–78.

24. Filipe Guamán Poma de Ayala, "Civdad," in "Nueva corónica," Det Kongelige Bibliotek, Copenhagen, fol. 1034 [1042]; http://www.kb.dk/permalink/2006/poma/1042/en/text/?open=id2978109.

25. *Recopilación de leyes de las indias*, libro 4, titulo 18, ley ii, "D. Felipe Segundo . . . 10 Noviembre de 1572." *Archivo digital de la legislación en el Perú*; http://www.congreso.gob.pe/ntley/LeyIndiaP.htm.

26. Archivo General de Indias, Seville, 1554, ES.41091.AGI/11//PASAJEROS,L.3,E.2373.

27. Gayle K. Brunelle, "Immigration, Assimilation and Success: Three Families of Spanish Origin in Sixteenth Century Rouen," *The Sixteenth Century Journal* 20, no. 2 (Summer 1989), pp. 203–20. See also Constance Jones Mathers, "Family Partnerships and International Trade in Early Modern Europe: Merchants from Burgos in England and France, 1470–1570," *Business History Review* 62, no. 3 (Autumn 1988), pp. 367–97. Rouen also has an interesting history in relation to the extensive import of dyewood from Brazil; see the author's essay on the dye trade in this publication.

28. "Prohibición de usar prendas de sedas en Indias," Archivo General de Indias, INDIFERENTE,418,L.2,F.87V-89V, 1509-11-12, Valladolid Real Pragmática ordenando que en las Indias no se puedan usar prendas de seda ni de otro material que suponga un gasto excesivo, bajo las penas que se indican.

29. Archivo General de Indias, 1554, ES.41091.AGI/11//PASAJEROS,L.3,E.2373.

30. Elena Phipps, "Woven Silver and Gold: Metallic Yarns in Colonial Andean Textiles," *Source: Notes in the History of Art* 29, no. 3 (Spring 2010), pp. 4–11.

31. Zavala, *El servicio personal de los indios en el Perú*, vol. 2, p. 97.

32. Silk imported from Valencia through Cádiz by the Compañia de Arte Mayor increased from 29 pieces of silk to Lima in 1771 to 14,346 in 1783. Vicente Ribes Iborra, *Los valencianos y America: El comercio valenciano con Indias en el siglo XVIII* (Valencia: Diputación Provincial de València, 1985), pp. 82, 87.

33. The 1591 prohibition against Chinese silk imports can be found in the *Recopilación de leyes de las indias*, libro 9, titulo 45, "Shipping and Commerce of the Philippine Islands, China, New Spain and Peru," and the same prohibitions are repeated in 1593, 1595, and 1604. See *Archivo digital de la legislación en el Perú*; http://www.congreso.gob.pe/ntley/LeyIndiaP.htm. Other references to the prohibitions are found, for example, in the Seville Archives in a 1737 letter from Manila that indicated the viceroy had reverted to the earlier 1720 royal cedula against shipments of silk to Mexico. Archivo General de Indias, ES.41091.AGI/22.14.824//FILIPINAS,209,N.1 1732/1737.

34. For further discussion of Asian-influenced Peruvian tapestry weaving, see Schuyler [van Rensselaer] Cammann, "Chinese Influence in Colonial Peruvian Tapestries," *Textile Museum Journal* 1, no. 3 (December 1964), pp. 21–34. See also Elena Phipps in *Colonial Andes*, pp. 250–54, nos. 75–76.

35. Ruth Corcuera, *Ponchos de las tierras del Plata* (Buenos Aires: Fondo Nacional de las Artes; Verstraeten Editores, [2000]), fig. p. 56.

36. Virginia Armella de Aspe and Guillermo Tovar y de Teresa, *Bordados y bordadores* (Mexico City: Grupo Gutsa, Fernández Cueto Editores, 1992), p. 130.

37. See Teresa Castelló Yturbide and Marita Martínez del Río de Redo, *Biombos mexicanos* (Mexico City: Instituto Nacional de Antropología e Historia, 1970).

38. Sophie Desrosiers brought this piece to my attention. Thanks to Milagritos Jiménez Moscoll Curadora, Museo de Arqueología "Josefina Ramos de Cox," Instituto Riva-Agüero, Lima, Peru, who supplied the excavation information and photo.

39. See Elisa Vargas Lugo de Bosch et al., *Imágenes de los naturales en el arte de la Nueva España: Siglos XVI–XVIII* (Mexico City: Fomento Cultural Banamex, 2005).

40. Bazant, "Evolution of the Textile Industry of Puebla," p. 69.

41. James Lockhart, *Spanish Peru, 1532–1560: A Colonial Society* (Madison: University of Wisconsin Press, 1968), p. 106.

42. Virginia Armella de Aspe, *Hilos del cielo: Las vestiduras litúrgicas de la Catedral Metropolitana de México* (Mexico City: Instituto Nacional de Antropología e Historia, Consejo Nacional para la Cultura y las Artes, 2007), pp. 172–73.

43. Ibid., p. 173. For what is considered to be one of the earliest embroideries in New Spain, see Dilys [E.] Blum, "Gremial of Archbishop Juan de Zumárraga," in *The Arts in Latin America, 1492–1820,* by Joseph J. Rishel et al., exh. cat. (New Haven and London: Yale University Press, 2006), p. 169, no. 11-4.

44. See Armella de Aspe, *Hilos del cielo,* and Armella de Aspe and Tovar y de Teresa, *Bordados y bordadores.*

45. Jorge Cornejo Bouroncle, *Derroteros de arte cuzqueño: Datos para una historia del arte en el Perú* (Cuzco: Editorial Garcilaso Ediciones Inca, 1960), p. 333.

46. "Aprendíz de bordador—Pedro Martín natural del pueblo de Santiago de Huánuco, con cierta con Baltazar Aucca Poma, maestro bordador para servirle de aprendíz y en todo lo concerniente al dicho oficio o arte, por el espacio de tres años durante los cuales le enseñará a border, dándole comida y curándole de sus enfermedades; por cada año le dará un vestido llano de paño de Quito, un sombrero, tres camisas, zapatos y al fín de los tres años un bastidor, unas tijeras, dedal y agujas y algunos padronos de buenas cortaduras y de cosas pulidas y curiosas de que se pueda valer y aprovechar en sus trabajos." Ibid., p. 335, 24–X–1600.

47. See Elena Phipps, "Cumbi to Tapestry: Collection, Innovation, and Transformation of the Colonial Andean Tapestry Tradition," in *Colonial Andes,* pp. 72–99.

48. See Isabel Iriarte in *Colonial Andes,* pp. 282–84, no. 93.

49. See Elena Phipps in *Colonial Andes,* pp. 235–37, no. 69, and Gauvin Alexander Bailey, *Art on the Jesuit Missions in Asia and Latin America, 1542–1773* (Toronto and Buffalo: University of Toronto Press, 1999), p. 49 and n. 192.

50. The presence of water-powered spinning in Arequipa is noted in Zavala, *El servicio personal de los indios en el Perú,* vol. 3, p. 88.

51. In 1559 Inez Muñoz, owner of one of the first *obrajes* in Peru—which had been established in 1545 in the town of Jauja—contracted with Spanish weavers, who brought their spinning wheels and looms with them. The reeds, leases, and other parts of the looms were then customized in Peru. Fernando Silva Santisteban, *Los obrajes en el virreinato del Perú* (Lima: Publicaciones del Museo Nacional de Historia, 1964), p. 19. Diego de Carvajal brought pins, needles, and iron scissors from Seville in 1554, along with his bales of *ruan* (noted above) and other silks and woolen textiles, ribbons, and laces. Archivo General de Indias, 1554 ES.41091.AGI/11//PASAJEROS,L.3,E.2373.

52. See Elena Phipps, "Textiles as Cultural Memory: Andean Garments in the Colonial Period," in *Converging Cultures: Art and Identity in Spanish America,* by Diana Fane et al., exh. cat. (Brooklyn: The Brooklyn Museum, 1996), pp. 144–56; and Eric Broudy, *The Book of Looms: A History of the Handloom from Ancient Times to the Present,* reprint ed. (1979; Hanover, N.H.: University Press of New England, 1993).

53. See Benjamin S. Orlove, *Alpacas, Sheep, and Men: The Wool Export Economy and Regional Society in Southern Peru* (1975; New York: Academic Press, 1977). See also Carlos Sempat Assadourian, "The Colonial Economy: The Transfer of the European System of Production to New Spain and Peru," *Journal of Latin American Studies* 24, Quincentenary Supplement [*The Colonial and Post-Colonial Experience: Five Centuries of Spanish and Portuguese America*] (1992), pp. 55–68.

54. This ordinance states "Obligación de Martín Cortés al virrey de Nueva España, Antonio de Mendoza, de plantar en las provincias de Huejotcingo, Cholula y Tlascala, cien mil pies de moreras, en 15 años, para la crianza del gusano de seda. Dice ser el primero que la cultivó en aquel reino tras su conquista. Tenoctitlan, 6 de octubre de 1536." (Obligation of Martín Cortés to the Viceroy of New Spain, Antonio de Mendoza, to plant in the provinces of Huejotzingo, Cholula and Tlascala, 100,000 mulberry trees, in 15 years for the raising of silkworms. It is said to be the first time that it is cultivated in this reign since the Conquest. Tenoctitlán, October 6, 1536.) "Ordenanzas de Antonio de Mendoza sobre géneros de seda," Archivo General de Indias, PATRONATO,181,R.3.

55. "Que los Virreyes y Governadores hagan sembrar, y beneficiar lino y cañamo. El Emperador D. Carlos, Donferrada a 13 junio 1545. Encargamos a los Virreyes, y Governadores, que hagan sembrar, y beneficiar en las Indias lino, y cañamo y procuren, que los Indios se apliquen à esta grangeria, y entiendan en hilar y texer lino." (That the viceroys and governors commence to grow and raise linen and hemp. Emperor D. Carlos, decreed June 13, 1545. We charge that the viceroys and governors grow and cultivate linen and hemp in the Indies and ensure that the Indians apply themselves to this cultivation and learn to spin and weave linen.) *Recopilación de leyes de las indias,* libro 4, titulo 18, ley xx; *Archivo digital de la legislación en el Perú;* http://www.congreso.gob.pe/ntley/LeyIndiaP.htm.

56. For more on *obrajes* in Mexico, see Manuel Miño Grijalva, *Obrajes y tejedores de Nueva España, 1700–1810: La industria urbana y rural de una economía colonial* (Mexico City: El Colegio de México, 1998). For Peru, see Silva Santisteban, *Los obrajes en el virreinato del Perú,* and Neus Escandell-Tur, *Producción y comercio de tejidos coloniales: Los obrajes y chorrillos del Cusco, 1570–1820,* Archivos de Historia Andina 23 (Cuzco: Centro de Estudios Regionales Andinos, "Bartolomé de Las Casas," 1997).

57. Bazant refers to the length. Bazant, "Evolution of the Textile Industry of Puebla," p. 69.

58. See Elena Phipps, *The Four-Selvaged Cloth* (Los Angeles: The Fowler Museum, forthcoming); Phipps, "Garments and Identity," pp. 16–39.

59. ". . . catorcenos, dieciochochenos, veinteno, veinticuartinos." Silva Santisteban, *Los obrajes en el virreinato del Perú,* p. 51. This classification system is similar to our measurement of thread count in cotton bedsheets.

60. Ibid., p. 19.

61. ". . . principalmente labran ropa que usan los indigenas y frazadas y no paños de valor." Miño Grijalva, *Obrajes y tejedores de Nueva España,* p. 207, citing Zavala, *El servicio personal de los indios en el Perú.*

62. Escandell-Tur, *Producción y comercio de tejidos colonials,* pp. 194–200, notes that in *obrajes* in Cuzco between 1778 and 1779 most of the indigo came from Lima and that by 1786–87 tax registers indicate that the merchants brought indigo from Guatemala.

Lima was certainly not a region that produced indigo, and it is likely that merchants purchased it in the markets there.

63. See http://peabody2.fas.harvard.edu/mcv/Project.htm. In 1980 the author also examined a small piece of red Spanish trade cloth recovered from the ceremonial site of Pachacamac, southeast of Lima, in the Museo del Sitio, Pachacamac.

64. Field Museum of Natural History, Chicago, no. 8400 (acc. 1445). "Book of textile samples . . . that are produced in ten towns in the province of Moxos in the present year of 1795" (from the handwritten front page). See Elena Phipps, "Textiles as Cultural Memory," p. 147, fig. 66.

65. Bazant, "Evolution of the Textile Industry of Puebla," pp. 56–69.

66. The fine "Pima cotton" that is now grown all over the world, notably in Egypt and other parts of Africa, for use in the high-end textile industry originated with this Peruvian species.

67. Manuel Miño Grijalva, "El camino hacia la fábrica en Nueva España: El caso de la 'Fábrica de Indianillas' de Francisco de Iglesias, 1801–1810," *Historia mexicana* 34, no. 1 (July–September 1984), pp. 135–48.

68. See Woodrow Wilson Borah, *Silk Raising in Colonial Mexico*, Ibero-Americana 20 (Berkeley and Los Angeles: University of California Press, 1943), pp. vii, 169.

69. Ibid. See also Bazant, "Evolution of the Textile Industry of Puebla," pp. 56–69.

70. "Se compró en México a Diego Gutiérrez quien hizo un frontal de terciopelo rojo y todo lo que se necessito par las frontaleras (franjas) bordadas con hilo de plata y raso Amarillo." Codex Sierra, fol. 15, 1555 (Nicolás León, trans. and ed., *Códice Sierra* [Mexico City: Impr. del Museo Nacional de Arqueología, Historia y Etnografía, 1933], p. 31). "Dos-cientos ochenta y un peso que importaran una capa de damasco blanco con orilla de terciopelo rojo y un paño de tafetán rojo que se pone sobre ella . . . Todo lo hizo Tomás de las Cuevas, igual a los que hay en Oaxaca." Codex Sierra, fol. 37, 1561 (León, *Códice Sierra*, p. 48).

71. Armella de Aspe, *Hilos del cielo*, p. 175.

72. See also León, *Códice Sierra*, above, which has multiple references to commissions for ecclesiastical garments made from white silk, which is presumably Chinese.

73. See also the author's essay on the dye trade in this publication, and Elena Phipps, "Cochineal Red: The Art History of a Color," *The Metropolitan Museum of Art Bulletin*, n.s., 67, no. 3 (Winter 2010), pp. 1–48.

74. In 1608 an unusual huaca was discovered in Lima: a European button covered in silk with a gold thread, which had been enshrined as an object of household worship. See Frank Salomon and Jorge Urioste, *The Huarochirí Manuscript: A Testament of Ancient and Colonial Andean Religion* (Austin: University of Texas Press, 1991), p. 17 (citing Francisco de Avila, "Prefación al libro de los sermons [1645]," in *Informaciones acerca de la religión y gobierno de los Incas*, edited by Horacio H. Urteaga and Carlos Romero [Lima, 1918], p. 74).

75. Sabine MacCormack, "'The Heart Has Its Reasons': Predicaments of Missionary Christianity in Early Colonial Peru," *Hispanic American Historical Review* 65, no. 3 (August 1985), pp. 443–66. The reference to the remaking of the altar frontal from indigenous clothing comes from p. 459 n. 50: "de la ropa de una huaca destruido hicieron frontales y doseles para las iglesias" (of the clothing from

a destroyed huaca they made frontals and hangings for the church). Another reference to the remaking of cloth from huacas into Christian frontals by Augustinian friars can be found in MacCormack, *Religion in the Andes*, p. 145.

76. Frank Salomon, "Indian Women of Early Colonial Quito as Seen through Their Testaments," *The Americas* 44, no. 3 (January 1988), pp. 325–41, esp. 334–35 n. 33.

77. See Elena Phipps and Isabel Iriarte in *Colonial Andes*, pp. 273–77, nos. 89–90.

78. "Les esta prohibido vestirse como nosotros." Viceroy Francisco de Toledo, from Juan de Solórzano y Pereyra, *Política indiana* (Madrid: Imprenta Real de la Gazeta, 1791), p. 200.

79. See Phipps, "Garments and Identity," pp. 27–33, 38 n. 47, 39 n. 71.

80. Bernabé Cobo, *Inca Religion and Customs*, translated and edited by Roland Hamilton (Austin: University of Texas Press, 1990), p. 188 (1653, bk. 13, chap. 2). The same regulation banned women's "disgusting" practice of nursing their children through an opening in the side of their dresses.

81. *Recopilación de leyes de las indias*, libro 7, titulo 5, ley xxvii; *Archivo digital de la legislación en el Perú*; http://www.congreso .gob.pe/ntley/LeyIndiaP.htm.

82. See Elena Phipps, "*Tornesol*: A Colonial Synthesis of European and Andean Textile Traditions," in *Approaching Textiles, Varying Viewpoints: Proceedings of the Seventh Biennial Symposium, Textile Society of America, Santa Fe, New Mexico, 2000* (Earleville, Md.: Textile Society of America, 2001), pp. 221–30.

83. This "marriage strategy" was also part of the Portuguese experience in Brazil. Portuguese traders married daughters of "headmen" of the Tupi tribes as a way to achieve legitimacy and to acquire material resources. See Monteiro, "Crisis and Transformations of Invaded Societies," p. 991.

84. Salomon, "Indian Women of Early Colonial Quito as Seen through Their Testaments," pp. 334–35.

85. The list continues with "la manta de Ruan; una camiseta de mediñaque labrada de azul; unas enaguas de blanco de algodon con cuatro ribetes; un jubon de mediñaque con varios zaragüellitos" (the shirt of Ruan; a *camiseta* of *mediñaque* worked with blue; some white petticoats of cotton with four edgings; a *jubon* of *mediñaque* with various breeches [drawers]). Jorge Zevallos Quiñones, "La ropa tributo de las encomiendas trujillanas en el siglo XVI," *Historia y cultura* 7 (1973), pp. 107–27.

86. The origin of the term *medriñaque* is unclear in the Andean context. The term was used in the sixteenth century to describe textiles in the Philippines, particularly a local fabric made of abaca (or some sources say palm or banana) fiber. It is mentioned multiple times in Blair and Robertson, eds., *The Philippine Islands 1493–1803*, in various volumes, including vols. 5, 14, and 16. Cloth made from palm or abaca fiber is not associated with garments from Peru. This type of leaf fiber would render the cloth with a certain stiffness. In the context of the embroidered waistcoat referred to in the colonial will, it is difficult to know whether the garment had in fact been made of this Philippine cloth, tailored in the European garment style, or perhaps had come via the Philippines from China as an embroidered silk, which would have been closer to the European model. In either case, the garment seems to have an association of having come from across the Pacific Ocean, via the Philippine trade.

87. Schurz, *Manila Galleon,* p. 365.

88. Amédée-François Frézier, *Voyage to the South-Sea, and along the Coasts of Chili and Peru, in the Years 1712, 1713, and 1714* (1717; London: Printed for Christian Bowyer, 1735), p. 219.

Chinese Textiles for Portuguese Tastes

I thank my colleagues Jessica Hallet, Carla Alferes Pinto, Nuno Senos, and Teresa Vale for their important contributions to this essay.

1. Chinese traders traveling among the ports of Southeast Asia guided the Portuguese in their journeys to the coast of Zhejiang and greatly contributed to the development of their maritime activities in Asia, even leading them to Japan, where they arrived in 1542; see J[ames] K. Chin, "The Portuguese on the Zhejiang and Fujian Coast prior to 1550 as Seen from Contemporary Chinese Private Records," in *Macau during the Ming Dynasty,* edited by Luís Filipe Barreto (Lisbon: Centro Científico e Cultural de Macau, 2009), pp. 119–37.

2. Other embassy missions would follow this one from the sixteenth to the eighteenth century, such as the ones led by Manuel Saldanha (1667), Alexandre Metelo de Sousa e Meneses (1725), Francisco de Assis Pacheco de Sampaio (1752), and Alexandre de Gouveia (1783).

3. John E. Wills, Jr., "Relations with Maritime Europeans, 1514–1662," in *The Cambridge History of China,* vol. 8, *The Ming Dynasty, 1368–1644, Part 2,* edited by Denis Twitchett and Frederick W. Mote (Cambridge and New York: Cambridge University Press, 1998), p. 336.

4. See Wu Zhiliang, "The Establishment of Macao as a Special Port City and the Ensuing Debates," in *Macau during the Ming Dynasty,* p. 299. Despite the success of the Portuguese and the maintenance of Macau over the years, the relationship between Portugal and China was tense and prone to conflict: the Portuguese presence reminded Chinese officials about foreigners and sea-trade policies, and China feared Portuguese intentions and actions, particularly in the religious context. For more on the trade between China and Japan, see the essay by Joyce Denney in this publication.

5. K[uzhippalli] S[karia] Mathew, *Portuguese Trade with India in the Sixteenth Century* (New Delhi: Manohar Publications, 1983), p. 133. The Portuguese, in fact, imported fabrics and commodities from India, China, and Persia. According to James Boyajian, "Silks from China were the exceptional shipment in the carreira da Índia. Persian and especially Indian silks were more common than the Chinese. . . . Of the cloth delivered to Lisbon, the overwhelming volume—perhaps 90 percent—was Indian cotton or cotton and silk mixtures of varying qualities." James C. Boyajian, *Portuguese Trade in Asia under the Habsburgs, 1580–1640* (Baltimore and London: Johns Hopkins University Press, 1993), p. 47.

6. Damião de Góis, *Chronica do felicissimo rei Dom Emanuel,* pt. 4, chap. 25 (Lisbon: Francisco Correa, 1567), fol. 31.

7. Anselmo Braamcamp Freire, "Inventário da guarda-roupa de D. Manuel," *Archivo histórico portuguez* 2 (1904), p. 388.

8. Anselmo Braamcamp Freire, "Inventário da casa de D. João III em 1534," *Archivo histórico portuguez* 8 (1910), pp. 276–77.

9. Arquivo Nacional da Torre do Tombo, Lisbon, Núcleo Antigo, no. 790, "Catalina de Austria, Inventario de joyas y guardarropa, 15 de Mayo de 1528," fol. 93.

10. Biblioteca da Ajuda (B.A.), Lisbon, Jesuítas na Ásia, 49-IV-50, doc. 133, p. 400; Maria João Pacheco Ferreira, "Entre a vivência religiosa cultural e académica: A presença de têxteis chineses nas festas do colégio de São Paulo de Goa em meados do século XVI," *Revista da Faculdade de Letras, Ciências e Técnicas do Património* 7–8 (2008–9), pp. 191–202; http://ler.letras.up.pt/uploads/ficheiros /9414.pdf.

11. Gauvin Alexander Bailey, "Incarnate Images: The Jesuits' Artistic Program in Portuguese Asia and Beyond," in *Encompassing the Globe: Portugal and the World in the 16th and 17th Centuries,* by Jay A. Levenson et al., exh. cat. (Lisbon: Instituto dos Museos e da Conservação, Museu Nacional de Arte Antiga, 2009), p. 228.

12. Verity Wilson, "China," in *5000 Years of Textiles,* by Jennifer Harris et al. (London: British Museum Press, 1993), p. 141.

13. Maria João Pacheco Ferreira, "Sino-Portuguese Embroidery: A Paradigm of Artistic and Cultural Exchanges between East and West," *Bulletin du CIETA* 82 (2005), pp. 108–18.

14. Michel Cazenave, ed., *Encyclopédie des symboles* (1996; Paris: Librairie Générale Française, 2004), pp. 12–13.

15. Chasuble (no. 3407); dalmatic (in Treasury without inventory number).

16. Jessica Rawson et al., *The British Museum Book of Chinese Art* (1992; London: British Museum Press, 1999), p. 265.

17. The motif of two birds circling one another has a long history in China. It first appears in the Tang dynasty (618–906) on metalwork, ceramics, and textiles, and thereafter becomes a standard motif in the decorative arts. See Shelagh Vainker, *Chinese Silk: A Cultural History* (London: British Museum Press, 2004), p. 158, and Young Yang Chung, *Silken Threads: A History of Embroidery in China, Korea, Japan, and Vietnam* (New York: Harry N. Abrams, 2004), p. 37.

18. John Irwin and Katharine B. Brett, *Origins of Chintz, with a Catalogue of Indo-European Cotton-Paintings in the Victoria and Albert Museum, London, and the Royal Ontario Museum, Toronto* (London: Her Majesty's Stationery Office, 1970), p. 19.

19. Lothar Ledderose, *Ten Thousand Things: Module and Mass Production in Chinese Art* (Princeton, N.J.: Princeton University Press, 2000).

20. In 1524 Cristovão Vieira wrote about the huge diversity and good quality of Chinese commodities in silk that had not yet been brought to Guangzhou because the Chinese feared that the Portuguese might not appreciate them or pay for their real value. Vieira noted in explanation that the emperor had decided that merchandise of the highest quality and greatest expense was to be forbidden to foreigners. *Cartas dos cativos de Cantão: Cristovão Vieira e Vasco Calvo (1524?),* edited by Rui Manuel Loureiro (Macau: Instituto Cultural de Macau, 1992), p. 48 (MS 1524). See also Maria João Pacheco Ferreira, "Notícias da Seda: Referências à seda chinesa na documentação impressa dos séculos XVI a XVIII e seu impacte na sociedade europeia," *Revista de Cultura* (Macao) 16 (2006), pp. 119–39.

21. Verity Wilson, "Silk," in *Chinese Export Art and Design,* by Craig Clunas et al. (London: Victoria and Albert Museum, 1987), p. 26.

22. G. F. Wingfield Digby, "Some Silks Woven under Portuguese Influence in the Far East," *The Burlington Magazine for Connoisseurs* 77, no. 449 (August 1940), p. 60.

23. Antonio de Morga, *Sucesos de las Islas Filipinas* (Mexico City: Geronymo Balli, 1609), p. 163, and C[harles] R. Boxer, *O grande*

navio de Amacau, 4th ed. (1959; Macau: Fundação Oriente, Museu e Centro de Estudos Marítimos de Macau, 1989), p. 5 n. 11.

24. Jorge Manuel Flores, "Macau: De surgidouro a cidade," in *História dos portugueses no Extremo Oriente,* vol. 1, pt. 2, *De Macau à periferia,* edited by António Henrique R. de Oliveira Marques (Lisbon: Fundação Oriente, 2000), p. 243.

25. Regina Krahl, "The Portuguese Presence in the Arts and Crafts of China," in *Encompassing the Globe,* pp. 312–13.

26. Siro Ulperni, *O forasteiro admirado: Relaçam panegyrica do trivnfo e festas, qve celebrou o Real Convento do Carmo de Lisboa pela canonização da seráfica virgem S. Maria Magdalena de Pazzi, religiosa da sua ordem,* pt. 1 (Lisbon: Off. de António Rodrigvez d'Abrev, 1672), p. 15.

27. Juan González de Mendoza, *Itinerario y compendio delas cosas notables que ay desde España hasta el reyno dela China, y dela China à España, bolviendo por la India Oriental, despues de auer dado buelta, à casi todo el mundo . . .* (Lisbon: S. Phelippe el Real, 1586), p. 61.

28. Maria João Pacheco Ferreira, "Os têxteis chineses em Portugal nas opções decorativas sacras de aparato (séculos XVI–XVIII)" (Chinese textiles in Portuguese decorative options for ecclesiastical apparatus [16th–18th centuries]), (Ph.D. diss., University of Oporto, 2011), vol. 1, pp. 337–45; http://repositorio-aberto.up.pt/handle /10216/56346, and Maria João Pacheco Ferreira, "Political Intentions of Chinese Textiles in Portuguese Sacred, Solemn, Celebratory Events of the 16th–18th Centuries," in *Textiles and Politics: Textile Society of America 13th Biennial Symposium Proceedings, Washington, D.C., September 18–22, 2012* (Earleville, Md.: Textile Society of America, 2013); http://digitalcommons.unl.edu/tsaconf/682.

29. António Caetano de Sousa, *História Genealógica da Casa Real Portuguesa,* vol. 3, pt. 1 (Coimbra: Atlântida-Livraria Editora, 1948), p. 521.

30. See Hugo Miguel Crespo, "Trajar as aparências, vestir para ser: O Testemunho da Pragmática de 1609" (Dressing for appearances, dress to be: The Testimonial of 1609 Guidelines), and Paula Monteiro, "Roupas de cama e outras cousas do lar" (Bed clothing and other things for the home), in *O luxo na região do Porto ao tempo de Filipe II de Portugal (1610)* (Luxury in Porto during the times of Felipe II of Portugal), edited by Gonçalo de Vasconcelos e Sousa (Porto: Universidade Católica Editora, Centro Interpretativo da Ourivesaria do Norte de Portugal, Centro de Investigação em Ciência e Tecnologia das Artes, 2012), pp. 93–148, 149–77.

31. Pacheco Ferreira, "Os têxteis chineses em Portugal," vol. 2, descriptions 12 and 14.

32. By the early seventeenth century slaves constituted about 9 percent of the total inhabitants of Lisbon; Asians made up 23 percent of the slave population. Unlike the African slaves, many of the Asians were manually skilled and trained as embroiderers. See Jorge Fonseca, *Escravos e senhores na Lisboa quinhentista* (Lisbon: Edições Colibri, 2010), pp. 90, 107, 245.

33. Filippo Sassetti, *Lettere edite e inedite,* edited and annotated by Ettore Marcucci (1835; Florence: Felice le Monnier, 1855), pp. 125–26.

34. "Das ilhas do Cubo e de outras de aquelle archipelago . . . boas obras de bastidor, escravas, perfeitas da mesma obra de bastir e broslar" (From the islands of Cubo [Cebu] and other islands in that archipelago . . . good tambour works, [and] slaves, perfect in producing the same sort of embroidery), Biblioteca Nacional de Madrid, MS 3015 (1602 or 1604), fol. 102, published in António da Silva Rego, ed., *Documentação ultramarina portuguesa,* vol. 2, *Bibl. Nac. Madrid, Ms. 3015; Mus. Brit., Col. Egerton Ms. 1131* (Lisbon: Centro de Estudos Históricos e Ultramarinos, 1962), p. 116.

35. Rank badges were hierarchical emblems of Chinese Empire officials and noblemen, bearing birds or animals as the main images: birds related to the civil category and were symbols of the literary refinement of scholars; animals were for the military, as elements invoking their courage. Valery M. Garrett, *Mandarin Squares: Mandarins and Their Insignia* (New York: Oxford University Press, 1990), p. 40. For more on this antependium, see Maria João Pacheco Ferreira, "Repercussions of Chinese Textiles in Portuguese Decorative Arts (16th–17th Centuries)," in *Face to Face: The Transcendence of the Arts in China and Beyond—Historical Perspectives,* edited by Rui Oliveira Lopes (Lisbon: CIEBA/FBAUL, forthcoming).

36. Gaspar da Cruz, *Tractado em que se cõtam muito por estẽso as cousas da China cõ suas particularidades, assi do reino d'Ormuz, cõposto por el. R. padre frei Gaspar da Cruz da orde de sam Domingos* [MS 1569], in *Enformação das cousas da China: Textos do século XVI,* edited by Raffaella D'Intino, Programa nacional de edições comemorativas dos descobrimentos portugueses (Lisbon: Imprensa Nacional, Casa da Moeda, 1989), pp. 210–11.

37. Between 1709 and 1760 the volume of finished imported pieces did not exceed 5 percent of the total amount of the Chinese commodities imported into England; Wilson, "Silk," p. 22. According to Vainker, *Chinese Silk,* p. 192, "in 1753, almost 70,000 kilos of raw silk and nearly 20,000 silk goods were exported to Europe, with approximately two thirds of the raw material and one third of the goods destined for England. Most of the remaining raw silk went equally to France and Holland, which also bought two fifths of the finished articles."

Japan and the Textile Trade

1. By far the largest portion of Japan's silk trade with China in the sixteenth and early seventeenth centuries was in reeled silk (silk filaments wound directly from several cocoons into skeins), neither dyed nor woven.

2. See Roderich Ptak, "Piracy along the Coasts of Southern India and Ming China: Comparative Notes on Two Sixteenth Century Cases," in *China and the Asian Seas: Trade, Travel, and Visions of the Other (1400–1750),* Variorum Collected Studies Series (Aldershot, U.K.: Ashgate, 1998), article 8, pp. 255–73.

3. See Roderich Ptak, "Sino-Japanese Maritime Trade, circa 1550: Merchants, Ports and Networks," in *China and the Asian Seas,* article 7, pp. 281–311.

4. The work of Charles Boxer, such as *The Great Ship from Amacon* (Lisbon: Centro de Estudos Históricos Ultramarinos, 1959), remains an important source for details of the early Sino-Japanese trade conducted by the Portuguese.

5. Madalena Ribeiro, "The Japanese Diaspora in the Seventeenth Century, According to Jesuit Sources," *Bulletin of Portuguese/ Japanese Studies* 3 (2001), pp. 53–83, surveys seventeenth-century Japanese communities in East and Southeast Asia. Two delegations

of high-ranking Japanese Christian converts went to Europe and Mexico during the period: the Tenshō mission of 1582–90 and the Keichō mission of 1613–20.

6. Derek Massarella and Izumi K. Tyler, "The Japonian Charters: The English and Dutch *Shuinjō*," *Monumenta Nipponica* 45, no. 2 (Summer 1990), p. 197.

7. This was true until 1715, when "they were placed under residential restrictions in Nagasaki somewhat similar to those for the Dutch." See Robert K. Sakai, "The Satsuma-Ryukyu Trade and the Tokugawa Seclusion Policy," *Journal of Asian Studies* 23, no. 3 (May 1964), p. 396.

8. Kazui Tashiro, "Tsushima Han's Korean Trade, 1684–1710," *Acta Asiatica* 30 (1976), pp. 85–86.

9. Sakai, "The Satsuma-Ryukyu Trade and the Tokugawa Seclusion Policy," pp. 391–92.

10. Yōko Nagazumi, "From Company to Individual Company Servants: Dutch Trade in Eighteenth-Century Japan," in *On the Eighteenth Century as a Category of Asian History: Van Leur in Retrospect,* edited by Leonard Blussé and Femme Gaastra (Aldershot, U.K.: Ashgate, 1998), pp. 147–72.

11. A breakthrough work on this aspect of seventeenth-century Japan was Ronald P. Toby's *State and Diplomacy in Early Modern Japan: Asia in the Development of the Tokugawa Bakufu* (Princeton, N.J.: Princeton University Press, 1984); the book reintegrates Japan into its Asian context, rather than allowing the theme of a "closed country" to focus attention solely on Japan's relations with Europe. For a useful summary, see also Kazui Tashiro, "Foreign Relations during the Edo Period: *Sakoku* Reexamined," *The Journal of Japanese Studies* 8, no. 2 (Summer 1982), pp. 283–306.

12. For English translations of some of these reports, see Yoneo Ishii, ed., *The Junk Trade from Southeast Asia: Translations from the Tōsen fūsetsu-gaki, 1674–1723* (Singapore: Institute of Southeast Asian Studies; Canberra: Research School of Pacific and Asian Studies, Australian National History, 1998).

13. See Morgan Pitelka, ed., *Japanese Tea Culture: Art, History, and Practice* (London and New York: Routledge Curzon, 2003); Paul Varley and Kumakura Isao, eds., *Tea in Japan: Essays on the History of Chanoyu* (Honolulu: University of Hawai'i Press, 1989); and Patricia J. Graham, *Tea of the Sages: The Art of Sencha* (Honolulu: University of Hawai'i Press, 1998).

14. Kimio Morita, *Meibutsu-gire no seiritsu* (The origins of *meibutsugire*), (Tokyo: Yoshikawa Kōbunkan, 1970), esp. pp. 23, 61, 68.

15. Graham, *Tea of the Sages*, p. 43.

16. Rumi Satoh et al., *Kowatari sarasa: Edo o someta Indo no hana/Sarasa: Flowers of the Textile Trade, The Gotoh Museum,* exh. cat. (Tokyo: Gotō Bijutsukan [The Gotoh Museum], 2008), pp. 172–73.

17. *Sencha, bi to sono katachi* (Sencha, its beauty and spirit), exh. cat. (Osaka: Osaka Shiritsu Bijutsukan [Osaka Municipal Museum of Art], 1997), pp. 82–83, 205, 240, 249.

18. Satoh et al., *Kowatari sarasa*, p. 130.

19. See ibid., p. 188, and *Sencha, bi to sono katachi*, pp. 96, 208, 238, 248.

20. Aki Yamakawa and Monica Bethe, *Kōsō to kesa: Koromo o tsutae, kokoro o tsunagu/Transmitting Robes, Linking Minds: The World of Buddhist Kasaya,* exh. cat. (Kyoto: Kyōto Kokuritsu Hakubutsukan [Kyoto National Museum], 2010), pp. xxvii, 200–203, 269–70.

21. Metropolitan Museum, acc. no. 19.93.50.

22. Masako Yoshida, "Saikyōji ya Honkokuji ni denrai suru kaki chōjū mon'yō shishū: Seisakuchi to seisaku mokuteki o megutte/Embroideries of Flower, Bird, and Animal Designs in Honkokuji and Saikyōji: Their Production Place and Purpose," *Genesis* (Bulletin of Kyoto University of Art and Design) 11 (September 2007), p. 102.

23. Nobuko Kajitani, *Gion matsuri yamaboko kensōhin chōsa hōkokusho: Torai senshoku no bu* (Report of the survey of items for decorating *yamaboko* of the Gion festival: Imported textiles), (Kyoto: Gion Matsuri Yamaboko Rengōkai [Gion Festival Yamaboko Association], 1992), pp. 119–20, 133.

24. Eiko Kamiya, "The *Dōbuku* in Patchwork of Gold Brocade, Silver Brocade and Other Cloths Reportedly Used by Uesugi Kenshin (I) [in Japanese]," *Bijutsu Kenkyū* (Journal of Art Studies), no. 216 (May 1961), pp. 2, 11–32, and Kamiya, "The *Dōbuku* in Patchwork of Gold Brocade, Silver Brocade and Other Cloths Reportedly Used by Uesugi Kenshin (II) [in Japanese]," *Bijutsu Kenkyū*, no. 219 (November 1961), pp. 2, 145–67.

25. Richard Cocks, *Diary of Richard Cocks, Cape-Merchant in the English Factory in Japan, 1615–1622, with Correspondence,* 2 vols., Works Issued by the Hakluyt Society 66–67 (London: Hakluyt Society, 1883), vol. 1, p. 259.

26. For the English term, see Florence M. Montgomery, *Textiles in America, 1650–1870: A Dictionary Based on Original Documents . . .* (New York: W. W. Norton, 1984), pp. 320–21, and the *Oxford English Dictionary*, s.v. "Perpetuana, n." For the Dutch, see the table of terms used by the Dutch for traded goods in Yōko Nagazumi, ed., *Tōsen yushutsunyūhin sūryō ichiran, 1637–1833-nen: Fukugen tōsen kamotsu aratamechō, kihan nimotsu kaiwatashichō* (Summary of imports and exports for the years 1637–1833), (Tokyo: Sōbunsha, 1987), p. 388.

27. Chihiro Ishida, *Nichiran bōeki no shiteki kenkyū* (A historical study of the Japanese Dutch trade), (Tokyo: Yoshikawa Kōbunkan, 2004), pp. 126, 145. See also Yuko Fukuoka Fukatsu, "Jinbaori no sozai to gihō ni kansuru kagakuteki bunseki to senshoku shiteki kenkyū/A Comprehensive Study on Jinbaori Based on the Scientific Analysis of Materials and Techniques" (Ph.D. diss., Kyōritsu Joshi Daigaku Daigakuin [Kyōritsu Women's University Graduate School], Tokyo, 2008), pp. 38–40, 68–71.

28. Kazuo Minami, "Edo bakufu okachigumi no fukusei ni tsuite" (Regarding the system of dress of the Edo shogunate's *okachigumi*), *Fūzoku* (Manners and customs) 5, no. 2 (1965), pp. 23–29.

29. Ishida, *Nichiran bōeki no shiteki kenkyū*, pp. 127, 129, 131–32.

30. Nagazumi, *Tōsen yushutsunyūhin sūryō ichiran, 1637–1833-nen*, pp. 331–32.

31. Satoh et al., *Kowatari sarasa*, p. 176.

32. For red the book suggests *enji*, lac, an insect dyestuff imported from India or Southeast Asia, and for blue it suggests *ai*, or indigo. In a departure from the tobacco pouch textile, however, the book suggests purple dye for the fine lines of the design, while the Indian textile used for the pouch features red lines probably produced using mordant dyeing.

33. Sae Ogasawara, *Hikone sarasa,* exh. cat. (Hikone: Hikonejō Hakubutsukan [Hikone Castle Museum], 1989), pp. 73–78. See also John Guy, *Woven Cargoes: Indian Textiles in the East* (London: Thames and Hudson, 1998), pp. 176–77.

Silk along the Seas

1. Niels Steensgaard, *The Asian Trade Revolution of the Seventeenth Century: The East India Companies and the Decline of the Caravan Trade* (Chicago: University of Chicago Press, 1974), p. 32.

2. Murat Çizakça, "Incorporation of the Middle East into the European World-Economy," in *Textiles: Production, Trade and Demand,* edited by Maureen Fennell Mazzaoui (Aldershot, U.K.: Ashgate, 1998), pp. 1–25, this reference p. 4 nn. 3, 7, and Nurhan Atasoy, Walter B. Denny, Louise W. Mackie, and Hülya Tezcan, *Ipek: The Crescent and the Rose; Imperial Ottoman Silks and Velvets* (London: Azimuth Editions, 2001), p. 175.

3. Atasoy, Denny, Mackie, and Tezcan, *Ipek,* p. 159.

4. Stanford J. Shaw and E[zel] K. Shaw, *History of the Ottoman Empire and Modern Turkey,* 2 vols. (Cambridge and New York: Cambridge University Press, 1976–77), vol. 1, pp. 62–68.

5. Steensgaard, *Asian Trade Revolution,* pp. 32–37.

6. R[obert] B. Serjeant, *The Portuguese off the South Arabian Coast: Hadramī Chronicles, with Yemeni and European Accounts of Dutch Pirates off Mocha in the Seventeenth Century* (Oxford: Clarendon Press, 1963), p. 5.

7. Halil İnalcık, "The Ottoman State: Economy and Society, 1300–1600; Trade," in *An Economic and Social History of the Ottoman Empire, 1300–1914,* edited by Halil İnalcık and Donald Quataert (Cambridge and New York: Cambridge University Press, 1994), pp. 245, 364–74.

8. Atasoy, Denny, Mackie, and Tezcan, *Ipek,* p. 176.

9. Andrew C. Hess, "The Evolution of the Ottoman Seaborne Empire in the Age of Oceanic Discoveries, 1453–1525," *The American Historical Review* 75, no. 7 (December 1970), pp. 1892–919.

10. Salih Özbaran, *The Ottoman Response to European Expansion: Studies on Ottoman-Portuguese Relations in the Indian Ocean and Ottoman Administration in the Arab Lands during the Sixteenth Century* (Istanbul: Isis Press, 1994), pp. 70–71.

11. Rudi Matthee, "Between Arabs, Turks and Iranians: The Town of Basra, 1600–1700," *Bulletin of the School of Oriental and African Studies* 69, pt. 1 (2006), pp. 53–78.

12. İnalcık, "Ottoman State," p. 194.

13. Suraiya Faroqhi, "Crisis and Change, 1590–1699," in *An Economic and Social History of the Ottoman Empire, 1300–1914,* pp. 482–502, 505.

14. Bruce McGowan, "The Age of the *Ayans,* 1699–1812," in *An Economic and Social History of the Ottoman Empire, 1300–1914,* p. 702.

15. Atasoy, Denny, Mackie, and Tezcan, *Ipek,* pp. 156–57.

16. İnalcık, "Ottoman State," pp. 231–34.

17. Atasoy, Denny, Mackie, and Tezcan, *Ipek,* pp. 156–57.

18. Rudi Matthee, "Anti-Ottoman Concerns and Caucasian Interests: Diplomatic Relations between Iran and Russia, 1587–1639," in *Safavid Iran and Her Neighbors,* edited by Michel Mazzaoui (Salt Lake City: The University of Utah Press, 2003), pp. 101–28, this reference pp. 105ff.

19. Willem Floor, "Hormuz, ii. Islamic Period," in *Encyclopaedia Iranica,* online edition (New York, 1996–), originally published December 15, 2004, last updated March 23, 2012; http://www.iranicaonline.org/articles/hormuz-ii.

20. Rudi Matthee, "Distant Allies: Diplomatic Contacts between Portugal and Iran in the Reign of Shah Tahmasb, 1524–1576," in *Portugal, The Persian Gulf and Safavid Persia,* edited by Rudi Matthee and Jorge Flores, Acta Iranica 52 ([Leuven]: Peeters, 2011), pp. 219–47, this reference pp. 223–25.

21. Linda K. Steinmann, "Sericulture and Silk: Production, Trade, and Export under Shah Abbas," in *Woven from the Soul, Spun from the Heart: Textile Arts of Safavid and Qajar Iran, 16th–19th Centuries,* by Carol Bier et al., exh. cat. (Washington, D.C.: The Textile Museum, 1987), pp. 12–19, this reference p. 13. See also T[homas] S. Willan, *The Early History of the Russia Company, 1553–1603* (Manchester: Manchester University Press, 1956).

22. Steinmann, "Sericulture and Silk," pp. 15–16.

23. Vahan Baibourtian, *International Trade and the Armenian Merchants in the Seventeenth Century* (New Delhi: Sterling Publishers, 2004), pp. 30–40, and Vartan Gregorian, "Minorities in Isfahan: The Armenian Community of Isfahan, 1587–1722," *Iranian Studies* 7, no. 3–4 [*Studies on Isfahan, Part II*] (Summer–Autumn 1974), pp. 652–80.

24. Steinmann, "Sericulture and Silk," pp. 16–17.

25. Linda [K.] Steinmann, "Shah 'Abbas and the Royal Silk Trade 1599–1629," *British Society for Middle Eastern Studies Bulletin* 14, no. 1 (198[7]), pp. 68–74, and X[avier] de Planhol, "Bandar-e 'Abbas," in *Encyclopaedia Iranica,* edited by Ehsan Yarshater (London and New York: Routledge & Kegan Paul, 1985–), vol. 3 (1989), pp. 685–87.

26. Steinmann, "Shah 'Abbas and the Royal Silk Trade," pp. 70–71.

27. Planhol, "Bandar-e 'Abbas," pp. 685–87.

28. Rudolph P. Matthee, *The Politics of Trade in Safavid Iran: Silk for Silver, 1600–1730* (Cambridge and New York: Cambridge University Press, 1999), pp. 105–11.

29. İnalcık, "Ottoman State," pp. 243–46.

30. Matthee, *Politics of Trade,* pp. 145–46, 173–75.

31. Ibid., p. 202.

32. *The American Magazine and Historical Chronicle* 1 (December 1743), pp. 146–52.

33. Halil İnalcık, "Harir; ii. The Ottoman Empire," in *The Encyclopedia of Islam,* new ed. (Leiden, London, and Boston: E. J. Brill, 1960–2009), vol. 3 (1971), pp. 211–18, this reference p. 218.

34. Atasoy, Denny, Mackie, and Tezcan, *Ipek,* p. 155.

35. Ibid., pp. 156, 162–63, 182–89.

36. This is in contrast to other types of Turkish goods—carpets, for instance—that were quite popular in Italy. See Walter B. Denny, "Oriental Carpets and Textiles in Venice," in *Venice and the Islamic World, 828–1797,* by Stefano Carboni et al., exh. cat. (New York: The Metropolitan Museum of Art, 2007), pp. 174–91.

37. Nurhan Atasoy and Lâle Uluç, *Impressions of Ottoman Culture in Europe, 1453–1699* (Istanbul: Armaggan Publications, 2012), pp. 35–36, 46–47, 80–81, 98–99.

38. Denny, "Oriental Carpets and Textiles in Venice," p. 189.

39. See Walter B. Denny, "Dating Ottoman Turkish Works in the Saz Style," *Muqarnas* 1 (1983), pp. 103–21.

40. Atasoy, Denny, Mackie, and Tezcan, *Ipek*, pp. 180–81.

41. Ibid., pp. 178–79, and Veronika Gervers, *The Influence of Ottoman Turkish Textiles and Costume in Eastern Europe, with Particular Reference to Hungary* (Toronto: Royal Ontario Museum, 1982).

42. Atasoy, Denny, Mackie, and Tezcan, *Ipek*, pp. 180–81.

43. Atasoy and Uluç, *Impressions of Ottoman Culture*, pp. 105–9, and Atasoy, Denny, Mackie, and Tezcan, *Ipek*, pp. 178–80.

44. Production of these special silks may have begun in the early 1500s, as suggested by a dalmatic preserved in the Dionysiou Monastery in Greece that is presumed to have entered the collection by 1508 because of its association with Nephon II, the patriarch of Constantinople, who died that year. See Atasoy, Denny, Mackie, and Tezcan, *Ipek*, p. 178.

45. This connection is suggested in ibid., pp. 178–80, and elaborated in Atasoy and Uluç, *Impressions of Ottoman Culture*, pp. 102–3.

46. Edmund M. Herzig, "The Volume of Iranian Raw Silk Exports in the Safavid Period," *Iranian Studies* 25, no. 1–2 [*The Carpets and Textiles of Iran: New Perspectives in Research*] (1992), pp. 61–79, this reference p. 79.

47. Willem Floor, *The Persian Textile Industry in Historical Perspective, 1500–1925* (Paris: Harmattan, 1999), pp. 13–15.

48. Ibid., pp. 31–33.

49. Carol Bier, "Islamic Art, VI: Textiles, 2. Fabrics, (iii) c. 1500 and after, (c) Iran," in *Grove Art Online*, Oxford Art Online; http://www.oxfordartonline.com/subscriber/article/grove/art/T041771pg34 (accessed October 11, 2012). See also Milton Sonday, "Pattern and Weaves: Safavid Lampas and Velvet," in *Woven from the Soul, Spun from the Heart*, pp. 57–83.

50. The story, recorded by Edward Terry, a chaplain in India from 1616 to 1619, is quoted in Carol Bier and Mogens Bencard, *The Persian Velvets at Rosenborg* (Copenhagen: De Danske Kongers Kronologiske Samling, 1995), pp. 12–13.

51. Susan Stronge, "Imperial Gifts at the Court of Hindustan," in *Gifts of the Sultan: The Arts of Giving at the Islamic Courts*, by Linda Komaroff et al., exh. cat. (Los Angeles: Los Angeles County Museum of Art, 2011), pp. 170–83, this reference p. 171.

52. Tadeusz Mańkowski, "Influence of Islamic Art in Poland," *Ars Islamica* 2, pt. 1 (1935), pp. 92–117, this reference pp. 105–6.

53. Willem Floor, "Economy and Society: Fibers, Fabrics, Factories," in *Woven from the Soul, Spun from the Heart*, pp. 20–32, this reference p. 23.

54. John Guy, *Indian Textiles in the East from Southeast Asia to Japan* (1998; London: Thames and Hudson, 2009), pp. 129–30. For more discussion of the Thai market and commissioning, see the essay by John Guy in this publication.

55. A Dutch East India Company letter in the Algemeen Rijks Archief [General State Archives], The Hague, VOC 1818 (27/4/1713), fol. 243, and translated by Floor in "Economy and Society," p. 22.

56. Alexey Konstantinovich Levykin et al., *The Tsars and the East: Gifts from Turkey and Iran in the Moscow Kremlin*, exh. cat. (Washington, D.C.: Arthur M. Sackler Gallery, Smithsonian Institution, 2009), p. 37, no. 9.

57. This was the fate of the ambassador Don Garcia de Silva y Figueroa. Marianna Shreve Simpson, "Gifts for the Shah: An Episode in Habsburg-Safavid Relations during the Reigns of Philip III and 'Abbas I," in *Gifts of the Sultan*, pp. 124–39, this reference p. 135.

58. This 1597 mission from Russia to Iran is discussed in Matthee, "Anti-Ottoman Concerns," p. 115.

59. Cornelis Haga thus waited in Istanbul. Alexander H. de Groot, *The Ottoman Empire and the Dutch Republic: A History of the Earliest Diplomatic Relations, 1610–1630* (Leiden: Nederlands Historisch-Archaeologisch Instituut Leiden/Istanbul, 1978), p. 206.

60. For the reasons behind this, see Gottfried Mraz, "The Role of Clocks in the Imperial Honoraria for the Turks," in *The Clockwork Universe: German Clocks and Automata 1550–1650*, edited by Klaus Maurice and Otto Mayr, exh. cat. (Washington, D.C.: Smithsonian Institution; New York: Neale Watson Academic Publications, 1980), pp. 37–48.

61. Jennifer Wearden, "Siegmund von Herberstein: An Italian Velvet in the Ottoman Court," *Costume: The Journal of the Costume Society* 19 (1985), pp. 22–29.

62. J. L. Nevinson, "Siegmund von Herberstein: Notes on 16th Century Dress," *Waffen- und Kostümkunde* 18 (1959), pp. 86–93.

63. Karin Ådahl, "Claes Brorson Rålamb's Embassy to the Sublime Porte in 1657–1658," in *The Sultan's Procession: The Swedish Embassy to Sultan Mehmed IV in 1657–1658 and the Rålamb Paintings,* edited by Karin Ådahl (Istanbul: Swedish Research Institute in Istanbul, 2006), pp. 8–25. Despite the unsatisfactory conclusion of this mission, Sweden maintained diplomatic contacts with the Ottomans through the 1700s as a safeguard against Russian aggression, and in 1709 the Swedish Levant Company was founded with the encouragement of Charles XII. See Atasoy, Denny, Mackie, and Tezcan, *Ipek*, pp. 179–80.

64. Margareta Nockert, "The Rålamb Caftan and Ottoman Textiles from the Rålamb Collection," in *The Sultan's Procession*, pp. 266–77.

65. Hüseyin Şen, Mehmet Tütüncü, and Hanno de Vries, *De prins en de pasja/The Prince and the Pasha/Prence ve paşa: 400 jaar Nederland Turkije* (The Hague: De Verdieping van Nederland, [2012]), pp. 12–16, with documents catalogued on pp. 58, 60, 68, 104.

66. Vanmour was permitted to observe such ceremonies in order to paint them, and, having spent thirty-seven years in the Ottoman capital, he would have been entirely familiar with the people depicted in his costumes series. Ol'ga Nefedova-Gruntova, *A Journey into the World of the Ottomans: The Art of Jean-Baptiste Vanmour, 1671–1737* (Milan: Skira, 2009).

67. Oliver Bast, "Germany. i. German-Persian Diplomatic Relations," in *Encyclopaedia Iranica*, vol. 10 (2001), pp. 506–19.

68. F[redrik] R[obert] Martin, *Die persischen Prachtstoffe im Schlosse Rosenborg in Kopenhagen* (Stockholm: G. Chelius in Commission, 1901), and Bier, *The Persian Velvets at Rosenborg*, pp. 61–75.

69. Rudi Matthee, "Anti-Ottoman Politics and Transit Rights: The Seventeenth Century Trade in Silk Between Safavid Iran and Muscovy," *Cahiers du monde russe* 35, no. 4 (October–December 1994), pp. 739–61, this reference pp. 744–48, 751–53.

70. Saleema Waraich in *Gifts of the Sultan*, pp. 270–71, no. 169.

71. S. N. Kologrivov, *Materialy dlia istorii snoshenii Rossii s inostrannymi derzhavami v XVII veke*, Vestnik arkheologii i istorii 2 (St. Petersburg: V. D. Smirnov, 1911), quoted in Inna Isidorovna Vishnevskaya, "Eastern Treasures of the Russian Tsars," in *The Tsars and the East,* p. 7.

72. The robe, dated about 1630, is made of velvet with a metal ground. It was likely from the 1639 embassy en route to visit Friedrich

III in Gottorp. Published in Agnes Geijer, *Oriental Textiles in Sweden* (Copenhagen: Rosenkilde and Bagger, 1951), p. 102 and pl. 15, and Guy Walton, "Diplomatic and Ambassadorial Gifts of the Sixteenth and Seventeenth Centuries," in *Gifts to the Tsars, 1500–1700: Treasures from the Kremlin,* edited by Barry Shifman and Guy Walton, exh. cat. (New York: Harry N. Abrams, 2001), pp. 74–95, these references pp. 78, 86–87.

73. R[oger] M. Savory, "The Sherley Myth," *Iran* 5 (1967), pp. 73–81, and Roger Stevens, "Robert Sherley: The Unanswered Questions," *Iran* 17 (1979), pp. 115–25.

74. R. W. Ferrier, "Charles I and the Antiquities of Persia: The Mission of Nicholas Wilford," *Iran* 8 (1970), pp. 51–56.

75. See the accounts quoted in Patricia L. Baker, "Wrought of Gold or Silver: Honorific Garments in Seventeenth Century Iran," in *Carpets and Textiles in the Iranian World, 1400–1700: Proceedings of the Conference Held at the Ashmolean Museum on 30–31 August 2003,* edited by Jon Thompson, Daniel Shaffer, and Pirjetta Mildh (Oxford: May Beattie Archive, Ashmolean Museum, Oxford; [Genoa]: Bruschettini Foundation for Islamic and Asian Art, 2010), pp. 158–67, this reference p. 161.

"Whims and Fancies"

1. See Godfrey Smith, *The Laboratory, or, School of Arts: In which are faithfully exhibited, and fully explained . . . with a great number of other scarce and valuable secrets. Volume II, compiled for the use, benefit, and entertainment of the curious; illustrated with a variety of curious copper-plates* (London, 1756), p. 44. This was the last of three editions and the only one to include a chapter on silk design. Peter Thornton proposes that this chapter was written by a professional silk designer, not by Smith; see Thornton, "An 18th Century Silk-Designer's Manual," *The Bulletin of the Needle and Bobbin Club* 42, no. 1–2 (1958), pp. 6–31.

2. The first recorded use of the word in English occurs in 1883; see the *Oxford English Dictionary,* s.v. "Chinois, n."

3. Hugh Honour's *Chinoiserie: The Vision of Cathay* (London: J. Murray, 1961) is considered the first significant text on this subject, followed by Oliver Impey's *Chinoiserie: The Impact of Oriental Styles on Western Art and Decoration* (London: Oxford University Press, 1977), Madeleine Jarry's *Chinoiserie: Chinese Influence on European Decorative Art, 17th and 18th Centuries* (New York: Vendome Press, 1981), Dawn Jacobson's *Chinoiserie* (London: Phaidon, 1993), and Francesco Morena's *Chinoiserie: The Evolution of the Oriental Style in Italy from the 14th to the 19th Century* (Florence: Centro Di, 2009), in which the author places the Italian taste for exotic goods and decor in the larger European context.

4. David M. Mitchell, "A Passion for the Exotic," in *City Merchants and the Arts, 1670–1720,* edited by Mireille Galinou (Wetherby, U.K.: Oblong for the Corporation of London, 2004), p. 69.

5. See David L. Porter, "Monstrous Beauty: Eighteenth-Century Fashion and the Aesthetics of the Chinese Taste," *Eighteenth-Century Studies* 35, no. 3 (Spring 2002), p. 395: "Chinoiserie, it should be noted at the outset, was a pan-European phenomenon, and most existing studies have considered it as such."

6. See Beverly Lemire, "Domesticating the Exotic: Floral Culture and the East India Calico Trade with England, c. 1600–1800,"

Textile: The Journal of Cloth and Culture 1, no. 1 (March 2003), pp. 65–85.

7. John Irwin, "Indian Textile Trade in the Seventeenth Century: I. Western India," *Journal of Indian Textile History,* no. 1 (1955), pp. 4–33, this reference pp. 6–7; Irwin quotes Richard Hakluyt, who stated that "our chief desire is to find ample vent of our woolen cloth," in *The Principal Navigations,* published between 1589 and 1600.

8. Irwin, "Indian Textile Trade in the Seventeenth Century: I. Western India," p. 7.

9. John Irwin and Katharine B. Brett, *Origins of Chintz, with a Catalogue of Indo-European Cotton-Paintings in the Victoria and Albert Museum, London, and the Royal Ontario Museum, Toronto* (London: Her Majesty's Stationery Office, 1970), p. 12; catalogue number 10A in this publication has an early company stamp with the initials G.C.E.

10. See K. N. Chaudhuri, *The Trading World of Asia and the English East India Company, 1660–1760* (London: Cambridge University Press, 1978), pp. 434–36, for a review of the financial crisis that led to the formation of the new EIC in Britain, and its eventual merger with the original company; these merged organizations became the United East India Company. The new name is rarely used; Chaudhuri refers to the company as either the English East India Company (to differentiate from the Dutch and French) or simply the East India Company.

11. For a history of the French companies, see Donald C. Wellington, *French East India Companies: A Historical Account and Record of Trade* (Lanham, Md.: Hamilton Books, 2006); the French company established in 1664 incorporated three earlier organizations that had been actively opposed by the Dutch and English traders.

12. See Sir John Chardin, *Travels in Persia, 1673–1677* (New York: Dover Publications, 1988), pp. 281–88.

13. Irwin, "Indian Textile Trade in the Seventeenth Century: I. Western India," pp. 9–10.

14. For the importation of Eastern raw silk for weaving in Europe, see Sjoukje Colenbrander, *When Weaving Flourished: The Silk Industry in Amsterdam and Haarlem, 1585–1750* (Amsterdam: Aronson Publishers, 2013), chaps. 1 and 2. I am grateful to Dr. Colenbrander for giving me access to an early draft of the English edition of this work.

15. See Audrey W. Douglas, "Cotton Textiles in England: The East India Company's Attempt to Exploit Developments in Fashion, 1660–1721," *The Journal of British Studies* 8, no. 2 (May 1969), pp. 28–43, this p. 29, and Beverly Lemire, *Fashion's Favourite: The Cotton Trade and the Consumer in Britain, 1660–1800,* Pasold Studies in Textile History 9 (Oxford and New York: Pasold Research Fund, Oxford University Press, 1991), pp. 14–15.

16. Christopher Morris, ed., *The Journeys of Celia Fiennes* (London: Cresset Press, 1947), quoted in Douglas, "Cotton Textiles in England," p. 29.

17. For example, the account of Indian cotton painting by the English botanist William Roxburgh (1750–1815) describes nineteen days of dyeing and cleaning, after which the cloth would be given a final finish, such as a starch, or calendered to create a glossy surface. See P[aul] R. Schwartz, "The Roxburgh Account of Indian Cotton-Painting, 1795," *Journal of Indian Textile History,* no. 4 (1959), pp. 47–56, and Irwin and Brett, *Origins of Chintz,* pp. 55–58.

18. Mitchell, "A Passion for the Exotic," pp. 80–81, 182 nn. 48–49. "Calico" was derived from the name Calicut, an Indian trading center on the west coast; "chintz" is probably derived from the Hindu *chint*, meaning "spotted cloth."

19. Chaudhuri, *Trading World of Asia*, p. 282.

20. Ibid., p. 291.

21. See, for example, Leanna Lee-Whitman, "The Silk Trade: Chinese Silks and the British East India Company," *Winterthur Portfolio* 17, no. 1 (Spring 1982), pp. 21–41, this p. 35, table 7, which indicates that the vast majority of silk taffetas imported from China between 1723 and 1753 were plain.

22. For the origins of this design, see Irwin and Brett, *Origins of Chintz*, chap. 5, pp. 16–22; for seventeenth-century English embroideries, see, for example, Victoria and Albert Museum (no. 816-1893), and Metropolitan Museum, acc. no. 64.101.1305. See also K[atharine] B. Brett, "The Flowering Tree in Indian Chintz," *Journal of Indian Textile History*, no. 3 (1957), pp. 45–57, and John Irwin, "Origins of 'Oriental' Chintz Design," *The Magazine Antiques* 75, no. 1 (1959), pp. 84–87.

23. Irwin, "Indian Textile Trade in the Seventeenth Century: I. Western India," p. 15; these palampores came in three sizes.

24. Victoria and Albert Museum (nos. IS.21-1956 and IS.137-1950).

25. I am grateful to Kirsten Toftegaard, curator, Designmuseum Danmark, for sharing images and information about this piece.

26. Chaudhuri, *Trading World of Asia*, pp. 282–95, provides a narrative of the vicissitudes of the market during the late seventeenth century.

27. See Colenbrander, *When Weaving Flourished*, p. 23.

28. Ibid., pp. 23–24. Not only were the weavers protesting, but silk throwers (thread makers or processors) protested the importation of finished thread, although all raw silk used in the Netherlands had to be imported, since sericulture never succeeded there.

29. Natalie Rothstein, "Dutch Silks—An Important but Forgotten Industry of the 18th Century or a Hypothesis?" *Oud Holland* 74, no. 3 (1964), pp. 152–71, p. 152 n. 2, quoted from Justin Godart, *L'ouvrier en soie . . .* (Lyon: Bernoux et Cumin, 1899), p. 356.

30. Irwin and Brett, *Origins of Chintz*, p. 5.

31. Josette Brédif, *Toiles de Jouy: Classic Printed Textiles from France, 1760–1843* (New York and London: Thames and Hudson, 1989), p. 17.

32. Chaudhuri, *Trading World of Asia*, p. 294.

33. Brédif, *Toiles de Jouy*, p. 18.

34. Daniel Defoe had a reputation for writing in support of any cause for which he was paid; he was, however, a patriotic Briton and believed that trade was the key to increased international power. See Paula R. Backscheider, "Defoe, Daniel (1660?–1731)," in *Oxford Dictionary of National Biography*, edited by H. C. G. Matthew, Brian Harrison, and Lawrence Goldman (Oxford: Oxford University Press, 2004; online ed., January 2008); http://www.oxforddnb.com.library .metmuseum.org/view/article/7421 (accessed February 12, 2013).

35. Daniel Defoe in *Weekly Review*, January 31, 1708, quoted in Lemire, *Fashion's Favourite*, p. 16.

36. *A Further Examination of the Weavers Pretences* (London: J. Roberts, 1719), quoted in Beverly Lemire, "Fashioning Cottons: Asian Trade, Domestic Industry and Consumer Demand, 1660–1780," in *The Cambridge History of Western Textiles*, 2 vols.

(Cambridge and New York: Cambridge University Press, 2003), vol. 1, pp. 493–512, this p. 503.

37. Jacobson, *Chinoiserie*, p. 35.

38. Emmanuelle Gaillard and Marc Walter, *Exotic Taste: Orientalist Interiors* (New York: Vendome Press, 2011), p. 60.

39. Quoted in Irwin, "Indian Textile Trade in the Seventeenth Century: I. Western India," p. 14, from Evelyn's diary dated August 30, 1655, also quoted in the *Oxford English Dictionary*, s.v. "Pintado." Irwin suggests that this was a textile from Golconda.

40. Joseph Breck compared Evelyn's comment with the Metropolitan Museum's hanging, acc. no. 20.79; see Joseph Breck, "Four Seventeenth-Century Pintadoes," *Metropolitan Museum Studies* 1, no. 1 (November 1928), pp. 3–15, p. 3 and n. 6. See also Marika Sardar, "A Seventeenth-Century *Kalamkari* Hanging at The Metropolitan Museum of Art," in *Sultans of the South: Arts of India's Deccan Courts, 1323–1687*, edited by Navina Najat Haidar and Marika Sardar (New York: The Metropolitan Museum of Art, 2011), pp. 148–61.

41. Samuel Pepys, *The Diary of Samuel Pepys: A New and Complete Transcription*, edited by Robert Latham and William Matthews, 11 vols. (1970–71; London: Harper Collins, 1995), vol. 4, p. 299, diary entry for September 5, 1663, quoted in Mitchell, "A Passion for the Exotic," p. 80.

42. For Prince Eugene's use of imported damask, probably acquired through his connections with England, see Clare Browne, "Silk Damask Bed Furnishings in the Early Eighteenth-Century—Influences on Choice in Colour and Design," in *Furnishing Textiles: Studies on Seventeenth- and Eighteenth-Century Interior Decoration*, edited by Anna Jolly, Riggisberger Berichte 17 (Riggisberg: Abegg-Stiftung, 2009), pp. 47–58, 223–36, esp. p. 58.

43. Angela Volker, "An Indian Chinoiserie from an Austrian Palace: Textile Furnishings for Prince Eugene's State Bedroom in Schloss Hof," in *Baroque Luxury Porcelain: The Manufactories of Du Paquier in Vienna and of Carlo Ginori in Florence*, by Johann Kräftner et al., exh. cat. (Munich: Prestel; Vienna: Liechtenstein Museum, 2005), pp. 62–63; Volker also suggests that this suite could have been made in India, rather than in Europe, as previously suggested.

44. See Santina M. Levey, *An Elizabethan Inheritance: The Hardwick Hall Textiles* (London: The National Trust, 1998), p. 29.

45. Lee-Whitman, "Silk Trade," p. 27.

46. Ibid., pp. 22–28; American consumers appear to have favored large patterns for both furnishings and dress.

47. Vecellio's first book, *Degli habiti antichi et moderni di diversi parti del mondo* (Venice, 1590), was updated and expanded in 1598 to include the Americas; see Margaret F. Rosenthal and Ann Rosalind Jones, *The Clothing of the Renaissance World—Europe, Asia, Africa, the Americas: Cesare Vecellio's* Habiti Antichi et Moderni (London: Thames and Hudson, 2008).

48. For a concise discussion of sumptuary legislation of the period as it pertains to fashion, and the reasons for its eventual failure, see Herman Freudenberger, "Fashion, Sumptuary Laws, and Business," *Business History Review* 37, no. 1–2 (Spring–Summer 1963), pp. 37–48.

49. See Irwin, "Indian Textile Trade in the Seventeenth Century: I. Western India," pp. 4–33; John Pollexfen (1636–1715) in a 1681 speech to the Board of Trade.

50. Douglas, "Cotton Textiles in England," p. 31.

51. Ibid., p. 31; one such advocate was Nicholas Barbon (ca. 1640–ca. 1698).

52. Chaudhuri, *Trading World of Asia,* p. 281 nn. 14–15, from the Despatch Book Records for 1683.

53. Mantua as defined in Randle Holme, *The Academy of Armory, or, A Storehouse of Armory and Blazon* (Chester, 1688), bk. 3, quoted in Janet Arnold, *Patterns of Fashion: Englishwomen's Dresses and Their Construction,* vol. 1, *C[irca] 1660–1860* (New York: Drama Books, 1977), pp. 3–4.

54. Chaudhuri, *Trading World of Asia,* p. 281, Despatch Book for 1687.

55. This fabric has been identified as both a chintz and a painted silk (for the painted silk attribution, see Aileen Ribeiro, *The Art of Dress: Fashion in England and France, 1750 to 1820* [New Haven and London: Yale University Press, 1995], p. 59). More recently, Rosemary Crill asserted that it was indeed a chintz; see Crill, *Chintz: Indian Textiles for the West* (London: V&A Publications, 2008), pp. 18–19.

56. See John Styles, *Threads of Feeling: The London Foundling Hospital's Textile Tokens, 1740–1770,* exh. cat. (London: The Foundling Museum, 2010). At least two samples appear to be Indian cottons; see pp. 27, 34, figs. 18 and 25.

57. For the practice of giving textiles and dress as part of diplomatic exchanges, see Lisa Monnas, "Textiles and Diplomacy: Ottoman Silks Entering Venice as Diplomatic Gifts in the Fifteenth and Sixteenth Centuries," conference paper presented at "Luxusgewebe des Orients im westlichen Mittelalter/Oriental Silks in Medieval Europe," Riggisberg, September 29–October 1, 2011 (Riggisberg: Abegg-Stiftung, forthcoming). I am grateful to Dr. Monnas for sharing a draft of the final article.

58. See Nicholas Tromans et al., *The Lure of the East: British Orientalist Painting,* exh. cat. (New Haven: Yale University Press, 2008), pp. 49, 62, fig. 49.

59. Paris, Jacques Le Hay, 1714; this work was commissioned by Charles Ferriol (1652–1722), the French ambassador to Constantinople with whom Vanmour was traveling.

60. In a letter dated May 17 (presumably 1718, on her return journey), she recounts a visit to the mosque of Sultan Selim in Adrianople (modern Edirne), where she thought she was recognized after all; *The Letters and Works of Lady Mary Wortley Montagu,* edited by Lord Wharncliffe, 2 vols. (Paris: A. and W. Galignani and Co., 1837), vol. 1, p. 265.

61. For a discussion of masquerade fashions based on foreign and historical dress and fashions, see Aileen Ribeiro, *Dress in Eighteenth-Century Europe, 1715–1789* (London: B. T. Batsford, 1984), p. 177, and Ribeiro, "The Exotic Diversion: The Dress Worn at Masquerades in Eighteenth Century London," *The Connoisseur* 197, no. 791 (January 1978), pp. 3–13, esp. p. 13.

62. See Aileen Ribeiro, "The Dress Worn at Masquerades in England," 1730 to 1790, and Its Relation to Fancy Dress in Portraiture" (Ph.D. diss., University of London, 1975; New York: Garland Publishing, 1984), pp. 222, 378 n. 11; the description was written by Horace Walpole in a letter to Richard Bentley dated February 8, 1755.

63. Maria Theresa was painted in Turkish dress for a masquerade by the court artist Martin van Meytens about 1744.

64. The letter was written by Lord Stafford, the Earl of Arundel's son, on September 24, 1643, from Amsterdam. See Mary F. S. Hervey, *The Life, Correspondence and Collections of Thomas Howard, Earl of Arundel, "Father of vertu in England"* (Cambridge: Cambridge University Press, 1921), p. 443, quoted in Margaret H. Swain, "Nightgown into Dressing Gown: A Study of Men's Nightgowns, Eighteenth Century," *Costume: The Journal of the Costume Society* 6 (1972), p. 11, and Patricia Wardle, *For Our Royal Person: Master of the Robes Bills of King-Stadholder William III* (Apeldoorn: Paleis Het Loo National Museum, 2002), p. 63.

65. See Aileen Ribeiro, *The Gallery of Fashion* (London: National Portrait Gallery, 2000), p. 12, pl. 3.

66. Quoted in Brédif, *Toiles de Jouy,* p. 14.

67. For this portrait and further references to Schloss Falkenlust, see *A Taste for the Exotic: Foreign Influences on Early Eighteenth-Century Silk Designs,* edited by Anna Jolly, Riggisberger Berichte 14 (Riggisberg: Abegg-Stiftung, 2007), pp. 7–10, 211–24. In her introduction, Jolly astutely chose this portrait to represent the theme of the 2002 colloquium, the place of textiles within the phenomenon of European consumption of Asian imports in the eighteenth century.

68. I am grateful to Jeffrey Munger, Curator, Department of European Sculpture and Decorative Arts at the Metropolitan Museum, for his comments on the porcelain.

69. See Edith A[ppleton] Standen, "The Story of the Emperor of China: A Beauvais Tapestry Series," *Metropolitan Museum Journal* 11 (1976), pp. 103–17.

70. See Johannes Nieuhof, *Legatio batavica ad magnum Tartariae chamum Sungteium . . .* (Amsterdam: J. Meursium, 1668), a translation of *Het gezantschap der Neêrlandtsche Ost-Indische Compagnie, aan den grooten Tartarischen cham, den tegenwoordigen keizer van China* of 1665. Nieuhof's work was the result of his participation in VOC embassies to Beijing.

71. Friederike Ulrichs, "Johan Nieuhof's and Olfert Dapper's Travel Accounts as Sources for European *Chinoiserie,*" in *A Taste for the Exotic,* p. 47 n. 6, and pp. 214, 223, lists all of the editions published in Amsterdam, Antwerp, and London up to 1679, when the Dutch publisher responsible for nine editions in Amsterdam, Jacob de Meurs, died.

72. See Charissa Bremer-David, *French Tapestries and Textiles in the J. Paul Getty Museum* (Los Angeles: The J. Paul Getty Museum, 1997), pp. 90–91.

73. Ulrichs, "Johan Nieuhof's and Olfert Dapper's Travel Accounts," pp. 45–56; the hangings also use the frontispiece, depicting the viceroy of Canton, who, Edith Standen suggests, inspired the depiction of the Chinese emperor in the Beauvais tapestries. See Standen, "The Story of the Emperor of China," pp. 104–6.

74. See Perrin Stein, "Boucher's Chinoiseries: Some New Sources," *The Burlington Magazine* 138, no. 1122 (September 1996), pp. 598–604, this pp. 601–2.

75. When Pillement lived in England, his patrons included the actor David Garrick and his Viennese wife. He also visited Italy and was in Austria at the court in Vienna between 1763 and 1765. See Maria Gordon-Smith, "Jean Pillement at the Imperial Court of Maria Theresa and Francis I in Vienna (1763 to 1765)," *Artibus et Historiae* 25, no. 50 (2004), pp. 187–213.

76. Some of the architectural drawings for garden facades are taken from William Chambers and Matthew Darly.

77. See Peter Thornton, *Baroque and Rococo Silks* (London: Faber and Faber, 1965), pp. 153–54, pls. 13A and B; the prints are after the French artist Paul Androuet Ducerceau (active 1660; died 1710).

78. I am grateful to Dr. Feng Zhao for introducing me to the group of related textiles in the National Palace Museum, Beijing, and to Joyce Denney and Mei Mei Rado for their additional comments on this group.

79. For an analysis of this textile and a list of others in European and American collections, see Anna Jolly, "Une soierie chinoise d'après un dessin anglais du XVIIIe siècle," *Bulletin du CIETA,* no. 80 (2003), pp. 75–83. Three similar silks are in the Palace Museum, Beijing; these may have been made for the Chinese emperor. The technical details that contribute to the Chinese attribution are the 7/1 satin weave and the use of gilt paper to create the metal-wrapped thread.

80. For a discussion of the degree to which cotton influenced consumption, see John Styles, "Indian Cottons and European Fashion, 1400–1800," in *Global Design History,* edited by Glenn Adamson et al. (London: Routledge, 2011), pp. 37–46.

81. S[tanley] D. Chapman and S[erge] Chassagne, *European Textile Printers in the Eighteenth Century: A Study of Peel and Oberkampf* (London: Heinemann Educational Books, The Pasold Fund, 1981), pp. 5–6.

82. See David [M.] Mitchell and Milton Sonday, "Printed Fustians: 1490–1600," *Bulletin du CIETA,* no. 77 (2000), pp. 99–118; see also Chapman and Chassagne, *European Textile Printers in the Eighteenth Century,* p. 11, for written accounts of printing on linen in Italy about 1400.

83. Antony Griffiths, *The Print in Stuart Britain, 1603–1689,* exh. cat. (London: British Museum Press, 1998), p. 105.

84. For Margaret van de Passe's work, see Nadine Orenstein, "Who Took the King of Sweden to Bed?" *Print Quarterly* 8, no. 1 (March 1991), pp. 44–47, where her nightcaps are described as being printed with popular political imagery. Not surprisingly, the maker was from a prominent and successful family of printers.

85. François de la Boullaye-le-Gouz, *Les voyages et observations du Sieur de la Boullaye-le-Gouz gentilhomme angeuin* (Paris: Gervais Clousier, 1653), cited in Giorgio Riello, "Asian Knowledge and the Development of Calico Printing in Europe in the Seventeenth and Eighteenth Centuries," *Journal of Global History* 5, no. 1 (March 2010), pp. 1–28, this pp. 2–3.

86. See Irwin and Brett, *Origins of Chintz,* pp. 36–41.

87. Brédif, *Toiles de Jouy,* p. 16. Marseille was declared a "free port" by Colbert in 1669, enabling Armenian merchants and craftspeople involved in the Levant trade to settle there and aid in the establishment of textile printworks. Records survive of textiles being printed in Marseille prior to this, as early as 1648; see Chapman and Chassagne, *European Textile Printers in the Eighteenth Century,* p. 6.

88. Chapman and Chassagne, *European Textile Printers in the Eighteenth Century,* p. 6. Sherwin's patent was for "a new and speedy way for printing broadcloth, which being the old true way of East India printing and stayning . . ."; see Parakunnel J. Thomas, "The Beginnings of Calico-Printing in England," *The English Historical Review* 39, no. 154 (April 1924), pp. 206–16, this reference p. 209.

89. Chapman and Chassagne, *European Textile Printers in the Eighteenth Century,* pp. 6–7.

90. Ibid., p. 18.

91. Ibid.; Brédif, *Toiles de Jouy,* p. 52.

92. A copperplate could print an area of more than one square yard as opposed to wood blocks that could conveniently print only about twelve square inches; see Chapman and Chassagne, *European Textile Printers in the Eighteenth Century,* p. 13.

93. See Metropolitan Museum, acc. no. 30.89, dated about 1790, and acc. no. 61.119.2, dated about 1800.

94. For a discussion of this as it refers to the consumption of cotton fabrics, see Lemire, "Domesticating the Exotic," pp. 65–85, esp. pp. 68–71.

95. Natalie Rothstein, ed., *Barbara Johnson's Album of Fashions and Fabrics* (London: Thames and Hudson, 1987).

96. See ibid., p. 29. Rothstein lists thirty-seven cottons and seven linens; her book was written before any of the fragments were tested for fiber content.

97. I thank John Styles, University of Hertfordshire, England, for this information. Personal communication, December 2012.

98. Chapman and Chassagne, *European Textile Printers in the Eighteenth Century,* p. 91.

99. See Starr Siegele, *Toiles for All Seasons: French and English Printed Textiles* (Boston: Bunker Hill Publishing, 2004), appendix, pp. 72–73; the design was based on sketches by Huet that were done on-site at the factory in Jouy-en-Josas.

"India Chints" and "China Taffaty"

1. The first Navigation Act in 1651 required that at least one-half of all ships' crews trading with the British colonies be British nationals and that most goods must travel back and forth on English or colonial ships. The goal of this act was to eliminate Dutch competition.

2. Subsequent British trade regulations included the 1660 Navigation Act, which required all colonial trade to be on English ships; the Staple Act of 1663, which stipulated that goods bound for the colonies shipped from Europe, Asia, or Africa first be landed in England before continuing to the colonies; the Navigation Act of 1696, which created a system of admiralty courts to enforce trade regulations and punish smugglers; and the Woolens Act of 1699, which prohibited export of colonial woolen cloth so as to prevent competition with English wool producers.

3. For more on British and European textiles in America, see especially Florence M. Montgomery's two seminal books *Printed Textiles: English and American Cottons and Linens, 1700–1850* (New York: The Viking Press, 1970) and *Textiles in America, 1650–1870: A Dictionary Based on Original Documents . . .* (New York: W. W. Norton, 1984). For an excellent survey of the types of clothing made from imported fabric, see Linda [R.] Baumgarten, *What Clothes Reveal: The Language of Clothing in Colonial and Federal America; The Colonial Williamsburg Collection* (Williamsburg, Va.: Colonial Williamsburg Foundation, 2002).

4. In Linda Baumgarten's groundbreaking work on the Boston textile trade from 1650 to 1700, amid the European wools and linens she found clear evidence, in the twenty-four merchants' inventories she studied, of Indian textile goods such as "painted calico," muslin, *pintadoes* (the Portuguese word for Indian painted cotton chintzes),

silk and cotton *romalls* (handkerchiefs), and even palampores (painted cotton bedcovers and hangings). Some bed quilts were listed simply as "East India," which could refer to a painted calico quilt or possibly a Chinese silk or Indian embroidered quilt. Linda R. Baumgarten, "The Textile Trade in Boston, 1650–1700," in *Arts of the Anglo-American Community in the Seventeenth Century*, edited by Ian M. G. Quimby, Winterthur Conference Report, 1974 (Winterthur, Del.: The Henry Francis du Pont Winterthur Museum; Charlottesville: The University Press of Virginia, 1975), pp. 219–73.

5. The information from 1630s port books from London, Barnstable, Bristol, Plymouth, Southampton, and Great Yarmouth were compiled by Norman C. P. Tyack in "English Exports to New England, 1632–1640: Some Records in the Port Books," *New England Historical and Genealogical Register* 135 (1981), pp. 213–38.

6. The woven silks listed in the port books, if they were not Asian, could have been made elsewhere in Europe, but likely not in England. The English silk-weaving industry did not start in earnest until after French Protestant silk weavers, fleeing France after the revocation of the Edict of Nantes (1685), settled in the Spitalfields area of London and soon produced silks to rival those of the other European countries with far longer silk-weaving traditions. For many years in the eighteenth century, even after the Spitalfields weavers were well established, basic silk taffetas, satins, and damasks were imported from China and India (discussed below in this essay).

7. With Richard Arkwright's 1768 invention of the spinning frame, strong cotton warps began to be produced. This enabled the weaving of all-cotton fabrics in the British Isles, thus cutting down on imports of some of the basic Indian cottons.

8. Although it is not always clear whether calicoes in eighteenth-century sources were Indian or English, "Callicoes" found in eighteenth-century merchants' orders that are listed side by side with other textiles of clear Indian origin are assumed to be Indian made.

9. When the merchant, butcher, and real estate entrepreneur Asser Levy died in New York City in 1682, his inventory listed "one Callico Cloath for a bed," likely a palampore. Leo Hershkowitz, "Original Inventories of Early New York Jews (1682–1763)," *American Jewish History* 90, no. 3 (September 2002), p. 258.

10. Sources include American Wing scholarship files, The Metropolitan Museum of Art; George Francis Dow, *Every Day Life in the Massachusetts Bay Colony* (Boston: The Society for the Preservation of New England Antiquities, 1935; reprint, New York: Dover Publications, 1988); Abbott Lowell Cummings, *Rural Household Inventories, Establishing the Names, Uses, and Furnishings of Rooms in the Colonial New England Home, 1675–1775* (Boston: The Society for the Preservation of New England Antiquities, 1964); Ruth Piwonka, "New York Colonial Inventories: Dutch Interiors as a Measure of Cultural Change," in *New World Dutch Studies: Dutch Arts and Culture in Colonial America, 1609–1776*, edited by Roderic H. Blackburn and Nancy A. Kelley (Albany: Albany Institute of History and Art, 1987), pp. 63–81; Deborah L. Krohn and Peter N. Miller, eds., *Dutch New York between East and West: The World of Margrieta van Varick*, exh. cat. (New York: Bard Graduate Center, 2009); and Hershkowitz, "Original Inventories of Early New York Jews," pp. 239–321, and "Original Inventories of Early New York Jews (1682–1763) (Concluded)," *American Jewish History* 90, no. 4 (December 2002), pp. 385–448. My enormous thanks to

Cynthia V. A. Schaffner for researching and compiling these sources.

11. In the December 17, 1651, inventory of the estate of Boston shopkeeper Henry Landis, "Red calico," "White calico," and "17 calico neckcloths" are listed. Dow, *Every Day Life in the Massachusetts Bay Colony*, p. 83. Merchant William Paine's Boston inventory of November 14, 1660, includes fabrics in several different rooms—in the "Warehouse Chamber," "8 peeces wt. calleco, 12 of blew calleco" and the intriguingly named "17 ½ (pieces) *east* cloath," while "In the Lower Room" there were "20 yrds. white calleco." Ibid., Appendix F, pp. 258–61. Jan Reyersen had "2 ½ els of red calico" that were auctioned off in July 1665, after his death in Albany, New York. Piwonka, "New York Colonial Inventories," p. 69.

12. The Bostonian shopkeeper Captain Bozone Allen's inventory of September 22, 1652. Dow, *Every Day Life in the Massachusetts Bay Colony*, Appendix D, pp. 244–45.

13. Cummings, *Rural Household Inventories*, p. 14. Banyans listed in inventories and ads in Boston are primarily wools such as *calamanco* or *cheney*, although there seems to have been a fashion for plaid banyans, likely also woven of wool.

14. Dow, *Every Day Life in the Massachusetts Bay Colony*, Appendix G, pp. 262–69.

15. For more on Corwin's trading patterns, see James E. McWilliams, *Building the Bay Colony: Local Economy and Culture in Early Massachusetts* (Charlottesville: The University of Virginia Press, 2007), pp. 75–83. Corwin's inventory also included "1 yd 3/4 bl. Calico, 28 yd ½ ell persian Silke, 17 yd bengall" in his store, and "1 Calico Counter pain, 1 Calico Carpet, 1 painted Couberd Cloth, 8 yd bengall, 1 yd wte Calico, 2 Calico Side bord clothes, 3 Calico ditto, 1 yd 3/4 persian Silke, 1 Calico Cuberd cloth" and "1 Quilt of Calico Colerd & flowred" in his home. Dow, *Every Day Life in the Massachusetts Bay Colony*, Appendix H, pp. 270–83.

16. Krohn and Miller, eds., *Dutch New York*, pp. 342–63.

17. Tores Nunes's inventory lists "11 pcs. Musleen 26 yds (per) pc," which were valued at 4 pounds sterling each. He also had "7 pieces stript Musleen" in fifteen-yard-long pieces as well as "5 pcs plain ditto," as well as "3 pieces ditto thin." Altogether 175 pieces of calico were listed, in white and a variety of colors such as "lead," "blue," and "sad." Some calicoes are differentiated as "printed" and "broad" vs. "narrow." The calicoes ranged in price from 10 to 30 shillings per piece. His nine cotton *romalls* were worth 35 shillings each. He also imported silks such as "34 yds Persian Silk" at 4 shillings per yard, "4 pcs & ½ East India Silk" that was 50 shillings per piece, "14 pcs pauncnes[?] East India silk" at only 20 shillings per piece, "2 pcs ditto 7 yd Each broad" at 25 shillings per piece, and "13 yds ½ Striped Silk" at 5 shillings per yard. Hershkowitz, "Original Inventories of Early New York Jews (1682–1763)," pp. 283–86.

18. While it cannot be assumed that every advertisement published in this time period was found, a total of 130 ads were surveyed from the three major shipping centers on the East Coast (Boston, 33 ads; New York, 58; and Philadelphia, 40). Most of these ads were accessed through the website *America's Historical Newspapers, Including Early American Newspapers*, Series 1–7, 1690–1922 (New York and Chester, Vt.: Readex, 2006–); http://infoweb.newsbank.com.

19. *The Boston Weekly Post-Boy*, no. 804, May 7, 1750, p. 2.

20. Robert and Richard Ray ad, *The New-York Gazette Revived in the Weekly Post-Boy*, no. 317, February 13, 1749, p. 3.

21. Robert G. Livingston ad, *The New-York Gazette Revived in the Weekly Post-Boy,* no. 315, January 30, 1749, p. 3.

22. *The Pennsylvania Gazette,* no. 830, November 8, 1744, p. 4.

23. Main sources for textile identification include Henry Yule and Arthur Coke Burnell, *Hobson-Jobson: Being a Glossary of Anglo-Indian Colloquial Words and Phrases, and of Kindred Terms; Etymological, Historical, Geographical, and Discursive* (London: John Murray, 1886); John Irwin, "Indian Textile Trade in the Seventeenth Century: I. Western India," *Journal of Indian Textile History,* no. 1 (1955), pp. 4–33; "II. Coromandel Coast," no. 2 (1956), pp. 24–42; "III. Bengal," no. 3 (1957), pp. 58–74; and Montgomery, *Textiles in America.*

24. "Persian silk," a frequently used textile description of EIC silks throughout the eighteenth century, could have actually referred to silk taffeta woven in Iran in the seventeenth century. See R. W. Ferrier, "An English View of Persian Trade in 1619: Reports from the Merchants Edward Pettus and Thomas Barker," *Journal of the Economic and Social History of the Orient* 19, no. 2 (May 1976), pp. 182–214.

25. Four ads specify "India Persians"; most list Persians after China taffetas with no specific place of origin attributed. However, a notice of EIC textiles, citing both types and number of pieces arriving from London that was posted in a New York newspaper in 1742, lists "Taffaties Bengal, 4630 pieces, Ditto China." The number of Chinese pieces is more than two thousand, but the precise number is illegible. *The New-York Weekly Journal,* no. 469, November 15, 1742, p. 1. For more on Bengali woven taffetas, see Irwin, "Indian Textile Trade in the Seventeenth Century: III. Bengal," pp. 61–62.

26. *The Pennsylvania Gazette,* no. 1415, February 5, 1756, p. 3.

27. Natalie Rothstein, "Silks for the American Market," *The Connoisseur* (American edition) 166, no. 668 (October 1967), pp. 90–94.

28. Eleven ads in the sampling refer to "India Damasks." English East India Company supercargo records of trade between Canton and London commonly list quantities of "Bed damasks," which were likely used in the colonies as dress damasks. See Leanna Lee-Whitman, "The Silk Trade: Chinese Silks and the British East India Company," *Winterthur Portfolio* 17, no. 1 (Spring 1982), pp. 27–28.

29. Ibid., pp. 21–41.

30. Susan S. Bean, "The Indian Origins of the Bandanna," *The Magazine Antiques* 156 (December 1999), pp. 832–39.

31. The Scottish-born James Alexander immigrated to the colonies in 1715 and was best known as a New York lawyer and statesman. In 1721 he married Mary Spratt Prevoost (1693–1760), an already established merchant with her late first husband, Samuel Prevoost, an importer. The Alexanders' dry-goods business was likely run mainly by Mary, even though James placed some of the orders.

32. Order from July 3, 1732, Alexander Papers, Box 5, Folder 1, The New-York Historical Society. This is a copy of an order that Alexander must have sent to Pacheco, as evidenced by correspondence from Pacheco to Alexander about parts of the order. There is also an earlier draft of this order, first dated May 26, 1732, then crossed out and redated June 19, in Box 2, Folder 1, Correspondence O–R.

33. See, for example, "Invoice of Goods requested of Mr. Pacheco balance in the Spring of 1739," which is dated March 20, 1738, as well as a shipping list written by Pacheco in London to Alexander for goods sent to New York on the ship *Aswoge* in September 1738. It lists sets of Chinese dinnerware in different decorative patterns, several cases of looking glasses, a case of dessert glasses of various types, and one trunk containing calicoes and *salempores* valued at more than £58. Alexander Papers, Box 5, Folder 1.

34. Irwin, "Indian Textile Trade in the Seventeenth Century: II. Coromandel Coast," pp. 35–36, 41.

35. It cannot be proven that the calicoes that Alexander was ordering were solely Indian products. Some could have been printed in England on Indian cotton fabric. The Alexander Papers contain a 1726 sample sheet of small-scale calicoes that look to be mostly English printed, though some could have been Indian printed. These were samples Mary Alexander sent to David Barclay & Sons in London to show the types of fabrics she wanted included in her next order (Alexander Papers, Box 10, Folder 4). In another letter from Mary Alexander to Barclay in 1749, she ordered "some patterns of Striped Callicoe" (fig. 106); some of the samples enclosed in the letter are clearly English products, whereas others are Indian (Box 10, Folder 2). There is no mention of their different origins. This seems to imply that the Alexanders did not distinguish between calicoes printed in India and England, as long as the product was printed on all-cotton Indian fabric and had pleasing patterns.

36. For further discussion of the source of this type of textile, see also the author's essay on trade textiles in the Metropolitan Museum in this publication.

37. There is an undated invoice from Pacheco, seemingly in response to this order, for "4 Demy Long Cloths two blews at 34/. . . £6:16/2 Do [ditto] Pencilwork at 38 . . . £3:16." Alexander Papers, Box 5, Folder 2.

38. See P[eter] C. Floud, "The English Contribution to the Early History of Indigo Printing," *The Journal of the Society of Dyers and Colourists* 76 (June 1960), pp. 344–49.

39. "Pencil Blue" was a short-lived indigo dyeing technique that was developed in Europe in the 1730s. Indigo mixed with arsenic trisulphide and a thickener could be kept from oxidizing long enough to be quickly brushed onto small areas on the surface of a fabric, stroke by stroke, but the technique was never known to yield good results for large areas of color or to be useful in block printing. It also proved quite dangerous to those who worked with the "enriched" dye. In the case of Alexander's order it is logical to interpret the mentioned "pencil work" as the resisted lines painted onto the fabric.

40. In *Printed Textiles,* p. 41, Florence Montgomery cites an order from 1739 that Philip Livingston of Albany sent to Samuel Storke in London for "blew penciled work'd calico two collours, All Large flowers," which sounds very similar to the fabric Alexander ordered. Montgomery speculates that this was blue-resist fabric, which, judging by the number of pieces found in the upper Hudson valley, was quite popular in the Albany area. Order of Philip Livingston, December 5, 1739, Albany, to Samuel Storke, London. Miscellaneous Manuscripts, V, p. 99, New York State Library, Albany.

41. Alexander requested forty-nine pieces of "China Taffaties" in black, blue, blue-and-white changeable, green, rose, light red, gold, lemon, changeable "cloth" colored (a tan or light brown color), plain "cloth" color, dove, and white. Chinese silks were ordered in lengths ("pieces") of either 38 or 45 *covids* (44 ft. 11 in. or 59 ft. 11 in.) and 2 or 2.2 *covids* wide (28 1/4 or 31 in.). A *covid* equaled slightly over

14 inches. He ordered nineteen pieces of single-color "india Damask" in the same colors as the taffetas, and five pieces of two-color damasks, all with white grounds and large blue, yellow, green, or red flowers. Additionally, he ordered thirty-two pieces of "Persians" (no country of origin named) in the same type of color array as the taffetas, although more black than the other colors.

42. Alexander also asked for nine pieces of *shagreen*, a silk taffeta with a pebbled surface often used for linings, in blue, dove, red, cloth, and black, and eight pieces of "Gorgoroons," a ribbed silk fabric woven in China, which may have been interchangeable with grograms.

43. These were likely "peniascoes," which Irwin defines as "Brightly coloured fabric, probably of mixed cotton-and-silk, usually striped." Irwin, "Indian Textile Trade in the Seventeenth Century: III. Bengal," p. 71.

44. At the end of the order is a long list of silk hose, for both men and women, silk gloves, and shoes, mainly of silk but some of wool "callemanco," velvet, as well as "1 Doz black leather mourning Shoes wt white heels" and "3 doz kid gloves." Whether these were made in China or India is hard to know.

45. The great-grandson of early Dutch settlers in New York, James Beekman was a successful merchant. He marked his status by building a country estate, Mount Pleasant, in 1763, which once overlooked the East River at what is now Fifty-First Street and Beekman Place in New York City. Beekman married Jane Keteltas in 1752; the couple were parents to ten children. Beekman remained a Whig throughout the American Revolution and moved to Ulster County when the British took possession of New York City. For an embroidered white Indian mull dress with a history of descent in Beekman's family, see catalogue number 76.

46. The business papers of James and his cousin Gerard G. Beekman have been published, making them the most accessible of merchants' papers of the period. Philip L. White, *The Beekman Mercantile Papers, 1746–1799*, 3 vols. (New York: The New-York Historical Society, 1956).

47. "I shall defer sending out any Orders for Goods for the present, as our City is overstocked with all kinds of Merchandize, and little or no Cash in Circulation, but as soon as I shall see a proper Encouragement, shall renew my Orders." However, it seems he never placed further orders with the firm after 1785. Beekman to Thomas Pomeroy, July 16, 1785. White, *Beekman Mercantile Papers*, vol. 3, p. 1188.

48. Beekman to Streatfeild and Mildred, August 26, 1784, acknowledges his debt to the firm for £1,456.8.4. Ibid., vol. 2, p. 1184. Until the mid-1760s, Beekman had used silver bullion to pay his bills. As the economy of the colonies destabilized in the years leading up to the war, Beekman wrote that he was having a hard time getting cash payments at home and was forced to take bonds for land as payment. Because these could not be translated into cash for his creditors in England, he racked up a huge debt to them. See letter to Pomeroys and Hodgkin, September 24, 1767. Ibid., p. 913.

49. Letter from Pomeroys and Streatfeild, London, March 7, 1753. Ibid., pp. 541–42. The reference to the "4 lungee romalls that contain 16 hanks" (handkerchiefs) explains that handkerchiefs were often printed in multiples on a single length of cloth (in this case,

sixteen to a length) that were cut and finished when they reached a merchant's shop.

50. Letter from Pomeroys and Streatfeild, September 3, 1753. Ibid., pp. 542–43.

51. East India House on Leadenhall Street was the London headquarters of the English East India Company. In addition to housing offices for executives, it had a large salesroom where merchants could purchase goods brought back on the company's ships.

52. Letter from Pomeroys and Streatfeild, March 31, 1757. White, *Beekman Mercantile Papers*, vol. 2, p. 632.

53. Letter from Pomeroys and Streatfeild, October 3, 1755. Ibid., pp. 548–49.

54. Order to Pomeroys and Hodgkin, September 24, 1767. Ibid., pp. 913–14.

55. For more on the short-lived "China Blue" process, as well as copperplate printing, see Montgomery, *Printed Textiles*, pp. 194–95, 212–86, and Floud, "The English Contribution to the Early History of Indigo Printing," pp. 344–49. For the order to Pomeroys and Hodgkin, see White, *Beekman Mercantile Papers*, vol. 2, pp. 942–46.

56. Letter from Pomeroys and Hodgkin, October 19, 1759. White, *Beekman Mercantile Papers*, vol. 2, pp. 644–45.

57. Letter from Pomeroys and Hodgkin, August 19, 1766. Ibid., p. 909.

58. Letter from Pomeroys and Hodgkin, October 22, 1768. Ibid., p. 917. All these are Chinese woven silks; a "Goshee" was likely a silk-and-cotton blend; "Powee" is perhaps a misspelling of *Poisee*, a satin painted with floral motifs, and *Gorgoron* (*gorgoroon*) was heavy ribbed silk. See Lee-Whitman, "The Silk Trade," pp. 21–41.

59. Letter from Pomeroys and Hodgkin, September 8, 1770. White, *Beekman Mercantile Papers*, vol. 2, p. 927. See note 6 above for Spitalfield silks.

60. Letter from Pomeroys and Hodgkin, February 6, 1771. White, *Beekman Mercantile Papers*, vol. 2, pp. 932–33.

61. Letter and order to T. Pomeroy, January 12, 1784. Ibid., vol. 3, pp. 1179–83.

62. Letter to B. Pomeroy & Son, May 30, 1775. Ibid., vol. 2, p. 948. In 1780, during the war, Beekman ordered some textiles from George Clifford and Company, a firm based in Amsterdam. Ibid., vol. 3, pp. 985–88.

63. Beekman placed his last large order on October 5, 1784. Ibid., vol. 3, pp. 1185–86. He seems to have taken his sons William and Abraham into the mercantile business with him that same year and changed the firm name to James Beekman and Sons. Judging from newspaper ads in which his name appears, James Beekman spent much of his time after the war selling real estate.

64. Although the British monopoly on trade with the United States ended in 1783, the English East India Company remained in business until 1874. The American market for EIC textiles shrank over time, and in fact the balance of trade completely shifted by the middle of the nineteenth century, when American-grown raw cotton accounted for approximately half the value of all United States exports. At this time, 77 percent of the 800 million pounds of cotton processed in Britain was from the American South. The impact of American cotton industrially spun and woven in both Europe and the United States had a devastating effect on the cotton textile producers of

India. For more on this subject, see Beverly Lemire, *Cotton* (Oxford and New York: Berg, 2011), pp. 83–98.

65. Diane L. Fagan Affleck, *Just New from the Mills: Printed Cottons in America, Late Nineteenth and Early Twentieth Centuries,* exh. cat. (North Andover, Mass.: The Museum of American Textile History, 1987), p. 11.

66. The Tariff Act of 1857 exempted all imported raw silk from duty, making it affordable to manufacturers, while successive tariff acts in 1861 and 1864 imposed steep duties on imported silk fabrics.

Global Colors

1. See Charles E. Pearson and Paul E. Hoffman, *The Last Voyage of El Nuevo Constante: The Wreck and Recovery of an Eighteenth-Century Spanish Ship off the Louisiana Coast* (Baton Rouge: Louisiana State University Press, 1995).

2. The ship, purchased by a Spanish merchant from the English trading firm Bewicke-Timmerman, originally left Spain with 1,200 boxes of mercury for use in the silver amalgamation process. Ibid., pp. 24–25.

3. Ibid., pp. 39–44.

4. See, for example, Jenny Balfour-Paul, *Indigo* (Chicago: Fitzroy Dearborn Publishers, 2000), and Dominique Cardon, *Natural Dyes: Sources, Tradition, Technology and Science* (London: Archetype, 2007), pp. 335–408. See also Florence H. Pettit, *America's Indigo Blues: Resist-Printed and Dyed Textiles of the Eighteenth Century* (New York: Hastings House, 1974).

5. For indigo cultivation in colonial North America, see David H. Rembert, Jr., "The Indigo of Commerce in Colonial North America," *Economic Botany* 33, no. 2 (April–June 1979), pp. 128–34.

6. See Elena Phipps, "Cochineal Red: The Art History of a Color," *The Metropolitan Museum of Art Bulletin,* n.s., 67, no. 3 (Winter 2010), pp. 1–48, cover illus.

7. Bernardino de Sahagún, "Historia general de las cosas de Nueva España," Mediceo Palatino 218–20, Biblioteca Medicea Laurenziana, Florence, MS 220, lib XI, cap 11, fol. 216v.

8. Cardon, *Natural Dyes,* pp. 263–300.

9. Ibid., p. 58; Kenneth G. Ponting, *A Dictionary of Dyes and Dyeing* (London: Bell and Hyman, 1980), p. 254.

10. See, for example, Joe Ben Wheat and Ann Lane Hedlund, *Blanket Weaving in the Southwest* (Tucson: University of Arizona Press, 2003), chap. 4, "Bayeta," pp. 69–89.

11. Raymond L. Lee, "Cochineal Production and Trade in New Spain to 1600," *The Americas* 4, no. 4 (April 1948), p. 453, citing Antonio de Herrera y Tordesillas, *Historia general de los hechos de los castellanos en las Islas y Tierrafirme del Mar Océano: Publicada por acuerdo de la academia de la historia,* 17 vols. (Madrid: [Tipografía de Archivos], 1934–57), vol. 7, p. 25. R[obin] A. Donkin includes the quotation in *Spanish Red: An Ethnogeographical Study of Cochineal and the Opuntia Cactus,* Transactions of the American Philosophical Society, n.s., 67, no. 5 (Philadelphia: American Philosophical Society, 1977), p. 23 n. 17.

12. Lee, "Cochineal Production and Trade," pp. 449–73.

13. Brian H. Davies, "Logwood under the Microscope," in *Dyes in History and Archaeology 21, Including Papers Presented at the 21st Meeting Held at Avignon and Lauris, France, 10–12 October 2002,* edited by Jo Kirby and Chris Cooksey (London: Archetype Publications, 2008), pp. 180, 186 n. 2; Mark Catesby, *The Natural History of Carolina, Florida and the Bahama Islands,* rev. ed., 2 vols. (1754; London, 1771), p. 66.

14. See Balfour-Paul, *Indigo,* pp. 63–64.

15. Spanish legislation also forbade locking spinners into enclosures. Archivo General de Indias, Seville, Legislao Book 6 tit 14 Law VI. April 6, 1563. See also Robert S. Smith, "Indigo Production and Trade in Colonial Guatemala," *The Hispanic American Historical Review* 39, no. 2 (May 1959), pp. 181–211.

16. Frederick P. Bowser, *The African Slave in Colonial Peru, 1524–1650* (Palo Alto: Stanford University Press, 1974).

17. See Robert S. Lopez, "The Trade in Medieval Europe: The South," in *The Cambridge Economic History of Europe,* vol. 2, *Trade and Industry in the Middle Ages,* edited by M[ichael] M. Postan and Edward Miller, 2nd ed. (1952; Cambridge: Cambridge University Press, 1987), pp. 306–401. See also Linda Komaroff et al., *Gifts of the Sultan: The Arts of Giving at the Islamic Courts,* exh. cat. (Los Angeles: Los Angeles County Museum of Art, 2011).

18. For a detailed discussion of the various red-producing insects worldwide, see Cardon, *Natural Dyes,* pp. 607–66.

19. "Matrícula de Tributos," Codex 35–52, Biblioteca del Museo Nacional de Antropología y Historia, Mexico City.

20. See Phipps, "Cochineal Red," pp. 18–21.

21. Bernardino de Sahagún, "Historia general de las cosas de Nueva España," Mediceo Palatino 218–20, Biblioteca Medicea Laurenziana, Florence, fol. 369r.

22. José Antonio de Alzate y Ramírez, "Memoria sobre la naturaleza, cultivo, y beneficio de la grana [Mexico City, 1777]," Ayer MS 1031, Edward E. Ayer Manuscript Collection, Newberry Library, Chicago, fols. 18r, 199.

23. Archivo General de Indias, COCHINILLA 1575; ES.41091 .AGI/28.5.15.3//PATRONATO,182,R.50.

24. Gonzalo Gómez Cervantes, *La vida económica y social de Nueva España al finalizar el siglo XVI,* edited and annotated by Alberto Maria Carreño, Biblioteca histórica mexicana de obras inéditas 19 (Mexico City: Antiqua librería Robredo, de J. Porrúa e hijos, 1944), p. 174. Alzate y Ramírez, "Memoria," fol. 198.

25. *Le teinturier parfait, ou, L'art de teindre les soyes . . . Suite des secrets concernant les arts et metiers* (Paris: Claude Jombert, 1716), p. 298.

26. [Jean] Hellot, [Pierre Joseph] Macquer, and [Le]pileur d'Apligny, *The Art of Dying Wool, Silk, and Cotton* (London: R. Baldwin, 1789), pp. 120–21.

27. For the salvage of cochineal, see Dorothy Dodd, "Jacob Housman of Indian Key," *Tequesta* 8 (1948), pp. 3–4; http://digitalcollections.fiu.edu/tequesta/files/1948/48_1_01.pdf.

28. Hellot, Macquer, and d'Apligny, *The Art of Dying Wool, Silk, and Cotton,* p. 125.

29. "Damaged cochineal is sometimes sold at Cádiz, either shipwrecked or by some mis-chance, wet with sea water," which lessens the price (ibid.).

30. Asa Ellis, *The Country Dyer's Assistant* (Brookfield, Mass., 1798), p. 15.

31. "The Evils of Cochineal, Tlaxcala, Mexico (1553)," in *Colonial Spanish America: A Documentary History,* edited by Kenneth Mills and William B. Taylor (Wilmington, Del.: Scholarly Resources, 1998), p. 92.

32. Nicolas-Joseph Thiéry de Menonville, *Traité de la culture du nopal, et de l'education de la cochenille . . .* (Cap-Français and Paris, 1787); published in English as *Travels to Guaxaca . . .* in 1812.

33. See Donkin, *Spanish Red,* p. 46.

34. Ibid., p. 49.

35. Ibid., pp. 50–51.

36. Ibid.

37. *Indigofera,* a member of the Leguminosae family, is the primary source of indigo dye. Other plant families, including Cruciferae (woads) and Polygonaceae (Asian indigo), also contain the indigo dye compound indican. For an extensive description of the plant sources and processes used for indigo dyeing around the world, see Cardon, *Natural Dyes,* chap. 8, pp. 355–408.

38. Rembert, "Indigo of Commerce," p. 128.

39. Cardon, *Natural Dyes,* p. 365.

40. Through the 1770s approximately 70 percent of Guatemalan indigo was shipped to Spain. A register from 1786–87 of the *alcabalas* (visiting merchants) to a Cuzco *obraje* indicates that most of the indigo consumed that year was imported from Guatemala. Neus Escandell-Tur, *Producción y comercio de tejidos coloniales: Los obrajes y chorrillos del Cusco, 1570–1820,* Archivos de Historia Andina 23 (Cuzco: Centro de Estudios Regionales Andinos, "Bartolomé de Las Casas," 1997), p. 196. For indigo commerce, see Troy S. Floyd, "The Indigo Merchant: Promoter of Central American Economic Development, 1750–1808," *Business History Review* 39, no. 4 (Winter 1965), pp. 466–88, esp. p. 474.

41. Rembert, "Indigo of Commerce," p. 129 (citing Dwight Jackson Huneycutt, "The Economics of the Indigo Industry in South Carolina" [M.A. thesis, University of South Carolina, Columbia, S.C., 1949]).

42. See Balfour-Paul, *Indigo,* chap. 3, esp. pp. 63–66, and Cardon, *Natural Dyes,* p. 365.

43. See Subhas Bhattacharya, "Indigo Planters, Ram Mohan Roy and the 1833 Charter Act," *Social Scientist* 4, no. 3 (October 1975), pp. 56–65. See also Raaj Sah, "Features of British Indigo in India," *Social Scientist* 9, no. 2–3 (September–October 1980), pp. 67–79.

44. Records of the Jewish merchant house of Ibn 'Awkal found in Fustat, Egypt, indicate that brazilwood from Sumatra was frequently imported, and in large quantities. R. J. Forbes, *Studies in Ancient Technology* (Leiden: E. J. Brill, 1955–64), vol. 4, p. 108. See Cardon, *Natural Dyes,* pp. 279–89, and Norman A. Stillman, "The Eleventh-Century Merchant House of Ibn 'Awkal (A Geniza Study)," *Journal of the Economic and Social History of the Orient* 16, no. 1 (April 1973), pp. 39–41.

45. Cardon, *Natural Dyes,* p. 297.

46. Ibid., p. 275 n. 106, citing Bernardino José de Sousa et al., *O pao-brasil na história nacional,* 2nd ed. (1939; São Paulo: Companhia Editora Nacional, 1978).

47. Cardon, *Natural Dyes,* p. 288.

48. Ibid., p. 280.

49. Ibid., p. 279.

50. *Instruction générale pour la teinture des laines . . .* (Paris: Impr. de François Muguet, 1671), p. 21, attributed to Colbert and M. d'Albo.

51. Hellot, Macquer, and d'Apligny, *The Art of Dying Wool, Silk, and Cotton,* p. 312.

52. Davies, "Logwood under the Microscope," pp. 181, 187 n. 6.

53. Pierre-Joseph Macquer, "Examination et comparaison de la solidité du teinture de soie en noir des principaux teinturierers de Lyon et Gênes," October 10, 1777, AN F/12/2259, in Sarah Lowengard, *The Creation of Color in Eighteenth-Century Europe* (New York: Gutenberg-e, [2006]); http://www.gutenberg-e.org/lowengard/B_Chap01.html#note21.

54. William Dampier, *A New Voyage Round the World* (London: James Knapton, 1699), p. 80, quoted in Michael A. Camille, "Historical Geography of the Belizean Logwood Trade," *Yearbook/Conference of Latin Americanist Geographers* 22 (1996), pp. 77–85.

55. See David Morgan McJunkin, "Logwood: An Inquiry into the Historical Biogeography of Haematoxylum Campechianum L. and Related Dyewoods of the Neotropics" (Ph.D. diss., University of California, Los Angeles, 1991).

56. Cardon, *Natural Dyes,* p. 198.

57. Edward Bancroft, *Experimental Researches Concerning the Philosophy of Permanent Colours . . . ,* 2nd ed. (1794; London: T. Cadell and W. Davies, 1813).

58. According to Jean Hellot, "for the scarletts, the *roucou* paste as imported from the Indies is added to the boiling of the silk . . . [which] gives it an *Isabella* color [orange with a yellowish tinge], tolerably permanent, yellowing [but] a little." Hellot, Macquer, and d'Apligny, *The Art of Dying Wool, Silk, and Cotton,* p. 307.

59. "La manière de nègotier dans les Indes orientales," section regarding agreements with the Indian painters translated and published in Paul R. Schwartz, *Printing on Cotton at Ahmedabad, India, in 1678, from an Unedited Manuscript in the Bibliothèque Nationale, Paris* [MS Français 14614], Museum Monograph 1 (Ahmedabad: Calico Museum of Textiles, 1969), p. 6.

60. Water is a critical component of dyeing, and regions that have pure, clean water generally achieve the best results. The Inca in Peru understood this and channeled especially pure water into Cuzco; see Elena Phipps, "Textile Colors and Colorants in the Andes," in *Colors between Two Worlds: The Florentine Codex of Bernardino de Sahagún,* edited by Gerhard Wolf, Joseph Connors, and Louis A. Waldman (Florence: Villa I Tatti, 2011), pp. 256–80. Georges Roques mentions in his 1678–80 manuscript cited above, note 59, that Indian dyers waited until the river had cleared sufficiently after the rainy season before beginning the dyeing process. Schwartz, *Printing on Cotton at Ahmedabad,* p. 5.

61. See the excellent chapter on mordants in Cardon, *Natural Dyes,* pp. 20–49. Schwartz, *Printing on Cotton at Ahmedabad,* p. 12, describes soured wheat flour being soaked in water along with myrobalans to produce black.

62. For more on shellfish dye in the Americas, see Peter Gerhard, "Shellfish Dye in America," in *xxxv Congreso Internacional de Americanistas, México, 1962: Actas y memorias,* 3 vols. (Mexico City: Editorial Libros de México, 1964), vol. 3, pp. 177–90.

63. The Sanskrit word *chitra* originated as the term for "spotted cloth"; see Schwartz, *Printing on Cotton at Ahmedabad,* p. 20 n. 8. The Portuguese term can also be related to a type of bird with polychrome feathers. See also John Irwin and Katharine B. Brett, *Origins of Chintz, with a Catalogue of Indo-European Cotton-Paintings in the Victoria and Albert Museum, London, and the Royal Ontario*

Museum, Toronto (London: Her Majesty's Stationery Office, 1970), and Mattiebelle Gittinger, *Master Dyers to the World: Technique and Trade in Early Indian Dyed Cotton Textiles,* exh. cat. (Washington, D.C.: The Textile Museum, 1982).

64. Beaulieu's manuscript as well as thirteen of his samples are in the Bibliothèque du Muséum National d'Histoire Naturelle, Paris (MS Beaulieu 193). For a transcription and translation, see P. R. Schwartz, Appendix A, in Irwin and Brett, *Origins of Chintz,* pp. 36–41.

65. As most dyes, such as madder, require a high temperature in the dyebath to be efficacious, the wax reserve can only be used for those dyes (including indigo) that do not require heat, since the wax would melt.

66. A similar practice devised by Inca dyers for use on camelid-hair weavings amazed the Spanish writer Bernabé Cobo (1582–1657), who observed in his *Historia del Nuevo Mundo* (1653) that the Inca master dyers were able to create purple cloth in a red dyebath, the red, in this case, being cochineal. See Bernabé Cobo, *Obras del P. Bernabé Cobo,* vol. 1, *Historia del Nuevo Mondo,* edited by Francisco Mateos (Madrid: Ediciones Atlas, 1956), pp. 113–16. This process is still used today, as confirmed by Ana Roquero's field observations of the cochineal dyers of Ecuador; Ana Roquero, *Tintes y tintoreros de América: Catálogo de materias primas y registro etnográfico . . .* (Madrid: Ministerio de Cultura, 2006), p. 149.

67. Another eyewitness account, with more accurate descriptions of the process, was provided to a colleague in Paris by Gaston Laurent Coeurdoux (1691–1799), a French Jesuit stationed in Pondicherry from 1742 to 1747: "I do not know whether the letter I wrote in 1742 on painted cottons in India can prove of any assistance in perfecting the art of dyeing in Europe: that at least was the aim I had in mind." For a transcription and translation of the Courdeaux letters, see P. R. Schwartz, Appendix B, in Irwin and Brett, *Origins of Chintz,* pp. 42–53 (quote from letter from December 22, 1747; Schwartz, Appendix B, p. 43). Another account of the block printing of fabrics in Ahmedabad, in northwestern India, was made by Georges Roques in 1678–80 and was translated and published in Schwartz, *Printing on Cotton at Ahmedabad.*

68. Delormois, *L'art de faire les indiennes* (Paris: Libraires Associés, 1786).

69. Cardon, *Natural Dyes,* p. 116. In 1746 dyers from Smyrna were brought to France to establish Turkey Red dyeing factories near Rouen and Langedoc. Anthony S. Travis et al., *From Turkey Red to Tyrian Purple: Textile Colours for the Industrial Revolution . . . ,* exh. cat. ([Jerusalem]: Jewish National and University Library, 1993). See also Robert Chenciner, *Madder Red: A History of Luxury and Trade . . .* (Richmond: Curzon Press, 2000), pp. 187–95. For more on the exact steps of dyeing Turkey Red, see J. N. Liles,

The Art and Craft of Natural Dyeing: Traditional Recipes for Modern Use (Knoxville: University of Tennessee Press, 1990), pp. 111–23.

70. Remarkably, the dye, which is insoluble in water, was preserved, and analysis of its components has identified the wood as *Pterocarpus santalinus.* Rex Cowen, "Shipwrecks, Dyestuffs and the India Trade," in *Textiles from India: The Global Trade; Papers Presented at a Conference on the Indian Textile Trade, Kolkata, 12–14 October 2003,* edited by Rosemary Crill (Calcutta: Seagull Books, 2006), pp. 374–88.

71. George W. Taylor, "A Jouy Calico Print Using Chay Root," *Dyes in History and Archaeology,* no. 9 (1990), pp. 32–34.

72. Ibid., p. 32.

73. Georges Roques, for example, recorded in 1678 that tests in Marseille had been successful in proving the efficacy of sappan-wood: "The dyers of France had proved the use of sappan wood sent to Le Havre by the Compagnie several years earlier, and that they had declared themselves satisfied." Schwartz, *Printing on Cotton at Ahmedabad,* p. 13.

74. Lowengard, *The Creation of Color in Eighteenth-Century Europe.*

75. Sidney M. Edelstein, "How Napoleon Aided the Early Dyeing Industry of France," in *Historical Notes on the Wet-Processing Industry,* rev. ed. ([New York]: Dexter Chemical Corporation, 1972), pp. 17–18.

76. They included José de Acosta (1540–1600) and Bernabé Cobo, who documented the natural world of the Andes, Alexander von Humboldt (1769–1859), who described the natural wonders of New Spain, and many others who traveled to Asia and Africa. These travelers also bore witness to the demise of indigenous cultures as they were transformed by the social and political events of the era. See, for example, Al[exander von] Humboldt, *Essai politique sur le royaume de la Nouvelle-Espagne,* 5 vols. (Paris: F. Schoell, 1811), bk. 4, chap. 10, on cochineal.

77. Another specimen of the same species in the Royal Botanic Gardens at Kew reportedly dates to 1761.

78. Jean Ryhiner, a Swiss maker of calico, published some of the first dye recipes that adapt Indian processes for European production; Schwartz, *Printing on Cotton at Ahmedabad,* p. 18. On the evolution of the scientific method in the dyeing industry from the Renaissance through the nineteenth century, see Franco Brunello, *The Art of Dyeing in the History of Mankind* (1968; Vicenza: N. Pozza, 1973), chaps. 5 and 6.

79. For a history of the development of soaps and bleaches in the dyeing industry, see Sidney M. Edelstein, "The Role of Chemistry in the Development of Dyeing and Bleaching," in *Historical Notes on the Wet-Processing Industry,* pp. 154–59.

BIBLIOGRAPHY

Abraham, Meera. *Two Medieval Merchant Guilds of South India.* New Delhi: Manohar Publications, 1988.

Ackermann, Hans Christoph, et al. *Seidengewebe des 18. Jahrhunderts.* Vol. 1, *Bizarre Seiden.* Riggisberg: Abegg-Stiftung, 2000.

Ådahl, Karin. "Claes Brorson Rålamb's Embassy to the Sublime Porte in 1657–1658." In *The Sultan's Procession: The Swedish Embassy to Sultan Mehmed IV in 1657–1658 and the Rålamb Paintings,* edited by Karin Ådahl, pp. 8–25. Istanbul: Swedish Research Institute in Istanbul, 2006.

Adenaike, Carolyn Keyes. "West African Textiles, 1500–1800." In *Textiles: Production, Trade and Demand,* edited by Maureen Fennell Mazzaoui, pp. 251–61. Aldershot, U.K., and Brookfield, Vt.: Ashgate, 1998.

Affleck, Diane L. Fagan. *Just New from the Mills: Printed Cottons in America, Late Nineteenth and Early Twentieth Centuries.* Exh. cat. North Andover, Mass.: The Museum of American Textile History, 1987.

Akveld, Leo [M.], and Els M. Jacobs, eds. *De kleurrijke wereld van de VOC: National Jubileumboek VOC 1602/2002.* Bussum: Thoth, 2002.

Alcalá, Luisa Elena. "Material Choices: Representing the Virgin's Domesticity in Colonial Mexico." Conference paper presented at "Contested Visions in the Spanish Colonial World," Los Angeles County Museum of Art and University of California, Los Angeles, December 2–4, 2011.

Alzate y Ramírez, José Antonio de. "Memoria sobre la naturaleza, cultivo, y beneficio de la grana [Mexico City, 1777]." Ayer MS 1031, Edward E. Ayer Manuscript Collection, Newberry Library, Chicago.

The American Magazine and Historical Chronicle 1 (December 1743), pp. 146–52.

America's Historical Newspapers, Including Early American Newspapers. Series 1–7, 1690–1922. New York and Chester, Vt.: Readex, 2006– ; http://infoweb.newsbank.com.

Andaya, Leonard Y. "Cultural State Formation in Eastern Indonesia." In *Southeast Asia in the Early Modern Era: Trade, Power, and Belief,* edited by Anthony Reid, pp. 23–41. Ithaca: Cornell University Press, 1993.

———. *The World of Maluku: Eastern Indonesia in the Early Modern Period.* Honolulu: University of Hawai'i Press, 1993.

Armella de Aspe, Virginia. *Hilos del cielo: Las vestiduras litúrgicas de la Catedral Metropolitana de México.* Mexico City: Instituto Nacional de Antropología e Historia, Consejo Nacional para la Cultura y las Artes, 2007.

Armella de Aspe, Virginia, and Guillermo Tovar y de Teresa. *Bordados y bordadores.* Mexico City: Grupo Gutsa, Fernández Cueto Editores, 1992.

Arnold, Janet. *Patterns of Fashion: Englishwomen's Dresses and Their Construction.* Vol. 1, *C[irca] 1660–1860.* New York: Drama Books, 1977.

———. *Patterns of Fashion: The Cut and Construction of Clothes for Men and Women c1560–1620.* London: Macmillan, 1985.

———. *Queen Elizabeth's Wardrobe Unlock'd: The Inventories of the Wardrobe of Robes Prepared in July 1600, Edited from Stowe MS 557 in the British Library, MS LR 2/121 in the Public Record Office, London, and MS V.B.72 in the Folger Shakespeare Library, Washington, D.C.* Leeds: Maney, 1988.

Arnolli, Gieneke. *Mode in Friesland/Moade yn Fryslân/Fashion in Friesland, 1750–1950.* Leeuwarden: Friese pers Boekerij, 2000.

Arthur, [E]liz[abeth]. *Embroidery 1600–1700 at the Burrell Collection.* Exh. cat. London: John Murray; Glasgow: Glasgow Museums, 1995.

Assadourian, Carlos Sempat. "The Colonial Economy: The Transfer of the European System of Production to New Spain and Peru." *Journal of Latin American Studies* 24, Quincentenary Supplement [*The Colonial and Post-Colonial Experience: Five Centuries of Spanish and Portuguese America*] (1992), pp. 55–68.

Atasoy, Nurhan, and Lâle Uluç. *Impressions of Ottoman Culture in Europe, 1453–1699.* Istanbul: Armaggan Publications, 2012.

Atasoy, Nurhan, Walter B. Denny, Louise W. Mackie, and Hülya Tezcan. *Ipek: The Crescent and the Rose; Imperial Ottoman Silks and Velvets.* London: Azimuth Editions, 2001.

Avila, Francisco de. "Prefación al libro de los sermons [1645]." In *Informaciones acerca de la religión y gobierno de los Incas,* edited by Horacio H. Urteaga and Carlos Romero. [Lima, 1918].

Backlin, Hedy. *The Four Continents from the Collection of James Hazen Hyde.* Exh. cat. New York: Cooper Union Museum, 1961.

Backscheider, Paula R. "Defoe, Daniel (1660?–1731)." In *Oxford Dictionary of National Biography,* edited by H. C. G. Matthew, Brian Harrison, and Lawrence Goldman. Oxford: Oxford University Press, 2004. Online ed., January 2008; http://www.oxforddnb.com.library. metmuseum.org/view/article/7421 (accessed February 12, 2013).

Baibourtian, Vahan. *International Trade and the Armenian Merchants in the Seventeenth Century.* New Delhi: Sterling Publishers, 2004.

Bailey, Gauvin Alexander. *Art on the Jesuit Missions in Asia and Latin America, 1542–1773.* Toronto, Buffalo, and London: University of Toronto Press, 1999.

———. "Incarnate Images: The Jesuits' Artistic Program in Portuguese Asia and Beyond." In *Encompassing the Globe: Portugal and the World in the 16th and 17th Centuries,* by Jay A. Levenson et al., pp. 213–31. Exh. cat. Lisbon: Instituto dos Museos e da Conservação, Museu Nacional de Arte Antiga, 2009.

Baker, Patricia L. "Wrought of Gold or Silver: Honorific Garments in Seventeenth Century Iran." In *Carpets and Textiles in the Iranian World, 1400–1700: Proceedings of the Conference Held at the Ashmolean Museum on 30–31 August 2003,* edited by Jon Thompson, Daniel Shaffer, and Pirjetta Mildh, pp. 158–67. Oxford: May Beattie Archive, Ashmolean Museum, Oxford; [Genoa]: Bruschettini Foundation for Islamic and Asian Art, 2010.

Baker, Patricia L., Hülya Tezcan, and Jennifer Wearden. *Silks for the Sultans: Ottoman Imperial Garments from the Topkapi Palace, Istanbul.* [Istanbul]: Ertuğ and Kocabiyik, 1996.

Balfour-Paul, Jenny. *Indigo.* Chicago: Fitzroy Dearborn Publishers, 2000.

Bancroft, Edward. *Experimental Researches Concerning the Philosophy of Permanent Colours . . .* 2nd ed. 1794. London: T. Cadell and W. Davies, 1813.

Barbier, Jacques A. "The Culmination of the Bourbon Reforms, 1787–1792." *The Hispanic American Historical Review* 57, no. 1 (February 1977), pp. 51–68.

Barbosa, Duarte. *The Book of Duarte Barbosa . . . 1518 A.D.* Edited by Mansel Longworth Dames. 2 vols. Works Issued by the Hakluyt Society, Second series 44, 49. London: Hakluyt Society, 1918–21.

Barnes, Ruth. *Indian Block-Printed Textiles in Egypt: The Newberry Collection in the Ashmolean Museum, Oxford.* 2 vols. Oxford and New York: Clarendon Press, 1997.

Barnes, Ruth, Steven Cohen, and Rosemary Crill. *Trade, Temple and Court: Indian Textiles from the TAPI Collection.* Mumbai: India Book House, 2002.

Barratt, Carrie Rebora. "Oriental Undress and the Artist." *Porticus: Journal of the Memorial Art Gallery of the University of Rochester* 20 (2001), pp. 18–31.

Bassani, Ezio, William B. Fagg, and Peter Mark. *Africa and the Renaissance: Art in Ivory.* Edited by Susan Vogel. Exh. cat. New York: The Center for African Art, 1988.

Bast, Oliver. "Germany. i. German-Persian Diplomatic Relations." In *Encyclopaedia Iranica,* edited by Ehsan Yarshater, vol. 10 (2001), pp. 506–19. London and New York: Routledge & Kegan Paul, 1985– .

Baugh, Daniel A. *The Global Seven Years War, 1754–1763: Britain and France in a Great Power Contest.* Harlow, U.K.: Longman, Peason Education, 2011.

Baumgarten, Linda R. "The Textile Trade in Boston, 1650–1700." In *Arts of the Anglo-American Community in the Seventeenth Century,* edited by Ian M. G. Quimby, pp. 219–73. Winterthur Conference Report, 1974. Winterthur, Del.: The Henry Francis du Pont Winterthur Museum; Charlottesville: The University Press of Virginia, 1975.

———. *What Clothes Reveal: The Language of Clothing in Colonial and Federal America; The Colonial Williamsburg Collection.* Williamsburg, Va.: Colonial Williamsburg Foundation, 2002.

Bayer, Andrea, et al. *Art and Love in Renaissance Italy.* Exh. cat. New York: The Metropolitan Museum of Art, 2008.

Bazant, Jan. "Evolución de la industria textil Poblana (1544–1845)." *Historia mexicana* 13, no. 4 (April–June 1964), pp. 473–516.

———. "Evolution of the Textile Industry of Puebla, 1544–1845." *Comparative Studies in Society and History* 7, no. 1 (October 1964), pp. 56–69.

[Beach, Moses Yale.] *Wealth and Biography of the Wealthy Citizens of New York City, Comprising an Alphabetical Arrangement of Persons Estimated to be Worth $100,000 and Upwards.* 6th ed. New York: The Sun Office, 1845.

Bean, Susan S. "The Indian Origins of the Bandanna." *The Magazine Antiques* 156 (December 1999), pp. 832–39.

Bedini, Silvio A. *The Pope's Elephant.* Manchester: Carcanet Press, 1997.

Beer, Alice Baldwin. *Trade Goods: A Study of Indian Chintz in the Collection of the Cooper-Hewitt Museum of Decorative Arts and Design, Smithsonian Institution.* Washington, D.C.: Smithsonian Institution Press, 1970.

Benson, Nancy C. *New Mexico Colcha Club: Spanish Colonial Embroidery and the Women Who Saved It.* Santa Fe: Museum of New Mexico Press, 2008.

Berg, Maxine. *Luxury and Pleasure in Eighteenth-Century Britain.* Oxford and New York: Oxford University Press, 2005.

Bernier, François. *Travels in the Mogul Empire*, A.D. *1656–1668*. Edited by Archibald Constable. London: Constable and Co., 1891.

Bhattacharya, Subhas. "Indigo Planters, Ram Mohan Roy and the 1833 Charter Act." *Social Scientist* 4, no. 3 (October 1975), pp. 56–65.

Bier, Carol. "Islamic Art, VI: Textiles, 2. Fabrics, (iii) c. 1500 and after, (c) Iran." In *Grove Art Online*, Oxford Art Online; http://www.oxfordartonline.com/subscriber/article/grove/art/T041771pg34 (accessed October 11, 2012).

Bier, Carol, and Mogens Bencard. *The Persian Velvets at Rosenborg*. Copenhagen: De Danske Kongers Kronologiske Samling, 1995.

Bier, Carol, et al. *Woven from the Soul, Spun from the Heart: Textile Arts of Safavid and Qajar Iran, 16th–19th Centuries*. Exh. cat. Washington, D.C.: The Textile Museum, 1987.

Bishop, LuAnn. "Campus Honors Man Who Gave Yale Its Name." *Yale Bulletin and Calendar* 27, no. 28 (April 12–19, 1999); http://www.yale.edu/opa/arc-ybc/v27.n28/story3.html.

Black, Christopher, and Pamela Gravestock, eds. *Early Modern Confraternities in Europe and the Americas: International and Interdisciplinary Perspectives*. Aldershot, U.K., and Brookfield, Vt.: Ashgate, 2006.

Blair, Emma Helen, and James Alexander Robertson, eds. *The Philippine Islands, 1493–1803: Explorations by Early Navigators, Descriptions . . .* 55 vols. Cleveland: A. H. Clark Co., 1903–9.

Blum, Dilys E. *The Fine Art of Textiles: The Collections of the Philadelphia Museum of Art*. Philadelphia: Philadelphia Museum of Art, 1997.

———. "Gremial of Archbishop Juan de Zumárraga." In *The Arts in Latin America, 1492–1820*, by Joseph J. Rishel et al., p. 169, no. 11-4. Exh. cat. New Haven and London: Yale University Press, 2006.

———. "Indo-Portuguese Bedcover, Late Seventeenth Century." *Philadelphia Museum of Art Bulletin* 86, no. 365–66 [*Gifts from The Friends of the Museum, 1985–90*] (Spring 1990), pp. 8–10.

Blum, Stella, ed. *Eighteenth-Century French Fashion Plates in Full Color: 64 Engravings from the "Galerie des modes," 1778–1787*. New York: Dover Publications, 1982.

Borah, Woodrow Wilson. *Silk Raising in Colonial Mexico*. Ibero-Americana 20. Berkeley and Los Angeles: University of California Press, 1943.

Born, Wolfgang. "Scarlet." *CIBA Review* 1, no. 7 (March 1938), pp. 206–27.

Boston Chronicle. See *America's Historical Newspapers*.

Boston Evening-Post. See *America's Historical Newspapers*.

Boston News-Letter. See *America's Historical Newspapers*.

Boston Post-Boy. See *America's Historical Newspapers*.

Boston Weekly Post-Boy. See *America's Historical Newspapers*.

Boucher, François, and Yvonne Deslandres. *20,000 Years of Fashion: The History of Costume and Personal Adornment*. Expanded ed. 1967. New York: Harry N. Abrams, 1987.

Boullaye-le-Gouz, François de la. *Les voyages et observations du Sieur de la Boullaye-le-Gouz gentilhomme angeuin*. Paris: Gervais Clousier, 1653.

Bowser, Frederick P. *The African Slave in Colonial Peru, 1524–1650*. Palo Alto: Stanford University Press, 1974.

Boxer, C[harles] R. *O grande navio de Amacau*. 4th ed. 1959. Macau: Fundação Oriente, Museu e Centro de Estudos Marítimos de Macau, 1989.

———. *The Great Ship from Amacon*. Lisbon: Centro de Estudos Historicos Ultramarinos, 1959.

Boyajian, James C. *Portuguese Trade in Asia under the Habsburgs, 1580–1640*. Baltimore and London: Johns Hopkins University Press, 1993.

Braamcamp Freire, Anselmo. "Inventário da casa de D. João III em 1534." *Archivo histórico portuguez* 8 (1910), pp. 261–80, 367–90.

———. "Inventário da guarda-roupa de D. Manuel." *Archivo histórico portuguez* 2 (1904), pp. 381–417.

Brand, Jan, and José Teunissen, eds. *Global Fashion/Local Tradition: Over de globalisering van mode*. Exh. cat. Warnsveld: Uitgeverij Terra Lannoo; Utrecht: Centraal Museum, 2005.

Bräutigam, Herbert, and Cornelia Morper. *Über den ziehenden Wolken der Fuji*. Exh. cat. Gotha: Gothaer Kultur- und Fremdenverkehrsbetriebe, 2000.

Breck, Joseph. "Four Seventeenth-Century Pintadoes." *Metropolitan Museum Studies* 1, no. 1 (November 1928), pp. 3–15.

———. "Resignation of Miss Frances Morris." *The Metropolitan Museum of Art Bulletin* 24, no. 10 (October 1929), p. 266.

Brédif, Josette. *Toiles de Jouy: Classic Printed Textiles from France, 1760–1843*. New York and London: Thames and Hudson, 1989.

Bremer-David, Charissa. *French Tapestries and Textiles in the J. Paul Getty Museum*. Los Angeles: The J. Paul Getty Museum, 1997.

Brett, K[atharine] B. "The Flowering Tree in Indian Chintz." *Journal of Indian Textile History*, no. 3 (1957), pp. 45–57.

———. "A French Source of Indian Chintz Design." *Journal of Indian Textile History*, no. 2 (1956), pp. 43–52.

———. "Variants of the Flowering Tree Design, Part II." *The Magazine Antiques* 77, no. 3 (March 1960), pp. 280–83.

Breukink-Peeze, Margaretha. "Japanese Robes: A Craze." In *Imitation and Inspiration: Japanese Influence on Dutch Art*, edited by Stefan van Raay, pp. 53–60. Amsterdam: Art Unlimited Books, 1989.

Briend, Christian. *Les objets d'art: Guide des collections*. Lyon: Musée des Beaux-Arts; Paris: Réunion des Musées Nationaux, 1993.

Brockey, Liam Matthew. *Journey to the East: The Jesuit Mission to China, 1579–1724*. Cambridge, Mass.: Belknap Press of Harvard University Press, 2007.

Broudy, Eric. *The Book of Looms: A History of the Handloom from Ancient Times to the Present*. Reprint ed. 1979. Hanover, N.H.: University Press of New England, 1993.

Browne, Clare. "Silk Damask Bed Furnishings in the Early Eighteenth Century—Influences on Choice in Colour and Design." In *Furnishing Textiles: Studies on Seventeenth- and Eighteenth-Century Interior Decoration*, edited by Anna Jolly, pp. 47–58, 223–36. Riggisberger Berichte 17. Riggisberg: Abegg-Stiftung, 2009.

Bruijn, J. R., F. S. Gaastra, and I. Schöffer. *Dutch-Asiatic Shipping in the 17th and 18th Centuries*. 3 vols. Rijks geschiedkundige publicatiën, Grote serie 165–67. The Hague: Martinus Nijhoff, 1987.

Brunelle, Gayle K. "Immigration, Assimilation and Success: Three Families of Spanish Origin in Sixteenth Century Rouen." *The Sixteenth Century Journal* 20, no. 2 (Summer 1989), pp. 203–20.

Brunello, Franco. *The Art of Dyeing in the History of Mankind*. 1968. Vicenza: N. Pozza, 1973.

Buckridge, Steeve O. *The Language of Dress: Resistance and Accommodation in Jamaica, 1760–1890*. Kingston, Jamaica: University of the West Indies Press, 2004.

Bühler, Alfred. "Patola Influences in Southeast Asia." *Journal of Indian Textile History*, no. 4 (1959), pp. 4–46.

Bühler, Alfred, and Eberhard Fischer. *Clamp Resist Dyeing of Fabrics: Towards an Interpretation of Large Wooden Printing-Blocks in the Calico Museum of Textiles, Ahmedabad*. Ahmedabad: Calico Museum of Textiles, 1977.

———. *The Patola of Gujarat: Double Ikat in India*. 2 vols. Basel: Krebs, 1979.

Buono, Amy J. "Winged Migrations: Tupinambá Featherwork and Its Ritual Performance from Brazil to Early Modern Europe." *Center: Record of Activities and Research Reports* [National Gallery of Art, Washington, D.C.] 27 (June 2006–June 2007), pp. 66–69.

Burbidge, Mary Elizabeth. "The Bower Textile Sample Book." *Textile History* 14, no. 2 (Autumn 1983), pp. 213–21.

Burnham, Harold B. *Chinese Velvets: A Technical Study*. Occasional paper (Royal Ontario Museum, Division of Art and Archaeology) 2. Toronto: University of Toronto Press, 1959.

Bushō no yosooi: Sendai-shi Hakubutsukan kaikan sanjisshūnen kinen/Armor and Costumes: Unique Style of the 16th and 17th Century Warlords. Exh. cat. Sendai: Sendai-shi Hakubutsukan (Sendai City Museum), 1991.

Buss, Chiara. *Seta oro Incarnadino: Lusso e devozione nella Lombardia spagnola*. Seta in Lombardia 2. Monza-Brianza, Italy: ISAL, 2011.

Butler, Nola, ed. *Los Angeles County Museum of Art*. World of Art. London: Thames and Hudson, 2003.

Callahan, Colleen R. "A Quilt and Its Pieces." *Metropolitan Museum Journal* 19–20 (1984–85), pp. 97–141.

Camille, Michael A. "Historical Geography of the Belizean Logwood Trade." *Yearbook/Conference of Latin Americanist Geographers* 22 (1996), pp. 77–85.

Cammann, Schuyler [van Rensselaer]. "Chinese Influence in Colonial Peruvian Tapestries." *Textile Museum Journal* 1, no. 3 (December 1964), pp. 21–34.

Cammann, Schuyler van R[ensselaer], and Karin Blomqvist. *Spansk korkåpa av kinesiskt broderi/A Spanish Cope Made from a XVIIth Century Chinese Embroidery*. Malmö: Malmö Museum, 1974.

Campbell, Myrtle. "Embroidered Bodices: An East India Company Connection?" *Costume: The Journal of the Costume Society*, no. 36 (2002), pp. 56–64.

Campbell, Thomas P., et al. *Tapestry in the Baroque: Threads of Splendor*. Exh. cat. New York: The Metropolitan Museum of Art, 2007.

———. *Tapestry in the Renaissance: Art and Magnificence*. Exh. cat. New York: The Metropolitan Museum of Art, 2002.

Campos, Joachim de. "Early Portuguese Accounts of Thailand." In *500 Years of Thai-Portuguese Relations: A Festschrift*, edited by Michael Smithies, pp. 15–36. Bangkok: Siam Society, 2011.

Canby, Sheila R. *The Rebellious Reformer: The Drawings and Paintings of Riza-yi Abbasi of Isfahan*. London: Azimuth Editions, 1996.

Cardon, Dominique. *Natural Dyes: Sources, Tradition, Technology and Science*. London: Archetype, 2007.

Carmichael, [A. C.] *Five Years in Trinidad and St. Vincent: A View of the Social Condition of the White, Coloured, and Negro Population of the West Indies*. 2 vols. London: Whittaker, 1834.

Carvalho, Pedro Moura. *Luxury for Export: Artistic Exchange between India and Portugal around 1600*. Exh. cat. Boston: Isabella Stewart Gardner Museum; Pittsburgh: Gutenberg Periscope Publishing, 2008.

Casale, Giancarlo. *The Ottoman Age of Exploration*. Oxford and New York: Oxford University Press, 2010.

Castelló Yturbide, Teresa, and Marita Martínez del Río de Redo. *Biombos mexicanos*. Mexico City: Instituto Nacional de Antropología e Historia, 1970.

———, eds. *Artes de México* 18, no. 142 [*El rebozo*] (1971), pp. 3–96, cover ill.

Castelló [Y]turbide, Teresa, and Patricia Meade. "Rebozos mexicanos en el extranjero/Mexican Rebozos Abroad." *Artes de México*, n.s., no. 90 [*El rebozo*] (2008), pp. 70–71, 88.

Catalogue of a Loan Exhibition of English Chintz: English Printed Furnishing Fabrics from their Origins until the Present Day. Exh. cat. London: Victoria and Albert Museum; H. M. Stationery Office, 1960.

Catesby, Mark. *The Natural History of Carolina, Florida and the Bahama Islands*. Rev. ed. 2 vols. 1754. London, 1771.

Cazenave, Michel, ed., *Encyclopédie des symboles*. 1996. Paris: Librairie Générale Française, 2004.

Chang, Sheng-ching. "The Pineapple Images by Michael Boym and the Circulation of Pineapple Images in Europe in the 17th Century [in Chinese]." *Gùgōng xuéshù jìkān* (The National Palace Museum Research Quarterly) 28, no. 1 (2010), pp. 79–140.

Chapman, S[tanley] D., and S[erge] Chassagne. *European Textile Printers in the Eighteenth Century: A Study of Peel and Oberkampf*. London: Heinemann Educational Books, The Pasold Fund, 1981.

Chardin, John. *Travels in Persia, 1673–1677*. New York: Dover Publications, 1988.

Charlton, David. "Caravane du Caire, La." In *The New Grove Dictionary of Opera*, edited by Stanley Sadie. *Grove Music Online. Oxford Music Online*. Oxford and New York: Oxford University Press; http://www.oxfordmusiconline.com.library.metmuseum.org/subscriber/article/grove/music/O008260 (accessed July 14, 2012).

Chaudhuri, K. N. *The Trading World of Asia and the English East India Company, 1660–1760*. Cambridge and New York: Cambridge University Press, 1978.

Chenciner, Robert. *Madder Red: A History of Luxury and Trade . . .* Richmond: Curzon Press, 2000.

Chin, J[ames] K. "The Portuguese on the Zhejiang and Fujian Coast prior to 1550 as Seen from Contemporary Chinese Private Records." In *Macau during the Ming Dynasty*, edited by Luís Filipe Barreto, pp. 119–37. Lisbon: Centro Científico e Cultural de Macau, 2009.

Chung, Young Yang. *Silken Threads: A History of Embroidery in China, Korea, Japan, and Vietnam*. New York: Harry N. Abrams, 2004.

Çizakça, Murat. "Incorporation of the Middle East into the European World-Economy." In *Textiles: Production, Trade and Demand*, edited by Maureen Fennell Mazzaoui, pp. 1–25. Aldershot, U.K.: Ashgate, 1998.

Clayton, Muriel, and Alma Oakes. "Early Calico Printers around London." *The Burlington Magazine* 96, no. 614 (May 1954), pp. 135–39.

Clouzot, Henri. *Painted and Printed Fabrics: The History of the Manufactory at Jouy and Other Ateliers in France, 1760–1815* [and] Morris, Frances. *Notes on the History of Cotton Printing, Especially in England and America*. New York: The Metropolitan Museum of Art, 1927.

Clunas, Craig, et al. *Chinese Export Art and Design*. London: Victoria and Albert Museum, 1987.

Cobo, Bernabé. *Inca Religion and Customs*. Translated and edited by Roland Hamilton. Austin: University of Texas Press, 1990.

———. *Obras del P. Bernabé Cobo*. Vol. 1, *Historia del Nuevo Mondo*. Edited by Francisco Mateos. Madrid: Ediciones Atlas, 1956.

Cocks, Richard. *Diary of Richard Cocks, Cape-Merchant in the English Factory in Japan, 1615–1622, with Correspondence*. 2 vols. Works Issued by the Hakluyt Society 66–67. London: Hakluyt Society, 1883.

Cohen, Steven. "The Unusual Textile Trade between India and Sri Lanka: Block Prints and Chintz 1550–1900." In *Textiles from India: The Global Trade; Papers Presented at a Conference on the Indian Textile Trade, Kolkata, 12–14 October 2003*, edited by Rosemary Crill, pp. 56–80. Calcutta: Seagull Books, 2006.

Coleção de várias receitas e segredos particulares da nossa companhia de Portugal, da Índia, de Macau e do Brasil: Compostas e experimentadas pelos melhores médicos e boticários mais celebres que tem havido nestas Partes; Aumentada com alguns índices e notícias muito curiosas as e necessárias para a boa direção e acerto contra as enfermidades. Rome, 1766.

Colenbrander, Sjoukje. "Dutch Silks, Narrow or . . . ?" *Bulletin du CIETA*, no. 79 (2002), pp. 59–65.

———. *When Weaving Flourished: The Silk Industry in Amsterdam and Haarlem, 1585–1750*. Amsterdam: Aronson Publishers, 2013.

Colenbrander, Sjoukje, and Clare Browne. "Indiennes: *Chinoiserie* Silks Woven in Amsterdam." In *A Taste for the Exotic: Foreign Influences on Early Eighteenth-Century Silk Designs*, edited by Anna Jolly, pp. 127–38, 211–24. Riggisberger Berichte 14. Riggisberg: Abegg-Stiftung, 2007.

Columbian Centinel. See *America's Historical Newspapers*.

Connecticut Courant. See *America's Historical Newspapers*.

Connecticut Journal. See *America's Historical Newspapers*.

Cooper, Arlene C. "Luxury Textiles from Feudal Workshops: 19th Century Russian Tapestry-Woven Shawls." In *Textiles in Daily Life: Proceedings of the Third Biennial Symposium of the Textile Society of America, September 24–26, 1992*, pp. 224–35. Earleville, Md.: Textile Society of America, 1993.

Cora Ginsburg LLC. *A Catalogue of Exquisite and Rare Works of Art, including 17th to 20th Century Costume, Textiles, Needlework, Winter 2010–2011*. Sale cat. New York, 2010.

———. *A Catalogue of Exquisite and Rare Works of Art, including 17th to 20th Century Costume, Textiles, and Needlework, Winter 2011–2012*. Sale cat. New York, 2011.

Corcuera, Ruth. *Ponchos de las tierras del Plata*. Buenos Aires: Fondo Nacional de las Artes; Verstraeten Editores, [2000].

Cornejo Bouroncle, Jorge. *Derroteros de arte cuzqueño: Datos para una historia del arte en el Perú*. Cuzco: Editorial Garcilaso Ediciones Inca, 1960.

Courtin, Nicolas, and David Langeois. *Steinitz*. Paris: Steinitz, 2002.

Couto, Dejanirah, et al. *Revisiting Hormuz: Portuguese Interactions in the Persian Gulf Region in the Early Modern Period*. Maritime Asia 19. Wiesbaden: Harrassowitz; Lisbon: Calouste Gulbenkian Foundation, 2008.

Cowen, Rex. "Shipwrecks, Dyestuffs and the India Trade." In *Textiles from India: The Global Trade; Papers Presented at a Conference on the Indian Textile Trade, Kolkata, 12–14 October 2003*, edited by Rosemary Crill, pp. 374–88. Calcutta: Seagull Books, 2006.

Crespo, Hugo Miguel. "Trajar as aparências, vestir para ser: O Testemunho da Pragmática de 1609" (Dressing for appearances, dress to be: The Testimonial of 1609 Guidelines). In *O luxo na região do Porto ao tempo de Filipe II de Portugal (1610)* (Luxury in Porto during the times of Felipe II of Portugal), edited by Gonçalo de Vasconcelos e Sousa, pp. 93–148. Porto: Universidade Católica Editora, Centro Interpretativo da Ourivesaria do Norte de Portugal, Centro de Investigação em Ciência e Tecnologia das Artes, 2012.

Crill, Rosemary. *Chintz: Indian Textiles for the West*. London: V&A Publications, 2008.

———. "The Earliest Survivors?: The Indian Embroideries at Hardwick Hall." In *Textiles from India: The Global Trade; Papers Presented at a Conference on the Indian Textile Trade, Kolkata, 12–14 October 2003*, edited by Rosemary Crill, pp. 245–60. Calcutta: Seagull Books, 2006.

———. *Indian Embroidery*. London: V&A Publications, 1999.

Cruysse, Dirk van der. *Siam and the West, 1500–1700*. Chiang Mai: Silkworm Books, 2001.

Cruz, Gaspar da. *Tractado em que se cõtam muito por estõso as cousas da China cõ suas particularidades, assi do reino d'Ormuz, cõposto por el. R. padre frei Gaspar da Cruz da orde de sam Domingos* [MS 1569], in *Enformação das cousas da China: Textos do século XVI*. Edited by Raffaella D'Intino. Programa nacional de edições comemorativas dos descobrimentos portugueses. Lisbon: Imprensa Nacional, Casa da Moeda, 1989.

Cummings, Abbott Lowell. *Rural Household Inventories, Establishing the Names, Uses, and Furnishings of Rooms in the Colonial New England Home, 1675–1775*. Boston: The Society for the Preservation of New England Antiquities, 1964.

Cunningham, Patricia A. "Eighteenth-Century Nightgowns: The Gentleman's Robe in Art and Fashion." *Dress* 10 (1984), pp. 2–11.

Dagnall, H. *The Marking of Textiles for Excise and Customs Duty: The Historical Background and Legislative Framework*. Edgware: Published by the author, 1996.

Dampier, William. *A New Voyage Round the World*. London: James Knapton, 1699.

Davies, Brian H. "Logwood under the Microscope." In *Dyes in History and Archaeology 21, Including Papers Presented at the 21st Meeting Held at Avignon and Lauris, France, 10–12 October 2002*, edited by Jo Kirby and Chris Cooksey, pp. 180–88. London: Archetype Publications, 2008.

De Britaine, William. *Humane Prudence; or, The Art by Which a Man May Raise Himself and Fortune to Grandeur*. 6th ed. 1680. London, 1693.

[Defoe, Daniel.] *A Brief State of the Question, between the Printed and Painted Callicoes, and the Woollen and Silk Manufactures, . . .* London: W. Boreham, 1719.

Deloche, Jean. *A Study in Nayaka-Period Social Life: Tiruppu-daimarudur Paintings and Carvings*. Collection Indologie 116. Pondicherry: Institut Français de Pondichéry, École Française d'Extrême-Orient, 2011.

Delormois, *L'art de faire les indienne*. Paris: Libraires Associés, 1786.

Denney, Joyce. "Mongol Dress in the Thirteenth and Fourteenth Centuries." In *The World of Khubilai Khan: Chinese Art in the Yuan Dynasty*, by James C. Y. Watt et al., pp. 74–83. Exh. cat. New York: The Metropolitan Museum of Art, 2010.

Denny, Walter B. "Dating Ottoman Turkish Works in the Saz Style." *Muqarnas* 1 (1983), pp. 103–21.

———. "Oriental Carpets and Textiles in Venice." In *Venice and the Islamic World, 828–1797*, by Stefano Carboni et al., pp. 174–91. Exh. cat. New York: The Metropolitan Museum of Art, 2007.

Denny, Walter B., and Sumru Belger Krody. *The Sultan's Garden: The Blossoming of Ottoman Art*. Exh. cat. Washington, D.C.: The Textile Museum, 2012.

Digby, G. F. Wingfield. "Some Silks Woven under Portuguese Influence in the Far East." *The Burlington Magazine for Connoisseurs* 77, no. 449 (August 1940), pp. 52–63.

Disney, Anthony, and Emily Booth, eds. *Vasco da Gama and the Linking of Europe and Asia*. Delhi and Oxford: Oxford University Press, 2000.

Dodd, Dorothy. "Jacob Housman of Indian Key." *Tequesta* 8 (1948), pp. 3–4; http://digitalcollections.fiu.edu/tequesta/files/1948/48_1_01.pdf.

Doniol, Henri. *Histoire de la participation de la France à l'établissement des États-Unis d'Amérique: Correspondance diplomatique et documents*. Paris: Picard, 1888.

Donkin, R[obin] A. *Spanish Red: An Ethnogeographical Study of Cochineal and the Opuntia Cactus*. Transactions of the American Philosophical Society, n.s., 67, no. 5. Philadelphia: American Philosophical Society, 1977.

Douglas, Audrey W. "Cotton Textiles in England: The East India Company's Attempt to Exploit Developments in Fashion, 1660–1721." *The Journal of British Studies* 8, no. 2 (May 1969), pp. 28–43.

Dow, George Francis. *Every Day Life in the Massachusetts Bay Colony*. Boston: The Society for the Preservation of New England Antiquities, 1935. Reprint, New York: Dover Publications, 1988.

Downs, Joseph. "The China Trade and Its Influences." *The Metropolitan Museum of Art Bulletin* 36, no. 4 (April 1941), pp. 81, 84–95.

Druesedow, Jean L. "In Style: Celebrating Fifty Years of the Costume Institute." *The Metropolitan Museum of Art Bulletin*, n.s., 45, no. 2 (Fall 1987), pp. 1–64, cover illus.

Dumas, Ann, et al. *Matisse, His Art and His Textiles: The Fabric of Dreams*. Exh. cat. London: The Royal Academy of Arts, 2004.

Dunne, George H., S.J. *Generation of Giants: The Story of the Jesuits in China in the Last Decades of the Ming Dynasty*. Notre Dame, Ind.: University of Notre Dame Press, 1962.

Eaton, Linda. *Quilts in a Material World: Selections from the Winterthur Collection*. New York: Harry N. Abrams; Winterthur, Del.: Henry Francis du Pont Winterthur Museum, 2007.

Edelstein, Sidney M. "How Napoleon Aided the Early Dyeing Industry of France." In *Historical Notes on the Wet-Processing Industry*, pp. 17–18. Rev. ed. [New York]: Dexter Chemical Corporation, 1972.

———. "The Role of Chemistry in the Development of Dyeing and Bleaching." In *Historical Notes on the Wet-Processing Industry*, pp. 154–59. Rev. ed. [New York]: Dexter Chemical Corporation, 1972.

Edwards, Bryan, and Sir William Young. *The History, Civil and Commercial, of the British Colonies in the West Indies*. Vol. 3. London, 1801.

Ekhtiar, Maryam D., Priscilla P. Soucek, Sheila R. Canby, and Navina Najat Haidar, eds. *Masterpieces from the Department of Islamic Art in The Metropolitan Museum of Art*. New York: The Metropolitan Museum of Art, 2011.

Ellis, Asa. *The Country Dyer's Assistant*. Brookfield, Mass., 1798.

Escandell-Tur, Neus. *Producción y comercio de tejidos coloniales: Los obrajes y chorrillos del Cusco, 1570–1820*. Archivos de Historia Andina 23. Cuzco: Centro de Estudios Regionales Andinos, "Bartolomé de Las Casas," 1997.

"The Evils of Cochineal, Tlaxcala, Mexico (1553)." In *Colonial Spanish America: A Documentary History*, edited by Kenneth Mills and William B. Taylor, pp. 90–93. Wilmington, Del.: Scholarly Resources, 1998.

Ezra, Kate. *Royal Art of Benin: The Perls Collection*. Exh. cat. New York: The Metropolitan Museum of Art, 1992.

Failla, Donatella. "Cielo di baldacchino processionale." In *La seta e la sua via*, by Maria Teresa Lucidi et al., p. 277, no. 156. Exh. cat. Rome: Edizioni De Luca, 1994.

Fane, Diana, et al. *Converging Cultures: Art and Identity in Spanish America*. Exh. cat. Brooklyn: The Brooklyn Museum, 1996.

Faroqhi, Suraiya. "Crisis and Change, 1590–1699." In *An Economic and Social History of the Ottoman Empire, 1300–1914*, edited by Halil İnalcık and Donald Quataert, pp. 411–636. Cambridge and New York: Cambridge University Press, 1994.

Ferrier, R. W. "Charles I and the Antiquities of Persia: The Mission of Nicholas Wilford." *Iran* 8 (1970), pp. 51–56.

———. "An English View of Persian Trade in 1619: Reports from the Merchants Edward Pettus and Thomas Barker." *Journal of the Economic and Social History of the Orient* 19, no. 2 (May 1976), pp. 182–214.

Fisher, John. "The Imperial Response to 'Free Trade': Spanish Imports from Spanish America, 1778–1796." *Journal of Latin American Studies* 17, pt. 1 (May 1985), pp. 35–78.

Floor, Willem. "Economy and Society: Fibers, Fabrics, Factories." In *Woven from the Soul, Spun from the Heart: Textile Arts of Safavid and Qajar Iran, 16th–19th Centuries*, by Carol Bier et al., pp. 20–32. Exh. cat. Washington, D.C.: The Textile Museum, 1987.

———. "Hormuz, ii. Islamic Period." In *Encyclopaedia Iranica*. Online edition. New York, 1996– , originally published December 15, 2004, last updated March 23, 2012; http://www.iranicaonline.org/articles/hormuz-ii.

———. *The Persian Textile Industry in Historical Perspective, 1500–1925*. Paris: Harmattan, 1999.

Flores, Jorge Manuel. "Macau: De surgidouro a cidade." In *História dos portugueses no Extremo Oriente*, vol. 1, pt. 2, *De Macau à periferia*, edited by António Henrique R. de Oliveira Marques, pp. 237–64. Lisbon: Fundação Oriente, 2000.

Floris, Peter. *Peter Floris, His Voyage to the East Indies in the Globe 1611–1615*. Edited by W. H. Moreland. Works Issued by the Hakluyt Society, Second series 74. London: Hakluyt Society, 1934.

Floud, P[eter] C. "The English Contribution to the Early History of Indigo Printing." *The Journal of the Society of Dyers and Colourists* 76 (June 1960), pp. 344–49.

Floyd, Troy S. "The Indigo Merchant: Promoter of Central American Economic Development, 1750–1808." *Business History Review* 39, no. 4 (Winter 1965), pp. 466–88.

Folliot, J., François-Léandre Regnault-Delalande, C.-F. Julliot, and François-Augustin Quillau. *Catalogue de tableaux, portraits peints depuis le quatorzième siècle jusqu'à nos jours, miniatures, gouaches . . . qui composoient le cabinet de feu M. le duc de Richelieu . . . la vente commencera le jeudi 18 décembre 1788 . . .* Paris, 1788.

Folsach, Kjeld von, and Anne-Marie Keblow Bernsted. *Woven Treasures: Textiles from the World of Islam*. Exh. cat. Copenhagen: The David Collection, 1993.

Fonseca, Jorge. *Escravos e senhores na Lisboa quinhentista*. Lisbon: Edições Colibri, 2010.

Forbes, R. J. *Studies in Ancient Technology*. 9 vols. Leiden: E. J. Brill, 1955–64.

Fortune, Brandon Brame. "'Studious Men are always Painted in Gowns': Charles Willson Peale's 'Benjamin Rush' and the Question of Banyans in Eighteenth-Century Anglo-American Portraiture." *Dress* 29 (2002), pp. 27–40.

Freudenberger, Herman. "Fashion, Sumptuary Laws, and Business." *Business History Review* 37, no. 1–2 (Spring–Summer 1963), pp. 37–48.

Frézier, Amédée François. *Relation du voyage de la mer du Sud aux côtes du Chili, du Pérou et de Brésil, fait pendant les années 1712, 1713, et 1714*. Amsterdam: Chez Pierre Humbert, 1717.

———. *Voyage to the South-Sea, and along the Coasts of Chili and Peru, in the Years 1712, 1713, and 1714*. 1717. London: Printed for Christian Bowyer, 1735.

Fukuoka Fukatsu, Yuko. "Jinbaori no sozai to gihō ni kansuru kagakuteki bunseki to senshoku shiteki kenkyū/A Comprehensive Study on Jinbaori Based on the Scientific Analysis of Materials and Techniques." Ph.D. diss., Kyōritsu Joshi Daigaku Daigakuin (Kyōritsu Women's University Graduate School), Tokyo, 2008.

A Further Examination of the Weavers Pretences. London: J. Roberts, 1719.

Gaillard, Emmanuelle, and Marc Walter. *Exotic Taste: Orientalist Interiors*. New York: Vendome Press, 2011.

Gale, Mary E[lizabeth], and Margaret T. Ordoñez. "Eighteenth-Century Indigo Resist Fabrics: Their Use in Quilts and Bedhangings." *Uncoverings: The Research Papers of the American Quilt Study Group* 25 (2004), pp. 157–79.

———. "Indigo-Resist Prints from Eighteenth-Century America: Technology and Technique." *Clothing and Textiles Research Journal* 22, no. 1–2 (January–March 2004), pp. 4–14.

Gámez Martínez, Ana Paulina. "El Rebozo: Estudio historiográfico, origen y uso." M.A. thesis, Universidad Nacional Autónoma de México, Mexico City, 2009; http://www.scribd.com/doc/63549624/L-REBO-ZO-ESTUDIO-HISTORIOGRAFICO-ORIGEN-Y-USO.

Garrett, Valery M. *Mandarin Squares: Mandarins and Their Insignia*. New York: Oxford University Press, 1990.

Geijer, Agnes. *Oriental Textiles in Sweden*. Copenhagen: Rosenkilde and Bagger, 1951.

Gerard Hawthorn Ltd. *Oriental Works of Art, 7 June–18 June 2004*. Exh. cat. London, 2004.

Gerhard, Peter. "Shellfish Dye in America." In *XXXV Congreso Internacional de Americanistas, México, 1962: Actas y memorias*, vol. 3, pp. 177–90. 3 vols. Mexico City: Editorial Libros de México, 1964.

Gervers, Veronika. *The Influence of Ottoman Turkish Textiles and Costume in Eastern Europe, with Particular Reference to Hungary*. Toronto: Royal Ontario Museum, 1982.

Geuter, Ruth. "Embroidered Biblical Narratives and Their Social Context." In *English Embroidery from The Metropolitan Museum of Art, 1580–1700: 'Twixt Art and Nature*, edited by Andrew Morrall and Melinda Watt, pp. 56–77. Exh. cat. New York: The Bard Graduate Center for Studies in the Decorative Arts, Design, and Culture; The Metropolitan Museum of Art, 2008.

Gillingham, Harrold E. "Calico and Linen Printing in Philadelphia." *The Pennsylvania Magazine of History and Biography* 52, no. 2 (1928), pp. 97–110, pls. 1–2.

Gittinger, Mattiebelle. *Master Dyers to the World: Technique and Trade in Early Indian Dyed Cotton Textiles*. Exh. cat. Washington, D.C.: The Textile Museum, 1982.

Gluckman, Dale Carolyn, and Sharon Sadako Takeda. *When Art Became Fashion: Kosode in Edo-Period Japan*. Exh. cat. Los Angeles: Los Angeles County Museum of Art; New York and Tokyo: Weatherhill, 1992.

Godart, Justin. *L'ouvrier en soie . . .* Lyon: Bernoux et Cumin, 1899.

Goetz, Hermann. "The History of Persian Costume." In *A Survey of Persian Art, from Prehistoric Times to the Present*, edited by Alexander Upham Pope and Phyllis Ackerman, vol. 3, pp. 2227–56; vols. 4–6, plates. London and New York: Oxford University Press, 1938–39.

Góis, Damião de. *Chronica do felicissimo rei Dom Emanuel*. Pt. 4. Lisbon: Francisco Correa, 1567.

Goitein, S. D. *A Mediterranean Society: The Jewish Communities of the Arab World as Portrayed in the Documents of the Cairo Geniza*. 6 vols. Berkeley and Los Angeles: University of California Press, 1967–93.

Goitein, S. D., and Mordechai Akiva Friedman. *India Traders of the Middle Ages: Documents from the Cairo Geniza, "India Book."* Études sur le judaïsme médiéval 31. Leiden: Brill, 2008.

Goldthorpe, Caroline. "Europe 1700–1900; Open Robe with Underskirt and Fichu." In "Recent Acquisitions: A Selection, 1991–1992." *The Metropolitan Museum of Art Bulletin*, n.s., 50, no. 2 (Fall 1992), p. 37.

Gómez Cervantes, Gonzalo. *La vida económica y social de Nueva España al finalizar el siglo XVI*. Edited and annotated by Alberto Maria Carreño. Biblioteca histórica mexicana de obras inéditas 19. Mexico City: Antiqua librería Robredo, de J. Porrúa e hijos, 1944.

González de Mendoza, Juan. *Itinerario y compendio delas cosas notables que ay desde España hasta la reyno dela China, y dela China à España, bolviendo por la India Oriental, despues de auer dado buelta, à casi todo el mundo . . .* Lisbon: S. Phelippe el Real, 1586.

Gordon-Smith, Maria. "Jean Pillement at the Imperial Court of Maria Theresa and Francis I in Vienna (1763 to 1765)." *Artibus et Historiae* 25, no. 50 (2004), pp. 187–213.

Gorguet Ballesteros, Pascale, et al. *Modes en miroir: La France et la Holland au temps des Lumières*. Exh. cat. Paris: Musée Galliéra, 2005.

Graham, Patricia J. *Tea of the Sages: The Art of Sencha*. Honolulu: University of Hawai'i Press, 1998.

Gregorian, Vartan. "Minorities in Isfahan: The Armenian Community of Isfahan, 1587–1722." *Iranian Studies* 7, no. 3–4 [*Studies on Isfahan, Part II*] (Summer–Autumn 1974), pp. 652–80.

Griffiths, Antony. *The Print in Stuart Britain, 1603–1689*. Exh. cat. London: British Museum Press, 1998.

Grimm, Ulrike. "Favorite, a Rare Place Exuding the Spirit of an Age when Chinoiserie Reigned Supreme." In *A Taste for the Exotic: Foreign Influences on Early Eighteenth-Century Silk Designs*, edited by Anna Jolly, pp. 77–90, 211–24. Riggisberger Berichte 14. Riggisberg: Abegg-Stiftung, 2007.

Griswold, Rufus Wilmot. *The Republican Court; or, American Society in the Days of Washington*. Rev. ed. New York: D. Appleton, 1867.

Groot, Alexander H. de. *The Ottoman Empire and the Dutch Republic: A History of the Earliest Diplomatic Relations, 1610–1630*. Leiden: Nederlands Historisch-Archaeologisch Instituut Leiden/Istanbul, 1978.

Gschwend, Annemarie Jordan, and Laura G. Bellet. *The Story of Süleyman: Celebrity Elephants and Other Exotica in Renaissance Portugal*. Zurich, 2010.

Guamán Poma de Ayala, Filipe. "Civdad." In "Nueva corónica." Det Kongelige Bibliotek, Copenhagen, fol. 1034 [1042]; http://www.kb.dk/permalink/2006/poma/1042/en/text/?open=id2978109.

Guy, John. "China in India." In *China and Southeast Asia: Historical Interactions*, edited by Geoffrey Wade and James K. Chin. Routledge Studies in the Modern History of Asia. Oxford and New York: Routledge, forthcoming.

———. "Choice Varied Flowers." *Hali*, no. 172 (Summer 2012), pp. 78–81.

———. "Cloth for the Gods: The Patola Trade to Kerala." *Asian Art and Culture* 9, no. 2 (1996), pp. 27–37.

———. "Indian Painting from 1100 to 1500." In *Masters of Indian Painting*, edited by Milo C. Beach, Eberhard Fischer, and B. N. Goswamy, vol. 1, pp. 14–28. 2 vols. Zurich: Artibus Asiae Publishers, 2011.

———. *Indian Textiles in the East from Southeast Asia to Japan*. 1998. London: Thames and Hudson, 2009.

———. "Quanzhou, Cosmopolitan City of Faiths." In *The World of Khubilai Khan: Chinese Art in the Yuan Dynasty*, by James C. Y. Watt et al., pp. 158–78. Exh. cat. New York: The Metropolitan Museum of Art, 2010.

———. "Rama, Rajas and Courtesans: Indian Figurative Textiles in Indonesia." In *The Secrets of Southeast Asian Textiles—Myth, Status and the Supernatural: The James H. W. Thompson Foundation Symposium Papers*, edited by Jane Puranananda, pp. 40–57. Bangkok: River Books, 2007.

———. "A Ruler and His Courtesans Celebrate Vasantotsava: Courtly and Divine Love in a Nayaka *Kalamkari*." In *Sultans of the South: Arts of India's Deccan Courts, 1323–1687*, edited by Navina Najat Haidar and Marika Sardar, pp. 162–75. New York: The Metropolitan Museum of Art, 2011.

———. "Tamil Merchant Guilds and the Quanzhou Trade." In *The Emporium of the World: Maritime Quanzhou, 1000–1400*, edited by Angela Schottenhammer, pp. 283–308. Leiden: Brill, 2001.

———. *Woven Cargoes: Indian Textiles in the East*. London: Thames and Hudson, 1998. Reissued as *Indian Textiles in the East from Southeast Asia to Japan*. London: Thames and Hudson, 2009.

Guy, John, and Deborah Swallow, eds. *Arts of India, 1550–1900*. London: Victoria and Albert Museum, 1990.

Guy, John, et al. *L'escultura en els temples indis: L'art de la devoció*. Exh. cat. Barcelona: Fundació la Caixa, 2007.

Hackenbroch, Yvonne. *English and Other Needlework, Tapestries and Textiles in the Irwin Untermyer Collection*. New York: The Metropolitan Museum of Art; Cambridge, Mass.: Harvard University Press, 1960.

Hakluyt, Richard. *The Principal Navigations . . .* 2nd ed. 3 vols. 1589. London: George Bishop, Ralph Newberie and Robert Barker, 1598–1600.

Hall, Linda B. *Mary, Mother and Warrior: The Virgin in Spain and the Americas*. Austin: University of Texas Press, 2004.

Hartkamp-Jonxis, Ebeltje. *Sitsen uit India/Indian Chintzes*. Aspecten van de verzameling beeldhouwkunst en kunstnijverheid 5. Amsterdam: Rijksmuseum; Zwolle: Waanders Uitgevers, 1994.

———. *Sits: Oost-west relaties in textiel*. Exh. cat. Zwolle: Waanders Uitgevers, 1987.

———. "Some Coromandel Chintzes." *The Bulletin of the Needle and Bobbin Club* 53, no. 1–2 (1970), pp. 37–57.

Hellot, [Jean], [Pierre Joseph] Macquer, and [Le]pileur d'Apligny. *The Art of Dying Wool, Silk, and Cotton*. London: R. Baldwin, 1789.

Henriques, Ana de Castro, et al. *Portugal and the World in the 16th and 17th Centuries*. Exh. cat. Lisbon: Museu Nacional de Arte Antiga, 2009.

Herbert, Thomas. *Travels in Persia, 1627–1629*. Abridged and edited by William Foster. New York: Robert M. McBride and Company, 1929.

Herrera y Tordesillas, Antonio de. *Historia general de los hechos de los castellanos en las Islas y Tierrafirme del Mar Oceìano: Publicada por acuerdo de la academia de la historia*. 17 vols. Madrid: [Tipografía de Archivos], 1934–57.

Hershkowitz, Leo. "Original Inventories of Early New York Jews (1682–1763)." *American Jewish History* 90, no. 3 (September 2002), pp. 239–321.

———. "Original Inventories of Early New York Jews (1682–1763) (Concluded)." *American Jewish History* 90, no. 4 (December 2002), pp. 385–448.

Hervey, Mary F. S. *The Life, Correspondence and Collections of Thomas Howard, Earl of Arundel, "Father of vertu in England."* Cambridge: Cambridge University Press, 1921.

Herzig, Edmund M. "The Volume of Iranian Raw Silk Exports in the Safavid Period." *Iranian Studies* 25, no. 1–2 [*The Carpets and Textiles of Iran: New Perspectives in Research*] (1992), pp. 61–79.

Hess, Andrew C. "The Evolution of the Ottoman Seaborne Empire in the Age of Oceanic Discoveries, 1453–1525." *The American Historical Review* 75, no. 7 (December 1970), pp. 1892–919.

Hirth, Friedrich, and W[illiam] W. Rockhill. *Chau Ju-kua: His Work on the Chinese and Arab Trade in the Twelfth and Thirteenth Centuries, entitled Chu-fan-chi*. Saint Petersburg: Imperial Academy of Sciences, 1911. Reprint, Taipei: Ch'eng-Wen Pub., 1967.

Holme, Randle. *The Academy of Armory, or, A Storehouse of Armory and Blazon*. Chester, 1688.

Honour, Hugh. *Chinoiserie: The Vision of Cathay*. London: J. Murray, 1961.

————. *The European Vision of America*. Exh. cat. Cleveland: Cleveland Museum of Art, 1975.

————. *The Image of the Black in Western Art*. Vol. 4, *From the American Revolution to World War I*. Part 1, *Slaves and Liberators*. Houston: Menil Foundation, 1989.

Humboldt, Al[exander von]. *Essai politique sur le royaume de la Nouvelle-Espagne*. 5 vols. Paris: F. Schoell, 1811.

Huneycutt, Dwight Jackson. "The Economics of the Indigo Industry in South Carolina." M.A. thesis, University of South Carolina, Columbia, S.C., 1949.

Hussey, Christopher. "Ashburnham of Ashburnham: I.—The Origins and End of a Great Sussex House." *Country Life* 113, no. 2935 (April 16, 1953), pp. 1158–60; "Ashburnham Place, Sussex—II." 113, no. 2936 (April 23, 1953), pp. 1246–50; "Ashburnham Place, Sussex—III." 113, no. 2937 (April 30, 1953), pp. 1334–38.

Ibn Battuta. *The Travels of Ibn Battuta, A.D. 1325–1354*. Translated by H. A. R. Gibb et al. 5 vols. Works Issued by the Hakluyt Society, Second series 110, 117, 141, 178, 190. London: Hakluyt Society, 1958–2000.

Impey, Oliver. *Chinoiserie: The Impact of Oriental Styles on Western Art and Decoration*. London: Oxford University Press, 1977.

İnalcık, Halil. "Harir; ii. The Ottoman Empire." In *The Encyclopedia of Islam*, vol. 3 (1971), pp. 211–18. New ed. Leiden, London, and Boston: E. J. Brill, 1960–2009.

————. "The Ottoman State: Economy and Society, 1300–1600." In *An Economic and Social History of the Ottoman Empire, 1300–1914*, edited by Halil İnalcık and Donald Quataert, pp. 9–409. Cambridge and New York: Cambridge University Press, 1994.

Inikori, Joseph E. "Slavery and the Revolution in Cotton Textile Production in England." *Social Science History* 13, no. 4 (Winter 1989), pp. 343–79.

Instruction générale pour la teinture des laines . . . Paris: Impr. de François Muguet, 1671.

Irwin, John. "The Commercial Embroidery of Gujerat [*sic*] in the Seventeenth Century." *Journal of the Indian Society of Oriental Art* 17 (1949), pp. 51–57.

————. "Indian Textile Trade in the Seventeenth Century: I. Western India." *Journal of Indian Textile History*, no. 1 (1955), pp. 4–33; "II. Coromandel Coast." no. 2 (1956), pp. 24–42; "III. Bengal." no. 3 (1957), pp. 58–74; "IV. Foreign Influences." no. 4 (1959), pp. 57–64.

————. "Indo-Portuguese Embroideries of Bengal." *Art and Letters: The Journal of the Royal India, Pakistan and Ceylon Society*, n.s., 26, no. 2 (1952), pp. 65–73.

————. *The Kashmir Shawl*. London: Her Majesty's Stationery Office, 1973.

————. "Origins of 'Oriental' Chintz Design." *The Magazine Antiques* 75, no. 1 (1959), pp. 84–87.

————. "Origins of the 'Oriental Style' in English Decorative Art." *The Burlington Magazine* 97, no. 625 (April 1955), pp. 106–14.

————. Review of *Bizarre Designs in Silks*, by Vilhelm Slomann. *The Burlington Magazine* 97, no. 626 (May 1955), pp. 153–54.

Irwin, John, and Katharine B. Brett. *Origins of Chintz, with a Catalogue of Indo-European Cotton-Paintings in the Victoria and Albert Museum, London, and the Royal Ontario Museum, Toronto*. London: Her Majesty's Stationery Office, 1970.

Ishida, Chihiro. *Nichiran bōeki no shiteki kenkyū* (A historical study of the Japanese-Dutch trade). Tokyo: Yoshikawa Kōbunkan, 2004.

Ishii, Yoneo, ed. *The Junk Trade from Southeast Asia: Translations from the Tōsen fūsetsu-gaki, 1674–1723*. Singapore: Institute of South-east Asian Studies; Canberra: Research School of Pacific and Asian Studies, Australian National History, 1998.

Jackson-Stops, Gervase, et al. *The Treasure Houses of Britain: Five Hundred Years of Private Patronage and Art Collecting*. Exh. cat. Washington, D.C.: National Gallery of Art; New Haven and London: Yale University Press, 1985.

Jacobson, Dawn. *Chinoiserie*. London: Phaidon, 1993.

Jacqué, Jacqueline, and Brigitte Nicolas. *Féerie indienne: Des rivages de l'Inde au royaume de France*. Exh. cat. Paris: Somogy Editions, 2008.

Japonisme et mode. Exh. cat. Paris: Les musées de la Ville de Paris, Palais Galliera, Musée de la mode et du costume, 1996.

Jarry, Madeleine. *Chinoiserie: Chinese Influence on European Decorative Art, 17th and 18th Centuries*. New York: Vendome Press, 1981.

Jennings, Lawrence C. *French Anti-Slavery: The Movement for the Abolition of Slavery in France, 1802–1848*. Cambridge and New York: Cambridge University Press, 2000.

Johnson, Thomas. *Animalium quadrupedum . . . /A Booke of Beast [sic], Birds, Flowers, Fruits, Flies and Wormes*. London, 1630.

Johnstone, Pauline. *High Fashion in the Church: The Place of Church Vestments in the History of Art from the Ninth to the Nineteenth Century*. Leeds: Maney, 2002.

Jolly, Anna. "Painted Silks from China: Problems of Attribution and Dating." In *Furnishing Textiles: Studies on Seventeenth- and Eighteenth-Century Interior Decoration*, edited by Anna Jolly, pp. 167–78, 223–36. Riggisberger Berichte 17. Riggisberg: Abegg-Stiftung, 2009.

————. "Une soierie chinoise d'après un dessin anglais du XVIIIe siècle." *Bulletin du CIETA*, no. 80 (2003), pp. 75–83.

Jolly, Anna, ed. *A Taste for the Exotic: Foreign Influences on Early Eighteenth-Century Silk Designs*. Riggisberger Berichte 14. Riggisberg: Abegg-Stiftung, 2007.

Jörg, Christiaan J. A. "Chinese Export Silks for the Dutch in the 18th Century." *Transactions of the Oriental Ceramic Society* 73 (2008–9), pp. 1–23.

Kaempfer, Engelbert. *Kaempfer's Japan: Tokugawa Culture Observed*. Edited, translated, and annotated by Beatrice M. Bodart-Bailey. Honolulu: University of Hawai'i Press, 1999.

Kajitani, Nobuko. *Gion matsuri yamaboko kensōhin chōsa hōkokusho: Torai senshoku no bu* (Report of the survey of items for decorating *yamaboko* of the Gion festival: Imported textiles). Kyoto: Gion Matsuri Yamaboko Rengōkai [Gion Festival Yamaboko Association], 1992.

Kamiya, Eiko. "The *Dōbuku* in Patchwork of Gold Brocade, Silver Brocade and Other Cloths Reportedly Used by Uesugi Kenshin (I) [in Japanese]." *Bijutsu Kenkyū* (Journal of Art Studies), no. 216 (May 1961), pp. 2, 11–32.

————. "The *Dōbuku* in Patchwork of Gold Brocade, Silver Brocade and Other Cloths Reportedly Used by Uesugi Kenshin (II) [in Japanese]." *Bijutsu Kenkyū*, no. 219 (November 1961), pp. 2, 145–67.

Karl, Barbara. "The Use of Growing Architecture as Propaganda: The Bengal Colcha at the Isabella Stewart Gardner Museum in Boston." In *O estado da Índia e os desafios Europeus: Actas do XII Seminário Internacional de História Indo-Portuguesa*, edited by João Paulo Oliveira e Costa and Vítor Luís Gaspar Rodrigues, pp. 231–44. Colecção Estudos e documentos 7. Lisbon: CHAM [Centro História de Além-Mar], 2010.

Katzew, Ilona. *Casta Painting: Images of Race in Eighteenth-Century Mexico*. New Haven and London: Yale University Press, 2004.

Kelemen, Pál. "Lenten Curtains from Colonial Peru." *Textile Museum Journal* 3, no. 1 (December 1970), pp. 4–14.

Kent, Henry Watson, and Florence N. Levy. *The Hudson-Fulton Celebration: Catalogue of an Exhibition Held in the Metropolitan Museum of Art*. Vol. 2, *Catalogue of an Exhibition of American Paintings, Furniture, Silver and Other Objects of Art, MDCXXV–MDCCCXXV*. Exh. cat. New York: The Metropolitan Museum of Art, 1909.

Kettering, Alison McNeil. "Gentlemen in Satin: Masculine Ideals in Later Seventeenth-Century Dutch Portraiture." *Art Journal* 56, no. 2 (Summer 1997), pp. 41–47.

King, Donald, and Santina Levey. *The Victoria and Albert Museum's Textile Collection: Embroidery in Britain from 1200 to 1750*. New York: Canopy Books, Abbeville Press, 1993.

King, Monique, and Donald King. *European Textiles in the Keir Collection 400 BC to 1800 AD*. The Keir Collection 6. London: Faber, 1990.

Kisluk-Grosheide, Daniëlle O. "Peregrinations of a *Lit à la Duchesse en Impériale* by George Jacob." *Metropolitan Museum Journal* 44 (2009), pp. 139–61.

Kologrivov, S. N. *Materialy dlia istorii snoshenii Rossii s inostrannymi derzhavami v XVII veke*. Vestnik arkheologii i istorii 2. St. Petersburg: V. D. Smirnov, 1911.

Komaroff, Linda, and Stefano Carboni, eds. *The Legacy of Genghis Khan: Courtly Art and Culture in Western Asia, 1256–1353*. Exh. cat. New York: The Metropolitan Museum of Art, 2002.

Komaroff, Linda, et al. *Gifts of the Sultan: The Arts of Giving at the Islamic Courts*. Exh. cat. Los Angeles: Los Angeles County Museum of Art, 2011.

Kornhauser, Elizabeth Mankin, et al. *Ralph Earl: The Face of the Young Republic*. Exh. cat. Hartford: The Wadsworth Atheneum; New Haven and London: Yale University Press, 1991.

Kowatari sarasa to wasarasa (Sarasa that came to Japan in early times and sarasa made in Japan). Exh. cat. Tokyo: Nezu Bijutsukan (Nezu Institute of Fine Arts), 1993.

Krahl, Regina. "The Portuguese Presence in the Arts and Crafts of China." In *Encompassing the Globe: Portugal and the World in the 16th and 17th Centuries*, by Jay A. Levenson et al., pp. 311–19. Exh. cat. Lisbon: Instituto dos Museos e da Conservação, Museu Nacional de Arte Antiga, 2009.

Kriger, Colleen E. *Cloth in West African History*. Lanham: Rowman and Littlefield Publishers, 2006.

Krohn, Deborah L., and Peter N. Miller, eds. *Dutch New York between East and West: The World of Margrieta van Varick*. Exh. cat. New York: Bard Graduate Center, 2009.

Krueger, Glee. *New England Samplers to 1840.* Sturbridge, Mass.: Old Sturbridge Village, 1978.

Lach, Donald F. "The Elephant." In *Asia in the Making of Europe,* vol. 2, *A Century of Wonder,* bk. 1, *The Visual Arts,* by Donald F. Lach, pp. 124–58. Chicago and London: The University of Chicago Press, 1970.

Lambourn, Elizabeth. "Carving and Communities: Marble Carving for Muslim Patrons at Khambhat and around the Indian Ocean Rim, Late Thirteenth–Mid-Fifteenth Centuries." *Ars Orientalis* 34 [*Communities and Commodities: Western India and the Indian Ocean Eleventh–Fifteenth Centuries*] (2004), pp. 99–133.

———. "From Cambay to Samudera-Pasai and Gresik: The Export of Gujarati Grave Memorials to Sumatra and Java in the Fifteenth Century C.E." *Indonesia and the Malay World* 31, no. 90 (July 2003), pp. 221–89.

Lavanha, João Baptista. *Viagem da Catholica Real Magestade del Rey D. Filipe II. N.S. ao reyno de Portvgal e rellação do solene recebimento que nelle se lhe fez. S. Magestade a mandou.* Madrid, 1622.

Leclercq, Jean-Paul. "From Threads to Pattern Composition, Technique, and Aesthetics." In *A Taste for the Exotic: Foreign Influences on Early Eighteenth-Century Silk Designs,* edited by Anna Jolly, pp. 139–54, 211–24. Riggisberger Berichte 14. Riggisberg: Abegg-Stiftung, 2007.

Ledderose, Lothar. *Ten Thousand Things: Module and Mass Production in Chinese Art.* Princeton, N.J.: Princeton University Press, 2000.

Lee, Raymond L. "Cochineal Production and Trade in New Spain to 1600." *The Americas* 4, no. 4 (April 1948), pp. 449–73.

Lee-Whitman, Leanna. "The Silk Trade: Chinese Silks and the British East India Company." *Winterthur Portfolio* 17, no. 1 (Spring 1982), pp. 21–41.

Lemire, Beverly. *Cotton.* Oxford and New York: Berg, 2011.

———. "Domesticating the Exotic: Floral Culture and the East India Calico Trade with England, c. 1600–1800." *Textile: The Journal of Cloth and Culture* 1, no. 1 (March 2003), pp. 65–85.

———. "Fashioning Cottons: Asian Trade, Domestic Industry and Consumer Demand, 1660–1780." In The *Cambridge History of Western Textiles,* vol. 1, pp. 493–512. 2 vols. Cambridge and New York: Cambridge University Press, 2003.

———. *Fashion's Favourite: The Cotton Trade and the Consumer in Britain, 1660–1800.* Pasold Studies in Textile History 9. Oxford and New York: Pasold Research Fund, Oxford University Press, 1991.

León, Nicolás, trans. and ed. *Códice Sierra* [Mexico City: Impr. del Museo Nacional de Arqueología, Historia y Etnografía, 1933].

Levenson, Jay A., et al. *Circa 1492: Art in the Age of Exploration.* Exh. cat. Washington, D.C.: National Gallery of Art; New Haven and London: Yale University Press, 1991.

———. *Encompassing the Globe: Portugal and the World in the 16th & 17th Centuries.* Exh. cat. Washington, D.C.: Arthur M. Sackler Gallery, Smithsonian Institution, 2007.

Levey, Santina M. *An Elizabethan Inheritance: The Hardwick Hall Textiles.* London: The National Trust, 1998.

———. *The Embroideries at Hardwick Hall: A Catalogue.* London: The National Trust, 2007.

———. *Lace: A History.* London: Victoria and Albert Museum; W. S. Maney and Son, 1983.

Levykin, Alexey Konstantinovich, et al. *The Tsars and the East: Gifts from Turkey and Iran in the Moscow Kremlin.* Exh. cat. Washington, D.C.: Arthur M. Sackler Gallery, Smithsonian Institution, 2009.

Li Chu-Tsing and James C. Y. Watt, eds. *The Chinese Scholar's Studio: Artistic Life in the Late Ming Period; An Exhibition from the Shanghai Museum.* Exh. cat. New York: The Asia Society Galleries; Thames and Hudson, 1987.

Liles, J. N. *The Art and Craft of Natural Dyeing: Traditional Recipes for Modern Use.* Knoxville: University of Tennessee Press, 1990.

Linschoten, Jan Huyghen van. *Itinerario, voyage ofte schipvaert . . . naer Oost ofte Portugaels Indien.* 2 pts. Amsterdam: Cornelis Claesz., 1595–96.

———. *The Voyage of John Huyghen van Linschoten to the East Indies from the Old English Translation of 1598.* Edited by Arthur Coke Burnell and P. A. Tiele. 2 vols. Works Issued by the Hakluyt Society 70–71. London: Hakluyt Society, 1885.

Liscia Bemporad, Dora. "Jewish Ceremonial Art in the Era of the Ghettos." In *Gardens and Ghettos: The Art of Jewish Life in Italy,* edited by Vivian B. Mann, pp. 111–35. Exh. cat. Berkeley and Los Angeles: University of California Press, 1989.

"List of Accessions and Loans." *The Metropolitan Museum of Art Bulletin* 21, no. 3 (March 1926), pp. 90–93.

Little, Frances. "Cotton Printing in Ireland in the Eighteenth Century." *The Bulletin of the Needle and Bobbin Club* 22, no. 1 (1938), pp. 14–23.

Locke, John. "Some Thoughts Concerning Education." In *The Works of John Locke in Nine Volumes,* vol. 8, pp. i–v, 6–205. 12th ed. London: Printed for C. and J. Rivington, 1824.

Lockhart, James. *Spanish Peru, 1532–1560: A Colonial Society.* Madison: University of Wisconsin Press, 1968.

Lockhart, James, and Stuart B. Schwartz. *Early Latin America: A History of Colonial Spanish America and Brazil.* Cambridge and New York: Cambridge University Press, 1983.

Logan, Anne-Marie, and Liam M. Brockey. "Nicolas Trigault, SJ: A Portrait by Peter Paul Rubens." *Metropolitan Museum Journal* 38 (2003), pp. 10, 157–67.

Lohuizen-de Leeuw, J[ohanna] E. van. "An Early 16th Century Link between Gujarat and Java." In *Essays Offered to G. H. Luce,* edited by Ba Shin et al., vol. 2, pp. 89–93. 2 vols. Ascona: Artibus Asiae, 1966.

Long, Edward. *The History of Jamaica.* London: Printed for T. Lowndes, 1774.

Loosley, Allyn A. "The Puerto Bello Fairs." *The Hispanic American Historical Review* 13, no. 3 (August 1933), pp. 314–35.

Lopez, Robert S. "The Trade in Medieval Europe: The South." In *The Cambridge Economic History of Europe,* vol. 2, *Trade and Industry in the Middle Ages,* edited by M[ichael] M. Postan and Edward Miller, pp. 306–401. 2nd ed. 1952. Cambridge: Cambridge University Press, 1987.

López de Gómara, Francisco. *Historia de las conquistas de Hernando Cortés.* Edited by Carlos María de Bustamante. 2 vols. Mexico City: Testamentaría de Ontiveros, 1826.

Loubère, Simon de la. *The Kingdom of Siam.* Introduction by David K. Wyatt. Reprint ed. 1693. Singapore and New York: Oxford University Press, 1986.

Loureiro, Rui Manuel, ed. *Cartas dos cativos de Cantão: Cristovão Vieira e Vasco Calvo (1524?).* Macau: Instituto Cultural de Macau, 1992.

Lowengard, Sarah. *The Creation of Color in Eighteenth-Century Europe.* New York: Gutenberg-e, [2006]; http://www.gutenberg-e.org/lowengard/B_Chap01.html#note21.

Lubberhuizen-van Gelder, A. M. "Japonsche Rocken." *Oud-Holland* 62 (1947), pp. 137–52.

MacCormack, Sabine. "Ethnography in South America: The First Two Hundred Years." In *The Cambridge History of the Native Peoples of the Americas,* vol. 3, *South America,* pt. 1, edited by Frank Salomon and Stuart B. Schwartz, pp. 98–187. Cambridge and New York: Cambridge University Press, 1999.

———. "From the Sun of the Incas to the Virgin of Copacabana." *Representations,* no. 8 (Fall 1984), pp. 30–60.

———. "'The Heart Has Its Reasons': Predicaments of Missionary Christianity in Early Colonial Peru." *Hispanic American Historical Review* 65, no. 3 (August 1985), pp. 443–66.

———. *Religion in the Andes: Vision and Imagination in Early Colonial Peru.* Princeton, N.J.: Princeton University Press, 1991.

Mahalingam, T. V. *Administration and Social Life under Vijayanagar.* Pt. 2, *Social Life.* 2nd ed. 1940. Madras: University of Madras, 1975.

Maia, Patrícia Albano. "Práticas de cura no encontro de culturas: Jesuítas e a circulação de receitas médicas." In *Anais do XXVI Simpósio Nacional de História—ANPUH, São Paulo, julho 2011*; http://www.snh2011.anpuh.org/resources/anais/14/1300867080_ARQUIVO_ANPUH2011-Praticas decuranoencontrodeculturas.pdf.

Mailey, Jean. "European Sculpture and Decorative Arts; The Abduction of Helen: From a Set of Hangings on the Trojan War." In *Notable Acquisitions [The Metropolitan Museum of Art], 1979 1980,* pp. 34–35. New York: The Metropolitan Museum of Art, 1980.

Majer, Michele [M]. "Costume Institute; Mantua and Petticoat." In "Recent Acquisitions: A Selection, 1990–1991." *The Metropolitan Museum of Art Bulletin,* n.s., 49, no. 2 (Fall 1991), p. 54.

———. "Europe 1700–1900; Casaquin and Petticoat." In "Recent Acquisitions: A Selection, 1992–1993." *The Metropolitan Museum of Art Bulletin,* n.s., 51, no. 2 (Fall 1993), p. 38.

Malekandathil, Pius. *Maritime India: Trade, Religion and Polity in the Indian Ocean.* Delhi: Primus Books, 2010.

Mańkowski, Tadeusz. "Influence of Islamic Art in Poland." *Ars Islamica* 2, pt. 1 (1935), pp. 92–117.

Marchese, Ronald T., and Marlene R. Breu. *Splendor and Pageantry: Textile Treasures from the Armenian Orthodox Churches of Istanbul.* Istanbul: Citlembik/Nettleberry Publications, 2010.

Marot, Daniel. *Nouveaux [sic] livre d'ornements propres pour faire en broderie et petit point.* Amsterdam, 1703.

———. *Oeuvres du Sr. D. Marot, architecte de Guillaume III, roy de la Grande Bretagne: Contenant plusieurs pensées utiles aux architectes, peintres, sculpteurs, orfeures, jardiniers et autres.* Amsterdam, 1712.

Martin, Emily. "Europe 1700–1900; Open Robe and Petticoat." In "Recent Acquisitions: A Selection, 1998–1999." *The Metropolitan Museum of Art Bulletin,* n.s., 57, no. 2 (Fall 1999), p. 35.

Martin, F[redrik] R. *A History of Oriental Carpets before 1800.* 3 vols. Vienna: Printed for the author in the I. and R. State and Court Print Office, 1908.

———. *Die persischen Prachtstoffe im Schlosse Rosenborg in Kopenhagen*. Stockholm: G. Chelius in Commission, 1901.

Martin, James S. "Unraveling the Material History of Painted Silk Textiles through Micro-Analysis." In *The Conservation of 18th-Century Painted Silk Dress*, edited by Chris Paulocik and Sean Flaherty, pp. 46–50. New York: The Costume Institute, The Metropolitan Museum of Art and the Graduate Program in Costume Studies, New York University, 1995.

Massachusetts Mercury. See *America's Historical Newspapers*.

Massachusetts Spy, Or, The Worcester Gazette. See *America's Historical Newspapers*.

Massarella, Derek, and Izumi K. Tyler. "The Japonian Charters: The English and Dutch *Shuinjo*." *Monumenta Nipponica* 45, no. 2 (Summer 1990), pp. 189–205.

Mastache, Alba Guadalupe. "El tejido en el México antiguo." *Arqueología mexicana* 19 [*Textiles del México de ayer y hoy*] (2005), pp. 20–31.

Mathers, Constance Jones. "Family Partnerships and International Trade in Early Modern Europe: Merchants from Burgos in England and France, 1470–1570." *Business History Review* 62, no. 3 (Autumn 1988), pp. 367–97.

Mathew, K[uzhippalli] S[karia]. *Portuguese Trade with India in the Sixteenth Century*. New Delhi: Manohar Publications, 1983.

Matsumoto, Kaneo. *Shōsōin-gire to Asuka Tenpyō no senshoku/ Jōdai Gire: 7th and 8th Century Textiles in Japan from the Shōsō-in and Hōryū-ji*. Kyoto: Shikōsha, 1984.

Matthee, Rudi. "Anti-Ottoman Concerns and Caucasian Interests: Diplomatic Relations between Iran and Russia, 1587–1639." In *Safavid Iran and Her Neighbors*, edited by Michel Mazzaoui, pp. 101–28. Salt Lake City: The University of Utah Press, 2003.

———. "Anti-Ottoman Politics and Transit Rights: The Seventeenth Century Trade in Silk Between Safavid Iran and Muscovy." *Cahiers du monde russe* 35, no. 4 (October–December 1994), pp. 739–61.

———. "Between Arabs, Turks and Iranians: The Town of Basra, 1600–1700." *Bulletin of the School of Oriental and African Studies* 69, pt. 1 (2006), pp. 53–78.

———. "Distant Allies: Diplomatic Contacts between Portugal and Iran in the Reign of Shah Tahmasb, 1524–1576." In *Portugal, The Persian Gulf and Safavid Persia*, edited by Rudi Matthee and Jorge Flores, pp. 219–47. Acta Iranica 52. [Leuven]: Peeters, 2011.

———. *The Politics of Trade in Safavid Iran: Silk for Silver, 1600–1730*. Cambridge and New York: Cambridge University Press, 1999.

Maxted, Ian. *Exeter Working Papers in Book History;* http://bookhistory.blogspot.com/.

May, Florence Lewis. *Silk Textiles of Spain, Eighth to Fifteenth Century*. Hispanic Notes and Monographs; Essays, Studies, and Brief Biographies, Peninsular Series. New York: Hispanic Society of America, 1957.

Mayer, Christa Charlotte. *Masterpieces of Western Textiles from the Art Institute of Chicago*. [Chicago]: The Art Institute of Chicago, 1969.

———, et al. *Raiment for the Lord's Service: A Thousand Years of Western Vestments*. Exh. cat. Chicago: The Art Institute of Chicago, 1975.

Mayer Thurman, Christa C[harlotte]. "Large Hanging with Crown and Escutcheon." In *European Tapestries in the Art Institute of Chicago*, edited by Koenraad Brosens et al., pp. 356–59, no. 60. Chicago: The Art Institute of Chicago, 2008.

McDonald, Roderick A. *The Economy and Material Culture of Slaves: Goods and Chattels on the Sugar Plantations of Jamaica and Louisiana*. Baton Rouge: Louisiana State University Press, 1993.

McGowan, Bruce. "The Age of the *Ayans*, 1699–1812." In *An Economic and Social History of the Ottoman Empire, 1300–1914*, edited by Halil İnalcık and Donald Quataert, pp. 637–758. Cambridge and New York: Cambridge University Press, 1994.

McJunkin, David Morgan. "Logwood: An Inquiry into the Historical Biogeography of Haematoxylum Campechianum L. and Related Dyewoods of the Neotropics." Ph.D. diss., University of California, Los Angeles, 1991.

McWilliams, James E. *Building the Bay Colony: Local Economy and Culture in Early Massachusetts*. Charlottesville: The University of Virginia Press, 2007.

Meibutsugire: Torai orimono e no akogare/From Loom to Heirloom: The World of Meibutsu-gire Textiles. Exh. cat. Tokyo: Gotō Bijutsukan (The Gotoh Museum), 2001.

Mendes Pinto, Maria Helena, et al. *Vasco da Gama et l'Inde*. Exh. cat. Lisbon: Fondation Calouste Gulbenkian; Paris: Chancellerie des Universités de Paris, 1998.

Mendonça, Maria José de. *Embroidered Quilts from the Museu Nacional de Arte Antiga Lisboa: India, Portugal, China, 16th/18th Century*. Exh. cat. London: Kensington Palace, 1978.

Mercantile Advertiser. See *America's Historical Newspapers*.

Mew, James, and Deborah Manley. "Baldwin, George (1744–1826)." In *Oxford Dictionary of National Biography*, edited by H. C. G. Matthew, Brian Harrison, and Lawrence Goldman. Oxford: Oxford University Press, 2004. Online ed., January 2008; http://www.oxforddnb.com.library.metmuseum.org/view/article/1165 (accessed April 8, 2013).

Meyer, Eve R. "*Turquerie* and Eighteenth-Century Music." *Eighteenth-Century Studies* 7, no. 4 (Summer 1974), pp. 474–88.

Middleton, Henry. *The Voyage of Sir Henry Middleton to the Moluccas, 1604–1606*. Edited by William Foster. Works Issued by the Hakluyt Society, Second series 88. London: Hakluyt Society, 1943.

Miller, Lesley Ellis. "Manufactures and the Man: A Reassessment of the Place of Jacques-Charles Dutillieu in the Silk Industry of Eighteenth-Century Lyon." *Textile History* 29, no. 1 (Spring 1998), pp. 19–40.

Miller, Susan. "Europe Looks East: Ceramics and Silk, 1680–1710." In *A Taste for the Exotic: Foreign Influences on Early Eighteenth-Century Silk Designs*, edited by Anna Jolly, pp. 155–73, 211–24. Riggisberger Berichte 14. Riggisberg: Abegg-Stiftung, 2007.

Mills, John. "The Coming of the Carpet to the West." In *The Eastern Carpet in the Western World from the 15th to the 17th Century: Hayward Gallery, London, 20 May–10 July 1983*, edited by Donald King and David Sylvester, pp. 10–23. London: Arts Council of Great Britain, 1983.

Minami, Kazuo. "Edo bakufu okachigumi no fukusei ni tsuite" (Regarding the system of dress of the Edo shogunate's *okachigumi*). *Fūzoku* (Manners and customs) 5, no. 2 (1965), pp. 23–29.

Miño Grijalva, Manuel. "El camino hacia la fábrica en Nueva España: El caso de la 'Fábrica de Indianillas' de Francisco de Iglesias, 1801–1810." *Historia mexicana* 34, no. 1 (July–September 1984), pp. 135–48.

———. *Obrajes y tejedores de Nueva España, 1700–1810: La industria urbana y rural de una economía colonial*. Mexico City: El Colegio de México, 1998.

Mitchell, David M. "The Influence of *Tartary* and the Indies on Social Attitudes and Material Culture in England and France, 1650–1730." In *A Taste for the Exotic: Foreign Influences on Early Eighteenth-Century Silk Designs*, edited by Anna Jolly, pp. 11–43, 211–24. Riggisberger Berichte 14. Riggisberg: Abegg-Stiftung, 2007.

———. "A Passion for the Exotic." In *City Merchants and the Arts, 1670–1720*, edited by Mireille Galinou, pp. 69–82. Wetherby, U.K.: Oblong for the Corporation of London, 2004.

Mitchell, David [M.], and Milton Sonday. "Printed Fustians: 1490–1600." *Bulletin du CIETA*, no. 77 (2000), pp. 99–118.

Mōdo no japonisumu/Japonism in Fashion, Tokyo. Exh. cat. Kyoto: Kyōto Fukushoku Bunka Kenkyū Zaidan (Kyoto Costume Institute), 1996.

Mōdo no japonisumu: Kimono kara umareta yutori no bi (Japonism in fashion: The beauty of space born from the kimono). Exh. cat. Kyoto: Kyōto Fukushoku Bunka Kenkyū Zaidan (Kyoto Costume Institute), 1994.

Monnas, Lisa. *Renaissance Velvets*. London: V&A Publishing, 2012.

———. "Textiles and Diplomacy: Ottoman Silks Entering Venice as Diplomatic Gifts in the Fifteenth and Sixteenth Centuries." Conference paper presented at "Luxusgewebe des Orients im westlichen Mittelalter/ Oriental Silks in Medieval Europe," Riggisberg, September 29– October 1, 2011. Riggisberger Berichte. Riggisberg: Abegg-Stiftung, forthcoming.

Montagu, Mary Wortley, Lady. *The Letters and Works of Lady Mary Wortley Montagu*. Edited by Lord Wharncliffe. 2 vols. Paris: A. and W. Galignani and Co., 1837.

Montebello, Philippe de. "Director's Foreword: Antonio Ratti Textile Center." *The Metropolitan Museum of Art Bulletin*, n.s., 53, no. 3 [*Textiles in The Metropolitan Museum of Art*] (Winter 1995–96), p. 5.

Monteiro, John M. "The Crisis and Transformations of Invaded Societies: Coastal Brazil in the Sixteenth Century." In *The Cambridge History of the Native Peoples of the Americas*, vol. 3, *South America*, pt. 1, edited by Frank Salomon and Stuart B. Schwartz, pp. 973–1023. Cambridge and New York: Cambridge University Press, 1999.

Monteiro, Paula. "Roupas de cama e outras cousas do lar" (Bed clothing and other things for the home). In *O luxo na região do Porto ao tempo de Filipe II de Portugal (1610)* (Luxury in Porto during the times of Felipe II of Portugal), edited by Gonçalo de Vasconcelos e Sousa, pp. 149–77. Porto: Universidade Católica Editora, Centro Interpretativo do Ourivesaria do Norte de Portugal, Centro de Investigação em Ciência e Tecnologia das Artes, 2012.

Montgomery, Florence M. *Printed Textiles: English and American Cottons and Linens, 1700–1850*. New York: The Viking Press, 1970.

———. *Textiles in America, 1650–1870: A Dictionary Based on Original Documents . . .* New York: W. W. Norton, 1984.

Montgomery, James. "The West Indies, A Poem in Four Parts." In *Poems on the Abolition of the Slave Trade*. London: Printed for R. Bowyer, 1809.

Moreland, W. H., ed. *Relations of Golconda in the Early Seventeenth Century.* Works Issued by the Hakluyt Society, Second series 66. London: Hakluyt Society, 1931.

Morena, Francesco. *Chinoiserie: The Evolution of the Oriental Style in Italy from the 14th to the 19th Century.* Florence: Centro Di, 2009.

Morga, Antonio de. *Sucesos de las Islas Filipinas.* Mexico City: Geronymo Balli, 1609.

Morita, Kimio. *Meibutsu-gire no seiritsu* (The origins of *meibutsugire*). Tokyo: Yoshikawa Kōbunkan, 1970.

Morrall, Andrew, and Melinda Watt, eds. *English Embroidery from The Metropolitan Museum of Art, 1580–1700: 'Twixt Art and Nature.* Exh. cat. New York: The Bard Graduate Center for Studies in the Decorative Arts, Design, and Culture; The Metropolitan Museum of Art, 2008.

Morris, Christopher, ed. *The Journeys of Celia Fiennes.* London: Cresset Press, 1947.

Morris, Frances. "Chinoiserie in Printed Fabrics." *The Metropolitan Museum of Art Bulletin* 22, no. 7 (July 1927), pp. 194–96.

———. "An Early Seventeenth-Century Cope." *The Metropolitan Museum of Art Bulletin* 9, no. 6 (June 1914), pp. 147–48.

———. "Indian Textiles in the Exhibition of Painted and Printed Fabrics." *The Metropolitan Museum of Art Bulletin* 22, no. 6 (June 1927), pp. 170–72.

Mott, Lawrence V. "Navigation Techniques." In *The Oxford Companion to World Exploration,* edited by David Buisseret. Online ed. Oxford and New York: Oxford University Press, 2007; http://www.oxfordreference.com.library.metmuseum.org/view/10.1093/acref/9780195149227.001.0001/acref-9780195149227-e-0456# (accessed February 16, 2013).

Mraz, Gottfried. "The Role of Clocks in the Imperial Honoraria for the Turks." In *The Clockwork Universe: German Clocks and Automata 1550–1650,* edited by Klaus Maurice and Otto Mayr, pp. 37–48. Exh. cat. Washington, D.C.: Smithsonian Institution; New York: Neale Watson Academic Publications, 1980.

Mujica, Ramon, et al. *Santa Rosa de Lima y su tiempo.* Lima: Banco de Crédito del Perú, 1995.

Murase, Miyeko, et al. *Jewel Rivers: Japanese Art from the Burke Collection.* Exh. cat. Richmond: Virginia Museum of Fine Arts, 1993.

Muro, Manuel. *História del Santuario de Guadalupe de San Luis Potosí.* San Luis Potosí: Tip. De Davalos, 1894.

Murra, John V., ed. *Visita de la provincia de León de Huánuco en 1562.* 2 vols. Huánuco, Peru: Universidad Nacional Hermilio Valdizán, Facultad de Letras y Educación, 1967–72.

Murúa, Martín de. *Historia general del Perú: Origen y descendencia de los Incas.* Introduction by Manuel Ballesteros Gaibrois. 2 vols. Bibliotheca americana vetus. 1611. Madrid, 1962–64.

Muyldermans, J. "Le costume liturgique arménien: Étude historique." *Le muséon: Revue d'études orientales* 39 (1926), pp. 253–324, pls. 1–9.

Nagazumi, Yōko. "From Company to Individual Company Servants: Dutch Trade in Eighteenth-Century Japan." In *On the Eighteenth Century as a Category of Asian History: Van Leur in Retrospect,* edited by Leonard Blussé and Femme Gaastra, pp. 147–72. Aldershot, U.K.: Ashgate, 1998.

N[agel], C[harles], Jr. "An Elihu Yale Tapestry." *Bulletin of the Associates in Fine Arts at Yale University* 4, no. 3 (October 1932), pp. 142–44.

Nefedova-Gruntova, Ol'ga. *A Journey into the World of the Ottomans: The Art of Jean-Baptiste Vanmour, 1671–1737.* Milan: Skira, 2009.

Nevinson, J. L. "Siegmund von Herberstein: Notes on 16th Century Dress." *Waffen- und Kostümkunde* 18 (1959), pp. 86–93.

New-York Gazette. See *America's Historical Newspapers.*

New-York Gazette Revived in the Weekly Post-Boy. See *America's Historical Newspapers.*

New-York Weekly Journal. See *America's Historical Newspapers.*

Nieuhof, Johannes. *Het gezantschap der Neêrlandtsche Ost-Indische Compagnie, aan den grooten Tartarischen cham, den tegenwoordigen keizer van China.* Amsterdam: Jacob van Meurs, 1665.

———. *Legatio batavica ad magnum Tartariae chamum Sungteium . . .* Amsterdam: J. Meursium, 1668.

———, et al. *An Embassy from the East-India Company of the United Provinces to the Grand Tartar Cham, Emperor of China . . .* 2nd ed. 1669. London: Printed by the author, 1673.

Nockert, Margareta. "The Rålamb Caftan and Ottoman Textiles from the Rålamb Collection." In *The Sultan's Procession: The Swedish Embassy to Sultan Mehmed IV in 1657–1658 and the Rålamb Paintings,* edited by Karin Ådahl, pp. 266–77. Istanbul: Swedish Research Institute in Istanbul, 2006.

Nooy-Palm, C. H[etty] M. "The Role of the Sacred Cloths in the Mythology and Ritual of the Sa'dan Toraja of Sulawesi, Indonesia." In *Indonesian Textiles: Irene Emery Roundtable on Museum Textiles,*

1979 Proceedings, edited by Mattiebelle Gittinger, pp. 81–95. Washington, D.C.: The Textile Museum, 1980.

———. "The Sacred Cloths of the Toraja: Unanswered Questions." In *To Speak with Cloth: Studies in Indonesian Textiles,* edited by Mattiebelle Gittinger, pp. 162–80. Los Angeles: Museum of Cultural History, University of California, Los Angeles, 1989.

North, Susan. "'An Instrument of profit, pleasure, and of ornament': Embroidered Tudor and Jacobean Dress Accessories." In *English Embroidery from The Metropolitan Museum of Art, 1580–1700: 'Twixt Art and Nature,* edited by Andrew Morrall and Melinda Watt, pp. 38–55. Exh. cat. New York: The Bard Graduate Center for Studies in the Decorative Arts, Design, and Culture; The Metropolitan Museum of Art, 2008.

Norwich Packet. See *America's Historical Newspapers.*

Ogasawara, Sae. *Hikone sarasa.* Exh. cat. Hikone: Hikonejō Hakubutsukan (Hikone Castle Museum), 1989.

———. *Sarasa.* Tokyo: Heibonsha, 2005.

———. *Some to ori no kanshō kiso chishiki* (Basic knowledge for appreciation of dyeing and weaving). Tokyo: Shibundō, 1998.

Orenstein, Nadine. "Who Took the King of Sweden to Bed?" *Print Quarterly* 8, no. 1 (March 1991), pp. 44–47.

Orlove, Benjamin S. *Alpacas, Sheep, and Men: The Wool Export Economy and Regional Society in Southern Peru.* 1975. New York: Academic Press, 1977.

Özbaran, Salih. *The Ottoman Response to European Expansion: Studies on Ottoman-Portuguese Relations in the Indian Ocean and Ottoman Administration in the Arab Lands during the Sixteenth Century.* Istanbul: Isis Press, 1994.

Pacheco Ferreira, Maria João. *As alfaias bordadas sinoportuguesas (séculos XVI a XVIII).* Lisbon: Colecção TESES, Universidade Lusíada Editora, 2007.

———. "Entre a vivência religiosa cultual e académica: A presença de têxteis chineses nas festas do colégio de São Paulo de Goa em meados do século XVI." *Revista da Faculdade de Letras, Ciências e Técnicas do Património* 7–8 (2008–9), pp. 191–202; http://ler.letras.up.pt/uploads/ficheiros/9414.pdf.

———. "Notícias da Seda: Referências à seda chinesa na documentação impressa dos séculos XVI a XVIII e seu impacte na sociedade europeia." *Revista de Cultura* (Macao) 16 (2006), pp. 119–39.

———. "Political Intentions of Chinese Textiles in Portuguese Sacred, Solemn, Celebratory Events of the 16th–18th Centuries." In *Textiles and Politics: Textile Society of America 13th Biennial Symposium Proceedings. Washington, D.C., September 18–22, 2012.* Earleville, Md.: Textile Society of America, 2013; http://digitalcommons.unl.edu/tsaconf/682.

———. "Repercussions of Chinese Textiles in Portuguese Decorative Arts (16th–17th Centuries)." In *Face to Face: The Transcendence of the Arts in China and Beyond—Historical Perspectives,* edited by Rui Oliveira Lopes. Lisbon: CIEBA/FBAUL, forthcoming.

———. "Sino-Portuguese Embroidery: A Paradigm of Artistic and Cultural Exchanges between East and West." *Bulletin du CIETA* 82 (2005), pp. 108–18.

———. *Os têxteis chineses em Portugal nas opções decorativas sacras de aparato (séculos XVI–XVIII)* (Chinese textiles in Portuguese decorative options for ecclesiastical apparatus [16th–18th centuries]). Ph.D. diss., University of Oporto, 2011; http://repositorio-aberto.up.pt/handle/10216/56346.

Palmer, Gabrielle, and Donna Pierce. *Cambios: The Spirit of Transformation in Spanish Colonial Art.* Santa Barbara: Santa Barbara Museum of Art, 1992.

Paulocik, Chris. "Investigating a Unique 18th-Century Painted Silk Costume: An Anomaly." In *The Conservation of 18th-Century Painted Silk Dress,* edited by Chris Paulocik and Sean Flaherty, pp. 37–45. New York: The Costume Institute, The Metropolitan Museum of Art and the Graduate Program in Costume Studies, New York University, 1995.

Paz, Octavio, et al. *Mexico: Splendors of Thirty Centuries.* Exh. cat. New York: The Metropolitan Museum of Art, 1990.

Pearson, Charles E., and Paul E. Hoffman. *The Last Voyage of El Nuevo Constante: The Wreck and Recovery of an Eighteenth-Century Spanish Ship off the Louisiana Coast.* Baton Rouge: Louisiana State University Press, 1995.

Peck, Amelia, with Cynthia V. A. Schaffner. *American Quilts and Coverlets in The Metropolitan Museum of Art.* Rev. ed. 1990. New York: The Metropolitan Museum of Art, 2007.

Pennsylvania Gazette. See *America's Historical Newspapers.*

Pennsylvania Packet. See *America's Historical Newspapers.*

Pepys, Samuel. *The Diary of Samuel Pepys: A New and Complete Transcription.* Edited by Robert Latham and William Matthews. 11 vols. 1970–71. London: Harper Collins, 1995.

Peter, Michael. "The Velvet Hanging of Albrecht of Brandenburg in Halberstadt Cathedral." Conference paper presented at 24ème Assemblée Générale du Centre International d'Étude des Textiles Anciens, Copenhagen, [October 3–5] 2011.

Peterson, Willard J. "What to Wear?: Observation and Participation by Jesuit Missionaries in Late Ming Society." In *Implicit Understandings: Observing, Reporting, and Reflecting on the Encounters between Europeans and Other Peoples in the Early Modern Era*, edited by Stuart B. Schwartz, pp. 403–21. Cambridge and New York: Cambridge University Press, 1994.

Pettit, Florence H. *America's Indigo Blues: Resist-Printed and Dyed Textiles of the Eighteenth Century*. New York: Hastings House, 1974.

———. *America's Printed and Painted Fabrics, 1600–1900*. New York: Hastings House, [1970].

Pfister, R. *Les toiles imprimées de Fostat et l'Hindoustan*. Paris: Les Éditions d'Art et d'Histoire, 1938.

Phipps, Elena. "Cochineal Red: The Art History of a Color." *The Metropolitan Museum of Art Bulletin*, n.s., 67, no. 3 (Winter 2010), pp. 1–48, cover illus.

———. "Cumbi to Tapestry: Collection, Innovation, and Transformation of the Colonial Andean Tapestry Tradition." In *The Colonial Andes: Tapestries and Silverwork, 1530–1830*, by Elena Phipps et al., pp. 72–99. Exh. cat. New York: The Metropolitan Museum of Art, 2004.

———. *The Four-Selvaged Cloth*. Los Angeles: The Fowler Museum, forthcoming.

———. "Garments and Identity in the Colonial Andes." In *The Colonial Andes: Tapestries and Silverwork, 1530–1830*, by Elena Phipps et al., pp. 16–39. Exh. cat. New York: The Metropolitan Museum of Art, 2004.

———. "Textile Colors and Colorants in the Andes." In *Colors between Two Worlds: The Florentine Codex of Bernardino de Sahagún*, edited by Gerhard Wolf, Joseph Connors, and Louis A. Waldman, pp. 256–80. Florence: Villa I Tatti, 2011.

———. "Textiles as Cultural Memory: Andean Garments in the Colonial Period." In *Converging Cultures: Art and Identity in Spanish America*, by Diana Fane et al., pp. 144–56. Exh. cat. Brooklyn: The Brooklyn Museum, 1996.

———. "*Tornesol*: A Colonial Synthesis of European and Andean Textile Traditions." In *Approaching Textiles, Varying Viewpoints: Proceedings of the Seventh Biennial Symposium, Textile Society of America, Santa Fe, New Mexico, 2000*, pp. 221–30. Earleville, Md.: Textile Society of America, 2001.

———. "Woven Silver and Gold: Metallic Yarns in Colonial Andean Textiles." *Source: Notes in the History of Art* 29, no. 3 (Spring 2010), pp. 4–11.

Phipps, Elena, and Lucy Commoner. "Investigation of a Colonial Latin American Textile." In *Textile Narratives and Conversations: Proceedings of the 10th Biennial Symposium of the Textile Society of America, October 11–14, Toronto, Ontario*, edited by Carol Bier and Ann Svenson Perlman, pp. 485–93. CD-ROM format; Middleton, Del.: Textile Society of America, 2007; http://digitalcommons.unl.edu/tsaconf/358/.

Phipps, Elena, et al. *The Colonial Andes: Tapestries and Silverwork, 1530–1830*. Exh. cat. New York: The Metropolitan Museum of Art, 2004.

Phipps, Elena, Florica Zaharia, and Nobuko Shibayama. "Conservation and Technical Study of a Colonial Andean Tapestry." *Met Objectives* 5, no. 2 (Spring 2004), pp. 1–6.

Pigafetta, Antonio. *Magellan's Voyage: A Narrative Account of the First Circumnavigation*. Translated by R. A. Skelton. 2 vols. New Haven: Yale University Press, 1969.

Pillement, Jean. *Oeuvres de fleurs, ornements, cartouches, figures et sujets chinois*. [Paris], 1771.

Pires, Tomé. *The Suma Oriental of Tomé Pires: An Account of the East, from the Red Sea to Japan, Written in Malacca and India in 1512–1515*. Translated and edited by Armando Cortesão. 2 vols. Works issued by the Hakluyt Society, Second series 89–90. London: Hakluyt Society, 1944.

Pitelka, Morgan, ed. *Japanese Tea Culture: Art, History, and Practice*. London and New York: Routledge Curzon, 2003.

Piwonka, Ruth. "New York Colonial Inventories: Dutch Interiors as a Measure of Cultural Change." In *New World Dutch Studies: Dutch Arts and Culture in Colonial America, 1609–1776*, edited by Roderic H. Blackburn and Nancy A. Kelley, pp. 63–81. Albany: Albany Institute of History and Art, 1987.

Planhol, X[avier] de. "Bandar-e ʿAbbas." In *Encyclopaedia Iranica*, edited by Ehsan Yarshater, vol. 3 (1989), pp. 685–87. London and New York: Routledge & Kegan Paul, 1985– .

Pombejra, Dhiravat na. "Conflict and Commerce in the Gulf of Siam, c. 1629–1642: Using Dutch Documents to 'De-centre' Ayutthayan History." In *Southeast Asian Historiography, Unravelling the Myths:*

Essays in Honour of Barend Jan Terwiel, edited by Volker Grabowsky, pp. 142–61. Bangkok: River Books, 2011.

Ponting, Kenneth G. *A Dictionary of Dyes and Dyeing*. London: Bell and Hyman, 1980.

Porter, David L. "Monstrous Beauty: Eighteenth-Century Fashion and the Aesthetics of the Chinese Taste." *Eighteenth-Century Studies* 35, no. 3 (Spring 2002), pp. 395–411.

Poskrobko-Strzęciwilk, Janina. "Polish Kontusz Sashes in the Collection of The Metropolitan Museum of Art." In *Crossroads of Costume and Textiles in Poland: Papers from the International Conference of the ICOM Costume Committee at the National Museum in Cracow, September 28–October 4, 2003*, edited by Beata Biedrońska-Słotowa, pp. 19–34. Cracow: The National Museum, 2005.

Ptak, Roderich. "Piracy along the Coasts of Southern India and Ming China: Comparative Notes on Two Sixteenth Century Cases." In *China and the Asian Seas: Trade, Travel, and Visions of the Other (1400–1750)*, article 8, pp. 255–73. Variorum Collected Studies Series. Aldershot, U.K.: Ashgate, 1998.

———. "Sino-Japanese Maritime Trade, circa 1550: Merchants, Ports and Networks." In *China and the Asian Seas: Trade, Travel, and Visions of the Other (1400–1750)*, article 7, pp. 281–311. Variorum Collected Studies Series. Aldershot, U.K.: Ashgate, 1998.

Rae, Janet, et al. *Quilt Treasures of Great Britain: The Heritage Search of the Quilters' Guild*. Nashville: Rutledge Hill Press, 1995.

Rainsford, Marcus. *An Historical Account of the Black Empire of Hayti*. [London], 1805.

Rawson, Jessica. *Chinese Ornament: The Lotus and the Dragon*. London: British Museum Publications, 1984.

Rawson, Jessica, et al. *The British Museum Book of Chinese Art*. 1992. London: British Museum Press, 1999.

Ray, Arthur J. "Indians as Consumers in the Eighteenth Century." In *Rethinking the Fur Trade: Cultures of Exchange in the Atlantic World*, edited by Susan Sleeper-Smith, pp. 320–43. Lincoln, Neb.: University of Nebraska Press, 2009.

Réal, Daniel. *Spanische und portugiesische gewebe*. Berlin: E. Wasmuth, 1926.

———. *Tissus espagnols et portugais*. Paris: Librairie des Arts Décoratifs; A. Calavas [1925].

Rebora, Carrie, et al. *John Singleton Copley in America*. Exh. cat. New York: The Metropolitan Museum of Art, 1995.

Records of the Relations between Siam and Foreign Countries in the 17th Century. 5 vols. Bangkok: Council of the Vajiranana National Library, 1915–21.

Rego, António da Silva, ed. *Documentação ultramarina portuguesa*. Vol. 2, *Bibl. Nac. Madrid, Ms. 3015; Mus. Brit., Col. Egerton Ms. 1131*. Lisbon: Centro de Estudos Históricos e Ultramarinos, 1962.

Rembert, David H., Jr. "The Indigo of Commerce in Colonial North America." *Economic Botany* 33, no. 2 (April–June 1979), pp. 128–34.

Renner Lidz, Margaret. "The Mystery of Seventeenth-Century Quilts." *The Magazine Antiques* 154, no. 6 (December 1998), pp. 834–43.

Ribeiro, Aileen. *The Art of Dress: Fashion in England and France, 1750 to 1820*. New Haven and London: Yale University Press, 1995.

———. *Dress in Eighteenth-Century Europe, 1715–1789*. 2nd ed. 1984. New Haven and London: Yale University Press, 2002.

———. "The Dress Worn at Masquerades in England, 1730 to 1790, and Its Relation to Fancy Dress in Portraiture." Ph.D. diss., University of London, 1975. New York: Garland Publishing, 1984.

———. "The Exotic Diversion: The Dress Worn at Masquerades in Eighteenth Century London." *The Connoisseur* 197, no. 791 (January 1978), pp. 3–13.

———. *Fashion and Fiction: Dress in Art and Literature in Stuart England*. New Haven: Paul Mellon Centre for Studies in British Art; Yale University Press, 2005.

———. *The Gallery of Fashion*. London: National Portrait Gallery, 2000.

Ribeiro, Madalena. "The Japanese Diaspora in the Seventeenth Century, According to Jesuit Sources." *Bulletin of Portuguese/Japanese Studies* 3 (2001), pp. 53–83.

Ribes Iborra, Vicente. *Los valencianos y America: El comercio valenciano con Indias en el siglo XVIII*. Valencia: Diputación Provincial de València, 1985.

Riello, Giorgio. "Asian Knowledge and the Development of Calico Printing in Europe in the Seventeenth and Eighteenth Centuries." *Journal of Global History* 5, no. 1 (March 2010), pp. 1–28.

Riffel, Mélanie, and Sophie Rouart. *Toile de Jouy: Printed Textiles in the French Classic Style*. London: Thames and Hudson, 2003.

Rishel, Joseph J., et al. *The Arts in Latin America, 1492–1820*. Exh. cat. Philadelphia: Philadelphia Museum of Art; New Haven and London: Yale University Press, 2006.

Roquero, Ana. *Tintes y tintoreros de América: Catálogo de materias primas y registro etnográfico . . .* Madrid: Ministerio de Cultura, 2006.

Rosenthal, Margaret F., and Ann Rosalind Jones. *The Clothing of the Renaissance World—Europe, Asia, Africa, the Americas: Cesare Vecellio's* Habiti Antichi et Moderni. London: Thames and Hudson, 2008.

Rothstein, Natalie. "Dutch Silks—An Important but Forgotten Industry of the 18th Century or a Hypothesis." *Oud Holland* 74, no. 3 (1964), pp. 152–71.

———. *Silk Designs of the Eighteenth Century in the Collection of the Victoria and Albert Museum, London, with a Complete Catalogue.* London: Thames and Hudson, 1990.

———. "Silks for the American Market." *The Connoisseur* (American edition) 166, no. 668 (October 1967), pp. 90–94.

Rothstein, Natalie, ed. *Barbara Johnson's Album of Fashions and Fabrics.* London: Thames and Hudson, 1987.

Rousmaniere, Nicole Coolidge, et al. *Kazari: Decoration and Display in Japan, 15th–19th Centuries.* Exh. cat. New York: Japan Society; London: British Museum Press, 2002.

Rousseau, Jean-Jacques. *Rousseau's Émile; or, Treatise on Education.* Abridged, translated, and annotated by William H[arold] Payne. 1892. New York: D. Appleton and Company, 1909.

Rowe, Ann Pollard. "Crewel Embroidered Bed Hangings in Old and New England." *Boston Museum Bulletin* 71, no. 365–66 (1973), pp. 102–64, cover ill.

Rowe, John Howland. "Standardization in Inca Tapestry Tunics." In *The Junius B. Bird Pre-Columbian Textile Conference, May 19 and 20, 1973,* edited by Ann Pollard Rowe, Elizabeth P. Benson, and Anne-Louise Schaffer, pp. 239–64. Washington, D.C.: The Textile Museum; Dumbarton Oaks, 1979.

Saavedra Fajárdo, Diego de. *Idea de un príncipe político christiano representada en cien empresas.* Monaco, 1640.

Safford, Frances Gruber. *American Furniture in The Metropolitan Museum of Art.* Vol. 1, *Early Colonial Period: The Seventeenth-Century and William and Mary Styles.* New York: The Metropolitan Museum of Art, 2007.

Sah, Raaj. "Features of British Indigo in India." *Social Scientist* 9, no. 2–3 (September–October 1980), pp. 67–79.

Sahagún, Bernardino de. "Historia general de las cosas de Nueva España." Mediceo Palatino 218–20, Biblioteca Medicea Laurenziana, Florence.

Sakai, Robert K. "The Satsuma-Ryukyu Trade and the Tokugawa Seclusion Policy." *Journal of Asian Studies* 23, no. 3 (May 1964), pp. 391–403.

Salomon, Frank. "Indian Women of Early Colonial Quito as Seen through Their Testaments." *The Americas* 44, no. 3 (January 1988), pp. 325–41.

Salomon, Frank, and Jorge Urioste. *The Huarochiri Manuscript: A Testament of Ancient and Colonial Andean Religion.* Austin: University of Texas Press, 1991.

Sarasa no sekai ten: Indo kara higashi e nishi e hanayaka na senshoku no bi tokubetsuten (The world of sarasa exhibition: Special exhibition of the beauty of brilliant textiles from India to the east and to the west). Exh. cat. Kobe: Kōbe Shiritsu Hakubutsukan (Kobe City Museum), [1984].

Sardar, Marika. "A Seventeenth-Century *Kalamkari* Hanging at The Metropolitan Museum of Art." In *Sultans of the South: Arts of India's Deccan Courts, 1323–1687,* edited by Navina Najat Haidar and Marika Sardar, pp. 148–61. New York: The Metropolitan Museum of Art, 2011.

Sarre, F[riederich], and F[redrik] R. Martin, eds. *Die Ausstellung von Meisterwerken muhammedanischer Kunst in München, 1910.* 3 vols. Exh. cat. Munich: F. Bruckman, 1910–12.

Sassetti, Filippo. *Lettere edite e inedite.* Edited and annotated by Ettore Marcucci. 1835. Florence: Felice le Monnier, 1855.

Satoh, Rumi, et al. *Kowatari sarasa: Edo o someta Indo no hana/Sarasa: Flowers of the Textile Trade, The Gotoh Museum.* Exh. cat. Tokyo: Gotō Bijutsukan (The Gotoh Museum), 2008.

Savory, R[oger] M. "The Sherley Myth." *Iran* 5 (1967), pp. 73–81.

Scarce, Jennifer M. "Vesture and Dress: Fashion, Function, and Impact." In *Woven from the Soul, Spun from the Heart: Textile Arts of Safavid and Qajar Iran, 16th–19th Centuries,* edited by Carol Bier, pp. 33–56. Exh. cat. Washington, D.C.: The Textile Museum, 1987.

Schaw, Janet. *Journal of a Lady of Quality: Being the Narrative of a Journey from Scotland to the West Indies, North Carolina, and Portugal, in the Years 1774 to 1776.* Edited by Evangeline Walker Andrews, with Charles McLean Andrews. Yale Historical Publications; Manuscripts and Edited Texts 6. New Haven: Yale University Press, 1921.

Schoelwer, Susan P[rendergast], et al. *Connecticut Needlework: Women, Art, and Family, 1740–1840.* Exh. cat. Hartford: The Connecticut Historical Society, 2010.

Schurz, William Lytle. *The Manila Galleon.* 1939. New York: E. P. Dutton & Co., 1959.

Schwartz, Paul R. *Printing on Cotton at Ahmedabad, India, in 1678, from an Unedited Manuscript in the Bibliothèque Nationale, Paris* [MS Français 14614]. Museum Monograph 1. Ahmedabad: Calico Museum of Textiles, 1969.

———. "The Roxburgh Account of Indian Cotton-Painting, 1795." *Journal of Indian Textile History,* no. 4 (1959), pp. 47–56.

Şen, Hüseyin, Mehmet Tütüncü, and Hanno de Vries. *De prins en de pasja/The Prince and the Pasha/Prence ve paşa: 400 jaar Nederland Turkije.* The Hague: De Verdieping van Nederland, [2012].

Sencha, bi to sono katachi (Sencha, its beauty and spirit). Exh. cat. Osaka: Osaka Shiritsu Bijutsukan [Osaka Municipal Museum of Art], 1997.

Serjeant, R[obert] B. *The Portuguese off the South Arabian Coast: Hadramī Chronicles, with Yemeni and European Accounts of Dutch Pirates off Mocha in the Seventeenth Century.* Oxford: Clarendon Press, 1963.

Serrão, Vítor. *A lenda de São Francisco Xavier pelo pintor André Reinoso: Estudo histórico, estético e iconológico de um ciclo barroco existente na Sacristía da Igreja de São Roque.* Colecção património artístico da Santa Casa da Misericórdia de Lisboa 1. Lisbon: Quetzal Editores; Santa Casa da Misericórdia de Lisboa, 2006.

Setterwall, Åke, Stig Fogelmarck, and Bo Gyllensvärd. *The Chinese Pavilion at Drottningholm.* Malmö: Allhems Förlag, 1974.

Seyller, John. "Pearls of the Parrot of India: The Walters Art Museum *Khamsa* of Amīr Khusraw of Delhi." *The Journal of the Walters Art Museum* 58 (2000), pp. 1–176.

Shah, Deepika. *Masters of the Cloth: Indian Textiles Traded to Distant Shores, TAPI Collection.* Exh. cat. New Delhi: National Museum, 2005.

Shan Guoqiang. *Zhixiu shuhua* (Embroidered pictures). Gùgōng bowuyuan cang wenwu zhenpin quanji (The complete collection of treasures of the Palace Museum) 52. Shanghai: Kexue jishu chubanshe, 2005.

Shaw, Stanford J., and E[zel] K. Shaw. *History of the Ottoman Empire and Modern Turkey.* 2 vols. Cambridge and New York: Cambridge University Press, 1976–77.

Sherburne, Edward Raymond. *Some Descendants of Henry and John Sherburne of Portsmouth, N.H.* Boston: New-England Historic Genealogy Society, 1904.

Siegele, Starr. *Toiles for All Seasons: French and English Printed Textiles.* Boston: Bunker Hill Publishing, 2004.

Silva, Nuno Vassallo e. *No caminho do Japão: Arte oriental nas colecções da Santa Casa da Misericórdia de Lisboa.* Exh. cat. Lisbon: Museu de São Roque, 1993.

Silva, R. K. de, and W. G. M. Beumer. *Illustrations and Views of Dutch Ceylon, 1602–1796: A Comprehensive Work of Pictorial Reference with Selected Eye-Witness Accounts.* London: Serendib Publications, 1988.

Silva Santisteban, Fernando. *Los obrajes en el virreinato del Perú.* Lima: Publicaciones del Museo Nacional de Historia, 1964.

Simpson, Marianna Shreve. "Gifts for the Shah: An Episode in Habsburg-Safavid Relations during the Reigns of Philip III and 'Abbas I." In *Gifts of the Sultan: The Arts of Giving at the Islamic Courts,* by Linda Komaroff et al., pp. 124–39. Exh. cat. Los Angeles: Los Angeles County Museum of Art, 2011.

Sims, Eleanor. "The European Print Sources of Paintings by the Seventeenth-Century Persian Painter Muhammad Zaman ibn Haji Yusuf of Qum." In *Le stampe e la diffusione delle immagini e degli stili,* edited by Henri Zerner, pp. 73–83 and figs. 75–85. C.I.H.A. atti . . . 1979, 8. Bologna: Editrice C.L.U.E.B. Bologna, [1983].

Sivaramamurti, C. *South Indian Paintings.* New Delhi: National Museum, 1968.

Slomann, Vilhelm. *Bizarre Designs in Silks: Trade and Traditions.* Copenhagen: Ejnar Munksgaard, 1953.

Slomann, Vilhelm, and John Irwin. "Letter: *Bizarre Designs in Silks.*" *The Burlington Magazine* 97, no. 631 (October 1955), pp. 322, 324–25.

Smith, Bernard. *Imagining the Pacific in the Wake of the Cook Voyages.* New Haven and London: Yale University Press, 1992.

Smith, C. Wayne, and J. Tom Cothren, eds. *Cotton: Origin, History, Technology, and Production.* Wiley Series in Crop Science. New York: John Wiley and Sons, 1999.

Smith, Godfrey. *The Laboratory, or, School of Arts: In which are faithfully exhibited, and fully explained . . . with a great number of other scarce and valuable secrets. Volume II, compiled for the use, benefit, and entertainment of the curious; illustrated with a variety of curious copper-plates.* London, 1756.

Smith, H. G. "Cornelius Drebbel and English Scarlet Dyeing." *CIBA Review* 1, no. 7 (March 1938), pp. 231–32.

Smith, Robert S. "Indigo Production and Trade in Colonial Guatemala." *The Hispanic American Historical Review* 39, no. 2 (May 1959), pp. 181–211.

Solórzano y Pereyra, Juan de. *Política indiana*. Madrid: Imprenta Real de la Gazeta, 1791.

Sonday, Milton. "Pattern and Weaves: Safavid Lampas and Velvet." In *Woven from the Soul, Spun from the Heart: Textile Arts of Safavid and Qajar Iran, 16th–19th Centuries*, by Carol Bier et al., pp. 57–83. Exh. cat. Washington, D.C.: The Textile Museum, 1987.

Soper, Alexander Coburn. "Literary Evidence for Early Buddhist Art in China." *Artibus Asiae*, Supplementum 19 (1959), pp. iii–v, vii, ix, xi–xvi, 1–121, 123–39, 141–257, 259–73, 275–96.

Sotheby's. *A Treasured Legacy: The Michael and Judy Steinhardt Judaica Collection*. Sale cat. New York, April 29, 2013.

Sousa, António Caetano de. *História Genealógica da Casa Real Portuguesa*. Vol. 3, pt. 1. Coimbra: Atlântida-Livraria Editora, 1948.

Sousa, Bernardino José de, et al. *O pao-brasil na história nacional*. 2nd ed. 1939. São Paulo: Companhia Editora Nacional, 1978.

Spink and Son Ltd. *The Glamour of Silk, to be Exhibited for Sale by Spink and Son Ltd., 28th May to 28th June 1996*. Exh. cat. London, 1996.

Stalker, John, and George Parker. *A Treatise of Japanning and Varnishing . . . 1688*. Introduction by H. D. Molesworth. London: Alec Tiranti, 1971.

Standen, Edith Appleton. "Embroideries in the French and Chinese Taste." *The Metropolitan Museum of Art Bulletin*, n.s., 13, no. 4 (December 1954), pp. 144–47.

———. "English Tapestries 'After the Indian Manner.'" *Metropolitan Museum Journal* 15 (1980), pp. 119–42.

———. *European Post-Medieval Tapestries and Related Hangings in The Metropolitan Museum of Art*. 2 vols. New York: The Metropolitan Museum of Art, 1985.

———. "Jean-Jacques-François Le Barbier and Two Revolutions." *Metropolitan Museum Journal* 24 [*Essays in Honor of Helmut Nickel*] (1989), pp. 255–74.

———. "The Story of the Emperor of China: A Beauvais Tapestry Series." *Metropolitan Museum Journal* 11 (1976), pp. 103–17.

Steensgaard, Niels. *The Asian Trade Revolution of the Seventeenth Century: The East India Companies and the Decline of the Caravan Trade*. Chicago: University of Chicago Press, 1974.

Stein, Perrin. "Amédée Van Loo's *Costume turc*: The French Sultana." *The Art Bulletin* 78, no. 3 (September 1996), pp. 417–38.

———. "Boucher's Chinoiseries: Some New Sources." *The Burlington Magazine* 138, no. 1122 (September 1996), pp. 598–604.

Stein, Stanley J., and Barbara H. Stein. *Silver, Trade, and War: Spain and America in the Making of Early Modern Europe*. Baltimore: The Johns Hopkins University Press, 2004.

Steinmann, Linda K. "Sericulture and Silk: Production, Trade, and Export under Shah Abbas." In *Woven from the Soul, Spun from the Heart: Textile Arts of Safavid and Qajar Iran, 16th–19th Centuries*, by Carol Bier et al., pp. 12–19. Exh. cat. Washington, D.C.: The Textile Museum, 1987.

———. "Shah 'Abbas and the Royal Silk Trade 1599–1629." *British Society for Middle Eastern Studies Bulletin* 14, no. 1 (198[7]), pp. 68–74.

Stevens, Roger. "Robert Sherley: The Unanswered Questions." *Iran* 17 (1979), pp. 115–25.

Stillman, Norman A. "The Eleventh-Century Merchant House of Ibn 'Awkal (A Geniza Study)." *Journal of the Economic and Social History of the Orient* 16, no. 1 (April 1973), pp. 39–41.

Stronge, Susan. "Imperial Gifts at the Court of Hindustan." In *Gifts of the Sultan: The Arts of Giving at the Islamic Courts*, by Linda Komaroff et al., pp. 170–83. Exh. cat. Los Angeles: Los Angeles County Museum of Art, 2011.

Styles, John. "Indian Cottons and European Fashion, 1400–1800." In *Global Design History*, edited by Glenn Adamson et al., pp. 37–46. London: Routledge, 2011.

———. *Threads of Feeling: The London Foundling Hospital's Textile Tokens, 1740–1770*. Exh. cat. London: The Foundling Museum, 2010.

Swain, Margaret H. "Nightgown into Dressing Gown: A Study of Men's Nightgowns, Eighteenth Century." *Costume: The Journal of the Costume Society* 6 (1972), pp. 10–21.

———. *Scottish Embroidery, Medieval to Modern*. London: Batsford, 1986.

Synge, Lanto. *Art of Embroidery: History of Style and Technique*. Woodbridge, U.K.: Antique Collectors' Club, 2001.

Takeda, Sharon Sadako, et al. *Fashioning Fashion: European Dress in Detail, 1700–1915*. Munich and London: Prestel; Los Angeles: Los Angeles County Museum of Art, 2010.

Tashiro, Kazui. "Foreign Relations during the Edo Period: *Sakoku* Reexamined." *The Journal of Japanese Studies* 8, no. 2 (Summer 1982), pp. 283–306.

———. "Tsushima Han's Korean Trade, 1684–1710." *Acta Asiatica* 30 (1976), pp. 85–105.

Tavernier, Jean-Baptiste. *Collections of Travels through Turky into Persia, and the East-Indies, Giving an Account of the State of those Countries . . . Being the Travels of Monsieur Tavernier, Bernier, and Other Great Men*. London: Moses Pitt, 1688.

Taylor, George W. "A Jouy Calico Print Using Chay Root." *Dyes in History and Archaeology*, no. 9 (1990), pp. 32–34.

Taylor, William B. *Our Lady of Guadalupe and Friends: The Virgin Mary in Colonial Mexico City*. Morrison Library Inaugural Address Series 15. Berkeley: The Doe Library, University of California, Berkeley, 1999; http://escholarship.org/uc/item/9nn001h8.

Le teinturier parfait, ou, L'art de teindre les soyes . . . Suite des secrets concernant les arts et metiers. Paris: Claude Jombert, 1716.

Terpstra, Heert. *Vestiging van de nederlanders aan de kust van Koromandel*. Groningen: De Waal, 1911.

"Textile Study Room at the Metropolitan Museum of Art." *Posselt's Textile Journal*, August 1923, p. 36.

Thiéry de Menonville, Nicolas-Joseph. *Traité de la culture du nopal, et de l'education de la cochenille . . .* Cap-Français and Paris, 1787.

———. "Travels to Guaxaca, Capital of the Province of the Same Name, in the Kingdom of Mexico." In *A General Collection of the Best and Most Interesting Voyages and Travels in All Parts of the World*, edited by John Pinkerton, vol. 13 (1812), pp. 753–876. London: Longman, Hurst, Rees, and Orme, 1808–14.

Thomas, Parakunnel J. "The Beginnings of Calico-Printing in England." *The English Historical Review* 39, no. 154 (April 1924), pp. 206–16.

Thornton, John. *Africa and Africans in the Making of the Atlantic World, 1400–1800*. 2nd ed. 1992. Cambridge and New York: Cambridge University Press, 1998.

Thornton, Peter. *Baroque and Rococo Silks*. London: Faber and Faber, 1965.

———. "An 18th Century Silk-Designer's Manual." *The Bulletin of the Needle and Bobbin Club* 42, no. 1–2 (1958), pp. 6–31.

———. *Seventeenth-Century Interior Decoration in England, France, and Holland*. New Haven: Paul Mellon Centre for Studies in British Art; Yale University Press, 1978.

Tillyard, Stella. *Aristocrats: Caroline, Emily, Louisa, and Sarah Lennox, 1740–1832*. New York: Farrar, Straus and Giroux, 1994.

Tobin, Beth F. *Picturing Imperial Power: Colonial Subjects in Eighteenth-Century British Painting*. Durham, N.C.: Duke University Press, 1999.

Toby, Ronald P. *State and Diplomacy in Early Modern Japan: Asia in the Development of the Tokugawa Bakufu*. Princeton, N.J.: Princeton University Press, 1984.

Toledo, Francisco de. "Instrucciones por los visitadores 1569–1579 Ciudad de los Reyes." In *Disposiciones gubernativas para el Virreinato del Perú, 1569–1574*. Vol. 1. Transcripts by María Justina Sarabia Viejo, edited by Guillermo Lohmann Villena. Publicaciones de la Escuela de Estudios Hispano-Americanos de la Universidad de Sevilla 320. Seville: Escuela de Estudios Hispano-Americanos, 1986.

Torres de Mendoza, Luis, Joaquín Francisco Pacheco, and Francisco de Cárdenas y Espejo, eds. *Colección de documentos inéditos, relativos al descubrimiento, conquista y organización de las antiguas posesiones españolas de América y Oceanía, sacados de los archivos del reino y muy especialmente del de Indias*. 42 vols. Madrid, 1864–84.

Tower, Walter Sheldon. *A History of the American Whale Fishery*. Philadelphia: University Press, 1907.

Travis, Anthony S., et al. *From Turkey Red to Tyrian Purple: Textile Colours for the Industrial Revolution . . .* Exh. cat. [Jerusalem]: Jewish National and University Library, 1993.

Trnek, Helmut, and Nuno Vassallo e Silva, eds. *Exotica: The Portuguese Discoveries and the Renaissance Kunstkammer*. Exh. cat. Lisbon: Calouste Gulbenkian Museum, 2001.

Tromans, Nicholas, et al. *The Lure of the East: British Orientalist Painting*. Exh. cat. New Haven: Yale University Press, 2008.

Tyack, Norman C. P. "English Exports to New England, 1632–1640: Some Records in the Port Books." *New England Historical and Genealogical Register* 135 (1981), pp. 213–38.

Ulperni, Siro. *O forasteiro admirado: Relaçam panegyrica do trivnfo e festas, qve celebrou o Real Convento do Carmo de Lisboa pela canon-ização da seráfica virgem S. Maria Magdalena de Pazzi, religiosa da sua ordem*. Pt. 1. Lisbon: Off. de António Rodrigvez d'Abrev, 1672.

Ulrichs, Friederike. "Johan Nieuhof's and Olfert Dapper's Travel Accounts as Sources for European *Chinoiserie*." In *A Taste for the Exotic: Foreign Influences on Early Eighteenth-Century Silk Designs*, edited by Anna Jolly, pp. 44–76, 211–24. Riggisberger Berichte 14. Riggisberg: Abegg-Stiftung, 2007.

Vainker, Shelagh. *Chinese Silk: A Cultural History*. London: British Museum Press, 2004.

Van Dyke, Paul A. *Merchants of Canton and Macao: Politics and Strategies in Eighteenth-Century Chinese Trade*. Hong Kong: Hong Kong University Press; Kyoto: Kyoto University Press, 2011.

———. "Weaver Suckin and the Canton Silk Trade, 1750–1781." *Revista de Cultura/Review of Culture* (Macao) 29 (January 2009), pp. 104–19.

Vanmour, Jean-Baptiste. *Recueil de cent estampes représentant différentes nations du Levant tirées sur les tableaux peints d'après nature en 1707 et 1708 par les ordres de M. de Ferriol, ambassadeur du roi à la Porte et gravées en 1712 et 1713 par les soins de Mr. Le Hay.* Paris, 1714.

Vargas Lugo de Bosch, Elisa, et al. *Imágenes de los naturales en el arte de la Nueva España: Siglos XVI–XVIII.* Mexico City: Fomento Cultural Banamex, 2005.

Varley, Paul, and Kumakura Isao, eds. *Tea in Japan: Essays on the History of Chanoyu.* Honolulu: University of Hawai'i Press, 1989.

Vaz Pinto, Clara. *Bordado de Castelo Branco: Catálogo de desenhos.* Vol. 1, *Colchas.* [Lisbon]: Instituto Português de Museus; [Castelo Branco]: Museu Francisco Tavares Proença Júnior, 1992.

Vecellio, Cesare. *Degli habiti antichi et moderni di diversi parti del mondo.* Venice: Damian Zenaro, 1590.

Ventura, Carol. "The Ikat Rebozos (Shawls) of Central Mexico." *Shuttle, Spindle, and Dyepot* 33, no. 4, issue 132 (Fall 2002), pp. 41–48.

Véron-Denise, Danièle. "Un mobilier à décor brodé de 'chinoiseries' au château de Fontainebleau." *La revue des musées de France: Revue du Louvre* 56, no. 2 (April 2006), pp. 63–71.

Vishnevskaya, Inna Isidorovna. "Eastern Treasures of the Russian Tsars." In *The Tsars and the East: Gifts from Turkey and Iran in the Moscow Kremlin,* pp. 1–13, 136, 138–41. Exh. cat. Washington, D.C.: Arthur M. Sackler Gallery, Smithsonian Institution, 2009.

Vliet, Jeremias van, translated by L. F. van Ravenswaay. "Description of the Kingdom of Siam." *Journal of the Siam Society* 7, pt. 1 (1910), pp. 1–105.

Vogelsang-Eastwood, G[illian] M. *Resist Dyed Textiles from Quseir al-Qadim, Egypt.* Paris: A.E.D.T.A., 1990.

Volker, Angela. "An Indian Chinoiserie from an Austrian Palace: Textile Furnishings for Prince Eugene's State Bedroom in Schloss Hof." In *Baroque Luxury Porcelain: The Manufactories of Du Paquier in Vienna and of Carlo Ginori in Florence,* by Johann Kräftner et al., pp. 54–63. Exh. cat. Munich: Prestel; Vienna: Liechtenstein Museum, 2005.

Vollmer, John E., and Izabella Krasuski. "Preserving the Past: An Indian Embroidered Coverlet." *Rotunda* 14, no. 2 (Summer 1981), pp. 24–31.

Vollmer, John E., E. J. Keall, and E. Nagai-Berthrong. *Silk Roads, China Ships.* Exh. cat. Toronto: Royal Ontario Museum, 1983.

Wadsworth, Alfred P., and Julia De Lacy Mann. *The Cotton Trade and Industrial Lancashire, 1600–1780.* Manchester: Manchester University Press, 1931.

Wagenaar, Lodewijk J. "The Castle of Batavia . . . " In *Dutch New York Between East and West: The World of Margrieta van Varick,* edited by Deborah L. Krohn and Peter N. Miller, p. 145, no. 8. Exh. cat. New York: Bard Graduate Center, 2009.

Walker, Stefanie, et al. *Life and the Arts in the Baroque Palaces of Rome: Ambiente Barocco.* Exh. cat. New Haven and London: Yale University Press for the Bard Graduate Center for Studies in the Decorative Arts, New York, 1999.

Walton, Guy. "Diplomatic and Ambassadorial Gifts of the Sixteenth and Seventeenth Centuries." In *Gifts to the Tsars, 1500–1700: Treasures from the Kremlin,* edited by Barry Shifman and Guy Walton, pp. 74–95. Exh. cat. New York: Harry N. Abrams, 2001.

Wang, Qi, and Siyi Wang. *Sancai tuhui* (Illustrated encyclopedia of the three realms). 3 vols. Facsimile ed. Wanli period (1573–1620). Shanghai: Shanghai guji chubanshe, 1988.

Wappenschmidt, Friederike. *Chinesische Tapeten für Europa vom Rollbild zur Bildtapete.* Veröffentlichung des Deutschen Vereins für Kunstwissenschaft. Berlin: Deutscher Verlag für Kunstwissenschaft, 1989.

Wardle, Patricia. *For Our Royal Person: Master of the Robes Bills of King-Stadholder William III.* Apeldoorn: Paleis Het Loo National Museum, 2002.

———. *75 x Lace.* Exh. cat. Amsterdam: Rijksmuseum; Zwolle: Waanders Uitgevers, 2000.

Warwick, Edward, Henry Clarence Pitz, and Alexander Wyckoff. *Early American Dress: The Colonial and Revolutionary Periods.* History of American Dress 2. New York: Benjamin Blom, 1965.

Watt, Melinda. "Exploring Pattern in Woven Design: A Comparison of Two Seventeenth Century Italian Textiles." In *Creating Textiles— Makers, Methods and Markets: Proceedings of the Sixth Biennial Symposium of the Textile Society of America, Inc., New York, New York, 1998,* pp. 446–55. Earleville, Md.: Textile Society of America, 1999.

Wearden, Jennifer. "Siegmund von Herberstein: An Italian Velvet in the Ottoman Court." *Costume: The Journal of the Costume Society* 19 (1985), pp. 22–29.

Weibel, Adèle Coulin. *Two Thousand Years of Textiles: The Figured Textiles of Europe and the Near East.* Detroit: The Detroit Institute of Arts; New York: Pantheon Books, 1952.

Weigert, Roger-Armand. *Textiles en Europe sous Louis XV: Les plus beaux spécimens de la collection Richelieu.* Fribourg: Office du livre, 1964.

Wellington, Donald C. *French East India Companies: A Historical Account and Record of Trade.* Lanham, Md.: Hamilton Books, 2006.

Wells-Cole, Anthony. *Art and Decoration in Elizabethan and Jacobean England: The Influence of Continental Prints, 1558–1625.* New Haven: Paul Mellon Centre for Studies in British Art; Yale University Press, 1997.

Wheat, Joe Ben, and Ann Lane Hedlund. *Blanket Weaving in the Southwest.* Tucson: University of Arizona Press, 2003.

Whitcomb, Donald S., and Janet H. Johnston. *Quseir al-Qadim 1980: Preliminary Report.* American Research Center in Egypt 7. Malibu: Undena Publications, 1982.

White, Philip L. *The Beekman Mercantile Papers, 1746–1799.* 3 vols. New York: The New-York Historical Society, 1956.

Wilckens, Leonie von. "Ein 'Haarmantel' des 16. Jahrhunderts." *Waffen- und Kostümkunde* 22, no. 1 (1980), pp. 39–44.

Willan, T[homas] S. *The Early History of the Russia Company, 1553–1603.* Manchester: Manchester University Press, 1956.

Wills, John E., Jr. "Relations with Maritime Europeans, 1514–1662." In *The Cambridge History of China,* vol. 8, *The Ming Dynasty, 1368–1644, Part 2,* edited by Denis Twitchett and Frederick W. Mote, pp. 333–75. Cambridge and New York: Cambridge University Press, 1998.

Wilson, Verity. "China." In *5000 Years of Textiles,* by Jennifer Harris et al., pp. 133–41. London: British Museum Press, 1993.

———. "Chinese Painted Silks for Export in the Victoria and Albert Museum." *Orientations* 18, no. 11 (October 1987), pp. 30–35.

———. "Silk." In *Chinese Export Art and Design,* by Craig Clunas et al. London: Victoria and Albert Museum, 1987.

Wingfield Digby, G. F. "Some Silks Woven under Portuguese Influence in the Far East." *The Burlington Magazine for Connoisseurs* 77, no. 449 (August 1940), pp. 52–53, 55–56, 58–60, 63.

Wulfert, Kimberly. "John Hewson and the French Connection." *The Magazine Antiques* 174, no. 2 (August 2008), pp. 78–85.

———. "The Man of Many Vases: John Hewson, Calico Printer." *Folk Art* 32 (Fall 2007), pp. 58–69.

Wu, Zhiliang. "The Establishment of Macao as a Special Port City and the Ensuing Debates." In *Macau during the Ming Dynasty,* edited by Luís Filipe Barreto, pp. 285–301. Lisbon: Centro Científico e Cultural de Macau, 2009.

Yamakawa, Aki, and Monica Bethe. *Kōsō to kesa: Koromo o tsutae kokoro o tsunagu/Transmitting Robes, Linking Minds: The World of Buddhist Kasaya.* Exh. cat. Kyoto: Kyōto Kokuritsu Hakubutsukan (Kyoto National Museum), 2010.

Yamanobe, Tomoyuki, and Saeko Ueno. *Kosode moyō hinagatabon shūsei* (Compendium of kimono design pattern books). Vols. [17–27], Facsimile of *Nishikawa yu momiji* (Evening maple leaves of west river [Kyoto, 1718]). Tokyo: Gakushū kenkyūsha, 1974.

Yoshida, Masako. "Chūgoku ni okeru berubetto no keisei/The Formation of Velvets in China." *Hata: Orimono bunka kenkyūkai kaishi* (Hata: Journal of the Textile Culture Research Group) 5 (1998), pp. 35–47.

———. "Metoroporitan bijutsukan shūzō no chaji sōka mon'yō birōdo jinbaori/The Warrior Jacket of Flower Pattern Velvet Preserved in the Metropolitan Museum of Art." *Kokusai fukushoku gakkai shi* (Journal of the International Association of Costume) 22 (2002), pp. 40–49.

———. "Saikyōji ya Honkokuji ni denrai suru kaki chōjū mon'yō shishū: Seisakuchi to seisaku mokuteki o megutte/Embroideries of Flower, Bird, and Animal Design in Honkokuji and Saikyōji: Their Production Place and Purpose." *Genesis* (Bulletin of Kyoto University of Art and Design) 11 (September 2007), pp. 101–19.

Yule, Henry, and Arthur Coke Burnell. *Hobson-Jobson: Being a Glossary of Anglo-Indian Colloquial Words and Phrases, and of Kindred Terms; Etymological, Historical, Geographical, and Discursive.* New ed. 1886. London: John Murray, 1903.

Zagorodnyaya, Irina A. "Russian Foreign Relations and Diplomacy." In *Gifts to the Tsars, 1500–1700: Treasures from the Kremlin,* edited by Barry Shifman and Guy Walton, pp. 20–41. Exh. cat. New York: Harry N. Abrams, 2001.

Zandvliet, Kees, et al. *The Dutch Encounter with Asia, 1600–1950.* Exh. cat. Amsterdam: Rijksmuseum; Zwolle: Waanders Uitgeverij, 2002.

Zavala, Silvio Arturo. *El servicio personal de los indios en el Perú: Extractos del siglo XVI–XVIII.* 3 vols. Mexico City: El Colegio de México, 1978–80.

Zevallos Quiñones, Jorge. "La ropa tributo de las encomiendas trujillanas en el siglo XVI." *Historia y cultura* 7 (1973), pp. 107–27.

INDEX

Page numbers in **boldface** refer to catalogue entries. Page numbers in *italics* refer to figures.

PHOTOGRAPHY CREDITS

The Metropolitan Museum of Art endeavors to respect copyright in a manner consistent with its nonprofit educational mission. If you feel any material has been included in this publication improperly, please contact the Editorial Department at The Metropolitan Museum of Art.

Fig. 1: © 2013 Succession H. Matisse / Artists Rights Society (ARS), New York; figs. 9, 46, 50, 53: © Museu Nacional de Arte Antiga, Lisbon, photographer: José Pessoa, Direção-Geral do Património Cultural / Arquivo de Documentação Fotográfica (DGPC/ADF); fig. 11: Spink & Son Ltd; fig. 13: Courtesy British Library, London; fig. 14: Kees Zandvliet et al., *The Dutch Encounter with Asia, 1600–1950* (Zwolle: Waanders Uitgeverij, 2002), p. 121; fig. 18: Courtesy Anna Seastrand; fig. 22: Ken Cheong, Singapore; figs. 31, 102, cat. 35 right: Cooper-Hewitt, National Design Museum, Smithsonian Institution / Art Resource, NY; fig. 32: Scala / Art Resource; figs. 33, 127, 142, cats. 44B, 74A, 74B, 75, 82, 93B, 104: Photograph © Museum of Fine Arts, Boston; figs. 36, 37: CONACULTA-INAH.-Mex, Reproduccíon Autorizada por el Instituto Nacinal de Antopología e Historia; fig. 39: Elena Phipps; figs. 40, 116: © Patrimonio Nacional, Madrid; fig. 44: Ilona Katzew, *Casta Painting: Images of Race in Eighteenth-Century Mexico* (New Haven and London: Yale University Press, 2004), p. 101; fig. 55: © Museu Nacional do Azulejo, Lisbon, Direção-Geral do Património Cultural/ Arquivo de

Documentação Fotográfica (DGPC/ADF); fig. 56: © Museu de Aveiro, Lisbon, Direção-Geral do Património Cultural / Arquivo de Documentação Fotográfica (DGPC/ADF); fig. 66: ©2013 State Historical and Cultural Museum-Preserve, Moscow Kremlin Museums; fig. 70: Photograph, Gabriel Hildebrand / National Historical Museum Stockholm; fig. 73: F. R. Martin, *Die persischen Prachtstoffe im Schlosse Rosenborg in Kopenhagen* (Stockholm: G. Chelius in Commission, 1901), plate 1; fig. 74: Photograph, Göran Schmidt, The Royal Armoury, Stockholm; fig. 75: National Trust Photo Library / Art Resource; fig. 79: Photograph, Pernille Klemp; fig. 80: © MAK / Georg Mayer; fig. 81: © National Gallery, London / Art Resource, NY; fig. 82: © National Portrait Gallery, London; fig. 84: Photograph, Klaus Wohlmann; fig. 89: © Les Arts Décoratifs, Paris / Jean-Paul Leclerc; fig. 91: © Abegg-Stiftung, photograph, Christoph von Viràg; fig. 135: Courtesy Openluchtmuseum, Arnhem; cat. 35 left: © The Cleveland Museum of Art; cat. 51A: © The Cleveland Museum of Art; cat. 21: © The Art Institute of Chicago; cat. 62: The Jewish Museum / Art Resource, NY; cats. 68, 95: Digital Image © 2013 Museum Associates / LACMA. Licensed by Art Resource, NY; fig. 148: The Lionel Pincus and Princess Firyal Map Division, The New York Public Library, Astor, Lenox and Tilden Foundations; cat. 96: © Centraal Museum, Utrecht, photograph, Ernst Moritz 2001

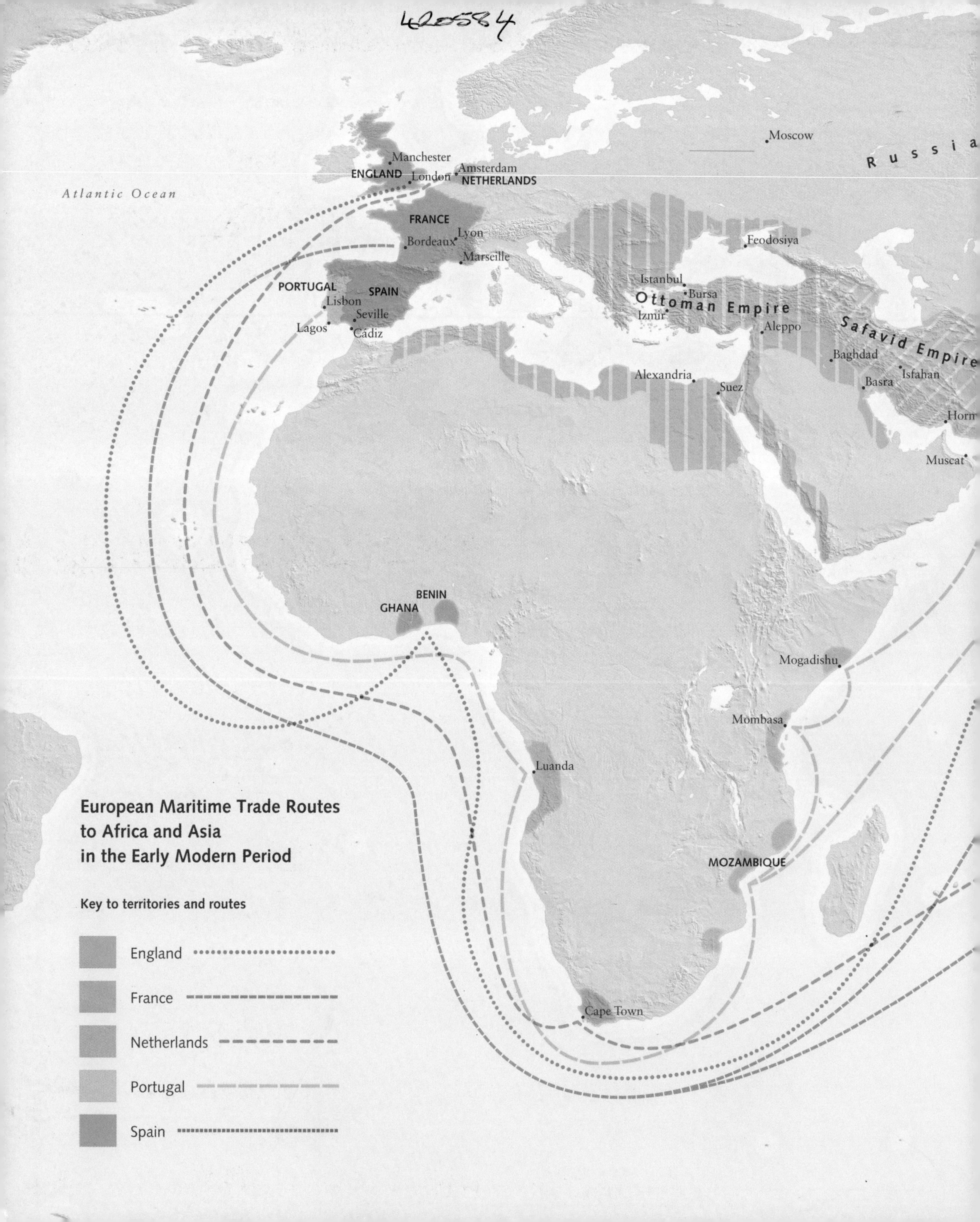

420584

Atlantic Ocean

Moscow

R u s s i a

Manchester
ENGLAND London
Amsterdam
NETHERLANDS

FRANCE
Bordeaux Lyon
Marseille

Feodosiya

Istanbul
PORTUGAL SPAIN
Lisbon
Lagos Seville
Cádiz

Ottoman Empire

Izmir Bursa
Aleppo

Safavid Empire

Alexandria
Suez

Baghdad
Basra Isfahan

Horn

Muscat

BENIN
GHANA

Mogadishu

Mombasa

Luanda

**European Maritime Trade Routes
to Africa and Asia
in the Early Modern Period**

MOZAMBIQUE

Key to territories and routes

England

France

Netherlands

Portugal

Spain

Cape Town